# MICROECONOMICS

For our other contributions to
the next generation:
Catherine, Nicholas and Peter;
and Benjamin, Oliver and Harriet

# MICROECONOMICS

**N. Gregory Mankiw and Mark P. Taylor**

Australia • Canada • Mexico • Singapore • Spain • United Kingdom • United States

**THOMSON**

*Microeconomics*
N. Gregory Mankiw and Mark P. Taylor

| | | |
|---|---|---|
| **Publishing Director**<br>John Yates | **Publisher**<br>Pat Bond | **Development Editor**<br>Anna Carter |
| **Production Editor**<br>Fiona Freel | **Manufacturing Manager**<br>Helen Mason | **Marketing Manager**<br>Anne-Marie Scoones |
| **Typesetter**<br>Saxon Graphics Ltd, Derby | **Cover Design**<br>Adam Renvoize | **Text Design**<br>Design Deluxe, Bath, UK |
| **Research Assistant**<br>Oliver Taylor | **Printer**<br>C&C Offset Printing Co., Ltd,<br>China | |

While the publisher has taken all reasonable care in the preparation of this book the publisher makes no representation, express or implied, with regard to the accuracy of the information contained in this book and cannot accept any legal responsibility or liability for any errors or omissions from the book or the consequences thereof.

Products and services that are referred to in this book may be either trademarks and/or registered trademarks of their respective owners. The publisher and author/s make no claim to these trademarks.

*British Library Cataloguing-in-Publication Data*
A catalogue record for this book is available from the British Library

# BRIEF CONTENTS

**v**

# CONTENTS

## PART 1

## INTRODUCTION 1

**PART 2**

# SUPPLY AND DEMAND I: HOW MARKETS WORK 61

**PART 3**

# SUPPLY AND DEMAND II: MARKETS AND WELFARE 129

# THE ECONOMICS OF THE PUBLIC SECTOR 187

## 10 Externalities 189

## 11 Public goods and common resources 207

## 12 The design of the tax system 223

**PART 5**

# FIRM BEHAVIOUR AND THE ORGANIZATION OF INDUSTRY 245

**PART 6**

# THE ECONOMICS OF LABOUR MARKETS 363

## 18 The markets for the factors of production 365

**The demand for labour** 366

The competitive profit-maximizing firm 366

**PART 7**

# TOPICS FOR FURTHER STUDY 417

**N. GREGORY MANKIW** is Professor of Economics at Harvard University. As a student, he studied economics at Princeton University and the Massachusetts Institute of Technology. As a teacher, he has taught macroeconomics, microeconomics, statistics and principles of economics. He even spent one summer long ago as a sailing instructor on Long Beach Island.

Professor Mankiw is a prolific writer and a regular participant in academic and policy debates. His work has been published in scholarly journals, such as the *American Economic Review,* the *Journal of Political Economy* and the *Quarterly Journal of Economics,* and in more popular forums, such as the *New York Times,* the *Financial Times,* the *Wall Street Journal* and *Fortune.* In addition to his teaching, research and writing, Professor Mankiw has been a research associate of the National Bureau of Economic Research, and an advisor to the Federal Reserve Bank of Boston and the Congressional Budget Office. From 2003 to 2005 he served as Chairman of the US President's Council of Economic Advisors.

Professor Mankiw lives in Wellesley, Massachusetts, with his wife Deborah, their three children, and their border terrier Tobin.

**MARK P. TAYLOR** is Professor of Economics at the University of Warwick. He obtained his first degree in philosophy, politics and economics from Oxford University. He then worked as a foreign exchange dealer in London for two years while simultaneously studying part-time for a master's degree in economics at London University, from where he also holds a doctorate in economics.

Professor Taylor has taught economics at various universities (including Warwick, Oxford, Marseille and New York), at various levels (from principles courses to advanced graduate and MBA courses) and in various fields (including macroeconomics, microeconomics and econometrics). He also worked for several years as a senior economist at the International Monetary Fund and before that at the Bank of England. His work has been extensively published in scholarly journals, such as the *Journal of Political Economy* and the *Economic Journal,* and he is today one of the most highly cited economists in the world in economic research. In addition, Professor Taylor has acted as an advisor to the International Monetary Fund, the World Bank, the Bank of England, the European Commission and to senior members of the UK government. He is a research fellow of the Centre for Economic Policy Research, a member of council of the Royal Economic Society, and a fellow of both the Royal Statistical Society and the Royal Society of Arts.

Professor Taylor lives (with his wife and three children and his three dogs named Byron, Shelley and Aphra) near Kenilworth, Warwickshire (where he collects clocks and keeps bees).

'Economics is a study of mankind in the ordinary business of life.' So wrote Alfred Marshall, the great 19th-century British economist, in his textbook, *Principles of Economics*. Although we have learned much about the economy since Marshall's time, this definition of economics is as true today as it was in 1890, when the first edition of his text was published.

Why should you, as a student at the beginning of the 21st century, embark on the study of economics? Here are three good reasons.

The first reason to study economics is that it will help you understand the world in which you live. There are many questions about the economy that might spark your curiosity. Why do airlines charge less for a return ticket if the traveller stays over a Saturday night? Why is Catherine Zeta Jones paid so much to star in films? Why are living standards so meagre in many African countries? Why do some countries have high rates of inflation while others have stable prices? Why have some European countries adopted a common currency? These are just a few of the questions that a course in economics will help you answer.

The second reason to study economics is that it will make you a more astute participant in the economy. As you go about your life, you make many economic decisions. While you are a student, you decide how many years to stay in full-time education. Once you take a job you decide how much of your income to spend, how much to save and how to invest your savings. One day you may find yourself running a small business or a large firm, and you will decide what prices to charge for your products. The insights developed in the coming chapters will give you a new perspective on how best to make these decisions. Studying economics will not by itself make you rich, but it will give you some tools that may help in that endeavour.

The third reason to study economics is that it will give you a better understanding of the potential and limits of economic policy. As a voter, you help choose the policies that guide the allocation of society's resources. When deciding which policies to support, you may find yourself asking various questions about economics. What are the burdens associated with alternative forms of taxation? What are the effects of free trade with other countries? What is the best way to protect the environment? How does the government budget deficit affect the economy? These and similar questions are always on the minds of policy makers.

Thus the principles of economics can be applied in many of life's situations. Whether the future finds you reading the newspaper, running a business or running the country, you will be glad that you studied economics.

## FOR WHOM IS THIS BOOK WRITTEN?

It is tempting for professional economists writing a textbook to take the economist's point of view and to emphasize those topics that fascinate them and other economists. We have done our best to avoid that temptation. We have tried to put ourselves in the position of someone seeing economics for the first time. Our goal has been to emphasize the material that *students* should and do find interesting about the study of the economy.

One result is that this book is briefer than many books used to introduce students to economics. Another is that more of this book is devoted to applications and policy – and less to formal economic theory – than is the case with many other books written for an introductory course. Throughout this book we have tried to return to applications and policy questions as often as possible. Most chapters include case studies illustrating how the principles of economics are applied. In addition, 'In the News' boxes offer excerpts from newspaper articles showing how economic ideas shed light on current issues facing society. After students finish their first course in economics, they should think about news items from a new perspective and with greater insight.

Something else worth pointing out is that the book has a distinctively European focus. This is not to say that it is an introduction to the economics of the European economy – it is not. Nor does the book ignore the importance of the US economy and the rest of the world – to do so would give a very lopsided view. But what it does attempt to do is to relate economic concepts to an environment that will be familiar and interesting to a European student, and we do examine some important issues relevant specifically to the European economy, such as the single European currency. The case studies and 'In the News' boxes also draw largely – but not exclusively – on European material. Since this is a book designed to teach students how to think about the world like an economist, analyses of particular institutional details are necessary primarily in order to illustrate the underlying economic principles, but we have used European institutional examples wherever possible. Where we have been forced to focus on a particular economy for reasons of space – for example in our discussion of the tax system – we have used the United Kingdom.

## HOW IS THIS BOOK ORGANIZED?

To write a brief and student-friendly book, we had to consider new ways to organize familiar material. What follows is a whirlwind tour of this text. The tour will, we hope, give instructors some sense of how the pieces fit together.

### Introductory Material

Chapter 1, 'Ten Principles of Economics', introduces students to the economists' view of the world. It previews some of the big ideas that recur throughout economics, such as opportunity cost, marginal decision making, the role of incentives, the gains from trade and the efficiency of market allocations. Throughout the book, we refer regularly to the *Ten Principles of Economics* introduced in Chapter 1 to remind students that these ideas are the foundation for all economics. An icon in the margin calls attention to these key, interconnected principles.

Chapter 2, 'Thinking Like an Economist', examines how economists approach their field of study. It discusses the role of assumptions in developing a theory and introduces the concept of an economic model. It also discusses the role of economists in making policy. The appendix to this chapter offers a brief refresher course on how graphs are used and how they can be abused.

Chapter 3, 'Interdependence and the Gains From Trade', presents the theory of comparative advantage. This theory explains why individuals trade with their neighbours, as well as why nations trade with other nations. Much of economics is about how market forces coordinate many individual production and consumption decisions. As a starting point for this analysis, students see in this chapter why specialization, interdependence and trade can benefit everyone.

## The Fundamental Tools of Supply and Demand

The next three chapters introduce the basic tools of supply and demand. Chapter 4, 'The Market Forces of Supply and Demand', develops the supply curve, the demand curve and the notion of market equilibrium. Chapter 5, 'Elasticity and Its Application', introduces the concept of elasticity and uses it to analyse events in three different markets. Chapter 6, 'Supply, Demand, and Government Policies', uses these tools to examine price controls, such as rent control and minimum wage laws, and tax incidence.

Chapter 7, 'Consumers, Producers and the Efficiency of Markets', extends the analysis of supply and demand using the concepts of consumer surplus and producer surplus. It begins by developing the link between consumers' willingness to pay and the demand curve, and the link between producers' costs of production and the supply curve. It then shows that the market equilibrium maximizes the sum of the producer and consumer surplus. Thus, students learn early about the efficiency of market allocations.

The next two chapters apply the concepts of producer and consumer surplus to questions of policy. Chapter 8, 'Application: The Costs of Taxation', shows why taxation results in deadweight losses and what determines the size of those losses. Chapter 9, 'Application: International Trade', considers who wins and who loses from international trade and presents the debate over protectionist trade policies.

## More Microeconomics

Having examined why market allocations are often desirable, the book then considers how the government can sometimes improve on them. Chapter 10, 'Externalities', explains how external effects such as pollution can render market outcomes inefficient and discusses the possible public and private solutions to those inefficiencies. Chapter 11, 'Public Goods and Common Resources', considers the problems that arise when goods, such as national defence, have no market price. Chapter 12, 'The Design of the Tax System', describes how the government raises the revenue necessary to pay for public goods. It presents some institutional background about the UK tax system and then discusses how the goals of efficiency and equity come into play when designing a tax system.

The next five chapters examine firm behaviour and industrial organization. Chapter 13, 'The Costs of Production', discusses what to include in a firm's costs, and it introduces cost curves. Chapter 14, 'Firms in Competitive Markets', analyses the behaviour of price-taking firms and derives the market supply curve. Chapter 15, 'Monopoly', discusses the behaviour of a firm that is the sole seller in its market. It discusses the inefficiency of monopoly pricing, the possible policy responses, and the attempts by monopolies to price discriminate. Chapter 16, 'Oligopoly', covers markets in which there are only a few sellers, using the prisoners' dilemma as the model for examining strategic interaction. Chapter 17, 'Monopolistic Competition', looks at behaviour in a market in which many sellers offer similar but differentiated products. It also discusses the debate over the effects of advertising.

The next three chapters present issues related to labour markets. Chapter 18, 'The Markets for the Factors of Production', emphasizes the link between factor prices and marginal productivity. Chapter 19, 'Earnings and Discrimination', discusses the determinants of equilibrium wages, including compensating differentials, human capital and discrimination. Chapter 20, 'Income Inequality and Poverty', examines the degree of inequality in UK society, alternative views about the government's role in changing the distribution of income and various policies aimed at helping society's poorest members.

The next two chapters present optional material. Chapter 21, 'The Theory of Consumer Choice', analyses individual decision making using budget constraints and indifference curves. Chapter 22, 'Frontiers of Microeconomics', introduces the topics of asymmetric information, political economy and behavioural economics. Many instructors may choose to omit all or some of this material. Instructors who do cover these topics may choose to assign these chapters earlier than they are presented in the book, and we have written them to give instructors flexibility.

## LEARNING TOOLS

The purpose of this book is to help students learn the fundamental lessons of economics and to show how such lessons can be applied to the world in which they live. Towards that end, we have used various learning tools that recur throughout the book:

- *Case studies.* Economic theory is useful and interesting only if it can be applied to understanding actual events and policies. This book, therefore, contains numerous case studies that apply the theory that has just been developed.
- *'In the News' boxes.* One benefit that students gain from studying economics is a new perspective and greater understanding about news from around the world. To highlight this benefit, we have included excerpts from many newspaper articles, some of which are opinion columns written by prominent economists. These articles, together with our brief introductions, show how basic economic theory can be applied.
- *'FYI' boxes.* These boxes provide additional material 'for your information'. Some of them offer a glimpse into the history of economic thought. Others clarify technical issues. Still others discuss supplementary topics that instructors might choose either to discuss or skip in their lectures.
- *Definitions of key concepts.* When key concepts are introduced in the chapter, they are presented in **bold** typeface. In addition, their definitions are placed in the margins. This treatment should aid students in learning and reviewing the material.
- *Quick quizzes.* After each major section, students are offered a 'quick quiz' to check their comprehension of what they have just learned. If students cannot readily answer these quizzes, they should stop and reread material before continuing.
- *Chapter summaries.* Each chapter ends with a brief summary that reminds students of the most important lessons that they have just learned. Later in their study it offers an efficient way to review for exams.
- *List of key concepts.* A list of key concepts at the end of each chapter offers students a way to test their understanding of the new terms that have been introduced. Page references are included so that students can review the terms they do not understand.
- *Questions for review.* At the end of each chapter are questions for review that cover the chapter's primary lessons. Students can use these questions to check their comprehension and to prepare for exams.
- *Problems and applications.* Each chapter also contains a variety of problems and applications that ask students to apply the material they have learned. Some professors may use these questions for homework assignments. Others may use them as a starting point for classroom discussions.

# WALK THROUGH TOUR

**Quick quizzes** are provided at the end of each section and allow students to check their comprehension of what they have just learned.

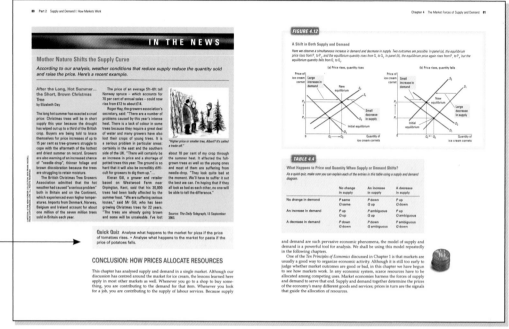

**Problems and applications** allow students to apply the material they have learned within the chapter. These can also be used for classroom discussions or homework assignments.

**Summaries** at the end of each chapter remind students of what they have learned so far, offering a useful way to review for exams.

**Questions for review** cover each chapter's primary lessons. These can be used to check comprehension and to prepare for exams.

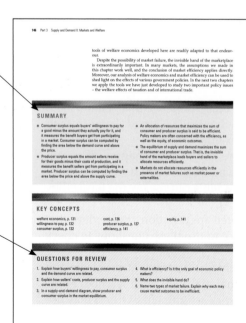

**FYI** provides additional material 'for your information'; the boxes offer a range of supplementary material, such as a glimpse into the history of economic thought, technical issues and current topics that can be discussed in lectures.

**Case studies** are provided throughout the text that apply the theory that has been developed to understanding events and policies.

**Ten Principles of Economics** references within the text are marked by a coin icon in the margin.

---

From these examples, you should now have a good understanding of how wages are set in competitive labour markets. Labour supply and labour demand together determine the equilibrium wage, and shifts in the supply or demand curve for labour cause the equilibrium wage to change. At the same time, profit maximization by the firms that demand labour ensures that the equilibrium wage always equals the value of the marginal product of labour.

### CASE STUDY

**Productivity and Wages**

One of the *Ten Principles of Economics* in Chapter 1 is that our standard of living depends on our ability to produce goods and services. We can now see how this principle works in the market for labour. In particular, our analysis of labour demand shows that wages equal productivity as measured by the value of the marginal product of labour. Put simply, highly productive workers are highly paid, and less productive workers are less highly paid.

This lesson is key to understanding why workers today are better off than workers in previous generations. Table 18.2 presents some data on growth in productivity and growth in real wages in the United Kingdom. From 1963 to 2003, productivity as measured by output per hour of work grew about 2.1 per cent per year. Real wages grew at almost the same rate: 2.0 per cent per year. With a growth rate of close to 2.0 per cent per year, productivity and real wages double about every 35 years.

Table 18.2 also shows the rates of growth for three shorter periods of time. Notice that from 1973 to 1995 growth in productivity, at 1.75 per cent per year, was slow compared to the period before 1973. Over the period 1995–2003, productivity growth slowed down even more, to about 1.6 per cent per year. The cause of the productivity slowdown in 1973 is not well understood, but the link between productivity and real wages that we find in the data is exactly as standard theory predicts. The slowdown in productivity growth from 2.8 to 1.75 per cent per year coincided with a slowdown in real wage growth from 3.1 to 1.5 per cent per year over the period 1973–95, and the growth in productivity over the more recent period of about 1.6 per cent was also reflected in a similar growth rate of real wages of 1.7 per cent per annum. Both theory and history confirm the close connection between productivity and real wages.

**TABLE 18.2**

Productivity and Wage Growth (%) in the United Kingdom

| Time period | Growth rate of productivity | Growth rate of real wages |
|---|---|---|
| 1963–2003 | 2.10 | 2.00 |
| 1963–1973 | 2.80 | 3.10 |
| 1973–1995 | 1.75 | 1.50 |
| 1995–2003 | 1.60 | 1.70 |

Source: UK Office for National Statistics. Growth in productivity is measured here as the annualized rate of change in output per worker. Growth in real wages is measured as the annualized change in average wages deflated by the Retail Price Index. These productivity data measure average productivity – the quantity of output divided by the quantity of labour – rather than marginal productivity, but average and marginal productivity are thought to move closely together.

**Quick Quiz** How does immigration of workers affect labour supply, labour demand, the marginal product of labour and the equilibrium wage?

### FYI

**Monopsony**

On the preceding pages, we built our analysis of the labour market with the tools of supply and demand. In doing so, we assumed that the labour market was competitive. That is, we assumed that there were many buyers of labour and many sellers of labour, so each buyer or seller had a negligible effect on the wage.

Yet imagine the labour market in a small town dominated by a single large employer. That employer can exert a large influence on the going wage, and it may well use that market power to alter the outcome. Such a market in which there is a single buyer is called a *monopsony*.

A monopsony (a market with one buyer) is in many ways similar to a monopoly (a market with one seller). Recall from Chapter 15 that a monopoly firm produces less of the good than would a competitive firm; by reducing the quantity offered for sale, the monopoly firm moves along the product's demand curve, raising the price and also its profits. Similarly, a monopsony firm in a labour market hires fewer workers than would a competitive firm; by reducing the number of jobs available, the monopsony firm moves along the labour supply curve, reducing the wage it pays and raising its profits. Thus, both monopolists and

monopsonists reduce economic activity in a market below the socially optimal level. In both cases, the existence of market power distorts the outcome and causes deadweight losses.

This book does not present the formal model of monopsony because, in the real world, monopsonies are rare. In most labour markets, workers have many possible employers, and firms compete with one another to attract workers. In this case, the model of supply and demand is the best one to use.

### THE OTHER FACTORS OF PRODUCTION: LAND AND CAPITAL

We have seen how firms decide how much labour to hire and how these decisions determine workers' wages. At the same time that firms are hiring workers, they are also deciding about other inputs to production. For example, our apple-producing firm might have to choose the size of its apple orchard and the number of ladders to make available to its apple pickers. We can think of the firm's factors of production as falling into three categories: labour, land and capital.

The meaning of the terms *labour* and *land* is clear, but the definition of *capital* is somewhat tricky. Economists use the term **capital** to refer to the stock of equipment and structures used for production. That is, the economy's capital represents the accumulation of goods produced in the past that are being used in the present to produce new goods and services. For our apple firm, the capital stock includes the ladders used to climb the trees, the trucks used to transport the apples, the buildings used to store the apples, and even the trees themselves.

**capital**
the equipment and structures used to produce goods and services

---

**'In the News'** excerpts from prominent world newspapers and magazines, include an introduction and show how basic economic theory can be applied.

in technological development were the Aztec and Mayan civilizations in the Americas, followed by the hunter-gatherers of Australia, and then the primitive people of Tasmania, who lacked even fire-making and most stone and bone tools.

The smallest isolated region was Flinders Island, a tiny island between Tasmania and Australia. With the smallest population, Flinders Island had the fewest opportunities for technological advance and, indeed, seemed to regress. Around 3000 B.C., human society on Flinders Island died out completely. A large population, Kremer concludes, is a prerequisite for technological advance.

At first sight this conclusion does seem to be at odds with casual empirical observation of the modern world: as we previously noted, in many rich, developed countries population growth has been only about 1 per cent per year in contrast to richer, while in many poor countries, such as those of sub-Saharan Africa, population growth is much higher. So why doesn't this higher population growth help these poor countries to grow, if Kremer's argument is right? The point is that Kremer was really analysing *world* economic growth, or rather, economic growth in isolated regions of the world. Nowadays, in a very poor country, it is unlikely that technological advances will be made that are not already known in developed countries; the problem is not lack of technological progress but difficulty in applying technology because of the scarcity of human capital and perhaps because of problems arising from political instability and corruption, as we discussed earlier. Moreover, because many talented people from less developed countries tend to emigrate to richer, developed countries where they may work, for example, as scientists or entrepreneurs – a phenomenon we referred to earlier as the *brain drain* – population growth in less developed countries may actually enhance economic growth in developed countries.

### IN THE NEWS

**A Solution to Africa's Problems**

*In 2000 the average income in sub-Saharan Africa was $480. Why? Here is the analysis of Jeffrey Sachs, an advisor to governments around the world and a critic of the World Bank and the International Monetary Fund (IMF), the international policy organizations that dispense advice and money to struggling countries.*

**Growth in Africa: It Can Be Done**
By Jeffrey Sachs

In the old story, the peasant goes to the priest for advice on saving his dying chickens. The priest recommends prayer, but the chickens continue to die. The priest then recommends music for the chicken coop, but the deaths continue unabated. Pondering again, the priest recommends repainting the

chicken coop in bright colors. Finally, all the chickens die. 'What a shame,' the priest tells the peasant. 'I had so many more good ideas.'

Since independence, African countries have looked to donor nations – often their former colonial rulers – and to the international finance institutions for guidance on growth. Indeed, since the onset of the African debt crisis of the 1980s, the guidance has provided a kind of economic receivership, with

the policies of many African nations decided in a seemingly endless cycle of advice from the IMF, the World Bank, donors and creditors.

What a shame. So many good ideas, so few results. ...

The IMF and World Bank would be absolved of shared responsibility for slow growth if Africa were structurally incapable of growth rates seen in other parts of the world or if the continent's low growth were an impenetrable

World leaders: can they help Africa?

mystery. But Africa's growth rates are not huge mysteries. ... Studies of cross-country growth show that per capita growth is related to:

- the initial income level of the country, with poorer countries tending to grow faster than richer ones;

- the extent of overall market orientation, including openness to trade, domestic market liberalization, private rather than state ownership, protection of private property rights, and low marginal tax rates;

- the national saving rate, which in turn is strongly affected by the government's own saving rate; and

- the geographic and resource structure of the economy. ...

These four factors can account broadly for Africa's long-term growth predicament. While it should have grown faster than other developing areas because of relatively low income per head (and hence larger opportunity for 'catch-up' growth), Africa grew more slowly. This was mainly because of much higher trade barriers; excessive tax rates; lower saving rates; and adverse structural conditions, including an unusually high incidence of inaccessibility to the sea (15 of 53 countries are landlocked). ...

provide modest support to African-based peacekeeping efforts.

'Easy taxes' are well within the ambit of the IMF and World Bank. But here, the IMF stands guilty of neglect, if not malfeasance. African nations need simple, low taxes, with modest revenue targets as a share of GDP. Easy taxes are most essential in international trade, since successful growth will depend, more than anything else, on economic integration with the rest of the world. Africa's largely self-imposed exile from world markets can end quickly by cutting import tariffs and ending export taxes on agricultural exports. Corporate tax rates should be cut. ...

Adam Smith spoke of a 'tolerable administration of justice, not perfect justice. Market liberalization is the primary key to strengthening the rule of law. Free trade, currency convertibility and automatic incorporation of business easily reduce the scope for official corruption and allow the government to focus on the real public goods – internal public order, the judicial system, basic public health and education, and monetary stability. ...

All of this is possible only if the government itself has held its own spending to the necessary minimum. ... Subsidies to publicly owned companies or marketing boards should be scrapped. Food and housing subsidies for urban workers cannot be financed. And, notably, interest payments on foreign debt are not budgeted for. This is because most bankrupt African states need a fresh start based on deep debt-reduction, which should be implemented in conjunction with far-reaching domestic reforms.

If the policies are largely to blame, why, then, were they adopted? The historical origins of Africa's antimarket orientation are not hard to discern. After almost a century of colonial depredations, African nations understandably if erroneously viewed open trade and foreign capital as a threat to national sovereignty. As in Sukarno's Indonesia, Nehru's India, and Peron's Argentina, 'self sufficiency' and 'state leadership', including state ownership of much of industry, became the guideposts of the economy. As a result, most of Africa went into a largely self-imposed economic exile.

Adam Smith in 1755 famously remarked that 'little else is requisite to carry a state to the highest degrees of opulence from the lowest barbarism, but peace, easy taxes, and tolerable administration of justice.' A growth agenda need not be long and complex. Take his points in turn.

Peace, of course, is not so easily guaranteed, but the conditions for peace on the continent are better than today's ghastly headlines would suggest. Several of the large-scale conflicts that have ravaged the continent are over or nearly so. ... The ongoing disasters, such as in Liberia, Rwanda and Somalia, would be better contained if the West were willing to

Source: *The Economist*, 29 June, 1996, pp. 19–21 Copyright ©1996 The Economist Newspaper Limited, London.

# SUPPLEMENTS

Thomson Learning offers various supplements for instructors and students who use this book. These resources make teaching the principles of economics easy for the professor and learning them easy for the student. The supplements have been written by Chris Downs of University College Chichester.

## FOR THE INSTRUCTOR

Teaching the principles of economics can be a demanding job. The supplements designed for the instructor make the job less difficult. All of the material listed below can be found on the supporting lecturers' side of the website which is password protected. The website can be found at www.thomsonlearning.co.uk/mankiw_taylor

### Instructor's Manual

For lecturer preparation, the Instructor's Manual offers a detailed outline for each chapter of the text that provides learning objectives, identifies stumbling blocks that students may face, offers helpful teaching tips and provides suggested in-classroom activities for a more cooperative learning experience. The Instructor's Manual also includes solutions to all end-of-chapter exercises, Quick Quizzes, Questions for Review, and Problems and Applications found in the text.

### PowerPoint Lecture and Exhibit Slides

Available only on the website are the two versions of the PowerPoint™ presentation. Professors can save valuable time as they prepare for class using this comprehensive lecture presentation. This supplement covers all the essential topics presented in each chapter of the book. Graphs, tables, lists and concepts are developed sequentially. Additional examples and applications are used to reinforce major lessons. Instructors may adapt or add slides to customize their lectures. A separate exhibit presentation provides instructors with all of the tables and graphs from the main text.

   Extra resources can also be found on the lecturers side of the site at www.thomsonlearning.co.uk/mankiw_taylor

## FOR THE STUDENT

The supplements designed for the student enrich and support the learning experience. All of the material listed below can be found on the student side of the website, which can be found at www.thomsonlearning.co.uk/mankiw_taylor

### Multiple Choice Questions

Allows the students to test their understanding of the key concepts learnt within the chapter. The questions provide the student with the correct/incorrect answer with instant feedback.

## Learning Objectives

Listed for each chapter, they help the student to monitor their understanding and progress through the chapter.

## Exhibit Slides

Provided in PowerPoint™ the exhibit presentation provides students with all of the tables and graphs from the main text.

## Glossary

A full glossary containing all key definitions within the text is included on the website.

Extra resources can also be found on the students' side of the site at www.thomsonlearning.co.uk/mankiw_taylor

# OTHER SUPPLEMENTARY RESOURCES

## Study Guide

Barry Harrison, of Nottingham Trent University, has prepared a guide that will enhance student success. Each chapter of the Study Guide includes learning objectives, a description of the chapter's context and purpose, a chapter review, key terms and definitions, advanced critical thinking questions, and helpful hints for understanding difficult concepts. Students can develop their understanding by doing the practice problems and short-answer questions and then assess their mastery of the key concepts with the self-test, which includes true/false and multiple-choice questions. Solutions to all problems are included in the Study Guide.

## CD Testbank

The computerized testing software contains numerous questions per chapter, which include multiple-choice, true/false and short-answer questions that assess students' critical thinking skills. Easy, medium and difficult questions outline the process that students must use to arrive at their answers: recall, application and integration. Questions are organized by text section to help instructors pick and choose their selections with ease. This program is easy-to-use test creation software compatible with Microsoft Windows. Instructors can add or edit questions, instructions and answers and can select questions by previewing them on the screen, selecting them randomly or selecting them by number. Instructors can also create and administer quizzes online, whether over the internet, a local area network (LAN) or a wide area network (WAN). This product is only available from your Thomson Learning sales representative.

## Virtual Learning Environment

All of the web material is available in a format that is compatible with virtual learning environments such as Blackboard and WebCT. This version of the product is only available from your Thomson Learning sales representative.

## TextChoice

TextChoice is the home of Thomson Learning's online digital content. It provides the fastest, easiest way for you to create your own learning materials. You may select content from hundreds of our best selling titles to make a custom text. Please contact your Thomson Learning sales representative to discuss further.

## Infotrac

This text is accompanied by a fully searchable on-line university library containing complete articles and their images. The database allows access to hundreds of scholarly and popular publications. Please contact your Thomson Learning sales representative to discuss how to access Infotrac.

## Mankiw Xtra!

**Mankiw Xtra! Website**  This site http://mankiwxtra.swlearning.com offers a robust set of on-line multimedia learning tools to help the student gain a deeper and richer understanding of economics.

- *Diagnostic Pretests* offer diagnostic self-assessment on student comprehension of each chapter and an individualized plan for directed study.
- *The MAP (Mankiw Learning Assistance Program)* privdes step-by-step instructions for each chapter's learning objectives to systematically guide the student to a deeper understanding of economic concepts.
- *The Graphic Workshop* is a one-stop learning resource for help in mastering the often difficult language of graphs. A unique learning system made up of graphing tutorials, interactive drawing tools, and exercises, it teaches the student how to interpret, reproduce, and explain graphs.
- *CNN Video Clips and Exercises* let the student see economics in action in the real world, to help learn theoretical material by applying it to current events.
- *Ask the Author Video Clips* provide the student with an opportunity for review and clarification of difficult material.
- *Xtra! Quizzing* allows the student to create and to take randomly generated quizzes on the chapter of his or her choice.
- *Economic Applications* (e-con apps), including EconNews Online, EconDebate Online, and EconData Online, features help to deepen student understanding of theoretical concepts through hands-on exploration and analysis of the latest economic news stories, policy debates and data.

This product is available through your Thomson Learning sales representative

## ExamView®

This testbank and test generator provides a huge amount of different types of questions, allowing lecturers to create online, paper and local area network (LAN) tests. This CD-based product is only available from your Thomson Learning sales representative.

## Virtual Learning Environment

All of the web material is available in a format that is compatible with virtual learning environments such as Blackboard and WebCT. This version of the product is only available from your Thomson Learning sales representative.

# ACCOMPANYING WEBSITE

Visit the *Economics* accompanying website at www.thomsonlearning.co.uk/mankiw_taylor to find the following further teaching and learning material.

## FOR STUDENTS

- Multiple Choice Questions for each chapter
- Glossary
- Exhibit Slides
- Learning Objectives

## FOR LECTURERS

- Instructors Manual
- PowerPoint™ Slides

Extra resources will also be added to the lecturers and students side of the site. Please bookmark and check regularly for updates.

# ACKNOWLEDGEMENTS

The authors would like to thank the following reviewers for their comments.

Robert Ackrill – Nottingham Trent University
Sverrir Arngīmsson – Iceland Engineering College
Michael Artis – European University Institute, Florence
Jürgen Bitzer –  Free University Berlin
Randy Bootland – Webster University
Phil Bowers – University of Edinburgh
Peter Clarke – University of Lincoln
Paul de Grauwe – Catholic University, Leuven
Kevin Denny – University College Dublin
Michael Devereux – University of Warwick
James Duncan – Robert Gordon University
Robert Eastwood – University of Sussex
Peter Else – University of Sheffield
Vanina Farber – Webster University, Geneva Campus
Heather Gage – University of Surrey
Erich Gundlach – Kiel Institute for World Economics/Helmut-Schmidt-
    University Hamburg
Bjarni Már Gylfason – Commercial College of Iceland
Heinz-Dieter Hardes – University of Trier
Bolli Héðinsson – Reykjavik University, Iceland
Andrew Henley – Swansea University
David Higgins – University of York
Hilary Ingham – Lancaster University
Ian Jackson – Staffordshire University
Brendan Kennelly – NUI Galway
Xander Koolman – Erasmus University Medical Centre
Richard Ledward – Staffordshire University
Michael J. McCrostie – University of Buckingham
Lukas Menkhoff – University of Hannover
Jonathan Michie – Professor of Management at the University of Birmingham
    and Director and Head of Birmingham Business School
Kerry Patterson – University of Reading
Martin Peitz – International University in Germany
Tom Segers – Group T Leuven Engineering School
Franz Seitz – University of Applied Sciences, Amberg-Weiden
Kunal Sen – University of East Anglia
Lorena Škuflic – University of Zagreb
Tilman Slembeck – University of St. Gallen and Zurich University of Applied Sciences
Ian Smith – University of St. Andrews
Remigiusez Smolinski – Leipzig Graduate School of Managment
Frank H. Stephen – Manchester School of Law
Kristan Sund – University of Applied Sciences, Chur
Benjamin Swalens – Vrije Universiteit Brussel
Oliver Taylor – University of Cambridge
Elise Tosi – Ceram EAItech
Linda Yueh – University of Oxford

The authors would like to thank Oliver Taylor for excellent research assistance.

1

# INTRODUCTION

# 1 TEN PRINCIPLES OF ECONOMICS

The word *economy* comes from the Greek word for 'one who manages a household'. At first, this origin might seem peculiar. But, in fact, households and economies have much in common.

A household faces many decisions. It must decide which members of the household do which tasks and what each member gets in return: Who cooks dinner? Who does the laundry? Who gets the extra slice of cake at tea time? Who chooses what TV programme to watch? In short, the household must allocate its scarce resources among its various members, taking into account each member's abilities, efforts and desires.

Like a household, a society faces many decisions. A society must decide what jobs will be done and who will do them. It needs some people to grow food, other people to make clothing and still others to design computer software. Once society has allocated people (as well as land, buildings and machines) to various jobs, it must also allocate the output of goods and services that they produce. It must decide who will eat caviar and who will eat potatoes. It must decide who will drive a Jaguar and who will take the bus.

The management of society's resources is important because resources are scarce. **Scarcity** means that society has limited resources and therefore cannot produce all the goods and services people wish to have. Just as a household cannot give every member everything he or she wants, a society cannot give every individual the highest standard of living to which he or she might aspire.

**Economics** is the study of how society manages its scarce resources. In most societies, resources are allocated not by a single central planner but through the

**scarcity**
the limited nature of society's resources

**economics**
the study of how society manages its scarce resources

3

combined actions of millions of households and firms. Economists therefore study how people make decisions: how much they work, what they buy, how much they save and how they invest their savings. Economists also study how people interact with one another. For instance, they examine how the multitude of buyers and sellers of a good together determine the price at which the good is sold and the quantity that is sold. Finally, economists analyse forces and trends that affect the economy as a whole, including the growth in average income, the fraction of the population that cannot find work and the rate at which prices are rising.

Although the study of economics has many facets, the field is unified by several central ideas. In the rest of this chapter we look at *Ten Principles of Economics*. Don't worry if you don't understand them all at first, or if you don't find them completely convincing. In the coming chapters we will explore these ideas more fully. The ten principles are introduced here just to give you an overview of what economics is all about. You can think of this chapter as a 'preview of coming attractions'.

## HOW PEOPLE MAKE DECISIONS

There is no mystery to what an 'economy' is. Whether we are talking about the economy of a group of countries such as the European Union, or the economy of one particular country, such as the United Kingdom, or of the whole world, an economy is just a group of people interacting with one another as they go about their lives. Because the behaviour of an economy reflects the behaviour of the individuals who make up the economy, we start our study of economics with four principles of individual decision making.

### Principle 1: People Face Trade-Offs

The first lesson about making decisions is summarized in an adage popular with economists: 'There is no such thing as a free lunch'. To get one thing that we like, we usually have to give up another thing that we also like. Making decisions requires trading off one goal against another.

Consider a student who must decide how to allocate her most valuable resource – her time. She can spend all of her time studying economics; she can spend all of her time studying psychology; or she can divide her time between the two fields. For every hour she studies one subject, she gives up an hour she could have used studying the other. And for every hour she spends studying, she gives up an hour that she could have spent in the gym, riding a bicycle, watching TV, napping or working at her part-time job for some extra spending money.

Or consider parents deciding how to spend their family income. They can buy food, clothing or a family holiday. Or they can save some of the family income for retirement or perhaps to help the children buy a house or a flat when they are grown up. When they choose to spend an extra euro on one of these goods, they have one less euro to spend on some other good.

When people are grouped into societies, they face different kinds of trade-offs. The classic trade-off is between 'guns and butter'. The more we spend on national defence (guns) to protect our shores from foreign aggressors, the less we can spend on consumer goods (butter) to raise our standard of living at home. Also important in modern society is the trade-off between a clean environment and a high level of income. Laws that require firms to reduce pollution raise the cost of producing goods and services. Because of the higher costs, these firms end up earning smaller profits, paying lower wages, charging higher prices, or some combination of these three. Thus, while pollution regulations give us the benefit of a cleaner environment and the improved levels of health that come with it, they have the cost of reducing the incomes of the firms' owners, workers and customers.

Another trade-off society faces is between efficiency and equity. **Efficiency** means that society is getting the most it can from its scarce resources. **Equity** means that the benefits of those resources are distributed fairly among society's members. In other words, efficiency refers to the size of the economic cake, and equity refers to how the cake is divided. Often, when government policies are being designed, these two goals conflict.

Consider, for instance, policies aimed at achieving a more equal distribution of economic well-being. Some of these policies, such as the social security system or unemployment insurance, try to help those members of society who are most in need. Others, such as the individual income tax, ask the financially successful to contribute more than others to support the government. Although these policies have the benefit of achieving greater equity, they have a cost in terms of reduced efficiency. When the government redistributes income from the rich to the poor, it reduces the reward for working hard; as a result, people work less and produce fewer goods and services. In other words, when the government tries to cut the economic cake into more equal slices, the cake gets smaller.

Recognizing that people face trade-offs does not by itself tell us what decisions they will or should make. A student should not abandon the study of psychology just because doing so would increase the time available for the study of economics. Society should not stop protecting the environment just because environmental regulations reduce our material standard of living. The poor should not be ignored just because helping them distorts work incentives. Nevertheless, acknowledging life's trade-offs is important because people are likely to make good decisions only if they understand the options that they have available.

**efficiency**
the property of society getting the most it can from its scarce resources
**equity**
the property of distributing economic prosperity fairly among the members of society

## Principle 2: The Cost of Something Is What You Give Up to Get It

Because people face trade-offs, making decisions requires comparing the costs and benefits of alternative courses of action. In many cases, however, the cost of some action is not as obvious as it might first appear.

Consider, for example, the decision whether to go to university. The benefit is intellectual enrichment and a lifetime of better job opportunities. But what is the cost? To answer this question, you might be tempted to add up the money you spend on tuition fees, books, room and board. Yet this total does not truly represent what you give up to spend a year at university.

The first problem with this answer is that it includes some things that are not really costs of going to university. Even if you decided to leave full-time education, you would still need a place to sleep and food to eat. Room and board are part of the costs of higher education only to the extent that they are more expensive at university than elsewhere. Indeed, the cost of room and board at your university might be less than the rent and food expenses that you would pay living on your own. In this case, the savings on room and board are actually a benefit of going to university.

The second problem with this calculation of costs is that it ignores the largest cost of a university education – your time. When you spend a year listening to lectures, reading text books and writing essays, you cannot spend that time working at a job. For most students, the wages given up to attend university are the largest single cost of their higher education.

**opportunity cost**
whatever must be given up to obtain some item

The **opportunity cost** of an item is what you give up to get that item. When making any decision, such as whether to go to university, decision makers should be aware of the opportunity costs that accompany each possible action. In fact, they usually are. University-age footballers who can earn millions if they opt out of higher education and play professional football are well aware that their opportunity cost of going to university is very high. It is not surprising that they often decide that the benefit is not worth the cost.

## Principle 3: Rational People Think at the Margin

Decisions in life are rarely black and white but usually involve shades of grey. At dinner time, the decision you face is not between fasting or eating like a pig, but whether to take that extra serving of chips. When examinations roll around, your decision is not between completely failing them or studying 24 hours a day, but whether to spend an extra hour revising your notes instead of watching TV. Economists use the term **marginal changes** to describe small incremental adjustments to an existing plan of action. Keep in mind that 'margin' means 'edge', so marginal changes are adjustments around the edges of what you are doing.

**marginal changes**
small incremental adjustments to a plan of action

In many situations, people make the best decisions by thinking at the margin. Suppose, for instance, that you asked a friend for advice about how many years to stay in education. If he were to compare for you the lifestyle of a person with a Ph.D. to that of someone who finished secondary school with no qualifications, you might complain that this comparison is not helpful for your decision. Perhaps you have already been at university for a few years but you're getting a little tired of studying and being broke and so you're deciding whether or not to stay on for that last year. To make this decision, you need to know the additional benefits that an extra year in education would offer (higher wages throughout your life and the sheer joy of learning) and the additional costs that you would incur (another year of tuition fees and another year of foregone wages). By comparing these *marginal benefits* and *marginal costs,* you can evaluate whether the extra year is worthwhile.

As another example, consider an airline company deciding how much to charge passengers who fly standby. Suppose that flying a 200-seat aeroplane from London to Warsaw costs the airline €100,000. In this case, the average cost of each seat is €100,000/200, which is €500. One might be tempted to conclude that the airline should never sell a ticket for less than €500. In fact, however, the airline can raise its profits by thinking at the margin. Imagine that a plane is about to take off with ten empty seats, and a standby passenger is waiting at the gate willing to pay €300 for a seat. Should the airline sell it to him? Of course it should. If the plane has empty seats, the cost of adding one more passenger is minuscule. Although the *average* cost of flying a passenger is €500, the *marginal* cost is merely the cost of the airline meal that the extra passenger will consume (which may have gone to waste in any case) and possibly an extremely slight increase in the amount of aircraft fuel used. As long as the standby passenger pays more than the marginal cost, selling him a ticket is profitable.

As these examples show, individuals and firms can make better decisions by thinking at the margin. A rational decision maker takes an action if and only if the marginal benefit of the action exceeds the marginal cost.

## Principle 4: People Respond to Incentives

Because people make decisions by comparing costs and benefits, their behaviour may change when the costs or benefits change. That is, people respond to incentives. When the price of an apple rises, for instance, people decide to eat more pears and fewer apples because the cost of buying an apple is higher. At the same time, apple orchards decide to hire more workers and harvest more apples, because the benefit of selling an apple is also higher. As we shall see, the effect of price on the behaviour of buyers and sellers in a market – in this case, the market for apples – is crucial for understanding how the economy works.

Public policy makers should never forget about incentives, because many policies change the costs or benefits that people face and, therefore, alter behaviour. A tax on petrol, for instance, encourages people to drive smaller, more fuel-efficient cars. It also encourages people to use public transport rather than drive and to live closer to where they work. If the tax were large enough, people would start driving electric cars.

When policy makers fail to consider how their policies affect incentives, they often end up with results they did not intend. For example, consider public policy regarding motor vehicle safety. Today all cars sold in the European Union have to have seat belts fitted by law (although actual seat belt use – especially by rear-seat passengers – varies widely, with official estimates ranging from about 30 per cent of car occupants in some member states to around 90 per cent in others, notably Sweden).

How does a seat belt law affect car safety? The direct effect is obvious: when a person wears a seat belt, the probability of surviving a major car accident rises. But that's not the end of the story, for the law also affects behaviour by altering incentives. The relevant behaviour here is the speed and care with which drivers operate their cars. Driving slowly and carefully is costly because it uses the driver's time and energy. When deciding how safely to drive, rational people compare the marginal benefit from safer driving to the marginal cost. They drive more slowly and carefully when the benefit of increased safety is high. It is no surprise, for instance, that people drive more slowly and carefully when roads are icy than when roads are clear.

Consider how a seat belt law alters a motorist's cost–benefit calculation. Seat belts make accidents less costly because they reduce the likelihood of injury or death. In other words, seat belts reduce the benefits to slow and careful driving. People respond to seat belts as they would to an improvement in road conditions – by faster and less careful driving. The end result of a seat belt law, therefore, is a larger number of accidents and so it will affect both motorists and pedestrians. The decline in safe driving has a clear, adverse impact on pedestrians, who are more likely to find themselves in an accident but (unlike the motorists) don't have the benefit of added protection.

At first, this discussion of incentives and seat belts might seem like idle speculation. Yet a 1981 study of seat belt laws in eight European countries commissioned by the UK Department of Transport showed that the laws did appear to have had many of these effects. Similar evidence was also presented in a 1975 study of US seat belt laws by the American economist Sam Peltzman. It does indeed seem that seat belt laws produce both fewer deaths per accident and more accidents. The net result is little change in the number of motorist deaths and an increase in the number of pedestrian deaths.

This is an example of the general principle that people respond to incentives. Many incentives that economists study are more straightforward than those of the car-safety laws. No one is surprised that people drive smaller cars in Europe, where petrol taxes are relatively high, than in the United States, where petrol

Rock star Mick Jagger understood opportunity cost and incentives. After doing well at school and studying economics for a year at the London School of Economics, he decided not to continue in full-time education and finish his degree but to concentrate on his music career with the Rolling Stones, and has earned millions.

PHOTO: COPYRIGHT © REUTERS/CORBIS

taxes are lower. Yet, as the seat belt example shows, policies can have effects that are not obvious in advance. When analysing any policy, we must consider not only the direct effects but also the indirect effects that work through incentives. If the policy changes incentives, it will cause people to alter their behaviour.

> **Quick Quiz** List and briefly explain the four principles of individual decision making.

## HOW PEOPLE INTERACT

The first four principles discussed how individuals make decisions. As we go about our lives, many of our decisions affect not only ourselves but other people as well. The next three principles concern how people interact with one another.

### Principle 5: Trade Can Make Everyone Better Off

The Americans and the Japanese are often mentioned in the news as being competitors to Europeans in the world economy. In some ways this is true, because American and Japanese firms do produce many of the same goods as European firms. Airbus and Boeing compete for the same customers in the market for aircraft. Toyota and Citroën compete for the same customers in the market for cars.

Yet it is easy to be misled when thinking about competition among countries. Trade between Europe and the United States or between Europe and Japan is not like a sports contest, where one side wins and the other side loses. In fact, the opposite is true: trade between two economies can make each economy better off.

To see why, consider how trade affects your family. When a member of your family looks for a job, he or she competes against members of other families who

*"You'll have to look harder than that to find a job, son."*

are looking for jobs. Families also compete against one another when they go shopping, because each family wants to buy the best goods at the lowest prices. So, in a sense, each family in the economy is competing with all other families.

Despite this competition, your family would not be better off isolating itself from all other families. If it did, your family would need to grow its own food, make its own clothes and build its own home. Clearly, your family gains much from its ability to trade with others. Trade allows each person to specialize in the activities he or she does best, whether it is farming, sewing or home building. By trading with others, people can buy a greater variety of goods and services at lower cost.

Countries as well as families benefit from the ability to trade with one another. Trade allows countries to specialize in what they do best and to enjoy a greater variety of goods and services. The Japanese and the Americans, as well as the Egyptians and the Brazilians, are as much our partners in the world economy as they are our competitors.

## Principle 6: Markets Are Usually a Good Way to Organize Economic Activity

The collapse of communism in the Soviet Union and Eastern Europe in the 1980s may be the most important change in the world during the past half century. Communist countries worked on the premise that central planners in the government were in the best position to guide economic activity. These planners decided what goods and services were produced, how much was produced, and who produced and consumed these goods and services. The theory behind central planning was that only the government could organize economic activity in a way that promoted economic well-being for the country as a whole.

Today, most countries that once had centrally planned economies have abandoned this system and are trying to develop market economies. In a **market economy,** the decisions of a central planner are replaced by the decisions of millions of firms and households. Firms decide whom to hire and what to make. Households decide which firms to work for and what to buy with their incomes. These firms and households interact in the marketplace, where prices and self-interest guide their decisions.

**market economy**
an economy that allocates resources through the decentralized decisions of many firms and households as they interact in markets for goods and services

At first glance, the success of market economies is puzzling. After all, in a market economy, no one is considering the economic well-being of society as a whole. Free markets contain many buyers and sellers of numerous goods and services, and all of them are interested primarily in their own well-being. Yet, despite decentralized decision making and self-interested decision makers, market economies have proven remarkably successful in organizing economic activity in a way that promotes overall economic well-being.

In his 1776 book *An Inquiry Into the Nature and Causes of the Wealth of Nations,* the British economist Adam Smith made the most famous observation in all of economics: households and firms interacting in markets act as if they are guided by an 'invisible hand' that leads them to desirable market outcomes. One of our goals in this book is to understand how this invisible hand works its magic. As you study economics, you will learn that prices are the instrument with which the invisible hand directs economic activity. Prices reflect both the value of a good to society and the cost to society of making the good. Because households and firms look at prices when deciding what to buy and sell, they unknowingly take into account the social benefits and costs of their actions. As a result, prices guide these individual decision makers to reach outcomes that, in many cases, maximize the welfare of society as a whole.

## Adam Smith and the Invisible Hand

Adam Smith's great work *The Wealth of Nations* was published in 1776 and is a landmark in economics. In its emphasis on the invisible hand of the market economy, it reflected a point of view that was typical of so-called 'enlightenment' writers at the end of the 18th century – that individuals are usually best left to their own devices, without the heavy hand of government guiding their actions. This political philosophy provides the intellectual basis for the market economy.

Why do decentralized market economies work so well? Is it because people can be counted on to treat one another with love and kindness? Not at all. Here is Adam Smith's description of how people interact in a market economy:

*Man has almost constant occasion for the help of his brethren, and it is vain for him to expect it from their benevolence only. He will be more likely to prevail if he can interest their self-love in his favour, and show them that it is for their own advantage to do for him what he requires of them. … It is not from the benevolence of the butcher, the brewer, or the baker that we expect our dinner, but from their regard to their own interest. …*

*Every individual … neither intends to promote the public interest, nor knows how much he is promoting it. … He*

*Adam Smith*

*intends only his own gain, and he is in this, as in many other cases, led by an invisible hand to promote an end which was no part of his intention. Nor is it always the worse for the society that it was no part of it. By pursuing his own interest he frequently promotes that of the society more effectually than when he really intends to promote it.*

Smith is saying that participants in the economy are motivated by self-interest and that the 'invisible hand' of the marketplace guides this self-interest into promoting general economic well-being.

Many of Smith's insights remain at the centre of modern economics. Our analysis in the coming chapters will allow us to express Smith's conclusions more precisely and to analyze fully the strengths and weaknesses of the market's invisible hand.

There is an important corollary to the skill of the invisible hand in guiding economic activity: when the government prevents prices from adjusting naturally to supply and demand, it impedes the invisible hand's ability to coordinate the millions of households and firms that make up the economy. This corollary explains why taxes adversely affect the allocation of resources: taxes distort prices and thus the decisions of households and firms. It also explains the even greater harm caused by policies that directly control prices, such as rent control. And it also explains the failure of communism. In communist countries, prices were not determined in the marketplace but were dictated by central planners. These planners lacked the information that gets reflected in prices when prices are free to respond to market forces. Central planners failed because they tried to run the economy with one hand tied behind their backs – the invisible hand of the marketplace.

### Principle 7: Governments Can Sometimes Improve Market Outcomes

If the invisible hand of the market is so wonderful, why do we need government? One answer is that the invisible hand needs government to protect it. Markets work only if property rights are enforced. A farmer won't grow food if he expects his crop to be stolen, and a restaurant won't serve meals unless it is assured that customers will pay before they leave. We all rely on government-provided police and courts to enforce our rights over the things we produce.

Yet there is another answer to why we need government: although markets are usually a good way to organize economic activity, this rule has some important exceptions. There are two broad reasons for a government to intervene in the economy – to promote efficiency and to promote equity. That is, most policies aim either to enlarge the economic cake or to change the way in which the cake is divided.

Although the invisible hand usually leads markets to allocate resources efficiently, that is not always the case. Economists use the term **market failure** to refer to a situation in which the market on its own fails to produce an efficient allocation of resources. One possible cause of market failure is an **externality**, which is the uncompensated impact of one person's actions on the well-being of a bystander. For instance, the classic example of an external cost is pollution. Another possible cause of market failure is **market power,** which refers to the ability of a single person (or small group) to unduly influence market prices. For example, if everyone in a remote village in the Scottish Highlands needs water but there is only one well, the owner of the well is not subject to the rigorous competition with which the invisible hand normally keeps self-interest in check. In the presence of externalities or market power, well designed public policy can enhance economic efficiency.

The invisible hand may also fail to ensure that economic prosperity is distributed equitably. A market economy rewards people according to their ability to produce things for which other people are willing to pay. The world's best footballer earns more than the world's best chess player simply because people are willing to pay more to watch football than chess. The invisible hand does not ensure that everyone has sufficient food, decent clothing and adequate health care. Many public policies, such as income tax and the social security system, aim to achieve a more equitable distribution of economic well-being.

To say that the government *can* improve on market outcomes at times does not mean that it always *will*. Public policy is made not by angels but by a political process that is far from perfect. Sometimes policies are designed simply to reward the politically powerful. Sometimes they are made by well intentioned leaders who are not fully informed. One goal of the study of economics is to help you judge when a government policy is justifiable to promote efficiency or equity, and when it is not.

**market failure**
a situation in which a market left on its own fails to allocate resources efficiently

**externality**
the uncompensated impact of one person's actions on the well-being of a bystander

**market power**
the ability of a single economic agent (or small group of agents) to have a substantial influence on market prices

> **Quick Quiz** List and briefly explain the three principles concerning economic interactions.

# HOW THE ECONOMY AS A WHOLE WORKS

We started by discussing how individuals make decisions and then looked at how people interact with one another. All these decisions and interactions together make up 'the economy'. The last three principles concern the workings of the economy as a whole.

## Principle 8: An Economy's Standard of Living Depends on Its Ability to Produce Goods and Services

In 2000 the average annual income per head of population in each of the UK, France and Germany was about €24,000, while it was somewhat lower in Spain (around €19,000) and in Greece (about €15,500), a little higher in Ireland (around €27,000) and an enviable €49,000 in Luxembourg. These figures compare with an income per person of about €36,000 in the USA and €28,700 in Canada in 2000. But once we move away from the prosperous economies of Western Europe and North America, we begin to see differences in income and living standards around the world that are quite staggering. For example, in the same year, 2000, average income in Argentina was slightly less than half the level in the UK, while in India it was about €2,700 and in Ethiopia it was only about €720 – about 1.5 per cent of the annual income per person in Luxembourg! Not surprisingly, this large variation in average income is reflected in various other measures of the quality of life and standard of living. Citizens of high-income countries have better nutrition, better health care and longer life expectancy than citizens of low-income countries, as well as more TV sets, more DVD players and more cars.

Changes in living standards over time are also large. Over the last 50 years, average incomes in Western Europe and North America have grown at about 2 per cent per year (after adjusting for changes in the cost of living). At this rate, average income doubles every 35 years, and over the last half-century average income in many of these prosperous economies has risen approximately three-fold. On the other hand, average income in Ethiopa rose by only a third over this period – an average annual growth rate of around only 0.6 per cent.

**productivity**
the quantity of goods and services produced from each hour of a worker's time

What explains these large differences in living standards among countries and over time? The answer is surprisingly simple. Almost all variation in living standards is attributable to differences in countries' **productivity** – that is, the amount of goods and services produced from each hour of a worker's time. In nations where workers can produce a large quantity of goods and services per unit of time, most people enjoy a high standard of living; in nations where workers are less productive, most people must endure a more meagre existence. Similarly, the growth rate of a nation's productivity determines the growth rate of its average income.

The fundamental relationship between productivity and living standards is simple, but its implications are far-reaching. If productivity is the primary determinant of living standards, other explanations must be of secondary importance. For example, it might be tempting to credit trades unions or minimum wage laws for the rise in living standards of European workers over the past 50 years. Yet the real hero of European workers is their rising productivity.

The relationship between productivity and living standards also has profound implications for public policy. When thinking about how any policy will affect living standards, the key question is how it will affect our ability to produce goods and services. To boost living standards, policy makers need to raise productivity by ensuring that workers are well educated, have the tools needed to produce goods and services, and have access to the best available technology.

## Principle 9: Prices Rise When the Government Prints Too Much Money

In Germany in January 1921, a daily newspaper cost 0.30 marks. Less than two years later, in November 1922, the same newspaper cost 70,000,000 marks. All other prices in the economy rose by similar amounts. This episode is one of history's most spectacular examples of **inflation,** an increase in the overall level of prices in the economy.

While inflation in Western Europe and North America has been much lower over the last 50 years than that experienced in Germany in the 1920s, inflation has at times been an economic problem. During the 1970s, for instance, the overall level of prices in the UK more than tripled. By contrast, UK inflation in the 1990s was about 3 per cent per year; at this rate it would take more than 20 years for prices to double. Because high inflation imposes various costs on society, keeping inflation at a low level is a goal of economic policy makers around the world.

What causes inflation? In almost all cases of high or persistent inflation, the culprit turns out to be the same – growth in the quantity of money. When a government creates large quantities of the nation's money, the value of the money falls. In Germany in the early 1920s, when prices were on average tripling every month, the quantity of money was also tripling every month. Although less dramatic, the economic history of other European and North American countries points to a similar conclusion: the high inflation of the 1970s was associated with rapid growth in the quantity of money and the low inflation of the 1990s was associated with slow growth in the quantity of money.

**inflation**
an increase in the overall level of prices in the economy

*"… but if daddy raised your allowance he'd be hurting the economy by stimulating inflation. You wouldn't want him to do that, would you?"*

## Principle 10: Society Faces a Short-Run Trade-Off Between Inflation and Unemployment

When the government increases the amount of money in the economy, one result is inflation. Another result, at least in the short run, is a lower level of unemployment. The curve that illustrates this short-run trade-off between inflation and unemployment is called the **Phillips curve**, after the economist who first examined this relationship while working at the London School of Economics.

**Phillips curve**
a curve that shows the short-run trade-off between inflation and unemployment

The Phillips curve remains a controversial topic among economists, but most economists today accept the idea that society faces a short-run trade-off between inflation and unemployment. This simply means that, over a period of a year or two, many economic policies push inflation and unemployment in opposite directions. Policy makers face this trade-off regardless of whether inflation and unemployment both start out at high levels (as they were in the early 1980s), at low levels (as they were in the late 1990s) or somewhere in between.

The trade-off between inflation and unemployment is only temporary, but it can last for several years. The Phillips curve is, therefore, crucial for understanding many developments in the economy. In particular, it is important for understanding the **business cycle** – the irregular and largely unpredictable fluctuations in economic activity, as measured by the number of people employed or the production of goods and services.

**business cycle**
fluctuations in economic activity, such as employment and production

Policy makers can exploit the short-run trade-off between inflation and unemployment using various policy instruments. By changing the amount that the government spends, the amount it taxes and the amount of money it prints, policy makers can influence the combination of inflation and unemployment that the economy experiences. Because these instruments of monetary and fiscal policy are potentially so powerful, how policy makers should use these instruments to control the economy, if at all, is a subject of continuing debate.

> **Quick Quiz** List and briefly explain the three principles that describe how the economy as a whole works.

**TABLE 1.1**

**Ten Principles of Economics**

| How people make decisions | 1. People face trade-offs |
| | 2. The cost of something is what you give up to get it |
| | 3. Rational people think at the margin |
| | 4. People respond to incentives |
| How people interact | 5. Trade can make everyone better off |
| | 6. Markets are usually a good way to organize economic activity |
| | 7. Governments can sometimes improve market outcomes |
| How the economy as a whole works | 8. A country's standard of living depends on its ability to produce goods and services |
| | 9. Prices rise when the government prints too much money |
| | 10. Society faces a short-run trade-off between inflation and unemployment |

## F Y I

### How To Read This Book

Economics is fun, but it can also be hard to learn. Our aim in writing this text has been to make it as easy and as much fun as possible. But you, the student, also have a role to play. Experience shows that if you are actively involved as you study this book, you will enjoy a better outcome, both in your exams and in the years that follow. Here are a few tips about how best to read this book.

1. *Summarize, don't highlight.* Running a yellow marker over the text is too passive an activity to keep your mind engaged. Instead, when you come to the end of a section, take a minute and summarize what you have just learnt in your own words, writing your summary in the wide margins we've provided. When you've finished the chapter, compare your summary with the one at the end of the chapter. Did you pick up the main points?

2. *Test yourself.* Throughout the book, Quick Quizzes offer instant feedback to find out if you've learned what you are supposed to. Take the opportunity. Write your answer in the book's margin. The quizzes are meant to test your basic comprehension. If you aren't sure your answer is right, you probably need to review the section.

3. *Practice, practice, practice.* At the end of each chapter, Questions for Review test your understanding, and Problems and Applications ask you to apply and extend the material. Perhaps your lecturer will assign some of these exercises as coursework. If so, do them. If not, do them anyway. The more you use your new knowledge, the more solid it becomes.

4. *Study in groups.* After you've read the book and worked through the problems on your own, get together with other students to discuss the material. You will learn from each other – an example of the gains from trade.

5. *Don't forget the real world.* In the midst of all the numbers, graphs and strange new words, it is easy to lose sight of what economics is all about. The Case Studies and In the News boxes sprinkled throughout this book should help remind you. Don't skip them. They show how the theory is tied to events happening in all of our lives. If your study is successful, you won't be able to read a newspaper again without thinking about supply, demand and the wonderful world of economics.

## CONCLUSION

You now have a taste of what economics is all about. In the coming chapters we will develop many specific insights about people, markets and economies. Mastering these insights will take some effort, but it is not an overwhelming task. The field of economics is based on a few basic ideas that can be applied in many different situations.

Throughout this book we will refer back to the *Ten Principles of Economics* highlighted in this chapter and summarized in Table 1.1. Whenever we do so, an icon will be displayed in the margin, as it is now. But even when that icon is absent, you should keep these building blocks in mind. Even the most sophisticated economic analysis is built using the ten principles introduced here.

## SUMMARY

- The fundamental lessons about individual decision making are that people face trade-offs among alternative goals, that the cost of any action is measured in terms of foregone opportunities, that rational people make decisions by comparing marginal costs and marginal benefits, and that people change their behaviour in response to the incentives they face.

- The fundamental lessons about interactions among people are that trade can be mutually beneficial, that markets are usually a good way of coordinating trade among people, and that the government can potentially improve market outcomes if there is some market failure or if the market outcome is inequitable.

- The fundamental lessons about the economy as a whole are that productivity is the ultimate source of living standards, that money growth is the ultimate source of inflation, and that society faces a short-run trade-off between inflation and unemployment.

## KEY CONCEPTS

scarcity, p. 3
economics, p. 3
efficiency, p. 5
equity, p. 5
opportunity cost, p. 6

marginal changes, p. 6
market economy, p. 9
market failure, p. 11
externality, p. 11
market power, p. 11

productivity, p. 12
inflation, p. 13
Phillips curve, p. 14
business cycle, p. 14

## QUESTIONS FOR REVIEW

1. Give three examples of important trade-offs that you face in your life.
2. What is the opportunity cost of going to the cinema to see a film?
3. Water is necessary for life. Is the marginal benefit of a glass of water large or small?
4. Why should policy makers think about incentives?
5. Why isn't trade among countries like a game, with some winners and some losers?
6. What does the 'invisible hand' of the marketplace do?
7. Explain the two main causes of market failure and give an example of each.
8. Why is productivity important?
9. What is inflation, and what causes it?
10. How are inflation and unemployment related in the short run?

## PROBLEMS AND APPLICATIONS

1. Describe some of the trade-offs faced by each of the following.
   a. A family deciding whether to buy a new car.
   b. A member of the government deciding how much to spend on building a new national football stadium.
   c. A company chief executive officer deciding whether to open a new factory.
   d. A university lecturer deciding how much to prepare for her lecture.

2. You are trying to decide whether to take a holiday. Most of the costs of the holiday (airfare, hotel, foregone wages) are measured in euros, but the benefits of the holiday are psychological. How can you compare the benefits to the costs?

3. You were planning to spend Saturday working at your part-time job, but a friend asks you to go to a football match. What is the true cost of going to the football match? Now suppose that you had been planning to spend the day studying in the library. What is the cost of going to the football match in this case? Explain.

4. You win €1,000 in the National Lottery. You have a choice between spending the money now or putting it away for a year in a bank account that pays 5 per cent interest. What is the opportunity cost of spending the €1,000 now?

5. The company that you manage has invested €5 million in developing a new product, but the development is not quite finished. At a recent meeting, your sales people report that the introduction of competing products has reduced the expected sales of your new product to €3 million. If it would cost €1 million to finish development and make the product, should you go ahead and do so? What is the most that you should pay to complete development?

6. Three managers of the Hubble Bubble Magic Potion Company are discussing a possible increase in production. Each suggests a way to make this decision.

   First Witch: When shall we three meet again? We need to decide how much Magic Potion to produce. Personally, I think we should examine whether our company's productivity – litres of potion per worker – would rise or fall if we increased output.

   Second Witch: We should examine whether our average cost – cost per worker – would rise or fall.

   Third Witch: We should examine whether the extra revenue from selling the additional potion would be greater or smaller than the extra costs.

   Who do you think is right? Why?

7. The social security system provides income for people over the age of 65. If a recipient of social security decides to work and earn some income, the amount he or she receives in social security benefits is typically reduced.
   a. How does the provision of social security affect people's incentive to save while working?
   b. How does the reduction in benefits associated with higher earnings affect people's incentive to work past age 65?

8. Your flat-mate is a better cook than you are, but you can clean more quickly than your flat-mate can. If your flat-mate did all of the cooking and you did all of the cleaning, would your household chores take you more or less time than if you divided each task evenly? Give a similar example of how specialization and trade can make two countries both better off.

9. Suppose the European Union adopted central planning for its economy, and you became the Chief Planner. Among the millions of decisions that you need to make for next year are how many CDs to produce, what artists to record and who should receive the CDs.
   a. To make these decisions intelligently, what information would you need about the CD industry? What information would you need about each of the people in the countries making up the European Union?
   b. How would your decisions about CDs affect some of your other decisions, such as how many CD players to make or cassette tapes to produce? How might some of your other decisions about the economy change your views about CDs?

10. Explain whether each of the following government activities is motivated by a concern about equity or a concern about efficiency. In the case of efficiency, discuss the type of market failure involved.
    a. Regulating water prices.
    b. Regulating electricity prices.
    c. Providing some poor people with vouchers that can be used to buy food.
    d. Prohibiting smoking in public places.
    e. Imposing higher personal income tax rates on people with higher incomes.
    f. Instituting laws against drunk driving.

11. Discuss each of the following statements from the standpoints of equity and efficiency.
    a. 'Everyone in society should be guaranteed the best health care possible.'

b. 'When workers are laid off, they should be able to collect unemployment benefits until they find a new job.'

12. In what ways is your standard of living different from that of your parents or grandparents when they were your age? Why have these changes occurred?

13. Suppose Europeans decide to save more of their incomes. If banks lend this extra saving to European businesses, which use the funds to build new European factories, how might this lead to faster growth in European productivity? Who do you suppose benefits from the higher productivity? Is society getting a free lunch?

14. Imagine that you are a policy maker trying to decide whether to reduce the rate of inflation in your country. To make an intelligent decision, what would you need to know about inflation, unemployment and the trade-off between them?

15. Look at a newspaper or at the website http://www.economist.com to find three stories about the economy that have been in the news lately. For each story, identify one (or more) of the *Ten Principles of Economics* discussed in this chapter that is relevant, and explain how it is relevant. Also, for each story, look through this book's table of contents and try to find a chapter that might shed light on the news event.

 For further resources, visit
http://www.thomsonlearning.co.uk/mankiw_taylor

# 2 THINKING LIKE AN ECONOMIST

Every field of study has its own language and its own way of thinking. Mathematicians talk about axioms, integrals and vector spaces. Psychologists talk about ego, id and cognitive dissonance. Medics talk about dyspnoea, claudication and myocardial infarction. Lawyers talk about venue, torts and promissory estoppel.

Economics is no different. Supply, demand, elasticity, comparative advantage, consumer surplus, deadweight loss – these terms are part of the economist's language. In the coming chapters, you will encounter many new terms and some familiar words that economists use in specialized ways. At first, this new language may seem needlessly arcane. But, as you will see, its value lies in its ability to provide you with a new and useful way of thinking about the world in which you live.

The single most important purpose of this book is to help you learn the economist's way of thinking. Of course, just as you cannot become a mathematician, psychologist, medical doctor or lawyer overnight, learning to think like an economist will take some time. Yet with a combination of theory, case studies and examples of economics in the news, this book will give you ample opportunity to develop and practise this skill.

Before delving into the substance and details of economics, it is helpful to have an overview of how economists approach the world. This chapter, therefore, discusses the field's methodology. What is distinctive about how economists confront a question? What does it mean to think like an economist?

# THE ECONOMIST AS SCIENTIST

Economists try to address their subject with a scientist's objectivity. They approach the study of the economy in much the same way as a physicist approaches the study of matter and a biologist approaches the study of life: they devise theories, collect data, and then analyse these data in an attempt to verify or refute their theories.

To beginners, it can seem odd to claim that economics is a science. After all, economists do not work with test tubes or telescopes. The essence of science, however, is the *scientific method* – the dispassionate development and testing of theories about how the world works. This method of inquiry is as applicable to studying a nation's economy as it is to studying the earth's gravity or a species' evolution. As Albert Einstein once put it, 'The whole of science is nothing more than the refinement of everyday thinking.'

Although Einstein's comment is as true for social sciences such as economics as it is for natural sciences such as physics, most people are not accustomed to looking at society through the eyes of a scientist. Let's therefore discuss some of the ways in which economists apply the logic of science to examine how an economy works.

## The Scientific Method: Observation, Theory and More Observation

Isaac Newton, the famous English 17th century scientist and mathematician, allegedly became intrigued one day when he saw an apple fall from a tree. This observation motivated Newton to develop a theory of gravity that applies not only to an apple falling to the earth but to any two objects in the universe. Subsequent testing of Newton's theory has shown that it works well in many circumstances (although, as Einstein would later emphasize, not in all circumstances). Because Newton's theory has been so successful at explaining observation, it is still taught today in undergraduate physics courses around the world.

This interplay between theory and observation also occurs in the field of economics. An economist might live in a country experiencing rapid increases in prices and be moved by this observation to develop a theory of inflation. The theory might assert that high inflation arises when the government prints too much money. (As you may recall, this was one of the *Ten Principles of Economics* in Chapter 1.) To test this theory, the economist could collect and analyse data on prices and money from many different countries. If growth in the quantity of money were not at all related to the rate at which prices are rising, the economist would start to doubt the validity of his theory of inflation. If money growth and inflation were strongly correlated in international data, as in fact they are, the economist would become more confident in his theory.

Although economists use theory and observation like other scientists, they do face an obstacle that makes their task especially challenging: experiments are often difficult in economics. Physicists studying gravity can drop many objects in their laboratories to generate data to test their theories. By contrast, economists studying inflation are not allowed to manipulate a nation's monetary policy simply to generate useful data. Economists, like astronomers and evolutionary biologists, usually have to make do with whatever data the world happens to give them.

To find a substitute for laboratory experiments, economists pay close attention to the natural experiments offered by history. When a war in the Middle East interrupts the flow of crude oil, for instance, oil prices shoot up around the world.

For consumers of oil and oil products, such an event depresses living standards. For economic policy makers, it poses a difficult choice about how best to respond. But for economic scientists, it provides an opportunity to study the effects of a key natural resource on the world's economies, and this opportunity persists long after the wartime increase in oil prices is over. Throughout this book, therefore, we consider many historical episodes. These episodes are valuable to study because they give us insight into the economy of the past and, more important, because they allow us to illustrate and evaluate economic theories of the present.

## The Role of Assumptions

If you ask a physicist how long it would take for a cannonball to fall from the top of the Leaning Tower of Pisa, she will probably answer the question by assuming that the cannonball falls in a vacuum. Of course, this assumption is false. In fact, the building is surrounded by air, which exerts friction on the falling cannonball and slows it down. Yet the physicist will correctly point out that friction on the cannonball is so small in relation to its weight that its effect is negligible. Assuming the cannonball falls in a vacuum greatly simplifies the problem without substantially affecting the answer.

Economists make assumptions for the same reason: assumptions can simplify the complex world and make it easier to understand. To study the effects of international trade, for example, we may assume that the world consists of only two countries and that each country produces only two goods. Of course, the real world consists of dozens of countries, each of which produces thousands of different types of goods. But by assuming two countries and two goods, we can focus our thinking. Once we understand international trade in an imaginary world with two countries and two goods, we are in a better position to understand international trade in the more complex world in which we live.

The art in scientific thinking – whether in physics, biology or economics – is deciding which assumptions to make. Suppose, for instance, that we were dropping a beach ball rather than a cannonball from the top of the building. Our physicist would realize that the assumption of no friction is far less accurate in this case: friction exerts a greater force on a beach ball than on a cannonball because a beach ball is much larger and, moreover, the effects of air friction may not be negligible relative to the weight of the ball because it is so light. The assumption that gravity works in a vacuum may, therefore, be reasonable for studying a falling cannonball but not for studying a falling beach ball.

Similarly, economists use different assumptions to answer different questions. Suppose that we want to study what happens to the economy when the government changes the amount of money in circulation. An important piece of this analysis, it turns out, is how prices respond. Many prices in the economy change infrequently; the prices of magazines and newspapers, for instance, are changed only every few years. Knowing this fact may lead us to make different assumptions when studying the effects of the policy change over different time horizons. For studying the short-run effects of the policy, we may assume that prices do not change much. We may even make the extreme and artificial assumption that all prices are completely fixed. For studying the long-run effects of the policy, however, we may assume that all prices are completely flexible. Just as a physicist uses different assumptions when studying falling cannonballs and falling beach balls, economists use different assumptions when studying the short-run and long-run effects of a change in the quantity of money.

*Economics is a science.*

## Economic Models

Secondary school biology teachers often teach basic anatomy with plastic replicas of the human body. These models have all the major organs – the heart, the liver, the kidneys and so on. The models allow teachers to show their students in a simple way how the important parts of the body fit together. Of course, these plastic models are not actual human bodies, and no one would mistake the model for a real person. These models are stylized, and they omit many details. Yet despite this lack of realism – indeed, because of this lack of realism – studying these models is useful for learning how the human body works.

Economists also use models to learn about the world, but instead of being made of plastic, they are most often composed of diagrams and equations. Like a biology teacher's plastic model, economic models omit many details to allow us to see what is truly important. Just as the biology teacher's model does not include all of the body's muscles and capillaries, an economist's model does not include every feature of the economy.

As we use models to examine various economic issues throughout this book, you will see that all the models are built with assumptions. Just as a physicist begins the analysis of a falling cannonball by assuming away the existence of friction, economists assume away many of the details of the economy that are irrelevant for studying the question at hand. All models – in physics, biology or economics – simplify reality in order to improve our understanding of it.

Another analogy that is useful in thinking about the role of assumptions in economic models has to do with maps. Maps are scaled-down representations of the world, but every map leaves out some features of the real world. Imagine what a map would look like that tried to describe every feature of the area it was supposed to represent: as well as standard features like roads and parks, it would, for example, have to represent all of the buildings, the rooms within the buildings, the furniture within each room, and so on. There would be so much detail that the scale would have to be very large and the map would be very hard to read. Of course, you might say that it would be ridiculous to have so much detail in a map, and you would be right. But how do you decide what details to leave out and what details to leave in? The answer depends on what you plan to do with the map.

Suppose a friend knocks on your door one day and asks whether you can lend her a map of London. In fact, you have three maps that would answer this general description: a road map showing the motorways and main roads going around and through the Greater London area, an A-to-Z street map of Central London and a tube map showing all of the lines and stations of the London Underground Railway system (or, as Londoners call it, the tube). Which should you give her? It all depends on the use to which your friend wants to put the map. If she is planning to travel around London on the tube, a tube map is indispensable. But if she wants to walk from Marble Arch to see Eros's statue in Piccadilly Circus, the tube map will be completely useless – it doesn't have a single street on it (unless the street name happens to coincide with a tube station) and she will need the A-to-Z. On the other hand, if she just wants to drive around Greater London, avoiding Central London, she will need the road map: the other two maps – since they do not show any major roads outside of Central London – will not help her. Now, each of the maps leaves out certain features of the real world and, as a result, each of them is indispensable for a particular purpose and useless for other purposes.

The same is true of economic models. Becoming a skilled economic modeller involves deciding what features of the real world to try to capture in the model and what features are just so much unnecessary detail. The decision as to which details are necessary to leave in and which details should be left out will depend crucially on the purpose for which you wish to use the model. In our first model of the economy, we shall try to understand in very general terms how the economy works and we shall therefore not try to explain within the model, for example, how firms decide exactly how many workers to employ or households decide how much milk to buy.

## Our First Model: The Circular-Flow Diagram

The economy consists of millions of people engaged in many activities – buying, selling, working, hiring, manufacturing and so on. To understand how the economy works, we must find some way to simplify our thinking about all these activities. In other words, we need a model that explains, in general terms, how the economy is organized and how participants in the economy interact with one another.

Figure 2.1 presents a visual model of the economy, called a **circular-flow diagram.** In this model, the economy is simplified to include only two types of decision makers – households and firms. Firms produce goods and services using inputs, such as labour, land and capital (buildings and machines). These inputs

**circular-flow diagram**
a visual model of the economy that shows how money and production inputs and outputs flow through markets among households and firms

---

### FIGURE 2.1

**The Circular Flow**

*This diagram is a schematic representation of the organization of the economy. Decisions are made by households and firms. Households and firms interact in the markets for goods and services (where households are buyers and firms are sellers) and in the markets for the factors of production (where firms are buyers and households are sellers). The outer set of arrows shows the flow of money, and the inner set of arrows shows the corresponding flow of inputs and outputs.*

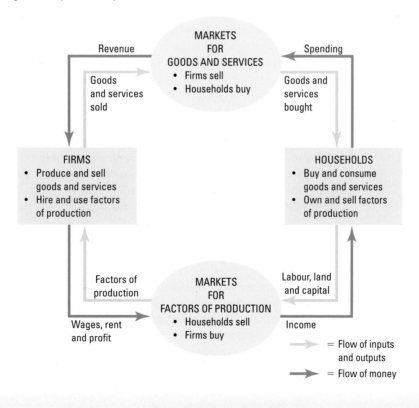

are called the *factors of production*. Households own the factors of production and consume all the goods and services that the firms produce.

Households and firms interact in two types of markets. In the *markets for goods and services*, households are buyers and firms are sellers. In particular, households buy the output of goods and services that firms produce. In the *markets for the factors of production,* households are sellers and firms are buyers. In these markets, households provide the inputs that the firms use to produce goods and services. The circular-flow diagram offers a simple way of organizing all of the economic transactions that occur between households and firms in the economy.

The inner loop of the circular-flow diagram represents the flows of inputs and outputs. The households sell the use of their labour, land and capital to the firms in the markets for the factors of production. The firms then use these factors to produce goods and services, which in turn are sold to households in the markets for goods and services. Hence, the factors of production flow from households to firms, and goods and services flow from firms to households.

The outer loop of the circular-flow diagram represents the corresponding flows of money. The households spend money to buy goods and services from the firms. The firms use some of the revenue from these sales to pay for the factors of production, such as the wages of their workers. What's left is the profit of the firm owners, who themselves are members of households. Hence, spending on goods and services flows from households to firms, and income in the form of wages, rent and profit flows from firms to households.

Let's take a tour of the circular flow by following a one euro coin as it makes its way from person to person through the economy. Imagine that the euro begins at a household, sitting in, say, your pocket. If you want to buy a cup of coffee, you take the euro to one of the economy's markets for goods and services, such as your local café. There you spend it on your favourite drink: a double espresso. When the euro moves into the café cash register, it becomes revenue for the owner of the café. The euro doesn't stay with the café owner for long, however, because he uses it to buy inputs in the markets for the factors of production. For instance, the café owner might use the euro to pay rent to the owner of the building that the café occupies or to pay the wages of its workers. In either case, the euro enters the income of some household and, once again, is back in someone's pocket. At that point, the story of the economy's circular flow starts once again.

The circular-flow diagram in Figure 2.1 is one simple model of the economy. As such, it is useful for developing some basic ideas as to how the economy works, but at the same time dispenses with details that, for some purposes, might be significant. A more complex and realistic circular-flow model would include, for instance, the roles of government and international trade. Yet these details are not crucial for a basic understanding of how the economy is organized. Because of its simplicity, this circular-flow diagram is useful to keep in mind when thinking about how the pieces of the economy fit together.

## Our Second Model: The Production Possibilities Frontier

Most economic models, unlike the purely visual circular-flow diagram, are built using the tools of mathematics. Here we consider one of the simplest such models, called the production possibilities frontier, and see how this model illustrates some basic economic ideas.

Although real economies produce thousands of goods and services, let's imagine an economy that produces only two goods – cars and computers. Together the car industry and the computer industry use all of the economy's factors of production. The **production possibilities frontier** is a graph that shows

**production possibilities frontier**
a graph that shows the combinations of output that the economy can possibly produce given the available factors of production and the available production technology

the various combinations of output – in this case, cars and computers – that the economy can possibly produce given the available factors of production and the available production technology that firms can use to turn these factors into output.

Figure 2.2 is an example of a production possibilities frontier. In this economy, if all resources were used in the car industry, the economy would produce 1,000 cars and no computers. If all resources were used in the computer industry, the economy would produce 3,000 computers and no cars. The two end points of the production possibilities frontier represent these extreme possibilities. If the economy were to divide its resources between the two industries, it could produce 700 cars and 2,000 computers, shown in the figure by point A. By contrast, the outcome at point D is not possible because resources are scarce: the economy does not have enough of the factors of production to support that level of output. In other words, the economy can produce at any point on or inside the production possibilities frontier, but it cannot produce at points outside the frontier.

An outcome is said to be *efficient* if the economy is getting all it can from the scarce resources it has available. Points on (rather than inside) the production possibilities frontier represent efficient levels of production. When the economy is producing at such a point, say point A, there is no way to produce more of one good without producing less of the other. Point B represents an *inefficient* outcome. For some reason, perhaps widespread unemployment, the economy is producing less than it could from the resources it has available: it is producing only 300 cars and 1,000 computers. If the source of the inefficiency were eliminated, the economy could move from point B to point A, increasing production of both cars (to 700) and computers (to 2,000).

One of the *Ten Principles of Economics* discussed in Chapter 1 is that people face trade-offs. The production possibilities frontier shows one trade-off that society faces. Once we have reached the efficient points on the frontier, the only way of

## FIGURE 2.2

### The Production Possibilities Frontier

*The production possibilities frontier shows the combinations of output – in this case, cars and computers – that the economy can possibly produce. The economy can produce any combination on or inside the frontier. Points outside the frontier are not feasible given the economy's resources.*

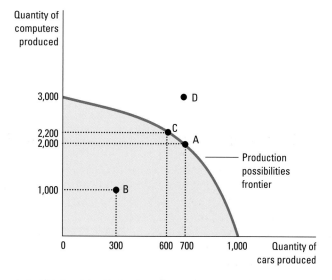

**opportunity cost**
whatever must be given up to obtain some item

getting more of one good is to get less of the other. When the economy moves from point A to point C, for instance, society produces more computers but at the expense of producing fewer cars.

Another of the *Ten Principles of Economics* is that the cost of something is what you give up to get it. This is called the **opportunity cost**. The production possibilities frontier shows the opportunity cost of one good as measured in terms of the other good. When society reallocates some of the factors of production from the car industry to the computer industry, moving the economy from point A to point C, it gives up 100 cars to get 200 additional computers. In other words, when the economy is at point A, the opportunity cost of 200 computers is 100 cars.

Notice that the production possibilities frontier in Figure 2.2 is bowed outward. This means that the opportunity cost of cars in terms of computers depends on how much of each good the economy is producing. When the economy is using most of its resources to make cars, the production possibilities frontier is quite steep. Because even workers and machines best suited to making computers are being used to make cars, the economy gets a substantial increase in the number of computers for each car it gives up. By contrast, when the economy is using most of its resources to make computers, the production possibilities frontier is quite flat. In this case, the resources best suited to making computers are already in the computer industry, and each car the economy gives up yields only a small increase in the number of computers.

The production possibilities frontier shows the trade-off between the production of different goods at a given time, but the trade-off can change over time. For example, if a technological advance in the computer industry raises the number of computers that a worker can produce per week, the economy can make more computers for any given number of cars. As a result, the production possibilities frontier shifts outward, as in Figure 2.3. Because of this economic growth, society might move production from point A to point E, enjoying more computers and more cars.

**FIGURE 2.3**

**A Shift in the Production Possibilities Frontier**

*An economic advance in the computer industry shifts the production possibilities frontier outward, increasing the number of cars and computers the economy can produce.*

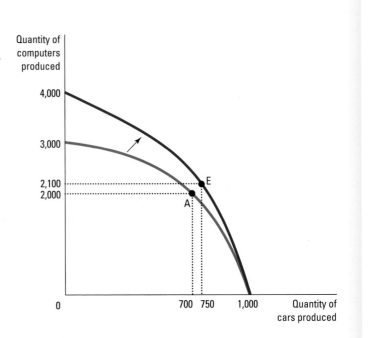

The production possibilities frontier simplifies a complex economy to highlight and clarify some basic ideas. We have used it to illustrate some of the concepts mentioned briefly in Chapter 1: scarcity, efficiency, trade-offs, opportunity cost and economic growth. As you study economics, these ideas will recur in various forms. The production possibilities frontier – our second economic model – offers one simple way of thinking about them.

## Microeconomics and Macroeconomics

Many subjects are studied on various levels. Consider biology, for example. Molecular biologists study the chemical compounds that make up living things. Cellular biologists study cells, which are made up of many chemical compounds and, at the same time, are themselves the building blocks of living organisms. Evolutionary biologists study the many varieties of animals and plants and how species change gradually over the centuries.

Economics is also studied on various levels. We can study the decisions of individual households and firms. Or we can study the interaction of households and firms in markets for specific goods and services. Or we can study the operation of the economy as a whole, which is just the sum of the activities of all these decision makers in all these markets.

Since roughly the 1930s, the field of economics has traditionally been divided into two broad subfields. **Microeconomics** is the study of how households and firms make decisions and how they interact in specific markets. **Macroeconomics** is the study of economy-wide phenomena. A microeconomist might study the effects of a congestion tax on the use of cars in Central London, the impact of foreign competition on the European car industry or the effects of attending university on a person's lifetime earnings. A macroeconomist might study the effects of borrowing by national governments, the changes over time in an economy's rate of unemployment or alternative policies to raise growth in national living standards.

Microeconomics and macroeconomics are closely intertwined. Because changes in the overall economy arise from the decisions of millions of individuals, it is impossible to understand macroeconomic developments without considering the associated microeconomic decisions. For example, a macroeconomist might study the effect of a cut in income tax on the overall production of goods and services in an economy. To analyse this issue, he or she must consider how the tax cut affects the decisions of households concerning how much to spend on goods and services.

Despite the inherent link between microeconomics and macroeconomics, the two fields are distinct. In economics, as in biology, it may seem natural to begin with the smallest unit and build up. Yet doing so is neither necessary nor always the best way to proceed. Evolutionary biology is, in a sense, built upon molecular biology, since species are made up of molecules. Yet molecular biology and evolutionary biology are separate fields, each with its own questions and its own methods. Similarly, because microeconomics and macroeconomics address different questions, they sometimes take quite different approaches and are often taught in separate courses.

**microeconomics**
the study of how households and firms make decisions and how they interact in markets

**macroeconomics**
the study of economy-wide phenomena, including inflation, unemployment and economic growth

**Quick Quiz** In what sense is economics like a science? • Draw a production possibilities frontier for a society that produces food and clothing. Show an efficient point, an inefficient point and an infeasible point. Show the effects of a drought. • Define *microeconomics* and *macroeconomics*.

# THE ECONOMIST AS POLICY ADVISOR

Often economists are asked to explain the causes of economic events. Why, for example, is unemployment higher for teenagers than for older workers? Sometimes economists are asked to recommend policies to improve economic outcomes. What, for instance, should the government do to improve the economic well-being of teenagers? When economists are trying to explain the world, they are scientists. When they are trying to help improve it, they are policy advisors.

## Positive Versus Normative Analysis

To help clarify the two roles that economists play, we begin by examining the use of language. Because scientists and policy advisors have different goals, they use language in different ways.

For example, suppose that two people are discussing minimum wage laws. Here are two statements you might hear:

HARRIET: Minimum wage laws cause unemployment.
SOPHIE: The government should raise the minimum wage.

Ignoring for now whether you agree with these statements, notice that Harriet and Sophie differ in what they are trying to do. Harriet is speaking like a scientist: she is making a claim about how the world works. Sophie is speaking like a policy advisor: she is making a claim about how she would like to change the world.

In general, statements about the world are of two types. One type, such as Harriet's, is positive. **Positive statements** are descriptive. They make a claim about how the world *is*. A second type of statement, such as Sophie's, is normative. **Normative statements** are prescriptive. They make a claim about how the world *ought to be*.

A key difference between positive and normative statements is how we judge their validity. We can, in principle, confirm or refute positive statements by examining evidence. An economist might evaluate Harriet's statement by analysing data on changes in minimum wages and changes in unemployment over time. By contrast, evaluating normative statements involves values as well as facts. Sophie's statement cannot be judged using data alone. Deciding what is good or bad policy is not merely a matter of science; it also involves our views on ethics, religion and political philosophy.

Of course, positive and normative statements may be related. Our positive views about how the world works affect our normative views about what policies are desirable. Harriet's claim that the minimum wage causes unemployment, if true, might lead us to reject Sophie's conclusion that the government should raise the minimum wage. Yet our normative conclusions cannot come from positive analysis alone; they involve value judgements as well.

As you study economics, keep in mind the distinction between positive and normative statements. Much of economics just tries to explain how the economy works. Yet often the goal of economics is to improve how the economy works. When you hear economists making normative statements, you know they have crossed the line from scientist to policy advisor.

**positive statements**
claims that attempt to describe the world as it is

**normative statements**
claims that attempt to prescribe how the world should be

## Economists in Governmental and Supra-Governmental Institutions

An old joke about economists concerns the politician who one day said that she would only employ economists with one hand: she was tired of receiving advice of the form, 'On the one hand, … On the other hand, ….'

Throughout Europe, North America and the world more generally, many government ministries dealing with economic issues – such as a country's finance ministry or Treasury – have large numbers of economists working for them, providing advice on alternative policy measures or forecasts of the economy. In the UK, the Government Economic Service is the biggest single employer of economists, with about 600 of them working in 30 government departments and agencies.

The joke about one-handed economists does reflect an element of truth concerning the nature of economic advice – namely that good economic advice is not always straightforward. This tendency is rooted in one of the *Ten Principles of Economics* in Chapter 1: people face trade-offs. Economists are aware that trade-offs are involved in most policy decisions. For example, a policy might, on the one hand, increase efficiency but, on the other hand, reduce equity. It might help future generations but hurt current generations. An economist who says that all policy decisions are easy is an economist not to be trusted.

Economists are also found outside the administrative branch of government. The Bank of England, the institution that implements the UK's monetary policy, employs a large staff of economists to analyse economic developments in the United Kingdom and throughout the world. At the time of writing this chapter, both the Governor of the Bank of England and its Chief Economist were former professors of the London School of Economics, while the President of the German central bank, the Bundesbank, was also a former professor of economics. Most of the central banks of other European countries also have economic research departments, as do the European Central Bank in Frankfurt and the US Federal Reserve in Washington (the US central bank).

*"Let's switch. I'll make the policy, you implement it, and he'll explain it."*

Economists are also employed to provide advice at the supra-governmental level. The International Monetary Fund, which was created in 1945 to help promote the health of the world economy, employs at its headquarters in Washington DC probably the largest number of economics Ph.D.s based at a single location anywhere in the world, originating from a very large proportion of the 184 countries that make up the IMF's near-global membership. Table 2.1 lists the websites of some of these agencies.

### TABLE 2.1

**Websites**

*Here are the websites for a few of the government and supra-governmental agencies that are responsible for collecting economic data and making or advising on economic policy.*

| | |
|---|---|
| European Central Bank | http://www.ecb.int |
| Organization for Economic Cooperation and Development | http://www.oecd.org |
| International Monetary Fund | http://www.imf.org |
| Bank of England | http://www.bankofengland.co.uk |
| UK Treasury | http://www.hm-treasury.gov.uk |
| UK Office of National Statistics | http://www.ons.gov.uk |
| US Federal Reserve Board | http://www.federalreserve.gov |

The influence of economists on policy goes beyond their role as advisors: their research and writings often affect policy indirectly. The great British economist John Maynard Keynes offered this observation:

> The ideas of economists and political philosophers, both when they are right and when they are wrong, are more powerful than is commonly understood. Indeed, the world is ruled by little else. Practical men, who believe themselves to be quite exempt from intellectual influences, are usually the slaves of some defunct economist. Madmen in authority, who hear voices in the air, are distilling their frenzy from some academic scribbler of a few years back.

Although these words were written in 1935, they remain true today. Indeed, the 'academic scribbler of a few years back' now influencing public policy is often Keynes himself.

> **Quick Quiz** Give an example of a positive statement and an example of a normative statement. • Name four government departments that regularly rely on advice from economists.

# WHY ECONOMISTS DISAGREE

'If all economists were laid end to end, they would not reach a conclusion.' This witticism from George Bernard Shaw is revealing. Economists as a group are often criticized for giving conflicting advice to policy makers. There are two basic reasons:

- Economists may disagree about the validity of alternative positive theories about how the world works.
- Economists may have different values and, therefore, different normative views about what policy should try to accomplish.

Let's discuss each of these reasons.

## Differences in Scientific Judgements

Several centuries ago, astronomers debated whether the earth or the sun was at the centre of the solar system. More recently, meteorologists have debated whether the earth is experiencing global warming and, if so, why. Science is a search for understanding about the world around us. It is not surprising that as the search continues, scientists can disagree about the direction in which truth lies.

Economists often disagree for the same reason. Economics is a young science, and there is still much to be learned. Economists sometimes disagree because they have different beliefs about the validity of alternative theories or about the size of important parameters.

For example, economists disagree about whether the government should levy taxes based on a household's income or based on its consumption (spending). Advocates of a switch from an income tax to a consumption tax believe that the change would encourage households to save more, because income that is saved would not be taxed. Higher saving, in turn, would lead to more rapid growth in productivity and living standards. Advocates of an income tax system believe that household saving would not respond much to a change in the tax laws. These two groups of economists hold different normative views about the tax system because they have different positive views about the responsiveness of saving to tax incentives.

## Differences in Values

Suppose that Hamish and Gavin both take the same amount of water from the town well. To pay for maintaining the well, the town imposes a property tax on its residents. Hamish lives in a large house worth £2 million and pays a property tax of £10,000 a year.  Gavin owns a small cottage worth £20,000 and pays a property tax of £1,000 a year.

Is this policy fair? If not, who pays too much and who pays too little? Would it be better to replace the tax based on the value of the property with a tax that was just a single payment from everyone living in the town (a poll tax) in return for using the well – say, £1,000 a year?  After all, Hamish lives on his own and actually uses much less water than Gavin and the other four bagpipe players in Gavin's band who live with him and bathe regularly before and after a bagpipe gig. Would that be a fairer policy?

In the 1980s, when the UK government attempted to replace the system of property tax in the UK with a poll tax, it resulted in riots in Trafalgar Square – many people clearly thought that it was indeed very unfair.

What about replacing the property tax not with a poll tax but with an income tax? Hamish has an income of £100,000 a year so that a 5 per cent income tax would present him with a tax bill of £5,000. Gavin, on the other hand, has an income of only £10,000 a year and so would pay only £500 a year in tax (although his four tenants, who earn about the same, would also have to pay a similar tax bill).  Does it matter whether Gavin's low income is due to his decision to pursue a career as a bagpipe player? Would it matter if it were due to a physical disability? Does it matter whether Hamish's high income is due to a large inheritance as the Laird of Loch Sporran?  What if it were due to his willingness to work long hours at a dreary job?

These are difficult questions on which people are likely to disagree. If the town hired two experts to study how the town should tax its residents to pay for the well, we should not be surprised if they offered conflicting advice.

This simple example shows why economists sometimes disagree about public policy. As we learned earlier in our discussion of normative and positive analysis, policies cannot be judged on scientific grounds alone. Economists give conflicting advice sometimes because they have different values. Perfecting the science of economics will not tell us whether it is Hamish or Gavin who pays too much.

## Perception Versus Reality

Because of differences in scientific judgements and differences in values, some disagreement among economists is inevitable. Yet one should not overstate the amount of disagreement. In many cases, economists do offer a united view.

Table 2.2 contains ten propositions about economic policy. In a survey of economists in business, government and academia, these propositions were endorsed by an overwhelming majority of respondents. Most of these propositions would fail to command a similar consensus among the general public.

One of the propositions in the table concerns tariffs and import quotas, two policies that restrict trade among nations. For reasons we will discuss more fully in later chapters, almost all economists oppose such barriers to free trade. This, in fact, is one of the major reasons why the European Union was set up and why countries are queuing up to join it:  tariffs and quotas are not imposed on trade between EU member countries. Tariffs and quotas *are*, however, often imposed by EU countries on goods coming from outside of the European Union.  In the USA, the president and Congress have, over the years, often chosen to restrict the

**TABLE 2.2**

**Proposition (and percentage of economists who agree)**

1. A ceiling on rents reduces the quantity and quality of housing available. (93%)
2. Tariffs and import quotas usually reduce general economic welfare. (93%)
3. Flexible and floating exchange rates offer an effective international monetary arrangement. (90%)
4. Fiscal policy (e.g., tax cut and/or government expenditure increase) has a significant stimulative impact on a less than fully employed economy. (90%)
5. If the government budget is to be balanced, it should be done over the business cycle rather than yearly. (85%)
6. Cash payments increase the welfare of recipients to a greater degree than do transfers-in-kind of equal cash value. (84%)
7. A large government budget deficit has an adverse effect on the economy. (83%)
8. A minimum wage increases unemployment among young and unskilled workers. (79%)
9. The government should restructure the welfare system along the lines of a 'negative income tax'. (79%)
10. Effluent taxes and marketable pollution permits represent a better approach to pollution control than imposition of pollution ceilings. (78%)

Ten Propositions About Which Most Economists Agree

Source: Adapted from Richard M. Alston, J.R. Kearl and Michael B. Vaughn, 'Is There Consensus among Economists in the 1990s?' *American Economic Review* (May 1992): 203–209. Used by permission.

import of certain goods. In 2002, for example, the Bush administration imposed large tariffs on steel to protect domestic steel producers from foreign competition – although they later had to drop the policy when the European Union threatened to retaliate by increasing the tariffs on US goods imported into EU countries from the US. In this case, economists did offer united advice, but policy makers chose to ignore it.

Another of the propositions concerns the imposition of a legal minimum wage – nearly 80 per cent of economists surveyed said that they thought that a minimum wage increases unemployment among unskilled and young workers. Nevertheless, the US and nine European Union countries, including the UK, now have a statutory minimum wage. Of course, these economists were not necessarily *against* the imposition of a minimum wage. Some of them might argue, for example, that while, on the one hand, introducing a minimum wage above a certain level may affect unemployment, on the other hand it may increase the average quality of goods and services produced in the economy by making it harder for producers of low-quality goods and services to compete by keeping wages and prices low, and this may lead to a net benefit to the economy overall. Remember: people face trade-offs.

**Quick Quiz** Why might economic advisors to the government disagree about a question of policy?

## LET'S GET GOING

The first two chapters of this book have introduced you to the ideas and methods of economics. We are now ready to get to work. In the next chapter we start learning in more detail the principles of economic behaviour and economic policy.

As you proceed through this book, you will be asked to draw on many of your intellectual skills. You might find it helpful to keep in mind some advice from the great John Maynard Keynes:

> The study of economics does not seem to require any specialised gifts of an unusually high order. Is it not … a very easy subject compared with the higher branches of philosophy or pure science? An easy subject, at which very few excel! The paradox finds its explanation, perhaps, in that the master-economist must possess a rare *combination* of gifts. He must be mathematician, historian, statesman, philosopher – in some degree. He must understand symbols and speak in words. He must contemplate the particular in terms of the general, and touch abstract and concrete in the same flight of thought. He must study the present in the light of the past for the purposes of the future. No part of man's nature or his institutions must lie entirely outside his regard. He must be purposeful and disinterested in a simultaneous mood; as aloof and incorruptible as an artist, yet sometimes as near the earth as a politician.

It is a tall order. But with practice you will become more and more accustomed to thinking like an economist.

## SUMMARY

- Economists try to address their subject with a scientist's objectivity. Like all scientists, they make appropriate assumptions and build simplified models in order to understand the world around them. Two simple economic models are the circular-flow diagram and the production possibilities frontier.

- The field of economics is divided into two subfields: microeconomics and macroeconomics. Microeconomists study decision making by households and firms and the interaction among households and firms in the marketplace. Macroeconomists study the forces and trends that affect the economy as a whole.

- A positive statement is an assertion about how the world *is*. A normative statement is an assertion about how the world *ought to be.* When economists make normative statements, they are acting more as policy advisors than scientists.

- Economists who advise policy makers offer conflicting advice either because of differences in scientific judgements or because of differences in values. At other times, economists are united in the advice they offer, but policy makers may choose to ignore it.

## KEY CONCEPTS

circular-flow diagram, p. 23
production possibilities frontier, p. 24
opportunity cost, p. 26

microeconomics, p. 27
macroeconomics, p. 27

positive statements, p. 28
normative statements, p. 28

## QUESTIONS FOR REVIEW

1. How is economics like a science?

2. Why do economists make assumptions?

3. Should an economic model describe reality exactly?

4. Draw and explain a production possibilities frontier for an economy that produces olive oil and milk. What happens to this frontier if disease kills half of the economy's cow population?

5. Use a production possibilities frontier to describe the idea of 'efficiency'.

6. What are the two subfields into which economics is divided? Explain what each subfield studies.

7. What is the difference between a positive and a normative statement? Give an example of each.

8. Why do economists sometimes offer conflicting advice to policy makers?

## PROBLEMS AND APPLICATIONS

1. Describe some unusual language used in one of the other fields that you are studying or have studied besides economics. Why are these special terms useful?

2. One common assumption in economics is that the products of different firms in the same industry are indistinguishable. For each of the following industries, discuss whether this is a reasonable assumption.
   a. steel
   b. novels
   c. wheat
   d. fast food.

3. Draw a circular-flow diagram. Identify the parts of the model that correspond to the flow of goods and services and the flow of euros for each of the following activities.
   a. Sam pays a shopkeeper €1 for a litre of milk.
   b. Georgia earns €4.50 per hour working at a fast food restaurant.
   c. Millie spends €7 to see a film.
   d. Owen earns €10,000 from his 10 per cent ownership of Pan-European Industrial.

4. Imagine a society that produces military goods and consumer goods, which we'll call 'guns' and 'butter'.
   a. Draw a production possibilities frontier for guns and butter. Explain why it most likely has a bowed-out shape.
   b. Show a point that is impossible for the economy to achieve. Show a point that is feasible but inefficient.
   c. Imagine that the society has two political parties, called the Hawks (who want a strong military) and the Doves (who want a smaller military sector). Show a point on your production possibilities frontier that the Hawks might choose and a point the Doves might choose.

   d. Imagine that an aggressive neighbouring country reduces the size of its military sector. As a result, both the Hawks and the Doves reduce their desired production of guns by the same amount. Which party would get the bigger 'peace dividend', measured by the increase in butter production? Explain.

5. The first principle of economics discussed in Chapter 1 is that people face trade-offs. Use a production possibilities frontier to illustrate society's trade-off between a clean environment and the quantity of industrial output. What do you suppose determines the shape and position of the frontier? Show what happens to the frontier if engineers develop an automobile engine with almost no emissions.

6. Classify the following topics as relating to microeconomics or macroeconomics.
   a. A family's decision about how much income to save.
   b. The effect of government regulations on car emissions.
   c. The impact of higher national saving on economic growth.
   d. A firm's decision about how many workers to recruit.
   e. The relationship between the inflation rate and changes in the quantity of money.

7. Classify each of the following statements as positive or normative. Explain.
   a. Society faces a short-run trade-off between inflation and unemployment.
   b. A reduction in the rate of growth of money will reduce the rate of inflation.
   c. The European Central Bank should reduce the rate of growth of money.

d.  Society ought to require welfare recipients to look for jobs.

e.  Lower tax rates encourage more work and more saving.

8.  Classify each of the statements in Table 2.2 as positive, normative or ambiguous. Explain.

9.  If you were prime minister, would you be more interested in your economic advisors' positive views or their normative views? Why?

10.  The *Bank of England Quarterly Bulletin* contains statistical information about the UK economy as well as analysis of current policy issues by the Bank's economic staff. Find a recent copy of this bulletin and read a chapter about an issue that interests you. Summarize the issue discussed and describe the Bank's recommended policy.

11.  Who is the current President of the European Central Bank? Who is the current Governor of the Bank of England? Who is the current UK Chancellor of the Exchequer?

12.  Would you expect economists to disagree less about public policy as time goes on? Why or why not? Can their differences be completely eliminated? Why or why not?

13.  Look up one of the websites listed in Table 2.1. What recent economic trends or issues are addressed there?

For further resources, visit
http://www.thomsonlearning.co.uk/mankiw_taylor

## APPENDIX  Graphing: A Brief Review

Many of the concepts that economists study can be expressed with numbers – the price of bananas, the quantity of bananas sold, the cost of growing bananas and so on. Often these economic variables are related to one another. When the price of bananas rises, people buy fewer bananas. One way of expressing the relationships among variables is with graphs.

Graphs serve two purposes. First, when developing economic theories, graphs offer a way to express visually ideas that might be less clear if described with equations or words. Secondly, when analysing economic data, graphs provide a way of finding how variables are in fact related in the world. Whether we are working with theory or with data, graphs provide a lens through which a recognizable forest emerges from a multitude of trees.

Numerical information can be expressed graphically in many ways, just as a thought can be expressed in words in many ways. A good writer chooses words that will make an argument clear, a description pleasing or a scene dramatic. An effective economist chooses the type of graph that best suits the purpose at hand.

In this appendix we discuss how economists use graphs to study the mathematical relationships among variables. We also discuss some of the pitfalls that can arise in the use of graphical methods.

### Graphs of a Single Variable

Three common graphs are shown in Figure 2A.1. The *pie chart* in panel (a) shows how total government expenditure in the UK in 2003 to 2004 was divided among the major categories such as social security, the National Health Service, education, defence and so on. A slice of the pie represents each category's share of total

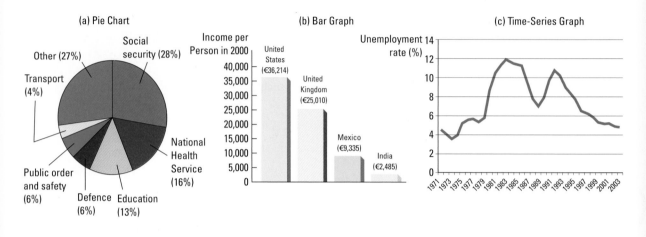

**FIGURE 2A.1**

### Types of Graph

*The pie chart in panel (a) shows how UK government expenditure was divided between the major spending categories in 2003 to 2004. The bar graph in panel (b) compares the average income in four countries in 2000. The time-series graph in panel (c) shows the UK unemployment rate from 1971 to 2004.*

government expenditure. The *bar graph* in panel (b) compares income per person for four countries in 2000, each expressed in Euros. The height of each bar represents the average income in each country. The *time-series graph* in panel (c) traces the course of unemployment in the UK over time. The height of the line shows the percentage of the work force that was out of work in each year. You have probably seen similar graphs presented in newspapers and magazines.

## Graphs of Two Variables: The Coordinate System

Although the three graphs in Figure 2A.1 are useful in showing how a variable changes over time or across individuals, such graphs are limited in how much they can tell us. These graphs display information only on a single variable. Economists are often concerned with the relationships between variables. Thus, they need to be able to display two variables on a single graph. The *coordinate system* makes this possible.

Suppose you want to examine the relationship between study time and examination marks. For each student attending your economics lectures, you could record a pair of numbers: hours per week spent studying and marks obtained in the final course examination. These numbers could then be placed in parentheses as an *ordered pair* and appear as a single point on the graph. Albert E. ('Young Einstein'), for instance, is represented by the ordered pair (25 hours/week, 70 per cent examination mark), while his classmate Alfred E. ('what, me worry?') is represented by the ordered pair (5 hours/week, 40 per cent examination mark).

We can graph these ordered pairs on a two-dimensional grid. The first number in each ordered pair, called the *x-coordinate*, tells us the horizontal location of the point. The second number, called the *y-coordinate*, tells us the vertical location of the point. The point with both an *x*-coordinate and a *y*-coordinate of zero is known as the *origin*. The two coordinates in the ordered pair tell us where the point is located in relation to the origin: *x* units to the right of the origin and *y* units above it.

**FIGURE 2A.2**

### Using the Coordinate System

*Final examination mark is measured on the vertical axis and study time on the horizontal axis. Albert E., Alfred E. and the other students on their course are represented by various points. We can see from the graph that students who study more tend to get higher marks.*

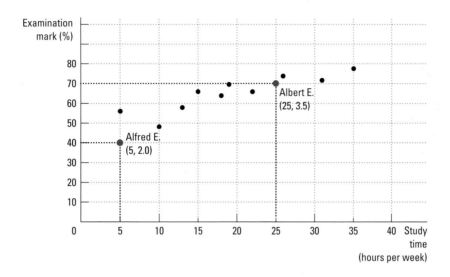

Figure 2A.2 graphs examination marks against study time for Albert E., Alfred E. and the rest of the students who attended the course. This type of graph is called a *scatterplot* because it plots scattered points. Looking at this graph, we immediately notice that points farther to the right (indicating more study time) also tend to be higher (indicating a better examination result). Because study time and examination mark typically move in the same direction, we say that these two variables have a *positive correlation*. By contrast, if we were to graph time spent partying per week and examination marks, we would probably find that higher party time is associated with lower marks; because these variables typically move in opposite directions, we would call this a *negative correlation*. In either case, the coordinate system makes the correlation between the two variables easy to see.

## Curves in the Coordinate System

Students who study more do tend to get higher marks, but other factors also influence a student's marks. Previous preparation is an important factor, for instance, as are talent, attention from teachers and even eating a good breakfast. A scatterplot like Figure 2A.2 does not attempt to isolate the effect that study has on grades from the effects of other variables. Often, however, economists prefer looking at how one variable affects another while holding everything else constant.

To see how this is done, let's consider one of the most important graphs in economics – the *demand curve*. The demand curve traces out the effect of a good's price on the quantity of the good consumers want to buy. Before showing a demand curve, however, consider Table 2A.1, which shows how the number of novels that Harriet buys depends on her income and on the price of novels. When novels are cheap, Harriet buys them in large quantities. As they become more expensive, she

## TABLE 2A.1

### Novels Purchased by Harriet

*This table shows the number of novels Harriet buys at various incomes and prices. For any given level of income, the data on price and quantity demanded can be graphed to produce Harriet's demand curve for novels, as shown in Figures 2A.3 and 2A.4.*

| | Income | | |
|---|---|---|---|
| Price | €20,000 | €30,000 | €40,000 |
| €10 | 2 novels | 5 novels | 8 novels |
| €9 | 6 | 9 | 12 |
| €8 | 10 | 13 | 16 |
| €7 | 14 | 17 | 20 |
| €6 | 18 | 21 | 24 |
| €5 | 22 | 25 | 28 |
| | Demand curve, $D_3$ | Demand curve, $D_1$ | Demand curve, $D_2$ |

borrows books from the library instead of buying them or chooses to go to the cinema instead of reading. Similarly, at any given price, Harriet buys more novels when she has a higher income. That is, when her income increases, she spends part of the additional income on novels and part on other goods.

We now have three variables – the price of novels, income and the number of novels purchased – which is more than we can represent in two dimensions. To put the information from Table 2A.1 in graphical form, we need to hold one of the three variables constant and trace out the relationship between the other two. Because the demand curve represents the relationship between price and quantity demanded, we hold Harriet's income constant and show how the number of novels she buys varies with the price of novels.

Suppose that Harriet's income is €30,000 per year. If we place the number of novels Harriet purchases on the *x*-axis and the price of novels on the *y*-axis, we can graphically represent the middle column of Table 2A.1. When the points that represent these entries from the table – (5 novels, €10), (9 novels, €9) and so on – are connected, they form a line. This line, pictured in Figure 2A.3, is known as Harriet's demand curve for novels; it tells us how many novels Harriet purchases at any given price. The demand curve is downward sloping, indicating that a higher price reduces the quantity of novels demanded. Because the quantity of novels demanded and the price move in opposite directions, we say that the two variables are *negatively related*. (Conversely, when two variables move in the same direction, the curve relating them is upward sloping, and we say the variables are *positively related*.)

Now suppose that Harriet's income rises to €40,000 per year. At any given price, Harriet will purchase more novels than she did at her previous level of income. Just as earlier we drew Harriet's demand curve for novels using the entries from the middle column of Table 2A.1, we now draw a new demand curve using the entries from the right-hand column of the table. This new demand curve (curve $D_2$) is pictured alongside the old one (curve $D_1$) in Figure 2A.4; the new curve is a similar line drawn farther to the right. We therefore say that Harriet's demand curve for novels *shifts* to the right when her income increases. Likewise, if Harriet's

## FIGURE 2A.3

### Demand Curve

The line D₁ shows how Harriet's purchases of novels depend on the price of novels when her income is held constant. Because the price and the quantity demanded are negatively related, the demand curve slopes downward.

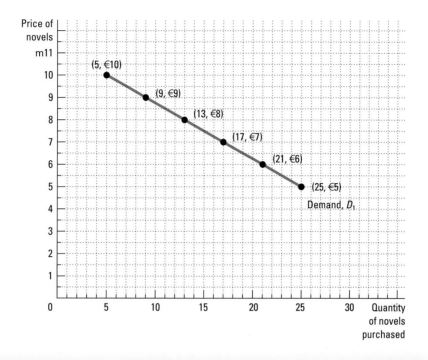

income were to fall to €20,000 per year, she would buy fewer novels at any given price and her demand curve would shift to the left (to curve $D_3$).

In economics, it is important to distinguish between *movements along a curve* and *shifts of a curve*. As we can see from Figure 2A.3, if Harriet earns €30,000 per year and novels cost €8 apiece, she will purchase 13 novels per year. If the price of novels falls to €7, Harriet will increase her purchases of novels to 17 per year. The demand curve, however, stays fixed in the same place. Harriet still buys the same number of novels *at each price,* but as the price falls she moves along her demand curve from left to right. By contrast, if the price of novels remains fixed at €8 but her income rises to €40,000, Harriet increases her purchases of novels from 13 to 16 per year. Because Harriet buys more novels *at each price,* her demand curve shifts out, as shown in Figure 2A.4.

There is a simple way to tell when it is necessary to shift a curve. When a variable that is not named on either axis changes, the curve shifts. Income is on neither the *x*-axis nor the *y*-axis of the graph, so when Harriet's income changes, her demand curve must shift. Any change that affects Harriet's purchasing habits, besides a change in the price of novels, will result in a shift in her demand curve. If, for instance, the public library closes and Harriet must buy all the books she wants to read, she will demand more novels at each price, and her demand curve will shift to the right. Or, if the price of going to the cinema falls and Harriet spends more time at the movies and less time reading, she will demand fewer novels at each price, and her demand curve will shift to the left. By contrast, when a variable on an axis of the graph changes, the curve does not shift. We read the change as a movement along the curve.

## Shifting Demand Curves

*The location of Harriet's demand curve for novels depends on how much income she earns. The more she earns, the more novels she will purchase at any given price, and the further to the right her demand curve will lie. Curve D₁ represents Harriet's original demand curve when her income is €30,000 per year. If her income rises to €40,000 per year, her demand curve shifts to D₂. If her income falls to €20,000 per year, her demand curve shifts to D₃.*

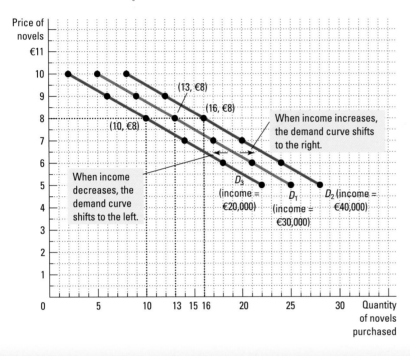

## Slope

One question we might want to ask about Harriet is how much her purchasing habits respond to price. Look at the demand curve pictured in Figure 2A.5. If this curve is very steep, Harriet purchases nearly the same number of novels regardless of whether they are cheap or expensive. If this curve is much flatter, Harriet purchases many fewer novels when the price rises. To answer questions about how much one variable responds to changes in another variable, we can use the concept of *slope*.

The slope of a line is the ratio of the vertical distance covered to the horizontal distance covered as we move along the line. This definition is usually written out in mathematical symbols as follows:

$$\text{slope} = \frac{\Delta y}{\Delta x}$$

where the Greek letter Δ (delta) stands for the change in a variable. In other words, the slope of a line is equal to the 'rise' (change in $y$) divided by the 'run' (change in $x$). The slope will be a small positive number for a fairly flat upward sloping line, a large positive number for a steep upward sloping line and a negative number for a downward sloping line. A horizontal line has a slope of zero because in this

## FIGURE 2A.5

**Calculating the Slope of a Line**

*To calculate the slope of the demand curve, we can look at the changes in the x- and y-coordinates as we move from the point (21 novels, €6) to the point (13 novels, €8). The slope of the line is the ratio of the change in the y-coordinate (–2) to the change in the x-coordinate (+8), which equals –1/4.*

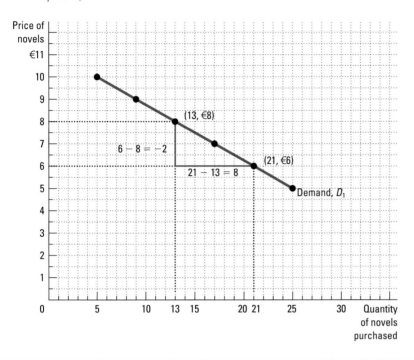

case the $y$-variable never changes; a vertical line is said to have an infinite slope because the $y$-variable can take any value without the $x$-variable changing at all.

What is the slope of Harriet's demand curve for novels? First of all, because the curve slopes down, we know the slope will be negative. To calculate a numerical value for the slope, we must choose two points on the line. With Harriet's income at €30,000, she will purchase 21 novels at a price of €6 or 13 novels at a price of €8. When we apply the slope formula, we are concerned with the change between these two points; in other words, we are concerned with the difference between them, which lets us know that we will have to subtract one set of values from the other, as follows:

$$\text{slope} = \frac{\Delta y}{\Delta x} = \frac{\text{first } y\text{-coordinate} - \text{second } y\text{-coordindate}}{\text{first } x\text{-coordinate} - \text{second } x\text{-coordinate}} = \frac{6-8}{21-13} = \frac{-2}{8} = \frac{-1}{4}$$

Figure 2A.5 shows graphically how this calculation works. Try computing the slope of Harriet's demand curve using two different points. You should get exactly the same result, –1/4. One of the properties of a straight line is that it has the same slope everywhere. This is not true of other types of curves, which are steeper in some places than in others.

The slope of Harriet's demand curve tells us something about how responsive her purchases are to changes in the price. A small slope (a number close to zero) means that Harriet's demand curve is relatively flat; in this case, she adjusts the number of novels she buys substantially in response to a price change. A larger slope (a number further from zero) means that Harriet's demand curve is relatively steep; in this case, she adjusts the number of novels she buys only slightly in response to a price change.

## Cause and Effect

Economists often use graphs to advance an argument about how the economy works. In other words, they use graphs to argue about how one set of events *causes* another set of events. With a graph like the demand curve, there is no doubt about cause and effect. Because we are varying price and holding all other variables constant, we know that changes in the price of novels cause changes in the quantity Harriet demands. Remember, however, that our demand curve came from a hypothetical example. When graphing data from the real world, it is often more difficult to establish how one variable affects another.

The first problem is that it is difficult to hold everything else constant when measuring how one variable affects another. If we are not able to hold variables constant, we might decide that one variable on our graph is causing changes in the other variable when actually those changes are caused by a third *omitted variable* not pictured on the graph. Even if we have identified the correct two variables to look at, we might run into a second problem – *reverse causality*. In other words, we might decide that A causes B when in fact B causes A. The omitted variable and reverse causality traps require us to proceed with caution when using graphs to draw conclusions about causes and effects.

**Omitted Variables** To see how omitting a variable can lead to a deceptive graph, let's consider an example. Imagine that the government, spurred by public concern about the large number of deaths from cancer, commissions an exhaustive study from Big Brother Statistical Services. Big Brother examines many of the items found in people's homes to see which of them are associated with the risk of cancer. Big Brother reports a strong relationship between two variables: the number of cigarette lighters that a household owns and the probability that someone in the household will develop cancer. Figure 2A.6 shows this relationship.

### FIGURE 2A.6

**Graph With an Omitted Variable**

*The upward sloping curve shows that members of households with more cigarette lighters are more likely to develop cancer. Yet we should not conclude that ownership of lighters causes cancer, because the graph does not take into account the number of cigarettes smoked.*

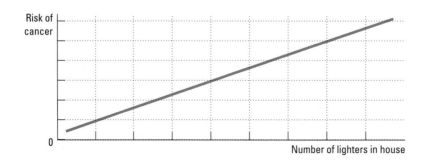

What should we make of this result? Big Brother advises a quick policy response. It recommends that the government discourages the ownership of cigarette lighters by taxing their sale. It also recommends that the government requires warning labels: 'Big Brother has determined that this lighter is dangerous to your health.'

In judging the validity of Big Brother's analysis, one question is paramount: has Big Brother held constant every relevant variable except the one under consideration? If the answer is no, the results are suspect. An easy explanation for Figure 2A.6 is that people who own more cigarette lighters are more likely to smoke cigarettes and that cigarettes, not lighters, cause cancer. If Figure 2A.6 does not hold constant the amount of smoking, it does not tell us the true effect of owning a cigarette lighter.

This story illustrates an important principle: when you see a graph being used to support an argument about cause and effect, it is important to ask whether the movements of an omitted variable could explain the results you see.

**Reverse Causality** Economists can also make mistakes about causality by misreading its direction. To see how this is possible, suppose the Association of European Anarchists commissions a study of crime in Eurovia and arrives at Figure 2A.7, which plots the number of violent crimes per 1,000 people in major Eurovian cities against the number of police officers per 1,000 people. The anarchists note the curve's upward slope and argue that because police increase rather than decrease the amount of urban violence, law enforcement should be abolished.

If we could run a controlled experiment, we would avoid the danger of reverse causality. To run an experiment, we would set the number of police officers in different cities randomly and then examine the correlation between police and crime. Figure 2A.7, however, is not based on such an experiment. We simply observe that more dangerous cities have more police officers. The explanation for this may be that more dangerous cities hire more police. In other words, rather than police causing crime, crime may cause police. Nothing in the graph itself allows us to establish the direction of causality.

It might seem that an easy way to determine the direction of causality is to examine which variable moves first. If we see crime increase and then the police

---

### FIGURE 2A.7

**Graph Suggesting Reverse Causality**

*The upward sloping curve shows that Eurovian cities with a higher concentration of police are more dangerous. Yet the graph does not tell us whether police cause crime or crime-plagued cities hire more police.*

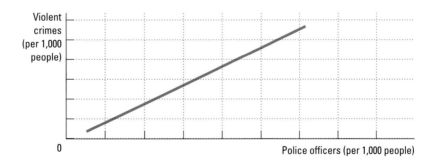

force expand, we reach one conclusion. If we see the police force expand and then crime increase, we reach the other. Yet there is also a flaw with this approach: often people change their behaviour not in response to a change in their present conditions but in response to a change in their *expectations* of future conditions. A city that expects a major crime wave in the future, for instance, might well hire more police now. This problem is even easier to see in the case of babies and baby cots. Couples often buy a baby cot in anticipation of the birth of a child. The cot comes before the baby, but we wouldn't want to conclude that the sale of cots causes the population to grow!

There is no complete set of rules that says when it is appropriate to draw causal conclusions from graphs. Yet just keeping in mind that cigarette lighters don't cause cancer (omitted variable) and baby cots do not cause larger families (reverse causality) will keep you from falling for many faulty economic arguments.

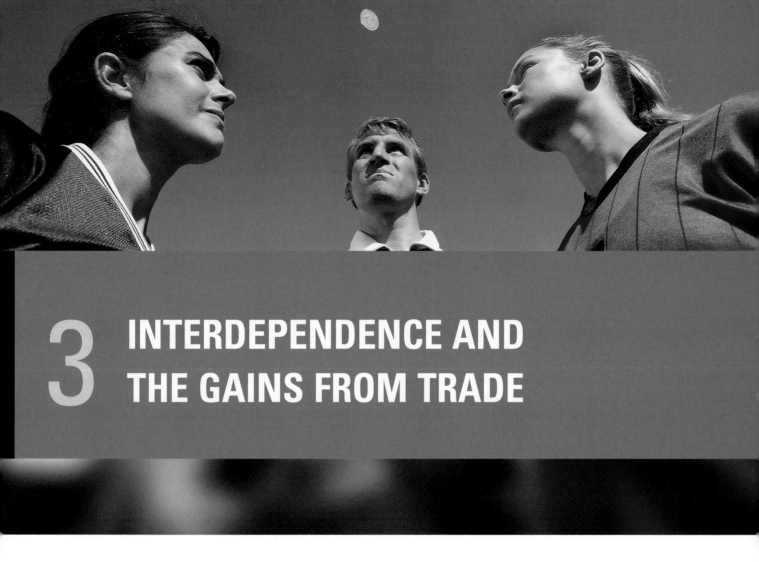

# 3 INTERDEPENDENCE AND THE GAINS FROM TRADE

onsider your typical day. You wake up in the morning and you make yourself some coffee from beans grown in Brazil, or tea from leaves grown in Sri Lanka. Over breakfast, you listen to a radio programme on your radio set made in Japan. You get dressed in clothes manufactured in Thailand. You drive to the university in a car made of parts manufactured in more than a dozen countries around the world. Then you open up your economics textbook written by two authors of whom one lives in the USA and the other lives in England, published by a company located in London and printed on paper made from trees grown in Finland.

Every day you rely on many people from around the world, most of whom you do not know, to provide you with the goods and services that you enjoy. Such interdependence is possible because people trade with one another. Those people who provide you with goods and services are not acting out of generosity or concern for your welfare. Nor is some government or supra-governmental agency directing them to make what you want and to give it to you. Instead, people provide you and other consumers with the goods and services they produce because they get something in return.

In subsequent chapters we will examine how our economy coordinates the activities of millions of people with varying tastes and abilities. As a starting point for this analysis, here we consider the reasons for economic interdependence. One of the *Ten Principles of Economics* highlighted in Chapter 1 is that trade can make everyone better off. This principle explains why people trade with their neighbours and why nations trade with other nations. In this chapter we examine this principle more closely. What exactly do people gain when they trade with one another? Why do people choose to become interdependent?

# A PARABLE FOR THE MODERN ECONOMY

To understand why people choose to depend on others for goods and services and how this choice improves their lives, let's look at a simple economy. Imagine that there are two goods in the world – beef and potatoes. And there are two people in the world – a cattle farmer named Connie and a market gardener named Mellors – each of whom would like to eat both beef and potatoes.

The gains from trade are most obvious if the cattle farmer can produce only meat and the market gardener can produce only potatoes. In one scenario, the farmer and the gardener could choose to have nothing to do with each other. But after several months of eating beef roasted, boiled, fried and grilled, the cattle farmer might decide that self-sufficiency is not all it's cracked up to be. The market gardener, who has been eating potatoes mashed, fried and baked, would most likely agree. It is easy to see that trade would allow them to enjoy greater variety: each could then have steak and chips.

Although this scene illustrates most simply how everyone can benefit from trade, the gains would be similar if the farmer and the gardener were each capable of producing the other good, but only at great cost. Suppose, for example, that the market gardener is able to rear cattle and produce meat, but that he is not very good at it. Similarly, suppose that the cattle farmer is able to grow potatoes, but that her land is not very well suited for it. In this case, it is easy to see that the gardener and the farmer can each benefit by specializing in what he or she does best and then trading with the other.

The gains from trade are less obvious, however, when one person is better at producing *every* good. For example, suppose that the cattle farmer is better at rearing cattle *and* better at growing potatoes than the market gardener. In this case, should the farmer or gardener choose to remain self-sufficient, or is there still reason for them to trade with each other? To answer this question, we need to look more closely at the factors that affect such a decision.

## Production Possibilities

Suppose that the gardener and the farmer each work eight hours a day six days a week (a working week of 48 hours) and take Sunday off. They can spend their time growing potatoes, rearing cattle, or a combination of the two. Table 3.1 shows the amount of time each person takes to produce 1 kilogram of each good. The gardener can produce 1 kilogram of meat in 6 hours and 1 kilogram of potatoes in an hour and a half. The farmer, who is more productive in both activities, can produce a kilogram of meat in 2 hours and a kilogram of potatoes in 1 hour. The last columns in Table 3.1 show the amounts of meat or potatoes the gardener and farmer can produce in a 48-hour working week, producing only that good.

Panel (a) of Figure 3.1 illustrates the amounts of meat and potatoes that the gardener can produce. If the gardener devotes all 48 hours of his time to potatoes, he produces 32 kilograms of potatoes (measured on the horizontal axis) and no meat. If he devotes all his time to meat, he produces 8 kilograms of meat (measured on the vertical axis) and no potatoes. If the gardener divides his time equally between the two activities, spending 24 hours a week on each, he produces 16 kilograms of potatoes and 4 kilograms of meat. The figure shows these three possible outcomes and all others in between.

This graph is the gardener's production possibilities frontier. As we discussed in Chapter 2, a production possibilities frontier shows the various mixes of output that an economy can produce. It illustrates one of the *Ten Principles of Economics* in Chapter 1: people face trade-offs. Here the gardener faces a trade-off between

## FIGURE 3.1

### The Production Possibilities Frontier

*Panel (a) shows the combinations of meat and potatoes that the gardener can produce. Panel (b) shows the combinations of meat and potatoes that the farmer can produce. Both production possibilities frontiers are derived from Table 3.1 and the assumption that the gardener and farmer each work 8 hours a day.*

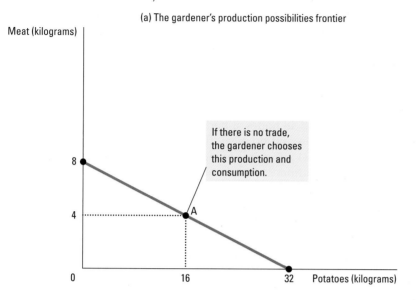

(a) The gardener's production possibilities frontier

If there is no trade, the gardener chooses this production and consumption.

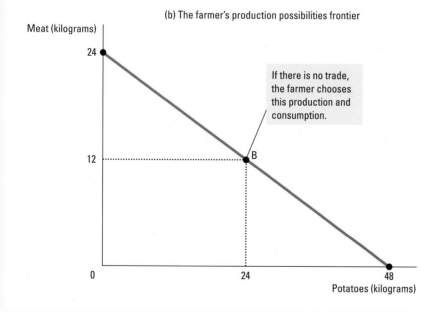

(b) The farmer's production possibilities frontier

If there is no trade, the farmer chooses this production and consumption.

producing meat and producing potatoes. You may recall that the production possibilities frontier in Chapter 2 was drawn bowed out; in that case, the trade-off between the two goods depended on the amounts being produced. Here, however, the gardener's technology for producing meat and potatoes (as summarized in Table 3.1) allows him to switch between one good and the other at a constant rate. In this case, the production possibilities frontier is a straight line.

## TABLE 3.1

**The Production Opportunities of the Gardener and the Farmer**

|  | Time needed to make 1 kg of: | | Amount of meat or potatoes produced in 48 hours | |
|---|---|---|---|---|
|  | **Meat** | **Potatoes** | **Meat** | **Potatoes** |
| Gardener | 6 hrs/kg | 1.5 hrs/kg | 8 kg | 32 kg |
| Farmer | 2 hrs/kg | 1 hr/kg | 24 kg | 48 kg |

Panel (b) of Figure 3.1 shows the production possibilities frontier for the farmer. If the farmer devotes all 48 hours of her working week to potatoes, she produces 48 kilograms of potatoes and no meat. If she devotes all of her time to meat production, she produces 24 kilograms of meat and no potatoes. If the farmer divides her time equally, spending 24 hours a week on each activity, she produces 24 kilograms of potatoes and 12 kilograms of meat. Once again, the production possibilities frontier shows all the possible outcomes.

If the gardener and farmer choose to be self-sufficient, rather than trade with each other, then each consumes exactly what he or she produces. In this case, the production possibilities frontier is also the consumption possibilities frontier. That is, without trade, Figure 3.1 shows the possible combinations of meat and potatoes that the gardener and farmer can each consume.

Although these production possibilities frontiers are useful in showing the trade-offs that the gardener and farmer face, they do not tell us what the gardener and farmer will actually choose to do. To determine their choices, we need to know the tastes of the gardener and the farmer. Let's suppose they choose the combinations identified by points A and B in Figure 3.1: the gardener produces and consumes 16 kilograms of potatoes and 4 kilograms of meat, while the farmer produces and consumes 24 kilograms of potatoes and 12 kilograms of meat.

## Specialization and Trade

After several years of feeding her family on combination B, the farmer gets an idea and she goes to talk to the gardener:

> FARMER: Mellors, my man, have I got a deal for you! I know how to improve life for both of us. I think you should stop producing meat altogether and devote all your time to growing potatoes. According to my calculations, if you devote all of your working week to growing potatoes, you'll produce 32 kilograms of potatoes. If you give me 15 of those 32 kilograms, I'll give you 5 kilograms of meat in return. In the end, you will enjoy 17 kilograms of potatoes and 5 kilograms of meat every week, instead of the 16 kilograms of potatoes and 4 kilograms of meat you now make do with. If you go along with my plan, you'll have more of *both* foods. [To illustrate her point, the farmer shows the gardener panel (a) of Figure 3.2.]
> 
> GARDENER: *(sounding sceptical)* That seems like a good deal for me, Connie, but I don't understand why you are offering it. If the deal is so good for me, it can't be good for you too.
> 
> FARMER: Oh, but it is, Mellors! Suppose I spend 12 hours a week growing potatoes and 36 hours rearing cattle. Then I can produce 18 kilograms of meat and 12 kilograms of potatoes. After I give you 5 kilograms of my

**FIGURE 3.2**

### How Trade Expands the Set of Consumption Opportunities

*The proposed trade between the gardener and the farmer offers each of them a combination of meat and potatoes that would be impossible in the absence of trade. In panel (a), the gardener consumes at point A\* rather than point A. In panel (b), the farmer consumes at point B\* rather than point B. Trade allows each to consume more meat and more potatoes.*

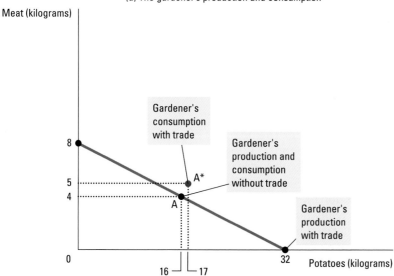

(a) The gardener's production and consumption

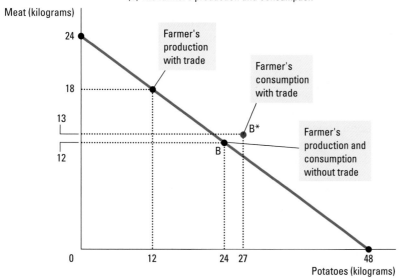

(b) The farmer's production and consumption

## TABLE 3.2

**The Gains from Trade: A Summary**

| | Gardener | | Farmer | |
|---|---|---|---|---|
| | Meat | Potatoes | Meat | Potatoes |
| **Without trade:** | | | | |
| Production and consumption | 4 kg | 16 kg | 12 kg | 24 kg |
| **With trade:** | | | | |
| Production | 0 kg | 32 kg | 18 kg | 12 kg |
| Trade | Gets 5 kg | Gives 15 kg | Gives 5 kg | Gets 15 kg |
| Consumption | 5 kg | 17 kg | 13 kg | 27 kg |
| **Gains from trade:** | | | | |
| Increase in consumption | +1 kg | +1 kg | +1 kg | +3 kg |

meat in exchange for 15 kilograms of your potatoes, I'll end up with 13 kilograms of meat and 27 kilograms of potatoes. So I will also be able to consume more of both foods than I do now. [She points out panel (b) of Figure 3.2.]

GARDENER: I don't know, Connie. … This sounds too good to be true.

FARMER: It's really not as complicated as it seems at first, my dear boy. Here – I've summarized my proposal for you in a simple table. [The farmer hands the gardener a copy of Table 3.2.]

GARDENER: *(after pausing to study the table)* These calculations seem correct, but I am puzzled. How can this deal make us both better off?

FARMER: We can both benefit because trade allows each of us to specialize in doing what we do best. You will spend more time growing potatoes and less time rearing cattle. I will spend more time rearing cattle and less time growing potatoes. As a result of specialization and trade, each of us can consume more meat and more potatoes without working any more hours.

**Quick Quiz** Draw an example of a production possibilities frontier for Robinson Crusoe, who is stranded on an island after a shipwreck and spends his time gathering coconuts and catching fish. Does this frontier limit Crusoe's consumption of coconuts and fish if he lives by himself? Does he face the same limits if he can trade with natives on the island?

## THE PRINCIPLE OF COMPARATIVE ADVANTAGE

The farmer's explanation of the gains from trade, though correct, poses a puzzle: if the farmer is better at both rearing cattle and growing potatoes, how can the gardener ever specialize in doing what he does best? The gardener doesn't seem to do anything best. To solve this puzzle, we need to look at the principle of *comparative advantage*.

As a first step in developing this principle, consider the following question: in our example, who can produce potatoes at lower cost – the gardener or the farmer? There are two possible answers, and in these two answers lie the solution to our puzzle and the key to understanding the gains from trade.

## Absolute Advantage

One way to answer the question about the cost of producing potatoes is to compare the inputs required by the two producers. Economists use the term **absolute advantage** when comparing the productivity of one person, firm, or nation to that of another. The producer that requires a smaller quantity of inputs to produce a good is said to have an absolute advantage in producing that good.

In our example, the farmer has an absolute advantage both in producing meat and in producing potatoes, because she requires less time than the gardener to produce a unit of either good. The farmer needs to input only 2 hours in order to produce a kilogram of meat, whereas the gardener needs 6 hours. Similarly, the farmer needs only 1 hour to produce a kilogram of potatoes, whereas the gardener needs 1.5 hours. Based on this information, we can conclude that the farmer has the lower cost of producing potatoes, if we measure cost in terms of the quantity of inputs.

**absolute advantage**
the comparison among producers of a good according to their productivity

## Opportunity Cost and Comparative Advantage

There is another way to look at the cost of producing potatoes. Rather than comparing inputs required, we can compare the opportunity costs. Recall from Chapter 1 that the **opportunity cost** of some item is what we give up to get that item. In our example, we assumed that the gardener and the farmer each spend 48 hours a week working. Time spent producing potatoes, therefore, takes away from time available for producing meat. As the farmer and gardener reallocate time between producing the two goods, they move along their production possibility frontiers; they give up units of one good to produce units of the other. The opportunity cost measures the trade-off between the two goods that each producer faces.

Let's first consider the farmer's opportunity cost. According to Table 3.1, producing 1 kilogram of potatoes takes her 1 hour of work. When the farmer spends that 1 hour producing potatoes, she spends 1 hour less producing meat. Because the farmer needs 2 hours to produce 1 kilogram of meat, 1 hour of work would yield ½ kilogram of meat. Hence, the farmer's opportunity cost of producing 1 kilogram of potatoes is ½ kilogram of meat.

Now consider the gardener's opportunity cost. Producing 1 kilogram of potatoes takes him 1½ hours. Because he needs 6 hours to produce 1 kilogram of meat, 1½ hours of work would yield ¼ kilogram of meat. Hence, the gardener's opportunity cost of 1 kilogram of potatoes is ¼ kilogram of meat.

Table 3.3 shows the opportunity costs of meat and potatoes for the two producers. Notice that the opportunity cost of meat is the inverse of the opportunity cost of potatoes. Because 1 kilogram of potatoes costs the farmer ½ kilogram of meat, 1 kilogram of meat costs the farmer 2 kilograms of potatoes. Similarly, because 1 kilogram of potatoes costs the gardener ¼ kilogram of meat, 1 kilogram of meat costs the gardener 4 kilograms of potatoes.

Economists use the term **comparative advantage** when describing the opportunity cost of two producers. The producer who gives up less of other goods to produce good X has the smaller opportunity cost of producing good X and is said to have a comparative advantage in producing it. In our example, the gardener has a lower opportunity cost of producing potatoes than does the farmer: a kilogram of potatoes costs the gardener only ¼ kilogram of meat, while it costs the farmer ½ kilogram of meat. Conversely, the farmer has a lower opportunity cost of producing meat than does the gardener: a kilogram of meat costs the farmer 2 kilograms of potatoes, while it costs the gardener 4 kilograms of potatoes. Thus,

**opportunity cost**
whatever must be given up to obtain some item

**comparative advantage**
the comparison among producers of a good according to their opportunity cost

### TABLE 3.3

**The Opportunity Cost of Meat and Potatoes**

|  | Opportunity cost of: | |
| --- | --- | --- |
|  | 1 kilogram of meat | 1 kilogram of potatoes |
| Gardener | 4 kg potatoes | 0.25 kg meat |
| Farmer | 2 kg potatoes | 0.5 kg meat |

the gardener has a comparative advantage in growing potatoes, and the farmer has a comparative advantage in producing meat.

Although it is possible for one person to have an absolute advantage in both goods (as the farmer does in our example), it is impossible for one person to have a comparative advantage in both goods. Because the opportunity cost of one good is the inverse of the opportunity cost of the other, if a person's opportunity cost of one good is relatively high, his opportunity cost of the other good must be relatively low. Comparative advantage reflects the relative opportunity cost. Unless two people have exactly the same opportunity cost, one person will have a

# FYI

## The Legacy of Adam Smith and David Ricardo

Economists have long understood the principle of comparative advantage. Here is how the great economist Adam Smith put the argument:

*It is a maxim of every prudent master of a family, never to attempt to make at home what it will cost him more to make than to buy. The tailor does not attempt to make his own shoes, but buys them of the shoemaker. The shoemaker does not attempt to make his own clothes but employs a tailor. The gardener attempts to make neither the one nor the other, but employs those different artificers. All of them find it for their interest to employ their whole industry in a way in which they have some advantage over their neighbours, and to purchase with a part of its produce, or what is the same thing, with the price of part of it, whatever else they have occasion for.*

This quotation is from Smith's 1776 book *An Inquiry into the Nature and Causes of the Wealth of Nations,* which was a landmark in the analysis of trade and economic interdependence.

Smith's book inspired David Ricardo – an Englishman born of Dutch parents – to become an economist, having already made his fortune as a stockbroker in the City of London. In his 1817 book *Principles of Political Economy and Taxation,* Ricardo developed the principle of comparative advantage as we

*David Ricardo*

know it today. His defence of free trade was not a mere academic exercise. Ricardo put his economic beliefs to work as a member of the British parliament, where he opposed the Corn Laws, which restricted the import of grain.

The conclusions of Adam Smith and David Ricardo on the gains from trade have held up well over time. Although economists often disagree on questions of policy, they are united in their support of free trade. Moreover, the central argument for free trade has not changed much in the past two centuries. Even though the field of economics has broadened its scope and refined its theories since the time of Smith and Ricardo, economists' opposition to trade restrictions is still based largely on the principle of comparative advantage.

comparative advantage in one good, and the other person will have a comparative advantage in the other good.

## Comparative Advantage and Trade

Differences in opportunity cost and comparative advantage create the gains from trade. When each person specializes in producing the good for which he or she has a comparative advantage, total production in the economy rises, and this increase in the size of the economic cake can be used to make everyone better off. In other words, as long as two people have different opportunity costs, each can benefit from trade by obtaining a good at a price that is lower than his or her opportunity cost of that good.

Consider the proposed deal from the viewpoint of the gardener. The gardener gets 5 kilograms of meat in exchange for 15 kilograms of potatoes. In other words, the gardener buys each kilogram of meat for a price of 3 kilograms of potatoes. This price of meat is lower than his opportunity cost for 1 kilogram of meat, which is 4 kilograms of potatoes. Thus, the gardener benefits from the deal because he gets to buy meat at a good price.

Now consider the deal from the farmer's viewpoint. The farmer buys 15 kilograms of potatoes for a price of 5 kilograms of meat. That is, the price of potatoes is ⅓ kilogram of meat. This price of potatoes is lower than her opportunity cost of 1 kilogram of potatoes, which is ½ kilogram of meat. The farmer benefits because she is able to buy potatoes at a good price.

These benefits arise because each person concentrates on the activity for which he or she has the lower opportunity cost: the gardener spends more time growing potatoes, and the farmer spends more time producing meat. As a result, the total production of potatoes and the total production of meat both rise. In our example, potato production rises from 40 to 44 kilograms, and meat production rises from 16 to 18 kilograms. The gardener and farmer share the benefits of this increased production. The moral of the story of the gardener and the farmer should now be clear: *trade can benefit everyone in society because it allows people to specialize in activities in which they have a comparative advantage.*

> **Quick Quiz** Robinson Crusoe can gather 10 coconuts or catch 1 fish per hour. His new friend, Man Friday, can gather 30 coconuts or catch 2 fish per hour. What is Crusoe's opportunity cost of catching one fish? What is Friday's? Who has an absolute advantage in catching fish? Who has a comparative advantage in catching fish?

# APPLICATIONS OF COMPARATIVE ADVANTAGE

The principle of comparative advantage explains interdependence and the gains from trade. Because interdependence is so prevalent in the modern world, the principle of comparative advantage has many applications. Here are two examples, one fanciful and one of great practical importance.

# IN THE NEWS

## What's The Advantage Of Trading With China?

*In recent years, the amount of trade that China transacts with the rest of the world has been growing rapidly. Some people have argued that this will make other countries poorer, since the Chinese are able to make some goods more cheaply. However, the principle of comparative advantage implies that, by allowing specialization, international trade should be to the benefit of everyone, as this article from* The Economist *newspaper makes clear.*

### China's Economic Success Should be Seen More as an Opportunity Than a Threat

Businesses all over the world have seen China gobble up the toy industry, and they now look on in horror as it does the same for shoes, fridges, microwaves and air conditioners. This country of 1.3 billion people has an apparently inexhaustible supply of workers, willing to work long hours for pitifully low pay. Boosted by its accession to the World Trade Organisation, China is sucking in foreign investment by the bucketload – last year, it became the world's biggest net recipient. How can anybody compete against this gigantic new workshop of the world?

There is no doubting the immense impact of a surging Chinese economy; or denying that for many, adjustment to the arrival of a new industrial goliath will be painful. But most of the economic fears that China arouses – that it will drive everybody else out of business, that it will always be super-competitive in everything, that it will cause mass unemployment – are plain wrong. They ignore all the benefits of China's growth. They also ignore elementary economics.

### As Scary as Japan

The world has been here before. In the 19th century, businessmen in many countries were convinced that Britain, the original workshop of the world, would steal their industries. Later, similar fears were expressed about the United States; as recently as the 1960s, the French were preoccupied with the economic *défi Americain*. Even closer parallels are the rise of Japan in the 1960s and 1970s and of South Korea in the 1980s and 1990s, both of which triggered worries about unfair competition. And remember Ross Perot's fears of a 'giant sucking sound' as a low-cost Mexico hoovered up jobs from the United States after the North American Free-Trade Agreement?

At their crudest, such concerns betray an abject failure to understand the economics of trade. Trade is never a zero-sum game; it profits buyers and sellers alike. It depends for its benefits not on competitive advantage, but on comparative advantage, a crucial distinction. Thus China may indeed be a cheaper place to manufacture everything than, say, Japan. But that does not mean that all manufacturing will or should shift from Japan to China. The central insight of trade theory is that, in such a situation, both countries will gain from specialising in goods in which they hold a comparative advantage (China in low-end manufacturing, Japan in higher value-added goods and services, say) and then trading with each other.

It is also easy for pessimists to overstate the magnitude of the problem. For all its rapid growth, China's share of world trade is only around 4% – about the same as Italy's. Its trade surplus, at around $30 billion, is similar to Canada's and smaller than Japan's, Germany's or even Russia's; and it has been shrinking. Although China has a big bilateral surplus with the United States – as which country does not? – it is running bilateral deficits with most of its supposedly threatened neighbours, including South Korea, Malaysia and Thailand.

Those deficits point to another factor that the fear-of-China brigade tends to ignore: the country's potential as an export market. Especially when other economies are stuttering, China's contribution to world demand is vital. Its share of world GDP, properly measured, is 12%; but its share of world GDP growth last year may have been as high as one-third. Although much foreign investment in China is aimed at exports, even more is intended to satisfy domestic demand. Far from being flattened by Chinese exports, the rest of East Asia is seeing fast-rising higher-value exports to China. Volkswagen counts China as its second-biggest market for cars after Germany. Legend Group, China's biggest computer-maker, is mostly supplying rising domestic demand. As WTO membership opens China's markets to competition, its importance as a source of demand will grow.

None of this is to say that China's rapid industrialisation will be problem-free for other countries. The shift from lower to higher value-added activities that it necessitates can be painful for companies and workers alike. It will be especially hard for the East Asian tigers that have only recently moved into low-end manufacturing. And some specific factors may obstruct China's own economic adjustment – and thus impose a bigger burden of adjustment on others. When a country's economy grows fast and its businesses grab markets from rivals, either real wages rise to match rising productivity, or the exchange rate starts to appreciate, or both. Japan and South Korea experienced both. The effect is to erode an initial cost advantage and to ease the burden of adjustment in other countries. But in China's case, the pool of underemployed labour in the countryside and in inefficient state-owned enterprises is so vast that real wages may rise only slowly. Meanwhile, its exchange rate is fixed against the dollar, and protected by capital controls.

Little can be done about real wages, although in practice it is certain that, even in China, they will eventually rise in line with higher productivity – as they have always done elsewhere. The exchange rate is trickier. China's price deflation and the dollar's weakness mean that the yuan is actually depreciating in real terms (though it is nonsense to accuse China of exporting deflation: its cheap exports are changing relative prices, not generating deflation overall). Some have urged China to scrap capital controls and float the currency. To do so immediately would be to invite a financial crisis, as China's banks, laden with bad debts, would collapse under the strain. A better idea would be to repeg the exchange rate at a higher parity, and move towards phasing out capital controls only after the banks' bad-debt problems are resolved.

**A Billion Blessings**
The focus, though, should not be on such obstacles, but on the great benefits of China's growth. Millions of consumers in other countries are gaining from the low prices and high quality of Chinese goods. A billion Chinese are escaping the dire poverty of the past. Businesses across the globe will profit from supplying a vast new market. These are wonders to be celebrated, not threats to be agonised over.

Source: *The Economist*, 13 February 2003. Copyright © The Economist Newspaper Limited, London.

## Should David Beckham Mow His Own Lawn?

David Beckham spends a lot of time on grass. One of the most talented footballers in the world, he can bend the ball around a defensive wall or pass it a hundred metres to land with deadly accuracy onto the boot of one of his team-mates in ways that most other professional footballers can only dream of doing. No one can bend it quite like Beckham. Most likely, he is talented at other activities too. For example, let's imagine that David Beckham can mow his lawn faster than anyone else. But just because he *can* mow his lawn fast, does this mean he *should*?

To answer this question, we can use the concepts of opportunity cost and comparative advantage. Let's say that David Beckham can mow his lawn in 2 hours. In that same 2 hours he could film a television advert for Adidas and earn, say, €10,000. By contrast, Alejandro, the boy next door, can mow David's lawn in 4 hours. In that same 4 hours, he could work at the local tapas bar and earn €20.

In this example, David's opportunity cost of mowing the lawn is €10,000 and Alejandro's opportunity cost is €20. David has an absolute advantage in mowing lawns because he can do the work in less time. Yet Alejandro has a comparative advantage in mowing lawns because he has the lower opportunity cost.

The gains from trade in this example are tremendous. Rather than mowing his own lawn, David should make the TV advert and hire Alejandro to mow the lawn. As long as David pays Alejandro more than €20 and less than €10,000, both of them are better off.

## Should the UK Trade With Other Countries?

Just as individuals can benefit from specialization and trade with one another, as the gardener and farmer did, so can populations of people in different countries.

**imports**
goods produced abroad and sold domestically

**exports**
goods produced domestically and sold abroad

Many of the goods that the British enjoy are produced abroad, and many of the goods produced in the United Kingdom are sold abroad. Goods produced abroad and sold domestically are called **imports**. Goods produced domestically and sold abroad are called **exports**.

To see how countries can benefit from trade, suppose there are two countries, the United Kingdom and Japan, and two goods, food and cars. Imagine that the two countries produce cars equally well: a UK worker and a Japanese worker can each produce 1 car per month. By contrast, because the UK has more land suitable for cultivation, it is better at producing food: a UK worker can produce 2 tonnes of food per month, whereas a Japanese worker can produce only 1 tonne of food per month.

The principle of comparative advantage states that each good should be produced by the country that has the smaller opportunity cost of producing that good. Because the opportunity cost of a car is 2 tonnes of food in the United Kingdom but only 1 tonne of food in Japan, Japan has a comparative advantage in producing cars. Japan should produce more cars than it wants for its own use and export some of them to the United Kingdom. Similarly, because the opportunity cost of a tonne of food is 1 car in Japan but only ½ car in the UK, the UK has a comparative advantage in producing food. The UK should produce more food than it wants to consume and export some of it to Japan. Through specialization and trade, both countries can have more food and more cars.

In reality, of course, the issues involved in trade among nations are more complex than this simple example suggests, as we will see later in the text. Most important among these issues is that each country has many citizens with different interests. International trade can make some individuals worse off, even as it makes the country as a whole better off. When the United Kingdom exports food and imports cars, the impact on a UK farmer is not the same as the impact on a UK car worker. Yet, contrary to the opinions sometimes voiced by politicians and political commentators, international trade is not like war, in which some countries win and others lose. Trade allows all countries to achieve greater prosperity.

**Quick Quiz** Suppose that the world's fastest typist happens to be trained in brain surgery. Should he do his own typing or hire a secretary? Explain.

## CONCLUSION

The principle of comparative advantage shows that trade can make everyone better off. You should now understand more fully the benefits of living in an interdependent economy. But having seen why interdependence is desirable, you might naturally ask how it is possible. How do free societies coordinate the diverse activities of all the people involved in their economies? What ensures that goods and services will get from those who should be producing them to those who should be consuming them?

In a world with only two people, such as the farmer and the gardener, the answer is simple: these two people can directly bargain and allocate resources between themselves. In the real world with billions of people, the answer is less obvious. We take up this issue in the next chapter, where we see that free societies allocate resources through the market forces of supply and demand.

# SUMMARY

- Each person consumes goods and services produced by many other people both in their country and around the world. Interdependence and trade are desirable because they allow everyone to enjoy a greater quantity and variety of goods and services.

- There are two ways to compare the ability of two people in producing a good. The person who can produce the good with the smaller quantity of inputs is said to have an *absolute advantage* in producing the good. The person who has the smaller opportunity cost of producing the good

is said to have a *comparative advantage*. The gains from trade are based on comparative advantage, not absolute advantage.

- Trade makes everyone better off because it allows people to specialize in those activities in which they have a comparative advantage.

- The principle of comparative advantage applies to countries as well as to people. Economists use the principle of comparative advantage to advocate free trade among countries.

# KEY CONCEPTS

absolute advantage, p. 51
opportunity cost, p. 51

comparative advantage, p. 51
imports, p. 56

exports, p. 56

# QUESTIONS FOR REVIEW

1. Explain how absolute advantage and comparative advantage differ.

2. Give an example in which one person has an absolute advantage in doing something but another person has a comparative advantage.

3. Is absolute advantage or comparative advantage more important for trade? Explain your reasoning using the example in your answer to Question 2.

4. Will a nation tend to export or import goods for which it has a comparative advantage? Explain.

5. Why do economists oppose policies that restrict trade among nations?

# PROBLEMS AND APPLICATIONS

1. Consider the gardener and the farmer from our example in this chapter. Explain why the gardener's opportunity cost of producing 1 kilogram of meat is 4 kilograms of potatoes. Explain why the farmer's opportunity cost of producing 1 kilogram of meat is 2 kilograms of potatoes.

2. Manuela can read 20 pages of economics in an hour. She can also read 50 pages of sociology in an hour. She spends 5 hours per day studying.
   a. Draw Manuela's production possibilities frontier for reading economics and sociology.
   b. What is Manuela's opportunity cost of reading 100 pages of sociology?

3. UK and Japanese workers can each produce 4 cars a year. A UK worker can produce 10 tonnes of grain a year, whereas a Japanese worker can produce 5 tonnes of grain a year. To keep things simple, assume that each country has 100 million workers.
   a. For this situation, construct a table analogous to Table 3.1.
   b. Graph the production possibilities frontier of the UK and Japanese economies.
   c. For the UK, what is the opportunity cost of a car? Of grain? For Japan, what is the opportunity cost of a car? Of grain? Put this information in a table analogous to Table 3.3.
   d. Which country has an absolute advantage in producing cars? In producing grain?
   e. Which country has a comparative advantage in producing cars? In producing grain?
   f. Without trade, half of each country's workers produce cars and half produce grain. What quantities of cars and grain does each country produce?
   g. Starting from a position without trade, give an example in which trade makes each country better off.

4. Victoria and David share a flat. They spend most of their time studying (of course), but they leave some time for their favourite activities: cooking pizza and making home-brew beer. Victoria takes 4 hours to produce 1 barrel of home-brew and 2 hours to make a pizza. David takes 6 hours to brew 1 barrel of beer and 4 hours to make a pizza.
   a. What is each flat-mate's opportunity cost of making a pizza? Who has the absolute advantage in making pizza? Who has the comparative advantage in making pizza?
   b. If Victoria and David trade foods with each other, who will trade away pizza in exchange for home-brew?

   c. The price of pizza can be expressed in terms of barrels of home-brew. What is the highest price at which pizza can be traded that would make both flat-mates better off? What is the lowest price? Explain.

5. Suppose that there are 10 million workers in Belgium, and that each of these workers can produce either 2 cars or 30 tonnes of wheat in a year.
   a. What is the opportunity cost of producing a car in Belgium? What is the opportunity cost of producing a tonne of wheat in Belgium? Explain the relationship between the opportunity costs of the two goods.
   b. Draw Belgium's production possibilities frontier. If Belgium chooses to consume 10 million cars, how much wheat can it consume without trade? Label this point on the production possibilities frontier.
   c. Now suppose that the United Kingdom offers to buy 10 million cars from Belgium in exchange for 20 tonnes of wheat per car. If Belgium continues to consume 10 million cars, how much wheat does this deal allow Belgium to consume? Label this point on your diagram. Should Belgium accept the deal?

6. Consider a professor who is writing a book. The professor can both write the chapters and gather the needed data faster than anyone else at his university. Still, he pays a student to collect data at the library. Is this sensible? Explain.

7. England and Scotland both produce scones and pullovers. Suppose that an English worker can produce 50 scones per hour or 1 pullover per hour. Suppose that a Scottish worker can produce 40 scones per hour or 2 pullovers per hour.
   a. Which country has the absolute advantage in the production of each good? Which country has the comparative advantage?
   b. If England and Scotland decide to trade, which commodity will Scotland trade to England? Explain.
   c. If a Scottish worker could produce only 1 pullover per hour, would Scotland still gain from trade? Would England still gain from trade? Explain.

8. The following table describes the production possibilities of two cities in the country of Footballia:

| | Pairs of red socks per worker per hour | Pairs of blue socks per worker per hour |
| --- | --- | --- |
| Manchester | 3 | 3 |
| Chelsea | 2 | 1 |

a. Without trade, what is the price of blue socks (in terms of red socks) in Manchester? What is the price in Chelsea?

b. Which city has an absolute advantage in the production of each colour sock? Which city has a comparative advantage in the production of each colour sock?

c. If the cities trade with each other, which colour sock will each export?

d. What is the range of prices at which trade can occur?

9. Suppose that all goods can be produced with fewer worker hours in Germany than in Belgium.

a. In what sense is the cost of all goods lower in Germany than in Belgium?

b. In what sense is the cost of some goods lower in Belgium?

c. If Germany and Belgium traded with each other, would both countries be better off as a result? Explain in the context of your answers to parts (a) and (b).

10. Are the following statements true or false? Explain in each case.

a. 'Two countries can achieve gains from trade even if one of the countries has an absolute advantage in the production of all goods.'

b. 'Certain very talented people have a comparative advantage in everything they do.'

c. 'If a certain trade is good for one person, it can't be good for the other one.'

 For further resources, visit
http://www.thomsonlearning.co.uk/mankiw_taylor

# 2

---

# SUPPLY AND DEMAND I:
# HOW MARKETS WORK

# 4 THE MARKET FORCES OF SUPPLY AND DEMAND

When there is a drought in southern Europe, the price of olive oil rises in supermarkets throughout Europe. When the Olympic games were held in Greece in 2004, the price of hotel rooms in Athens rocketed. When a war breaks out in the Middle East, the price of petrol in Europe rises and the price of a used Mercedes falls. What do these events have in common? They all show the workings of supply and demand.

*Supply* and *demand* are the two words that economists use most often – and for good reason. Supply and demand are the forces that make market economies work. They determine the quantity of each good produced and the price at which it is sold. If you want to know how any event or policy will affect the economy, you must think first about how it will affect supply and demand.

This chapter introduces the theory of supply and demand. It considers how buyers and sellers behave and how they interact with one another. It shows how supply and demand determine prices in a market economy and how prices, in turn, allocate the economy's scarce resources.

## MARKETS AND COMPETITION

The terms *supply* and *demand* refer to the behaviour of people as they interact with one another in markets. A **market** is a group of buyers and sellers of a particular good or service. The buyers as a group determine the demand for the product, and the sellers as a group determine the supply of the product. Before discussing

**market**
a group of buyers and sellers of a particular good or service

how buyers and sellers behave, let's first consider more fully what we mean by a 'market' and the various types of markets we observe in the economy.

## Competitive Markets

Markets take many forms. Sometimes markets are highly organized, such as the markets for many agricultural commodities. In these markets, buyers and sellers meet at a specific time and place, where an auctioneer helps set prices and arrange sales.

More often, markets are less organized. For example, consider the market for ice cream in a particular town. Buyers of ice cream do not meet together at any one time. The sellers of ice cream are in different locations and offer somewhat different products. There is no auctioneer calling out the price of ice cream. Each seller posts a price for a cornet of ice cream in their shop, and each buyer decides how much ice cream to buy at each shop.

Even though it is not organized, the group of ice cream buyers and ice cream sellers forms a market. Each buyer knows that there are several sellers from which to choose, and each seller is aware that his product is similar to that offered by other sellers. The price of ice cream and the quantity of ice cream sold are not determined by any single buyer or seller. Rather, price and quantity are determined by all buyers and sellers as they interact in the marketplace.

**competitive market**
a market in which there are many buyers and many sellers so that each has a negligible impact on the market price

The market for ice cream, like most markets in the economy, is highly competitive. A **competitive market** is a market in which there are many buyers and many sellers so that each has a negligible impact on the market price. Each seller of ice cream has limited control over the price because other sellers are offering similar products. A seller has little reason to charge less than the going price, and if he or she charges more, buyers will make their purchases elsewhere. Similarly, no single buyer of ice cream can influence the price of ice cream because each buyer purchases only a small amount.

In this chapter we examine how buyers and sellers interact in competitive markets. We see how the forces of supply and demand determine both the quantity of the good sold and its price.

## Competition: Perfect and Otherwise

We assume in this chapter that markets are *perfectly competitive*. Perfectly competitive markets are defined by two primary characteristics: (1) the goods being offered for sale are all the same, and (2) the buyers and sellers are so numerous that no single buyer or seller can influence the market price. Because buyers and sellers in perfectly competitive markets must accept the price the market determines, they are said to be *price takers*.

There are some markets in which the assumption of perfect competition applies perfectly. In the wheat market, for example, there are thousands of farmers who sell wheat and millions of consumers who use wheat and wheat products. Because no single buyer or seller can influence the price of wheat, each takes the price as given.

Not all goods and services, however, are sold in perfectly competitive markets. Some markets have only one seller, and this seller sets the price. Such a seller is called a *monopoly*. Your local water company, for instance, may be a monopoly. Residents in your area probably have only one water company from which to buy this service.

Some markets fall between the extremes of perfect competition and monopoly. One such market, called an *oligopoly,* has a few sellers that do not always compete aggressively. Airline routes are an example. If a route between two cities is serviced by only two or three carriers, the carriers may avoid rigorous competition so they can keep prices high. Another type of market is *monopolistically competitive;* it contains many sellers but each offers a slightly different product. Because the products are not exactly the same, each seller has some ability to set the price for its own product. An example is the market for magazines. Magazines compete with one another for readers and anyone can enter the market by starting a new one, but each magazine offers different articles and can set its own price.

Despite the diversity of market types we find in the world, we begin by studying perfect competition. Perfectly competitive markets are the easiest to analyse. Moreover, because some degree of competition is present in most markets, many of the lessons that we learn by studying supply and demand under perfect competition apply in more complicated markets as well.

**Quick Quiz**  What is a market?  •  What are the characteristics of a competitive market?

# DEMAND

We begin our study of markets by examining the behaviour of buyers. To focus our thinking, let's keep in mind a particular good – ice cream.

## The Demand Curve: The Relationship Between Price and Quantity Demanded

The **quantity demanded** of any good is the amount of the good that buyers are willing and able to purchase. As we shall see, many things determine the quantity demanded of any good, but when analysing how markets work, one determinant plays a central role – the price of the good. If the price of ice cream rose to €20 per scoop, you would buy less ice cream. You might buy a frozen ice lolly instead. If the price of ice cream fell to €0.20 per scoop, you would buy more. Because the quantity demanded falls as the price rises and rises as the price falls, we say that the quantity demanded is *negatively related* to the price. This relationship between price and quantity demanded is true for most goods in the economy and, in fact, is so pervasive that economists call it the **law of demand**: other things equal, when the price of a good rises, the quantity demanded of the good falls, and when the price falls, the quantity demanded rises.

The table in Figure 4.1 shows how many cornets of ice cream Harriet buys each month at different prices of ice cream. If ice cream is free, Harriet eats 12 cornets. At €0.50 per cornet, Harriet buys 10 cornets. As the price rises further, she buys fewer and fewer cornets. When the price reaches €3.00, Harriet doesn't buy any ice cream at all. This table is a **demand schedule,** a table that shows the relationship between the price of a good and the quantity demanded, holding constant everything else that influences how much consumers of the good want to buy.

The graph in Figure 4.1 uses the numbers from the table to illustrate the law of demand. By convention, the price of ice cream is on the vertical axis, and the quantity of ice cream demanded is on the horizontal axis. The downward sloping line relating price and quantity demanded is called the **demand curve**.

**quantity demanded**
the amount of a good that buyers are willing and able to purchase

**law of demand**
the claim that, other things equal, the quantity demanded of a good falls when the price of the good rises

**demand schedule**
a table that shows the relationship between the price of a good and the quantity demanded

**demand curve**
a graph of the relationship between the price of a good and the quantity demanded

### Harriet's Demand Schedule and Demand Curve

*The demand schedule shows the quantity demanded at each price. The demand curve, which graphs the demand schedule, shows how the quantity demanded of the good changes as its price varies. Because a lower price increases the quantity demanded, the demand curve slopes downward.*

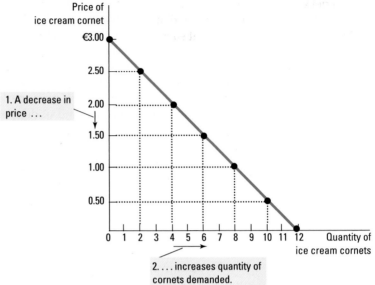

| Price of ice cream cornet | Quantity of cornets demanded |
|---|---|
| €0.00 | 12 |
| 0.50 | 10 |
| 1.00 | 8 |
| 1.50 | 6 |
| 2.00 | 4 |
| 2.50 | 2 |
| 3.00 | 0 |

1. A decrease in price ...

2. ... increases quantity of cornets demanded.

### Market Demand as the Sum of Individual Demands

*The quantity demanded in a market is the sum of the quantities demanded by all the buyers at each price. Thus, the market demand curve is found by adding horizontally the individual demand curves. At a price of €2, Harriet demands 4 ice cream cornets and Oliver demands 3 ice cream cornets. The quantity demanded in the market at this price is 7 cornets.*

| Price of ice cream cornet | Harriet | | Oliver | | Market |
|---|---|---|---|---|---|
| €0.00 | 12 | + | 7 | = | 19 |
| 0.50 | 10 | | 6 | | 16 |
| 1.00 | 8 | | 5 | | 13 |
| 1.50 | 6 | | 4 | | 10 |
| 2.00 | 4 | | 3 | | 7 |
| 2.50 | 2 | | 2 | | 4 |
| 3.00 | 0 | | 1 | | 1 |

Harriet's demand    +    Oliver's demand    =    Market demand

$D_{Harriet}$

$D_{Oliver}$

$D_{Market}$

Quantity of ice cream cornets

## Market Demand Versus Individual Demand

The demand curve in Figure 4.1 shows an individual's demand for a product. To analyse how markets work, we need to determine the *market demand*, which is the sum of all the individual demands for a particular good or service.

The table in Figure 4.2 shows the demand schedules for ice cream of two individuals – Harriet and Oliver. At any price, Harriet's demand schedule tells us how much ice cream she buys, and Oliver's demand schedule tells us how much ice cream he buys. The market demand at each price is the sum of the two individual demands.

The graph in Figure 4.2 shows the demand curves that correspond to these demand schedules. Notice that we sum the individual demand curves *horizontally* to obtain the market demand curve. That is, to find the total quantity demanded at any price, we add the individual quantities found on the horizontal axis of the individual demand curves. Because we are interested in analysing how markets work, we shall work most often with the market demand curve. The market demand curve shows how the total quantity demanded of a good varies as the price of the good varies, while all the other factors that affect how much consumers want to buy are held constant.

## Shifts in the Demand Curve

The demand curve for ice cream shows how much ice cream people buy at any given price, holding constant the many other factors beyond price that influence consumers' buying decisions. As a result, this demand curve need not be stable over time. If something happens to alter the quantity demanded at any given price, the demand curve shifts. For example, suppose the British Medical Association discovered that people who regularly eat ice cream live longer, healthier lives. The discovery would raise the demand for ice cream. At any given price, buyers would now want to purchase a larger quantity of ice cream and the demand curve for ice cream would shift.

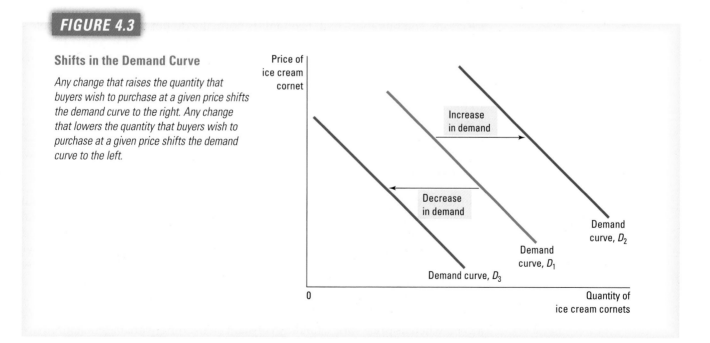

**FIGURE 4.3**

**Shifts in the Demand Curve**

*Any change that raises the quantity that buyers wish to purchase at a given price shifts the demand curve to the right. Any change that lowers the quantity that buyers wish to purchase at a given price shifts the demand curve to the left.*

Figure 4.3 illustrates shifts in demand. Any change that increases the quantity demanded at every price, such as our imaginary discovery by the British Medical Association, shifts the demand curve to the right and is called *an increase in demand*. Any change that reduces the quantity demanded at every price shifts the demand curve to the left and is called *a decrease in demand*.

There are many variables that can shift the demand curve. Here are the most important.

**Income** What would happen to your demand for ice cream if you lost your job one summer? Most likely, it would fall. A lower income means that you have less to spend in total, so you would have to spend less on some – and probably most – goods. If the demand for a good falls when income falls, the good is called a **normal good**.

Not all goods are normal goods. If the demand for a good rises when income falls, the good is called an **inferior good**. An example of an inferior good might be bus rides. As your income falls, you are less likely to buy a car or take a taxi and more likely to take the bus.

**Prices of Related Goods** Suppose that the price of ice lollies falls. The law of demand says that you will buy more ice lollies. At the same time, you will probably buy less ice cream. Because ice cream and ice lollies are both frozen, sweet confectionary, they satisfy similar desires. When a fall in the price of one good reduces the demand for another good, the two goods are called **substitutes**. Substitutes are often pairs of goods that are used in place of each other, such as beef steak and Wiener schnitzel, pullovers and sweatshirts, and cinema tickets and DVD rentals.

Now suppose that the price of chocolate flake bars falls. According to the law of demand, you will buy more chocolate flakes. Yet, in this case, you will buy more ice cream as well, because ice cream and chocolate flakes are often used together. When a fall in the price of one good raises the demand for another good, the two goods are called **complements**. Complements are often pairs of goods that are used together, such as petrol and cars, computers and software, bread and cheese, strawberries and cream, and bacon and eggs.

**Tastes** The most obvious determinant of your demand is your tastes. If you like ice cream, you buy more of it. Economists normally do not try to explain people's tastes because tastes are based on historical and psychological forces that are beyond the realm of economics. Economists do, however, examine what happens when tastes change.

**Expectations** Your expectations about the future may affect your demand for a good or service today. For example, if you expect to earn a higher income next month, you may be more willing to spend some of your current savings buying ice cream. As another example, if you expect the price of ice cream to fall tomorrow, you may be less willing to buy an ice cream cornet at today's price.

**Number of Buyers** Because market demand is derived from individual demands, it depends on all those factors that determine the demand of individual buyers, including buyers' incomes, tastes, expectations and the prices of related goods. In addition, it depends on the number of buyers. If Ben, another consumer of ice cream, were to join Harriet and Oliver, the quantity demanded in the market would be higher at every price and the demand curve would shift to the right.

**Summary** The demand curve shows what happens to the quantity demanded of a good when its price varies, holding constant all the other variables that influence

**normal good**
a good for which, other things equal, an increase in income leads to an increase in demand

**inferior good**
a good for which, other things equal, an increase in income leads to a decrease in demand

**substitutes**
two goods for which an increase in the price of one leads to an increase in the demand for the other

**complements**
two goods for which an increase in the price of one leads to a decrease in the demand for the other

## TABLE 4.1

**Variables That Influence Buyers**

*This table lists the variables that affect how much consumers choose to buy of any good. Notice the special role that the price of the good plays: a change in the good's price represents a movement along the demand curve, whereas a change in one of the other variables shifts the demand curve.*

| Variable | A change in this variable . . . |
|---|---|
| Price | Represents a movement along the demand curve |
| Income | Shifts the demand curve |
| Prices of related goods | Shifts the demand curve |
| Tastes | Shifts the demand curve |
| Expectations | Shifts the demand curve |
| Number of buyers | Shifts the demand curve |

buyers. When one of these other variables changes, the demand curve shifts. Table 4.1 lists all the variables that influence how much consumers choose to buy of a good.

## CASE STUDY

### Two Ways to Reduce the Quantity of Smoking Demanded

Public policy makers often want to reduce the amount that people smoke. There are two ways that policy can attempt to achieve this goal.

One way to reduce smoking is to shift the demand curve for cigarettes and other tobacco products. Anti-smoking campaigns on television, mandatory health warnings on cigarette packages and the prohibition of cigarette advertising are all policies aimed at reducing the quantity of cigarettes demanded at any given price. If successful, these policies shift the demand curve for cigarettes to the left, as in panel (a) of Figure 4.4.

Alternatively, policy makers can try to raise the price of cigarettes. If the government taxes the manufacture of cigarettes, for example, cigarette companies pass much of this tax on to consumers in the form of higher prices. A higher price encourages smokers to reduce the numbers of cigarettes they smoke. In this case, the reduced amount of smoking does not represent a shift in the demand curve. Instead, it represents a movement along the same demand curve to a point with a higher price and lower quantity, as in panel (b) of Figure 4.4.

How much does the amount of smoking respond to changes in the price of cigarettes? Economists have attempted to answer this question by studying what happens when the tax on cigarettes changes. They have found that a 10 per cent increase in the price causes about a 4 per cent reduction in the quantity demanded. Teenagers are found to be especially sensitive to the price of cigarettes: a 10 per cent increase in the price causes about a 12 per cent drop in teenage smoking.

A related question is how the price of cigarettes affects the demand for illicit drugs, such as marijuana. Opponents of cigarette taxes often argue that tobacco and marijuana are substitutes, so that high cigarette prices encourage marijuana use. By contrast, many experts on substance abuse view tobacco as a 'gateway drug' leading the young to experiment with other harmful substances. Most studies of the data are consistent with this view: they find that lower cigarette prices are associated with greater use of marijuana. In other words, tobacco and marijuana appear to be complements rather than substitutes.

PHOTO: COPYRIGHT © STOCK IMAGE/ALAMY

*What is the best way to reduce smoking?*

**FIGURE 4.4**

### Shifts in the Demand Curve Versus Movements Along the Demand Curve

*If health warnings on cigarette packets convince smokers to smoke less, the demand curve for cigarettes shifts to the left. In panel (a), the demand curve shifts from D$_1$ to D$_2$. At a price of €2 per pack, the quantity demanded falls from 20 to 10 cigarettes per day, as reflected by the shift from point A to point B. By contrast, if a tax raises the price of cigarettes, the demand curve does not shift. Instead, we observe a movement to a different point on the demand curve. In panel (b), when the price rises from €2 to €4, the quantity demanded falls from 20 to 12 cigarettes per day, as reflected by the movement from point A to point C.*

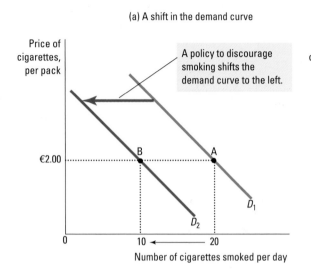

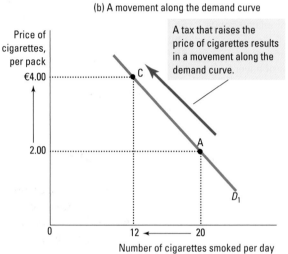

**Quick Quiz** Make up an example of a demand schedule for pizza, and graph the implied demand curve • Give an example of something that would shift this demand curve • Would a change in the price of pizza shift this demand curve?

## SUPPLY

We now turn to the other side of the market and examine the behaviour of sellers. Once again, to focus our thinking, let's consider the market for ice cream.

### The Supply Curve: The Relationship Between Price and Quantity Supplied

**quantity supplied**
the amount of a good that sellers are willing and able to sell

The **quantity supplied** of any good or service is the amount that sellers are willing and able to sell. There are many determinants of quantity supplied, but once again price plays a special role in our analysis. When the price of ice cream is high, selling ice cream is profitable, and so the quantity supplied is large. Sellers of ice cream work long hours, buy many ice cream machines and hire many workers. By contrast, when the price of ice cream is low, the business is less profitable, and so sellers produce less ice cream. At a low price, some sellers may even choose to shut down, and their quantity supplied falls to zero. Because the quantity supplied rises as the price rises and falls as the price falls, we say that the quantity supplied is *positively related* to the price of the good. This relationship between price and quantity supplied is called the **law of supply**: other things equal, when the price of a good rises, the quantity supplied of the good also rises, and when the price falls, the quantity supplied falls as well.

The table in Figure 4.5 shows the quantity supplied by Häagen, an ice cream seller, at various prices of ice cream. At a price below €1.00 per cornet of ice cream, Häagen does not supply any ice cream at all. As the price rises, he supplies a greater and greater quantity. This is the **supply schedule,** a table that shows the relationship between the price of a good and the quantity supplied, holding constant everything else that influences how much producers of the good want to sell.

The graph in Figure 4.5 uses the numbers from the table to illustrate the law of supply. The curve relating price and quantity supplied is called the **supply curve.** The supply curve slopes upward because, other things equal, a higher price means a greater quantity supplied.

**law of supply**
the claim that, other things equal, the quantity supplied of a good rises when the price of the good rises

**supply schedule**
a table that shows the relationship between the price of a good and the quantity supplied

**supply curve**
a graph of the relationship between the price of a good and the quantity supplied

## Market Supply Versus Individual Supply

Just as market demand is the sum of the demands of all buyers, market supply is the sum of the supplies of all sellers. The table in Figure 4.6 shows the supply schedules for two ice cream producers – Häagen and Dazs. At any price, Häagen's supply schedule tells us the quantity of ice cream Häagen supplies, and Dazs's supply

---

**FIGURE 4.5**

**Häagen's Supply Schedule and Supply Curve**

*The supply schedule shows the quantity supplied at each price. This supply curve, which graphs the supply schedule, shows how the quantity supplied of the good changes as its price varies. Because a higher price increases the quantity supplied, the supply curve slopes upward.*

| Price of ice cream cornet | Quantity of cornets demanded |
|---|---|
| €0.00 | 0 |
| 0.50 | 0 |
| 1.00 | 1 |
| 1.50 | 2 |
| 2.00 | 3 |
| 2.50 | 4 |
| 3.00 | 5 |

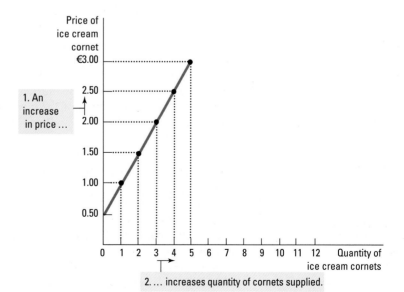

**FIGURE 4.6**

### Market Supply as the Sum of Individual Supplies

*The quantity supplied in a market is the sum of the quantities supplied by all the sellers at each price. Thus, the market supply curve is found by adding horizontally the individual supply curves. At a price of €2, Häagen supplies 3 ice cream cornets, and Dazs supplies 4 ice cream cornets. The quantity supplied in the market at this price is 7 cornets.*

| Price of ice cream cornet | Häagen | | Dazs | | Market |
|---|---|---|---|---|---|
| €0.00 | 0 | + | 0 | = | 0 |
| 0.50 | 0 | | 0 | | 0 |
| 1.00 | 1 | | 0 | | 1 |
| 1.50 | 2 | | 2 | | 4 |
| 2.00 | 3 | | 4 | | 7 |
| 2.50 | 4 | | 6 | | 10 |
| 3.00 | 5 | | 8 | | 13 |

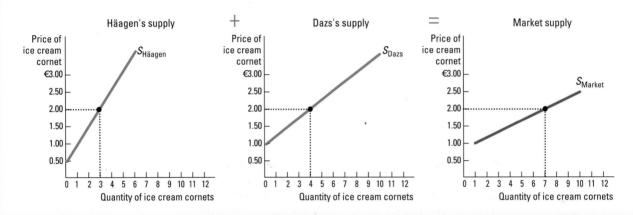

schedule tells us the quantity of ice cream Dazs supplies. The market supply is the sum of the two individual supplies.

The graph in Figure 4.6 shows the supply curves that correspond to the supply schedules. As with demand curves, we sum the individual supply curves *horizontally* to obtain the market supply curve. That is, to find the total quantity supplied at any price, we add the individual quantities found on the horizontal axis of the individual supply curves. The market supply curve shows how the total quantity supplied varies as the price of the good varies.

## Shifts in the Supply Curve

The supply curve for ice cream shows how much ice cream producers offer for sale at any given price, holding constant all the other factors beyond price that influence producers' decisions about how much to sell. This relationship can change over time, which is represented by a shift in the supply curve. For example, suppose the price of sugar falls. Because sugar is an input into producing ice cream, the fall in the price of sugar makes selling ice cream more profitable. This raises the supply of ice cream: at any given price, sellers are now willing to produce a larger quantity. Thus, the supply curve for ice cream shifts to the right.

## FIGURE 4.7

**Shifts in the Supply Curve**

*Any change that raises the quantity that sellers wish to produce at a given price shifts the supply curve to the right. Any change that lowers the quantity that sellers wish to produce at a given price shifts the supply curve to the left.*

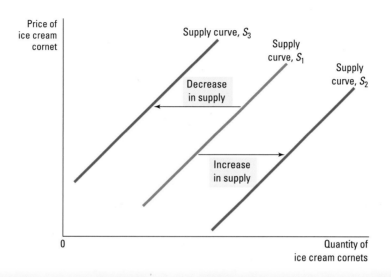

Figure 4.7 illustrates shifts in supply. Any change that raises quantity supplied at every price, such as a fall in the price of sugar, shifts the supply curve to the right and is called *an increase in supply*. Similarly, any change that reduces the quantity supplied at every price shifts the supply curve to the left and is called *a decrease in supply*.

There are many variables that can shift the supply curve. Here are some of the most important.

**Input Prices** To produce its output of ice cream, sellers use various inputs: cream, sugar, flavouring, ice cream machines, the buildings in which the ice cream is made, and the labour of workers to mix the ingredients and operate the machines. When the price of one or more of these inputs rises, producing ice cream is less profitable and firms supply less ice cream. If input prices rise substantially, a firm might shut down and supply no ice cream at all. Thus, the supply of a good is negatively related to the price of the inputs used to make the good.

**Technology** The technology for turning the inputs into ice cream is yet another determinant of supply. The invention of the mechanized ice cream machine, for example, reduced the amount of labour necessary to make ice cream. By reducing firms' costs, the advance in technology raised the supply of ice cream.

**Expectations** The amount of ice cream a firm supplies today may depend on its expectations of the future. For example, if it expects the price of ice cream to rise in the future, it will put some of its current production into storage and supply less to the market today.

**Number of Sellers** Market supply depends on all those factors that influence the supply of individual sellers, such as the prices of inputs used to produce the

## TABLE 4.2

**Variables That Influence Sellers**

*This table lists the variables that affect how much producers choose to sell of any good. Notice the special role that the price of the good plays: a change in the good's price represents a movement along the supply curve, whereas a change in one of the other variables shifts the supply curve.*

| Variable | A change in this variable . . . |
| --- | --- |
| Price | Represents a movement along the supply curve |
| Input prices | Shifts the supply curve |
| Technology | Shifts the supply curve |
| Expectations | Shifts the supply curve |
| Number of sellers | Shifts the supply curve |

good, the available technology and expectations. In addition, the supply in a market depends on the number of sellers. If Häagen or Dazs were to retire from the ice cream business, the supply in the market would fall.

**Summary** The supply curve shows what happens to the quantity supplied of a good when its price varies, holding constant all the other variables that influence sellers. When one of these other variables changes, the supply curve shifts. Table 4.2 lists all the variables that influence how much producers choose to sell of a good.

**Quick Quiz** Make up an example of a supply schedule for pizza, and graph the implied supply curve • Give an example of something that would shift this supply curve • Would a change in the price of pizza shift this supply curve?

# SUPPLY AND DEMAND TOGETHER

Having analysed supply and demand separately, we now combine them to see how they determine the quantity of a good sold in a market and its price.

## Equilibrium

**equilibrium**
a situation in which the price has reached the level where quantity supplied equals quantity demanded

**equilibrium price**
the price that balances quantity supplied and quantity demanded

**equilibrium quantity**
the quantity supplied and the quantity demanded at the equilibrium price

Figure 4.8 shows the market supply curve and market demand curve together. Notice that there is one point at which the supply and demand curves intersect. This point is called the market's **equilibrium.** The price at this intersection is called the **equilibrium price,** and the quantity is called the **equilibrium quantity.** Here the equilibrium price is €2.00 per cornet, and the equilibrium quantity is 7 ice cream cornets.

The dictionary defines the word *equilibrium* as a situation in which various forces are in balance – and this also describes a market's equilibrium. At the equilibrium price, the quantity of the good that buyers are willing and able to buy exactly balances the quantity that sellers are willing and able to sell. The equilibrium price is sometimes called the *market-clearing price* because, at this price, everyone in the market has been satisfied: buyers have bought all they want to buy, and sellers have sold all they want to sell.

**FIGURE 4.8**

### The Equilibrium of Supply and Demand

*The equilibrium is found where the supply and demand curves intersect. At the equilibrium price, the quantity supplied equals the quantity demanded. Here the equilibrium price is €2: at this price, 7 ice cream cornets are supplied and 7 ice cream cornets are demanded.*

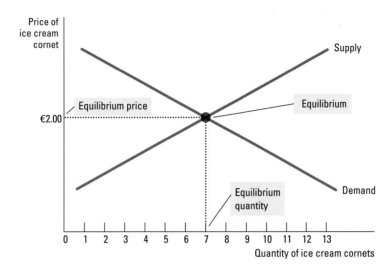

The actions of buyers and sellers naturally move markets towards the equilibrium of supply and demand. To see why, consider what happens when the market price is not equal to the equilibrium price.

Suppose first that the market price is above the equilibrium price, as in panel (a) of Figure 4.9. At a price of €2.50 per cornet, the quantity of the good supplied (10 cornets) exceeds the quantity demanded (4 cornets). There is a **surplus** of the good: suppliers are unable to sell all they want at the going price. A surplus is sometimes called a situation of *excess supply*. When there is a surplus in the ice cream market, sellers of ice cream find their freezers increasingly full of ice cream they would like to sell but cannot. They respond to the surplus by cutting their prices. Falling prices, in turn, increase the quantity demanded and decrease the quantity supplied. Prices continue to fall until the market reaches the equilibrium.

**surplus**
a situation in which quantity supplied is greater than quantity demanded

Suppose now that the market price is below the equilibrium price, as in panel (b) of Figure 4.9. In this case, the price is €1.50 per cornet, and the quantity of the good demanded exceeds the quantity supplied. There is a **shortage** of the good: demanders are unable to buy all they want at the going price. A shortage is sometimes called a situation of *excess demand*. When a shortage occurs in the ice cream market, buyers have to wait in long queues for a chance to buy one of the few cornets that are available. With too many buyers chasing too few goods, sellers can respond to the shortage by raising their prices without losing sales. As the price rises, quantity demanded falls, quantity supplied rises and the market once again moves toward the equilibrium.

**shortage**
a situation in which quantity demanded is greater than quantity supplied

Thus, the activities of the many buyers and sellers automatically push the market price towards the equilibrium price. Once the market reaches its equilibrium, all buyers and sellers are satisfied, and there is no upward or downward pressure on the price. How quickly equilibrium is reached varies from market to

**Markets Not in Equilibrium**

*In panel (a), there is a surplus. Because the market price of €2.50 is above the equilibrium price, the quantity supplied (10 cornets) exceeds the quantity demanded (4 cornets). Suppliers try to increase sales by cutting the price of a cornet, and this moves the price toward its equilibrium level. In panel (b), there is a shortage. Because the market price of €1.50 is below the equilibrium price, the quantity demanded (10 cornets) exceeds the quantity supplied (4 cornets). With too many buyers chasing too few goods, suppliers can take advantage of the shortage by raising the price. Hence, in both cases, the price adjustment moves the market towards the equilibrium of supply and demand.*

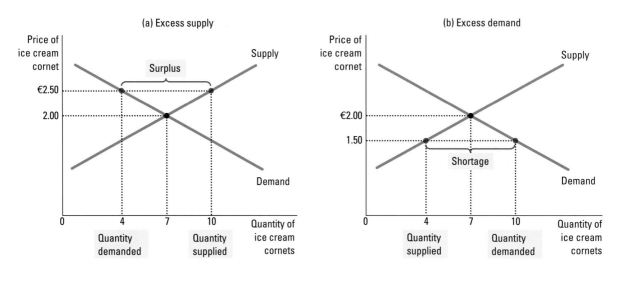

market, depending on how quickly prices adjust. In most free markets, surpluses and shortages are only temporary because prices eventually move towards their equilibrium levels. Indeed, this phenomenon is so pervasive that it is called the **law of supply and demand:** the price of any good adjusts to bring the quantity supplied and quantity demanded for that good into balance.

**law of supply and demand**
the claim that the price of any good adjusts to bring the quantity supplied and the quantity demanded for that good into balance

## Three Steps to Analysing Changes in Equilibrium

So far we have seen how supply and demand together determine a market's equilibrium, which in turn determines the price of the good and the amount of the good that buyers purchase and sellers produce. Of course, the equilibrium price and quantity depend on the position of the supply and demand curves. When some event shifts one of these curves, the equilibrium in the market changes. The analysis of such a change is called *comparative statics* because it involves comparing two unchanging situations – an initial and a new equilibrium.

When analysing how some event affects a market, we proceed in three steps. First, we decide whether the event shifts the supply curve, the demand curve or, in some cases, both curves. Secondly, we decide whether the curve shifts to the right or to the left. Thirdly, we use the supply and demand diagram to compare the initial and the new equilibrium, which shows how the shift affects the equilibrium price and quantity. Table 4.3 summarizes these three steps. To see how this recipe is used, let's consider various events that might affect the market for ice cream.

**TABLE 4.3**

**A Three-Step Programme for Analysing Changes in Equilibrium**

1. Decide whether the event shifts the supply or demand curve (or perhaps both).
2. Decide in which direction the curve shifts.
3. Use the supply and demand diagram to see how the shift changes the equilibrium price and quantity.

**Example: A Change in Demand** Suppose that one summer the weather is very hot. How does this event affect the market for ice cream? To answer this question, let's follow our three steps.

1. The hot weather affects the demand curve by changing people's taste for ice cream. That is, the weather changes the amount of ice cream that people want to buy at any given price. The supply curve is unchanged because the weather does not directly affect the firms that sell ice cream.
2. Because hot weather makes people want to eat more ice cream, the demand curve shifts to the right. Figure 4.10 shows this increase in demand as the shift in the demand curve from $D_1$ to $D_2$. This shift indicates that the quantity of ice cream demanded is higher at every price.
3. As Figure 4.10 shows, the increase in demand raises the equilibrium price from €2.00 to €2.50 and the equilibrium quantity from 7 to 10 cornets. In other words, the hot weather increases the price of ice cream and the quantity of ice cream sold.

**FIGURE 4.10**

**How an Increase in Demand Affects the Equilibrium**

*An event that raises quantity demanded at any given price shifts the demand curve to the right. The equilibrium price and the equilibrium quantity both rise. Here, an abnormally hot summer causes buyers to demand more ice cream. The demand curve shifts from D$_1$ to D$_2$, which causes the equilibrium price to rise from €2.00 to €2.50 and the equilibrium quantity to rise from 7 to 10 cornets.*

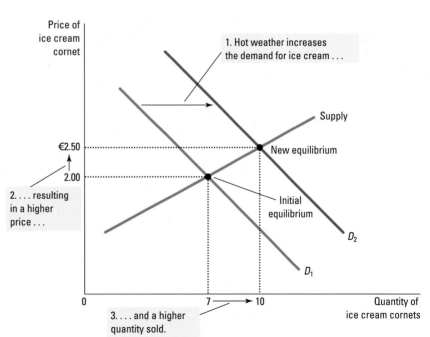

**Shifts in Curves Versus Movements Along Curves** Notice that when hot weather drives up the price of ice cream, the quantity of ice cream that firms supply rises, even though the supply curve remains the same. In this case, economists say there has been an increase in 'quantity supplied' but no change in 'supply'.

'Supply' refers to the position of the supply curve, whereas the 'quantity supplied' refers to the amount suppliers wish to sell. In this example, supply does not change because the weather does not alter firms' desire to sell at any given price. Instead, the hot weather alters consumers' desire to buy at any given price and thereby shifts the demand curve. The increase in demand causes the equilibrium price to rise. When the price rises, the quantity supplied rises. This increase in quantity supplied is represented by the movement along the supply curve.

To summarize, a shift *in* the supply curve is called a 'change in supply', and a shift *in* the demand curve is called a 'change in demand'. A movement *along* a fixed supply curve is called a 'change in the quantity supplied', and a movement *along* a fixed demand curve is called a 'change in the quantity demanded'.

**Example: A Change in Supply** Suppose that, during another summer, a hurricane destroys part of the South American sugar cane crop and drives up the world price of sugar. How does this event affect the market for ice cream? Once again, to answer this question, we follow our three steps.

1. The change in the price of sugar, an input into making ice cream, affects the supply curve. By raising the costs of production, it reduces the amount of ice cream that firms produce and sell at any given price. The demand curve does not change because the higher cost of inputs does not directly affect the amount of ice cream households wish to buy.
2. The supply curve shifts to the left because, at every price, the total amount that firms are willing and able to sell is reduced. Figure 4.11 illustrates this decrease in supply as a shift in the supply curve from $S_1$ to $S_2$.
3. As Figure 4.11 shows, the shift in the supply curve raises the equilibrium price from €2.00 to €2.50 and lowers the equilibrium quantity from 7 to 4 cornets. As a result of the sugar price increase, the price of ice cream rises, and the quantity of ice cream sold falls.

**Example: A Change in Both Supply and Demand** Now suppose that the heat wave and the hurricane occur during the same summer. To analyse this combination of events, we again follow our three steps.

1. We determine that both curves must shift. The hot weather affects the demand curve because it alters the amount of ice cream that households want to buy at any given price. At the same time, when the hurricane drives up sugar prices, it

## FIGURE 4.11

### How a Decrease in Supply Affects the Equilibrium

*An event that reduces quantity supplied at any given price shifts the supply curve to the left. The equilibrium price rises, and the equilibrium quantity falls. Here, an increase in the price of sugar (an input) causes sellers to supply less ice cream. The supply curve shifts from $S_1$ to $S_2$, which causes the equilibrium price of ice cream to rise from €2.00 to €2.50 and the equilibrium quantity to fall from 7 to 4 cornets.*

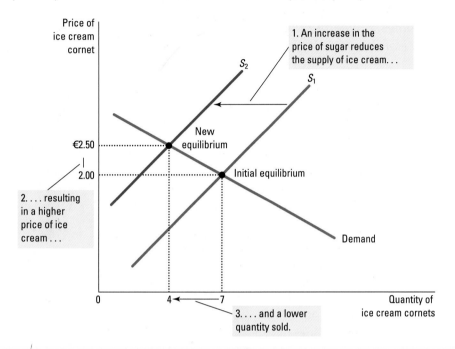

alters the supply curve for ice cream because it changes the amount of ice cream that firms want to sell at any given price.
2. The curves shift in the same directions as they did in our previous analysis: the demand curve shifts to the right, and the supply curve shifts to the left. Figure 4.12 illustrates these shifts.
3. As Figure 4.12 shows, there are two possible outcomes that might result, depending on the relative size of the demand and supply shifts. In both cases, the equilibrium price rises. In panel (a), where demand increases substantially while supply falls just a little, the equilibrium quantity also rises. By contrast, in panel (b), where supply falls substantially while demand rises just a little, the equilibrium quantity falls. Thus, these events certainly raise the price of ice cream, but their impact on the amount of ice cream sold is ambiguous (that is, it could go either way).

**Summary** We have just seen three examples of how to use supply and demand curves to analyse a change in equilibrium. Whenever an event shifts the supply curve, the demand curve, or perhaps both curves, you can use these tools to predict how the event will alter the amount sold in equilibrium and the price at which the good is sold. Table 4.4 shows the predicted outcome for any combination of shifts in the two curves. To make sure you understand how to use the tools of supply and demand, pick a few entries in this table and make sure you can explain to yourself why the table contains the prediction it does.

# IN THE NEWS

## Mother Nature Shifts the Supply Curve

*According to our analysis, weather conditions that reduce supply reduce the quantity sold and raise the price. Here's a recent example.*

### After the Long, Hot Summer… the Short, Brown Christmas Tree

by Elizabeth Day

The long hot summer has exacted a cruel price: Christmas trees will be in short supply this year because the drought has wiped out up to a third of the British crop. Buyers are being told to brace themselves for price increases of up to 15 per cent as tree-growers struggle to cope with the aftermath of the hottest and driest summer on record. Growers are also warning of an increased chance of "needle-drop", thinner foliage and brown discoloration because the trees are struggling to retain moisture.

The British Christmas Tree Growers Association admitted that the hot weather had caused "a serious problem" both in Britain and on the Continent, which experienced even higher temperatures. Imports from Denmark, Norway, Belgium and Ireland account for about one million of the seven million trees sold in Britain each year.

The price of an average 5ft–6ft tall Norway spruce – which accounts for 70 per cent of annual sales – could now rise from £12 to about £14.

Roger Hay, the growers association's secretary, said: "There are a number of problems caused by this year's intense heat. There is a lack of colour in some trees because they require a great deal of water and many growers have also lost their crops of young trees. It is a serious problem in particular areas: certainly in the east and the southern side of the UK. "There will certainly be an increase in price and a shortage of potted trees this year. The ground is so hard that it will also be incredibly difficult for growers to dig them up."…

Kieran Gill, a grower and retailer based on Westwood Farm near Orpington, Kent, said that his 30,000 trees had been badly affected by the summer heat. "We are suffering serious losses," said Mr Gill, who has been growing Christmas trees for 22 years. "The trees are already going brown and some will be unsaleable. I've lost

*"Higher price or smaller tree, Albert? It's called a trade-off."*

about 10 per cent of my crop through the summer heat. It affected the full-grown trees as well as the young ones and most of them are suffering from needle-drop. "They look quite bad at the moment. We'll have to suffer it out the best we can. I'm hoping that if they all look as bad as each other, no one will be able to tell the difference."

Source: *The Daily Telegraph*, 13 September 2003.

**Quick Quiz** Analyse what happens to the market for pizza if the price of tomatoes rises. • Analyse what happens to the market for pasta if the price of potatoes falls.

## CONCLUSION: HOW PRICES ALLOCATE RESOURCES

This chapter has analysed supply and demand in a single market. Although our discussion has centred around the market for ice cream, the lessons learned here apply in most other markets as well. Whenever you go to a shop to buy something, you are contributing to the demand for that item. Whenever you look for a job, you are contributing to the supply of labour services. Because supply

## FIGURE 4.12

### A Shift in Both Supply and Demand

*Here we observe a simultaneous increase in demand and decrease in supply. Two outcomes are possible. In panel (a), the equilibrium price rises from $P_1$ to $P_2$, and the equilibrium quantity rises from $Q_1$ to $Q_2$. In panel (b), the equilibrium price again rises from $P_1$ to $P_2$, but the equilibrium quantity falls from $Q_1$ to $Q_2$.*

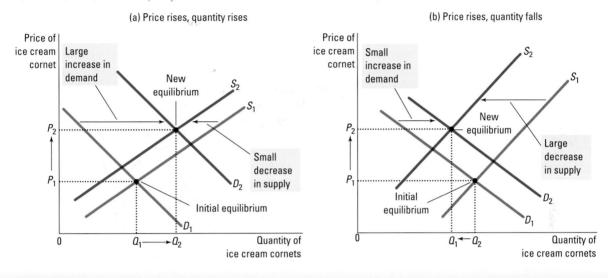

(a) Price rises, quantity rises

(b) Price rises, quantity falls

## TABLE 4.4

### What Happens to Price and Quantity When Supply or Demand Shifts?

*As a quick quiz, make sure you can explain each of the entries in this table using a supply and demand diagram.*

|  | No change in supply | An increase in supply | A decrease in supply |
|---|---|---|---|
| No change in demand | P same<br>Q same | P down<br>Q up | P up<br>Q down |
| An increase in demand | P up<br>Q up | P ambiguous<br>Q up | P up<br>Q ambiguous |
| A decrease in demand | P down<br>Q down | P down<br>Q ambiguous | P ambiguous<br>Q down |

and demand are such pervasive economic phenomena, the model of supply and demand is a powerful tool for analysis. We shall be using this model repeatedly in the following chapters.

One of the *Ten Principles of Economics* discussed in Chapter 1 is that markets are usually a good way to organize economic activity. Although it is still too early to judge whether market outcomes are good or bad, in this chapter we have begun to see how markets work. In any economic system, scarce resources have to be allocated among competing uses. Market economies harness the forces of supply and demand to serve that end. Supply and demand together determine the prices of the economy's many different goods and services; prices in turn are the signals that guide the allocation of resources.

*"I see the businessman's lunch is up 50p."*

For example, consider the allocation of property on the seafront in a seaside resort. Because the amount of this property is limited, not everyone can enjoy the luxury of living by the beach. Who gets this resource? The answer is: whoever is willing and able to pay the price. The price of seafront property adjusts until the quantity of property demanded exactly balances the quantity supplied. Thus, in market economies, prices are the mechanism for rationing scarce resources.

Similarly, prices determine who produces each good and how much is produced. For instance, consider farming. Because we need food to survive, it is crucial that some people work on farms. What determines who is a farmer and who is not? In a free society, there is no government planning agency making this decision and ensuring an adequate supply of food. Instead, the allocation of workers to farms is based on the job decisions of millions of workers. This decentralized system works well because these decisions depend on prices. The prices of food and the wages of farm workers (the price of their labour) adjust to ensure that enough people choose to be farmers.

If a person had never seen a market economy in action, the whole idea might seem preposterous. Economies are large groups of people engaged in many interdependent activities. What prevents decentralized decision making from degenerating into chaos? What coordinates the actions of the millions of people with their varying abilities and desires? What ensures that what needs to get done does in fact get done? The answer, in a word, is *prices.* If market economies are guided by an invisible hand, as Adam Smith famously suggested, then prices are the baton that the invisible hand uses to conduct the economic orchestra.

## SUMMARY

- Economists use the model of supply and demand to analyse competitive markets. In a competitive market, there are many buyers and sellers, each of whom has little or no influence on the market price.

- The demand curve shows how the quantity of a good demanded depends on the price. According to the law of demand, as the price of a good falls, the quantity demanded rises. Therefore, the demand curve slopes downward.

- In addition to price, other determinants of how much consumers want to buy include income, the prices of substitutes and complements, tastes, expectations and the number of buyers. If one of these factors changes, the demand curve shifts.

- The supply curve shows how the quantity of a good supplied depends on the price. According to the law of supply, as the price of a good rises, the quantity supplied rises. Therefore, the supply curve slopes upward.

- In addition to price, other determinants of how much producers want to sell include input prices, technology, expectations and the number of sellers. If one of these factors changes, the supply curve shifts.

- The intersection of the supply and demand curves determines the market equilibrium. At the equilibrium price, the quantity demanded equals the quantity supplied.

- The behaviour of buyers and sellers naturally drives markets toward their equilibrium. When the market price is above the equilibrium price, there is a surplus of the good, which causes the market price to fall. When the market price is below the equilibrium price, there is a shortage, which causes the market price to rise.

- To analyse how any event influences a market, we use the supply and demand diagram to examine how the event affects the equilibrium price and quantity. To do this we follow three steps. First, we decide whether the event shifts the supply curve or the demand curve (or both). Secondly, we decide which direction the curve shifts. Thirdly, we compare the new equilibrium with the initial equilibrium.

- In market economies, prices are the signals that guide economic decisions and thereby allocate scarce resources. For every good in the economy, the price ensures that supply and demand are in balance. The equilibrium price then determines how much of the good buyers choose to purchase and how much sellers choose to produce.

# KEY CONCEPTS

market, p. 63
competitive market, p. 64
quantity demanded, p. 65
law of demand, p. 65
demand schedule, p. 65
demand curve, p. 65
normal good, p. 68

inferior good, p. 68
substitutes, p. 68
complements, p. 68
quantity supplied, p. 70
law of supply, p. 71
supply schedule, p. 71
supply curve, p. 71

equilibrium, p. 74
equilibrium price, p. 74
equilibrium quantity, p. 74
surplus, p. 75
shortage, p. 75
law of supply and demand, p. 76

# QUESTIONS FOR REVIEW

1. What is a competitive market? Briefly describe the types of markets other than perfectly competitive markets.

2. What determines the quantity of a good that buyers demand?

3. What are the demand schedule and the demand curve, and how are they related? Why does the demand curve slope downward?

4. Does a change in consumers' tastes lead to a movement along the demand curve or a shift in the demand curve? Does a change in price lead to a movement along the demand curve or a shift in the demand curve?

5. Popeye's income declines and, as a result, he buys more spinach. Is spinach an inferior or a normal good? What happens to Popeye's demand curve for spinach?

6. What determines the quantity of a good that sellers supply?

7. What are the supply schedule and the supply curve, and how are they related? Why does the supply curve slope upward?

8. Does a change in producers' technology lead to a movement along the supply curve or a shift in the supply curve? Does a change in price lead to a movement along the supply curve or a shift in the supply curve?

9. Define the equilibrium of a market. Describe the forces that move a market toward its equilibrium.

10. Cheese and wine are complements because they are often enjoyed together. When the price of wine rises, what happens to the supply, demand, quantity supplied, quantity demanded and the price in the market for cheese?

11. Describe the role of prices in market economies.

# PROBLEMS AND APPLICATIONS

1. Explain each of the following statements using supply and demand diagrams.
   a. When there is a drought in southern Europe, the price of olive oil rises in supermarkets throughout Europe.
   b. When the Olympic games were held in Greece in 2004, the price of hotel rooms in Athens rocketed.
   c. When a war breaks out in the Middle East, the price of petrol in Europe rises and the price of a used Mercedes falls.

2. 'An increase in the demand for mozzarella cheese raises the quantity of mozzarella demanded, but not the quantity supplied.' Is this statement true or false? Explain.

3. Consider the market for large family saloon cars. For each of the events listed here, identify which of the determinants of demand or supply are affected. Also indicate whether demand or supply is increased or decreased. Then show the effect on the price and quantity of large family saloon cars.
   a. People decide to have more children.
   b. A strike by steel workers raises steel prices.
   c. Engineers develop new automated machinery for the production of cars.
   d. The price of estate cars rises.
   e. A stock market crash lowers people's wealth.

4. During the 1990s, technological advances reduced the cost of computer chips. How do you think this affected the market for computers? For computer software? For typewriters?

5. Using supply and demand diagrams, show the effect of the following events on the market for sweatshirts.
   a. A drought in Egypt damages the cotton crop.
   b. The price of leather jackets falls.
   c. All universities require students to attend morning exercise classes in appropriate attire.
   d. New knitting machines are invented.

6. Suppose that in the year 2005 the number of births is temporarily high. How does this baby boom affect the price of baby-sitting services in 2010 and 2020? (Hint: 5-year-olds need baby-sitters, whereas 15-year-olds can be baby-sitters.)

7. Vinegar is a complement (as well as a condiment) for chips (at least in the UK and Ireland). If the price of chips rises, what happens to the market for vinegar? For ketchup? For fish? For orange juice?

8. The case study presented in the chapter discussed cigarette taxes as a way to reduce smoking. Now think about the market for cigars.

a. Are cigars substitutes or complements for cigarettes?
b. Using a supply and demand diagram, show what happens in the markets for cigars if the tax on cigarettes is increased.
c. If policy makers wanted to reduce total tobacco consumption, what policies could they combine with the cigarette tax?

9. The market for pizza has the following demand and supply schedules:

| Price | Quantity demanded | Quantity supplied |
| --- | --- | --- |
| €4 | 135 | 26 |
| 5 | 104 | 53 |
| 6 | 81 | 81 |
| 7 | 68 | 98 |
| 8 | 53 | 110 |
| 9 | 39 | 121 |

Graph the demand and supply curves. What is the equilibrium price and quantity in this market? If the actual price in this market were *above* the equilibrium price, what would drive the market towards the equilibrium? If the actual price in this market were *below* the equilibrium price, what would drive the market towards the equilibrium?

10. Because bacon and eggs are often eaten together, they are complements.
    a. We observe that both the equilibrium price of eggs and the equilibrium quantity of bacon have risen. What could be responsible for this pattern – a fall in the price of chicken feed or a fall in the price of pig feed? Illustrate and explain your answer.
    b. Suppose instead that the equilibrium price of bacon has risen but the equilibrium quantity of eggs has fallen. What could be responsible for this pattern – a rise in the price of chicken feed or a rise in the price of pig feed? Illustrate and explain your answer.

11. Suppose that the price of tickets to see your local football team play at home is determined by market forces. Currently, the demand and supply schedules are as follows:

| Price | Quantity demanded | Quantity supplied |
|-------|-------------------|-------------------|
| €10 | 50,000 | 30,000 |
| 20 | 40,000 | 30,000 |
| 30 | 30,000 | 30,000 |
| 40 | 20,000 | 30,000 |
| 50 | 10,000 | 30,000 |

a.  Draw the demand and supply curves. What is unusual about this supply curve? Why might this be true?

b.  What are the equilibrium price and quantity of tickets?

c.  Your team plans to increase total capacity in its stadium by 5,000 seats next season. What admission price should it charge?

12. An article in *The New York Times* described a successful marketing campaign by the French champagne industry. The article noted that 'many executives felt giddy about the stratospheric champagne prices. But they also feared that such sharp price increases would cause demand to decline, which would then cause prices to plunge.' What mistake are the executives making in their analysis of the situation? Illustrate your answer with a graph.

13. Market research has revealed the following information about the market for chocolate bars: the demand schedule can be represented by the equation $Q^D = 1,600 - 300P$, where $Q^D$ is the quantity demanded and P is the price. The supply schedule can be represented by the equation $Q^S = 1,400 + 700P$, where $Q^S$ is the quantity supplied. Calculate the equilibrium price and quantity in the market for chocolate bars.

14. What do we mean by a perfectly competitive market? Do you think that the example of ice cream used in this chapter fits this description? Is there another type of market that better characterizes the market for ice cream?

   For further resources, visit
http://www.thomsonlearning.co.uk/mankiw_taylor

# 5 ELASTICITY AND ITS APPLICATION

I magine yourself as a wheat farmer. Because you earn all your income from selling wheat, you devote much effort to making your land as productive as it can be. You monitor weather and soil conditions, check your fields for pests and disease, and study the latest advances in farm technology. You know that the more wheat you grow, the more you will have to sell after the harvest, and the higher will be your income and your standard of living.

One day your local university announces a major discovery. Scientists have devised a new hybrid of wheat that raises the amount farmers can produce from each hectare of land by 20 per cent. How should you react to this news? Should you use the new hybrid? Does this discovery make you better off or worse off than you were before? In this chapter we will see that these questions can have surprising answers. The surprise will come from applying the most basic tools of economics – supply and demand – to the market for wheat.

The previous chapter introduced supply and demand. In any competitive market, such as the market for wheat, the upward sloping supply curve represents the behaviour of sellers, and the downward sloping demand curve represents the behaviour of buyers. The price of the good adjusts to bring the quantity supplied and quantity demanded of the good into balance. To apply this basic analysis to understand the impact of the agronomists' discovery, we must first develop one more tool: the concept of *elasticity*. Elasticity, a measure of how much buyers and sellers respond to changes in market conditions, allows us to analyse supply and demand with greater precision. When studying how some event or policy affects a market, we can discuss not only the direction of the effects but their magnitude as well.

# THE ELASTICITY OF DEMAND

When we introduced demand in Chapter 4, we noted that consumers usually buy more of a good when its price is lower, when their incomes are higher when the prices of substitutes for the good are higher or when the prices of complements of the good are lower. Our discussion of demand was qualitative, not quantitative. That is, we discussed the direction in which quantity demanded moves, but not the size of the change. To measure how much consumers respond to changes in these variables, economists use the concept of **elasticity.**

**elasticity**
a measure of the responsiveness of quantity demanded or quantity supplied to one of its determinants

## The Price Elasticity of Demand and Its Determinants

The law of demand states that a fall in the price of a good raises the quantity demanded. The **price elasticity of demand** measures how much the quantity demanded responds to a change in price. Demand for a good is said to be *elastic* if the quantity demanded responds substantially to changes in the price. Demand is said to be *inelastic* if the quantity demanded responds only slightly to changes in the price.

**price elasticity of demand**
a measure of how much the quantity demanded of a good responds to a change in the price of that good, computed as the percentage change in quantity demanded divided by the percentage change in price

The price elasticity of demand for any good measures how willing consumers are to move away from the good as its price rises. Thus, the elasticity reflects the many economic, social and psychological forces that influence consumer tastes. Based on experience, however, we can state some general rules about what determines the price elasticity of demand.

**Availability of Close Substitutes** Goods with close substitutes tend to have more elastic demand because it is easier for consumers to switch from that good to others. For example, butter and margarine are easily substitutable. A small increase in the price of butter, assuming the price of margarine is held fixed, causes the quantity of butter sold to fall by a large amount. By contrast, because eggs are a food without a close substitute, the demand for eggs is less elastic than the demand for butter.

**Necessities Versus Luxuries** Necessities tend to have inelastic demands, whereas luxuries have elastic demands. People use gas and electricity to heat their homes and cook their food. If the price of gas and electricity rose together, people would not demand dramatically less of them. They might try and be more energy-efficient and reduce their demand a little, but they would still need hot food and warm homes. By contrast, when the price of sailing dinghies rises, the quantity of sailing dinghies demanded falls substantially. The reason is that most people view hot food and warm homes as necessities and a sailing dinghy as a luxury. Of course, whether a good is a necessity or a luxury depends not on the intrinsic properties of the good but on the preferences of the buyer. For an avid sailor with little concern over her health, sailing dinghies might be a necessity with inelastic demand and hot food and a warm place to sleep a luxury with elastic demand.

**Definition of the Market** The elasticity of demand in any market depends on how we draw the boundaries of the market. Narrowly defined markets tend to have more elastic demand than broadly defined markets, because it is easier to find close substitutes for narrowly defined goods. For example, food, a broad category, has a fairly inelastic demand because there are no good substitutes for food. Ice cream, a narrower category, has a more elastic demand because it is easy to substitute other desserts for ice cream. Vanilla ice cream, a very narrow category, has a very elastic demand because other flavours of ice cream are almost perfect substitutes for vanilla.

**Time Horizon** Goods tend to have more elastic demand over longer time horizons. When the price of petrol rises, the quantity of petrol demanded falls only slightly in the first few months. Over time, however, people buy more fuel-efficient cars, switch to public transport and move closer to where they work. Within several years, the quantity of petrol demanded falls substantially. Similarly, if the price of a unit of electricity rises much above an equivalent energy unit of gas, demand may fall only slightly in the short run because many people already have electric cookers or electric heating appliances installed in their homes and cannot easily switch. If the price difference persists over several years, however, people may find it worth their while to replace their old electric heating and cooking appliances with new gas appliances and the demand for electricity will fall.

## Computing the Price Elasticity of Demand

Now that we have discussed the price elasticity of demand in general terms, let's be more precise about how it is measured. Economists compute the price elasticity of demand as the percentage change in the quantity demanded divided by the percentage change in the price. That is:

$$\text{Price elasticity of demand} = \frac{\text{Percentage change in quantity demanded}}{\text{Percentage change in price}}$$

For example, suppose that a 10 per cent increase in the price of an ice cream cornet causes the amount of ice cream you buy to fall by 20 per cent. We calculate your elasticity of demand as:

$$\text{Price elasticity of demand} = \frac{20\%}{10\%} = 2$$

In this example, the elasticity is 2, reflecting that the change in the quantity demanded is proportionately twice as large as the change in the price.

Because the quantity demanded of a good is negatively related to its price, the percentage change in quantity will always have the opposite sign to the percentage change in price. In this example, the percentage change in price is a *positive* 10 per cent (reflecting an increase), and the percentage change in quantity demanded is a *negative* 20 per cent (reflecting a decrease). For this reason, price elasticities of demand are sometimes reported as negative numbers. In this book we follow the common practice of dropping the minus sign and reporting all price elasticities as positive numbers. (Mathematicians call this the *absolute value.*) With this convention, a larger price elasticity implies a greater responsiveness of quantity demanded to price.

## The Midpoint Method: A Better Way to Calculate Percentage Changes and Elasticities

If you try calculating the price elasticity of demand between two points on a demand curve, you will quickly notice an annoying problem: the elasticity from point A to point B seems different from the elasticity from point B to point A. For example, consider these numbers:

Point A:    Price = €4    Quantity = 120
Point B:    Price = €6    Quantity =   80

Going from point A to point B, the price rises by 50 per cent, and the quantity falls by 33 per cent, indicating that the price elasticity of demand is 33/50, or 0.66. By contrast, going from point B to point A, the price falls by 33 per cent, and the quantity rises by 50 per cent, indicating that the price elasticity of demand is 50/33, or 1.5.

One way to avoid this problem is to use the *midpoint method* for calculating elasticities. The standard way to compute a percentage change is to divide the change by the initial level. By contrast, the midpoint method computes a percentage change by dividing the change by the midpoint (or average) of the initial and final levels. For instance, €5 is the midpoint of €4 and €6. Therefore, according to the midpoint method, a change from €4 to €6 is considered a 40 per cent rise, because $(6 - 4)/5 \times 100 = 40$. Similarly, a change from €6 to €4 is considered a 40 per cent fall.

Because the midpoint method gives the same answer regardless of the direction of change, it is often used when calculating the price elasticity of demand between two points. In our example, the midpoint between point A and point B is:

Midpoint:    Price = €5    Quantity = 100

According to the midpoint method, when going from point A to point B, the price rises by 40 per cent, and the quantity falls by 40 per cent. Similarly, when going from point B to point A, the price falls by 40 per cent, and the quantity rises by 40 per cent. In both directions, the price elasticity of demand equals 1.

We can express the midpoint method with the following formula for the price elasticity of demand between two points, denoted $(Q_1, P_1)$ and $(Q_2, P_2)$:

$$\text{Price elasticity of demand} = \frac{(Q_2 - Q_1)/[(Q_2 + Q_1)/2]}{(P_2 - P_1)/[(P_2 + P_1)/2]}$$

The numerator is the percentage change in quantity computed using the midpoint method, and the denominator is the percentage change in price computed using the midpoint method. If you ever need to calculate elasticities, you should use this formula.

In this book, however, we rarely perform such calculations. For most of our purposes, what elasticity represents – the responsiveness of quantity demanded to price – is more important than how it is calculated.

## The Variety of Demand Curves

Economists classify demand curves according to their elasticity. Demand is *elastic* when the elasticity is greater than 1, so that quantity moves proportionately more than the price. Demand is *inelastic* when the elasticity is less than 1, so that quantity moves proportionately less than the price. If the elasticity is exactly 1, so that quantity moves the same amount proportionately as price, demand is said to have *unit elasticity*.

Because the price elasticity of demand measures how much quantity demanded responds to changes in the price, it is closely related to the slope of the demand curve. The following rule of thumb is a useful guide: the flatter the demand curve

*FIGURE 5.1*

## The Price Elasticity of Demand

*The price elasticity of demand determines whether the demand curve is steep or flat. Note that all percentage changes are calculated using the midpoint method.*

(a) Perfectly inelastic demand: Elasticity equals 0

(b) Inelastic demand: Elasticity is less than 1

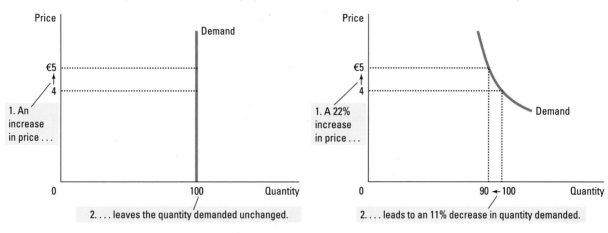

(c) Unit elastic demand: Elasticity equals 1

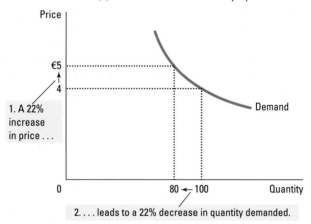

(d) Elastic demand: Elasticity is greater than 1

(e) Perfectly elastic demand: Elasticity equals infinity

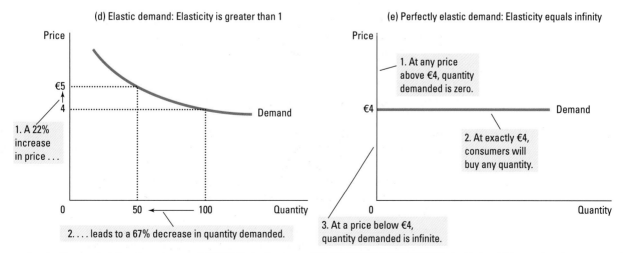

that passes through a given point, the greater the price elasticity of demand. The steeper the demand curve that passes through a given point, the smaller the price elasticity of demand.

Figure 5.1 shows five cases. In the extreme case of a zero elasticity shown in panel (a), demand is *perfectly inelastic,* and the demand curve is vertical. In this case, regardless of the price, the quantity demanded stays the same. As the elasticity rises, the demand curve gets flatter and flatter, as shown in panels (b), (c) and (d). At the opposite extreme shown in panel (e), demand is *perfectly elastic.* This occurs as the price elasticity of demand approaches infinity and the demand curve becomes horizontal, reflecting the fact that very small changes in the price lead to huge changes in the quantity demanded.

Finally, if you have trouble keeping straight the terms *elastic* and *inelastic,* here's a memory trick for you: *I*nelastic curves, such as in panel (a) of Figure 5.1, look like the letter *I. E*lastic curves, as in panel (e), look like the middle bar of the letter *E.* This is not a deep insight, but it might help in your next economics exam.

## Total Revenue and the Price Elasticity of Demand

**total revenue**

the amount paid by buyers and received by sellers of a good, computed as the price of the good times the quantity sold

When studying changes in supply or demand in a market, one variable we often want to study is **total revenue,** the amount paid by buyers and received by sellers of the good. In any market, total revenue is $P \times Q$, the price of the good times the quantity of the good sold. We can show total revenue graphically, as in Figure 5.2. The height of the box under the demand curve is $P$, and the width is $Q$. The area of this box, $P \times Q$, equals the total revenue in this market. In Figure 5.2, where $P = €4$ and $Q = 100$, total revenue is $€4 \times 100$, or $€400$.

How does total revenue change as one moves along the demand curve? The answer depends on the price elasticity of demand. If demand is inelastic, as in

## FIGURE 5.2

### Total Revenue

*The total amount paid by buyers, and received as revenue by sellers, equals the area of the box under the demand curve, P × Q. Here, at a price of €4, the quantity demanded is 100, and total revenue is €400.*

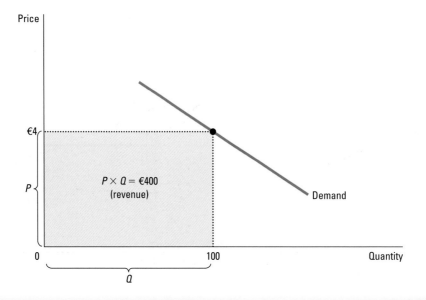

## FIGURE 5.3

### How Total Revenue Changes When Price Changes: Inelastic Demand

*With an inelastic demand curve, an increase in the price leads to a decrease in quantity demanded that is proportionately smaller. Therefore, total revenue (the product of price and quantity) increases. Here, an increase in the price from €1 to €3 causes the quantity demanded to fall from 100 to 80, and total revenue rises from €100 to €240.*

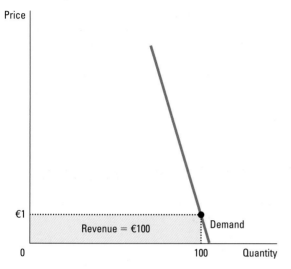
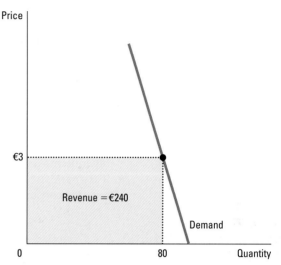

## FIGURE 5.4

### How Total Revenue Changes When Price Changes: Elastic Demand

*With an elastic demand curve, an increase in the price leads to a decrease in quantity demanded that is proportionately larger. Therefore, total revenue (the product of price and quantity) decreases. Here, an increase in the price from €4 to €5 causes the quantity demanded to fall from 50 to 20, so total revenue falls from €200 to €100.*

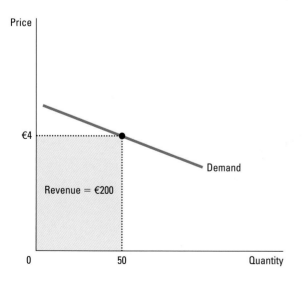
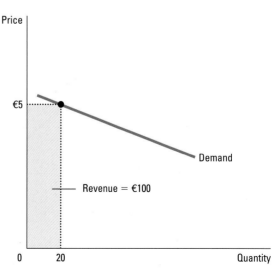

Figure 5.3, then an increase in the price causes an increase in total revenue. Here an increase in price from €1 to €3 causes the quantity demanded to fall only from 100 to 80, and so total revenue rises from €100 to €240. An increase in price raises $P \times Q$ because the fall in $Q$ is proportionately smaller than the rise in $P$.

We obtain the opposite result if demand is elastic: an increase in the price causes a decrease in total revenue. In Figure 5.4, for instance, when the price rises from €4 to €5, the quantity demanded falls from 50 to 20, and so total revenue falls from €200 to €100. Because demand is elastic, the reduction in the quantity demanded is so great that it more than offsets the increase in the price. That is, an increase in price reduces $P \times Q$ because the fall in $Q$ is proportionately greater than the rise in $P$.

Although the examples in these two figures are extreme, they illustrate a general rule:

- When demand is inelastic (a price elasticity less than 1), price and total revenue move in the same direction.
- When demand is elastic (a price elasticity greater than 1), price and total revenue move in opposite directions.
- If demand is unit elastic (a price elasticity exactly equal to 1), total revenue remains constant when the price changes.

## FIGURE 5.5

### Elasticity of a Linear Demand Curve

*The slope of a linear demand curve is constant, but its elasticity is not. The demand schedule in the table was used to calculate the price elasticity of demand by the midpoint method. At points with a low price and high quantity, the demand curve is inelastic. At points with a high price and low quantity, the demand curve is elastic.*

|  |  | Total revenue (Price × Quantity) | Percent change in price | Percent change in quantity | Price elasticity | Quantity description |
|---|---|---|---|---|---|---|
| €7 | 0 | €0 |  |  |  |  |
|  |  |  | 15 | 200 | 13.0 | Elastic |
| 6 | 2 | 12 |  |  |  |  |
|  |  |  | 18 | 67 | 3.7 | Elastic |
| 5 | 4 | 20 |  |  |  |  |
|  |  |  | 22 | 40 | 1.8 | Elastic |
| 4 | 6 | 24 |  |  |  |  |
|  |  |  | 29 | 29 | 1.0 | Unit elastic |
| 3 | 8 | 24 |  |  |  |  |
|  |  |  | 40 | 22 | 0.6 | Inelastic |
| 2 | 10 | 20 |  |  |  |  |
|  |  |  | 67 | 18 | 0.3 | Inelastic |
| 1 | 12 | 12 |  |  |  |  |
|  |  |  | 200 | 15 | 0.1 | Inelastic |
| 0 | 14 | 0 |  |  |  |  |

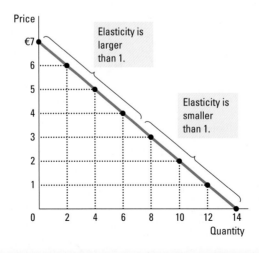

## Elasticity and Total Revenue along a Linear Demand Curve

Although some demand curves have an elasticity that is the same along the entire curve, that is not always the case. An example of a demand curve along which elasticity changes is a straight line, as shown in Figure 5.5. A linear demand curve has a constant slope. Recall that slope is defined as 'rise over run', which here is the ratio of the change in price ('rise') to the change in quantity ('run'). This particular demand curve's slope is constant because each €1 increase in price causes the same 2-unit decrease in the quantity demanded.

Even though the slope of a linear demand curve is constant, the elasticity is not. The reason is that the slope is the ratio of *changes* in the two variables, whereas the elasticity is the ratio of *percentage changes* in the two variables. You can see this by looking at the table in Figure 5.5, which shows the demand schedule for the linear demand curve in the graph. The table uses the midpoint method to calculate the price elasticity of demand. At points with a low price and high quantity,

# IN THE NEWS

## On the Road with Elasticity

*How should a firm that operates a private toll road set a price for its service? As the following article makes clear, answering this question requires an understanding of the demand curve and its elasticity.*

### Tolled Motorway Charge Criticised as High but Road's Operator Says the Price is Right
By Juliette Jowit

Britain's first tolled motorway will charge double the amount of those in Europe, but the road's operator said the price was right for the amount of time saved. M6 Toll, which cost £600m, runs north of the existing M6 from junctions four to seven, north of Birmingham. It bypasses one of the most congested sections of road in Europe and will charge £11 for trucks and £3 for cars during the day when it opens next year.

Midland Expressway, which built the 27-mile road and has a concession to run it for 50 years, also announced a £1 discount for the first 10m vehicles. Charges will be lower at night and for vehicles joining at the third junction. Even taking off the discount and value added tax, which businesses reclaim, the charge is 32p a mile – the most expensive toll road in Europe, said the Freight Transport Association. The FTA said the figure compared with 16p–18p a mile for motorway tolls and truck taxes in France, Spain and Germany, although bridges and tunnels were more expensive. 'I don't think anyone else can think of anything as expensive in Europe,' said James Hookham, FTA policy director.

The Road Haulage Association said the level was 'too high for regular users', particularly with many hauliers on the 'tightest' profit margins. However, the RAC Foundation motoring lobby group said it was 'a fair charge for a high-quality alternative'. Robert Bain, an associate in infrastructure finance for Standard & Poor's credit rating agency, said the charge was 'shrewd pricing' to attract long-distance business and commercial traffic but deter local drivers and commuters. 'If it was too cheap it would be as congested as the M6,' he said. Tom Fanning, Midland Expressway managing director, said the charges were set after 'extensive' consultation with users and were intended to balance the needs of financing the investment and running of the road and keeping traffic moving.

The company previously forecast the road could attract 100,000 vehicles a day, but yesterday Mr Fanning said it was too soon to predict user numbers. He declined to specify what level of service users would get, but the company said average speeds on the equivalent section of the M6 were 17mph. 'We're offering drivers the choice to avoid the misery on the M6,' said Mr Fanning.

Source: *The Financial Times*, 7 May 2003.

the demand curve is inelastic. At points with a high price and low quantity, the demand curve is elastic.

The table also presents total revenue at each point on the demand curve. These numbers illustrate the relationship between total revenue and elasticity. When the price is €1, for instance, demand is inelastic and a price increase to €2 raises total revenue. When the price is €5, demand is elastic, and a price increase to €6 reduces total revenue. Between €3 and €4, demand is exactly unit elastic and total revenue is the same at these two prices.

## CASE STUDY

### Pricing Admission to a Public Aquarium

*Aquarium in Valencia – if the price of admission was higher would the number of visitors decline?*

You are the manager of a large public aquarium, 'Fish World'. Your accountant tells you that the aquarium is running short of funds and suggests that you consider changing the price of admission to increase total revenue. What do you do? Do you raise the price of admission, or do you lower it?

The answer depends on the elasticity of demand. If the demand for visits to the aquarium is inelastic, then an increase in the price of admission would increase total revenue. But if the demand is elastic, then an increase in price would cause the number of visitors to fall by so much that total revenue would decrease. In this case, you should cut the price. The number of visitors would rise by so much that total revenue would increase.

To estimate the price elasticity of demand, you would need to turn to your statisticians. They might use historical data to study how aquarium attendance varied from year to year as the admission price changed. Or they might use data on attendance at the aquariums around the country to see how the admission price affects attendance. In studying either of these sets of data, the statisticians would need to take account of other factors that affect attendance – weather, population, size and variety of fish on view, and so forth – to isolate the effect of price. In the end, such data analysis would provide an estimate of the price elasticity of demand, which you could use in deciding how to respond to your financial problem.

## Other Demand Elasticities

In addition to the price elasticity of demand, economists also use other elasticities to describe the behaviour of buyers in a market.

**income elasticity of demand**
a measure of how much the quantity demanded of a good responds to a change in consumers' income, computed as the percentage change in quantity demanded divided by the percentage change in income

**The Income Elasticity of Demand** The **income elasticity of demand** measures how the quantity demanded changes as consumer income changes. It is calculated as the percentage change in quantity demanded divided by the percentage change in income. That is,

$$\text{Income elasticity of demand} = \frac{\text{Percentage change in quantity demanded}}{\text{Percentage change in income}}$$

As we discussed in Chapter 4, most goods are *normal goods*: higher income raises quantity demanded. Because quantity demanded and income move in the same direction, normal goods have positive income elasticities. A few goods, such as bus rides, are *inferior goods*: higher income lowers the quantity demanded. Because quantity demanded and income move in opposite directions, inferior goods have negative income elasticities.

Even among normal goods, income elasticities vary substantially in size. Necessities, such as food and clothing, tend to have small income elasticities because consumers, regardless of how low their incomes, choose to buy some of these goods. Luxuries, such as caviar and diamonds, tend to have large income elasticities because consumers feel that they can do without these goods altogether if their income is too low.

**The Cross-Price Elasticity of Demand** The **cross-price elasticity of demand** measures how the quantity demanded of one good changes as the price of another good changes. It is calculated as the percentage change in quantity demanded of good 1 divided by the percentage change in the price of good 2. That is:

$$\text{Cross-price elasticity of demand} = \frac{\text{Percentage change in quantity demanded of good 1}}{\text{Percentage change in the price of good 2}}$$

**cross-price elasticity of demand**
a measure of how much the quantity demanded of one good responds to a change in the price of another good, computed as the percentage change in quantity demanded of the first good divided by the percentage change in the price of the second good

Whether the cross-price elasticity is a positive or negative number depends on whether the two goods are substitutes or complements. As we discussed in Chapter 4, substitutes are goods that are typically used in place of one another, such as beef steak and Wiener schnitzel. An increase in the price of beef steak induces people to eat Wiener schnitzel instead. Because the price of beef steak and the quantity of Wiener schnitzel demanded move in the same direction, the cross-price elasticity is positive. Conversely, complements are goods that are typically used together, such as computers and software. In this case, the cross-price elasticity is negative, indicating that an increase in the price of computers reduces the quantity of software demanded. As with price elasticity of demand, cross-price elasticity may increase over time: a change in the price of electricity will have little effect on demand for gas in the short run but much stronger effects over several years.

**Quick Quiz** Define the price elasticity of demand. • Explain the relationship between total revenue and the price elasticity of demand.

# THE ELASTICITY OF SUPPLY

When we introduced supply in Chapter 4, we noted that producers of a good offer to sell more of it when the price of the good rises, when their input prices fall or when their technology improves. To turn from qualitative to quantitative statements about quantity supplied, we once again use the concept of elasticity.

## The Price Elasticity of Supply and Its Determinants

The law of supply states that higher prices raise the quantity supplied. The **price elasticity of supply** measures how much the quantity supplied responds to changes in the price. Supply of a good is said to be *elastic* if the quantity supplied responds substantially to changes in the price. Supply is said to be *inelastic* if the quantity supplied responds only slightly to changes in the price.

The price elasticity of supply depends on the flexibility of sellers to change the amount of the good they produce. For example, seafront property has an inelastic supply because it is almost impossible to produce more of it. By contrast,

**price elasticity of supply**
a measure of how much the quantity supplied of a good responds to a change in the price of that good, computed as the percentage change in quantity supplied divided by the percentage change in price

manufactured goods, such as books, cars and television sets, have elastic supplies because the firms that produce them can run their factories longer in response to a higher price.

In most markets, a key determinant of the price elasticity of supply is the time period being considered. Supply is usually more elastic in the long run than in the short run. Over short periods of time, firms cannot easily change the size of their factories to make more or less of a good. Thus, in the short run, the quantity supplied is not very responsive to the price. By contrast, over longer periods, firms can build new factories or close old ones. In addition, new firms can enter a market and old firms can shut down. Thus, in the long run, the quantity supplied can respond substantially to price changes.

## Computing the Price Elasticity of Supply

Now that we have some idea about what the price elasticity of supply is, let's be more precise. Economists compute the price elasticity of supply as the percentage change in the quantity supplied divided by the percentage change in the price. That is:

$$\text{Price elasticity of supply} = \frac{\text{Percentage change in quantity supplied}}{\text{Percentage change in price}}$$

For example, suppose that an increase in the price of milk from €2.85 to €3.15 a litre raises the amount that dairy farmers produce from 90,000 to 110,000 litres per month. Using the midpoint method, we calculate the percentage change in price as:

$$\text{Percentage change in price} = (3.15 - 2.85)/3.00 \times 100 = 10\%$$

Similarly, we calculate the percentage change in quantity supplied as:

$$\text{Percentage change in quantity supplied} = (110{,}000 - 90{,}000)/100{,}000 \times 100 = 20\%$$

In this case, the price elasticity of supply is:

$$\text{Price elasticity of supply} = \frac{20\%}{10\%} = 2$$

In this example, the elasticity of 2 reflects the fact that the quantity supplied moves proportionately twice as much as the price.

## The Variety of Supply Curves

Because the price elasticity of supply measures the responsiveness of quantity supplied to the price, it is reflected in the appearance of the supply curve. Figure 5.6 shows five cases. In the extreme case of a zero elasticity, as shown in panel (a), supply is *perfectly inelastic* and the supply curve is vertical. In this case, the quantity supplied is the same regardless of the price. As the elasticity rises, the supply curve gets flatter, which shows that the quantity supplied responds more to changes in the price. At the opposite extreme, shown in panel (e), supply is *perfectly elastic*. This occurs as the price elasticity of supply approaches infinity and the supply curve becomes horizontal, meaning that very small changes in the price lead to very large changes in the quantity supplied.

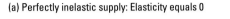

## The Price Elasticity of Supply

*The price elasticity of supply determines whether the supply curve is steep or flat. Note that all percentage changes are calculated using the midpoint method.*

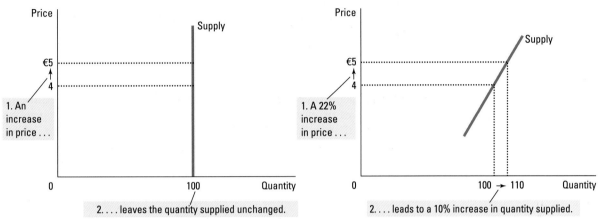

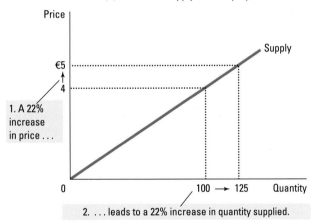

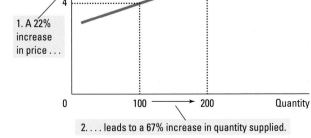

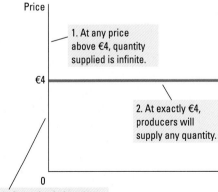

In some markets, the elasticity of supply is not constant but varies over the supply curve. Figure 5.7 shows a typical case for an industry in which firms have factories with a limited capacity for production. For low levels of quantity supplied, the elasticity of supply is high, indicating that firms respond substantially to changes in the price. In this region, firms have capacity for production that is not being used, such as buildings and machinery sitting idle for all or part of the day. Small increases in price make it profitable for firms to begin using this idle capacity. As the quantity supplied rises, firms begin to reach capacity. Once capacity is fully used, increasing production further requires the construction of new factories. To induce firms to incur this extra expense, the price must rise substantially, so supply becomes less elastic.

Figure 5.7 presents a numerical example of this phenomenon. When the price rises from €3 to €4 (a 29 per cent increase, according to the midpoint method), the quantity supplied rises from 100 to 200 (a 67 per cent increase). Because quantity supplied moves proportionately more than the price, the supply curve has elasticity greater than 1. By contrast, when the price rises from €12 to €15 (a 22 per cent increase), the quantity supplied rises from 500 to 525 (a 5 per cent increase). In this case, quantity supplied moves proportionately less than the price, so the elasticity is less than 1.

> **Quick Quiz** Define the price elasticity of supply • Explain why the price elasticity of supply might be different in the long run from in the short run.

---

## FIGURE 5.7

### How the Price Elasticity of Supply Can Vary

*Because firms often have a maximum capacity for production, the elasticity of supply may be very high at low levels of quantity supplied and very low at high levels of quantity supplied. Here, an increase in price from €3 to €4 increases the quantity supplied from 100 to 200. Because the increase in quantity supplied of 67 per cent (computed using the midpoint method) is larger than the increase in price of 29 per cent, the supply curve is elastic in this range. By contrast, when the price rises from €12 to €15, the quantity supplied rises only from 500 to 525. Because the increase in quantity supplied of 5 per cent is smaller than the increase in price of 22 per cent, the supply curve is inelastic in this range.*

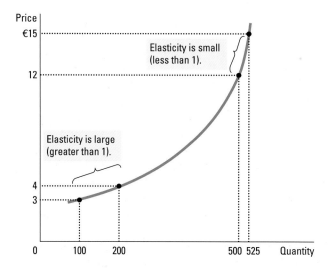

# THREE APPLICATIONS OF SUPPLY, DEMAND AND ELASTICITY

Can good news for farming be bad news for farmers? Why did OPEC fail to keep the price of oil high? Does drug prohibition increase or decrease drug-related crime? At first, these questions might seem to have little in common. Yet all three questions are about markets and all markets are subject to the forces of supply and demand. Here we apply the versatile tools of supply, demand and elasticity to answer these seemingly complex questions.

## Can Good News for Farming Be Bad News for Farmers?

Let's now return to the question posed at the beginning of this chapter: what happens to wheat farmers and the market for wheat when scientists discover a new wheat hybrid that is more productive than existing varieties? Recall from Chapter 4 that we answer such questions in three steps. First, we examine whether the supply or demand curve shifts. Secondly, we consider which direction the curve shifts. Thirdly, we use the supply and demand diagram to see how the market equilibrium changes.

In this case, the discovery of the new hybrid affects the supply curve. Because the hybrid increases the amount of wheat that can be produced on each acre of land, farmers are now willing to supply more wheat at any given price. In other words, the supply curve shifts to the right. The demand curve remains the same because consumers' desire to buy wheat products at any given price is not affected by the introduction of a new hybrid. Figure 5.8 shows an example of such a change. When the supply curve shifts from $S_1$ to $S_2$, the quantity of wheat sold increases from 100 to 110, and the price of wheat falls from €3 to €2.

But does this discovery make farmers better off? As a first stab at answering this question, consider what happens to the total revenue received by farmers. Farmers' total revenue is $P \times Q$, the price of the wheat times the quantity sold. The discovery affects farmers in two conflicting ways. The hybrid allows farmers to produce more wheat ($Q$ rises), but now each tonne of wheat sells for less ($P$ falls).

Whether total revenue rises or falls depends on the elasticity of demand. In practice, the demand for basic foodstuffs such as wheat is usually inelastic, for these items are relatively inexpensive and have few good substitutes. When the demand curve is inelastic, as it is in Figure 5.8, a decrease in price causes total revenue to fall. You can see this in the figure: the price of wheat falls substantially, whereas the quantity of wheat sold rises only slightly. Total revenue falls from €300 to €220. Thus, the discovery of the new hybrid lowers the total revenue that farmers receive for the sale of their crops.

If farmers are made worse off by the discovery of this new hybrid, why do they adopt it? The answer to this question goes to the heart of how competitive markets work. Because each farmer is a small part of the market for wheat, he or she takes the price of wheat as given. For any given price of wheat, it is better to use the new hybrid in order to produce and sell more wheat. Yet when all farmers do this, the supply of wheat rises, the price falls and farmers are worse off.

Although this example may at first seem only hypothetical, in fact it helps to explain a major change in the European economy over the past two centuries. Two hundred years ago, most Europeans worked on farms. Agricultural methods were sufficiently primitive that most of us had to work the land in order to produce enough food to sustain the population. Yet, over time, advances in farm technology increased the amount of food that each farm could produce. This

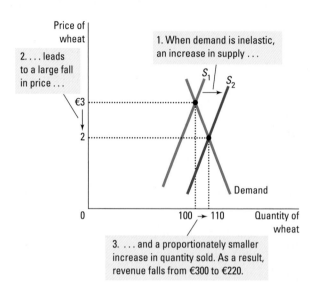

**FIGURE 5.8**

**An Increase in Supply in the Market for Wheat**

*When an advance in farm technology increases the supply of wheat from S₁ to S₂, the price of wheat falls. Because the demand for wheat is inelastic, the increase in the quantity sold from 100 to 110 is proportionately smaller than the decrease in the price from €3 to €2. As a result, farmers' total revenue falls from €300 (€3 × 100) to €220 (€2 × 110).*

*"I get so much subsidy I don't know what to do with it!"*

increase in food supply, together with inelastic food demand, caused farm revenues to fall, which in turn encouraged people to leave the agricultural sector as farmers' profits and agricultural workers' wages fell.

This analysis of the market for farm products also helps to explain a seeming paradox of public policy: certain agricultural policies such as the Common Agricultural Policy of the European Union try to help farmers by inducing them not to plant crops on all of their land. Why do these programmes do this? Their purpose is to reduce the supply of farm products and thereby raise prices. With inelastic demand for their products, farmers as a group receive greater total revenue if they supply a smaller crop to the market. No single farmer would choose to leave his land fallow on his own because each takes the market price as given. But if all farmers do so together, each of them can be better off.

When analysing the effects of farm technology or farm policy, it is important to keep in mind that what is good for farmers is not necessarily good for society as a whole. Improvement in farm technology can be bad for farmers who become increasingly unnecessary, but it is surely good for consumers who pay less for food. Similarly, a policy aimed at reducing the supply of farm products may raise the incomes of farmers, but it does so at the expense of consumers.

## Why Did OPEC Fail to Keep the Price of Oil High?

Many of the most disruptive events for the world's economies over the past several decades have originated in the world market for oil. In the 1970s members of the Organization of Petroleum Exporting Countries (OPEC) decided to raise the world price of oil in order to increase their incomes. These countries accomplished this goal by jointly reducing the amount of oil they supplied. From 1973 to 1974, the price of oil (adjusted for overall inflation) rose more than 50 per cent. Then, a few years later, OPEC did the same thing again. The price of oil rose 14 per cent in 1979, followed by 34 per cent in 1980, and another 34 per cent in 1981.

Yet OPEC found it difficult to maintain a high price. From 1982 to 1985 the price of oil steadily declined at about 10 per cent per year. Dissatisfaction and disarray soon prevailed among the OPEC countries. In 1986 cooperation among OPEC members completely broke down, and the price of oil plunged 45 per cent. In 1990 the price of oil (adjusted for overall inflation) was back to where it began in 1970 and it stayed at that low level throughout most of the 1990s.

This episode shows how supply and demand can behave differently in the short run and in the long run. In the short run, both the supply and demand for oil are relatively inelastic. Supply is inelastic because the quantity of known oil reserves and the capacity for oil extraction cannot be changed quickly. Demand is inelastic because buying habits do not respond immediately to changes in price. Many drivers with old petrol-thirsty cars, for instance, will just pay the higher price. Thus, as panel (a) of Figure 5.9 shows, the short-run supply and demand curves are steep. When the supply of oil shifts from $S_1$ to $S_2$, the price increase from $P_1$ to $P_2$ is large.

The situation is very different in the long run. Over long periods of time, producers of oil outside of OPEC respond to high prices by increasing oil exploration and by building new extraction capacity. Consumers respond with greater conservation, for instance by replacing old inefficient cars with newer efficient ones. Thus, as panel (b) of Figure 5.9 shows, the long-run supply and demand curves are more elastic. In the long run, the shift in the supply curve from $S_1$ to $S_2$ causes a much smaller increase in the price.

## FIGURE 5.9

### A Reduction in Supply in the World Market for Oil

*When the supply of oil falls, the response depends on the time horizon. In the short run, supply and demand are relatively inelastic, as in panel (a). Thus, when the supply curve shifts from $S_1$ to $S_2$, the price rises substantially. By contrast, in the long run, supply and demand are relatively elastic, as in panel (b). In this case, the same size shift in the supply curve ($S_1$ to $S_2$) causes a smaller increase in the price.*

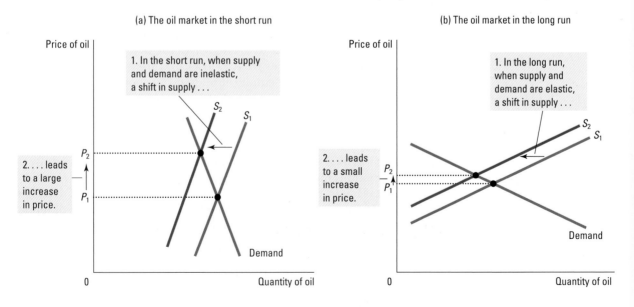

This analysis shows why OPEC succeeded in maintaining a high price of oil only in the short run. When OPEC countries agreed to reduce their production of oil, they shifted the supply curve to the left. Even though each OPEC member sold less oil, the price rose by so much in the short run that OPEC incomes rose. By contrast, in the long run when supply and demand are more elastic, the same reduction in supply, measured by the horizontal shift in the supply curve, caused a smaller increase in the price. Thus, OPEC's coordinated reduction in supply proved less profitable in the long run.

OPEC still exists today, and it has from time to time succeeded at reducing supply and raising prices. But the price of oil (adjusted for overall inflation) has never returned to the peak reached in 1981. The cartel now seems to understand that raising prices is easier in the short run than in the long run.

## Does Drug Prohibition Increase or Decrease Drug-Related Crime?

A persistent problem facing society is the use of illegal drugs, such as heroin, cocaine, marijuana and ecstasy. Drug use has several adverse effects. One is that drug dependency can ruin the lives of drug users and their families. Another is that drug addicts often turn to robbery and other violent crimes in order to obtain the money needed to support their habit. To discourage the use of illegal drugs, European and North American governments devote billions of euros each year to reduce the flow of drugs into their countries. Let's use the tools of supply and demand to examine this policy of drug prohibition.

Suppose the government increases the number of undercover police devoted to the war on drugs. What happens in the market for illegal drugs? As is usual, we answer this question in three steps. First, we consider whether the supply or demand curve shifts. Secondly, we consider the direction of the shift. Thirdly, we see how the shift affects the equilibrium price and quantity.

Although the purpose of drug prohibition is to reduce drug use, its direct impact is on the sellers of drugs rather than the buyers. When the government stops some drugs from entering the country and arrests more smugglers, it raises the cost of selling drugs and, therefore, reduces the quantity of drugs supplied at any given price. The demand for drugs – the amount buyers want at any given price – is not changed. As panel (a) of Figure 5.10 shows, prohibition shifts the supply curve to the left from $S_1$ to $S_2$ and leaves the demand curve the same. The equilibrium price of drugs rises from $P_1$ to $P_2$, and the equilibrium quantity falls from $Q_1$ to $Q_2$. The fall in the equilibrium quantity shows that drug prohibition does reduce drug use.

But what about the amount of drug-related crime? To answer this question, consider the total amount that drug users pay for the drugs they buy. Because few drug addicts are likely to break their self-destructive habits in response to a higher price, it is likely that the demand for drugs is inelastic, as it is drawn in the figure. If demand is inelastic, then an increase in price raises total revenue in the drug market. That is, because drug prohibition raises the price of drugs proportionately more than it reduces drug use, it raises the total amount of money that drug users pay for drugs. Addicts who already had to steal to support their habits would have an even greater need for quick cash. Thus, drug prohibition could increase drug-related crime.

Because of this adverse effect of drug prohibition, some analysts argue for alternative approaches to the drug problem. Rather than trying to reduce the supply of drugs, policy makers might try to reduce the demand by pursuing a policy of drug education. Successful drug education has the effects shown in panel (b)

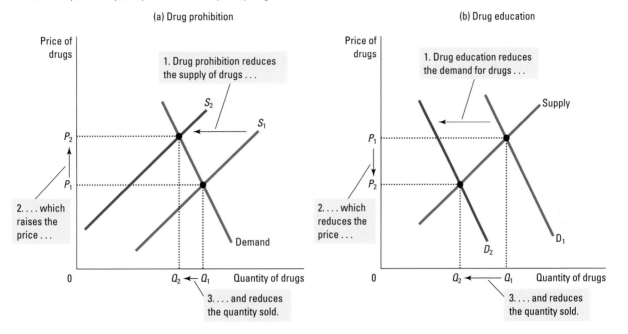

**FIGURE 5.10**

**Policies to Reduce the Use of Illegal Drugs**

*Drug prohibition reduces the supply of drugs from $S_1$ to $S_2$, as in panel (a). If the demand for drugs is inelastic, then the total amount paid by drug users rises, even as the amount of drug use falls. By contrast, drug education reduces the demand for drugs from $D_1$ to $D_2$, as in panel (b). Because both price and quantity fall, the amount paid by drug users falls.*

**(a) Drug prohibition**

Price of drugs

1. Drug prohibition reduces the supply of drugs . . .

$S_2$

$S_1$

$P_2$

$P_1$

2. . . . which raises the price . . .

Demand

0       $Q_2$ ← $Q_1$    Quantity of drugs

3. . . . and reduces the quantity sold.

**(b) Drug education**

Price of drugs

1. Drug education reduces the demand for drugs . . .

Supply

$P_1$

$P_2$

2. . . . which reduces the price . . .

$D_2$

$D_1$

0       $Q_2$ ← $Q_1$    Quantity of drugs

3. . . . and reduces the quantity sold.

of Figure 5.10. The demand curve shifts to the left from $D_1$ to $D_2$. As a result, the equilibrium quantity falls from $Q_1$ to $Q_2$, and the equilibrium price falls from $P_1$ to $P_2$. Total revenue, which is price times quantity, also falls. Thus, in contrast to drug prohibition, drug education can reduce both drug use and drug-related crime.

Advocates of drug prohibition might argue that the effects of this policy are different in the long run from what they are in the short run, because the elasticity of demand may depend on the time horizon. The demand for drugs is probably inelastic over short periods of time because higher prices do not substantially affect drug use by established addicts. But demand may be more elastic over longer periods of time because higher prices would discourage experimentation with drugs among the young and, over time, lead to fewer drug addicts. In this case, drug prohibition would increase drug-related crime in the short run while decreasing it in the long run.

**Quick Quiz** How might a drought that destroys half of all farm crops be good for farmers? If such a drought is good for farmers, why don't farmers destroy their own crops in the absence of a drought?

# CONCLUSION

According to an old quip, even a parrot can become an economist simply by learning to say 'supply and demand'. These last two chapters should have convinced you that there is much truth in this statement. The tools of supply and demand allow you to analyse many of the most important events and policies that shape the economy. You are now well on your way to becoming an economist (or, at least, a well educated parrot).

## SUMMARY

- The price elasticity of demand measures how much the quantity demanded responds to changes in the price. Demand tends to be more elastic if close substitutes are available, if the good is a luxury rather than a necessity, if the market is narrowly defined or if buyers have substantial time to react to a price change.

- The price elasticity of demand is calculated as the percentage change in quantity demanded divided by the percentage change in price. If the elasticity is less than 1, so that quantity demanded moves proportionately less than the price, demand is said to be inelastic. If the elasticity is greater than 1, so that quantity demanded moves proportionately more than the price, demand is said to be elastic.

- Total revenue, the total amount paid for a good, equals the price of the good times the quantity sold. For inelastic demand curves, total revenue rises as price rises. For elastic demand curves, total revenue falls as price rises.

- The income elasticity of demand measures how much the quantity demanded responds to changes in consumers'

income. The cross-price elasticity of demand measures how much the quantity demanded of one good responds to changes in the price of another good.

- The price elasticity of supply measures how much the quantity supplied responds to changes in the price. This elasticity often depends on the time horizon under consideration. In most markets, supply is more elastic in the long run than in the short run.

- The price elasticity of supply is calculated as the percentage change in quantity supplied divided by the percentage change in price. If the elasticity is less than 1, so that quantity supplied moves proportionately less than the price, supply is said to be inelastic. If the elasticity is greater than 1, so that quantity supplied moves proportionately more than the price, supply is said to be elastic.

- The tools of supply and demand can be applied in many different kinds of markets. This chapter uses them to analyse the market for wheat, the market for oil and the market for illegal drugs.

## KEY CONCEPTS

elasticity, p. 88
price elasticity of demand, p. 88

total revenue, p. 92
income elasticity of demand, p. 96

cross-price elasticity of demand, p. 97
price elasticity of supply, p. 97

# QUESTIONS FOR REVIEW

1. Define the price elasticity of demand and the income elasticity of demand.

2. List and explain some of the determinants of the price elasticity of demand.

3. If the elasticity is greater than 1, is demand elastic or inelastic? If the elasticity equals 0, is demand perfectly elastic or perfectly inelastic?

4. On a supply and demand diagram, show equilibrium price, equilibrium quantity and the total revenue received by producers.

5. If demand is elastic, how will an increase in price change total revenue? Explain.

6. What do we call a good whose income elasticity is less than 0?

7. How is the price elasticity of supply calculated? Explain what this measures.

8. What is the price elasticity of supply of Picasso paintings?

9. Is the price elasticity of supply usually larger in the short run or in the long run? Why?

10. In the 1970s, OPEC caused a dramatic increase in the price of oil. What prevented it from maintaining this high price through the 1980s?

# PROBLEMS AND APPLICATIONS

1. For each of the following pairs of goods, which good would you expect to have more elastic demand and why?
   a. Required text books or mystery novels.
   b. Beethoven recordings or classical music recordings in general.
   c. Heating oil during the next six months or heating oil during the next five years.
   d. Lemonade or water.

2. Suppose that business travellers and holidaymakers have the following demand for airline tickets from Birmingham to Naples:

| Price | Quantity demanded (business travellers) | Quantity demanded (holidaymakers) |
|---|---|---|
| €150 | 2,100 | 1,000 |
| 200 | 2,000 | 800 |
| 250 | 1,900 | 600 |
| 300 | 1,800 | 400 |

   a. As the price of tickets rises from €200 to €250, what is the price elasticity of demand for (i) business travellers and (ii) holidaymakers? (Use the midpoint method in your calculations.)
   b. Why might holidaymakers have a different elasticity from business travellers?

3. Suppose that your demand schedule for compact discs is as follows:

| Price | Quantity demanded (income = €10,000) | Quantity demanded (income = €12,000) |
|---|---|---|
| €8 | 40 | 50 |
| 10 | 32 | 45 |
| 12 | 24 | 30 |
| 14 | 16 | 20 |
| 16 | 8 | 12 |

   a. Use the midpoint method to calculate your price elasticity of demand as the price of compact discs increases from €8 to €10 if (i) your income is €10,000, and (ii) your income is €12,000.
   b. Calculate your income elasticity of demand as your income increases from €10,000 to €12,000 if (i) the price is €12, and (ii) the price is €16.

4. Xanthe has decided always to spend one-third of her income on clothing in the Portobello Road.
   a. What is her income elasticity of clothing demand?
   b. What is her price elasticity of clothing demand?
   c. If Xanthe's tastes change and she decides to spend only one-quarter of her income on clothing, how does

her demand curve change? What are her income elasticity and price elasticity now?

5. Two drivers – Tom and Jerry – each drive up to a petrol station. Before looking at the price, each places an order. Tom says, 'I'd like 30 litres of petrol.' Jerry says, 'I'd like €30-worth of petrol.' What is each driver's price elasticity of demand?

6. Economists have observed that spending on restaurant meals declines more during economic downturns than does spending on food to be eaten at home. How might the concept of elasticity help to explain this phenomenon?

7. Consider public policy aimed at smoking.
   a. Studies indicate that the price elasticity of demand for cigarettes is about 0.4. If a packet of cigarettes currently costs €2 and the government wants to reduce smoking by 20 per cent, by how much should it increase the price?
   b. If the government permanently increases the price of cigarettes, will the policy have a larger effect on smoking one year from now or five years from now?
   c. Studies also find that teenagers have a higher price elasticity than do adults. Why might this be true?

8. Would you expect the price elasticity of *demand* to be larger in the market for all ice cream or the market for vanilla ice cream? Would you expect the price elasticity of *supply* to be larger in the market for all ice cream or the market for vanilla ice cream? Be sure to explain your answers.

9. Pharmaceutical drugs have an inelastic demand, and computers have an elastic demand. Suppose that technological advance doubles the supply of both products (that is, the quantity supplied at each price is twice what it was).
   a. What happens to the equilibrium price and quantity in each market?
   b. Which product experiences a larger change in price?
   c. Which product experiences a larger change in quantity?

d. What happens to total consumer spending on each product?

10. Seafront properties along the promenade at Brighton have an inelastic supply, and cars have an elastic supply. Suppose that a rise in population doubles the demand for both products (that is, the quantity demanded at each price is twice what it was).
    a. What happens to the equilibrium price and quantity in each market?
    b. Which product experiences a larger change in price?
    c. Which product experiences a larger change in quantity?
    d. What happens to total consumer spending on each product?

11. Suppose that there is severe flooding in a region in which there is a high concentration of wheat farmers.
    a. Farmers whose crops were destroyed by the floods were much worse off, but farmers whose crops were not destroyed benefited from the floods. Why?
    b. What information would you need about the market for wheat to assess whether farmers as a group were hurt or helped by the floods?

12. Explain why the following might be true: a drought around the world raises the total revenue that farmers receive from the sale of grain, but a drought only in France reduces the total revenue that French farmers receive.

13. Because better weather makes farmland more productive, farmland in regions with good weather conditions is more expensive than farmland in regions with bad weather conditions. Over time, however, as advances in technology have made all farmland more productive, the price of farmland (adjusted for overall inflation) has fallen. Use the concept of elasticity to explain why productivity and farmland prices are positively related across space but negatively related over time.

For further resources, visit
http://www.thomsonlearning.co.uk/mankiw_taylor

# 6 SUPPLY, DEMAND AND GOVERNMENT POLICIES

Economists have two roles. As scientists, they develop and test theories to explain the world around them. As policy advisors, they use their theories to help change the world for the better. The focus of the preceding two chapters has been scientific. We have seen how supply and demand determine the price of a good and the quantity of the good sold. We have also seen how various events shift supply and demand and thereby change the equilibrium price and quantity.

This chapter offers our first look at policy. Here we analyse various types of government policy using only the tools of supply and demand. As you will see, the analysis yields some surprising insights. Policies often have effects that their architects did not intend or anticipate.

We begin by considering policies that directly control prices. For example, some countries have rent-control laws that dictate a maximum rent that landlords may charge tenants or minimum wage laws that dictate the lowest wage that firms may pay workers. Price controls are usually enacted when policy makers believe that the market price of a good or service is unfair to buyers or sellers. Yet, as we will see, these policies can generate inequities of their own.

After our discussion of price controls, we next consider the impact of taxes. Policy makers use taxes both to influence market outcomes and to raise revenue for public purposes. Although the prevalence of taxes in a developed economy is obvious, their effects are not. For example, when the government levies a tax on the amount that firms pay their workers, do the firms or the workers bear the burden of the tax? The answer is not at all clear – until we apply the powerful tools of supply and demand.

# CONTROLS ON PRICES

To see how price controls affect market outcomes, let's look once again at the market for ice cream. As we saw in Chapter 4, if ice cream is sold in a competitive market free of government regulation, the price of ice cream adjusts to balance supply and demand: at the equilibrium price, the quantity of ice cream that buyers want to buy exactly equals the quantity that sellers want to sell. To be concrete, suppose the equilibrium price is €3 per cornet.

Not everyone may be happy with the outcome of this free-market process. Let's say the National Association of Ice Cream Eaters complains that the €3 price is too high for everyone to enjoy a cornet a day (their recommended diet). Meanwhile, the National Organization of Ice Cream Producers complains that the €3 price – the result of 'cut-throat competition' – is too low and is depressing the incomes of its members. Each of these groups lobbies the government to pass laws that alter the market outcome by directly controlling the price of an ice cream cornet.

Of course, because buyers of any good always want a lower price while sellers want a higher price, the interests of the two groups conflict. If the Ice Cream Eaters are successful in their lobbying, the government imposes a legal maximum on the price at which ice cream can be sold. Because the price is not allowed to rise above this level, the legislated maximum is called a **price ceiling** or a price cap. By contrast, if the Ice Cream Makers are successful, the government imposes a legal minimum on the price. Because the price cannot fall below this level, the legislated minimum is called a **price floor.** Let us consider the effects of these policies in turn.

## How Price Ceilings Affect Market Outcomes

When the government, moved by the complaints and campaign contributions of the Ice Cream Eaters, imposes a price ceiling on the market for ice cream, two outcomes are possible. In panel (a) of Figure 6.1, the government imposes a price ceiling of €4 per cornet. In this case, because the price that balances supply and demand (€3) is below the ceiling, the price ceiling is *not binding*. Market forces naturally move the economy to the equilibrium, and the price ceiling has no effect on the price or the quantity sold.

Panel (b) of Figure 6.1 shows the other, more interesting, possibility. In this case, the government imposes a price ceiling of €2 per cornet. Because the equilibrium price of €3 is above the price ceiling, the ceiling is a *binding constraint* on the market. The forces of supply and demand tend to move the price towards the equilibrium price, but when the market price hits the ceiling, it can rise no further. Thus, the market price equals the price ceiling. At this price, the quantity of ice cream demanded (125 cornets in the figure) exceeds the quantity supplied (75 cornets). There is a shortage of ice cream, so some people who want to buy ice cream at the going price are unable to.

When a shortage of ice cream develops because of this price ceiling, some mechanism for rationing ice cream will naturally develop. The mechanism could simply be long queues: buyers who are willing to arrive early and queue get a cornet, while those unwilling to wait do not. Alternatively, sellers could ration ice cream according to their own personal biases, selling it only to friends, relatives, or members of their own racial or ethnic group. Notice that even though the price ceiling was motivated by a desire to help buyers of ice cream, not all buyers benefit from the policy. Some buyers do get to pay a lower price, although they may have to queue a long time to do so, but other buyers cannot get any ice cream at all.

**price ceiling**
a legal maximum on the price at which a good can be sold
**price floor**
a legal minimum on the price at which a good can be sold

## FIGURE 6.1

**A Market With a Price Ceiling**

*In panel (a), the government imposes a price ceiling of €4. Because the price ceiling is above the equilibrium price of €3, the price ceiling has no effect, and the market can reach the equilibrium of supply and demand. In this equilibrium, quantity supplied and quantity demanded both equal 100 cornets. In panel (b), the government imposes a price ceiling of €2. Because the price ceiling is below the equilibrium price of €3, the market price equals €2. At this price, 125 cornets are demanded and only 75 are supplied, so there is a shortage of 50 cornets.*

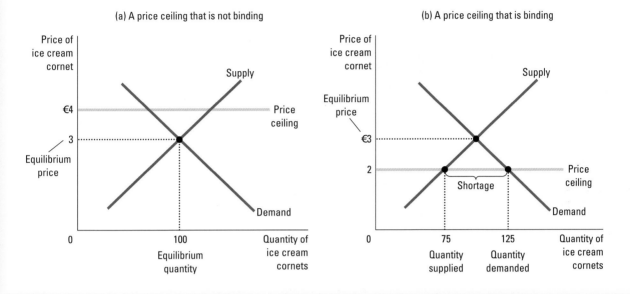

This example in the market for ice cream shows a general result: when the government imposes a binding price ceiling on a competitive market, a shortage of the good arises, and sellers must ration the scarce goods among the large number of potential buyers. The rationing mechanisms that develop under price ceilings are rarely desirable. Long queues are inefficient because they waste buyers' time. Discrimination according to seller bias is both inefficient (because the good does not necessarily go to the buyer who values it most highly) and potentially unfair. By contrast, the rationing mechanism in a free, competitive market is both efficient and impersonal. When the market for ice cream reaches its equilibrium, anyone who wants to pay the market price can get a cornet. Free markets ration goods with prices.

## CASE STUDY

### Rent Control in the Short Run and Long Run

It is sometimes argued that governments should help the poor find more affordable housing by placing a ceiling on the rents that landlords may charge their tenants. Economists often criticize rent control, arguing that it is a highly inefficient way to help the poor raise their standard of living. One economist called rent control 'the best way to destroy a city, other than bombing.'

The adverse effects of rent control are less apparent to the general population because these effects occur over many years. In the short run, landlords have a fixed number of housing units (houses and flats) to rent, and they cannot adjust this number quickly as market conditions change. Moreover, the number of people searching for housing in a city may not be highly responsive to rents in the short run because people take time to adjust their housing arrangements. Therefore, the short-run supply and demand for housing are relatively inelastic.

Panel (a) of Figure 6.2 shows the short-run effects of rent control on the housing market. As with any binding price ceiling, rent control causes a shortage. Yet because supply and demand are inelastic in the short run, the initial shortage caused by rent control is small. The primary effect in the short run is to reduce rents.

The long-run story is very different because the buyers and sellers of rental housing respond more to market conditions as time passes. On the supply side, landlords respond to low rents by not building new housing and by failing to maintain existing housing. On the demand side, low rents encourage people to find their own housing (rather than living with their parents or sharing with friends) and induce more people to move into a city. Therefore, both supply and demand are more elastic in the long run.

Panel (b) of Figure 6.2 illustrates the housing market in the long run. When rent control depresses rents below the equilibrium level, the quantity of housing units supplied falls substantially, and the quantity of housing units demanded rises substantially. The result is a large shortage of housing.

In cities with rent control, landlords use various mechanisms to ration housing. Some landlords keep long waiting lists. Others give a preference to tenants without children. Still others discriminate on the basis of race. Sometimes, apartments are allocated to those willing to offer under-the-table payments. In essence, these bribes bring the total price of an apartment (including the bribe) closer to the equilibrium price.

## FIGURE 6,2

### Rent Control in the Short Run and in the Long Run

*Panel (a) shows the short-run effects of rent control: because the supply and demand for housing units are relatively inelastic, the price ceiling imposed by a rent-control law causes only a small shortage of housing. Panel (b) shows the long-run effects of rent control: because the supply and demand for housing units are more elastic, rent control causes a large shortage.*

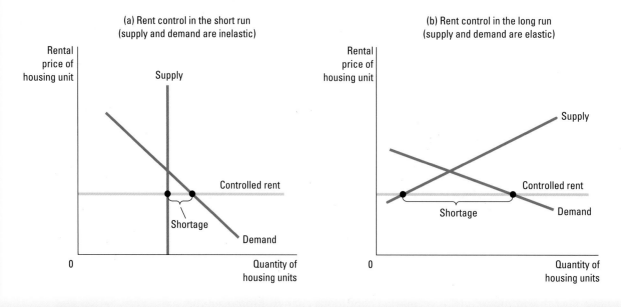

To understand fully the effects of rent control, we have to remember one of the *Ten Principles of Economics* from Chapter 1: people respond to incentives. In free markets, landlords try to keep their buildings clean and safe because desirable apartments command higher prices. By contrast, when rent control creates shortages and waiting lists, landlords lose their incentive to respond to tenants' concerns. Why should a landlord spend his money to maintain and improve his property when people are waiting to get in as it is? In the end, tenants get lower rents, but they also get lower-quality housing.

Policy makers often react to the effects of rent control by imposing additional regulations. For example, there are laws that make racial discrimination in housing illegal and require landlords to provide minimally adequate living conditions. These laws, however, are difficult and costly to enforce. By contrast, when rent control is eliminated and a market for housing is regulated by the forces of competition, such laws are less necessary. In a free market, the price of housing adjusts to eliminate the shortages that give rise to undesirable landlord behaviour.

## How Price Floors Affect Market Outcomes

To examine the effects of another kind of government price control, let's return to the market for ice cream. Imagine now that the government is persuaded by the pleas of the National Organization of Ice Cream Producers. In this case, the government might institute a price floor. Price floors, like price ceilings, are an attempt by the government to maintain prices at other than equilibrium levels.

### FIGURE 6.3

**A Market With a Price Floor**

*In panel (a), the government imposes a price floor of €2. Because this is below the equilibrium price of €3, the price floor has no effect. The market price adjusts to balance supply and demand. At the equilibrium, quantity supplied and quantity demanded both equal 100 cornets. In panel (b), the government imposes a price floor of €4, which is above the equilibrium price of €3. Therefore, the market price equals €4. Because 120 cornets are supplied at this price and only 80 are demanded, there is a surplus of 40 cornets.*

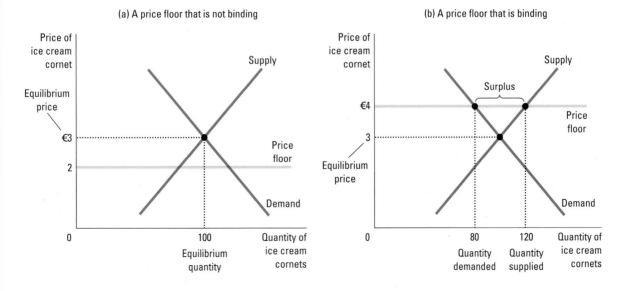

# IN THE NEWS

## Rent Controls in the Big Apple

*Price ceilings rarely, if ever, lead to economically efficient outcomes. In particular, rent controls, while they may lead to only a small initial shortage, generally have more pernicious long-term effects. However, sometimes politics can be a greater force than economics. This article looks at the rental market in Manhattan, where rent controls have been imposed for about 60 years.*

### The Great Manhattan Rip-Off; Rent Controls, New York's Particular Bane, are Poised to Receive Yet Another Unwelcome Extension

IT WAS one of many price controls brought in during the grim, panicky period between the attack on Pearl Harbour in 1941 and America's move to a full wartime economy in 1943. The housing market was seen as another thing that needed to be rationed or, at least, regulated – alongside rubber, petrol, coffee and shoes. By 1947 all these controls were phased out, except property-price regulations. Most cities have since scrapped these market distortions; the capital of capitalism has not.

Only one-third of New York City's 2m rental apartments are free of some kind of price restraint. A city board sets annual increases and administers an ever more complicated system. In some buildings, people live in similar apartments but pay wildly different levels of rent. In others, lone grandmothers sit in huge apartments, aware that moving would mean paying more for a smaller place elsewhere.

The oldest controls cover pre-1947 buildings (including any number of lovely houses on the city's most fashionable streets): these have average rents of $500 a month. A second tier, covered by rent stabilisation, rent for $760. Unregulated apartments cost an average of $850, but this number is deceptive, since it includes the worst buildings in the outer boroughs.

Technically, new construction is free from these constraints. In fact, a complex system of tax inducements persuades most clever builders 'voluntarily' to agree to rent-stabilisation restraints. Not surprisingly under these conditions, building is anaemic; even with the largest surge in construction since the 1960s, the number of building permits issued in the past year will add less than 1% to New York's housing supply. Needless to say, in such a sclerotic system, the poor suffer most.

On June 15th, 60 years after this 'temporary' measure was introduced in New York City, rent control once again comes up for renewal by the state government in Albany. It will almost certainly pass. Back in 1997, the then free-market-friendly Republican state Senate and the then free-market-friendly state governor, George Pataki, tried to get rid of rent restraints, but ran into fierce resistance from the Democrat-controlled assembly. 'What exactly is "homeland security" if your homes are not secure?' cried Sheldon Silver, the Assembly speaker, at a recent rally.

A compromise 'reform', won in 1997 against the odds, removed only 23,000 renters from a pool of almost 1m. The wretched 23,000, cruelly deprived of price controls, qualified for this punishment either by having income of more than $175,000 for two consecutive years and living in apartments whose rent was above $2,000 a month, or by moving into empty apartments costing more than $2,000 a month.

Buried in the 1997 agreement, however, was a detail that moved the next re-approval date to a time when no elections were due. If any time was right for debating the issue on economic rather than emotional grounds, it should be now.

In the intervening years, however, New York's politics have changed. A grinding recession and the sharp drop on Wall Street seem to have blunted state politicians' enthusiasm for market forces. The same governor and state Senate that fought for the cause in 1997 have lost their nerve. At best, they will keep the reforms won six years ago. Truly opening up New York's housing market is no longer on the table.

This is odd, because there is growing evidence that the transition from a strictly regulated to an unregulated market is less painful than people like Mr Silver make out. The most striking example has been in Cambridge, Massachusetts, where tight restrictions were lifted in 1994 after 23 years. A study by Henry Pollakowski, an economist at the MIT Center for Real Estate, shows no dire consequences. Instead there has been a huge surge in housing investment, even allowing for the 1990s housing boom.

It is hard to find any economist who supports rent restraints. Price controls, even if laboriously tweaked, inevitably produce inefficiencies, reduce supply and cause bad side-effects. Black markets and bribery thrive. Building maintenance is often ignored. Landlords and tenants find themselves in poisonous relationships, since they are linked by law rather than by voluntarily renewable contracts. Unscrupulous property owners go to dangerous lengths to evict tenants in order to get higher-paying replacements; as a result, tenant-protection laws have been enacted that make it almost impossible to evict even a scoundrel.

Meanwhile, a vast bureaucracy has grown up to administer the price controls, supported by volunteers and litigators. The property owner who misses a filing deadline, or has his paperwork mislaid, can be blocked from even permissible rent increases. Given all this, most sane New Yorkers would rather eat their money than join the rentier class.

Oddly enough, for those landlords adept at navigating the system, returns are likely to be unaffected by price caps, as long as properties were acquired after they had been imposed and the potential for income is understood. Indeed, although the press depicts the fight over price restraints as tenants versus landlords, it is more accurate to see it as tenants paying a below-market rent versus tenants who, in effect, pay the cost of this subsidy, says Peter Salins, the provost of the State University of New York and co-author of a book on New York's housing market (*Scarcity by Design,* Harvard University Press, 1992).

Who, then, are the lucky tenants? According to another study by Mr Pollakowski, most benefits go to tenants in lower and mid-Manhattan, where the residents are relatively wealthy. The city's poorer folk, most of whom live in the outer boroughs, receive little or nothing. Perhaps the strongest argument offered by supporters of rent control is that it promotes stability; but, typically, long-term tenants in unregulated markets receive similar concessions, since it is in a property-owner's interest to retain dependable renters in his buildings.

Mr Salins says the members of the state legislature are well aware of all the basic arguments about the evil effects of price controls on the property market. They believe even more strongly, however, that voters do not like getting socked with rent increases. For New York's politicians, it is a time of small thoughts.

Source: *The Economist* , 5 June 2003.

Whereas a price ceiling places a legal maximum on prices, a price floor places a legal minimum.

When the government imposes a price floor on the ice cream market, two outcomes are possible. If the government imposes a price floor of €2 per cornet when the equilibrium price is €3, we obtain the outcome in panel (a) of Figure 6.3. In this case, because the equilibrium price is above the floor, the price floor is not binding. Market forces naturally move the economy to the equilibrium, and the price floor has no effect.

Panel (b) of Figure 6.3 shows what happens when the government imposes a price floor of €4 per cornet. In this case, because the equilibrium price of €3 is below the floor, the price floor is a binding constraint on the market. The forces of supply and demand tend to move the price towards the equilibrium price, but when the market price hits the floor, it can fall no further. The market price equals the price floor. At this floor, the quantity of ice cream supplied (120 cornets) exceeds the quantity demanded (80 cornets). Some people who want to sell ice cream at the going price are unable to. Thus, a binding price floor causes a surplus.

Just as price ceilings and shortages can lead to undesirable rationing mechanisms, so can price floors and surpluses. In the case of a price floor, some sellers are unable to sell all they want at the market price. The sellers who appeal to the personal biases of the buyers, perhaps due to racial or familial ties, are better able to sell their goods than those who do not. By contrast, in a free market, the price serves as the rationing mechanism, and sellers can sell all they want at the equilibrium price.

# CASE STUDY

## The Minimum Wage

An important example of a price floor is the minimum wage. Minimum wage laws dictate the lowest price for labour that any employer may pay. The US and nine European Union countries – including, since April 1999, the UK – now have a statutory minimum wage.

To examine the effects of a minimum wage, we must consider the market for labour. Panel (a) of Figure 6.4 shows the labour market, which, like all markets, is subject to the forces of supply and demand. Workers determine the supply of labour, and firms determine the demand. If the government doesn't intervene, the wage normally adjusts to balance labour supply and labour demand.

Panel (b) of Figure 6.4 shows the labour market with a minimum wage. If the minimum wage is above the equilibrium level, as it is here, the quantity of labour supplied exceeds the quantity demanded. The result is unemployment. Thus, the minimum wage raises the incomes of those workers who have jobs, but it lowers the incomes of those workers who cannot find jobs.

To understand fully the minimum wage, keep in mind that the economy contains not a single labour market, but many labour markets for different types of workers. The impact of the minimum wage depends on the skill and experience of the worker. Workers with high skills and much experience are not affected, because their equilibrium wages are well above the minimum. For these workers, the minimum wage is not binding. One would therefore expect a diagram such as that in Panel (b) of Figure 6.4, where the minimum wage is above the equilibrium wage and unemployment results, to apply primarily to the market for low-skilled and teenage labour. Note, however, that the *extent* of the unemployment that results depends upon the elasticities of the supply and demand for labour. In Panel (c) of Figure 6.4 we have redrawn the diagram with a more elastic demand curve for labour and we can see that this results in a higher level of unemployment. It is often argued that the demand for unskilled labour is in fact likely to be highly elastic with respect to the price of labour because employers of unskilled labour, such as fast food restaurants usually face highly price-elastic demand curves for their own product and so cannot easily pass on wage rises in the form of higher prices without seeing their revenue fall.

This is only true, however, if one firm raises its price while others do not. If all fast food companies are forced to raise prices slightly in order to pay the minimum wage to their staff, this may result in a much smaller fall in the demand for the output (e.g. hamburgers) of any one firm. If this is the case, then the imposition of a statutory minimum wage may actually lead to a right-ward shift in the segment of the labour demand curve at or above the statutory minimum wage: a firm is able to pay the higher wage without drastically reducing its labour demand because it can pass on the higher wage costs by charging a higher price for its product, safe in the knowledge that other firms in the industry will have to do the same and hence that it will not suffer a dramatic fall in demand for its output. In this case – as in panel (d) of Figure 6.4 – although there is an increase in unemployment relative to the case with no minimum wage, this is mainly because the supply of labour is higher with the minimum wage imposed. This is because some workers will be attracted by the higher wage to enter the labour market – second earners, for example, or young people who otherwise would have stayed in full-time education.

**FIGURE 6.4**

### How the Minimum Wage Affects the Labour Market

*Panel (a) shows a labour market in which the wage adjusts to balance labour supply and demand. Panel (b) shows the impact of a binding minimum wage. Because the minimum wage is a price floor, it causes a surplus: the quantity of labour supplied exceeds the quantity demanded. The result is unemployment. Panel (c) shows that the more elastic labour demand is, the higher will be ensuing unemployment. In panel (d), because the minimum wage is binding across the whole industry, firms are able to pass a higher proportion of the wage costs onto higher prices without a drastic fall in demand for output, and so the labour demand curve for an individual firm actually shifts to the right at or above the minimum wage, so that the impact on employment is much less.*

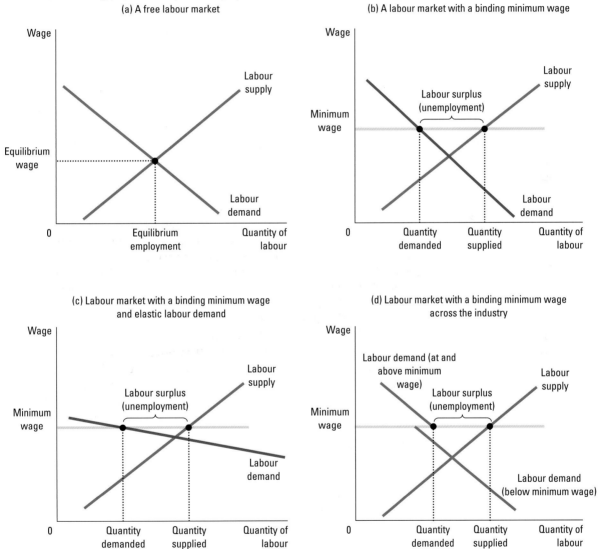

Advocates of minimum wage laws view the policy as one way to raise the income of the working poor. They correctly point out that workers who earn the minimum wage can afford only a meagre standard of living. They admit that it may have some adverse effects, including a possible rise in unemployment, but they believe that these effects are small and that, all things considered, a higher minimum wage makes the poor better off.

Opponents of the minimum wage contend that it is not the best way to combat poverty since it affects only the income of those in employment and may raise unemployment, and because not all minimum wage workers are heads of households trying to help their families escape poverty – some may be second earners or even third earners in relatively well-off households.

In short, the effects of the minimum wage on the labour market are complicated. It is one of those cases where there are no clear-cut answers: it all depends on what assumptions you make. At this point you may throw up your hands in despair and ask 'so what's the point of studying economics if it can't tell me one way or the other if introducing a minimum wage benefits the poor or not?' But all our brief economic analysis of the minimum wage has shown is that the issue is very complex: don't shoot the messenger for telling you so.

### Evaluating Price Controls

One of the *Ten Principles of Economics* discussed in Chapter 1 is that markets are usually a good way to organize economic activity. This principle explains why economists usually oppose price ceilings and price floors. To economists, prices are not the outcome of some haphazard process. Prices, they contend, are the result of the millions of business and consumer decisions that lie behind the supply and demand curves. Prices have the crucial job of balancing supply and demand and, thereby, coordinating economic activity. When policy makers set prices by legal decree, they obscure the signals that normally guide the allocation of society's resources.

Another one of the *Ten Principles of Economics* is that governments can sometimes improve market outcomes. Indeed, policy makers are led to control prices because they view the market's outcome as unfair. Price controls are often aimed at helping the poor. For instance, rent-control laws try to make housing affordable for everyone, and minimum wage laws try to help people escape poverty.

Yet price controls often hurt those they are trying to help. Rent control may keep rents low, but it also discourages landlords from maintaining their buildings and makes housing hard to find. Minimum wage laws may raise the incomes of some workers, but they also cause other workers to be unemployed.

Helping those in need can be accomplished in ways other than controlling prices. For instance, the government can make housing more affordable by paying a fraction of the rent for poor families. Unlike rent control, such rent subsidies do not reduce the quantity of housing supplied and, therefore, do not lead to housing shortages.

Although these alternative policies are often better than price controls, they are not perfect. Rent and wage subsidies cost the government money and, therefore, require higher taxes. As we see in the next section, taxation has costs of its own.

**Quick Quiz** Define *price ceiling* and *price floor*, and give an example of each. Which leads to a shortage? Which leads to a surplus? Why?

## TAXES

All governments, whether national or local, use taxes to raise revenue for public projects, such as roads, schools and national defence. Because taxes are such an important policy instrument, and because they affect our lives in many ways, the study of taxes is a topic to which we return several times throughout this book. In this section we begin our study of how taxes affect the economy.

To set the stage for our analysis, imagine that the government decides to hold a national annual ice cream festival – with a parade, fireworks and speeches by leading politicians. To raise revenue to pay for the event, it decides to place a €0.50 tax on the sale of ice cream cornets. When the plan is announced, our two lobbying groups swing into action. The National Organization of Ice Cream Producers claims that its members are struggling to survive in a competitive market, and it argues that *buyers* of ice cream should have to pay the tax. The National Association of Ice Cream Eaters claims that consumers of ice cream are having trouble making ends meet, and it argues that *sellers* of ice cream should pay the tax. The prime minister, hoping to reach a compromise, suggests that half the tax be paid by the buyers and half be paid by the sellers.

To analyse these proposals, we need to address a simple but subtle question: when the government levies a tax on a good, who bears the burden of the tax? The people buying the good? The people selling the good? Or, if buyers and sellers share the tax burden, what determines how the burden is divided? Can the government simply legislate the division of the burden, as the prime minister is suggesting, or is the division determined by more fundamental forces in the economy? Economists use the term **tax incidence** to refer to the distribution of a tax burden. As we will see, some surprising lessons about tax incidence arise just by applying the tools of supply and demand.

**tax incidence**
the manner in which the burden of a tax is shared among participants in a market

## How Taxes on Buyers Affect Market Outcomes

We first consider a tax levied on buyers of a good. Suppose, for instance, that the government passes a law requiring buyers of ice cream cornets to send €0.50 to the Treasury for each ice cream cornet they buy. How does this law affect the buyers and sellers of ice cream? To answer this question, we can follow the three steps in Chapter 4 for analysing supply and demand: (1) we decide whether the law affects the supply curve or demand curve; (2) we decide which way the curve shifts; (3) we examine how the shift affects the equilibrium.

**Step One**  The initial impact of the tax is on the demand for ice cream. The supply curve is not affected because, for any given price of ice cream, sellers have the same incentive to provide ice cream to the market. By contrast, buyers now have to pay a tax to the government (as well as the price to the sellers) whenever they buy ice cream. Thus, the tax shifts the demand curve for ice cream.

**Step Two**  The direction of the shift is easy to determine. Because the tax on buyers makes buying ice cream less attractive, buyers demand a smaller quantity of ice cream at every price. As a result, the demand curve shifts to the left (or, equivalently, downward), as shown in Figure 6.5.

We can, in this case, be precise about how much the curve shifts. Because of the €0.50 tax levied on buyers, the effective price to buyers is now €0.50 higher than the market price (whatever the market price happens to be). For example, if the market price of a cornet happened to be €2.00, the effective price to buyers would be €2.50. Because buyers look at their total cost including the tax, they demand a quantity of ice cream as if the market price were €0.50 higher than it actually is. In other words, to induce buyers to demand any given quantity, the market price must now be €0.50 lower to make up for the effect of the tax. Thus, the tax shifts the demand curve *downward* from $D_1$ to $D_2$ by exactly the size of the tax (€0.50).

**FIGURE 6.5**

**A Tax on Buyers**

*When a tax of €0.50 is levied on buyers, the demand curve shifts down by €0.50 from D$_1$ to D$_2$. The equilibrium quantity falls from 100 to 90 cornets. The price that sellers receive falls from €3.00 to €2.80. The price that buyers pay (including the tax) rises from €3.00 to €3.30. Even though the tax is levied on buyers, buyers and sellers share the burden of the tax.*

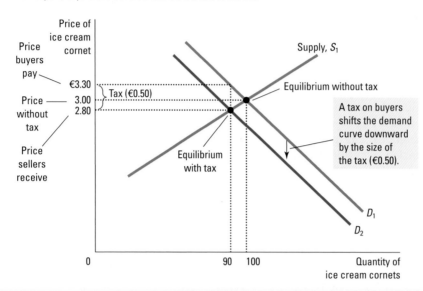

**Step Three**  Having determined how the demand curve shifts, we can now see the effect of the tax by comparing the initial equilibrium and the new equilibrium. You can see in the figure that the equilibrium price of ice cream falls from €3.00 to €2.80 and the equilibrium quantity falls from 100 to 90 cornets. Because sellers sell less and buyers buy less in the new equilibrium, the tax on ice cream reduces the size of the ice cream market.

**Implications**  We can now return to the question of tax incidence: who pays the tax? Although buyers send the entire tax to the government, buyers and sellers share the burden. Because the market price falls from €3.00 to €2.80 when the tax is introduced, sellers receive €0.20 less for each ice cream cornet than they did without the tax. Thus, the tax makes sellers worse off. Buyers pay sellers a lower price (€2.80), but the effective price including the tax rises from €3.00 before the tax to €3.30 with the tax (€2.80 + €0.50 = €3.30). Thus, the tax also makes buyers worse off.

To sum up, the analysis yields two lessons:

● Taxes discourage market activity. When a good is taxed, the quantity of the good sold is smaller in the new equilibrium.
● Buyers and sellers share the burden of taxes. In the new equilibrium, buyers pay more for the good, and sellers receive less.

## How Taxes on Sellers Affect Market Outcomes

Now consider a tax levied on sellers of a good. Suppose the government passes a law requiring sellers of ice cream cornets to send €0.50 to the Treasury for each cornet they sell. What are the effects of this law? Again, we apply our three steps.

**Step One** In this case, the immediate impact of the tax is on the sellers of ice cream. Because the tax is not levied on buyers, the quantity of ice cream demanded at any given price is the same; thus, the demand curve does not change. By contrast, the tax on sellers makes the ice cream business less profitable at any given price, so it shifts the supply curve.

**Step Two** Because the tax on sellers raises the cost of producing and selling ice cream, it reduces the quantity supplied at every price. The supply curve shifts to the left (or, equivalently, upward).

Once again, we can be precise about the magnitude of the shift. For any market price of ice cream, the effective price to sellers – the amount they get to keep after paying the tax – is €0.50 lower. For example, if the market price of a cornet happened to be €2.00, the effective price received by sellers would be €1.50. Whatever the market price, sellers will supply a quantity of ice cream as if the price were €0.50 lower than it is. Put differently, to induce sellers to supply any given quantity, the market price must now be €0.50 higher to compensate for the effect of the tax. Thus, as shown in Figure 6.6, the supply curve shifts *upward* from $S_1$ to $S_2$ by exactly the size of the tax (€0.50).

**Step Three** Having determined how the supply curve shifts, we can now compare the initial and the new equilibrium. The figure shows that the equilibrium price of ice cream rises from €3.00 to €3.30, and the equilibrium quantity falls from 100 to 90 cornets. Once again, the tax reduces the size of the ice cream market. And once again, buyers and sellers share the burden of the tax. Because the market

---

### FIGURE 6.6

**A Tax on Sellers**

*When a tax of €0.50 is levied on sellers, the supply curve shifts up by €0.50 from $S_1$ to $S_2$. The equilibrium quantity falls from 100 to 90 cornets. The price that buyers pay rises from €3.00 to €3.30. The price that sellers receive (after paying the tax) falls from €3.00 to €2.80. Even though the tax is levied on sellers, buyers and sellers share the burden of the tax.*

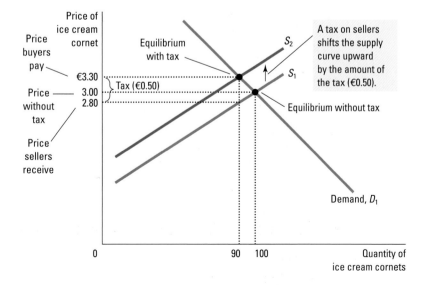

price rises, buyers pay €0.30 more for each cornet of ice cream than they did before the tax was enacted. Sellers receive a higher price than they did without the tax, but the effective price (after paying the tax) falls from €3.00 to €2.80.

**Implications** If you compare Figures 6.5 and 6.6, you will notice a surprising conclusion: taxes on buyers and taxes on sellers are equivalent. In both cases, the tax places a wedge between the price that buyers pay and the price that sellers receive. The wedge between the buyers' price and the sellers' price is the same, regardless of whether the tax is levied on buyers or sellers. In either case, the wedge shifts the relative position of the supply and demand curves. In the new equilibrium, buyers and sellers share the burden of the tax. The only difference between taxes on buyers and taxes on sellers is who sends the money to the government.

The equivalence of these two taxes is easy to understand if we imagine that the government collects the €0.50 ice cream tax in a bowl on the counter of each ice cream parlour. When the government levies the tax on buyers, the buyer is required to place €0.50 in the bowl every time a cornet is bought. When the government levies the tax on sellers, the seller is required to place €0.50 in the bowl after the sale of each cornet. Whether the €0.50 goes directly from the buyer's pocket into the bowl or indirectly from the buyer's pocket into the seller's hand and then into the bowl, does not matter. Once the market reaches its new equilibrium, buyers and sellers share the burden, regardless of how the tax is levied.

## *CASE STUDY*

### Can the Government Distribute the Burden of a Payroll Tax?

If you have ever received a pay cheque, you probably noticed that taxes were deducted from the amount you earned. In the United Kingdom, one of these taxes is called National Insurance Contributions (NICs). In theory, the UK government uses the revenue from NICs to pay for social security and state pensions (in practice, the money goes into the government coffers without being earmarked for any particular use). NICs are an example of a *payroll tax*, which is a tax on the wages that firms pay their workers.

Who do you think bears the burden of this payroll tax – firms or workers? In fact, if you read official UK government documents, it seems that the burden is split fairly clearly: in 2003–4, for example, average-paid workers paid 11 per cent of their income above a basic level in NICs, while the workers' employer paid 12.8 per cent.

Our analysis of tax incidence, however, shows that politicians cannot so easily dictate the distribution of a tax burden. To illustrate, we can analyse a payroll tax as merely a tax on a good, where the good is labour and the price is the wage. The key feature of the payroll tax is that it places a wedge between the wage that firms pay and the wage that workers receive. Figure 6.7 shows the outcome. When a payroll tax is enacted, the wage received by workers falls, and the wage paid by firms rises. In the end, workers and firms share the burden of the tax, much as the legislation requires. Yet this division of the tax burden between workers and firms has nothing to do with the legislated division. Moreover, the same outcome would prevail if the law levied the entire tax on workers or if it levied the entire tax on firms.

This example shows that the most basic lesson of tax incidence is often overlooked in public debate. Politicians can decide whether a tax comes from the buyer's pocket or from the seller's, but they cannot legislate the true burden of a tax. Rather, tax incidence depends on the forces of supply and demand.

## FIGURE 6.7

**A Payroll Tax**

*A payroll tax places a wedge between the wage that workers receive and the wage that firms pay. Comparing wages with and without the tax, you can see that workers and firms share the tax burden. This division of the tax burden between workers and firms does not depend on whether the government levies the tax on workers, levies the tax on firms or divides the tax equally between the two groups.*

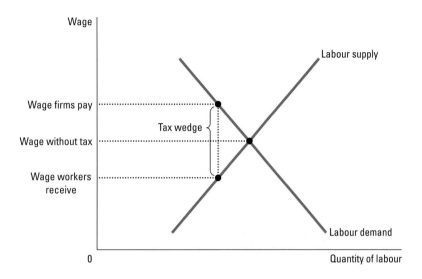

## Elasticity and Tax Incidence

When a good is taxed, buyers and sellers of the good share the burden of the tax. But how exactly is the tax burden divided? Only rarely will it be shared equally. To see how the burden is divided, consider the impact of taxation in the two markets in Figure 6.8. In both cases, the figure shows the initial demand curve, the initial supply curve, and a tax that drives a wedge between the amount paid by buyers and the amount received by sellers. (Not drawn in either panel of the figure is the new supply or demand curve. Which curve shifts depends on whether the tax is levied on buyers or sellers. As we have seen, this is irrelevant for the incidence of the tax.) The difference in the two panels is the relative elasticity of supply and demand.

Panel (a) of Figure 6.8 shows a tax in a market with very elastic supply and relatively inelastic demand. That is, sellers are very responsive to changes in the price of the good (so the supply curve is relatively flat), whereas buyers are not very responsive (so the demand curve is relatively steep). When a tax is imposed on a market with these elasticities, the price received by sellers does not fall much, so sellers bear only a small burden. By contrast, the price paid by buyers rises substantially, indicating that buyers bear most of the burden of the tax.

Panel (b) of Figure 6.8 shows a tax in a market with relatively inelastic supply and very elastic demand. In this case, sellers are not very responsive to changes in the price (so the supply curve is steeper), while buyers are very responsive (so the demand curve is flatter). The figure shows that when a tax is imposed, the price paid by buyers does not rise much, while the price received by sellers falls substantially. Thus, sellers bear most of the burden of the tax.

The two panels of Figure 6.8 show a general lesson about how the burden of a tax is divided: a tax burden falls more heavily on the side of the market that is

### FIGURE 6.8

#### How the Burden of a Tax Is Divided

*In panel (a), the supply curve is elastic and the demand curve is inelastic. In this case, the price received by sellers falls only slightly, while the price paid by buyers rises substantially. Thus, buyers bear most of the burden of the tax. In panel (b), the supply curve is inelastic and the demand curve is elastic. In this case, the price received by sellers falls substantially, while the price paid by buyers rises only slightly. Thus, sellers bear most of the burden of the tax.*

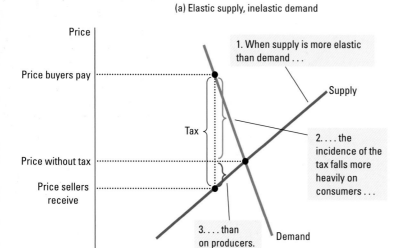

(a) Elastic supply, inelastic demand

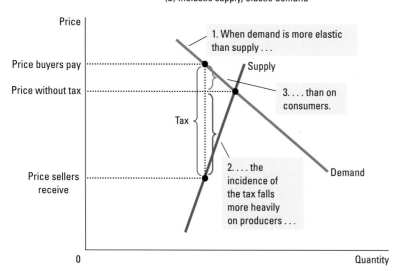

(b) Inelastic supply, elastic demand

less elastic. Why is this true? In essence, the elasticity measures the willingness of buyers or sellers to leave the market when conditions become unfavourable. A small elasticity of demand means that buyers do not have good alternatives to consuming this particular good. A small elasticity of supply means that sellers do not have good alternatives to producing this particular good. When the good is taxed, the side of the market with fewer good alternatives cannot easily leave the market and must, therefore, bear more of the burden of the tax.

We can apply this logic to the payroll tax discussed in the previous case study. Most labour economists believe that the supply of labour is much less elastic than the demand. This means that workers, rather than firms, bear most of the burden of any payroll tax, whatever the official split.

## *CASE STUDY*

### Who Pays the Luxury Tax?

In 1990, the US Congress adopted a new luxury tax on items such as yachts, private aeroplanes, furs, jewellery and expensive cars. The goal of the tax was to raise revenue from those who could most easily afford to pay. Because only the rich could afford to buy such extravagances, taxing luxuries seemed a logical way of taxing the rich.

Yet, when the forces of supply and demand took over, the outcome was quite different from what the US Congress had intended. Consider, for example, the market for yachts. The demand for yachts is quite elastic. A millionaire can easily not buy a yacht; she can use the money to buy a bigger house, go on holiday to Europe or leave a larger bequest to her heirs. By contrast, the supply of yachts is relatively inelastic, at least in the short run. Yacht factories are not easily converted to alternative uses, and workers who build yachts are not eager to change careers in response to changing market conditions.

Our analysis makes a clear prediction in this case. With elastic demand and inelastic supply, the burden of a tax falls largely on the suppliers. That is, a tax on yachts places a burden largely on the firms and workers who build yachts because they end up getting a lower price for their product. The workers, however, are not wealthy. Thus, the burden of a luxury tax falls more on the middle class than on the rich.

The mistaken assumptions about the incidence of the luxury tax quickly became apparent after the tax became effective. Suppliers of luxuries made their congressional representatives well aware of the economic hardship they experienced, and the US Congress repealed most of the luxury tax in 1993.

PHOTO: COPYRIGHT © IMAGESTATE/ALAMY

*A taxing pastime?*

**Quick Quiz** In a supply and demand diagram, show how a tax on car buyers of €1,000 per car affects the quantity of cars sold and the price of cars. In another diagram, show how a tax on car sellers of €1,000 per car affects the quantity of cars sold and the price of cars. In both of your diagrams, show the change in the price paid by car buyers and the change in price received by car sellers.

## CONCLUSION

The economy is governed by two kinds of laws: the laws of supply and demand and the laws enacted by governments. In this chapter we have begun to see how these laws interact. Price controls and taxes are common in various markets in the economy, and their effects are frequently debated in the press and among policy makers. Even a little bit of economic knowledge can go a long way towards understanding and evaluating these policies.

In subsequent chapters we shall analyse many government policies in greater detail. We shall examine the effects of taxation more fully, and we shall consider a broader range of policies than we considered here. Yet the basic lessons of this chapter will not change: when analysing government policies, supply and demand are the first and most useful tools of analysis.

## SUMMARY

- A price ceiling is a legal maximum on the price of a good or service. An example is rent control. If the price ceiling is below the equilibrium price, the quantity demanded exceeds the quantity supplied. Because of the resulting shortage, sellers must in some way ration the good or service among buyers.

- A price floor is a legal minimum on the price of a good or service. An example is the minimum wage. If the price floor is above the equilibrium price, the quantity supplied exceeds the quantity demanded. Because of the resulting surplus, buyers' demands for the good or service must in some way be rationed among sellers.

- When the government levies a tax on a good, the equilibrium quantity of the good falls. That is, a tax on a market shrinks the size of the market.

- A tax on a good places a wedge between the price paid by buyers and the price received by sellers. When the market moves to the new equilibrium, buyers pay more for the good and sellers receive less for it. In this sense, buyers and sellers share the tax burden. The incidence of a tax (that is, the division of the tax burden) does not depend on whether the tax is levied on buyers or sellers.

- The incidence of a tax depends on the price elasticities of supply and demand. The burden tends to fall on the side of the market that is less elastic because that side of the market can respond less easily to the tax by changing the quantity bought or sold.

## KEY CONCEPTS

price ceiling, p. 110        price floor, p. 110        tax incidence, p. 119

## QUESTIONS FOR REVIEW

1. Give an example of a price ceiling and an example of a price floor.

2. Which causes a shortage of a good – a price ceiling or a price floor? Which causes a surplus?

3. What mechanisms allocate resources when the price of a good is not allowed to bring supply and demand into equilibrium?

4. Explain why economists usually oppose rent controls.

5. What is the difference between a tax paid by buyers and a tax paid by sellers?

6. How does a tax on a good affect the price paid by buyers, the price received by sellers and the quantity sold?

7. What determines how the burden of a tax is divided between buyers and sellers? Why?

# PROBLEMS AND APPLICATIONS

1. Lovers of classical music persuade the government to impose a price ceiling of €40 per ticket at classical music concerts. Does this policy get more or fewer people to attend?

2. The government has decided that the free market price of cheese is too low.
   a. Suppose the government imposes a binding price floor in the cheese market. Use a supply and demand diagram to show the effect of this policy on the price of cheese and the quantity of cheese sold. Is there a shortage or surplus of cheese?
   b. Farmers complain that the price floor has reduced their total revenue. Is this possible? Explain.
   c. In response to farmers' complaints, the government agrees to purchase all of the surplus cheese at the price floor. Compared to the basic price floor, who benefits from this new policy? Who loses?

3. A recent study found that the demand and supply schedules for frisbees are as follows:
   a. What are the equilibrium price and quantity of frisbees?
   b. Frisbee manufacturers persuade the government that frisbee production improves scientists' understanding of aerodynamics and thus is important for national security. The government decides to impose a price floor €2 above the equilibrium price. What is the new market price? How many frisbees are sold?
   c. Irate university students march on Westminster and demand a reduction in the price of frisbees. The government decides to repeal the price floor and impose a price ceiling €1 below the former price floor. What is the new market price? How many frisbees are sold?

4. Suppose that in the absence of any tax whatsoever, the equilibrium price of beer is €1.50 per pint. Now suppose that the government requires beer drinkers to pay a total tax (sales tax plus alcohol duty) of €0.50 on every pint of beer purchased.
   a. Draw a supply and demand diagram of the market for beer without the tax. Show the price paid by consumers, the price received by producers and the quantity of beer sold. What is the difference between the price paid by consumers and the price received by producers?
   b. Now draw a supply and demand diagram for the beer market with the tax. Show the price paid by consumers, the price received by producers and the quantity of beer sold. What is the difference between

the price paid by consumers and the price received by producers? Has the quantity of beer sold increased or decreased?

5. The employment minister wants to raise tax revenue and at the same time make workers better off. A civil servant suggests raising the payroll tax paid by firms and using part of the extra revenue to reduce the payroll tax paid by workers. Would this accomplish the minister's goal?

6. If the government places a €500 tax on luxury cars, will the price paid by consumers rise by more than €500, less than €500 or exactly €500? Explain.

7. The government decides to reduce air pollution by reducing the use of petrol. It imposes €0.50 tax for each litre of petrol sold.
   a. Should it impose this tax on petrol companies or motorists? Explain carefully, using a supply and demand diagram.
   b. If the demand for petrol were more elastic, would this tax be more effective or less effective in reducing the quantity of petrol consumed? Explain with both words and a diagram.
   c. Are consumers of petrol helped or hurt by this tax? Why?
   d. Are workers in the oil industry helped or hurt by this tax? Why?

8. A case study in this chapter discusses the minimum wage law.
   a. Suppose the minimum wage is above the equilibrium wage in the market for unskilled labour. Using a supply and demand diagram of the market for unskilled labour, show the market wage, the number of workers who are employed and the number of workers who are unemployed. Also show the total wage payments to unskilled workers.
   b. Now suppose the minister for employment proposes an increase in the minimum wage. What effect would this increase have on employment? Does the change in employment depend on the elasticity of demand, the elasticity of supply, both elasticities, or neither?
   c. What effect would this increase in the minimum wage have on unemployment? Does the change in unemployment depend on the elasticity of demand, the elasticity of supply, both elasticities, or neither?
   d. If the demand for unskilled labour were inelastic, would the proposed increase in the minimum wage raise or lower total wage payments to unskilled workers? Would your answer change if the demand for unskilled labour were elastic?

9. A subsidy is the opposite of a tax. With a €0.50 tax on the buyers of ice cream cornets, the government collects €0.50 for each cornet purchased; with a €0.50 subsidy for the buyers of ice cream cornets, the government pays buyers €0.50 for each cornet purchased.

   a. Show the effect of a €0.50 per cornet subsidy on the demand curve for ice cream cornets, the effective price paid by consumers, the effective price received by sellers and the quantity of cornets sold.

   b. Do consumers gain or lose from this policy? Do producers gain or lose? Does the government gain or lose?

For further resources, visit
http://www.thomsonlearning.co.uk/mankiw_taylor

# 3

# SUPPLY AND DEMAND II: MARKETS AND WELFARE

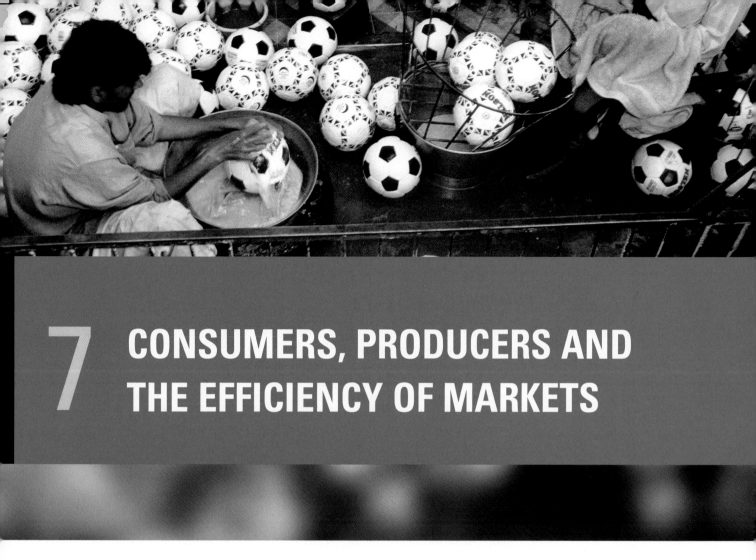

# 7 CONSUMERS, PRODUCERS AND THE EFFICIENCY OF MARKETS

When consumers go to the butcher's shop or the supermarket to buy their turkeys for Christmas dinner, they may be disappointed that the price of turkey is as high as it is. At the same time, when farmers bring to market the turkeys they have reared, they wish the price of turkey were even higher. These views are not surprising: buyers always want to pay less and sellers always want to get paid more. But is there a 'right price' for turkey from the standpoint of society as a whole?

In previous chapters we saw how, in market economies, the forces of supply and demand determine the prices of goods and services and the quantities sold. So far, however, we have described the way markets allocate scarce resources without directly addressing the question of whether these market allocations are desirable. In other words, our analysis has been *positive* (what is) rather than *normative* (what should be). We know that the price of turkey adjusts to ensure that the quantity of turkey supplied equals the quantity of turkey demanded. But, at this equilibrium, is the quantity of turkey produced and consumed too small, too large or just right?

In this chapter we take up the topic of **welfare economics,** the study of how the allocation of resources affects economic well-being. We begin by examining the benefits that buyers and sellers receive from taking part in a market. We then examine how society can make these benefits as large as possible. This analysis leads to a profound conclusion: the equilibrium of supply and demand in a market maximizes the total benefits received by buyers and sellers.

As you may recall from Chapter 1, one of the *Ten Principles of Economics* is that markets are usually a good way to organize economic activity. The study of

**welfare economics**
the study of how the allocation of resources affects economic well-being

welfare economics explains this principle more fully. It also answers our question about the right price of turkey: the price that balances the supply and demand for turkey is, in a particular sense, the best one because it maximizes the total welfare of turkey consumers and turkey producers.

# CONSUMER SURPLUS

We begin our study of welfare economics by looking at the benefits buyers receive from participating in a market.

## Willingness to Pay

Imagine that you own a mint-condition recording of the Rolling Stones first album. Because you are not a Stones fan, you decide to sell it. One way to do so is to hold an auction.

Four Stones fans show up for your auction: John, Paul, George and Ringo. Each of them would like to own the album, but there is a limit to the amount that each is willing to pay for it. Table 7.1 shows the maximum price that each of the four possible buyers would pay. Each buyer's maximum is called his **willingness to pay,** and it measures how much that buyer values the good. Each buyer would be eager to buy the album at a price less than his willingness to pay, would refuse to buy the album at a price more than his willingness to pay, and would be indifferent about buying the album at a price exactly equal to his willingness to pay.

To sell your album, you begin the bidding at a low price, say €10. Because all four buyers are willing to pay much more, the price rises quickly. The bidding stops when John bids €80 (or slightly more). At this point, Paul, George and Ringo have dropped out of the bidding because they are unwilling to bid any more than €80. John pays you €80 and gets the album. Note that the album has gone to the buyer who values the album most highly.

What benefit does John receive from buying the Rolling Stones album? In a sense, John has found a real bargain: he is willing to pay €100 for the album but pays only €80 for it. We say that John receives *consumer surplus* of €20. **Consumer surplus** is the amount a buyer is willing to pay for a good minus the amount the buyer actually pays for it.

Consumer surplus measures the benefit to buyers of participating in a market. In this example, John receives a €20 benefit from participating in the auction because he pays only €80 for a good he values at €100. Paul, George and Ringo get no consumer surplus from participating in the auction because they left without the album and without paying anything.

**willingness to pay**
the maximum amount that a buyer will pay for a good

**consumer surplus**
a buyer's willingness to pay minus the amount the buyer actually pays

---

### TABLE 7.1

**Four Possible Buyers' Willingness to Pay**

| Buyer | Willingness to pay |
|---|---|
| John | €100 |
| Paul | 80 |
| George | 70 |
| Ringo | 50 |

Now consider a somewhat different example. Suppose that you had two identical Rolling Stones albums to sell. Again, you auction them off to the four possible buyers. To keep things simple, we assume that both albums are to be sold for the same price and that no buyer is interested in buying more than one album. Therefore, the price rises until two buyers are left.

In this case, the bidding stops when John and Paul bid €70 (or slightly higher). At this price, John and Paul are each happy to buy an album and George and Ringo are not willing to bid any higher. John and Paul each receive consumer surplus equal to his willingness to pay minus the price. John's consumer surplus is €30 and Paul's is €10. John's consumer surplus is higher now than it was previously, because he gets the same album but pays less for it. The total consumer surplus in the market is €40.

## Using the Demand Curve to Measure Consumer Surplus

Consumer surplus is closely related to the demand curve for a product. To see how they are related, let's continue our example and consider the demand curve for this rare Rolling Stones album.

We begin by using the willingness to pay of the four possible buyers to find the demand schedule for the album. The table in Figure 7.1 shows the demand schedule that corresponds to Table 7.1. If the price is above €100, the quantity demanded in the market is 0, because no buyer is willing to pay that much. If the price is between €80 and €100, the quantity demanded is 1, because only John is willing to pay such a high price. If the price is between €70 and €80, the quantity demanded is 2, because both John and Paul are willing to pay the price. We can continue this analysis for other prices as well. In this way, the demand schedule is derived from the willingness to pay of the four possible buyers.

### FIGURE 7.1

**The Demand Schedule and the Demand Curve**

*The table shows the demand schedule for the buyers in Table 7.1. The graph shows the corresponding demand curve. Note that the height of the demand curve reflects buyers' willingness to pay.*

| Price | Buyers | Quantity demanded |
|---|---|---|
| More than €100 | None | 0 |
| €80 to €100 | John | 1 |
| €70 to €80 | John, Paul | 2 |
| €50 to €70 | John, Paul, George | 3 |
| €50 or less | John, Paul, George, Ringo | 4 |

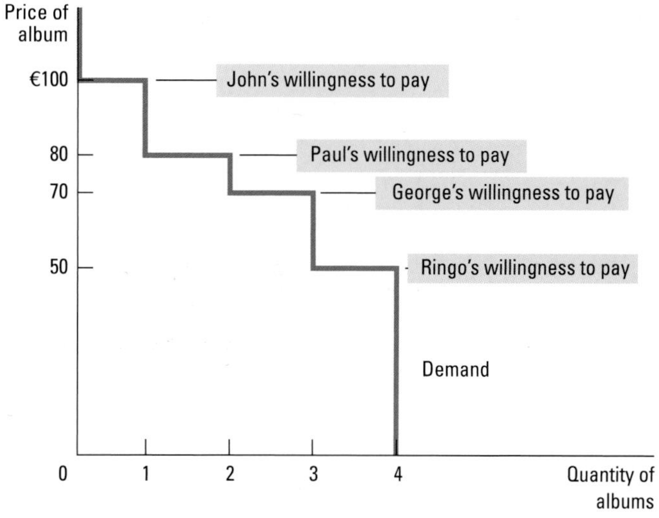

The graph in Figure 7.1 shows the demand curve that corresponds to this demand schedule. Note the relationship between the height of the demand curve and the buyers' willingness to pay. At any quantity, the price given by the demand curve shows the willingness to pay of the *marginal buyer*, the buyer who would leave the market first if the price were any higher. At a quantity of 4 albums, for instance, the demand curve has a height of €50, the price that Ringo (the marginal buyer) is willing to pay for an album. At a quantity of 3 albums, the demand curve has a height of €70, the price that George (who is now the marginal buyer) is willing to pay.

Because the demand curve reflects buyers' willingness to pay, we can also use it to measure consumer surplus. Figure 7.2 uses the demand curve to compute consumer surplus in our example. In panel (a), the price is €80 (or slightly above) and the quantity demanded is 1. Note that the area above the price and below the demand curve equals €20. This amount is exactly the consumer surplus we computed earlier when only 1 album is sold.

Panel (b) of Figure 7.2 shows consumer surplus when the price is €70 (or slightly above). In this case, the area above the price and below the demand curve equals the total area of the two rectangles: John's consumer surplus at this price is €30 and Paul's is €10. This area equals a total of €40. Once again, this amount is the consumer surplus we computed earlier.

The lesson from this example holds for all demand curves: the area below the demand curve and above the price measures the consumer surplus in a market. The reason is that the height of the demand curve measures the value buyers place on the good, as measured by their willingness to pay for it. The difference between this willingness to pay and the market price is each buyer's consumer surplus. Thus, the total area below the demand curve and above the price is the sum of the consumer surplus of all buyers in the market for a good or service.

## FIGURE 7.2

**Measuring Consumer Surplus with the Demand Curve**

*In panel (a) the price of the good is €80 and the consumer surplus is €20. In panel (b) the price of the good is €70 and the consumer surplus is €40.*

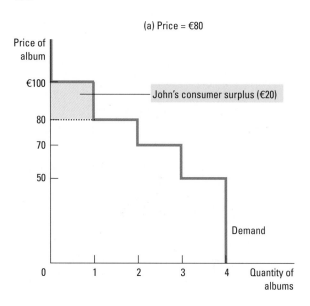

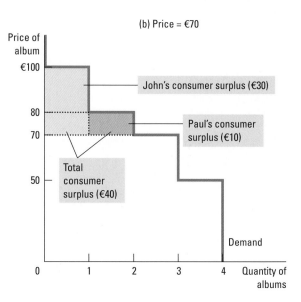

## How a Lower Price Raises Consumer Surplus

Because buyers always want to pay less for the goods they buy, a lower price makes buyers of a good better off. But how much does buyers' well-being rise in response to a lower price? We can use the concept of consumer surplus to answer this question precisely.

Figure 7.3 shows a typical downward sloping demand curve. Although this demand curve appears somewhat different in shape from the step-like demand curves in our previous two figures, the ideas we have just developed apply nevertheless: consumer surplus is the area above the price and below the demand curve. In panel (a), consumer surplus at a price of $P_1$ is the area of triangle ABC.

Now suppose that the price falls from $P_1$ to $P_2$, as shown in panel (b). The consumer surplus now equals area ADF. The increase in consumer surplus attributable to the lower price is the area BCFD.

This increase in consumer surplus is composed of two parts. First, those buyers who were already buying $Q_1$ of the good at the higher price $P_1$ are better off because they now pay less. The increase in consumer surplus of existing buyers is the reduction in the amount they pay; it equals the area of the rectangle BCED. Secondly, some new buyers enter the market because they are now willing to buy the good at the lower price. As a result, the quantity demanded in the market increases from $Q_1$ to $Q_2$. The consumer surplus these newcomers receive is the area of the triangle CEF.

---

### FIGURE 7.3

**How the Price Affects Consumer Surplus**

*In panel (a) the price is $P_1$, the quantity demanded is $Q_1$ and consumer surplus equals the area of the triangle ABC. When the price falls from $P_1$ to $P_2$, as in panel (b), the quantity demanded rises from $Q_1$ to $Q_2$, and the consumer surplus rises to the area of the triangle ADF. The increase in consumer surplus (area BCFD) occurs in part because existing consumers now pay less (area BCED) and in part because new consumers enter the market at the lower price (area CEF).*

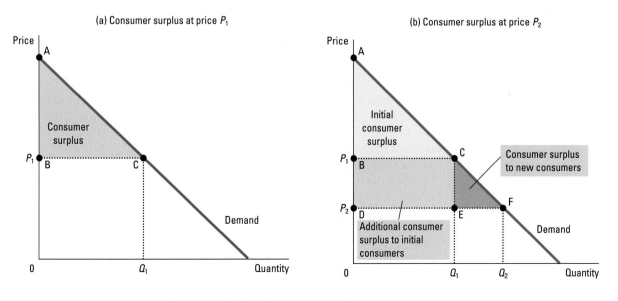

## What Does Consumer Surplus Measure?

Our goal in developing the concept of consumer surplus is to make normative judgements about the desirability of market outcomes. Now that you have seen what consumer surplus is, let's consider whether it is a good measure of economic well-being.

Imagine that you are a policy maker trying to design a good economic system. Would you care about the amount of consumer surplus? Consumer surplus, the amount that buyers are willing to pay for a good minus the amount they actually pay for it, measures the benefit that buyers receive from a good *as the buyers themselves perceive it*. Thus, consumer surplus is a good measure of economic well-being if policy makers want to respect the preferences of buyers.

In some circumstances, policy makers might choose not to care about consumer surplus because they do not respect the preferences that drive buyer behaviour. For example, drug addicts are willing to pay a high price for heroin. Yet we would not say that addicts get a large benefit from being able to buy heroin at a low price (even though addicts might say they do). From the standpoint of society, willingness to pay in this instance is not a good measure of the buyers' benefit, and consumer surplus is not a good measure of economic well-being, because addicts are not looking after their own best interests.

In most markets, however, consumer surplus does reflect economic well-being. Economists normally presume that buyers are rational when they make decisions and that their preferences should be respected. In this case, consumers are the best judges of how much benefit they receive from the goods they buy.

> **Quick Quiz** Draw a demand curve for turkey. In your diagram, show a price of turkey and the consumer surplus that results from that price. Explain in words what this consumer surplus measures.

# PRODUCER SURPLUS

We now turn to the other side of the market and consider the benefits sellers receive from participating in a market. As you will see, our analysis of sellers' welfare is similar to our analysis of buyers' welfare.

## Cost and the Willingness to Sell

Imagine now that you own a house and you need to get it painted externally. You turn to four sellers of house painting services: Millie, Georgia, Julie and Nana. Each painter is willing to do the work for you if the price is right. You decide to take bids from the four painters and auction off the job to the painter who will do the work for the lowest price.

**cost**
the value of everything a seller must give up to produce a good

Each painter is willing to take the job if the price she would receive exceeds her **cost** of doing the work. Here the term **cost** should be interpreted as the painter's opportunity cost: it includes the painter's out-of-pocket expenses (for paint, brushes and so on) as well as the value that the painter places on her own time. Table 7.2 shows each painter's cost. Because a painter's cost is the lowest price she would accept for her work, cost is a measure of her willingness to sell her services. Each painter would be eager to sell her services at a price greater than her cost, would refuse to sell her services at a price less than her cost, and would be indifferent about selling her services at a price exactly equal to her cost.

> ### TABLE 7.2
>
> **The Costs of Four Possible Sellers**
>
> | Seller | Cost |
> | --- | --- |
> | Millie | €900 |
> | Julie | 800 |
> | Georgia | 600 |
> | Nana | 500 |

When you take bids from the painters, the price might start off high, but it quickly falls as the painters compete for the job. Once Nana has bid €600 (or slightly less), she is the sole remaining bidder. Nana is happy to do the job for this price, because her cost is only €500. Millie, Georgia and Julie are unwilling to do the job for less than €600. Note that the job goes to the painter who can do the work at the lowest cost.

What benefit does Nana receive from getting the job? Because she is willing to do the work for €500 but gets €600 for doing it, we say that she receives *producer surplus* of €100. **Producer surplus** is the amount a seller is paid minus the cost of production. Producer surplus measures the benefit to sellers of participating in a market.

Now consider a somewhat different example. Suppose that you have two houses that need painting. Again, you auction off the jobs to the four painters. To keep things simple, let's assume that no painter is able to paint both houses and that you will pay the same amount to paint each house. Therefore, the price falls until two painters are left.

In this case, the bidding stops when Georgia and Nana each offer to do the job for a price of €800 (or slightly less). At this price, Georgia and Nana are willing to do the work, and Millie and Julie are not willing to bid a lower price. At a price of €800, Nana receives producer surplus of €300, and Georgia receives producer surplus of €200. The total producer surplus in the market is €500.

## Using the Supply Curve to Measure Producer Surplus

Just as consumer surplus is closely related to the demand curve, producer surplus is closely related to the supply curve. To see how, let's continue our example.

We begin by using the costs of the four painters to find the supply schedule for painting services. The table in Figure 7.4 shows the supply schedule that corresponds to the costs in Table 7.2. If the price is below €500, none of the four painters is willing to do the job, so the quantity supplied is zero. If the price is between €500 and €600, only Nana is willing to do the job, so the quantity supplied is 1. If the price is between €600 and €800, Nana and Georgia are willing to do the job, so the quantity supplied is 2, and so on. Thus, the supply schedule is derived from the costs of the four painters.

The graph in Figure 7.4 shows the supply curve that corresponds to this supply schedule. Note that the height of the supply curve is related to the sellers' costs. At any quantity, the price given by the supply curve shows the cost of the *marginal seller*, the seller who would leave the market first if the price were any lower. At a quantity of 4 houses, for instance, the supply curve has a height of €900, the cost that Millie (the marginal seller) incurs to provide her painting services. At a quantity of 3 houses, the supply curve has a height of €800, the cost that Julie (who is now the marginal seller) incurs.

**producer surplus**
the amount a seller is paid for a good minus the seller's cost

## FIGURE 7.4

### The Supply Schedule and the Supply Curve

*The table shows the supply schedule for the sellers in Table 7.2. The graph shows the corresponding supply curve. Note that the height of the supply curve reflects sellers' costs.*

| Price | Sellers | Quantity supplied |
|---|---|---|
| €900 or more | Millie, Julie, Georgia, Nana | 4 |
| €800 to €900 | Julie, Georgia, Nana | 3 |
| €600 to €800 | Georgia, Nana | 2 |
| €500 to €600 | Nana | 1 |
| Less than €500 | None | 0 |

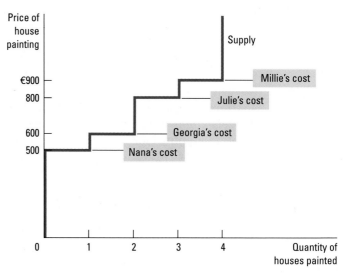

## FIGURE 7.5

### Measuring Producer Surplus with the Supply Curve

*In panel (a) the price of the good is €600 and the producer surplus is €100. In panel (b) the price of the good is €800 and the producer surplus is €500.*

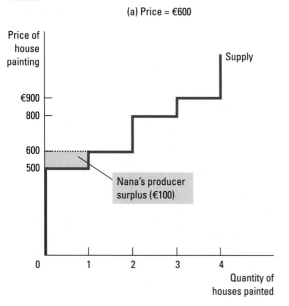

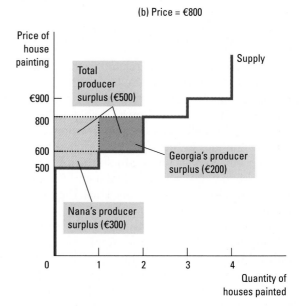

Because the supply curve reflects sellers' costs, we can use it to measure producer surplus. Figure 7.5 uses the supply curve to compute producer surplus in our example. In panel (a) we assume that the price is €600. In this case, the quantity supplied is 1. Note that the area below the price and above the supply curve equals €100. This amount is exactly the producer surplus we computed earlier for Nana.

Panel (b) of Figure 7.5 shows producer surplus at a price of €800. In this case, the area below the price and above the supply curve equals the total area of the two rectangles. This area equals €500, the producer surplus we computed earlier for Georgia and Nana when two houses needed painting.

The lesson from this example applies to all supply curves: the area below the price and above the supply curve measures the producer surplus in a market. The logic is straightforward: the height of the supply curve measures sellers' costs, and the difference between the price and the cost of production is each seller's producer surplus. Thus, the total area is the sum of the producer surplus of all sellers.

## How a Higher Price Raises Producer Surplus

You will not be surprised to hear that sellers always want to receive a higher price for the goods they sell. But how much does sellers' well-being rise in response to a higher price? The concept of producer surplus offers a precise answer to this question.

Figure 7.6 shows a typical upward sloping supply curve. Even though this supply curve differs in shape from the step-like supply curves in the previous figure, we measure producer surplus in the same way: producer surplus is the

### FIGURE 7.6

**How the Price Affects Producer Surplus**

*In panel (a) the price is $P_1$, the quantity demanded is $Q_1$ and producer surplus equals the area of the triangle ABC. When the price rises from $P_1$ to $P_2$, as in panel (b), the quantity supplied rises from $Q_1$ to $Q_2$ and the producer surplus rises to the area of the triangle ADF. The increase in producer surplus (area BCFD) occurs in part because existing producers now receive more (area BCED) and in part because new producers enter the market at the higher price (area CEF).*

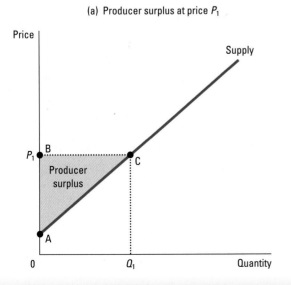

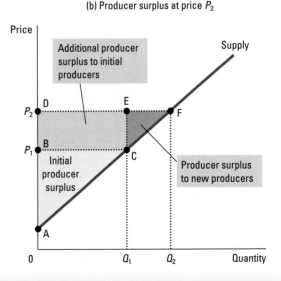

area below the price and above the supply curve. In panel (a), the price is $P_1$ and producer surplus is the area of triangle ABC.

Panel (b) shows what happens when the price rises from $P_1$ to $P_2$. Producer surplus now equals area ADF. This increase in producer surplus has two parts. First, those sellers who were already selling $Q_1$ of the good at the lower price $P_1$ are better off because they now get more for what they sell. The increase in producer surplus for existing sellers equals the area of the rectangle BCED. Secondly, some new sellers enter the market because they are now willing to produce the good at the higher price, resulting in an increase in the quantity supplied from $Q_1$ to $Q_2$. The producer surplus of these newcomers is the area of the triangle CEF.

As this analysis shows, we use producer surplus to measure the well-being of sellers in much the same way as we use consumer surplus to measure the well-being of buyers. Because these two measures of economic welfare are so similar, it is natural to use them together. And, indeed, that is exactly what we do in the next section.

> **Quick Quiz** Draw a supply curve for turkey. In your diagram show a price of turkey and the producer surplus that results from that price. Explain in words what this producer surplus measures.

# MARKET EFFICIENCY

Consumer surplus and producer surplus are the basic tools that economists use to study the welfare of buyers and sellers in a market. These tools can help us address a fundamental economic question: is the allocation of resources determined by free markets in any way desirable?

## The Benevolent Social Planner

To evaluate market outcomes, we introduce into our analysis a new, hypothetical character, the benevolent social planner – the BSP. The BSP is an omniscient, omnipotent, benign dictator. He wants to maximize the economic well-being of everyone in society. What do you suppose this planner should do? Should he just leave buyers and sellers at the equilibrium that they reach naturally on their own? Or can he increase economic well-being by altering the market outcome in some way?

To answer this question, the planner must first decide how to measure the economic well-being of a society. One possible measure is the sum of consumer and producer surplus, which we call *total surplus*. Consumer surplus is the benefit that buyers receive from participating in a market, and producer surplus is the benefit that sellers receive. It is therefore natural to use total surplus as a measure of society's economic well-being.

To better understand this measure of economic well-being, recall how we measure consumer and producer surplus. We define consumer surplus as:

Consumer surplus = Value to buyers – Amount paid by buyers

Similarly, we define producer surplus as:

Producer surplus = Amount received by sellers − Cost to sellers

When we add consumer and producer surplus together, we obtain:

$$\text{Total surplus} = \text{Value to buyers} - \text{Amount paid by buyers}$$
$$+ \text{Amount received by sellers} - \text{Cost to sellers}$$

The amount paid by buyers equals the amount received by sellers, so the middle two terms in this expression cancel each other. As a result, we can write total surplus as:

$$\text{Total surplus} = \text{Value to buyers} - \text{Cost to sellers}$$

Total surplus in a market is the total value to buyers of the goods, as measured by their willingness to pay, minus the total cost to sellers of providing those goods.

If an allocation of resources maximizes total surplus, we say that the allocation exhibits **efficiency.** If an allocation is not efficient, then some of the gains from trade among buyers and sellers are not being realized. For example, an allocation is inefficient if a good is not being produced by the sellers with lowest cost. In this case, moving production from a high-cost producer to a low-cost producer will lower the total cost to sellers and raise total surplus. Similarly, an allocation is inefficient if a good is not being consumed by the buyers who value it most highly. In this case, moving consumption of the good from a buyer with a low valuation to a buyer with a high valuation will raise total surplus. In Chapter 1, we defined *efficiency* as 'the property of society getting the most it can from its scarce resources'. Now that we have the concept of total surplus, we can be more precise about what we mean by 'getting the most it can'. In this context, society will be getting the most it can from its scarce resources if it allocates them so as to maximize total surplus.

**efficiency**
the property of a resource allocation of maximizing the total surplus received by all members of society

In addition to efficiency, the BSP might also care about **equity** – the property of distibuting economic prosperity fairly among the members of society. In essence, the gains from trade in a market are like a cake to be distributed among the market participants. The question of efficiency is whether the cake is as big as possible. The question of equity is whether the cake is divided fairly. Evaluating the equity of a market outcome is more difficult than evaluating the efficiency. Whereas efficiency is an objective goal that can be judged on strictly positive grounds, equity involves normative judgements that go beyond economics and enter into the realm of political philosophy.

**equity**
the property of distributing economic prosperity fairly among the members of society

In this chapter we concentrate on efficiency as the social planner's goal. Keep in mind, however, that real policy makers often care about equity as well. That is, they care about both the size of the economic cake and how the cake gets sliced and distributed among members of society.

## Evaluating the Market Equilibrium

Figure 7.7 shows consumer and producer surplus when a market reaches the equilibrium of supply and demand. Recall that consumer surplus equals the area above the price and under the demand curve and producer surplus equals the area below the price and above the supply curve. Thus, the total area between the supply and demand curves up to the point of equilibrium represents the total surplus in this market.

Is this equilibrium allocation of resources efficient? Does it maximize total surplus? To answer these questions, keep in mind that when a market is in equilibrium, the price determines which buyers and sellers participate in the market. Those buyers who value the good more than the price (represented by the segment AE on the demand curve) choose to buy the good; those buyers who value it less than the price (represented by the segment EB) do not. Similarly, those sellers whose costs are less than the price (represented by the segment CE

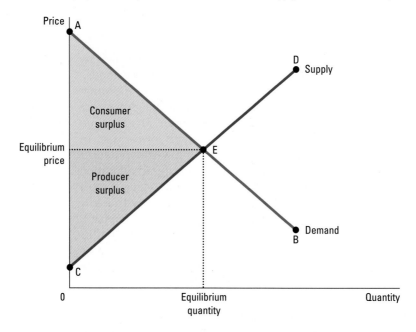

**FIGURE 7.7**

**Consumer and Producer Surplus in the Market Equilibrium**

*Total surplus – the sum of consumer and producer surplus – is the area between the supply and demand curves up to the equilibrium quantity.*

on the supply curve) choose to produce and sell the good; those sellers whose costs are greater than the price (represented by the segment ED) do not.

These observations lead to two insights about market outcomes:

1. Free markets allocate the supply of goods to the buyers who value them most highly, as measured by their willingness to pay.
2. Free markets allocate the demand for goods to the sellers who can produce them at least cost.

Thus, given the quantity produced and sold in a market equilibrium, the BSP cannot increase economic well-being by changing the allocation of consumption among buyers or the allocation of production among sellers.

But can the BSP raise total economic well-being by increasing or decreasing the quantity of the good? The answer is no, as stated in this third insight about market outcomes:

3. Free markets produce the quantity of goods that maximizes the sum of consumer and producer surplus.

To see why this is true, consider Figure 7.8. Recall that the demand curve reflects the value to buyers and that the supply curve reflects the cost to sellers. At quantities below the equilibrium level, the value to buyers exceeds the cost to sellers. In this region, increasing the quantity raises total surplus, and it continues to do so until the quantity reaches the equilibrium level. Beyond the equilibrium quantity, however, the value to buyers is less than the cost to sellers. Producing more than the equilibrium quantity would, therefore, lower total surplus.

These three insights about market outcomes tell us that the equilibrium of supply and demand maximizes the sum of consumer and producer surplus. In

---

**FIGURE 7.8**

### The Efficiency of the Equilibrium Quantity

*At quantities less than the equilibrium quantity, the value to buyers exceeds the cost to sellers. At quantities greater than the equilibrium quantity, the cost to sellers exceeds the value to buyers. Therefore, the market equilibrium maximizes the sum of producer and consumer surplus.*

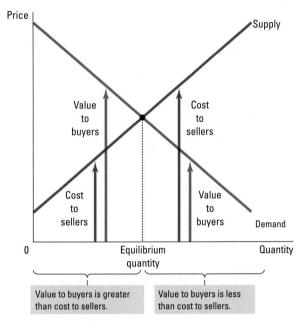

---

other words, the equilibrium outcome is an efficient allocation of resources. The job of the BSP is, therefore, very easy: he can leave the market outcome just as he finds it. This policy of leaving well enough alone goes by the French expression *laissez-faire*, which literally translated means 'leave them to do'.

We can now better appreciate Adam Smith's invisible hand of the marketplace, which we first discussed in Chapter 1. The BSP doesn't need to alter the market outcome because the invisible hand has already guided buyers and sellers to an allocation of the economy's resources that maximizes total surplus. This conclusion explains why economists often advocate free markets as the best way to organize economic activity.

## CASE STUDY

### Should There Be a Market in Human Organs?

As a matter of public policy, people are not allowed to sell their organs in Europe and North America. In essence, in the market for organs, the governments of these countries have imposed a price ceiling of zero. The result, as with any binding price ceiling, is a shortage of the good.

Many economists believe that there would be large benefits to allowing a free market in organs. People are born with two kidneys, but they usually need only one. Meanwhile, a few people suffer from illnesses that leave them without any working kidney. Despite the obvious gains from trade, the current situation is dire. In the UK in 2003 there were around 5,500 people waiting for a transplant but only about 1,700 transplant operations were performed because of the shortage of donor kidneys. The average time spent waiting for a kidney transplant in the UK is about 1½ years, during which time about 15 in every 100 of those waiting die. If those needing a kidney were allowed to buy one from those who have two, the price would rise to balance supply and demand. Sellers would be better off with the extra cash in their pockets. Buyers would be better off with the organ they need to save their lives. The shortage of kidneys would disappear.

Such a market would lead to an efficient allocation of resources, but critics of this plan worry about fairness. A market for organs, they argue, would benefit the rich at the expense of the poor, because organs would then be allocated to those most willing and able to pay. But you can also question the fairness of the current system. Now, most of us walk around with an extra organ that we don't really need, while some of our fellow citizens are dying to get one. Is that fair? Moreover, there is evidence that some people in relatively rich European and North American countries are already, in desperation, going to less developed countries where legislation is less stringent and it is easier to find live donors. But a donor in a less developed country is likely to receive a lower standard of screening to make sure his or her other kidney is good enough to function on its own, and is also likely to receive a lower level of medical care after the kidney has been removed, so the donor's life is put at much higher risk. Is that fair?

> **Quick Quiz** Draw the supply and demand for turkey. In the equilibrium, show producer and consumer surplus. Explain why producing more turkey would lower total surplus.

## CONCLUSION: MARKET EFFICIENCY AND MARKET FAILURE

This chapter introduced the basic tools of welfare economics – consumer and producer surplus – and used them to evaluate the efficiency of free markets. We showed that the forces of supply and demand allocate resources efficiently. That is, even though each buyer and seller in a market is concerned only about his or her own welfare, they are together led by an invisible hand to an equilibrium that maximizes the total benefits to buyers and sellers.

A word of warning is in order. To conclude that markets are efficient, we made several assumptions about how markets work. When these assumptions do not hold, our conclusion that the market equilibrium is efficient may no longer be true. As we close this chapter, let's consider briefly two of the most important of these assumptions.

First, our analysis assumed that markets are perfectly competitive. In the real world, however, competition is sometimes far from perfect. In some markets a single buyer or seller (or a small group of them) may be able to control market prices. This ability to influence prices is called *market power*. Market power can cause markets to be inefficient because it keeps the price and quantity away from the equilibrium of supply and demand.

Second, our analysis assumed that the outcome in a market matters only to the buyers and sellers in that market. Yet, in the real world, the decisions of buyers and sellers sometimes affect people who are not participants in the market at all. Pollution is the classic example of a market outcome that affects people not in the market. Such side effects, called *externalities,* cause welfare in a market to depend

# IN THE NEWS

## Ticket Touting

*To allocate resources efficiently, an economy must get goods to the consumers who value them most highly. Sometimes this job falls to ticket touts.*

### Touts Out

Ticket touts, along with gypsies, squatters and new age travellers, rank high in current [government] demonology. This seems odd, given their obvious social utility in matching supply and demand in markets which have been distorted by bureaucratic pricing. Yet touts at Wimbledon or Wembley can suffer a variety of indignities ranging from prosecution under local authority by-laws to arrest by the police for obstruction. Now the Department of Trade and Industry is proposing to introduce regulations under Section 26 of the Consumer Protection Act 1987 to crack down on ticket agencies selling tickets for theatre, concerts, sporting and other events.

It is not clear why, in dealing with these areas of the arts and leisure industries, the principle of caveat emptor should be cast aside in favour of intervention by the state. At many sporting events touts are simply jobbers operating in a competitive over-the-counter market. Their existence reflects the reluctance or inability of the organisers

of sporting events to establish a more formal secondary market to permit the privileged insiders who initially receive the tickets to pass them on to others at close to their real economic value. People who are prepared to buy from touts usually know what risks they run.

In the case of ticket agencies the argument is less clear cut. The agencies are, in the main, selling tickets for performances – *Cats*, the *Phantom of the*

*Opera* – that are booked out for months ahead. To the extent that foreign or out-of-town tourists might find it difficult to book so far in advance, they do provide a service. The snag is that they can be unforthcoming about the original price of the ticket and other details of what the customer is receiving for the premium paid. Many theatres remain unconvinced that the agencies' operations really extend the run of any given performance.

The merit of the DTI's proposals is that they are confined to requirements for disclosure of the original price and the details of seating, which will at least make for more transparency. Since the agencies are identifiable businesses, local authority trading standards departments should be able to follow up complaints. Yet the people arguably most in need of protection – foreign tourists – are the ones least likely to complain. It says something about the priorities of [the present] government that it thought this game worth the candle.

Source: The *Financial Times,* 6 April 1994.

on more than just the value to the buyers and the cost to the sellers. Because buyers and sellers do not take these side effects into account when deciding how much to consume and produce, the equilibrium in a market can be inefficient from the standpoint of society as a whole.

Market power and externalities are examples of a general phenomenon called *market failure* – the inability of some unregulated markets to allocate resources efficiently. When markets fail, public policy can potentially remedy the problem and increase economic efficiency. Microeconomists devote much effort to studying when market failure is likely and what sorts of policies are best at correcting market failures. As you continue your study of economics, you will see that the tools of welfare economics developed here are readily adapted to that endeavour.

Despite the possibility of market failure, the invisible hand of the marketplace is extraordinarily important. In many markets, the assumptions we made in this chapter work well, and the conclusion of market efficiency applies directly. Moreover, our analysis of welfare economics and market efficiency can be used to shed light on the effects of various government policies. In the next two chapters we apply the tools we have just developed to study two important policy issues – the welfare effects of taxation and of international trade.

## SUMMARY

- Consumer surplus equals buyers' willingness to pay for a good minus the amount they actually pay for it, and it measures the benefit buyers get from participating in a market. Consumer surplus can be computed by finding the area below the demand curve and above the price.

- Producer surplus equals the amount sellers receive for their goods minus their costs of production, and it measures the benefit sellers get from participating in a market. Producer surplus can be computed by finding the area below the price and above the supply curve.

- An allocation of resources that maximizes the sum of consumer and producer surplus is said to be efficient. Policy makers are often concerned with the efficiency, as well as the equity, of economic outcomes.

- The equilibrium of supply and demand maximizes the sum of consumer and producer surplus. That is, the invisible hand of the marketplace leads buyers and sellers to allocate resources efficiently.

- Markets do not allocate resources efficiently in the presence of market failures such as market power or externalities.

## KEY CONCEPTS

welfare economics, p. 131
willingness to pay, p. 132
consumer surplus, p. 132

cost, p. 136
producer surplus, p. 137
efficiency, p. 141

equity, p. 141

## QUESTIONS FOR REVIEW

1. Explain how buyers' willingness to pay, consumer surplus and the demand curve are related.

2. Explain how sellers' costs, producer surplus and the supply curve are related.

3. In a supply-and-demand diagram, show producer and consumer surplus in the market equilibrium.

4. What is efficiency? Is it the only goal of economic policy makers?

5. What does the invisible hand do?

6. Name two types of market failure. Explain why each may cause market outcomes to be inefficient.

# PROBLEMS AND APPLICATIONS

1. An early freeze in Normandy ruins half of the apple harvest. What happens to consumer surplus in the market for apples? What happens to consumer surplus in the market for cider? Illustrate your answers with diagrams.
2. Suppose the demand for French bread rises. What happens to producer surplus in the market for French bread? What happens to producer surplus in the market for flour? Illustrate your answer with diagrams.
3. It is a hot day, and Oliver is thirsty. Here is the value he places on a bottle of water:

   | | |
   |---|---|
   | Value of first bottle | €7 |
   | Value of second bottle | 5 |
   | Value of third bottle | 3 |
   | Value of fourth bottle | 1 |

   a. From this information, derive Oliver's demand schedule. Graph his demand curve for bottled water.
   b. If the price of a bottle of water is €4, how many bottles does Oliver buy? How much consumer surplus does Oliver get from his purchases? Show Oliver's consumer surplus in your graph.
   c. If the price falls to €2, how does quantity demanded change? How does Oliver's consumer surplus change? Show these changes in your graph.
4. Ben owns a water pump. Because pumping large amounts of water is harder than pumping small amounts, the cost of producing a bottle of water rises as he pumps more. Here is the cost he incurs to produce each bottle of water:

   | | |
   |---|---|
   | Cost of first bottle | €1 |
   | Cost of second bottle | 3 |
   | Cost of third bottle | 5 |
   | Cost of fourth bottle | 7 |

   a. From this information, derive Ben's supply schedule. Graph his supply curve for bottled water.
   b. If the price of a bottle of water is €4, how many bottles does Ben produce and sell? How much producer surplus does Ben get from these sales? Show Ben's producer surplus in your graph.
   c. If the price rises to €6, how does quantity supplied change? How does Ben's producer surplus change? Show these changes in your graph.
5. Consider a market in which Oliver from Problem 3 is the buyer and Ben from Problem 4 is the seller.
   a. Use Ben's supply schedule and Oliver's demand schedule to find the quantity supplied and quantity demanded at prices of €2, €4 and €6. Which of these prices brings supply and demand into equilibrium?

   b. What are consumer surplus, producer surplus and total surplus in this equilibrium?
   c. If Ben produced and Oliver consumed one fewer bottle of water, what would happen to total surplus?
   d. If Ben produced and Oliver consumed one additional bottle of water, what would happen to total surplus?
6. The cost of producing stereo systems has fallen over the past several decades. Let's consider some implications of this fact.
   a. Use a supply-and-demand diagram to show the effect of falling production costs on the price and quantity of stereos sold.
   b. In your diagram, show what happens to consumer surplus and producer surplus.
   c. Suppose the supply of stereos is very elastic. Who benefits most from falling production costs – consumers or producers of stereos?
7. There are four consumers willing to pay the following amounts for haircuts:
   Roberto: €7    Ronaldo: €2    David: €8    Zinadin: €5
   There are four haircutting businesses with the following costs:
   Firm A: €3    Firm B: €6    Firm C: €4    Firm D: €2
   Each firm has the capacity to produce only one haircut. For efficiency, how many haircuts should be given? Which businesses should cut hair, and which consumers should have their hair cut? How large is the maximum possible total surplus?
8. Suppose a technological advance reduces the cost of making computers.
   a. Use a supply and demand diagram to show what happens to price, quantity, consumer surplus and producer surplus in the market for computers.
   b. Computers and adding machines are substitutes. Use a supply-and-demand diagram to show what happens to price, quantity, consumer surplus and producer surplus in the market for adding machines. Should adding machine producers be happy or sad about the technological advance in computers?
   c. Computers and software are complements. Use a supply-and-demand diagram to show what happens to price, quantity, consumer surplus and producer surplus in the market for software. Should software producers be happy or sad about the technological advance in computers?
   d. Does this analysis help explain why software producer Bill Gates is one of the world's richest men?

For further resources, visit
http://www.thomsonlearning.co.uk/mankiw_taylor

# 8 APPLICATION: THE COSTS OF TAXATION

axes have been around a long time. In the Bible, for example, we can read how Jesus's parents had to return to Nazareth to be taxed and how, later, Jesus converted a prominent tax collector to become one of his disciples. Since taxes, by definition, are a means of legally extracting money from individuals or organizations, it is not surprising that they have often been a source of heated political debate throughout history. In 1776 the anger of the American colonies over British taxes sparked the American Revolution. More recently, the issue of whether and how tax systems should be harmonized within the European Union has been the source of much debate.

We began our study of taxes in Chapter 6. There we saw how a tax on a good affects its price and the quantity sold and how the forces of supply and demand divide the burden of a tax between buyers and sellers. In this chapter we extend this analysis and look at how taxes affect welfare, the economic well-being of participants in a market.

The effects of taxes on welfare might at first seem obvious. The government imposes taxes in order to raise revenue, and that revenue must come out of someone's pocket. As we saw in Chapter 6, both buyers and sellers are worse off when a good is taxed: a tax raises the price buyers pay and lowers the price sellers receive. Yet to understand fully how taxes affect economic well-being, we must compare the reduced welfare of buyers and sellers to the amount of revenue the government raises. The tools of consumer and producer surplus allow us to make this comparison. The analysis will show that the costs of taxes to buyers and sellers exceeds the revenue raised by the government.

# THE DEADWEIGHT LOSS OF TAXATION

We begin by recalling one of the surprising lessons from Chapter 6: it does not matter whether a tax on a good is levied on buyers or sellers of the good. When a tax is levied on buyers, the demand curve shifts downward by the size of the tax; when it is levied on sellers, the supply curve shifts upward by that amount. In

"DON'T WORRY! SINCE 28% OF MY SALARY GOES TO THE GOVERNMENT, I'VE DECIDED TO WORK 72% OF THE TIME."

**FIGURE 8.1**

**The Effects of a Tax**

*A tax on a good places a wedge between the price that buyers pay and the price that sellers receive. The quantity of the good sold falls.*

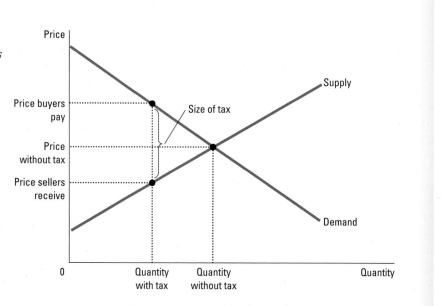

either case, when the tax is imposed, the price paid by buyers rises, and the price received by sellers falls. In the end, buyers and sellers share the burden of the tax, regardless of how it is levied.

Figure 8.1 shows these effects. To simplify our discussion, this figure does not show a shift in either the supply or demand curve, although one curve must shift. Which curve shifts depends on whether the tax is levied on sellers (the supply curve shifts) or buyers (the demand curve shifts). In this chapter, we can simplify the graphs by not bothering to show the shift. The key result for our purposes here is that the tax places a wedge between the price buyers pay and the price sellers receive. Because of this tax wedge, the quantity sold falls below the level that would be sold without a tax. In other words, a tax on a good causes the size of the market for the good to shrink. These results should be familiar from Chapter 6.

## How a Tax Affects Market Participants

Now let's use the tools of welfare economics to measure the gains and losses from a tax on a good. To do this, we must take into account how the tax affects buyers, sellers and the government. The benefit received by buyers in a market is measured by consumer surplus – the amount buyers are willing to pay for the good minus the amount they actually pay for it. The benefit received by sellers in a market is measured by producer surplus – the amount sellers receive for the good minus their costs. These are precisely the measures of economic welfare we used in Chapter 7.

What about the third interested party, the government? If $T$ is the size of the tax and $Q$ is the quantity of the good sold, then the government gets total tax revenue of $T \times Q$. It can use this tax revenue to provide services, such as roads, police and education, or to help the needy. Therefore, to analyse how taxes affect economic well-being, we use tax revenue to measure the government's benefit from the tax. Keep in mind, however, that this benefit actually accrues not to government but to those on whom the revenue is spent.

Figure 8.2 shows that the government's tax revenue is represented by the rectangle between the supply and demand curves. The height of this rectangle is the size of the tax, $T$, and the width of the rectangle is the quantity of the good sold, $Q$. Because a rectangle's area is its height times its width, this rectangle's area is $T \times Q$, which equals the tax revenue.

**Welfare Without a Tax** To see how a tax affects welfare, we begin by considering welfare before the government has imposed a tax. Figure 8.3 shows the supply and demand diagram and marks the key areas with the letters A through F.

Without a tax, the price and quantity are found at the intersection of the supply and demand curves. The price is $P_1$, and the quantity sold is $Q_1$. Because the demand curve reflects buyers' willingness to pay, consumer surplus is the area between the demand curve and the price, A + B + C. Similarly, because the supply curve reflects sellers' costs, producer surplus is the area between the supply curve and the price, D + E + F. In this case, because there is no tax, tax revenue equals zero.

Total surplus – the sum of consumer and producer surplus – equals the area A + B + C + D + E + F. In other words, as we saw in Chapter 7, total surplus is the area between the supply and demand curves up to the equilibrium quantity. The first column of the table in Figure 8.3 summarizes these conclusions.

**Welfare With a Tax** Now consider welfare after the tax is imposed. The price paid by buyers rises from $P_1$ to $P_B$, so consumer surplus now equals only area A (the area below the demand curve and above the buyer's price). The price received

### FIGURE 8.2

#### Tax Revenue

*The tax revenue that the government collects equals T × Q, the size of the tax T times the quantity sold Q. Thus, tax revenue equals the area of the rectangle between the supply and demand curves.*

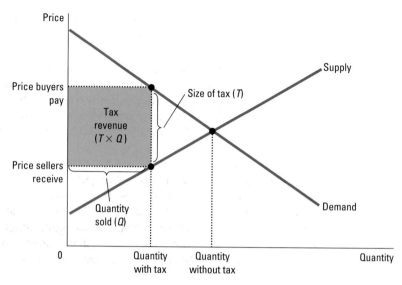

### FIGURE 8.3

#### How a Tax Affects Welfare

*A tax on a good reduces consumer surplus (by the area B + C) and producer surplus (by the area D + E). Because the fall in producer and consumer surplus exceeds tax revenue (area B + D), the tax is said to impose a deadweight loss (area C + E).*

|  | Without tax | With tax | Change |
|---|---|---|---|
| Consumer surplus | A + B + C | A | −(B + C) |
| Producer surplus | D + E + F | F | −(D + E) |
| Tax revenue | None | B + D | +(B + D) |
| Total surplus | A + B + C + D + E + F | A + B + D + F | −(C + E) |

The area C + E shows the fall in total surplus and is the deadweight loss of the tax.

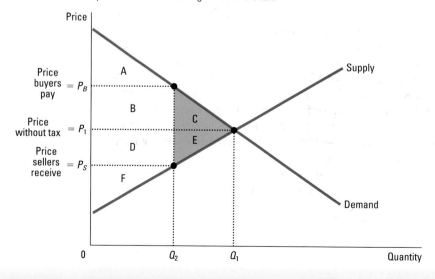

by sellers falls from $P_1$ to $P_{s'}$ so producer surplus now equals only area F (the area above the supply curve and below the seller's price). The quantity sold falls from $Q_1$ to $Q_2$, and the government collects tax revenue equal to the area B + D.

To compute total surplus with the tax, we add consumer surplus producer surplus and tax revenue. Thus, we find that total surplus is area A + B + D + F. The second column of the table provides a summary.

**Changes in Welfare** We can now see the effects of the tax by comparing welfare before and after the tax is imposed. The third column in the table in Figure 8.3 shows the changes. The tax causes consumer surplus to fall by the area B + C and producer surplus to fall by the area D + E. Tax revenue rises by the area B + D. Not surprisingly, the tax makes buyers and sellers worse off and the government better off.

The change in total welfare includes the change in consumer surplus (which is negative), the change in producer surplus (which is also negative), and the change in tax revenue (which is positive). When we add these three pieces together, we find that total surplus in the market falls by the area C + E. Thus, the losses to buyers and sellers from a tax exceed the revenue raised by the government. The fall in total surplus that results when a tax (or some other policy) distorts a market outcome is called the **deadweight loss.** The area C + E measures the size of the deadweight loss.

To understand why taxes impose deadweight losses, recall one of the *Ten Principles of Economics* in Chapter 1: people respond to incentives. In Chapter 7 we saw that markets normally allocate scarce resources efficiently. That is, the equilibrium of supply and demand maximizes the total surplus of buyers and sellers in a market. When a tax raises the price to buyers and lowers the price to sellers, however, it gives buyers an incentive to consume less and sellers an incentive to produce less than they otherwise would. As buyers and sellers respond to these incentives, the size of the market shrinks below its optimum. Thus, because taxes distort incentives, they cause markets to allocate resources inefficiently.

**deadweight loss**
the fall in total surplus that results from a market distortion, such as a tax

## Deadweight Losses and the Gains From Trade

To gain some intuition for why taxes result in deadweight losses, consider an example. Imagine that Ted cleans Kay's house each week for €100. The opportunity cost of Ted's time is €80, and the value of a clean house to Kay is €120. Thus, Ted and Kay each receive a €20 benefit from their deal. The total surplus of €40 measures the gains from trade in this particular transaction.

Now suppose that the government levies a €50 tax on the providers of cleaning services. There is now no price that Kay can pay Ted that will leave both of them better off after paying the tax. The most Kay would be willing to pay is €120, but then Ted would be left with only €70 after paying the tax, which is less than his €80 opportunity cost. Conversely, for Ted to receive his opportunity cost of €80, Kay would need to pay €130, which is above the €120 value she places on a clean house. As a result, Kay and Ted cancel their arrangement. Ted goes without the income, and Kay lives in a dirtier house.

The tax has made Ted and Kay worse off by a total of €40, because they have lost this amount of surplus. At the same time, the government collects no revenue from Ted and Kay because they decide to cancel their arrangement. The €40 is pure deadweight loss: it is a loss to buyers and sellers in a market not offset by an increase in government revenue. From this example, we can see the ultimate source of deadweight losses: taxes cause deadweight losses because they prevent buyers and sellers from realizing some of the gains from trade.

## FIGURE 8.4

### The Deadweight Loss

*When the government imposes a tax on a good, the quantity sold falls from $Q_1$ to $Q_2$. As a result, some of the potential gains from trade among buyers and sellers do not get realized. These lost gains from trade create the deadweight loss.*

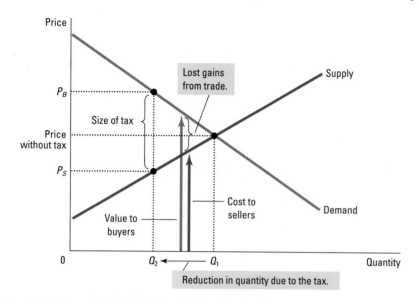

The area of the triangle between the supply and demand curves (area C + E in Figure 8.3) measures these losses. This loss can be seen most easily in Figure 8.4 by recalling that the demand curve reflects the value of the good to consumers and that the supply curve reflects the costs of producers. When the tax raises the price to buyers to $P_B$ and lowers the price to sellers to $P_S$, the marginal buyers and sellers leave the market, so the quantity sold falls from $Q_1$ to $Q_2$. Yet, as the figure shows, the value of the good to these buyers still exceeds the cost to these sellers. As in our example with Ted and Kay, the gains from trade – the difference between buyers' value and sellers' cost – is less than the tax. Thus, these trades do not get made once the tax is imposed. The deadweight loss is the surplus lost because the tax discourages these mutually advantageous trades.

**Quick Quiz** Draw the supply and demand curve for ham-and-cheese sandwiches. If the government imposes a tax on sandwiches, show what happens to the quantity sold, the price paid by buyers and the price paid by sellers. In your diagram, show the deadweight loss from the tax. Explain the meaning of the deadweight loss.

## THE DETERMINANTS OF THE DEADWEIGHT LOSS

What determines whether the deadweight loss from a tax is large or small? The answer is the price elasticities of supply and demand, which measure how much the quantity supplied and quantity demanded respond to changes in the price.

## FIGURE 8.5

### Tax Distortions and Elasticities

*In panels (a) and (b) the demand curve and the size of the tax are the same, but the price elasticity of supply is different. Notice that the more elastic the supply curve, the larger the deadweight loss of the tax. In panels (c) and (d) the supply curve and the size of the tax are the same, but the price elasticity of demand is different. Notice that the more elastic the demand curve, the larger the deadweight loss of the tax.*

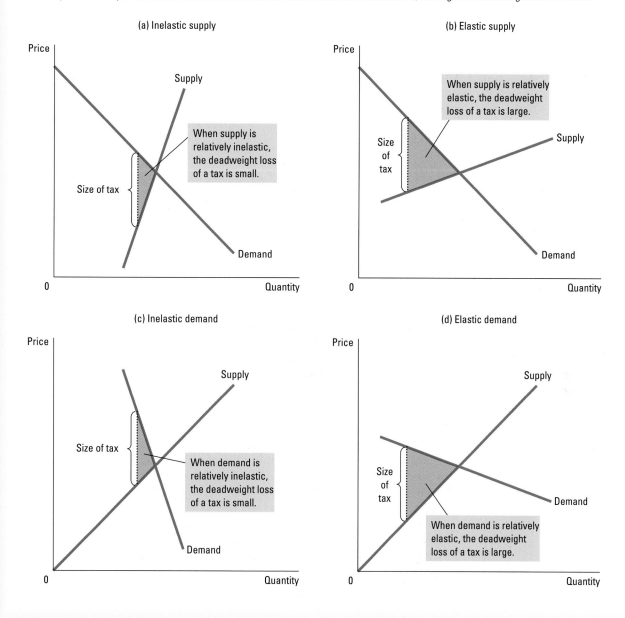

Let's consider first how the elasticity of supply affects the size of the dead-weight loss. In the top two panels of Figure 8.5, the demand curve and the size of the tax are the same. The only difference in these figures is the elasticity of the supply curve. In panel (a), the supply curve is relatively inelastic: quantity supplied responds only slightly to changes in the price. In panel (b), the supply curve is relatively elastic: quantity supplied responds substantially to changes in the price. Notice that the deadweight loss, the area of the triangle between the supply and demand curves, is larger when the supply curve is more elastic.

Similarly, the bottom two panels of Figure 8.5 show how the elasticity of demand affects the size of the deadweight loss. Here the supply curve and the size of the tax are held constant. In panel (c) the demand curve is relatively inelastic, and the deadweight loss is small. In panel (d) the demand curve is more elastic, and the deadweight loss from the tax is larger.

The lesson from this figure is easy to explain. A tax has a deadweight loss because it induces buyers and sellers to change their behaviour. The tax raises the price paid by buyers, so they consume less. At the same time, the tax lowers the price received by sellers, so they produce less. Because of these changes in behaviour, the size of the market shrinks below the optimum. The elasticities of supply and demand measure how much sellers and buyers respond to the changes in the price and, therefore, determine how much the tax distorts the market outcome. Hence, the greater the elasticities of supply and demand, the greater the deadweight loss of a tax.

## CASE STUDY

### The Deadweight Loss Debate

Supply, demand, elasticity, deadweight loss – all this economic theory is enough to make your head spin. But believe it or not, these ideas go to the heart of a profound political question: how big should the government sector be? The debate hinges on these concepts because the larger the deadweight loss of taxation, the larger the welfare cost of any government expenditure programme such as providing public health services or national defence. If taxation entails large deadweight losses, then these losses are a strong argument for a leaner government that does less and taxes less. But if taxes impose small deadweight losses, then government programmes are less costly than they otherwise might be.

So how big are the deadweight losses of taxation? This is a question about which economists disagree. To see the nature of this disagreement, consider one of the most important taxes in most advanced economies – the tax on labour. In the UK, for example, National Insurance Contributions and, to a large extent, income tax are taxes on labour. A labour tax places a wedge between the wage that firms pay and the wage that workers receive. If we add both forms of labour taxes together, the *marginal tax rate* on labour income – the tax on the last pound of earnings – is around 33 per cent for most UK manual workers. In some European countries – particularly Scandinavian countries – the marginal rate is even higher.

Although the size of the labour tax is easy to determine, the deadweight loss of this tax is less straightforward. Economists disagree about whether this 33 per cent labour tax has a small or a large deadweight loss. This disagreement arises because economists hold different views about the elasticity of labour supply.

Economists who argue that labour taxes are not very distorting believe that labour supply is fairly inelastic. Most people, they claim, would work full-time regardless of the wage. If so, the labour supply curve is almost vertical, and a tax on labour has a small deadweight loss.

Economists who argue that labour taxes are highly distorting believe that labour supply is more elastic. They admit that some groups of workers may supply their labour inelastically but claim that many other groups respond more to incentives. Here are some examples:

● Many workers can adjust the number of hours they work – for instance, by working overtime. The higher the wage, the more hours they choose to work.

● Some families have second earners – often married women with children – with some discretion over whether to do unpaid work at home or paid work in the marketplace. When deciding whether to take a job, these second earners compare the benefits of being at home (including savings on the cost of child care) with the wages they could earn.

● Many people can choose when to retire, and their decisions are partly based on the wage. Once they are retired, the wage determines their incentive to work part-time.

● Some people consider engaging in illegal economic activity, such as the drug trade, or working at jobs that pay 'under the table' to evade taxes. Economists call this the *black economy* (or sometimes the *underground economy*). In deciding whether to work in the black economy or at a legitimate job, these potential criminals compare what they can earn by breaking the law with the wage they can earn legally.

In each of these cases, the quantity of labour supplied responds to the wage (the price of labour). Thus, the decisions of these workers are distorted when their labour earnings are taxed. Labour taxes encourage workers to work fewer hours, second earners to stay at home, the elderly to retire early and the unscrupulous to enter the black economy.

These two views of labour taxation persist to this day. Indeed, whenever you see two political candidates debating whether the government should provide more services or reduce the tax burden, keep in mind that part of the disagreement may rest on different views about the elasticity of labour supply and the deadweight loss of taxation.

**Quick Quiz** The demand for beer is more elastic than the demand for milk. Would a tax on beer or a tax on milk have larger deadweight loss? Why?

## DEADWEIGHT LOSS AND TAX REVENUE AS TAXES VARY

Taxes rarely stay the same for long periods of time. Policy makers are always considering raising one tax or lowering another. Here we consider what happens to the deadweight loss and tax revenue when the size of a tax changes.

Figure 8.6 shows the effects of a small, medium and large tax, holding constant the market's supply and demand curves. The deadweight loss – the reduction in total surplus that results when the tax reduces the size of a market below the optimum – equals the area of the triangle between the supply and demand curves. For the small tax in panel (a), the area of the deadweight loss triangle is quite small. But as the size of a tax rises in panels (b) and (c), the deadweight loss grows larger and larger.

Indeed, the deadweight loss of a tax rises even more rapidly than the size of the tax. The reason is that the deadweight loss is an area of a triangle, and an area of a triangle depends on the *square* of its size. If we double the size of a tax, for

**FIGURE 8.6**

**Deadweight Loss and Tax Revenue From Three Taxes of Different Size**

*The deadweight loss is the reduction in total surplus due to the tax. Tax revenue is the amount of the tax times the amount of the good sold. In panel (a) a small tax has a small deadweight loss and raises a small amount of revenue. In panel (b) a somewhat larger tax has a larger deadweight loss and raises a larger amount of revenue. In panel (c) a very large tax has a very large deadweight loss, but because it has reduced the size of the market so much, the tax raises only a small amount of revenue.*

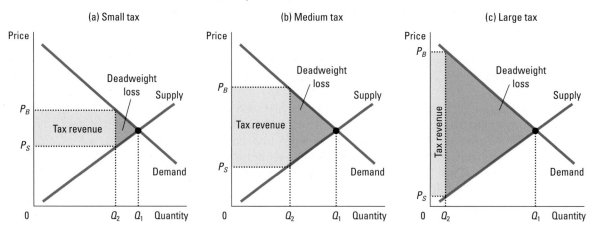

instance, the base and height of the triangle double, so the deadweight loss rises by a factor of 4. If we triple the size of a tax, the base and height triple, so the deadweight loss rises by a factor of 9.

The government's tax revenue is the size of the tax times the amount of the good sold. As Figure 8.6 shows, tax revenue equals the area of the rectangle between the supply and demand curves. For the small tax in panel (a), tax revenue is small. As the size of a tax rises from panel (a) to panel (b), tax revenue grows. But as the size of the tax rises further from panel (b) to panel (c), tax revenue falls because the higher tax drastically reduces the size of the market. For a very large tax, no revenue would be raised, because people would stop buying and selling the good altogether.

Figure 8.7 summarizes these results. In panel (a) we see that as the size of a tax increases, its deadweight loss quickly gets larger. By contrast, panel (b) shows that tax revenue first rises with the size of the tax; but then, as the tax gets larger, the market shrinks so much that tax revenue starts to fall.

## CASE STUDY

### The Laffer Curve and Supply-Side Economics

One day in 1974, the American economist Arthur Laffer sat in a Washington restaurant with some prominent journalists and politicians. He took out a napkin and drew a figure on it to show how tax rates affect tax revenue. It looked much like panel (b) of our Figure 8.7. Laffer then suggested that the United States was on the downward sloping side of this curve. Tax rates were so high, he argued, that reducing them would actually raise tax revenue.

Most economists were sceptical of Laffer's suggestion. The idea that a cut in tax rates could raise tax revenue was correct as a matter of economic theory,

## FYI

## Henry George and the Land Tax

Is there an ideal tax? Henry George, the 19th-century American economist and social philosopher, thought so. In his 1879 book *Progress and Poverty,* George argued that the government should raise all its revenue from a tax on land. This 'single tax' was, he claimed, both equitable and efficient. George's ideas won him a large political following, and in 1886 he lost a close race for mayor of New York City.

George's proposal to tax land was motivated largely by a concern over the distribution of economic well-being. He deplored the 'shocking contrast between monstrous wealth and debasing want' and thought landowners benefited more than they should from the rapid growth in the overall economy.

George's arguments for the land tax can be understood using the tools of modern economics. Consider first supply and demand in the market for renting land. As immigration causes the population to rise and technological progress causes incomes to grow, the demand for land rises over time. Yet because the amount of land is fixed, the supply is perfectly inelastic. Rapid increases in demand together with inelastic supply

lead to large increases in the equilibrium rents on land, so that economic growth makes rich landowners even richer.

Now consider the incidence of a tax on land. As we first saw in Chapter 6, the burden of a tax falls more heavily on the side of the market that is less elastic. A tax on land takes this principle to an extreme. Because the elasticity of supply is zero, the landowners bear the entire burden of the tax.

Consider next the question of efficiency. As we just discussed, the deadweight loss of a tax depends on the elasticities of supply and demand. Again, a tax on land is an extreme case. Because supply is perfectly inelastic, a tax on land does not alter the market allocation. There is no deadweight loss, and the

*Henry George*

government's tax revenue exactly equals the loss of the landowners.

Although taxing land may look attractive in theory, it is not as straightforward in practice as it may appear. For a tax on land not to distort economic incentives, it must be a tax on raw land. Yet the value of land often comes from improvements, such as clearing trees, providing sewers and building roads. Unlike the supply of raw land, the supply of improvements has an elasticity greater than zero. If a land tax were imposed on improvements, it would distort incentives. Landowners would respond by devoting fewer resources to improving their land.

Today, few economists support George's proposal for a single tax on land. Not only is taxing improvements a potential problem, but the tax would not raise enough revenue to pay for the much larger government we have today. Yet many of George's arguments remain valid. Here is the assessment of the eminent economist Milton Friedman a century after George's book: 'In my opinion, the least bad tax is the property tax on the unimproved value of land, the Henry George argument of many, many years ago.'

but there was more doubt about whether it would do so in practice. There was little evidence for Laffer's view that tax rates – in the United States or elsewhere – had in fact reached such extreme levels.

Nevertheless, the thinking underlying the *Laffer curve* (as it became known) became very influential in policy circles during the 1980s, particularly in the USA during the years of President Ronald Reagan's administration and in the UK during Prime Minister Margaret Thatcher's government. Tax rates – particularly income tax rates – were cut aggressively in both countries during the 1980s.

In the UK, for example, under Prime Minister Thatcher the top marginal rate of income tax was cut from 83 per cent to 60 per cent in 1980 and then again to 40 per cent in 1988. Economists have, however, found it hard to trace

## FIGURE 8.7

### How Deadweight Loss and Tax Revenue Vary With the Size of a Tax

*Panel (a) shows that as the size of a tax grows larger, the deadweight loss grows larger. Panel (b) shows that tax revenue first rises, then falls. This relationship is sometimes called the Laffer curve.*

(a) Deadweight loss | (b) Revenue (the Laffer curve)

Deadweight loss — 0 — Tax size

Tax revenue — 0 — Tax size

*Prime Minister Margaret Thatcher: tax cutter.*

PHOTO: COPYRIGHT © REUTERS/CORBIS

any strong incentive effects of these tax cuts leading to increases in total tax revenue, as the Laffer curve would suggest. A study by the UK Institute for Fiscal Studies, for example, concluded that at most about 3 per cent of the increase in tax revenue between 1980 and 1986 could be attributed to the 1980 income tax cut.

In the USA, President Reagan also cut taxes aggressively, but the result was less tax revenue, not more. Revenue from personal income taxes in the United States (per person, adjusted for inflation) fell by 9 per cent from 1980 to 1984, even though average income (per person, adjusted for inflation) grew by 4 per cent over this period. The tax cut, together with policy makers' unwillingness to restrain spending, began a long period during which the US government spent more than it collected in taxes. Throughout Reagan's two terms in office, and for many years thereafter, the US government ran large budget deficits.

Yet Laffer's argument is not completely without merit. Although an overall cut in tax rates normally reduces revenue, some taxpayers at some times may be on the wrong side of the Laffer curve. The idea that cutting taxes can raise revenue may be correct if applied to those taxpayers facing the highest tax rates, but most people face lower marginal rates. Where the *typical* worker is on the top end of the Laffer curve, it may be more appropriate. In Sweden in the early 1980s, for instance, the typical worker faced a marginal tax rate of about 80 per cent. Such a high tax rate provides a substantial disincentive to work. Studies have suggested that Sweden would indeed have raised more tax revenue if it had lowered its tax rates.

Policy makers disagree about these issues in part because they disagree about the size of the relevant elasticities. The more elastic that supply and demand are in any market, the more taxes in that market distort behaviour, and the more likely it is that a tax cut will raise tax revenue. There is no debate, however, about the general lesson: how much revenue the government gains or loses from a tax change cannot be computed just by looking at tax rates. It also depends on how the tax change affects people's behaviour.

**Quick Quiz** If the government doubles the tax on petrol, can you be sure that revenue from the petrol tax will rise? Can you be sure that the deadweight loss from the petrol tax will rise? Explain.

## CONCLUSION

Taxes, someone once said, are the price we pay for a civilized society. Indeed, our society cannot exist without some form of taxes. We all expect the government to provide us with certain services, such as roads, parks, police and national defence. These public services require tax revenue.

This chapter has shed some light on how high the price of civilized society can be. One of the *Ten Principles of Economics* discussed in Chapter 1 is that markets are usually a good way to organize economic activity. When the government imposes taxes on buyers or sellers of a good, however, society loses some of the benefits of market efficiency. Taxes are costly to market participants not only because taxes transfer resources from those participants to the government, but also because they alter incentives and distort market outcomes.

### SUMMARY

- A tax on a good reduces the welfare of buyers and sellers of the good, and the reduction in consumer and producer surplus usually exceeds the revenue raised by the government. The fall in total surplus – the sum of consumer surplus, producer surplus and tax revenue – is called the deadweight loss of the tax.

- Taxes have deadweight losses because they cause buyers to consume less and sellers to produce less, and this change in behaviour shrinks the size of the market

below the level that maximizes total surplus. Because the elasticities of supply and demand measure how much market participants respond to market conditions, larger elasticities imply larger deadweight losses.

- As a tax grows larger, it distorts incentives more, and its deadweight loss grows larger. Tax revenue first rises with the size of a tax. Eventually, however, a larger tax reduces tax revenue because it reduces the size of the market.

### KEY CONCEPT

deadweight loss, p. 153

## QUESTIONS FOR REVIEW

1. What happens to consumer and producer surplus when the sale of a good is taxed? How does the change in consumer and producer surplus compare to the tax revenue? Explain.

2. Draw a supply and demand diagram with a tax on the sale of the good. Show the deadweight loss. Show the tax revenue.

3. How do the elasticities of supply and demand affect the deadweight loss of a tax? Why do they have this effect?

4. Why do experts disagree about whether labour taxes have small or large deadweight losses?

5. What happens to the deadweight loss and tax revenue when a tax is increased?

## PROBLEMS AND APPLICATIONS

1. The market for pizza is characterized by a downward sloping demand curve and an upward sloping supply curve.
   a. Draw the competitive market equilibrium. Label the price, quantity, consumer surplus and producer surplus. Is there any deadweight loss? Explain.
   b. Suppose that the government forces each pizzeria to pay a €1 tax on each pizza sold. Illustrate the effect of this tax on the pizza market, being sure to label the consumer surplus, producer surplus, government revenue and deadweight loss. How does each area compare to the pre-tax case?
   c. If the tax were removed, pizza eaters and sellers would be better off, but the government would lose tax revenue. Suppose that consumers and producers voluntarily transferred some of their gains to the government. Could all parties (including the government) be better off than they were with a tax? Explain using the labelled areas in your graph.

2. Evaluate the following two statements. Do you agree? Why or why not?
   a. 'If the government taxes land, wealthy landowners will pass the tax on to their poorer renters.'
   b. 'If the government taxes blocks of flats, wealthy landlords will pass the tax on to their poorer renters.'

3. Evaluate the following two statements. Do you agree? Why or why not?
   a. 'A tax that has no deadweight loss cannot raise any revenue for the government.'
   b. 'A tax that raises no revenue for the government cannot have any deadweight loss.'

4. Consider the market for rubber bands.
   a. If this market has very elastic supply and very inelastic demand, how would the burden of a tax on

rubber bands be shared between consumers and producers? Use the tools of consumer surplus and producer surplus in your answer.
   b. If this market has very inelastic supply and very elastic demand, how would the burden of a tax on rubber bands be shared between consumers and producers? Contrast your answer with your answer to part (a).

5. Suppose that the government imposes a tax on heating oil.
   a. Would the deadweight loss from this tax likely be greater in the first year after it is imposed or in the fifth year? Explain.
   b. Would the revenue collected from this tax likely be greater in the first year after it is imposed or in the fifth year? Explain.

6. After your economics lecture one day, your friend suggests that taxing food would be a good way to raise revenue because the demand for food is quite inelastic. In what sense is taxing food a 'good' way to raise revenue? In what sense is it not a 'good' way to raise revenue?

7. The government places a tax on the purchase of socks.
   a. Illustrate the effect of this tax on equilibrium price and quantity in the sock market. Identify the following areas both before and after the imposition of the tax: total spending by consumers; total revenue for producers; and government tax revenue.
   b. Does the price received by producers rise or fall? Can you tell whether total receipts for producers rise or fall? Explain.
   c. Does the price paid by consumers rise or fall? Can you tell whether total spending by consumers rises or falls? Explain carefully. (Hint: think about elasticity.) If total consumer spending falls, does consumer surplus rise? Explain.

8. Suppose the government currently raises €100 million through a €0.01 tax on widgets, and another €100 million through a €0.10 tax on gadgets. If the government doubled the tax rate on widgets and eliminated the tax on gadgets, would it raise more money than today, less money or the same amount of money? Explain.

9. In the 1980s the UK government imposed a 'poll tax' that required each person to pay a flat amount to the government independent of his or her income or wealth. What is the effect of such a tax on economic efficiency? What is the effect on economic equity? Do you think this was a popular tax?

10. This chapter analysed the welfare effects of a tax on a good. Consider now the opposite policy. Suppose that the government *subsidizes* a good: for each unit of the good sold, the government pays €2 to the buyer. How does the subsidy affect consumer surplus, producer surplus, tax revenue and total surplus? Does a subsidy lead to a deadweight loss? Explain.

11. (This problem uses some secondary school algebra and is challenging.) Suppose that a market is described by the following supply and demand equations:

$$Q^S = 2P$$
$$Q^D = 300 - P$$

a. Solve for the equilibrium price and the equilibrium quantity.

b. Suppose that a tax of $T$ is placed on buyers, so the new demand equation is:

$$Q^D = 300 - (P + T).$$

Solve for the new equilibrium. What happens to the price received by sellers, the price paid by buyers and the quantity sold?

c. Tax revenue is $T \times Q$. Use your answer to part (b) to solve for tax revenue as a function of $T$. Graph this relationship for $T$ between 0 and 300.

d. The deadweight loss of a tax is the area of the triangle between the supply and demand curves. Recalling that the area of a triangle is $1/2 \times$ base $\times$ height, solve for deadweight loss as a function of $T$. Graph this relationship for $T$ between 0 and 300. (Hint: looking sideways, the base of the deadweight loss triangle is $T$, and the height is the difference between the quantity sold with the tax and the quantity sold without the tax.)

e. The government now levies a tax on this good of €200 per unit. Is this a good policy? Why or why not? Can you propose a better policy?

   For further resources, visit
http://www.thomsonlearning.co.uk/mankiw_taylor

# 9 APPLICATION: INTERNATIONAL TRADE

I f you check the labels on the clothes you are now wearing, you will probably find that some of your clothes were made in another country. A century ago the textiles and clothing industry was a major part of the UK economy and of many other European economies. In fact, when Ricardo first developed his argument about the principle of comparative advantage back in the early 19th century, he used an example of cloth being produced in England and wine in Portugal. Portugal still has a comparative advantage in producing wine relative to many countries in the world, but England no longer has a comparative advantage in producing cloth. Faced with foreign competitors that could produce quality goods at low cost, many European firms have found it increasingly difficult to produce and sell textiles and clothing at a profit. As a result, they have laid off their workers and shut down their factories. Today, much of the textiles and clothing that Europeans consume is imported from outside of Europe.

The story of the textiles industry raises important questions for economic policy: how does international trade affect economic well-being? Who gains and who loses from free trade among countries, and how do the gains compare to the losses?

Chapter 3 introduced the study of international trade by applying the principle of comparative advantage. According to this principle, all countries can benefit from trading with one another because trade allows each country to specialize in doing what it does best. But the analysis in Chapter 3 was incomplete. It did not explain how the international marketplace achieves these gains from trade or how the gains are distributed among various economic actors.

We now return to the study of international trade and take up these questions. Over the past several chapters we have developed many tools for analysing how markets work: supply, demand, equilibrium, consumer surplus, producer surplus and so on. With these tools we can learn more about the effects of international trade on economic well-being.

# THE DETERMINANTS OF TRADE

Consider the market for steel. The steel market is well suited to examining the gains and losses from international trade: steel is made in many countries around the world, and there is much world trade in steel. Moreover, the steel market is one in which policy makers often consider (and sometimes implement) trade restrictions to protect domestic steel producers from foreign competitors. We examine here the steel market in the imaginary country of Isoland.

## The Equilibrium Without Trade

As our story begins, the Isolandian steel market is isolated from the rest of the world. By government decree, no one in Isoland is allowed to import or export steel, and the penalty for violating the decree is so large that no one dares try.

Because there is no international trade, the market for steel in Isoland consists solely of Isolandian buyers and sellers. As Figure 9.1 shows, the domestic price adjusts to balance the quantity supplied by domestic sellers and the quantity demanded by domestic buyers. The figure shows the consumer and producer surplus in the equilibrium without trade. The sum of consumer and producer surplus measures the total benefits that buyers and sellers receive from the steel market.

Now suppose that, in an election upset, Isoland elects a new president. The president campaigned on a platform of 'change' and promised the voters bold

---

**FIGURE 9.1**

**The Equilibrium Without International Trade**

*When an economy cannot trade in world markets, the price adjusts to balance domestic supply and demand. This figure shows consumer and producer surplus in an equilibrium without international trade for the steel market in the imaginary country of Isoland.*

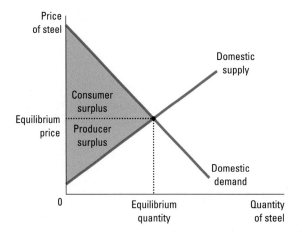

new ideas. Her first act is to assemble a team of economists to evaluate Isolandian trade policy. She asks them to report back on three questions:

- If the government allowed Isolandians to import and export steel, what would happen to the price of steel and the quantity of steel sold in the domestic steel market?
- Who would gain from free trade in steel and who would lose, and would the gains exceed the losses?
- Should a tariff (a tax on steel imports) or an import quota (a limit on steel imports) be part of the new trade policy?

After reviewing supply and demand in their favourite textbook (this one, of course), the Isolandian economics team begins its analysis.

## The World Price and Comparative Advantage

The first issue our economists take up is whether Isoland is likely to become a steel importer or a steel exporter. In other words, if free trade were allowed, would Isolandians end up buying or selling steel in world markets?

To answer this question, the economists compare the current Isolandian price of steel to the price of steel in other countries. We call the price prevailing in world markets the **world price.** If the world price of steel is higher than the domestic price, then Isoland would become an exporter of steel once trade is permitted. Isolandian steel producers would be eager to receive the higher prices available abroad and would start selling their steel to buyers in other countries. Conversely, if the world price of steel is lower than the domestic price, then Isoland would become an importer of steel. Because foreign sellers offer a better price, Isolandian steel consumers would quickly start buying steel from other countries.

**world price**
the price of a good that prevails in the world market for that good

In essence, comparing the world price and the domestic price before trade indicates whether Isoland has a comparative advantage in producing steel. The domestic price reflects the opportunity cost of steel: it tells us how much an Isolandian must give up to get one unit of steel. If the domestic price is low, the cost of producing steel in Isoland is low, suggesting that Isoland has a comparative advantage in producing steel relative to the rest of the world. If the domestic price is high, then the cost of producing steel in Isoland is high, suggesting that foreign countries have a comparative advantage in producing steel.

As we saw in Chapter 3, trade among nations is ultimately based on comparative advantage. That is, trade is beneficial because it allows each nation to specialize in doing what it does best. By comparing the world price and the domestic price before trade, we can determine whether Isoland is better or worse at producing steel than the rest of the world.

> **Quick Quiz** The country Autarka does not allow international trade. In Autarka, you can buy a wool suit for 300 grams of gold. Meanwhile, in neighbouring countries, you can buy the same suit for 200 grams of gold. If Autarka were to allow free trade, would it import or export suits?

# THE WINNERS AND LOSERS FROM TRADE

To analyse the welfare effects of free trade, the Isolandian economists begin with the assumption that Isoland is a small economy compared to the rest of the world so that its actions have a negligible effect on world markets. The small economy assumption has a specific implication for analysing the steel market: if Isoland is a small economy, then the change in Isoland's trade policy will not affect the world price of steel. The Isolandians are said to be *price takers* in the world economy. That is, they take the world price of steel as given. They can sell steel at this price and be exporters, or buy steel at this price and be importers.

The small economy assumption is not necessary to analyse the gains and losses from international trade. But the Isolandian economists know from experience that this assumption greatly simplifies the analysis. They also know that the basic lessons do not change in the more complicated case of a large economy.

## The Gains and Losses of an Exporting Country

Figure 9.2 shows the Isolandian steel market when the domestic equilibrium price before trade is below the world price. Once free trade is allowed, the domestic price rises to equal the world price. No seller of steel would accept less than the world price, and no buyer would pay more than the world price.

With the domestic price now equal to the world price, the domestic quantity supplied differs from the domestic quantity demanded. The supply curve shows the quantity of steel supplied by Isolandian sellers. The demand curve shows the quantity of steel demanded by Isolandian buyers. Because the domestic quantity supplied is greater than the domestic quantity demanded, Isoland sells steel to other countries. Thus, Isoland becomes a steel exporter.

Although domestic quantity supplied and domestic quantity demanded differ, the steel market is still in equilibrium because there is now another participant in the market: the rest of the world. One can view the horizontal line at the world price as representing the demand for steel from the rest of the world. This

### FIGURE 9.2

**International Trade in an Exporting Country**

*Once trade is allowed, the domestic price rises to equal the world price. The supply curve shows the quantity of steel produced domestically, and the demand curve shows the quantity consumed domestically. Exports from Isoland equal the difference between the domestic quantity supplied and the domestic quantity demanded at the world price.*

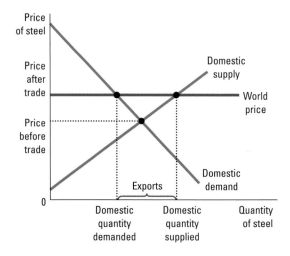

demand curve is perfectly elastic because Isoland, as a small economy, can sell as much steel as it wants at the world price.

Now consider the gains and losses from opening up trade. Clearly, not everyone benefits. Trade forces the domestic price to rise to the world price. Domestic producers of steel are better off because they can now sell steel at a higher price, but domestic consumers of steel are worse off because they have to buy steel at a higher price.

To measure these gains and losses, we look at the changes in consumer and producer surplus, which are shown in the graph and table in Figure 9.3. Before trade is allowed, the price of steel adjusts to balance domestic supply and domestic demand. Consumer surplus, the area between the demand curve and the before-trade price, is area A + B. Producer surplus, the area between the supply curve and the before-trade price, is area C. Total surplus before trade, the sum of consumer and producer surplus, is area A + B + C.

After trade is allowed, the domestic price rises to the world price. Consumer surplus is area A (the area between the demand curve and the world price). Producer surplus is area B + C + D (the area between the supply curve and the world price). Thus, total surplus with trade is area A + B + C + D.

These welfare calculations show who wins and who loses from trade in an exporting country. Sellers benefit because producer surplus increases by the area B + D. Buyers are worse off because consumer surplus decreases by the area B. Because the gains of sellers exceed the losses of buyers by the area D, total surplus in Isoland increases.

This analysis of an exporting country yields two conclusions:

## FIGURE 9.3

### How Free Trade Affects Welfare in an Exporting Country

*When the domestic price rises to equal the world price, sellers are better off (producer surplus rises from C to B + C + D), and buyers are worse off (consumer surplus falls from A + B to A). Total surplus rises by an amount equal to area D, indicating that trade raises the economic well-being of the country as a whole.*

|  | Before trade | After trade | Change |
|---|---|---|---|
| Consumer surplus | A + B | A | −B |
| Producer surplus | C | B + C + D | +(B + D) |
| Total surplus | A + B + C | A + B + C + D | +D |

The area D shows the increase in total surplus and represents the gains from trade.

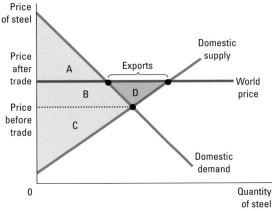

- When a country allows trade and becomes an exporter of a good, domestic producers of the good are better off, and domestic consumers of the good are worse off.
- Trade raises the economic well-being of a nation in the sense that the gains of the winners exceed the losses of the losers.

## The Gains and Losses of an Importing Country

Now suppose that the domestic price before trade is above the world price. Once again, after free trade is allowed, the domestic price must equal the world price. As Figure 9.4 shows, the domestic quantity supplied is less than the domestic quantity demanded. The difference between the domestic quantity demanded and the domestic quantity supplied is bought from other countries, and Isoland becomes a steel importer.

In this case, the horizontal line at the world price represents the supply of the rest of the world. This supply curve is perfectly elastic because Isoland is a small economy and, therefore, can buy as much steel as it wants at the world price.

Now consider the gains and losses from trade. Once again, not everyone benefits. When trade forces the domestic price to fall, domestic consumers are better off (they can now buy steel at a lower price), and domestic producers are worse off (they now have to sell steel at a lower price). Changes in consumer and producer surplus measure the size of the gains and losses, as shown in the graph and table in Figure 9.5. Before trade, consumer surplus is area A, producer surplus is area B + C, and total surplus is area A + B + C. After trade is allowed, consumer surplus is area A + B + D, producer surplus is area C and total surplus is area A + B + C + D.

These welfare calculations show who wins and who loses from trade in an importing country. Buyers benefit because consumer surplus increases by the

---

### FIGURE 9.4

**International Trade in an Importing Country**

*Once trade is allowed, the domestic price falls to equal the world price. The supply curve shows the amount produced domestically, and the demand curve shows the amount consumed domestically. Imports equal the difference between the domestic quantity demanded and the domestic quantity supplied at the world price.*

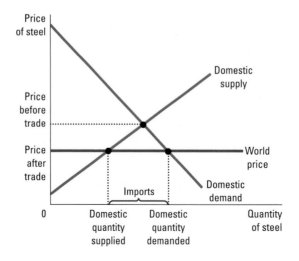

## FIGURE 9.5

### How Free Trade Affects Welfare in an Importing Country

*When the domestic price falls to equal the world price, buyers are better off (consumer surplus rises from A to A + B + D), and sellers are worse off (producer surplus falls from B + C to C). Total surplus rises by an amount equal to area D, indicating that trade raises the economic well-being of the country as a whole.*

|  | Before trade | After trade | Change |
|---|---|---|---|
| Consumer surplus | A | A + B + D | +(B + D) |
| Producer surplus | B + C | C | −B |
| Total surplus | A + B + C | A + B + C + D | +D |

The area D shows the increase in total surplus and represents the gains from trade.

area B + D. Sellers are worse off because producer surplus falls by the area B. The gains of buyers exceed the losses of sellers, and total surplus increases by the area D.

This analysis of an importing country yields two conclusions parallel to those for an exporting country:

- When a country allows trade and becomes an importer of a good, domestic consumers of the good are better off, and domestic producers of the good are worse off.
- Trade raises the economic well-being of a nation in the sense that the gains of the winners exceed the losses of the losers.

Having completed our analysis of trade, we can better understand one of the *Ten Principles of Economics* in Chapter 1: trade can make everyone better off. If Isoland opens up its steel market to international trade, that change will create winners and losers, regardless of whether Isoland ends up exporting or importing steel. In either case, however, the gains of the winners exceed the losses of the losers, so the winners could compensate the losers and still be better off. In this sense, trade *can* make everyone better off. But *will* trade make everyone better off? Probably not. In practice, compensation for the losers from international trade is rare. Without such compensation, opening up to international trade is a policy that expands the size of the economic cake, while perhaps leaving some participants in the economy with a smaller slice.

We can now see why the debate over trade policy is so often contentious. Whenever a policy creates winners and losers, the stage is set for a political battle. Nations sometimes fail to enjoy the gains from trade simply because the losers from free trade have more political clout than the winners. The losers lobby for trade restrictions, such as tariffs and import quotas.

## The Effects of a Tariff

**tariff**

a tax on goods produced abroad and sold domestically

The Isolandian economists next consider the effects of a **tariff** – a tax on imported goods. The economists quickly realize that a tariff on steel will have no effect if Isoland becomes a steel exporter. If no one in Isoland is interested in importing steel, a tax on steel imports is irrelevant. The tariff matters only if Isoland becomes a steel importer. Concentrating their attention on this case, the economists compare welfare with and without the tariff.

The graph in Figure 9.6 shows the Isolandian market for steel. Under free trade, the domestic price equals the world price. A tariff raises the price of imported steel above the world price by the amount of the tariff. Domestic suppliers of steel, who compete with suppliers of imported steel, can now sell their steel for the

**FIGURE 9.6**

### The Effects of a Tariff

*A tariff reduces the quantity of imports and moves a market closer to the equilibrium that would exist without trade. Total surplus falls by an amount equal to area D + F. These two triangles represent the deadweight loss from the tariff.*

|  | Before tariff | After tariff | Change |
|---|---|---|---|
| Consumer surplus | A + B + C + D + E + F | A + B | −(C + D + E + F) |
| Producer surplus | G | C + G | +C |
| Government revenue | None | E | +E |
| Total surplus | A + B + C + D + E + F + G | A + B + C + E + G | −(D + F) |

The area D + F shows the fall in total surplus and represents the deadweight loss of the tariff.

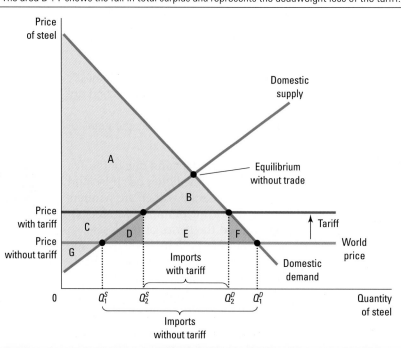

world price plus the amount of the tariff. Thus, the price of steel – both imported and domestic – rises by the amount of the tariff and is, therefore, closer to the price that would prevail without trade.

The change in price affects the behaviour of domestic buyers and sellers. Because the tariff raises the price of steel, it reduces the domestic quantity demanded from $Q_1^D$ to $Q_2^D$ and raises the domestic quantity supplied from $Q_1^S$ to $Q_2^S$. Thus, the tariff reduces the quantity of imports and moves the domestic market closer to its equilibrium without trade.

Now consider the gains and losses from the tariff. Because the tariff raises the domestic price, domestic sellers are better off, and domestic buyers are worse off. In addition, the government raises revenue. To measure these gains and losses, we look at the changes in consumer surplus, producer surplus and government revenue. These changes are summarized in the table in Figure 9.6.

Before the tariff, the domestic price equals the world price. Consumer surplus, the area between the demand curve and the world price, is area A + B + C + D + E + F. Producer surplus, the area between the supply curve and the world price, is area G. Government revenue equals zero. Total surplus – the sum of consumer surplus, producer surplus and government revenue – is area A + B + C + D + E + F + G.

Once the government imposes a tariff, the domestic price exceeds the world price by the amount of the tariff. Consumer surplus is now area A + B. Producer surplus is area C + G. Government revenue, which is the quantity of after-tariff imports times the size of the tariff, is the area E. Thus, total surplus with the tariff is area A + B + C + E + G.

To determine the total welfare effects of the tariff, we add the change in consumer surplus (which is negative), the change in producer surplus (positive) and the change in government revenue (positive). We find that total surplus in the market decreases by the area D + F. This fall in total surplus is called the *deadweight loss* of the tariff.

A tariff causes a deadweight loss simply because a tariff is a type of tax. Like most taxes, it distorts incentives and pushes the allocation of scarce resources away from the optimum. In this case, we can identify two effects. First, the tariff on steel raises the price of steel that domestic producers can charge above the world price and, as a result, encourages them to increase production of steel (from $Q_1^S$ to $Q_2^S$). Second, the tariff raises the price that domestic steel buyers have to pay and, therefore, encourages them to reduce consumption of steel (from $Q_1^D$ to $Q_2^D$). Area D represents the deadweight loss from the overproduction of steel, and area F represents the deadweight loss from the underconsumption. The total deadweight loss of the tariff is the sum of these two triangles.

## The Effects of an Import Quota

The Isolandian economists next consider the effects of an **import quota** – a limit on the quantity of imports. In particular, imagine that the Isolandian government distributes a limited number of import licences. Each licence gives the licence holder the right to import 1 tonne of steel into Isoland from abroad. The Isolandian economists want to compare welfare under a policy of free trade and welfare with the addition of this import quota.

The graph and table in Figure 9.7 show how an import quota affects the Isolandian market for steel. Because the import quota prevents Isolandians from buying as much steel as they want from abroad, the supply of steel is no longer perfectly elastic at the world price. Instead, as long as the price of steel in Isoland is above the world price, the licence holders import as much as they are permitted,

**import quota**
a limit on the quantity of a good that can be produced abroad and sold domestically

# IN THE NEWS

## Life in Isoland

*Our story about the steel industry and the debate over trade policy in Isoland is just a parable. Or is it?*

**George Bush, Protectionist: The President's Decision to Place High Tariffs on Imports of Steel is Disgraceful**

Nobody was surprised, despite affectations of shock in some quarters, when George Bush announced this week his plans to protect the American steel industry. The proposals had been trailed; they were regarded in Washington as politically inescapable. The fact that the president did what everybody expected him to makes this decision no less damaging, and no less stupid.

This steel-tariff plan, it is important to remember, lies well outside the ordinary run of bad economic policy: it is so wrong it makes other kinds of wealth-destroying intervention feel inadequate. And was it really politically inescapable? What a depressingly feeble excuse from a president who has promised, and shown, strong leadership in other respects, and who had claimed, by the way, to be a champion of liberal trade. Mr Bush and his advisers should be ashamed.

### More Hat, No Cattle

The administration has announced a complicated schedule of supposedly temporary high tariffs (ranging up to 30%) on different kinds of steel. Something like $8 billion of imports from Europe, Japan, South Korea and other countries will be affected, about 10% of the world market. It would be bad enough if things stopped there. The policy as it stands will make most Americans worse off, by forcing them to pay more for their steel. Except in the

short term it will also do little to help the people it is intended to help – namely, workers in the parts of America's steel industry that cannot compete with foreign suppliers or with America's own more productive mini-mills.

The day after the tariffs were announced, National Steel joined the many other American steel makers already in bankruptcy. Tariffs fail to address the real problem – high costs, including 'legacy liabilities' in health-care and pension benefits. Many companies will fold anyway. When they do, putting workers out of a job and rendering those promised benefits null, the tariffs will only make the victims, as consumers, even worse off than they would have been.

But the rot does not stop there. Europe now expects to face a surge in steel imports, and may well adopt the same self-destructive remedy. The damage will scale up globally, possibly spreading to other kinds of trade, and a good part of the cost will end up with developing-country producers. The leaders of Europe and the United States love to preach liberal trade to the benighted rulers of the developing world, and never tire of promising better access to their own markets. Fine words.

The outrage in Europe's governments over the tariffs, like the shock at the news, is synthetic. Europe has forgotten more than America will ever know about trade protection (common agricultural policy, *passim*). The linkage now being advanced in Europe between, on one side, America's need

for allies and, on the other, its protectionist affront to those friends, is also largely bogus. There is a long tradition in transatlantic relations of allowing mutually burdensome trade illiteracy to flourish in its own separate domain. But there is no need for additional unpersuasive criticisms of American policy. The straightforward case against what the administration has done is shaming enough on its own.

What then should Mr Bush have done? As we argued last week, the principle should be 'protect the worker, not the industry'. The government should improve its assistance programmes for workers who lose their health-care benefits and pensions when firms fail, and it should look at new and more generous ways of helping workers find new jobs. These policies cost money, of course – but so does shutting out imports, and far more so, the only other difference being that the effect is disguised. It requires political spine, sometimes, to do the right thing. Mr Bush was supposed to have one.

Source: *The Economist*, 7 March 2002.
Copyright © The Economist Newspaper Limited, London.

### The Effects of an Import Quota

*An import quota, like a tariff, reduces the quantity of imports and moves a market closer to the equilibrium that would exist without trade. Total surplus falls by an amount equal to area D + F. These two triangles represent the deadweight loss from the quota. In addition, the import quota transfers E' + E'' to whoever holds the import licences.*

|  | Before quota | After quota | Change |
|---|---|---|---|
| Consumer surplus | A + B + C + D + E' + E'' + F | A + B | −(C + D + E' + E'' + F) |
| Producer surplus | G | C + G | +C |
| Licence-holder surplus | None | E' + E'' | +(E' + E'') |
| Total surplus | A + B + C + D + E' + E'' + F + G | A + B + C + E' + E'' + G | −(D + F) |

| The area D + F shows the fall in total surplus and represents the deadweight loss of the quota. |
|---|

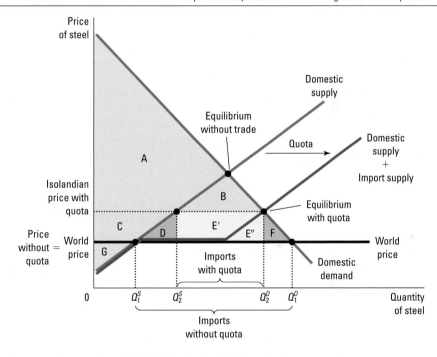

and the total supply of steel in Isoland equals the domestic supply plus the quota amount. That is, the supply curve above the world price is shifted to the right by exactly the amount of the quota. (The supply curve below the world price does not shift because, in this case, importing is not profitable for the licence holders.)

The price of steel in Isoland adjusts to balance supply (domestic plus imported) and demand. As the figure shows, the quota causes the price of steel to rise above the world price. The domestic quantity demanded falls from $Q_1^D$ to $Q_2^D$, and the domestic quantity supplied rises from $Q_1^S$ to $Q_2^S$. Not surprisingly, the import quota reduces steel imports.

Now consider the gains and losses from the quota. Because the quota raises the domestic price above the world price, domestic sellers are better off, and domestic buyers are worse off. In addition, the licence holders are better off because they make a profit from buying at the world price and selling at the higher domestic price. To measure these gains and losses, we look at the changes in consumer surplus, producer surplus and licence-holder surplus.

Before the government imposes the quota, the domestic price equals the world price. Consumer surplus, the area between the demand curve and the world price, is area A + B + C + D + E′ + E″ + F. Producer surplus, the area between the supply curve and the world price, is area G. The surplus of licence holders equals zero because there are no licences. Total surplus, the sum of consumer, producer and licence-holder surplus, is area A + B + C + D + E′ + E″ + F + G.

After the government imposes the import quota and issues the licences, the domestic price exceeds the world price. Domestic consumers get surplus equal to area A + B, and domestic producers get surplus equal to area C + G. The licence holders make a profit on each unit imported equal to the difference between the Isolandian price of steel and the world price. Their surplus equals this price differential times the quantity of imports. Thus, it equals the area of the rectangle E′ + E″. Total surplus with the quota is the area A + B + C + E′ + E″ + G.

To see how total welfare changes with the imposition of the quota, we add the change in consumer surplus (which is negative), the change in producer surplus (positive) and the change in licence-holder surplus (positive). We find that total surplus in the market decreases by the area D + F. This area represents the deadweight loss of the import quota.

This analysis should seem somewhat familiar. Indeed, if you compare the analysis of import quotas in Figure 9.7 with the analysis of tariffs in Figure 9.6, you will see that they are essentially identical. Both tariffs and import quotas raise the domestic price of the good, reduce the welfare of domestic consumers, increase the welfare of domestic producers and cause deadweight losses. There is only one difference between these two types of trade restriction: a tariff raises revenue for the government (area E in Figure 9.6), whereas an import quota creates surplus for licence holders (area E′ + E″ in Figure 9.7).

Tariffs and import quotas can be made to look even more similar. Suppose that the government tries to capture the licence-holder surplus for itself by charging a fee for the licences. A licence to sell 1 tonne of steel is worth exactly the difference between the Isolandian price of steel and the world price, and the government can set the licence fee as high as this price differential. If the government does this, the licence fee for imports works exactly like a tariff: Consumer surplus, producer surplus and government revenue are exactly the same under the two policies.

In practice, however, countries that restrict trade with import quotas rarely do so by selling the import licences. For example, in 1991 the European Union reached an agreement with Japan to 'voluntarily' limit the sale of Japanese cars in member countries of the EU. In this case, the Japanese government allocates the import licences to Japanese firms, and the surplus from these licences (area E′ + E″) accrues to those firms. This kind of import quota is, from the standpoint of the welfare of the European Union, strictly worse than an EU tariff on imported cars. Both a tariff and an import quota raise prices, restrict trade and cause deadweight losses, but at least the tariff produces revenue for the European Union rather than for Japanese auto companies. It is perhaps not surprising, therefore, that this arrangement was terminated at the end of 1999.

Although in our analysis so far import quotas and tariffs appear to cause similar deadweight losses, a quota can potentially cause an even larger deadweight loss, depending on the mechanism used to allocate the import licences. Suppose that when Isoland imposes a quota, everyone understands that the licences will go to those who spend the most resources lobbying the Isolandian government. In this case, there is an implicit licence fee – the cost of lobbying. The revenues from this fee, however, rather than being collected by the government, are spent on lobbying expenses. The deadweight losses from this type of quota include not only the losses from overproduction (area D) and underconsumption (area F) but also whatever part of the licence-holder surplus (area E′ + E″) is wasted on the cost of lobbying.

## The Lessons for Trade Policy

The team of Isolandian economists can now write to the new president:

Dear Madam President,

You asked us three questions about opening up trade. After much hard work, we have the answers.

*Question:* If the government allowed Isolandians to import and export steel, what would happen to the price of steel and the quantity of steel sold in the domestic steel market?
*Answer:* Once trade is allowed, the Isolandian price of steel would be driven to equal the price prevailing around the world.

If the world price is now higher than the Isolandian price, our price would rise. The higher price would reduce the amount of steel Isolandians consume and raise the amount of steel that Isolandians produce. Isoland would, therefore, become a steel exporter. This occurs because, in this case, Isoland would have a comparative advantage in producing steel.

Conversely, if the world price is now lower than the Isolandian price, our price would fall. The lower price would raise the amount of steel that Isolandians consume and lower the amount of steel that Isolandians produce. Isoland would, therefore, become a steel importer. This occurs because, in this case, other countries would have a comparative advantage in producing steel.

*Question:* Who would gain from free trade in steel and who would lose, and would the gains exceed the losses?
*Answer:* The answer depends on whether the price rises or falls when trade is allowed. If the price rises, producers of steel gain, and consumers of steel lose. If the price falls, consumers gain, and producers lose. In both cases, the gains are larger than the losses. Thus, free trade raises the total welfare of Isolandians.

*Question:* Should a tariff or an import quota be part of the new trade policy?
*Answer:* A tariff, like most taxes, has deadweight losses: the revenue raised would be smaller than the losses to the buyers and sellers. In this case, the deadweight losses occur because the tariff would move the economy closer to our current no-trade equilibrium. An import quota works much like a tariff and would cause similar deadweight losses. The best policy, from the standpoint of economic efficiency, would be to allow trade without a tariff or an import quota.

We hope you find these answers helpful as you decide on your new policy.

Your obedient servants,<br>Isolandian economics team

**Quick Quiz** Draw the supply and demand curve for wool suits in the country of Autarka. When trade is allowed, the price of a suit falls from 300 to 200 grams of gold. In your diagram, what is the change in consumer surplus, the change in producer surplus and the change in total surplus? How would a tariff on suit imports alter these effects?

## F Y I

## Other Benefits of International Trade

Our conclusions so far have been based on the standard analysis of international trade. As we have seen, there are winners and losers when a nation opens itself up to trade, but the gains to the winners exceed the losses of the losers. Yet the case for free trade can be made even stronger. There are several other economic benefits of trade beyond those emphasized in the standard analysis. Here, in a nutshell, are some of these other benefits:

● *Increased variety of goods*. Goods produced in different countries are not exactly the same. German beer, for instance, is not the same as American beer. Free trade gives consumers in all countries greater variety from which to choose.

● *Lower costs through economies of scale*. Some goods can be produced at low cost only if they are produced in large quantities – a phenomenon called *economies of scale*. A firm in a small country cannot take full advantage of economies of scale if it can sell only in a small domestic market. Free trade gives firms access to larger world markets and allows them to realize economies of scale more fully.

● *Increased competition*. A company shielded from foreign competitors is more likely to have market power, which in turn gives it the ability to raise prices above competitive levels. This is a type of market failure. Opening up trade fosters competition and gives the invisible hand a better chance to work its magic.

● *Enhanced flow of ideas*. The transfer of technological advances around the world is often thought to be linked to international trade in the goods that embody those advances. The best way for a poor, agricultural nation to learn about the computer revolution, for instance, is to buy some computers from abroad, rather than trying to make them domestically.

Thus, free international trade increases variety for consumers, allows firms to take advantage of economies of scale, makes markets more competitive and facilitates the spread of technology. If the Isolandian economists thought these effects were important, their advice to their president would be even more forceful.

## THE ARGUMENTS FOR RESTRICTING TRADE

The letter from the economics team persuades the new president of Isoland to consider opening up trade in steel. She notes that the domestic price is now high compared to the world price. Free trade would, therefore, cause the price of steel to fall and hurt domestic steel producers. Before implementing the new policy, she asks Isolandian steel companies to comment on the economists' advice.

Not surprisingly, the steel companies are opposed to free trade in steel. They believe that the government should protect the domestic steel industry from foreign competition. Let's consider some of the arguments they might give to support their position and how the economics team would respond.

### The Jobs Argument

Opponents of free trade often argue that trade with other countries destroys domestic jobs. In our example, free trade in steel would cause the price of steel to fall, reducing the quantity of steel produced in Isoland and thus reducing employment in the Isolandian steel industry. Some Isolandian steelworkers would lose their jobs.

Yet free trade creates jobs at the same time that it destroys them. When Isolandians buy steel from other countries, those countries obtain the resources to buy other goods from Isoland. Isolandian workers would move from the steel industry to those industries in which Isoland has a comparative advantage. Although the transition may impose hardship on some workers in the short run, it allows Isolandians as a whole to enjoy a higher standard of living.

Opponents of trade are often sceptical that trade creates jobs. They might respond that *everything* can be produced more cheaply abroad. Under free trade, they might argue, Isolandians could not be profitably employed in any industry. As Chapter 3 explains, however, the gains from trade are based on comparative advantage, not absolute advantage. Even if one country is better than another country at producing everything, each country can still gain from trading with the other. Workers in each country will eventually find jobs in the industry in which that country has a comparative advantage.

## The National Security Argument

When an industry is threatened with competition from other countries, opponents of free trade often argue that the industry is vital for national security. In our example, Isolandian steel companies might point out that steel is used to make guns and tanks. Free trade would allow Isoland to become dependent on foreign countries to supply steel. If a war later broke out, Isoland might be unable to produce enough steel and weapons to defend itself.

Economists acknowledge that protecting key industries may be appropriate when there are legitimate concerns over national security. Yet they fear that this argument may be used too quickly by producers eager to gain at consumers' expense. Certainly, it is tempting for those in an industry to exaggerate their role in national defence to obtain protection from foreign competition.

## The Infant Industry Argument

New industries sometimes argue for temporary trade restrictions to help them get started. After a period of protection, the argument goes, these industries will mature and be able to compete with foreign competitors. Similarly, older industries sometimes argue that they need protection to help them adjust to new conditions. In 2002, for example, when US President George Bush imposed steep tariffs on the import of steel from the European Union, he argued that the industry needed protection in order to be able to afford to pay the pensions and health care costs of its retired workers and while it was going through a period of adjustment in terms of making its production more efficient in order to be able to cope with intense foreign competition.

Economists are often sceptical about such claims. The primary reason is that the infant industry argument is difficult to implement in practice. To apply protection successfully, the government would need to decide which industries will eventually be profitable and decide whether the benefits of establishing these industries exceed the costs to consumers of protection. Yet 'picking winners' is extraordinarily difficult. It is made even more difficult by the political process, which often awards protection to those industries that are politically powerful. And once a powerful industry is protected from foreign competition, the 'temporary' policy is hard to remove.

In addition, many economists are sceptical about the infant industry argument even in principle. Suppose, for instance, that the Isolandian steel industry is young and unable to compete profitably against foreign rivals. Yet there is reason to believe that the industry can be profitable in the long run. In this case, the owners of the firms should be willing to incur temporary losses to obtain the

# Berry's World

"You like protectionism as a 'working man.' How about as a consumer?"

# IN THE NEWS

## The Gains From Free Trade

*Restrictive trade policies are often adopted by rich and poor countries alike. The World Bank thinks that this makes all countries poorer.*

### Preaching the Universal Benefits of Freer Trade: This Year's *Global Economic Prospects* Study Carries the Message that Opening Markets and Scrapping Tariffs Bring Gains For Rich and Poor

By Guy De Jonquieres

Trade negotiators obey a perverse logic. They call improved access to other countries' markets 'gains', and cuts in their trade barriers 'concessions'. Yet, as the World Bank points out in this year's *Global Economic Prospects*, they are talking economic nonsense.

In reality, countries gain most by opening their own markets. Lowering import costs and exposing their economies to competition increases productivity and exports. 'Study after study has shown that trade reforms rebound first and fastest to the reformer,' the bank says.

Somewhat optimistically, it urges World Trade Organisation members to ... renounce mercantilist thinking and adopt a new strategy .... It says bold reciprocal liberalisation that slashed tariffs over five years to no more than 15 per cent in developing countries and 10 per cent in industrialised ones could raise incomes by $350bn (€323bn, £223bn) in the former and by $170bn in the latter by 2015. It could also lift as many as 140m people out of extreme poverty. World trade would grow by an extra 10 per cent and developing countries' exports by 20 per cent. However, most of the growth in income would be

due to reforms that trade liberalisation spurred in countries' own economies, not to higher exports.

The bank's prescriptions, published a week before the WTO's ministerial meeting in Cancun, Mexico, challenge developing countries' insistence on maintaining many trade barriers, which are often much higher than in the industrialised world.

The bank urges rich countries to lead by reforming their agricultural policies, the biggest obstacle to development. It says reducing protection would yield two thirds of the gains from liberalising all merchandise trade – but removing border barriers is more important than cutting subsidies.

The report says rich countries' industrial tariffs also penalise poor ones. The former collected from developing countries more than twice the tariff revenues per dollar of imports levied on trade with each other.

It calls for reform of trade preference schemes, saying they penalise developing nations that are excluded from them. The arrangements did little to help the poorest economies. The bank also wants looser restrictions on temporary movement of workers. If rich countries allowed immigration equal to only 3 per cent of their labour forces, it says, developing countries could gain $160bn in extra income.

However, it also criticises middle-income developing countries' determination to keep their trade barriers high, saying these harm their own and other poorer countries' growth. 'Middle-

income countries have ample scope for undertaking reductions in their protection that will accelerate their growth,' it says.

Developing countries should also open their services markets to competition. Liberalising sectors such as finance and transport would raise their overall performance.

The bank dismisses suggestions that liberalisation deprives governments of the right to regulate, but underlines the importance of sound national regulatory frameworks. In many countries, privatisations had left monopolies intact.

The report is sceptical about proposals for WTO investment rules, backed by the EU and Japan, saying they would contribute little to development. It also expresses concern about tighter border security measures since September 11, saying every 1 per cent of costs they imposed on trade cut world income by $75bn.

The bank sugars its free-market pill by saying that developing countries which open their markets will incur adjustment costs that require more technical assistance and development aid.

A greater effort is also needed to build sound institutions that would enable poor countries to take advantage of trade liberalisation by implementing effective domestic reforms.

Source: The *Financial Times,* 4 September 2003.

eventual profits. Protection is not necessary for an industry to grow. Firms in various industries – such as many internet firms today – incur temporary losses in the hope of growing and becoming profitable in the future. And many of them succeed, even without protection from foreign competition.

## The Unfair Competition Argument

A common argument is that free trade is desirable only if all countries play by the same rules. If firms in different countries are subject to different laws and regulations, then it is unfair (the argument goes) to expect the firms to compete in the international marketplace. For instance, suppose that the government of Neighbourland subsidizes its steel industry by giving steel companies large tax breaks. The Isolandian steel industry might argue that it should be protected from this foreign competition because Neighbourland is not competing fairly.

Would it, in fact, hurt Isoland to buy steel from another country at a subsidized price? Certainly, Isolandian steel producers would suffer, but Isolandian steel consumers would benefit from the low price. Moreover, the case for free trade is no different: the gains of the consumers from buying at the low price would exceed the losses of the producers. Neighbourland's subsidy to its steel industry may be a bad policy, but it is the taxpayers of Neighbourland who bear the burden. Isoland can benefit from the opportunity to buy steel at a subsidized price.

## The Protection as a Bargaining Chip Argument

Another argument for trade restrictions concerns the strategy of bargaining. Many policy makers claim to support free trade but, at the same time, argue that trade restrictions can be useful when we bargain with our trading partners. They claim that the threat of a trade restriction can help remove a trade restriction already imposed by a foreign government. For example, Isoland might threaten to impose a tariff on steel unless Neighbourland removes its tariff on wheat. If Neighbourland responds to this threat by removing its tariff, the result can be freer trade.

The problem with this bargaining strategy is that the threat may not work. If it doesn't work, the country has a difficult choice. It can carry out its threat and implement the trade restriction, which would reduce its own economic welfare. Or it can back down from its threat, which would cause it to lose prestige in international affairs. Faced with this choice, the country would probably wish that it had never made the threat in the first place.

## *CASE STUDY*

### Trade Agreements and the World Trade Organization

A country can take one of two approaches to achieving free trade. It can take a *unilateral* approach and remove its trade restrictions on its own. This is the approach that the United Kingdom took in the 19th century and that Chile and South Korea have taken in recent years. Alternatively, a country can take a *multilateral* approach and reduce its trade restrictions while other countries do the same. In other words, it can bargain with its trading partners in an attempt to reduce trade restrictions around the world.

**customs union**
a group of countries that agree not to impose any restrictions at all on trade between their own economies, but to impose the same restrictions as one another on goods imported from countries outside the group

Perhaps the most important example of the multilateral approach is the European Union (EU), which in 2004 expanded to a total membership of 25. The EU is an example of a **customs union**. A customs union is a group of countries that agree not to impose any restrictions at all on trade between their own economies, but to impose the same restrictions as one another on goods imported from outside the group.

Two other examples of the multilateral approach are the North American Free Trade Agreement (NAFTA) – which in 1993 lowered trade barriers among the United States, Mexico and Canada – and the General Agreement on Tariffs and Trade (GATT), which is a continuing series of negotiations among many of the world's countries with the goal of promoting free trade. The United States helped to found GATT after World War II in response to the high tariffs imposed during the Great Depression of the 1930s. Many economists believe that the high tariffs contributed to the economic hardship during that period. GATT has successfully reduced the average tariff among member countries from about 40 per cent after World War II to about 5 per cent today.

The rules established under GATT are now enforced by an international institution called the World Trade Organization (WTO). The WTO was established in 1995 and has its headquarters in Geneva, Switzerland. As of June 2005, 148 countries have joined the organization, accounting for about 98 per cent of world trade. The functions of the WTO are to administer trade agreements, provide a forum for negotiations, and handle disputes that arise among member countries.

What are the pros and cons of the multilateral approach to free trade? One advantage is that the multilateral approach has the potential to result in freer trade than a unilateral approach because it can reduce trade restrictions abroad as well as at home. If international negotiations fail, however, the result could be more restricted trade than under a unilateral approach.

In addition, the multilateral approach may have a political advantage. In most markets, producers are fewer and better organized than consumers – and thus wield greater political influence. Reducing the Isolandian tariff on steel, for example, may be politically difficult if considered by itself. The steel companies would oppose free trade, and the users of steel who would benefit are so numerous that organizing their support would be difficult. Yet suppose that Neighbourland promises to reduce its tariff on wheat at the same time that Isoland reduces its tariff on steel. In this case, the Isolandian wheat farmers, who are also politically powerful, would back the agreement. Thus, the multilateral approach to free trade can sometimes win political support when a unilateral reduction cannot.

**Quick Quiz** The textile industry of Autarka advocates a ban on the import of wool suits. Describe five arguments its lobbyists might make. Give a response to each of these arguments.

# IN THE NEWS

## Globalization

*The movement towards free trade – sometimes called globalization – has some vocal opponents. As this article discusses, governments need to resist these pressures towards restricting trade if the huge benefits that free trade has brought are to be maintained.*

### Storm over Globalization

Breaking down barriers is controversial work. That will be clear on November 30th, when as many as 100,000 demonstrators will march through Seattle, ostensibly to protest at the launch, at a World Trade Organisation summit, of a new round of trade-liberalizing talks. But their real target is globalization, broadly defined. This in a city that thrives on trade: a port, near Canada, home to Microsoft and Boeing, two of America's biggest exporters, and birthplace of such global crazes as 'Frasier' and fancy coffee.

Around the world, support for free trade is weak at best; and the WTO is copping the blame for the perceived evils of globalization. It is under attack from trade unions, greens and even consumer groups, all of whom say its rules advance big companies' global ambitions at the expense of jobs and the environment. They also attack the WTO for being secretive and unaccountable. Such arguments will gain ground unless the case for globalization is made with renewed vigour.

The economic benefits of the greater openness – faster growth, cheaper imports, new technologies, the spur of foreign competition – that the world has enjoyed in recent years are too easily taken for granted. Greater prosperity is also the best way to improve working conditions and the environment. Yet for all the gains that globalization brings, it can also create losers, who naturally dislike change. Their concerns should

not be dismissed. But shutting out the rest of the world would make everyone worse off.

For all the storm over globalisation, too many trade barriers remain – one reason that a new round of trade talks is needed. Despite huge strides towards open markets over the past 50 years, big swathes of the world economy, such as agriculture, textiles and shipping, remain highly protected. Many tariffs are still high. New trade barriers keep appearing too. Booming industries such as computing and telecoms are vulnerable, notably through standards that handicap foreign firms. Even e-commerce can be subject to trade restrictions.

All around the world, protectionist sentiment is alive and well. There has been a surge in anti-dumping duties on imports deemed 'unfairly' cheap. Such duties are rarely lifted, so their burden grows each year. America now has around 300 in place. Even illegal 'voluntary export restraints' are re-emerging: Japan has privately agreed to limit steel exports to America. Merely to stand still, a new effort to open markets is needed. It is also the surest way to deflect protectionist pressure, because the prospect of greater access to foreign markets should rally export lobbies to the free-trade cause....

America and Europe urgently need to show more genuine commitment to free trade. Mike Moore, the WTO's pugnacious new boss, has started the long fight to win over sceptics on globalisation. But he cannot succeed without

governments' help. All too often, they appease protectionists rather than confront them. By trying to force labour rights on to the agenda for the new round, for instance, America and Europe are playing with fire. Globalisation is not irreversible. Unless governments come out fighting for free trade in Seattle and beyond, the huge gains it has brought could be lost.

Source: *The Economist*, 25 November 1999. Copyright © The Economist Newspaper Limited, London.

# CONCLUSION

Economists and the general public often disagree about free trade. In particular, economists are usually opposed to trade restrictions while the general public often wants to see restrictions on trade in order to 'protect' the domestic economy from 'cut-throat' foreign competition.

To understand better the economists' view of trade, let's continue our parable. Suppose that the country of Isoland ignores the advice of its economics team and decides not to allow free trade in steel. The country remains in the equilibrium without international trade.

Then, one day, some Isolandian inventor discovers a new way to make steel at very low cost. The process is quite mysterious, however, and the inventor insists on keeping it a secret. What is odd is that the inventor doesn't need any workers or iron ore to make steel. The only input he requires is wheat.

The inventor is hailed as a genius. Because steel is used in so many products, the invention lowers the cost of many goods and allows all Isolandians to enjoy a higher standard of living. Workers who had previously produced steel do suffer when their factories close, but eventually they find work in other industries. Some become farmers and grow the wheat that the inventor turns into steel. Others enter new industries that emerge as a result of higher Isolandian living standards. Everyone understands that the displacement of these workers is an inevitable part of progress.

After several years, a newspaper reporter decides to investigate this mysterious new steel process. She sneaks into the inventor's factory and learns that the inventor is a fraud. The inventor has not been making steel at all. Instead, he has been smuggling wheat abroad in exchange for steel from other countries. The only thing that the inventor had discovered was the gains from international trade.

When the truth is revealed, the government shuts down the inventor's operation. The price of steel rises and workers return to jobs in steel factories. Living standards in Isoland fall back to their former levels. The inventor is jailed and held up to public ridicule. After all, he was no inventor. He was just an economist.

## SUMMARY

- The effects of free trade can be determined by comparing the domestic price without trade to the world price. A low domestic price indicates that the country has a comparative advantage in producing the good and that the country will become an exporter. A high domestic price indicates that the rest of the world has a comparative advantage in producing the good and that the country will become an importer.

- When a country allows trade and becomes an exporter of a good, producers of the good are better off, and consumers of the good are worse off. When a country allows trade and becomes an importer of a good, consumers are better off, and producers are worse off. In both cases, the gains from trade exceed the losses.

- A tariff – a tax on imports – moves a market closer to the

equilibrium that would exist without trade and, therefore, reduces the gains from trade. Although domestic producers are better off and the government raises revenue, the losses to consumers exceed these gains.

- An import quota – a limit on imports – has effects that are similar to those of a tariff. Under a quota, however, the holders of the import licences receive the revenue that the government would collect with a tariff.

- There are various arguments for restricting trade: protecting jobs, defending national security, helping infant industries, preventing unfair competition and responding to foreign trade restrictions. Although some of these arguments have some merit in some cases, economists believe that free trade is usually the better policy.

## KEY CONCEPTS

world price, p. 167

import quota, p. 173

customs union, p. 182

tariff, p. 172

## QUESTIONS FOR REVIEW

1. What does the domestic price that prevails without international trade tell us about a nation's comparative advantage?

2. When does a country become an exporter of a good? An importer?

3. Draw the supply-and-demand diagram for an importing country. What is consumer surplus and producer surplus before trade is allowed? What is consumer surplus and producer surplus with free trade? What is the change in total surplus?

4. Describe what a tariff is, and describe its economic effects.

5. What is an import quota? Compare its economic effects with those of a tariff.

6. List five arguments often given to support trade restrictions. How do economists respond to these arguments?

7. What is the difference between the unilateral and multilateral approaches to achieving free trade? Give an example of each.

## PROBLEMS AND APPLICATIONS

1. France represents a small part of the world apple market.
   a. Draw a diagram depicting the equilibrium in the French apple market without international trade. Identify the equilibrium price, equilibrium quantity, consumer surplus and producer surplus.
   b. Suppose that the world apple price is below the French price before trade, and that the French apple market is now opened to trade. Identify the new equilibrium price, quantity consumed, quantity produced domestically and quantity imported. Also show the change in the surplus of domestic consumers and producers. Has domestic total surplus increased or decreased?

2. The world price of wine is below the price that would prevail in France in the absence of trade.
   a. Assuming that French imports of wine are a small part of total world wine production, draw a graph for the French market for wine under free trade. Identify consumer surplus, producer surplus and total surplus in an appropriate table.
   b. Now suppose that an outbreak of phyloxera in California and South America destroys much of the

grape harvest there. What effect does this shock have on the world price of wine? Using your graph and table from part (a), show the effect on consumer surplus, producer surplus and total surplus in France. Who are the winners and losers? Is France better or worse off?

3. The world price of cotton is below the no-trade price in country A and above the no-trade price in country B. Using supply and demand diagrams and welfare tables such as those in the chapter, show the gains from trade in each country. Compare your results for the two countries.

4. Suppose that European Union countries impose a common tariff on imported cars to protect the European car industry from foreign competition. Assuming that Europe is a price taker in the world car market, show on a diagram: the change in the quantity of imports, the loss to European consumers, the gain to European car manufacturers, government revenue and the deadweight loss associated with the tariff. The loss to consumers can be decomposed into three pieces: a transfer to domestic producers, a transfer to the government and a deadweight loss. Use your diagram to identify these three pieces.

5. Write a brief essay advocating or criticizing each of the following policy positions.
   a. The government should not allow imports if foreign firms are selling below their costs of production (a phenomenon called 'dumping').
   b. The government should temporarily stop the import of goods for which the domestic industry is new and struggling to survive.
   c. The government should not allow imports from countries with weaker environmental regulations than ours.

6. Suppose that a technological advance in Japan lowers the world price of televisions.
   a. Assume the UK is an importer of televisions and there are no trade restrictions. How does the technological advance affect the welfare of UK consumers and UK producers? What happens to total surplus in the United Kingdom?
   b. Now suppose the United Kingdom has a quota on television imports. How does the Japanese technological advance affect the welfare of UK consumers, UK producers and the holders of import licences?

7. When the government of Tradeland decides to impose an import quota on foreign cars, three proposals are suggested: (1) Sell the import licences in an auction. (2) Distribute the licences randomly in a lottery. (3) Let people wait in line and distribute the licences on a first-come, first-served basis. Compare the effects of these policies. Which policy do you think has the largest deadweight losses? Which policy has the smallest deadweight losses? Why? (Hint: the government's other ways of raising tax revenue themselves all cause deadweight losses.)

8. (This question is challenging.) Consider a small country that exports steel. Suppose that a 'pro-trade' government decides to subsidize the export of steel by paying a certain amount for each tonne sold abroad. How does this export subsidy affect the domestic price of steel, the quantity of steel produced, the quantity of steel consumed and the quantity of steel exported? How does it affect consumer surplus, producer surplus, government revenue and total surplus? (Hint: the analysis of an export subsidy is similar to the analysis of a tariff.)

9. Examine a trade dispute or trade agreement that has been in the news lately. In this case, who do you think are the winners and losers from free trade? Which group has more political clout? Note: a good place to look for this information is the website of the World Trade Organization (http://www.wto.org).

 For further resources, visit
http://www.thomsonlearning.co.uk/mankiw_taylor

# 4

# THE ECONOMICS
# OF THE PUBLIC SECTOR

# 10 EXTERNALITIES

F irms that make and sell paper also create, as a by-product of the manufacturing process, a chemical called dioxin. Scientists believe that once dioxin enters the environment it raises the population's risk of cancer, birth defects and other health problems.

Is the production and release of dioxin a problem for society? In Chapters 4 through 9 we examined how markets allocate scarce resources with the forces of supply and demand, and we saw that the equilibrium of supply and demand is typically an efficient allocation of resources. To use Adam Smith's famous metaphor, the 'invisible hand' of the marketplace leads self-interested buyers and sellers in a market to maximize the total benefit that society derives from that market. This insight is the basis for one of the *Ten Principles of Economics* in Chapter 1: markets are usually a good way to organize economic activity. Should we conclude, therefore, that the invisible hand prevents firms in the paper market from emitting too much dioxin?

Markets do many things well, but they do not do everything well. In this chapter we begin our study of another one of the *Ten Principles of Economics:* governments can sometimes improve market outcomes. We examine why markets sometimes fail to allocate resources efficiently, how government policies can potentially improve the market's allocation and what kinds of policies are likely to work best.

The market failures examined in this chapter fall under a general category called *externalities*. An **externality** arises when a person engages in an activity that influences the well-being of a bystander and yet neither pays nor receives any compensation for that effect. If the impact on the bystander is adverse, it is called

**externality**
the uncompensated impact of one person's actions on the well-being of a bystander

189

a *negative externality;* if it is beneficial, it is called a *positive externality.* In the presence of externalities, society's interest in a market outcome extends beyond the well-being of buyers and sellers who participate in the market; it also includes the well-being of bystanders who are affected indirectly. Because buyers and sellers neglect the external effects of their actions when deciding how much to demand or supply, the market equilibrium is not efficient when there are externalities. That is, the equilibrium fails to maximize the total benefit to society as a whole. The release of dioxin into the environment, for instance, is a negative externality. Self-interested paper firms will not consider the full cost of the pollution they create and, therefore, will emit too much pollution unless the government prevents or discourages them from doing so.

Externalities come in many varieties, as do the policy responses that try to deal with the market failure. Here are some examples:

● The exhaust from cars is a negative externality because it creates smog that other people have to breathe. As a result of this externality, drivers tend to pollute too much. The government attempts to solve this problem by setting emission standards for cars. It also taxes petrol in order to reduce the amount that people drive.

● Restored historic buildings convey a positive externality because people who walk or drive by them can enjoy their beauty and the sense of history that these buildings provide. Building owners do not get the full benefit of restoration and, therefore, tend to discard older buildings too quickly. Many national governments respond to this problem by regulating the destruction of historic buildings and by providing tax incentives to owners who restore them.

● Barking dogs create a negative externality because neighbours are disturbed by the noise. Dog owners do not bear the full cost of the noise and, therefore, tend to take too few precautions to prevent their dogs from barking. The government may address this problem by making it illegal to 'disturb the peace'.

● Research into new technologies provides a positive externality because it creates knowledge that other people can use. Because inventors cannot capture the full benefits of their inventions, they tend to devote too few resources to research. The government addresses this problem partially through the patent system, which gives inventors an exclusive use over their inventions for a period of time.

In each of these cases, some decision maker fails to take account of the external effects of his or her behaviour. The government responds by trying to influence this behaviour to protect the interests of bystanders.

## EXTERNALITIES AND MARKET INEFFICIENCY

In this section we use the tools from Chapter 7 to examine how externalities affect economic well-being. The analysis shows precisely why externalities cause markets to allocate resources inefficiently. Later in the chapter we examine various ways in which private actors and public policy makers may remedy this type of market failure.

### Welfare Economics: A Recap

We begin by recalling the key lessons of welfare economics from Chapter 7. To make our analysis concrete, we will consider a specific market – the market for

FIGURE 10.1

### The Market for Aluminium

*The demand curve reflects the value to buyers, and the supply curve reflects the costs of sellers. The equilibrium quantity, $Q_{MARKET}$, maximizes the total value to buyers minus the total costs of sellers. In the absence of externalities, therefore, the market equilibrium is efficient.*

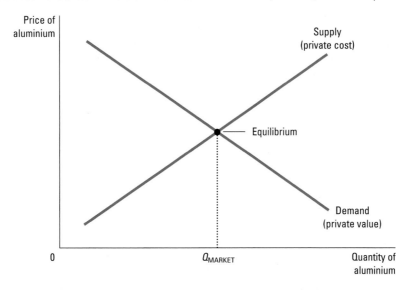

aluminium. Figure 10.1 shows the supply and demand curves in the market for aluminium.

As you should recall from Chapter 7, the supply and demand curves contain important information about costs and benefits. The demand curve for aluminium reflects the value of aluminium to consumers, as measured by the prices they are willing to pay. At any given quantity, the height of the demand curve shows the willingness to pay of the marginal buyer. In other words, it shows the value to the consumer of the last unit of aluminium bought. Similarly, the supply curve reflects the costs of producing aluminium. At any given quantity, the height of the supply curve shows the cost of the marginal seller. In other words, it shows the cost to the producer of the last unit of aluminium sold.

In the absence of government intervention, the price adjusts to balance the supply and demand for aluminium. The quantity produced and consumed in the market equilibrium, shown as $Q_{MARKET}$ in Figure 10.1, is efficient in the sense that it maximizes the sum of producer and consumer surplus. That is, the market allocates resources in a way that maximizes the total value to the consumers who buy and use aluminium minus the total costs to the producers who make and sell aluminium.

## Negative Externalities

Now let's suppose that aluminium factories emit pollution: for each unit of aluminium produced, a certain amount of smoke enters the atmosphere. Because this smoke creates a health risk for those who breathe the air, it is a negative externality. How does this externality affect the efficiency of the market outcome?

Because of the externality, the cost to *society* of producing aluminium is larger than the cost to the aluminium producers. For each unit of aluminium produced,

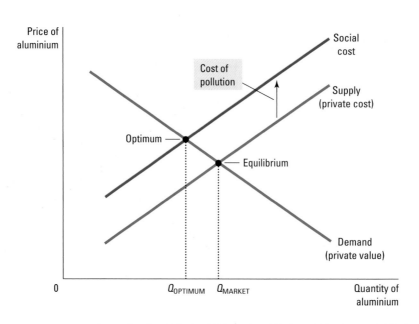

*"I've been nominated 'Industrialist of the Year' and the Dept of Environment are going to prosecute me for pollution."*

the *social cost* includes the private costs of the aluminium producers plus the costs to those bystanders affected adversely by the pollution. Figure 10.2 shows the social cost of producing aluminium. The social cost curve is above the supply curve because it takes into account the external costs imposed on society by aluminium producers. The difference between these two curves reflects the cost of the pollution emitted.

What quantity of aluminium should be produced? To answer this question, we once again consider what a benevolent social planner would do. The planner wants to maximize the total surplus derived from the market – the value to consumers of aluminium minus the cost of producing aluminium. The planner understands, however, that the cost of producing aluminium includes the external costs of the pollution.

The planner would choose the level of aluminium production at which the demand curve crosses the social cost curve. This intersection determines the optimal amount of aluminium from the standpoint of society as a whole. Below this level of production, the value of the aluminium to consumers (as measured by the height of the demand curve) exceeds the social cost of producing it (as measured by the height of the social cost curve). The planner does not produce more than this level because the social cost of producing additional aluminium exceeds the value to consumers.

Note that the equilibrium quantity of aluminium, $Q_{MARKET}$, is larger than the socially optimal quantity, $Q_{OPTIMUM}$. The reason for this inefficiency is that the market equilibrium reflects only the private costs of production. In the market equilibrium, the marginal consumer values aluminium at less than the social cost of producing it. That is, at $Q_{MARKET}$ the demand curve lies below the social cost

---

**FIGURE 10.2**

**Pollution and the Social Optimum**

*In the presence of a negative externality, such as pollution, the social cost of the good exceeds the private cost. The optimal quantity, $Q_{OPTIMUM}$, is therefore smaller than the equilibrium quantity, $Q_{MARKET}$.*

curve. Thus, reducing aluminium production and consumption below the market equilibrium level raises total economic well-being.

How can the social planner achieve the optimal outcome? One way would be to tax aluminium producers for each tonne of aluminium sold. The tax would shift the supply curve for aluminium upward by the size of the tax. If the tax accurately reflected the social cost of smoke released into the atmosphere, the new supply curve would coincide with the social cost curve. In the new market equilibrium, aluminium producers would produce the socially optimal quantity of aluminium.

The use of such a tax is called **internalizing an externality** because it gives buyers and sellers in the market an incentive to take account of the external effects of their actions. Aluminium producers would, in essence, take the costs of pollution into account when deciding how much aluminium to supply because the tax would make them pay for these external costs. The policy is based on one of the *Ten Principles of Economics:* people respond to incentives. Later in this chapter we consider other ways in which policy makers can deal with externalities.

**internalizing an externality**
altering incentives so that people take account of the external effects of their actions

## Positive Externalities

Although some activities impose costs on third parties, others yield benefits. For example, consider education. Education yields positive externalities because a more educated population leads to better government, which benefits everyone. Notice that the productivity benefit of education is not necessarily an externality: the consumer of education reaps most of the benefit in the form of higher wages. But if some of the productivity benefits of education spill over and benefit other people, then this effect would count as a positive externality as well.

The analysis of positive externalities is similar to the analysis of negative externalities. As Figure 10.3 shows, the demand curve does not reflect the value to society of the good. Because the social value is greater than the private value, the social value curve lies above the demand curve. The optimal quantity is found where the social value curve and the supply curve (which represents costs)

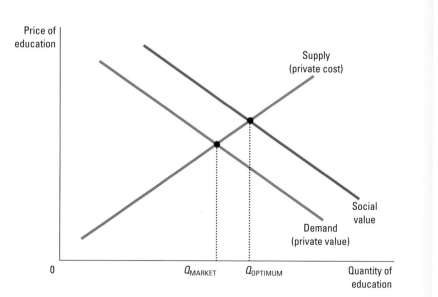

### FIGURE 10.3

**Education and the Social Optimum**

*In the presence of a positive externality, the social value of the good exceeds the private value. The optimal quantity, $Q_{OPTIMUM}$, is therefore larger than the equilibrium quantity, $Q_{MARKET}$.*

intersect. Hence, the socially optimal quantity is greater than the quantity determined by the private market.

Once again, the government can correct the market failure by inducing market participants to internalize the externality. The appropriate response in the case of positive externalities is exactly the opposite to the case of negative externalities. To move the market equilibrium closer to the social optimum, a positive externality requires a subsidy. In fact, that is exactly the policy the government follows by heavily subsidizing education.

To summarize: negative externalities lead markets to produce a larger quantity than is socially desirable. Positive externalities lead markets to produce a smaller quantity than is socially desirable. To remedy the problem, the government can internalize the externality by taxing goods that have negative externalities and subsidizing goods that have positive externalities.

## CASE STUDY

### Technology Spillovers and Industrial Policy

Consider the market for industrial robots. Robots are at the frontier of a rapidly changing technology. Whenever a firm builds a robot, there is some chance that it will discover a new and better design. This new design will benefit not only this firm but society as a whole because the design will enter society's pool of technological knowledge. This type of positive externality is called a *technology spillover.*

In this case, the government can internalize the externality by subsidizing the production of robots. If the government paid firms a subsidy for each robot produced, the supply curve would shift down by the amount of the subsidy, and this shift would increase the equilibrium quantity of robots. To ensure that the market equilibrium equals the social optimum, the subsidy should equal the value of the technology spillover.

How large are technology spillovers, and what do they imply for public policy? This is an important question because technological progress is the key to why living standards rise over time. Yet it is also a difficult question on which economists often disagree.

Some economists believe that technology spillovers are pervasive and that the government should encourage those industries that yield the largest spillovers. For instance, these economists argue that if making computer chips yields greater spillovers than making fish and chips, then the government should use the tax laws to encourage the production of computer chips relative to the production of fish and chips. Government intervention in the economy that aims to promote technology-enhancing industries is sometimes called *industrial policy.*

Other economists are sceptical about industrial policy. Even if technology spillovers are common, the success of an industrial policy requires that the government be able to measure the size of the spillovers from different markets. This measurement problem is difficult at best. Moreover, without precise measurements, the political system may end up subsidizing those industries with the most political clout, rather than those that yield the largest positive externalities.

Another way to deal with technology spillovers is patent protection. The patent laws protect the rights of inventors by giving them exclusive use of their inventions for a period of time. When a firm makes a technological breakthrough, it can patent the idea and capture much of the economic benefit for itself. The patent is said to internalize the externality by giving the firm a *property right* over its invention. If other firms want to use the new technology, they would have to obtain permission from the inventing firm and pay it some royalty. Thus, the patent system gives firms a greater incentive to engage in research and other activities that advance technology.

**Quick Quiz** Give an example of a negative externality and a positive externality • Explain why market outcomes are inefficient in the presence of externalities.

# PRIVATE SOLUTIONS TO EXTERNALITIES

We have discussed why externalities lead markets to allocate resources inefficiently, but have mentioned only briefly how this inefficiency can be remedied. In practice, both private actors and public policy makers respond to externalities in various ways. All of the remedies share the goal of moving the allocation of resources closer to the social optimum. In this section we examine private solutions.

## The Types of Private Solutions

Although externalities tend to cause markets to be inefficient, government action is not always needed to solve the problem. In some circumstances, people can develop private solutions.

Sometimes, the problem of externalities is solved with moral codes and social sanctions. Consider, for instance, why most people do not litter. Although there are laws against littering, these laws are not vigorously enforced. Most people do not litter just because it is the wrong thing to do. The Golden Rule taught to children says, 'Do unto others as you would have them do unto you.' This moral injunction tells us to take account of how our actions affect other people. In economic terms, it tells us to internalize externalities.

Another private solution to externalities is charities, many of which are established to deal with externalities. For example, Greenpeace, whose goal is to protect the environment, is a non-profit organization funded with private donations. As another example, colleges and universities sometimes receive gifts from alumni, corporations and foundations in part because education has positive externalities for society.

The private market can often solve the problem of externalities by relying on the self-interest of the relevant parties. Sometimes the solution takes the form of integrating different types of business. For example, consider an apple grower and a beekeeper who are located next to each other. Each business confers a positive externality on the other: by pollinating the flowers on the trees, the bees help the orchard produce apples. At the same time, the bees use the nectar they get from the apple trees to produce honey. Nevertheless, when the apple grower is deciding how many trees to plant and the beekeeper is deciding how many bees to keep, they neglect the positive externality. As a result, the apple grower plants too few trees and the beekeeper keeps too few bees. These externalities could be internalized if the beekeeper bought the apple orchard or if the apple grower bought the beehives: both activities would then take place within the same firm, and this single firm could choose the optimal number of trees and bees.

Internalizing externalities is one reason that some firms are involved in different types of business.

Another way for the private market to deal with external effects is for the interested parties to enter into a contract. In the foregoing example, a contract between the apple grower and the beekeeper can solve the problem of too few trees and too few bees. The contract can specify the number of trees, the number of bees, and perhaps a payment from one party to the other. By setting the right number of trees and bees, the contract can solve the inefficiency that normally arises from these externalities and make both parties better off.

## The Coase Theorem

**Coase theorem**
the proposition that if private parties can bargain without cost over the allocation of resources, they can solve the problem of externalities on their own

How effective is the private market in dealing with externalities? A famous result, called the **Coase theorem** after British economist Ronald Coase, suggests that it can be very effective in some circumstances. According to the Coase theorem, if private parties can bargain without cost over the allocation of resources, then the private market will always solve the problem of externalities and allocate resources efficiently.

To see how the Coase theorem works, consider an example. Suppose that Lizzie owns a dog (a corgi, in fact) named Brandy. Brandy barks and disturbs Phil, Lizzie's neighbour. Lizzie gets a benefit from owning the dog, but the dog confers a negative externality on Phil. Should Lizzie be forced to send Brandy to the dogs' home, or should Phil have to suffer sleepless nights because of Brandy's barking?

Consider first what outcome is socially efficient. A social planner, considering the two alternatives, would compare the benefit that Lizzie gets from the dog to the cost that Phil bears from the barking. If the benefit exceeds the cost, it is efficient for Lizzie to keep the dog and for Phil to live with the barking. Yet if the cost exceeds the benefit, then Lizzie should get rid of the dog.

According to the Coase theorem, the private market will reach the efficient outcome on its own. How? Phil can simply offer to pay Lizzie to get rid of the dog. Lizzie will accept the deal if the amount of money Phil offers is greater than the benefit of keeping the dog.

By bargaining over the price, Lizzie and Phil can always reach the efficient outcome. For instance, suppose that Lizzie gets a €500 benefit from the dog and Phil bears an €800 cost from the barking. In this case, Phil can offer Lizzie €600 to get rid of the dog, and Lizzie will gladly accept. Both parties are better off than they were before, and the efficient outcome is reached.

It is possible, of course, that Phil would not be willing to offer any price that Lizzie would accept. For instance, suppose that Lizzie gets a €1,000 benefit from the dog and Phil bears an €800 cost from the barking. In this case, Lizzie would turn down any offer below €1,000, while Phil would not offer any amount above €800. Therefore, Lizzie ends up keeping the dog. Given these costs and benefits, however, this outcome is efficient.

So far, we have assumed that Lizzie has the legal right to keep a barking dog. In other words, we have assumed that Lizzie can keep Brandy unless Phil pays her enough to induce her to give up the dog voluntarily. How different would the outcome be, on the other hand, if Phil had the legal right to peace and quiet?

According to the Coase theorem, the initial distribution of rights does not matter for the market's ability to reach the efficient outcome. For instance, suppose that Phil can legally compel Lizzie to get rid of the corgi. Although having this right works to Phil's advantage, it probably will not change the outcome. In this case, Lizzie can offer to pay Phil to allow her to keep the dog. If the benefit of the dog to Lizzie exceeds the cost of the barking to Phil, then Lizzie and Phil will strike a bargain in which Lizzie keeps the dog.

Although Lizzie and Phil can reach the efficient outcome regardless of how rights are initially distributed, the distribution of rights is not irrelevant: it determines the distribution of economic well-being. Whether Lizzie has the right to a barking dog or Phil the right to peace and quiet determines who pays whom in the final bargain. But, in either case, the two parties can bargain with each other and solve the externality problem. Lizzie will end up keeping the dog only if the benefit exceeds the cost.

To sum up: the Coase theorem says that private economic actors can solve the problem of externalities among themselves. Whatever the initial distribution of rights, the interested parties can always reach a bargain in which everyone is better off and the outcome is efficient.

## Why Private Solutions Do Not Always Work

Despite the appealing logic of the Coase theorem, private actors on their own often fail to resolve the problems caused by externalities. The Coase theorem applies only when the interested parties have no trouble reaching and enforcing an agreement. In the world, however, bargaining does not always work, even when a mutually beneficial agreement is possible.

Sometimes the interested parties fail to solve an externality problem because of **transaction costs,** the costs that parties incur in the process of agreeing to and following through on a bargain. In our example, imagine that Lizzie and Phil speak different languages so that, to reach an agreement, they will need to hire a translator. If the benefit of solving the barking problem is less than the cost of the translator, Lizzie and Phil might choose to leave the problem unsolved. In more realistic examples, the transaction costs are the expenses not of translators but of the lawyers required to draft and enforce contracts.

At other times bargaining simply breaks down. The recurrence of wars and labour strikes shows that reaching agreement can be difficult and that failing to reach agreement can be costly. The problem is often that each party tries to hold out for a better deal. For example, suppose that Lizzie gets a €500 benefit from the dog, and Phil bears an €800 cost from the barking. Although it is efficient for Phil to pay Lizzie to get rid of the dog, there are many prices that could lead to this outcome. Lizzie might demand €750, and Phil might offer only €550. As they haggle over the price, the inefficient outcome with the barking dog persists.

Reaching an efficient bargain is especially difficult when the number of interested parties is large because coordinating everyone is costly. For example, consider a factory that pollutes the water of a nearby lake. The pollution confers a negative externality on the local fishermen. According to the Coase theorem, if the pollution is inefficient, then the factory and the fishermen could reach a bargain in which the fishermen pay the factory not to pollute. If there are many fishermen, however, trying to coordinate them all to bargain with the factory may be almost impossible.

When private bargaining does not work, the government can sometimes play a role. The government is an institution designed for collective action. In this example, the government can act on behalf of the fishermen, even when it is impractical for the fishermen to act for themselves. In the next section, we examine how the government can try to remedy the problem of externalities.

**transaction costs**
the costs that parties incur in the process of agreeing and following through on a bargain

# PUBLIC POLICIES TOWARDS EXTERNALITIES

When an externality causes a market to reach an inefficient allocation of resources, the government can respond in one of two ways. *Command-and-control policies* regulate behaviour directly. *Market-based policies* provide incentives so that private decision makers will choose to solve the problem on their own.

## Regulation

The government can remedy an externality by making certain behaviours either required or forbidden. For example, it is a crime in any European country to dump poisonous chemicals into the water supply. In this case, the external costs to society far exceed the benefits to the polluter. The government therefore institutes a command-and-control policy that prohibits this act altogether.

In most cases of pollution, however, the situation is not this simple. Despite the stated goals of some environmentalists, it would be impossible to prohibit all polluting activity. For example, virtually all forms of transport – even the horse – produce some undesirable polluting by-products. But it would not be sensible for the government to ban all transport. Thus, instead of trying to eradicate pollution altogether, society has to weigh the costs and benefits to decide the kinds and quantities of pollution it will allow.

Environmental regulations can take many forms. Sometimes the government may dictate a maximum level of pollution that a factory may emit. Other times the government requires that firms adopt a particular technology to reduce emissions. In all cases, to design good rules, the government regulators need to know the details about specific industries and about the alternative technologies that those industries could adopt. This information is often difficult for government regulators to obtain.

## Pigovian Taxes and Subsidies

Instead of regulating behaviour in response to an externality, the government can use market-based policies to align private incentives with social efficiency. For instance, as we saw earlier, the government can internalize the externality by taxing activities that have negative externalities and subsidizing activities that have positive externalities. Taxes enacted to correct the effects of negative externalities are called **Pigovian taxes,** after the English economist Arthur Pigou (1877–1959), an early advocate of their use.

**Pigovian tax**
a tax enacted to correct the effects of a negative externality

Economists usually prefer Pigovian taxes over regulations as a way to deal with pollution because such taxes can reduce pollution at a lower cost to society. To see why, let us consider an example.

Suppose that two factories – a paper mill and a steel mill – are each dumping 500 tonnes of effluent into a river each year. The government decides that it wants to reduce the amount of pollution. It considers two solutions:

- *Regulation.* The government could tell each factory to reduce its pollution to 300 tonnes of effluent per year.
- *Pigovian tax.* The government could levy a tax on each factory of €50,000 for each tonne of effluent it emits.

The regulation would dictate a level of pollution, whereas the tax would give factory owners an economic incentive to reduce pollution. Which solution do you think is better?

Most economists would prefer the tax. They would first point out that a tax is just as effective as a regulation in reducing the overall level of pollution. The government can achieve whatever level of pollution it wants by setting the tax at the appropriate level. The higher the tax, the larger the reduction in pollution. Indeed, if the tax is high enough, the factories will close down altogether, reducing pollution to zero.

The reason why economists would prefer the tax is that it reduces pollution more efficiently. The regulation requires each factory to reduce pollution by the same amount, but an equal reduction is not necessarily the least expensive way to clean up the water. It is possible that the paper mill can reduce pollution at lower cost than the steel mill. If so, the paper mill would respond to the tax by reducing pollution substantially to avoid the tax, whereas the steel mill would respond by reducing pollution less and paying the tax.

In essence, the Pigovian tax places a price on the right to pollute. Just as markets allocate goods to those buyers who value them most highly, a Pigovian tax allocates pollution to those factories that face the highest cost of reducing it. Whatever the level of pollution the government chooses, it can achieve this goal at the lowest total cost using a tax.

Economists also argue that Pigovian taxes are better for the environment. Under the command-and-control policy of regulation, the factories have no reason to reduce emission further once they have reached the target of 300 tonnes of effluent. By contrast, the tax gives the factories an incentive to develop cleaner technologies, because a cleaner technology would reduce the amount of tax the factory has to pay.

Pigovian taxes are unlike most other taxes. As we discussed in Chapter 8, most taxes distort incentives and move the allocation of resources away from the social optimum. The reduction in economic well-being – that is, in consumer and producer surplus – exceeds the amount of revenue the government raises, resulting in a deadweight loss. By contrast, when externalities are present, society also cares about the well-being of the bystanders who are affected. Pigovian taxes correct incentives for the presence of externalities and thereby move the allocation of resources closer to the social optimum. Thus, while Pigovian taxes raise revenue for the government, they also enhance economic efficiency.

# CASE STUDY

## Why Is Petrol Taxed So Heavily?

In European countries, petrol is among the most heavily taxed goods in the economy. In the United Kingdom, for instance, more than three-quarters of what motorists pay for petrol is tax.

Why is this tax so common? One possible answer is that tax on petrol is a Pigovian tax aimed at correcting three negative externalities associated with driving:

*Petrol tax: payable 24 hours a day.*

- *Congestion.* If you have ever been stuck in bumper-to-bumper traffic, you have probably wished that there were fewer cars on the road. A petrol tax keeps congestion down by encouraging people to take public transport, participate in carpools and live closer to work.
- *Accidents.* Whenever a person buys a large car or 4×4 vehicle like a Range Rover, he makes himself safer, but he puts his neighbours at risk. Statistical research has shown that a person driving a typical car is much more likely to die if hit by a 4×4 vehicle than if hit by another car. The petrol tax is an indirect way of making people pay when their large, petrol-thirsty vehicles impose risk on others, which in turn makes them take account of this risk when choosing what vehicle to purchase.
- *Pollution.* The burning of fossil fuels such as petrol is widely believed to be the cause of global warming. Experts disagree about how dangerous this threat is, but there is no doubt that the petrol tax reduces the risk by reducing the use of petrol.

So the tax on petrol, rather than causing deadweight losses like most taxes, actually makes the economy work better. It means less traffic congestion, safer roads and a cleaner environment.

## Tradable Pollution Permits

Returning to our example of the paper mill and the steel mill, let us suppose that, despite the advice of its economists, the government adopts the regulation and requires each factory to reduce its pollution to 300 tonnes of effluent per year. Then one day, after the regulation is in place and both mills have complied, the two firms go to the government with a proposal. The steel mill wants to increase its emission of effluent by 100 tonnes. The paper mill has agreed to reduce its emission by the same amount if the steel mill pays it €5 million. Should the government allow the two factories to make this deal?

From the standpoint of economic efficiency, allowing the deal is good policy. The deal must make the owners of the two factories better off, because they are voluntarily agreeing to it. Moreover, the deal does not have any external effects because the total amount of pollution remains the same. Thus, social welfare is enhanced by allowing the paper mill to sell its right to pollute to the steel mill.

The same logic applies to any voluntary transfer of the right to pollute from one firm to another. If the government allows firms to make these deals, it will, in essence, have created a new scarce resource: pollution permits. A market to trade these permits will eventually develop, and that market will be governed by the forces of supply and demand. The invisible hand will ensure that this new market efficiently allocates the right to pollute. The firms that can reduce pollution only at high cost will be willing to pay the most for the pollution permits. The firms that can reduce pollution at low cost will prefer to sell whatever permits they have.

One advantage of allowing a market for pollution permits is that the initial allocation of pollution permits among firms does not matter from the standpoint of economic efficiency. The logic behind this conclusion is similar to that behind the Coase theorem. Those firms that can reduce pollution most easily would be willing to sell whatever permits they get, and those firms that can reduce pollution only at high cost would be willing to buy whatever permits they need. As long as there is a free market for the pollution rights, the final allocation will be efficient whatever the initial allocation.

Although reducing pollution using pollution permits may seem quite different from using Pigovian taxes, in fact the two policies have much in common. In both cases, firms pay for their pollution. With Pigovian taxes, polluting firms must pay a tax to the government. With pollution permits, polluting firms must pay to buy the permit. (Even firms that already own permits must pay to pollute: the opportunity cost of polluting is what they could have received by selling their permits on the open market.) Both Pigovian taxes and pollution permits internalize the externality of pollution by making it costly for firms to pollute.

The similarity of the two policies can be seen by considering the market for pollution. Both panels in Figure 10.4 show the demand curve for the right to pollute. This curve shows that the lower the price of polluting, the more firms will choose to pollute. In panel (a) the government uses a Pigovian tax to set a price for pollution. In this case, the supply curve for pollution rights is perfectly elastic (because firms can pollute as much as they want by paying the tax), and the position of the demand curve determines the quantity of pollution. In panel (b) the government sets a quantity of pollution by issuing pollution permits. In this case, the supply curve for pollution rights is perfectly inelastic (because the quantity of pollution is fixed by the number of permits), and the position of the demand curve determines the price of pollution. Hence, for any given demand curve for pollution, the government can achieve any point on the demand curve either by setting a price with a Pigovian tax or by setting a quantity with pollution permits.

In some circumstances, however, selling pollution permits may be better than levying a Pigovian tax. Suppose the government wants no more than 600 tonnes of effluent to be dumped into the river. But, because the government does not know the demand curve for pollution, it is not sure what size tax would achieve that goal. In this case, it can simply auction off 600 pollution permits. The auction price would yield the appropriate size of the Pigovian tax.

## FIGURE 10.4

### The Equivalence of Pigovian Taxes and Pollution Permits

*In panel (a) the government sets a price on pollution by levying a Pigovian tax, and the demand curve determines the quantity of pollution. In panel (b) the government limits the quantity of pollution by limiting the number of pollution permits, and the demand curve determines the price of pollution. The price and quantity of pollution are the same in the two cases.*

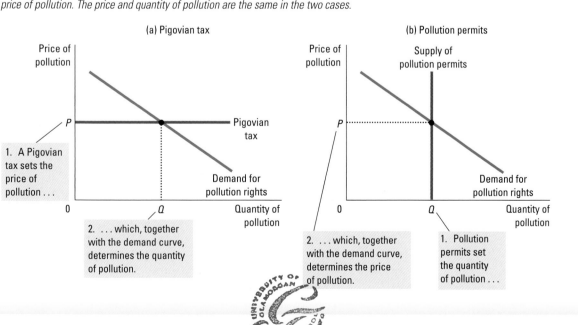

The idea of the government auctioning off the right to pollute may at first sound like a creature of some economist's imagination. And, in fact, that is how the idea began. But a number of governments around the world – in particular the US government – have used such a system as a way to control pollution. In 2002, European Union environment ministers unanimously agreed to set up a market to trade pollution permits for carbon dioxide ($CO_2$), the main so-called greenhouse gas of concern. Pollution permits, like Pigovian taxes, are increasingly being viewed as a cost-effective way to keep the environment clean.

## Objections to the Economic Analysis of Pollution

Some environmentalists argue that it is in some sense morally wrong to allow any one to pollute the environment in return for paying a fee. Clean air and clean water, they argue, are fundamental human rights that should not be debased by considering them in economic terms. How can you put a price on clean air and clean water? The environment is so important, they claim, that we should protect it as much as possible, regardless of the cost.

Economists have little sympathy with this type of argument. To economists, good environmental policy begins by acknowledging the first of the *Ten Principles of Economics* in Chapter 1: people face trade-offs. Certainly, clean air and clean water have value. But their value must be compared to their opportunity cost – that is, to what one must give up to obtain them. Eliminating all pollution is impossible. Trying to eliminate all pollution would reverse many of the technological advances that allow us to enjoy a high standard of living. Few people would be willing to accept poor nutrition, inadequate medical care or shoddy housing to make the environment as clean as possible.

Economists argue that some environmental activists hurt their own cause by not thinking in economic terms. A clean environment is a good like other goods. Like all normal goods, it has a positive income elasticity: rich countries can afford a cleaner environment than poor ones and, therefore, usually have more rigorous environmental protection. In addition, like most other goods, clean air and water obey the law of demand: the lower the price of environmental protection, the more the public will want. The economic approach of using pollution permits and Pigovian taxes reduces the cost of environmental protection and should, therefore, increase the public's demand for a clean environment.

**Quick Quiz** A glue factory and a steel mill emit smoke containing a chemical that is harmful if inhaled in large amounts. Describe three ways the town government might respond to this externality. What are the pros and cons of each of your solutions?

# IN THE NEWS

## Children As Externalities

*This tongue-in-cheek editorial from* The Economist *calls attention to a common externality that is not fully appreciated.*

### Mum's the Word: When Children Should Be Screened and Not Heard

We live in increasingly intolerant times. Signs proliferate demanding no smoking, no spitting, no parking, even no walking. ... Posh clubs and restaurants have long had 'no jeans' rules, but these days you can be too smart. Some London hostelries have 'no suits' policies, for fear that boisterous city traders in suits might spoil the atmosphere. Environmentalists have long demanded all sorts of bans on cars. Mobile telephones are the latest target: some trains, airline lounges, restaurants, and even golf courses are being designated 'no phone' areas.

If intolerance really has to be the spirit of this age, *The Economist* would like to suggest restrictions on another source of noise pollution: children. Lest you dismiss this as mere prejudice, we can even produce a good economic argument for it. Smoking, driving, and mobile phones all cause what economists call 'negative externalities.' That is, the costs of these activities to other people tend to exceed the costs to the individuals of their proclivities. The invisible hand of the market fumbles, leading resources astray. Thus, because a driver's private motoring costs do not reflect the costs he imposes on others in

the form of pollution and congestion, he uses the car more than is socially desirable. Likewise, it is argued, smokers take too little care to ensure that their acrid fumes do not damage other people around them.

Governments typically respond to such market failures in two ways. One is higher taxes, to make polluters pay the full cost of their anti-social behaviour. The other is regulation, such as emission standards or bans on smoking in public places. Both approaches might work for children.

For children, just like cigarettes or mobile phones, clearly impose a negative externality on people who are near them. Anybody who has suffered a 12-hour flight with a bawling baby in the row immediately ahead, or a bored youngster viciously kicking their seat from behind, will grasp this as quickly as they would love to grasp the youngster's neck. Here is a clear case of market failure: parents do not bear the full costs (indeed young babies travel free), so they are too ready to take their noisy brats with them. Where is the invisible hand when it is needed to administer a good smack?

The solution is obvious. All airlines, trains, and restaurants should create child-free zones. Put all those children at the back of the plane and parents might make more effort to minimise

their noise pollution. And instead of letting children pay less and babies go free, they should be charged (or taxed) more than adults, with the revenues used to subsidise seats immediately in front of the war-zone.

Passengers could then request a no-children seat, just as they now ask for a no-smoking one. As more women choose not to have children and the number of older people without young children increases, the demand for child-free travel will expand. Well, yes, it is a bit intolerant – but why shouldn't parents be treated as badly as smokers? And at least there is an obvious airline to pioneer the scheme: Virgin.

## CONCLUSION

The invisible hand is powerful but not omnipotent. A market's equilibrium maximizes the sum of producer and consumer surplus. When the buyers and sellers in the market are the only interested parties, this outcome is efficient from the standpoint of society as a whole. But when there are external effects, such as pollution, evaluating a market outcome requires taking into account the well-being of third parties as well. In this case, the invisible hand of the marketplace may fail to allocate resources efficiently.

In some cases, people can solve the problem of externalities on their own. The Coase theorem suggests that the interested parties can bargain among themselves and agree on an efficient solution. Sometimes, however, an efficient outcome cannot be reached, perhaps because the large number of interested parties makes bargaining difficult.

When people cannot solve the problem of externalities privately, the government often steps in. Yet, even now, society should not abandon market forces entirely. Rather, the government can address the problem by requiring decision makers to bear the full costs of their actions. Pigovian taxes on emissions and pollution permits, for instance, are designed to internalize the externality of pollution. Increasingly, they are being seen as effective policies for those interested in protecting the environment. Market forces, properly redirected, are often the best remedy for market failure.

## SUMMARY

- When a transaction between a buyer and seller directly affects a third party, the effect is called an externality. Negative externalities, such as pollution, cause the socially optimal quantity in a market to be less than the equilibrium quantity. Positive externalities, such as technology spillovers, cause the socially optimal quantity to be greater than the equilibrium quantity.

- Those affected by externalities can sometimes solve the problem privately. For instance, when one business confers an externality on another business, the two businesses can internalize the externality by merging. Alternatively, the interested parties can solve the problem by negotiating a contract. According to the Coase theorem, if people can bargain without cost, then they

can always reach an agreement in which resources are allocated efficiently. In many cases, however, reaching a bargain among the many interested parties is difficult, so the Coase theorem does not apply.

- When private parties cannot adequately deal with external effects, such as pollution, the government often steps in. Sometimes the government prevents socially inefficient activity by regulating behaviour. At other times it internalizes an externality using Pigovian taxes. Another public policy is to issue permits. For instance, the government could protect the environment by issuing a limited number of pollution permits. The end result of this policy is largely the same as imposing Pigovian taxes on polluters.

## KEY CONCEPTS

externality, p. 189
internalizing an externality, p. 193

Coase theorem, p. 196
transaction costs, p. 197

Pigovian tax, p. 198

# QUESTIONS FOR REVIEW

1. Give an example of a negative externality and an example of a positive externality.

2. Use a supply and demand diagram to explain the effect of a negative externality in production.

3. In what way does the patent system help society solve an externality problem?

4. List some of the ways that the problems caused by externalities can be solved without government intervention.

5. Imagine that you are a non-smoker sharing a room with a smoker. According to the Coase theorem, what determines whether your roommate smokes in the room? Is this outcome efficient? How do you and your roommate reach this solution?

6. What are Pigovian taxes? Why do economists prefer them over regulations as a way to protect the environment from pollution?

# PROBLEMS AND APPLICATIONS

1. Do you agree with the following statements? Why or why not?
   a. 'The benefits of Pigovian taxes as a way to reduce pollution have to be weighed against the deadweight losses that these taxes cause.'
   b. 'When deciding whether to levy a Pigovian tax on consumers or producers, the government should be careful to levy the tax on the side of the market generating the externality.'

2. Consider the market for fire extinguishers.
   a. Why might fire extinguishers exhibit positive externalities?
   b. Draw a graph of the market for fire extinguishers, labelling the demand curve, the social value curve, the supply curve and the social cost curve.
   c. Indicate the market equilibrium level of output and the efficient level of output. Give an intuitive explanation for why these quantities differ.
   d. If the external benefit is €10 per extinguisher, describe a government policy that would result in the efficient outcome.

3. In many countries, contributions to charitable organizations are deductible from income tax. In what way does this government policy encourage private solutions to externalities?

4. Mick loves playing rock music at high volume. Luciano loves opera and hates rock music. Unfortunately, they are next-door neighbours in an apartment building with paper-thin walls.
   a. What is the externality here?
   b. What command-and-control policy might the landlord impose? Could such a policy lead to an inefficient outcome?

   c. Suppose the landlord lets the tenants do whatever they want. According to the Coase theorem, how might Mick and Luciano reach an efficient outcome on their own? What might prevent them from reaching an efficient outcome?

5. It is rumoured that the Swiss government subsidizes cattle farming, and that the subsidy is larger in areas with more tourist attractions. Can you think of a reason why this policy might be efficient?

6. Greater consumption of alcohol leads to more motor vehicle accidents and, thus, imposes costs on people who do not drink and drive.
   a. Illustrate the market for alcohol, labelling the demand curve, the social value curve, the supply curve, the social cost curve, the market equilibrium level of output and the efficient level of output.
   b. On your graph, shade the area corresponding to the deadweight loss of the market equilibrium. (Hint: the deadweight loss occurs because some units of alcohol are consumed for which the social cost exceeds the social value.) Explain.

7. Many observers believe that the levels of pollution in our economy are too high.
   a. If society wishes to reduce overall pollution by a certain amount, why is it efficient to have different amounts of reduction at different firms?
   b. Command-and-control approaches often rely on uniform reductions among firms. Why are these approaches generally unable to target the firms that should undertake bigger reductions?
   c. Economists argue that appropriate Pigovian taxes or tradable pollution rights will result in efficient pollution

reduction. How do these approaches target the firms that should undertake bigger reductions?

8. The Pristine River (or the 'Blue Pristine', as it is affectionately known) has two polluting firms on its banks. European Industrial and Creative Chemicals each dump 100 tonnes of effluent into the river each year. The cost of reducing effluent emissions per tonne equals €10 for European Industrial and €100 for Creative. The government wants to reduce overall pollution from 200 tonnes to 50 tonnes.

   a. If the government knew the cost of reduction for each firm, what reductions would it impose to reach its overall goal? What would be the cost to each firm and the total cost to the firms together?

   b. In a more typical situation, the government would not know the cost of pollution reduction at each firm. If the government decided to reach its overall goal by imposing uniform reductions on the firms, calculate the reduction made by each firm, the cost to each firm and the total cost to the firms together.

   c. Compare the total cost of pollution reduction in parts (a) and (b). If the government does not know the cost of reduction for each firm, is there still some way for it to reduce pollution to 50 tonnes at the total cost you calculated in part (a)? Explain.

9. 'A fine is a tax for doing something wrong. A tax is a fine for doing something right.' Discuss.

10. Figure 10.4 shows that for any given demand curve for the right to pollute, the government can achieve the same outcome either by setting a price with a Pigovian tax or by setting a quantity with pollution permits. Suppose there is a sharp improvement in the technology for controlling pollution.

   a. Using graphs similar to those in Figure 10.4, illustrate the effect of this development on the demand for pollution rights.

   b. What is the effect on the price and quantity of pollution under each regulatory system? Explain.

11. Suppose that the government decides to issue tradable permits for a certain form of pollution.

   a. Does it matter for economic efficiency whether the government distributes or auctions the permits? Does it matter in any other ways?

   b. If the government chooses to distribute the permits, does the allocation of permits among firms matter for efficiency? Does it matter in any other ways?

12. The primary cause of global warming is carbon dioxide, which enters the atmosphere in varying amounts from different countries but is distributed equally around the globe within a year. In order to solve this problem, some economists have argued that carbon dioxide emissions should be reduced in countries where the costs are least, with the countries that bear that burden being compensated by the rest of the world.

   a. Why is international cooperation necessary to reach an efficient outcome?

   b. Is it possible to devise a compensation scheme such that all countries would be better off than under a system of uniform emission reductions? Explain.

13. Some people object to market-based policies to reduce pollution, claiming that they place a monetary value on cleaning our air and water. Economists reply that society *implicitly* places a monetary value on environmental clean-up even under command-and-control policies. Discuss why this is true.

14. (This problem is challenging.) There are three industrial firms in Eurovia.

| Firm | Initial pollution level | Cost of reducing pollution by 1 unit |
|------|-------------------------|--------------------------------------|
| A | 70 units | €20 |
| B | 80 | 25 |
| C | 50 | 10 |

The government wants to reduce pollution to 120 units, so it gives each firm 40 tradable pollution permits.

   a. Who sells permits and how many do they sell? Who buys permits and how many do they buy? Briefly explain why the sellers and buyers are each willing to do so. What is the total cost of pollution reduction in this situation?

   b. How much higher would the costs of pollution reduction be if the permits could not be traded?

For further resources, visit
http://www.thomsonlearning.co.uk/mankiw_taylor

# 11 PUBLIC GOODS AND COMMON RESOURCES

An old song lyric maintains that 'the best things in life are free.' A moment's thought reveals a long list of goods that the songwriter could have had in mind. Nature provides some of them, such as rivers, mountains, beaches, lakes and oceans. The government provides others, such as playgrounds, parks and parades. In each case, people do not pay a fee when they choose to enjoy the benefit of the good.

Free goods provide a special challenge for economic analysis. Most goods in our economy are allocated in markets, where buyers pay for what they receive and sellers are paid for what they provide. For these goods, prices are the signals that guide the decisions of buyers and sellers. When goods are available free of charge, however, the market forces that normally allocate resources in our economy are absent.

In this chapter we examine the problems that arise for goods without market prices. Our analysis will shed light on one of the *Ten Principles of Economics* in Chapter 1: governments can sometimes improve market outcomes. When a good does not have a price attached to it, private markets cannot ensure that the good is produced and consumed in the proper amounts. In such cases, government policy can potentially remedy the market failure and raise economic well-being.

## THE DIFFERENT KINDS OF GOODS

How well do markets work in providing the goods that people want? The answer to this question depends on the good being considered. As we discussed in

Chapter 7, we can rely on the market to provide the efficient number of ice cream cornets: the price of ice cream cornets adjusts to balance supply and demand, and this equilibrium maximizes the sum of producer and consumer surplus. Yet, as we discussed in Chapter 10, we cannot rely on the market to prevent aluminium manufacturers from polluting the air we breathe: buyers and sellers in a market typically do not take account of the external effects of their decisions. Thus, markets work well when the good is ice cream, but they work badly when the good is clean air.

In thinking about the various goods in the economy, it is useful to group them according to two characteristics:

**excludability**
the property of a good whereby a person can be prevented from using it
**rivalry**
the property of a good whereby one person's use diminishes other people's use
**private goods**
goods that are both excludable and rival

- Is the good **excludable?** Can people be prevented from using the good?
- Is the good **rival?** Does one person's use of the good diminish another person's ability to use it?

Using these two characteristics, Figure 11.1 divides goods into four categories:

1. **Private goods** are both excludable and rival. Consider an ice cream cornet, for example. An ice cream cornet is excludable because it is possible to prevent someone from eating an ice cream cornet – you just don't give it to him. An ice cream cornet is rival because if one person eats an ice cream cornet, another person cannot eat the same cornet. Most goods in the economy are private goods like ice cream cornets. When we analysed supply and demand in Chapters 4, 5 and 6 and the efficiency of markets in Chapters 7, 8 and 9, we implicitly assumed that goods were both excludable and rival.

**public goods**
goods that are neither excludable nor rival

2. **Public goods** are neither excludable nor rival. That is, people cannot be prevented from using a public good, and one person's use of a public good does not reduce another person's ability to use it. For example, a country's national defence system: it protects all of the country's citizens equally and the fact that one person is being defended does not affect whether or not another citizen is defended.

---

**FIGURE 11.1**

**Four Types of Goods**

*Goods can be grouped into four categories according to two questions: (1) Is the good excludable? That is, can people be prevented from using it? (2) Is the good rival? That is, does one person's use of the good diminish other people's use of it? This diagram gives examples of goods in each of the four categories.*

|  |  | Rival? | |
|---|---|---|---|
|  |  | Yes | No |
| **Excludable?** | Yes | Private goods<br><br>• Ice cream cornets<br>• Clothing<br>• Congested toll roads | Natural monopolies<br><br>• The fire service<br>• Cable TV<br>• Uncongested toll roads |
|  | No | Common resources<br><br>• Fish in the ocean<br>• The environment<br>• Congested non-toll roads | Public goods<br><br>• Flood-control dams<br>• National defence<br>• Uncongested non-toll roads |

3. **Common resources** are rival but not excludable. For example, fish in the ocean are a rival good: when one person catches fish, there are fewer fish for the next person to catch. Yet these fish are not an excludable good because, given the vast size of an ocean, it is difficult to stop fishermen from taking fish out of it.

4. When a good is excludable but not rival, it is an example of a *natural monopoly*. For instance, consider fire protection in a small town. It is easy to exclude people from using this good: the fire service can just let their house burn down. Yet fire protection is not rival. Firefighters spend much of their time waiting for a fire, so protecting an extra house is unlikely to reduce the protection available to others. In other words, once a town has paid for the fire service, the additional cost of protecting one more house is small. In Chapter 15 we give a more complete definition of natural monopolies and study them in some detail.

**common resources**
goods that are rival but not excludable

In this chapter we examine goods that are not excludable and, therefore, are available to everyone free of charge: public goods and common resources. As we will see, this topic is closely related to the study of externalities. For both public goods and common resources, externalities arise because something of value has no price attached to it. If one person were to provide a public good, such as a national defence system, other people would be better off, and yet they could not be charged for this benefit. Similarly, when one person uses a common resource, such as the fish in the ocean, other people are worse off, and yet they are not compensated for this loss. Because of these external effects, private decisions about consumption and production can lead to an inefficient allocation of resources, and government intervention can potentially raise economic well-being.

> **Quick Quiz**  Define *public goods* and *common resources*, and give an example of each.

# PUBLIC GOODS

To understand how public goods differ from other goods and what problems they present for society, let's consider an example: a fireworks display. This good is not excludable because it is impossible to prevent someone from seeing fireworks, and it is not rival because one person's enjoyment of fireworks does not reduce anyone else's enjoyment of them.

## The Free Rider Problem

The citizens of a small English town, Little Hamlet, like seeing fireworks on 5 November, Guy Fawkes' Night. Each of the town's 500 residents places a £10 value on the experience. The cost of putting on a fireworks display is £1,000. Because the £5,000 of benefits exceed the £1,000 of costs, it is efficient for Little Hamlet residents to have a fireworks display on the 5 November.

Would the private market produce the efficient outcome? Probably not. Imagine that Gertrude, a Little Hamlet entrepreneur, decided to put on a fireworks display. Gertrude would surely have trouble selling tickets to the event because her potential customers would quickly figure out that they could see the fireworks even without a ticket. Because fireworks are not excludable, people have an incentive to be free riders. A **free rider** is a person who receives the benefit of a good but avoids paying for it.

**free rider**
a person who receives the benefit of a good but avoids paying for it

One way to view this market failure is that it arises because of an externality. If Gertrude did put on the fireworks display, she would confer an external benefit on those who saw the display without paying for it. When deciding whether to put on the display, Gertrude ignores these external benefits. Even though a fireworks display is socially desirable, it is not privately profitable. As a result, Gertrude makes the socially inefficient decision not to put on the display.

Although the private market fails to supply the fireworks display demanded by Little Hamlet residents, the solution to Little Hamlet's problem is obvious: the local government can sponsor a Guy Fawkes' Night celebration. The town council raises revenue by levying taxes on property in the area (in the UK these local property taxes are known as local rates). Suppose that the council uses this mechanism so as to raise on average an extra £2 from every resident of Little Hamlet and then uses the resulting revenue to hire Gertrude to produce the fireworks. Everyone in Little Hamlet is better off by £8 – the £10 in value from the fireworks minus the £2 tax bill. Gertrude can help Little Hamlet reach the efficient outcome as a public employee even though she could not do so as a private entrepreneur.

The story of Little Hamlet is simplified, but it is also realistic. In fact, many local councils in the United Kingdom do pay for fireworks on 5 November, just as many local governments in France pay for fireworks on 14 July (Bastille Day) and many local governments in the USA pay for fireworks on 4 July (Independence Day). Moreover, the story shows a general lesson about public goods: because public goods are not excludable, the free-rider problem prevents the private market from supplying them. The government, however, can potentially remedy the problem. If the government decides that the total benefits exceed the costs, it can provide the public good and pay for it with tax revenue, making everyone better off.

## Some Important Public Goods

There are many examples of public goods. Here we consider three of the most important.

**National Defence** The defence of the country from foreign aggressors is a classic example of a public good. Once the country is defended, it is impossible to prevent any single person from enjoying the benefit of this defence. Moreover, when one person enjoys the benefit of national defence, he does not reduce the benefit to anyone else. Thus, national defence is neither excludable nor rival.

National defence is also one of the most expensive public goods. In the UK in 2002 it accounted for about £25 billion of government expenditure – the fourth largest category (behind social security, the National Health Service and education). People disagree about whether this amount is too small or too large, but almost no one doubts that some government spending on national defence is necessary. Even economists who advocate small government agree that the national defence is a public good the government should provide.

**Basic Research** The creation of knowledge is a public good. If a mathematician proves a new theorem, the theorem enters the general pool of knowledge that anyone can use without charge. Because knowledge is a public good, profit-seeking firms tend to free ride on the knowledge created by others and, as a result, devote too few resources to creating new knowledge.

In evaluating the appropriate policy towards knowledge creation, it is important to distinguish general knowledge from specific, technological knowledge. Specific, technological knowledge, such as the invention of a better battery, can be patented. The inventor thus obtains much of the benefit of his invention, although

*"I like the concept if we can do it with no new taxes."*

certainly not all of it. By contrast, a mathematician cannot patent a theorem; such general knowledge is freely available to everyone. In other words, the patent system makes specific, technological knowledge excludable, whereas general knowledge is not excludable.

The government tries to provide the public good of general knowledge in various ways. Government agencies such as the UK's Research Councils subsidize basic research in many academic disciplines, including medicine, mathematics, science and even economics. Some people justify government funding of space exploration programmes – for example by public funding of the European Space Agency (ESA) or the US National Aeronautics and Space Administration (NASA) – on the grounds that it adds to society's pool of knowledge. Certainly, many private goods, including bullet-proof vests and the instant drink Tang, use materials that were first developed by scientists and engineers trying to land a man on the moon. Determining the appropriate level of governmental support for these endeavours is difficult because the benefits are hard to measure. Moreover, the politicians who appropriate funds for research usually have little expertise in science and, therefore, are not in the best position to judge what lines of research will produce the largest benefits.

**Fighting Poverty** Many government expenditure programmes are aimed at helping the poor. These anti-poverty programmes are financed by taxes on families that are financially more successful.

Economists disagree among themselves about what role the government should play in fighting poverty. Here we note one important argument: Advocates of anti-poverty programmes claim that fighting poverty is a public good.

Suppose that everyone prefers to live in a society without poverty. Even if this preference is strong and widespread, fighting poverty is not a 'good' that the private market can provide. No single individual can eliminate poverty because the problem is so large. Moreover, private charity is hard pressed to solve the problem: people who do not donate to charity can free ride on the generosity of others. In this case, taxing the wealthy to raise the living standards of the poor can make everyone better off. The poor are better off because they now enjoy a higher standard of living, and those paying the taxes are better off because they enjoy living in a society with less poverty.

# CASE STUDY

## Are Lighthouses Public Goods?

Some goods can switch between being public goods and being private goods depending on the circumstances. For example, a fireworks display is a public good if performed in a town with many residents. Yet if performed at a private amusement park, such as Disneyland Paris, a fireworks display is more like a private good because visitors to the park pay for admission.

Another example is a lighthouse. Economists have long used lighthouses as an example of a public good. Lighthouses are used to mark specific locations so that passing ships can avoid treacherous waters. The benefit that the lighthouse provides to the ship captain is neither excludable nor rival, so each captain has an incentive to free ride by using the lighthouse to navigate without paying for the service. Because of this free rider problem, private markets usually fail to provide the lighthouses that ship captains need. As a result, most lighthouses today are operated by the government.

In some cases, however, lighthouses may be closer to private goods. On the coast of England in the 19th century, some lighthouses were privately owned and operated. Instead of trying to charge ship captains for the service, however, the owner of the lighthouse charged the owner of the nearby port. If the port owner did not pay, the lighthouse owner turned off the light and ships avoided that port.

In deciding whether something is a public good, one must determine the number of beneficiaries and whether these beneficiaries can be excluded from using the good. A free rider problem arises when the number of beneficiaries is large and exclusion of any one of them is impossible. If a lighthouse benefits many ship captains, it is a public good. Yet if it primarily benefits a single port owner, it is more like a private good.

*What kind of good?*

## The Difficult Job of Cost–Benefit Analysis

So far we have seen that the government provides public goods because the private market on its own will not produce an efficient quantity. Yet deciding that the government must play a role is only the first step. The government must then determine what kinds of public goods to provide and in what quantities.

Suppose that the government is considering a public project, such as building a new motorway. To judge whether to build the motorway, it must compare the total benefits of all those who would use it to the costs of building and maintaining it. To make this decision, the government might hire a team of economists and engineers to conduct a study, called a **cost–benefit analysis,** the goal of which is to estimate the total costs and benefits of the project to society as a whole.

**cost–benefit analysis**
a study that compares the costs and benefits to society of providing a public good

Cost–benefit analysts have a tough job. Because the motorway will be available to everyone free of charge, there is no price with which to judge the value of the motorway. Simply asking people how much they would value the motorway is not reliable: quantifying benefits is difficult using the results from a questionnaire, and respondents have little incentive to tell the truth. Those who would use the motorway have an incentive to exaggerate the benefit they receive to get the motorway built. Those who would be harmed by the motorway have an incentive to exaggerate the costs to them to prevent the motorway from being built.

The efficient provision of public goods is, therefore, intrinsically more difficult than the efficient provision of private goods. Private goods are provided in the market. Buyers of a private good reveal the value they place on it by the prices they are willing to pay. Sellers reveal their costs by the prices they are willing to accept. By contrast, cost–benefit analysts do not observe any price signals when evaluating whether the government should provide a public good. Their findings on the costs and benefits of public projects are, therefore, rough approximations at best.

## CASE STUDY

### How Much is a Life Worth?

Imagine that you have been elected to serve as a member of your local town council. The town engineer comes to you with a proposal: the town can spend €10,000 to build and operate a traffic light at the intersection of Main Street (the town's busy main road) and Easy Street (the much quieter, leafy road where the stockbrokers live). At present, there are only signs instructing motorists entering Main Street from Easy Street that they must stop and give way to Main Street traffic. The benefit of the traffic light is increased safety. The engineer estimates, based on data from similar intersections, that the traffic light would reduce the risk of a fatal traffic accident over the lifetime of the traffic light from 1.6 to 1.1 per cent. Should you spend the money for the new light?

To answer this question, you turn to cost–benefit analysis. But you quickly run into an obstacle: the costs and benefits must be measured in the same units if you are to compare them meaningfully. The cost is measured in euros, but the benefit – the possibility of saving a person's life – is not directly monetary. To make your decision, you have to put a monetary value on a human life.

At first, you may be tempted to conclude that a human life is priceless. After all, there is probably no amount of money that you could be paid to voluntarily give up your life or that of a loved one. This suggests that a human life has an infinite monetary value.

For the purposes of cost–benefit analysis, however, this answer leads to nonsensical results. If we truly placed an infinite value on human life, we should be placing traffic lights on every street corner. Similarly, we should all be driving large cars with all the latest safety features, instead of smaller ones with fewer safety features. Yet traffic lights are not at every corner, and people sometimes choose to buy small cars without side-impact air bags or antilock brakes. In both our public and private decisions, we are at times willing to risk our lives to save some money.

Once we have accepted the idea that a person's life does have an implicit monetary value, how can we determine what that value is? One approach, sometimes used by courts to award damages in wrongful death suits, is to look at the total amount of money a person would have earned if he or she had lived. This approach was also used by the US government in deciding what amount of damages to award to the families of people killed in the terrorist attack on the World Trade Center in September 2001. Economists are often critical of this approach. It has the bizarre implication that the life of a retired or disabled person has no value.

Perhaps a better way to value human life is to look at the risks that people are voluntarily willing to take and how much they must be paid for taking them. Mortality risk varies across jobs, for example. Construction workers in high-rise buildings face greater risk of death on the job than office workers do. By comparing wages in risky and less risky occupations, controlling for education, experience and other determinants of wages, economists can get some sense about what value people put on their own lives. Studies using this approach conclude that the value of a human life is about €10 million.

We can now return to our original example and respond to the town engineer. The traffic light reduces the risk of fatality by 0.5 percentage points. Thus, the expected benefit from having the traffic light is 0.005 × €10 million, or €50,000. This estimate of the benefit well exceeds the cost of €10,000, so you should approve the project.

**Quick Quiz** What is the free rider problem? • Why does the free rider problem induce the government to provide public goods? • How should the government decide whether to provide a public good?

# COMMON RESOURCES

Common resources, like public goods, are not excludable: they are available free of charge to anyone who wants to use them. Common resources are, however, rival: one person's use of the common resource reduces other people's ability to use it. Thus, common resources give rise to a new problem. Once the good is provided, policy makers need to be concerned about how much it is used. This problem is best understood from the classic parable called the **Tragedy of the Commons.**

**Tragedy of the Commons**
a parable that illustrates why common resources get used more than is desirable from the standpoint of society as a whole

## The Tragedy of the Commons

Consider life in a small medieval town. Of the many economic activities that take place in the town, one of the most important is raising sheep. Many of the town's families own flocks of sheep and support themselves by selling the sheep's wool, which is used to make clothing.

As our story begins, the sheep spend much of their time grazing on the land surrounding the town, called the Town Common. No family owns the land. Instead, the town residents own the land collectively, and all the residents are allowed to graze their sheep on it. Collective ownership works well because land is plentiful. As long as everyone can get all the good grazing land they want, the Town Common is not a rival good, and allowing residents' sheep to graze for free causes no problems. Everyone in town is happy.

As the years pass, the population of the town grows, and so does the number of sheep grazing on the Town Common. With a growing number of sheep and a fixed amount of land, the land starts to lose its ability to replenish itself. Eventually, the land is grazed so heavily that it becomes barren. With no grass left on the Town Common, raising sheep is impossible, and the town's once prosperous wool industry disappears and, tragically, many families lose their source of livelihood.

What causes the tragedy? Why do the shepherds allow the sheep population to grow so large that it destroys the Town Common? The reason is that social and private incentives differ. Avoiding the destruction of the grazing land depends on the collective action of the shepherds. If the shepherds acted together, they could reduce the sheep population to a size that the Town Common could support. Yet no single family has an incentive to reduce the size of its own flock because each flock represents only a small part of the problem.

In essence, the Tragedy of the Commons arises because of an externality. When one family's flock grazes on the common land, it reduces the quality of the land

# IN THE NEWS

## A Free Market Solution, I Presume?

*Left-wing Mayor Ken Livingstone introduced a radical free-market scheme in an attempt to solve London's traffic congestion, as this article from The Economist discusses.*

### Traffic Decongestant: Charging is the Right Way To Go, Even If London's Scheme Is Flawed

Threaten a man's freedom to drive and you strike at the core of his being. Anybody who doubts that has not been to a London dinner party lately. In the run-up to its introduction on February 17th, the congestion charge has overtaken the war as a topic of conversation and a cause for complaint.

From February 17th, drivers entering an eight-square-mile patch bounded by Park Lane, Euston Road, Commercial Street and Vauxhall will have to pay £5 ($8) between 7am and 6.30pm on weekdays. Ken Livingstone, London's mayor, hopes to cut traffic by 15%, leading to a 25% reduction in traffic delays. The net proceeds – expected to be around £120m a year – are to be used to improve public transport. Other cities have tried similar schemes, but nothing on London's scale. It is a measure of the city's desperation that a socialist mayor is introducing a practice – road pricing – normally advocated by free-market rightwingers, from Adam Smith in 1776 to Milton Friedman in 1951. Mr Livingstone is brave. If the scheme works, it will be taken for granted, and if it fails, he will probably lose the next mayoral election.

All over the world, people are finding themselves increasingly bogged down in congestion. Governments can either choose to leave people fuming in their cars (which wastes people's time and pollutes the air) or they can ration road space by regulation or by

price. Regulation – banning people from driving in certain areas at certain times – is relatively clumsy. Rationing by price is more efficient because it allocates road space to those who value it most.

Charging people for new, fast roads (the French autoroutes, for instance, which were built alongside crowded *routes nationales*) is uncontentious. But governments fear that if they introduce charges on existing roads, drivers will revolt at the idea of paying for something they have been getting for free. The Dutch, for example, have been discussing a scheme for crowded motorways for years, but no coalition government has ever felt that it could hold together in the turbulence that would follow such a radical scheme. Even in highly disciplined Singapore, home of the most sophisticated road-pricing system in the world, citizens have had to be cajoled into accepting the latest flexible charging system with reductions on other motor taxes.

Still, if congestion charging can work anywhere, London is probably the place. It is the most congested part of Europe's most congested country. Since the idea of a motorway box inside the city was abandoned because of local opposition in the 1960s, nobody has put forward a better idea for what to do. And Mr Livingstone can claim a mandate to try congestion charging: it was part of his pitch to the voters before he was elected two years ago.

Some criticize the charge on the grounds that it is a flat tax, and therefore regressive. That doesn't wash. Most weekday drivers in central

London are affluent. Poorer people tend to use the public transport systems that will benefit from extra spending. Other critics complain that the charge is unfair on particular groups – small businesses, for instance, and parents living just outside the zone who find themselves paying £25 a week just to take their children to school. That's true, but if the overall effect is good enough, it is worth a bit of injustice.

There are more serious grounds for worry. The crude technology, based on cameras reading number-plates, may not work. The charge may have little impact, since people who have company parking-spaces or are prepared to pay parking fees of as much as £20 a day will hardly balk at another £5. If it makes a difference, it is likely to divert cars from central London (where the traffic is already inhibited by high

▶

◀

parking charges) to areas that are even more crowded outside the zone.

Even some of those who support road pricing argue against Mr Livingstone's scheme on the grounds that its flaws could lead to failure, and that if it is abandoned it will set the cause of road pricing back by ten years. But if it does not work at first, the correct response is not to give it up, but to change it – raise the charge, widen the area it covers, switch to better, satellite-based technology, which would allow flexible charges everywhere within the M25 motorway encircling London, and indeed on that overcrowded motorway too.

With their awful commuter trains and creaking underground, Londoners are used to failures in their transport system. That is no reason to shirk a bold attempt to make things better, nor to retreat if it does not work at the first go.

Source: *The Economist*, 13 February 2003. Copyright © The Economist Newspaper Limited, London.

available for other families. Because people neglect this negative externality when deciding how many sheep to own, the result is an excessive number of sheep.

If the tragedy had been foreseen, the town could have solved the problem in various ways. It could have regulated the number of sheep in each family's flock, internalized the externality by taxing sheep, or auctioned off a limited number of sheep-grazing permits. That is, the medieval town could have dealt with the problem of overgrazing in the way that modern society deals with the problem of pollution.

In the case of land, however, there is a simpler solution. The town can divide up the land among town families. Each family can enclose its allotment of land with a fence and then protect it from excessive grazing. In this way, the land becomes a private good rather than a common resource. This outcome in fact occurred during the enclosure movement in England in the 17th century.

The Tragedy of the Commons is a story with a general lesson: when one person uses a common resource, he diminishes other people's enjoyment of it. Because of this negative externality, common resources tend to be used excessively. The government can solve the problem by reducing use of the common resource through regulation or taxes. Alternatively, the government can sometimes turn the common resource into a private good.

This lesson has been known for thousands of years. The ancient Greek philosopher Aristotle pointed out the problem with common resources: 'What is common to many is taken least care of, for all men have greater regard for what is their own than for what they possess in common with others.'

## Some Important Common Resources

There are many examples of common resources. In almost all cases, the same problem arises as in the Tragedy of the Commons: private decision makers use the common resource too much. Governments often regulate behaviour or impose fees to mitigate the problem of overuse.

**Clean Air and Water**  As we discussed in Chapter 10, markets do not adequately protect the environment. Pollution is a negative externality that can be remedied with regulations or with Pigovian taxes on polluting activities. One can view this market failure as an example of a common-resource problem. Clean air and clean water are common resources like open grazing land, and excessive pollution is like excessive grazing. Environmental degradation is a modern Tragedy of the Commons.

**Congested Roads**  Roads can be either public goods or common resources. If a road is not congested, then one person's use does not affect anyone else. In this case, use is not rival, and the road is a public good. Yet if a road is congested, then use of that road yields a negative externality. When one person drives on the road, it becomes more crowded, and other people must drive more slowly. In this case, the road is a common resource.

One way for the government to address the problem of road congestion is to charge drivers a toll. A toll is, in essence, a Pigovian tax on the externality of congestion. Often, as in the case of local roads, tolls are not a practical solution because the cost of collecting them is too high. Nevertheless, tolls are often charged on stretches of motorways in continental Europe and the USA, and occasionally in the UK (on the M6, for example).

Sometimes congestion is a problem only at certain times of day. If a bridge is heavily travelled only during rush hour, for instance, the congestion externality is larger during this time than during other times of day. The efficient way to deal with these externalities is to charge higher tolls during rush hour. This toll would provide an incentive for drivers to alter their schedules and would reduce traffic when congestion is greatest.

Another policy that responds to the problem of road congestion, discussed in a case study in the previous chapter, is the tax on petrol. Petrol is a complementary good to driving: an increase in the price of petrol tends to reduce the quantity of driving demanded. Therefore, a petrol tax reduces road congestion. A petrol tax, however, is an imperfect solution to road congestion. The problem is that the petrol tax affects other decisions besides the amount of driving on congested roads. For example, the petrol tax discourages driving on non-congested roads, even though there is no congestion externality for these roads.

**Fish, Whales and Other Wildlife** Many species of animals are common resources. Fish and whales, for instance, have commercial value, and anyone can go to the ocean and catch whatever is available. Each person has little incentive to maintain the species for the next year. Just as excessive grazing can destroy the Town Common, excessive fishing and whaling can destroy commercially valuable marine populations.

The ocean remains one of the least regulated common resources. Two problems prevent an easy solution. First, many countries have access to the oceans, so any solution would require international cooperation among countries that hold different values. Secondly, because the oceans are so vast, enforcing any agreement is difficult. As a result, fishing rights have been a frequent source of international tension among normally friendly countries.

Within the United Kingdom and other European countries, various laws aim to protect fish and other wildlife. For example, the government charges for fishing and hunting licences, and it restricts the lengths of the fishing and hunting seasons. Fishermen are often required to throw back small fish, and hunters can kill only a limited number of animals or shoot certain wild birds such as pheasant or grouse during specified periods of the year. All these laws reduce the use of a common resource and help maintain animal populations.

## CASE STUDY

### Why the Cow is Not Extinct

Throughout history, many species of animals have been threatened with extinction. When Europeans first arrived in North America, more than 60 million buffalo roamed the continent. Yet hunting the buffalo was so popular during the 19th century that by 1900 the animal's population fell to about 400

*"Can the market become my friend too?"*

before the government stepped in to protect the species. In some African countries today, the elephant faces a similar challenge, as poachers kill the animals for the ivory in their tusks.

Yet not all animals with commercial value face this threat. The cow, for example, is a valuable source of food, but no one worries that the cow will soon be extinct. Indeed, the great demand for beef seems to ensure that the species will continue to thrive.

Why is the commercial value of ivory a threat to the elephant, while the commercial value of beef is a guardian of the cow? The reason is that elephants are a common resource, whereas cows are a private good. Elephants roam freely without any owners. Each poacher has a strong incentive to kill as many elephants as he can find. Because poachers are numerous, each poacher has only a slight incentive to preserve the elephant population. By contrast, cows live on farms that are privately owned. Each farmer takes great effort to maintain the cow population on his farm because he reaps the benefit of these efforts.

Governments have tried to solve the elephant's problem in two ways. Some countries, such as Kenya, Tanzania and Uganda, have made it illegal to kill elephants and sell their ivory. Yet these laws have been hard to enforce, and elephant populations have continued to dwindle. By contrast, other countries, such as Botswana, Malawi, Namibia and Zimbabwe, have made elephants a private good by allowing people to kill elephants, but only those on their own property. Landowners now have an incentive to preserve the species on their own land, and as a result, elephant populations have started to rise. With private ownership and the profit motive now on its side, the African elephant might someday be as safe from extinction as the cow.

**Quick Quiz** Why do governments try to limit the use of common resources?

# IN THE NEWS

## Greens Turn To the Market

*The 'green movement' – the set of groups that make up the broadly environmentalist lobby – has traditionally seen free market economics as the villain of the piece. Now there is some sign that the greens may be utilizing economic analysis to see that free markets need not be environmentally unfriendly, as this article discusses.*

**The Invisible Green Hand: Markets Could Be a Potent Force For Greenery – If Only Greens Could Learn to Love Them**

'Mandate, regulate and litigate.' That has been the environmentalists' rallying cry for ages. Nowhere in the green manifesto has there been much mention of the market. And, oddly, it was market-minded America that led the dirigiste trend. Three decades ago, Congress passed a sequence of laws, including the Clean Air Act, which set lofty goals and generally set rigid technological standards. Much of the world followed America's lead. ...

But times may be changing. ...

In recent years, market-based greenery has taken off in several ways. With emissions trading, officials decide on a pollution target and then allocate tradable credits to companies based on that target. Those that find it expensive to cut emissions can buy credits from those that find it cheaper, so the target is achieved at the minimum cost and disruption.

The greatest green success story of the past decade is probably America's innovative scheme to cut emissions of sulphur dioxide ($SO_2$). Dan Dudek of Environmental Defence, a most unusual green group, and his market-minded colleagues persuaded the elder George Bush to agree to an amendment to the sacred Clean Air Act that would introduce an emissions-trading system to achieve sharp cuts in $SO_2$. ... Europe, meanwhile, is forging ahead with another sort of market-based instrument: pollution taxes. The idea is to levy charges on goods and services so that their price reflects their 'externalities' – jargon for how much harm they do to the environment and human health. Sweden introduced a sulphur tax a decade ago, and found that the sulphur content of fuels dropped 50% below legal requirements.

Though 'tax' still remains a dirty word in America, other parts of the world are beginning to embrace green tax reform by shifting taxes from employment to pollution. Robert Williams of Princeton University has looked at energy use (especially the terrible effects on health of particulate pollution) and concluded that such externalities are comparable in size to the direct economic costs of producing that energy.

Externalities are only half the battle in fixing market distortions. The other half involves scrapping environmentally harmful subsidies. These range from prices below market levels for electricity and water to shameless cash handouts for industries such as coal. The boffins at the OECD reckon that stripping away harmful subsidies, along with introducing taxes on carbon-based fuels and chemicals use, would result in dramatically lower emissions by 2020

than current policies would be able to achieve. If the revenues raised were then used to reduce other taxes, the cost of these virtuous policies would be less than 1% of the OECD's economic output in 2020.

Such subsidies are nothing short of perverse, in the words of Norman Myers of Oxford University. They do double damage, by distorting markets and by encouraging behaviour that harms the environment. Development banks say such subsidies add up to $700 billion a year, but Mr Myers reckons the true sum is closer to $2 trillion a year. Moreover, the numbers do not fully reflect the harm done. For example, EU countries subsidise their fishing fleets to the tune of $1 billion a year, but that has encouraged enough overfishing to drive many North Atlantic fishing grounds to near-collapse.

Fishing is an example of the 'tragedy of the commons', which pops up frequently in the environmental debate. A resource such as the ocean is common to many, but an individual 'free rider' can benefit from plundering that commons or dumping waste into it, knowing that the costs of his actions will probably be distributed among many neighbours. In the case of shared fishing grounds, the absence of individual ownership drives each fisherman to snatch as many fish as he can – to the detriment of all.

Assigning property rights can help, because providing secure rights (set at a sustainable level) aligns the interests of the individual with the wider good of preserving nature. This is what sceptical conservationists have observed in New Zealand and Iceland, where schemes for tradable quotas have helped revive fishing stocks. Similar rights-based approaches have led to revivals in stocks of African elephants in southern Africa, for example, where

the authorities stress property rights and private conservation. ...

Economic liberals argue that the market itself is the greatest price-discovery mechanism known to man. Allow it to function freely and without government meddling, goes the argument, and prices are discovered and internalised automatically. Jerry Taylor of the Cato Institute, a libertarian think-tank, insists that 'The world today is already sustainable – except those parts where western capitalism doesn't exist.' He notes that countries that have relied on central planning, such as the Soviet Union, China and India, have invariably misallocated investment, stifled innovation and fouled their environment far more than the prosperous market economies of the world have done.

All true. Even so, markets are currently not very good at valuing environmental goods. ... The World Bank's Ian Johnson argues that conventional economic measures such as gross domestic product are not measuring wealth creation properly because they ignore the effects of environmental degradation. He points to the positive contribution to China's GDP from the logging industry, arguing that such a calculation completely ignores the billions of dollars-worth of damage from devastating floods caused by over-logging. He advocates a more comprehensive measure the Bank is working on, dubbed 'genuine GDP', that tries (imperfectly, he accepts) to measure depletion of natural resources.

That could make a dramatic difference to how the welfare of the poor is assessed. ...

Source: *The Economist*, 4 July 2002.
Copyright © The Economist Newspaper Limited, London.

# CONCLUSION: THE IMPORTANCE OF PROPERTY RIGHTS

In this chapter and the previous one, we have seen there are some 'goods' that the market does not provide adequately. Markets do not ensure that the air we breathe is clean or that our country is defended from foreign aggressors. Instead, societies rely on the government to protect the environment and to provide for the national defence.

Although the problems we considered in these chapters arise in many different markets, they share a common theme. In all cases, the market fails to allocate resources efficiently because *property rights* are not well established. That is, some item of value does not have an owner with the legal authority to control it. For example, although no one doubts that the 'good' of clean air or national defence is valuable, no one has the right to attach a price to it and profit from its use. A factory pollutes too much because no one charges the factory for the pollution it emits. The market does not provide for national defence because no one can charge those who are defended for the benefit they receive.

When the absence of property rights causes a market failure, the government can potentially solve the problem. Sometimes, as in the sale of pollution permits, the solution is for the government to help define property rights and thereby unleash market forces. Other times, as in the restriction on hunting seasons, the solution is for the government to regulate private behaviour. Still other times, as in the provision of national defence, the solution is for the government to supply a good that the market fails to supply. In all cases, if the policy is well planned and well run, it can make the allocation of resources more efficient and thus raise economic well-being.

## SUMMARY

- Goods differ in whether they are excludable and whether they are rival. A good is excludable if it is possible to prevent someone from using it. A good is rival if one person's use of the good reduces other people's ability to use the same unit of the good. Markets work best for private goods, which are both excludable and rival. Markets do not work as well for other types of goods.

- Public goods are neither rival nor excludable. Examples of public goods include fireworks displays, national defence and the creation of fundamental knowledge. Because people are not charged for their use of the public good,

they have an incentive to free ride when the good is provided privately. Therefore, governments provide public goods, making their decision about the quantity based on cost–benefit analysis.

- Common resources are rival but not excludable. Examples include common grazing land, clean air and congested roads. Because people are not charged for their use of common resources, they tend to use them excessively. Therefore, governments try to limit the use of common resources.

## KEY CONCEPTS

# QUESTIONS FOR REVIEW

1. Explain what is meant by a good being 'excludable'. Explain what is meant by a good being 'rival'. Is a pizza excludable? Is it rival?

2. Define and give an example of a public good. Can the private market provide this good on its own? Explain.

3. What is cost–benefit analysis of public goods? Why is it important? Why is it hard?

4. Define and give an example of a common resource. Without government intervention, will people use this good too much or too little? Why?

# PROBLEMS AND APPLICATIONS

1. The text says that both public goods and common resources involve externalities.
   a. Are the externalities associated with public goods generally positive or negative? Use examples in your answer. Is the free market quantity of public goods generally greater or less than the efficient quantity?
   b. Are the externalities associated with common resources generally positive or negative? Use examples in your answer. Is the free market use of common resources generally greater or less than the efficient use?

2. Think about the goods and services provided by your local government.
   a. Using the classification in Figure 11.1, explain what category each of the following goods falls into:
      • police protection
      • road gritting
      • education
      • rural roads
      • city streets.
   b. Why do you think the government provides items that are not public goods?

3. One of the UK's major broadcasting companies, the British Broadcasting Corporation (BBC) is funded largely by the sale of annual licences. Charles loves watching football matches on TV when the BBC broadcasts them, but he never buys a TV licence.
   a. What name do economists have for Charles?
   b. How can the government solve the problem caused by people like Charles?
   c. Can you think of ways the private market can solve this problem? How does the existence of cable or satellite TV alter the situation?

4. The text states that private firms will not undertake the efficient amount of basic scientific research.

   a. Explain why this is so. In your answer, classify basic research in one of the categories shown in Figure 11.1.
   b. What sort of policy has the United Kingdom adopted in response to this problem?
   c. It is often argued that this policy increases the technological capability of British producers relative to that of foreign firms. Is this argument consistent with your classification of basic research in part (a)? (Hint: can excludability apply to some potential beneficiaries of a public good and not others?)

5. Why is there litter along most motorways but rarely in people's gardens?

6. An *Economist* article (19 March 1994) states: 'In the past decade, most of the rich world's fisheries have been exploited to the point of near-exhaustion.' The article continues with an analysis of the problem and a discussion of possible private and government solutions.
   a. 'Do not blame fishermen for overfishing. They are behaving rationally, as they have always done.' In what sense is 'overfishing' rational for fishermen?
   b. 'A community, held together by ties of obligation and mutual self-interest, can manage a common resource on its own.' Explain how such management can work in principle, and what obstacles it faces in the real world.
   c. 'Until 1976 most world fish stocks were open to all comers, making conservation almost impossible. Then an international agreement extended some aspects of [national] jurisdiction from 12 to 200 miles offshore.' Using the concept of property rights, discuss how this agreement reduces the scope of the problem.
   d. The article notes that many governments come to the aid of suffering fishermen in ways that encourage increased fishing. How do such policies encourage a vicious cycle of overfishing?

e. 'Only when fishermen believe they are assured a long-term and exclusive right to a fishery are they likely to manage it in the same far-sighted way as good farmers manage their land.' Defend this statement.

f. What other policies to reduce overfishing might be considered?

7. In a market economy, information about the quality or function of goods and services is a valuable good in its own right. How does the private market provide this information? Can you think of any way in which the government plays a role in providing this information?

8. Do you think the internet is a public good? Why or why not?

9. High-income people are willing to pay more than lower-income people to avoid the risk of death. For example, they are more likely to pay for safety features on cars. Do you think cost–benefit analysts should take this fact into account when evaluating public projects? Consider, for instance, a rich town and a poor town, both of which are considering the installation of a traffic light. Should the rich town use a higher monetary value for a human life in making this decision? Why or why not?

For further resources, visit
http://www.thomsonlearning.co.uk/mankiw_taylor

# 12 THE DESIGN OF THE TAX SYSTEM

Al 'Scarface' Capone, the notorious 1920s Chicago gangster and crime boss, was never convicted for his many violent crimes. Yet eventually he did go to jail – for tax evasion. Capone could, quite literally, get away with murder, but he couldn't get away with not paying his taxes.

Taxes are inevitable because we as citizens expect the government to provide us with various goods and services. The previous two chapters have started to shed light on one of the *Ten Principles of Economics* from Chapter 1: the government can sometimes improve market outcomes. When the government remedies an externality (such as air pollution), provides a public good (such as national defence) or regulates the use of a common resource (such as fish in a public lake), it can raise economic well-being. Yet the benefits of government come with costs. For the government to perform these and its many other functions, it needs to raise revenue through taxation.

We began our study of taxation in earlier chapters, where we saw how a tax on a good affects supply and demand for that good. In Chapter 6 we saw that a tax reduces the quantity sold in a market, and we examined how the burden of a tax is shared by buyers and sellers, depending on the elasticities of supply and demand. In Chapter 8 we examined how taxes affect economic well-being. We learned that taxes cause *deadweight losses:* the reduction in consumer and producer surplus resulting from a tax exceeds the revenue raised by the government.

In this chapter we build on these lessons to discuss the design of a tax system. In particular, we consider the fundamental principles of taxation. Most people agree that taxes should impose as small a cost on society as possible and that the burden of taxes should be distributed fairly. That is, the tax system should be both *efficient* and *equitable*. As we will see, however, stating these goals is easier than achieving them.

When thinking about the tax system, it is useful to have in mind some basic facts about a particular tax system and so, for illustrative purposes, we'll start with a financial overview of the UK system.

## A FINANCIAL OVERVIEW OF THE UK GOVERNMENT

How much of the nation's income does the government take as taxes? Figure 12.1 shows UK government revenue and spending since 1900 as a percentage of GDP. It shows that, over time, the government has taken a larger and larger share of total income. In 1910, the government collected about 10 per cent of total income; in the early 2000s, it collected around 40 per cent. In other words, as the economy's income has grown, the government has grown even more. Perhaps the most striking feature of Figure 12.1, however, is the role of wars. The 20th century began with relatively high spending reflecting the costs of the Boer War. The World Wars I and II both led to very large increases in public spending and rather smaller increases in tax. After both of these wars, public spending fell back when hostilities ceased, but to levels much higher than those that had preceded the war.

### FIGURE 12.1

**UK Government Revenue and Expenditure as a Percentage of GDP**

*This figure shows the expenditure and revenue of the UK government as a percentage of GDP, which measures the total income in the economy. It shows that the government plays a large role in the UK economy and that its role has grown over time.*

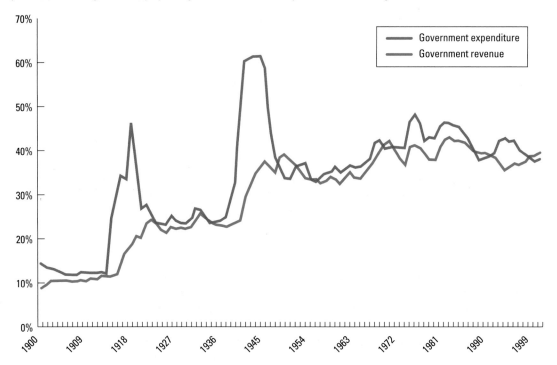

Source: Tom Clark and Andrew Dilnot, *Long-Term Trends in British Taxation and Spending*, June 2002, Institute for Fiscal Studies Briefing Note BN25.

**TABLE 12.1**

Government Revenue as a Percentage of GDP in the G7 Countries, 2005

| | |
|---|---|
| France | 49.8% |
| Italy | 45.1 |
| Germany | 44.1 |
| Canada | 41.2 |
| United Kingdom | 40.4 |
| United States | 31.4 |
| Japan | 30.0 |

Source: Institute for Fiscal Studies.

Table 12.1 compares the tax burden for seven major economies – the so-called 'Group of Seven', or G7 – as measured by the government's tax revenue as a percentage of the nation's total income in 2005. The United Kingdom comes out at just below the median level for these industrialized economies: the UK tax burden is low compared to other European countries such as France, Italy and Germany, but high compared to Japan and the United States.

The overall size of government tells only part of the story, however. Behind the total figures lie thousands of individual decisions about taxes and spending. To understand the government's finances more fully, let's look at how the total breaks down into some broad categories.

## Receipts

Table 12.2 shows the sources of UK government revenue in the financial year 2003–04 (in the UK, the tax year or 'fiscal year' runs from 6 April in one calendar year to 5 April in the next calendar year). (Here we are defining government in a wide sense to include, for example, local government as well as the central government based in London. Taxes are collected by a government agency, Her Majesty's Revenue and Customs.) Total receipts in 2003–04 were £418.9 billion, a number so large that it is hard to comprehend. To bring this astronomical figure down to earth, we can divide it by the size of the UK population – just under 60 million. We then find that the total amount of taxes levied amounted to £7,000 for every man, woman and child in the United Kingdom.

The largest source of revenue for the government is personal income tax. This represents receipts on a tax on individuals' income from all sources: wages from working, interest on savings, dividends from corporations in which the person owns shares, profits from any small businesses he or she operates, and so on. The individual's *tax liability* (how much he or she owes) is then based on total income for the year.

A person's income tax liability is not simply proportional to their income. Instead, the law requires a more complicated calculation. Taxable income is computed as total income minus a 'personal allowance' – a basic amount of income that is not taxed – and minus certain expenses that policy makers have deemed 'deductible' (such as the costs of operating an office in order to run a small business). Then the tax liability is calculated from taxable income (income minus personal allowance and deductibles) using a schedule like that shown in Table 12.3 (although the Chancellor of the Exchequer has the power to change this schedule from time to time, and usually does so annually).

**TABLE 12.2**

**Sources of UK Government Revenue, 2003–04**

| Tax | Amount (billions) | Amount per person | Percentage of receipts |
| --- | --- | --- | --- |
| Personal income tax | £113.9 | £1,902 | 27.2% |
| National Insurance contributions | 72.5 | 1,211 | 17.3 |
| Value-added tax | 69.1 | 1,155 | 16.5 |
| Other indirect taxes | 46.6 | 778 | 11.1 |
| Company taxes | 46.4 | 776 | 11.1 |
| Council tax | 18.8 | 314 | 4.5 |
| Capital taxes | 12.2 | 203 | 2.9 |
| Other taxes and receipts | 39.4 | 658 | 9.4 |
| Total | £418.9 | £7,000 | 100% |

Source: HM Treasury, *Financial Statement and Budget Report, 2005,* and authors' calculations.

**TABLE 12.3**

**UK Income Tax Bands and Rates, 2005–06**

*This table shows the marginal tax rates for a taxpayer under the age of 65. For 2005–06 the personal allowance was £4,895, so that taxable income is any income in excess of this amount. The taxes levied on a taxpayer depend on all the marginal tax rates up to his or her income level. For example, a taxpayer with an income of £35,000 pays nothing on the first £4,895 of income, 10 per cent of the next £2,090 and then 22 per cent of the rest.*

| Taxable income | Tax rate |
| --- | --- |
| Up to £2,090 | 10% |
| From £2,091 to £32,400 | 22 |
| Over £32,400 | 40 |

Source: HM Revenue and Customs.

This table presents the *marginal tax rate* – the tax rate applied to each additional amount of income. Because the marginal tax rate rises as income rises, higher-income individuals pay a larger percentage of their income in taxes. Note that each tax rate in the table applies only to income within the associated range, not to a person's entire income. For example, in 2005–06, a person with an income of a million pounds a year still paid nothing on the first £4,895 of income and 10 per cent of the next £2,090. (We discuss the concept of marginal tax rate more fully later in this chapter.)

Almost as important to the UK government as individual income tax are National Insurance contributions. National Insurance contributions, or NICs, are a peculiarity of the UK tax system in that they are part income tax, part payroll tax (a *payroll tax* is a tax on the wages that a firm pays its workers). NICs work like this: the level of the employee's NICs is based on income, similar to income tax, except that it is usually worked out on weekly rather than annual earnings. The earnings limits and NIC rates for 2005–06 are shown in Table 12.4. Up to a weekly earned income of £94, nothing is paid. Once a worker earns more than £94 a week, however, he pays 11 per cent of weekly income above £94 and less than £630. On the balance of his weekly earnings in excess of £630 he pays 1 per

## TABLE 12.4

**UK National Insurance Contribution Earnings Limits and Rates, 2005–06**

*This table shows UK standard rate National Insurance contribution rates in 2005–06. They are worked out on weekly earnings and comprise both an employee's contribution and an employer's contribution. For example, a worker with an Income of £700 a week (about £36,400 a year) would pay nothing on the first £94 of weekly income, 11 per cent of what he earned between £94 and £630, and 1 per cent on the remaining £70. In addition, his employer would also have to pay 12.8 per cent of his weekly earnings in excess of £94.*

| Weekly earnings | Employee's contribution | Employer's contribution |
| --- | --- | --- |
| Up to £94 | 0% | 0% |
| From £94 to £630 | 11 | 12.8 |
| Over £630 | 1 | 12.8 |

Source: HM Revenue and Customs.

cent. The payroll tax part of NICs, the employer's NIC, is more straightforward: the employer pays 12.8 per cent of all earnings paid to the employee above £94 a week. These rates will be lower if the worker has 'contracted out' of the state pension scheme (i.e. elected not to receive a state pension).

NICs are a form of *social insurance tax*, because a worker's entitlement to certain benefits such as unemployment benefit and a state pension, depends upon the amount of NICs paid (for this reason they are termed 'contributory' benefits). The revenue from these taxes is paid into a National Insurance fund. A small, fixed proportion of this is allocated to the National Health Service and the remainder is used to fund spending on contributory benefits. However, the link between National Insurance contributions paid and eligibility for benefits is quite weak, and has been getting weaker over time.

Almost as large in magnitude as National Insurance contributions are the receipts from value-added tax, or VAT. Value-added tax is a proportional sales tax, and in the UK is levied at the rate of 17.5 per cent of the selling price of many goods and services. It is called 'value-added' tax because the person producing the good or service is able to deduct any VAT he or she has already paid on goods or services used in producing it before paying the tax bill, so that the tax paid is actually a tax on the value added to the product at each stage of production. To make this clearer, let's consider an example. Suppose a sculptor wants £800 for a stone sculpture. She will charge £800 plus VAT of £140 (= 17.5 per cent of £800), or £940 in total. Before paying her VAT bill to HM Revenue and Customs, however, she will deduct from the £140 any VAT she paid in the production of the sculpture. In fact, she bought a block of stone from a local quarry for £200 plus VAT of £35 (= 17.5 per cent of £200), so she will deduct the £35 VAT she has already paid and send £105 (= £140 – £35) to HM Revenue and Customs. How much VAT will the Revenue and Customs receive in total? They get £35 when the stone is sold to the sculptor; this represents a tax on the value added at this stage of production – digging the stone up from the quarry, where it was worth nothing, and delivering it to the sculptor's studio, where it was worth £200. Then Revenue and Customs received £105 when the sculptor sold the sculpture. This again represents a tax on the value added at this stage of production: selling price of £800 minus cost of marble of £200 equals value added of £600, and 17.5 per cent of £600 is £105. Adding the £35 the Revenue and Customs received when the block of stone was sold to the sculptor and the £105 they received when the sculptor sold the final sculpture, they have received £140. This is 17.5 per cent of the total value added in the whole production process – from a value of zero when the stone was in the ground, to £800 when the sculpture was sold (£140 = 17.5 per cent of £800).

VAT is an example of an **indirect tax**, as opposed to income tax, which is a **direct tax**. A direct tax is levied directly on a person's income or wealth, while an indirect tax is levied on the price of something sold. Other indirect taxes besides VAT – the next most important category in UK government revenue, at about 11 per cent – include taxes on fuel and on cigarettes and alcoholic drinks.

Almost equal in magnitude to indirect taxes excluding VAT are company taxes. These include taxes such as local taxes levied on the value of a company's buildings, as well as corporation tax, which is a tax on a company's profits. A *corporation* is a business that is set up as a separate legal entity. The government taxes each corporation based on its profit – the amount the corporation receives for the goods or services it sells minus the costs of producing those goods or services. Notice that corporate profits are, in essence, taxed twice. They are taxed once by corporation tax when the corporation earns the profits; they are taxed a second time by the individual income tax when the corporation uses its profits to pay dividends to its shareholders.

Council taxes, accounting for about 4.5 per cent of total receipts, are local taxes paid by individuals – in the UK, usually levied on the value of residential property owned – in order to pay for local amenities such as refuse collection and local roads.

Capital taxes, accounting for just under 3 per cent of total tax revenue, are composed of inheritance tax, capital gains tax and stamp duty. Inheritance tax is the tax paid by an individual when he or she inherits money or property. Capital gains tax is paid when an individual makes a profit from investments – for example if he or she buys shares in a company and later sells them at a profit, capital gains tax will be payable on that profit. Stamp duty is a tax levied by the government on capital transactions: for example, when a person buys shares in a company or a house to live in, they will normally be liable to pay a certain percentage of the price as stamp duty. (The term 'stamp duty' is a reminder of years gone by when a government official would have used a rubber stamp on the transaction document as proof that the tax had been paid.)

## Spending

Table 12.5 shows the spending of the UK government in 2003–04. Total spending in that year was £454 billion, or £7,600 per person. This table also shows how the government's spending was divided among major categories.

The largest category in Table 12.5 is social security, which represents transfer payments to the elderly (i.e. pensions) as well as unemployment benefits and other forms of social benefits. (A *transfer payment* is a government payment not made in exchange for a good or service.) This category made up 28.5 per cent of spending by the UK government in 2003–04.

The second largest category of spending is on the National Health Service. Since 1948, the UK has offered health care to UK residents free at the point of delivery. The term 'free at the point of delivery' is important here. It means that at the time the service is delivered – when you go to see your GP or you have your appendix taken out in hospital – there is no charge made. At a total cost of £72.1 billion to taxpayers in 2003–04, however, or £1,205 for every man, woman and child in the United Kingdom, it should be clear that health care has to be paid for like everything else.

Next in importance in terms of the amount spent is education, accounting for almost £60 billion in 2003–04, or about 13 per cent of total spending. This includes

**indirect tax**
a tax that is levied on goods and services bought
**direct tax**
a tax that is levied directly on a person's income

## TABLE 12.5

### UK Government Spending, 2003–04

| Category | Amount (billions) | Amount per person | Percentage of spending |
|---|---|---|---|
| Social security | £129.5 | £2,164 | 28.5% |
| National Health Service | 72.1 | 1,205 | 15.9 |
| Education | 59.5 | 994 | 13.1 |
| Defence | 28.0 | 468 | 6.2 |
| Public order and safety | 27.7 | 463 | 6.1 |
| Transport | 15.9 | 266 | 3.5 |
| Other | 121.3 | 2,027 | 26.7 |
| Total | £454.0 | £7,600 | 100% |

Source: Institute for Fiscal Studies

spending on all forms of primary, secondary and higher education, as well as government training programmes.

Expenditure on national defence, weighing in at £28 billion, or £468 per person, is the fourth largest category. This includes both the salaries of military personnel and purchases of military equipment such as guns, fighter jets and warships.

The fifth category, only slightly smaller than defence spending, is public order and safety, which includes, for example, the cost of maintaining a police force and a fire service, as well as the criminal justice system. Government spending on transport – for example the cost of maintaining national motorways and the cost of subsidies paid to rail operators for maintaining the rail network – makes up the sixth largest category, at just under £16 billion, or about 3.5 per cent of total spending.

(The category labelled 'other' in Table 12.5 is comprised of a range of smaller categories of expenditure, such as environmental protection, housing, culture, science and technology, and agriculture, as well as items such as debt interest.)

In Table 12.6, we show how the main categories of UK government expenditure have changed over time, measured as a percentage of GDP. It is striking how expenditure on social security and the NHS have both increased strongly and steadily over the past four decades, while defence expenditure has shown a steady decline. The decline in defence expenditure is even more marked as a percentage of total government expenditure: as shown in Table 12.5, defence spending in 2003–04 amounted to about 6 per cent of the total, but in the mid-1980s it was about 11 per cent of total government spending. This reflects changing shifts in international political tensions, from the height of the Cold War in the 1960s to its effective end with the collapse of communism in the late 1980s and early 1990s.

The increase in spending on the NHS over time, also evident in Table 12.6, reflects at least three factors: changes in the population, which means that there is an increasing proportion of elderly people; the general tendency for an increase in demand for health services as countries become richer; and finally the increase in the range of treatable ailments over time as medical science has become more advanced.

You might have noticed that total receipts of the UK government shown in Table 12.2 fall short of total spending shown in Table 12.5 by £35.1 billion. Such a shortfall of receipts compared with spending is called a **budget deficit.** When receipts exceed spending, the government is said to run a **budget surplus.** The government finances a budget deficit by borrowing from the public. When the

**budget deficit**
an excess of government spending over government receipts
**budget surplus**
an excess of government receipts over government spending

### TABLE 12.6

**UK Government Spending as a Percentage of GDP in the Six Main Areas**

|  | 1963–64 | 1978–79 | 1996–97 | 2003–04 |
| --- | --- | --- | --- | --- |
| Social security | 6.2 | 9.8 | 12.5 | 11.6 |
| NHS | 3.4 | 4.5 | 5.3 | 6.5 |
| Education | 3.9 | 5.3 | 4.7 | 5.3 |
| Defence | 5.6 | 4.4 | 2.9 | 2.5 |
| Transport | n/a | 1.7 | 1.3 | 1.4 |
| Public order and safety | n/a | 1.5 | 2.1 | 2.5 |

Source: Institute for Fiscal Studies.

government runs a budget surplus, it uses the excess receipts to reduce its outstanding debts.

**Quick Quiz** What are the three most important sources of tax revenue for the UK government? • What are the three most important expenditure categories?

# IN THE NEWS

## In Favour of a Flat Tax

*Tax systems are usually very complicated. However, some countries have adopted very simple tax systems: a flat rate of tax on all income. This article argues in favour of flat-tax systems.*

**The Flat-Tax Revolution: Fine in Theory, But It Will Never Happen. Oh Really?**

The more complicated a country's tax system becomes, the easier it is for governments to make it more complicated still, in an accelerating process of proliferating insanity – until, perhaps, a limit of madness is reached and a spasm of radical simplification is demanded. In 2005, many of the world's rich countries seem far along this curve. The United States, which last simplified its tax code in 1986, and which spent the

next two decades feverishly unsimplifying it, may soon be coming to a point of renewed fiscal catharsis. Other rich countries, with a tolerance for tax-code sclerosis even greater than America's, may not be so far behind. Revenue must be raised, of course. But is there no realistic alternative to tax codes which, as they discharge that sad but necessary function, squander resources on an epic scale and grind the spirit of the helpless taxpayer as well?

The answer is yes: there is indeed an alternative, and experience is proving that it is an eminently realistic one. The

experiment started in a small way in 1994, when Estonia became the first country in Europe to introduce a 'flat tax' on personal and corporate income. Income is taxed at a single uniform rate of 26%: no schedule of rates, no deductions. The economy has flourished. Others followed: first, Latvia and Lithuania, Estonia's Baltic neighbours; later Russia (with a rate of 13% on personal income), then Slovakia (19% on personal and corporate income). One of Poland's centre-right opposition parties is campaigning for a similar code (with a rate of 15%). So far eight countries have followed Estonia's example. An old idea that for decades elicited the response, 'Fine in theory, just not practical in the real world,' seems to be working as well in practice as it does on the blackboard.

Practical types who said that flat taxes cannot work offer a further instant objection, once they are shown such taxes working – namely, that they are unfair. Enlightened countries, it is argued, have 'progressive' tax systems, requiring the rich to forfeit a bigger share of their incomes in tax than the poor are called upon to pay. A flat tax seems to rule this out in principle.

Not so. A flat tax on personal incomes combines a threshold (that is, an exempt amount) with a single rate of tax on all income above it. The progressivity of such a system can be varied within wide limits using just these two variables. Under systems such as America's, or those operating in most of western Europe, the incentives for the rich to avoid tax (legally or otherwise) are enormous; and the opportunities to do so, which arise from the very complexity of the codes, are commensurately large. So it is unsurprising to discover, as experience suggests, that the rich usually pay about as much tax under a flat-tax regime as they do under an orthodox code.

So much for the two main objections. What then are the advantages of being very simple-minded when it comes to tax? Simplicity of course is a boon in its own right. The costs merely of administering a conventionally clotted tax system are outrageous. Estimates for the United States, whose tax regime, despite the best efforts of Congress, is by no means the world's

most burdensome, put the costs of compliance, administration and enforcement between 10% and 20% of revenue collected. (That sum, by the way, is equivalent to between one-quarter and one-half of the government's budget deficit.)

Though it is impossible to be precise, that direct burden is almost certainly as nothing compared with the broader economic costs caused by the government's interfering so pervasively in the allocation of resources. A pathological optimist, or somebody nostalgic for Soviet central planning, might argue that the whole point of the myriad breaks, deductions, allowances, concessions, reliefs and assorted other tax expenditures that clog rich countries' tax systems – requiring total revenues to be gathered from a narrower base of taxpayers at correspondingly higher and more distorting rates – is to improve economic efficiency. The whole idea, you see, is to allocate resources more intelligently. Yes, well. Take a look at the current United States tax code, or just at one session of Congress's worth of tax-gifts to favourite constituencies, and try to keep a straight face while saying that.

Once tax codes have degenerated to the extent they have in most rich countries, laden with so many breaks and exceptions that they retain nothing of their original shape, even the pretence of any interior logic can be dispensed with. No tax break is too narrow, too squalid, too funny, to be excluded on those grounds: everybody is at it, so why not join in? At the other extreme, the simpler the system, the more such manoeuvres offend, and the easier it is to retain the simplicity.

In Britain, election notwithstanding, tax simplification is nowhere on the agenda: why not? George Bush has at least appointed a commission to look into tax reform. But its terms of reference are so narrow that it could not suggest a flat tax even if it wanted to. This is a great pity. A flat tax would not eliminate the need for spending control; it would not deal with the impending financial distress of Social Security and Medicare; it would not even settle the arguments about the so-called consumption tax (since in principle a flat tax could take as its base either all income, or income net of savings, in which case it would act as a consumption tax). There are things it cannot do and questions it does not answer. But the gains from a radical simplification of the tax system would be very great. The possibility should not be excluded at the outset.

It is true that the flat-tax revolutionaries of central and eastern Europe are more inclined to radicalism than their politically maturer neighbours to the west and across the Atlantic. Mobilising support for sensible change is far harder in those more advanced places – but not impossible. In tax reform, as 1986 showed, the radical programme can suddenly look easier to implement than the timid package of piecemeal changes. Now and then, the bigger the idea, and the simpler the idea, the easier it is to roll over the opposition. The flat-tax idea is big enough and simple enough to be worth taking seriously.

Source: *The Economist,* 16 April 2005. Copyright © The Economist Newspaper Limited, London.

## TAXES AND EFFICIENCY

Now that we have seen how the UK government raises and spends money, let's consider how one might evaluate its tax policy. Obviously, the aim of a tax system is to raise revenue for the government. But there are many ways to raise any given amount of money. In designing a tax system, policy makers have two objectives: efficiency and equity.

One tax system is more efficient than another if it raises the same amount of revenue at a smaller cost to taxpayers. What are the costs of taxes to taxpayers? The most obvious cost is the tax payment itself. This transfer of money from the taxpayer to the government is an inevitable feature of any tax system. Yet taxes also impose two other costs, which well designed tax policy tries to avoid or, at least, minimize:

- The deadweight losses that result when taxes distort the decisions that people make.
- The administrative burdens that taxpayers bear as they comply with the tax laws.

An efficient tax system is one that imposes small deadweight losses and small administrative burdens.

## Deadweight Losses

One of the *Ten Principles of Economics* is that people respond to incentives, and this includes incentives provided by the tax system. If the government taxes tea, people drink less tea and drink more coffee. If the government taxes housing, people live in smaller houses and spend more of their income on other things. If the government taxes labour earnings, people work less and enjoy more leisure.

Because taxes distort incentives, they entail deadweight losses. As we first discussed in Chapter 8, the deadweight loss of a tax is the reduction in economic well-being of taxpayers in excess of the amount of revenue raised by the government. The deadweight loss is the inefficiency that a tax creates as people allocate resources according to the tax incentive rather than the true costs and benefits of the goods and services that they buy and sell.

To recall how taxes cause deadweight losses, consider an example. Suppose that Ian places an €8 value on a pizza, and Dawn places a €6 value on it. If there is no tax on pizza, the price of pizza will reflect the cost of making it. Let's suppose that the price of pizza is €5, so both Ian and Dawn choose to buy one. Both consumers get some surplus of value over the amount paid. Ian gets consumer surplus of €3, and Dawn gets consumer surplus of €1. Total surplus is €4.

Now suppose that the government levies a €2 tax on pizza and the price of pizza rises to €7. Ian still buys a pizza, but now he has consumer surplus of only €1. Dawn now decides not to buy a pizza because its price is higher than its value to her. The government collects tax revenue of €2 on Ian's pizza. Total consumer surplus has fallen by €3 (from €4 to €1). Because total surplus has fallen by more than the tax revenue, the tax has a deadweight loss. In this case, the deadweight loss is €1.

Notice that the deadweight loss comes not from Ian, the person who pays the tax, but from Dawn, the person who doesn't. The reduction of €2 in Ian's surplus exactly offsets the amount of revenue the government collects. The deadweight loss arises because the tax causes Dawn to alter her behaviour. When the tax raises the price of pizza, Dawn is worse off, and yet there is no offsetting revenue to the government. This reduction in Dawn's welfare is the deadweight loss of the tax.

# CASE STUDY

## Should Income or Consumption Be Taxed?

When taxes induce people to change their behaviour – such as inducing Dawn to buy less pizza – the taxes cause deadweight losses and make the allocation of resources less efficient. As we have already seen, much government revenue comes from personal income tax. In a case study in Chapter 8 we discussed how this tax discourages people from working as hard as they otherwise might. Another inefficiency caused by this tax is that it discourages people from saving.

Consider a person 25 years old who is considering saving €100. If he puts this money in a savings account that earns 8 per cent and leaves it there, he would have €2,172 when he retires at age 65. Yet if the government taxes one quarter of his interest income each year, the effective interest rate is only 6 per cent. After 40 years of earning 6 per cent, the €100 grows to only €1,029, less than half of what it would have been without taxation. Thus, because interest income is taxed, saving is much less attractive.

Some economists advocate eliminating the current tax system's disincentive towards saving by changing the basis of taxation. Rather than taxing the amount of income that people *earn*, the government could tax the amount that people *spend*. Under this proposal, all income that is saved would not be taxed until the saving is later spent. This alternative system, called a *consumption tax*, would not distort people's saving decisions.

## Administrative Burden

In the UK, anyone paying (or who should pay) the highest rate of income tax (in 2004–05, those with taxable income of £32,400 or more) is required to fill in a tax return and send it to HM Revenue and Customs. This is a long form which Revenue and Customs use to determine tax liability. If you ask the typical person required to do this for an opinion about the tax system, the opinion is unlikely to be favourable. The administrative burden of any tax system is part of the inefficiency it creates. This burden includes not only the time spent filling out forms but also the time spent throughout the year keeping records for tax purposes and the resources the government has to use to enforce the tax laws.

Many taxpayers – especially those in higher tax brackets – hire accountants or tax lawyers to help them with their taxes. These experts in the complex tax laws fill out the tax forms for their clients and help clients arrange their affairs in a way that reduces the amount of taxes owed. This behaviour is avoidance (optimizing your affairs so that you pay as little tax as possible without breaking the law, which is different from tax evasion – i.e lying about your affairs in order to reduce the amount of tax paid). Tax avoidance is perfectly legal. Tax evasion is illegal, as Scarface Capone discovered.

Critics of the tax system say that these advisors help their clients avoid taxes by abusing some of the detailed provisions of the tax system (or, as it is sometimes termed, the tax code). These detailed provisions are often dubbed 'loopholes'. In some cases, loopholes are government mistakes: they arise from ambiguities or omissions in the tax laws. More often, they arise because the government has chosen to give special treatment to specific types of behaviour. For example, the UK tax system allows money spent on a personal pension plan to be exempt from income tax, up to certain limit. This is because the government wants to encourage people to save for their retirement.

The resources devoted to complying with the tax laws are a type of deadweight loss. The government gets only the amount of taxes paid. By contrast, the taxpayer loses not only this amount but also the time and money spent documenting, computing and avoiding taxes.

The administrative burden of the tax system could be reduced by simplifying the tax laws. Yet simplification is often politically difficult. Most people are ready to simplify the tax code by eliminating the loopholes that benefit others, yet few are eager to give up the loopholes that they use. In the end, the complexity of the tax law results from the political process as various taxpayers with their own special interests lobby for their causes.

## Marginal Tax Rates Versus Average Tax Rates

**average tax rate**
total taxes paid divided by total income
**marginal tax rate**
the extra taxes paid on an additional unit of income

When discussing the efficiency and equity of income taxes, economists distinguish between two notions of the tax rate: the average and the marginal. The **average tax rate** is total taxes paid divided by total income. The **marginal tax rate** is the extra taxes paid on an additional unit of income.

For example, suppose that the government taxes 20 per cent of the first €50,000 of income and 50 per cent of all income above €50,000. Under this tax, a person who earns €60,000 pays a tax of €15,000: 20 per cent of the first €50,000 (0.20 × €50,000 = €10,000) plus 50 per cent of the next €10,000 (0.50 × €10,000 = €5,000). For this person, the average tax rate is €15,000/€60,000, or 25 per cent. But the marginal tax rate is 50 per cent. If the taxpayer earned an additional euro of income, that euro would be subject to the 50 per cent tax rate, so the amount the taxpayer would owe to the government would rise by €0.50.

The marginal and average tax rates each contain a useful piece of information. If we are trying to gauge the sacrifice made by a taxpayer, the average tax rate is more appropriate because it measures the fraction of income paid in taxes. By contrast, if we are trying to gauge how much the tax system distorts incentives, the marginal tax rate is more meaningful. One of the *Ten Principles of Economics* in Chapter 1 is that rational people think at the margin. A corollary to this principle is that the marginal tax rate measures how much the tax system discourages people from working. If you are thinking of working an extra few hours, the marginal tax rate determines how much the government takes of your additional earnings. It is the marginal tax rate, therefore, that determines the deadweight loss of an income tax.

## CASE STUDY

### Iceland's Natural Experiment

In the 1980s, Iceland changed its tax system in a way that, as a side effect, provided a natural experiment to show how taxes affect an economy. Before the reform, people paid taxes based on their *previous* year's income. After the reform, people paid taxes based on their *current* income. Thus, taxes in 1987 were based on 1986 income, but taxes in 1988 were based on 1988 income. Income earned in 1987 was never taxed. For this one year of transition, the marginal income tax rate fell to zero.

As reported in a December 2001 article in the *American Economic Review*, the citizens of Iceland took advantage of this tax holiday. Total hours worked rose by about 3 per cent in 1987 and then fell back to its normal level in 1988. The production of goods and services in 1987 (as measured by real GDP) was 4 per cent higher than the average of the year before and the year after. This episode confirms one of the *Ten Principles of Economics:* people respond to incentives.

The fall in the Icelandic marginal tax rate was for one year only, and this fact surely influenced the response. On the one hand, some people may have put off vacations and worked overtime to take advantage of the temporary incentive. On the other hand, no one would alter career plans, and no business would restructure its work environment, in response to an incentive that would soon disappear. A permanent change in a marginal tax rate could have either a smaller or a larger incentive effect than a temporary change.

## Lump-Sum Taxes

Suppose the government imposes a tax of €4,000 on everyone. That is, everyone owes the same amount, regardless of earnings or any actions that a person might take. Such a tax is called a **lump-sum tax.**

**lump-sum tax**
a tax that is the same amount for every person

A lump-sum tax shows clearly the difference between average and marginal tax rates. For a taxpayer with income of €20,000, the average tax rate of a €4,000 lump-sum tax is 20 per cent; for a taxpayer with income of €40,000, the average tax rate is 10 per cent. For both taxpayers, the marginal tax rate is zero because no tax is owed on an additional unit of income.

A lump-sum tax is the most efficient tax possible. Because a person's decisions do not alter the amount owed, the tax does not distort incentives and, therefore, does not cause deadweight losses. Because everyone can easily compute the amount owed and because there is no benefit to hiring tax lawyers and accountants, the lump-sum tax imposes a minimal administrative burden on taxpayers.

If lump-sum taxes are so efficient, why do we rarely observe them in the real world? The reason is that efficiency is only one goal of the tax system. A lump-sum tax would take the same amount from the poor and the rich, an outcome most people would view as unfair. To understand the tax systems that we observe, in the next section, we consider the other major goal of tax policy: equity.

> **Quick Quiz** What is meant by the efficiency of a tax system? • What can make a tax system inefficient?

# TAXES AND EQUITY

In any country, tax policy always generates some of the most heated political debates. The heat is rarely fuelled by questions of efficiency. Instead, it usually arises from disagreements over how the tax burden should be distributed. Of course, if we are to rely on the government to provide some of the goods and services we want, taxes must fall on someone. In this section we consider the equity of a tax system. How should the burden of taxes be divided among the population? How do we evaluate whether a tax system is fair? Everyone agrees that the tax system should be equitable, but there is much disagreement about what equity means and how the equity of a tax system can be judged.

## The Benefits Principle

**benefits principle**
the idea that people should pay taxes based on the benefits they receive from government services

One principle of taxation, called the **benefits principle,** states that people should pay taxes based on the benefits they receive from government services. This principle tries to make public goods similar to private goods. It seems fair that a person who often goes to the cinema pays more in total for cinema tickets than a person who rarely goes. Similarly, a person who gets great benefit from a public good should pay more for it than a person who gets little benefit.

The duty on petrol, for instance, is sometimes justified using the benefits principle, since in some countries, revenues from the tax on petrol are used to build and maintain roads. Because those who buy petrol are the same people who use the roads, this tax might be viewed as a fair way to pay for this government service.

The benefits principle can also be used to argue that wealthy citizens should pay higher taxes than poorer ones. Why? Simply because the wealthy benefit more from public services. Consider, for example, the benefits of police protection from theft. Citizens with much to protect get greater benefit from the police than do those with less to protect. Therefore, according to the benefits principle, the wealthy should contribute more than the poor to the cost of maintaining the police force. The same argument can be used for many other public services, such as fire protection, national defence and the criminal justice system.

It is even possible to use the benefits principle to argue for anti-poverty programmes funded by taxes on the wealthy. As we discussed in Chapter 11, people prefer living in a society without poverty, suggesting that anti-poverty programmes are a public good. If the wealthy place a greater value on this public good than other members of society, perhaps just because the wealthy have more to spend, then, according to the benefits principle, they should be taxed more heavily to pay for these programmes.

## The Ability-to-Pay Principle

**ability-to-pay principle**
the idea that taxes should be levied on a person according to how well that person can shoulder the burden

Another way to evaluate the equity of a tax system is called the **ability-to-pay principle,** which states that taxes should be levied on a person according to how well that person can shoulder the burden. This principle is sometimes justified by the claim that all citizens should make an 'equal sacrifice' to support the government. The magnitude of a person's sacrifice, however, depends not only on the size of his tax payment but also on his income and other circumstances. A €1,000 tax paid by a poor person may require a larger sacrifice than a €10,000 tax paid by a rich one.

The ability-to-pay principle leads to two corollary notions of equity: vertical equity and horizontal equity. **Vertical equity** states that taxpayers with a greater ability to pay taxes should contribute a larger amount. **Horizontal equity** states that taxpayers with similar abilities to pay should contribute the same amount. Although these notions of equity are widely accepted, applying them to evaluate a tax system is rarely straightforward.

**vertical equity**
the idea that taxpayers with a greater ability to pay taxes should pay larger amounts
**horizontal equity**
the idea that taxpayers with similar abilities to pay taxes should pay the same amount
**proportional tax**
a tax for which high-income and low-income taxpayers pay the same fraction of income
**regressive tax**
a tax for which high-income taxpayers pay a smaller fraction of their income than do low-income taxpayers

**Vertical Equity**   If taxes are based on ability to pay, then richer taxpayers should pay more than poorer taxpayers. But how much more should the rich pay? Much of the debate over tax policy concerns this question.

Consider the three tax systems in Table 12.7. In each case, taxpayers with higher incomes pay more. Yet the systems differ in how quickly taxes rise with income. The first system is called **proportional** because all taxpayers pay the same fraction of income. The second system is called **regressive** because high-income

### TABLE 12.7

**Three Tax Systems**

| Income | Proportional tax | | Regressive tax | | Progressive tax | |
|---|---|---|---|---|---|---|
| | Amount of tax | Percentage of income | Amount of tax | Percentage of income | Amount of tax | Percentage of income |
| €50,000 | €12,500 | 25% | €15,000 | 30% | €10,000 | 20% |
| 100,000 | 25,000 | 25 | 25,000 | 25 | 25,000 | 25 |
| 200,000 | 50,000 | 25 | 40,000 | 20 | 60,000 | 30 |

taxpayers pay a smaller fraction of their income, even though they pay a larger amount. The third system is called **progressive** because high-income taxpayers pay a larger fraction of their income.

Which of these three tax systems is most fair? There is no obvious answer, and economic theory does not offer any help in trying to find one. Equity, like beauty, is in the eye of the beholder.

**progressive tax**
a tax for which high-income taxpayers pay a larger fraction of their income than do low-income taxpayers

## CASE STUDY

### UK Income Tax and the Laffer Curve

Much debate over tax policy concerns whether the rich pay their fair share. There is no objective way to make this judgement. In evaluating the issue for yourself, however, it is useful to know how much individuals of different incomes pay under the current tax system.

Table 12.8 presents some data on what proportion of total UK income tax received by the government is paid by people receiving incomes in the top 1 per cent, 10 per cent and 50 per cent of the population, and how these proportions have shifted over time. The table shows that about 22 per cent of all income tax is paid for by people who are in the very top percentile of income. While this figure has been stable for several years, it is double the proportion paid by the top 1 per cent in the late 1970s and early 1980s (despite the fact that the top rate of income tax was reduced from 60 per cent to 40 per cent in the late 1980s). Note also that the top 10 per cent of the highest paid pay more than half of all income tax paid, and while this figure has also stabilized in recent years it is much higher than it was 25 years ago, when the top 10 per cent paid about 35 per cent of all income tax receipts. Overall, one might be tempted to conclude from Table 12.8 that the UK system of income tax is progressive and that its progressivity has been increasing over time. The UK income tax code is certainly progressive in that higher earners pay a higher proportion of their income in tax, but the degree of progressivity of the UK system has not in fact been increasing over this period. In fact, during the 1980s, the top rates of tax were cut quite dramatically – from 83 per cent to 60 per cent in 1980 and then to 40 per cent in 1988.

In a case study in Chapter 8 (p. 158) we discussed the Laffer curve – the idea that reducing tax rates may induce people to work more so that they earn more and actually end up paying more tax. Is this an example of the Laffer curve in action? As we noted in our earlier discussion, it is not easy to say, because untangling the incentive effects of tax cuts from other factors is extremely difficult.

### TABLE 12.8

**Shares of Total UK Income Tax Paid By Groups Ranked According to Income**

| Year | Top 1% | Top 10% | Top 50% |
| --- | --- | --- | --- |
| 1978–79 | 11 | 35 | 82 |
| 1981–82 | 11 | 35 | 81 |
| 1986–87 | 14 | 39 | 84 |
| 1990–91 | 15 | 42 | 85 |
| 1993–94 | 16 | 44 | 87 |
| 1996–97 | 20 | 48 | 88 |
| 1998–99 | 21 | 49 | 88 |
| 2000–01 | 22 | 52 | 89 |
| 2001–02 | 22 | 52 | 89 |
| 2002–03 | 22 | 52 | 89 |
| 2003–04 | 22 | 52 | 90 |
| 2004–05 | 22 | 52 | 89 |

Source: Institute for Fiscal Studies.

**Horizontal Equity** If taxes are based on ability to pay, then similar taxpayers should pay similar amounts of taxes. But what determines if two taxpayers are similar? Individuals' circumstances can differ in many ways. To evaluate whether a tax system is horizontally equitable, one must determine which differences are relevant for a person's ability to pay and which differences are not.

Suppose Mr Smith and Ms Jones each have an income of €50,000 a year. Mr Smith is unmarried and has no children, but he has an illness that means that he has to employ someone to be with him while he is at work and getting to and from his place of business. This costs him €20,000 a year. Ms Jones is in good health and is a lone parent with a child aged three. Ms Jones has to pay €15,000 a year for child care while she is at work. Would it be fair for Mr Smith and Ms Jones to

"...IN SICKNESS OR HEALTH, INFLATION OR DEFLATION, MARRIAGE TAX CREDIT OR DEBIT..."

pay the same tax because they have the same income? Would it be fairer to give Mr Smith a tax break to help him offset the costs of a caring assistant? Would it be fairer to give Ms Jones a tax break to compensate her for the cost of child care?

There are no easy answers to these questions.

## Tax Incidence and Tax Equity

Tax incidence – the study of who bears the burden of taxes – is central to evaluating tax equity. As we first saw in Chapter 6, the person who bears the burden of a tax is not always the person who gets the tax bill from the government. Because taxes alter supply and demand, they alter equilibrium prices. As a result, they affect people beyond those who, according to statute, actually pay the tax. When evaluating the vertical and horizontal equity of any tax, it is important to take account of these indirect effects.

Many discussions of tax equity ignore the indirect effects of taxes and are based on what economists mockingly call the *flypaper theory* of tax incidence. According to this theory, the burden of a tax, like a fly on flypaper, sticks wherever it first lands. This assumption, however, is rarely valid.

For example, a person not trained in economics might argue that a tax on expensive fur coats is vertically equitable because most buyers of furs are wealthy. Yet if these buyers can easily substitute other luxuries for furs, then a tax on furs might only reduce the sale of furs. In the end, the burden of the tax will fall more on those who make and sell furs than on those who buy them. Because most workers who make furs are not wealthy, the equity of a fur tax could be quite different from what the flypaper theory indicates.

## CASE STUDY

### Who Pays Corporation Tax?

Corporation tax provides a good example of the importance of tax incidence for tax policy. Corporation tax is popular among voters. After all, corporations are not people. Voters are always eager to have their taxes reduced and have some impersonal corporation pick up the tab. In a sense, corporation tax appears to be a tax that is imposed on nobody. No wonder it's popular with policy makers also.

But before deciding that corporation tax is a good way for the government to raise revenue, we should consider who bears the burden of corporation tax. This is a difficult question on which economists disagree, but one thing is certain: *people pay all taxes.* When the government levies a tax on a corporation, the corporation is more like a tax collector than a taxpayer. The burden of the tax ultimately falls on people – the owners, customers or workers of the corporation.

Many economists believe that workers and customers bear much of the burden of corporation tax. To see why, consider an example. Suppose that the government decides to raise the tax on the income earned by car companies. At first, this tax hurts the owners of the car companies, who receive less profit. But, over time, these owners will respond to the tax. Because producing cars is less profitable, they invest less in building new car factories. Instead, they invest their wealth in other ways – for example, by buying larger houses or by building factories in other industries or other countries. With fewer car factories, the supply of cars declines, as does the demand for car workers. Thus, a

*Workers pay part of corporation tax.*

tax on corporations making cars causes the price of cars to rise and the wages of car workers to fall.

Corporation tax shows how dangerous the flypaper theory of tax incidence can be. Corporation tax is popular in part because it appears to be paid by rich corporations. Yet those who bear the ultimate burden of the tax – the customers and workers of corporations – are often not rich. If the true incidence of corporation tax were more widely known, this tax might be less popular among voters – and policy makers.

**Quick Quiz** Explain the benefits principle and the ability-to-pay principle. • What are vertical equity and horizontal equity? • Why is studying tax incidence important for determining the equity of a tax system?

# IN THE NEWS

## Equity Versus Efficiency

*Deciding on a system of government taxation and spending always involves a trade-off between equity and efficiency. This article argues that many European systems are heavily biased towards efficiency.*

### Taxing the Poor to Pay the Poor: Europe's big welfare states are surprisingly efficient – and surprisingly inequitable

Economists, who prize efficiency above equity, have long given warning of the dangers of redistribution. England's poor laws, which paid a pittance to the destitute out of taxes, earned David Ricardo's condemnation in the early 19th century. 'The principle of gravitation is not more certain than the tendency of such laws to change wealth and power into misery and weakness,' he claimed. Modern economists have raised similar concerns about today's redistributive welfare states: by subtracting from the rewards of work and adding to the consolations of idleness, social transfers sap economies of their vigour. Some American conservatives have sought to 'starve the beast', cutting the taxes that feed social spending.

In the Nordic countries and much of Europe, however, the beast remains well fed. According to the OECD, Sweden, Denmark and Finland devote almost a third of their GDP to social transfers. Germany and France devote about a quarter. America redirects only 14% or so of its national income in this way.

The costs to Europe of overgrown welfare systems are plain: its citizens pay for redistribution with high taxes, which may be one reason why Europe's economic performance has lagged behind America's. The average French worker produces 5% more per hour than his American counterpart, but produces less in total because he works fewer hours – in part because those high taxes reduce his incentive to work. Yet Europe's redistribution has not led to the 'plague of universal poverty' predicted by Ricardo. Far from it: European countries are rich.

How can this be? Peter Lindert, of the University of California, Davis, offers an answer towards the end of his new book, *Growing Public*, a monumental history of two centuries of social spending. The big European and Nordic welfare states are undoubtedly expensive. But their economic costs are held down by the perhaps surprisingly efficient tax systems with which they are financed. Once the means of finance are taken into account, they are also less redistributive than you might expect.

Economic theory has a lot to say about efficient systems of taxation. One guiding principle is that it is better to tax consumption than income, because taxing what is spent rather than what is earned does less damage to incentives to save. If wages are taxed, and the interest on savings is taxed also, then anything saved out of your wages is, in effect, taxed twice. Compared with the Americans, the Europeans place far more of their tax burden on consumption than income.

A second principle dates from a 1927 paper by Frank Ramsey, a Cambridge polymath. In essence, Ramsey's theory says that those goods or services most sensitive to price should be taxed the least; those least sensitive to price should be taxed the most. Scandinavian tax systems, in particular, are close to the spirit of the Ramsey rule. They lean on labour rather than on capital, because capitalists are deterred from investing more easily than workers are discouraged from labouring. They tax habits, such as smoking and drinking, more than luxuries, because the addicted or habituated will buy at almost any price.

In general, Europe's big social spenders tax capital relatively lightly. On some measures, indeed, Europeans treat capital better than supposedly more sympathetic Americans. According to an OECD study, the grabbing hand of the American state took an average of 31% of capital income between 1991 and 1997. The corresponding figure was about 20% in Germany, Norway and Finland, and 24% in France. In 1998, rich Americans faced a marginal tax rate on dividends of over 46%. Rich Belgians, Finns and Norwegians paid much lower rates. While Americans were arguing about Reaganomics in the 1980s, Swedish households were enjoying a negative tax rate on capital

income, once generous deductions and adjustments for inflation were taken into account.

This style of taxation is efficient, but it is clearly inequitable. Taxing luxuries less heavily than, say, alcohol is likely to be regressive. Suppliers of capital, who tend to be richer, get off lightly, while labour carries a heavier burden, through both lower net income and higher unemployment. The income and payroll taxes that support Europe's large welfare states drive a deep wedge between a worker's take-home wage and the much higher cost of employing him. Generous minimum wages and unemployment benefits also put a floor under wages, pricing many people out of the labour market. The result is that just 68% of the European Union's working-age citizens are employed, compared with 77% of America's.

But surely this is evidence of the inefficiency of Europe's welfare systems and the taxes needed to finance them? Mr Lindert, however, is keen to stress the other side of the tax-and-spend ledger. Returns to some of Europe's social expenditures, such as child-care

subsidies, are probably quite high, he says. He also claims, rather unkindly, that unemployment benefits and generous retirement schemes both 'harvest lemons' – ie, they pluck the least productive out of the labour force. Discarding these workers subtracts little from the nation's output, he argues; it also flatters the productivity figures of those with jobs.

America, Mr Lindert conjectures, can get away with an inefficient tax code because its tax burden is quite low. Bigger welfare states have to be smarter, because the stakes are so much higher. The 'Swedish model', for example, has been declared dead more than once, but each time has reinvented itself and survived. Europe's other welfare states are now ailing, blamed for weak growth and high unemployment. Some foresee their slow demise. Survival through adaptation seems more likely.

Source: *The Economist*, 3 April 2004, p. 80. Copyright © The Economist Newspaper Limted, London.

## CONCLUSION: THE TRADE-OFF BETWEEN EQUITY AND EFFICIENCY

Almost everyone agrees that equity and efficiency are the two most important goals of the tax system. But often these two goals conflict. Many proposed changes in the tax laws increase efficiency while reducing equity, or increase equity while reducing efficiency. People disagree about tax policy often because they attach different weights to these two goals.

Economics alone cannot determine the best way to balance the goals of efficiency and equity. This issue involves political philosophy as well as economics. But economists do have an important role in the political debate over tax policy: they can shed light on the trade-offs that society faces and can help us avoid policies that sacrifice efficiency without any benefit in terms of equity.

## SUMMARY

- Governments raises revenue using various taxes. In many countries, the most important taxes for the government are personal income taxes and social insurance taxes.

- The efficiency of a tax system refers to the costs that it imposes on taxpayers. There are two costs of taxes beyond the transfer of resources from the taxpayer to the government. The first is the distortion in the allocation of resources that arises as taxes alter incentives and behaviour. The second is the administrative burden of complying with the tax laws.

- The equity of a tax system concerns whether the tax burden is distributed fairly among the population.

- According to the benefits principle, it is fair for people to pay taxes based on the benefits they receive from the government. According to the ability-to-pay principle, it is fair for people to pay taxes based on their capability to handle the financial burden. When evaluating the equity of a tax system, it is important to remember a lesson from the study of tax incidence: the distribution of tax burdens is not the same as the distribution of tax bills.

- When considering changes in the tax laws, policy makers often face a trade-off between efficiency and equity. Much of the debate over tax policy arises because people give different weights to these two goals.

## KEY CONCEPTS

indirect tax, p. 228
direct tax, p. 228
budget deficit, p. 229
budget surplus, p. 229
average tax rate, p. 234

marginal tax rate, p. 234
lump-sum tax, p. 235
benefits principle, p. 236
ability-to-pay principle, p. 237
vertical equity, p. 236

horizontal equity, p. 236
proportional tax, p. 236
regressive tax, p. 236
progressive tax, p. 237

## QUESTIONS FOR REVIEW

1. Over the past century, has the size of government, as measured by tax receipts or government spending, grown more or less slowly than the rest of the economy?

2. What are the two most important sources of revenue for the government?

3. Explain how corporate profits are taxed twice.

4. Why is the burden of a tax to taxpayers greater than the revenue received by the government?

5. Why do some economists advocate taxing consumption rather than income?

6. Give two arguments why wealthy taxpayers should pay more taxes than poor taxpayers.

7. What is the concept of horizontal equity, and why is it hard to apply?

# PROBLEMS AND APPLICATIONS

1. Government spending in most industrialized countries has grown as a share of national income over time. What changes in our economy and our society might explain this trend? Do you expect the trend to continue?

2. In a published source or on the internet, find out whether the government had a budget deficit or surplus last year. What do policy makers expect to happen over the next few years?

3. In many industrialized countries, the elderly population is growing more rapidly than the total population. This is partly because of historical movements in the birth rate ('baby booms') and partly due to the fact that people are now living longer on average.  Because the elderly are eligible for state retirement pensions, this places an increasing burden on the working age population to pay for those retirement pensions.  Discuss the merits of each of the following proposed policies for dealing with this problem. Which do you think would be the best policy or combination of policies? Explain.
   a. Making exempt from income tax any money paid into a private retirement pension fund.
   b. Making exempt from income tax any money paid into a private retirement pension fund so long as the person involved gives up his or her right to a state pension.
   c. Reducing the amount of state retirement pension by 50 per cent.
   d. Raising the minimum age of retirement from 65 to 70 years of age.
   e. Raising the basic rate of income tax.
   f. Raising the higher rate of income tax.
   g. A drive to increase immigration in order to increase the working age population.

4. Suppose you are a typical person in the UK economy. Refer to Tables 12.3 and 12.4 for income tax and employer's National Insurance contribution rates. How much income tax do you pay if you earn £25,000 a year? How much do you pay in National Insurance contributions? Taking both of these taxes into account, what are your average and marginal tax rates? What happens to your total tax bill and to your average and marginal tax rates if your income rises to £40,000?

5. In the UK, value-added tax is levied at the rate of 17.5 per cent on most goods and services, although it is not levied on a range of items, such as food, books, and water and sewerage systems. Discuss the merits of this policy. Consider the principles of equity and efficiency.

6. VAT is not levied in the UK on children's clothing but it is levied on adult's clothing. Discuss the merits of this distinction, considering both efficiency and equity.

7. Suppose that the tax system had the following features. Explain how individuals' behaviour is affected.
   a. Contributions to charity are tax-deductible.
   b. Sales of beer are taxed.
   c. Realized capital gains are taxed, but accrued gains are not. (When someone owns a share of stock that rises in value, she has an 'accrued' capital gain. If she sells the share, she has a 'realized' gain.)

8. The tax on cigarettes and other smoking products is very high in many countries (in the UK it is over 80 per cent of the selling price) and has been rising over time. Discuss the merits of this policy, considering the principles of equity and efficiency.

9. Categorize each of the following funding schemes as examples of the benefits principle or the ability-to-pay principle.
   a. Visitors to public museums are required to pay an entrance fee.
   b. Local property taxes support elementary and secondary schools.
   c. An airport trust fund collects a tax on each plane ticket sold and uses the money to improve airports and the air traffic control system.

10. Any income tax schedule embodies two types of tax rates – average tax rates and marginal tax rates.
    a. The average tax rate is defined as total taxes paid divided by income. For the proportional tax system presented in Table 12.7, what are the average tax rates for people earning €50,000, €100,000 and €200,000? What are the corresponding average tax rates in the regressive and progressive tax systems?
    b. The marginal tax rate is defined as the extra taxes paid on additional income divided by the increase in income. Calculate the marginal tax rate for the proportional tax system as income rises from €50,000 to €100,000. Calculate the marginal tax rate as income rises from €100,000 to €200,000. Calculate the corresponding marginal tax rates for the regressive and progressive tax systems.
    c. Describe the relationship between average tax rates and marginal tax rates for each of these three systems. In general, which rate is relevant for someone deciding whether to accept a job that pays slightly more than her current job? Which rate is relevant for judging the vertical equity of a tax system?

11. As we noted in the text, the employer's contribution element of UK National Insurance contributions (NICs) are effectively a form of income tax. Consider the figures

on tax rates and NIC rates given in Tables 12.3 and 12.4. Work out a complete schedule showing the total amount of tax (income tax and employee's NIC combined) payable on income over all ranges.

12. What is the efficiency justification for taxing consumption rather than income? If your country were to adopt a consumption tax, do you think that would make the tax system more or less progressive? Explain.

For further resources, visit
http://www.thomsonlearning.co.uk/mankiw_taylor

# 5

## FIRM BEHAVIOUR AND THE ORGANIZATION OF INDUSTRY

# 13 THE COSTS OF PRODUCTION

The economy is made up of thousands of firms that produce the goods and services we enjoy every day: Mercedes Benz produces cars, British Petroleum (BP) produces energy products such as petrol and domestic gas, and Nestlé produces food and drink. Some firms, such as these three, are large; they employ thousands of workers and have thousands of shareholders who share in the firms' profits. Other firms, such as the local hairdresser's shop or pizzeria, are small; they employ only a few workers and may be owned by a single person or family.

In previous chapters we used the supply curve to summarize firms' production decisions. According to the law of supply, firms are willing to produce and sell a greater quantity of a good when the price of the good is higher, and this response leads to a supply curve that slopes upward. For analysing many questions, the law of supply is all you need to know about firm behaviour.

In this chapter and the ones that follow, we examine firm behaviour in more detail. This topic will give you a better understanding of what decisions lie behind the supply curve in a market. In addition, it will introduce you to a part of economics called *industrial organization* – the study of how firms' decisions regarding prices and quantities depend on the market conditions they face. The town in which you live, for instance, may have several pizzerias but only one cable television company. How does this difference in the number of firms affect the prices in these markets and the efficiency of the market outcomes? The field of industrial organization addresses exactly this question.

Before we turn to these issues, however, we need to discuss the costs of production. All firms, from Air France to your local baker's shop, incur costs as they make the goods and services that they sell. As we will see in the coming chapters, a firm's costs are a key determinant of its production and pricing decisions. In this chapter, we define some of the variables that economists use to measure a firm's costs, and we consider the relationships among them. A word of warning: this topic can seem dry and technical. But it provides a crucial foundation for the fascinating topics that follow.

# WHAT ARE COSTS?

We begin our discussion of costs at Hungry Horace's Pizza Factory. Horace, the owner of the firm, buys flour, tomatoes, mozzarella cheese, salami and other pizza ingredients. He also buys the mixers and ovens and hires workers to run this equipment. He then sells the resulting pizzas to consumers. By examining some of the issues that Horace faces in his business, we can learn some lessons about costs that apply to all firms in the economy.

## Total Revenue, Total Cost and Profit

We begin with the firm's objective. To understand what decisions a firm makes, we must understand what it is trying to do. It is conceivable that Horace started his firm because of an altruistic desire to provide the world with pizza or, perhaps, out of love for the pizza business. More likely, Horace started his business to make money. Economists normally assume that the goal of a firm is to maximize profit, and they find that this assumption works well in most cases.

What is a firm's profit? The amount that the firm receives for the sale of its output (pizzas) is called its **total revenue.** The amount that the firm pays to buy inputs (flour, mozzarella cheese, workers, ovens, etc.) is called its **total cost.** Horace keeps any revenue that is not needed to cover costs. **Profit** is a firm's total revenue minus its total cost. That is:

$$\text{Profit} = \text{Total revenue} - \text{Total cost}$$

Horace's objective is to make his firm's profit as large as possible.

To see how a firm goes about maximizing profit, we must consider fully how to measure its total revenue and its total cost. Total revenue is the easy part: it equals the quantity of output the firm produces times the price at which it sells its output. If Horace produces 10,000 pizzas and sells them at €2 a pizza, his total revenue is €20,000. By contrast, the measurement of a firm's total cost is more subtle.

**total revenue**
the amount a firm receives for the sale of its output
**total cost**
the market value of the inputs a firm uses in production
**profit**
total revenue minus total cost

## Costs as Opportunity Costs

When measuring costs at Hungry Horace's Pizza Factory, or any other firm, it is important to keep in mind one of the *Ten Principles of Economics* from Chapter 1: the cost of something is what you give up to get it. Recall that the *opportunity cost* of an item refers to all those things that must be forgone to acquire that item. When economists speak of a firm's cost of production, they include all the opportunity costs of making its output of goods and services.

A firm's opportunity costs of production are sometimes obvious and sometimes less so. When Horace pays €1,000 for flour, that €1,000 is an opportunity cost because Horace can no longer use that €1,000 to buy something else. Similarly, when Horace hires workers to make the pizzas, the wages he pays are part of the firm's costs. Because these costs require the firm to pay out some money, they are called **explicit costs.** By contrast, some of a firm's opportunity costs, called **implicit costs,** do not require a cash outlay. Imagine that Horace is skilled with computers and could earn €100 per hour working as a programmer. For every hour that Horace works at his pizza factory, he gives up €100 in income, and this forgone income is also part of his costs.

This distinction between explicit and implicit costs highlights an important difference between how economists and accountants analyse a business. Economists are interested in studying how firms make production and pricing decisions. Because these decisions are based on both explicit and implicit costs, economists include both when measuring a firm's costs. By contrast, accountants have the job of keeping track of the money that flows into and out of firms. As a result, they measure the explicit costs but often ignore the implicit costs.

The difference between economists and accountants is easy to see in the case of Hungry Horace's Pizza Factory. When Horace gives up the opportunity to earn money as a computer programmer, his accountant will not count this as a cost of his pizza business. Because no money flows out of the business to pay for this cost, it never shows up on the accountant's financial statements. An economist, however, will count the foregone income as a cost because it will affect the decisions that Horace makes in his pizza business. For example, if Horace's wage as a computer programmer rises from €100 to €500 per hour, he might decide that running his pizza business is too costly and choose to shut down the factory to become a full-time computer programmer.

## The Cost of Capital as an Opportunity Cost

An important implicit cost of almost every business is the opportunity cost of the financial capital that has been invested in the business. Suppose, for instance, that Horace used €300,000 of his savings to buy his pizza factory from the previous owner. If Horace had instead left this money deposited in a savings account that pays an interest rate of 5 per cent, he would have earned €15,000 per year. To own his pizza factory, therefore, Horace has given up €15,000 a year in interest income. This forgone €15,000 is one of the implicit opportunity costs of Horace's business.

As we have already noted, economists and accountants treat costs differently, and this is especially true in their treatment of the cost of capital. An economist views the €15,000 in interest income that Horace gives up every year as a cost of his business, even though it is an implicit cost. Horace's accountant, however, will not show this €15,000 as a cost because no money flows out of the business to pay for it.

To explore further the difference between economists and accountants, let's change the example slightly. Suppose now that Horace did not have the entire €300,000 to buy the factory but, instead, used €100,000 of his own savings and borrowed €200,000 from a bank at an interest rate of 5 per cent. Horace's accountant, who only measures explicit costs, will now count the €10,000 interest paid on the bank loan every year as a cost because this amount of money now flows out of the firm. By contrast, according to an economist, the opportunity cost of owning the business is still €15,000. The opportunity cost equals the interest on the bank loan (an explicit cost of €10,000) plus the forgone interest on savings (an implicit cost of €5,000).

## Economic Profit Versus Accounting Profit

Now let's return to the firm's objective – profit. Because economists and accountants measure costs differently, they also measure profit differently. An

**explicit costs**
input costs that require an outlay of money by the firm

**implicit costs**
input costs that do not require an outlay of money by the firm

**FIGURE 13.1**

**Economists Versus Accountants**

*Economists include all opportunity costs when analysing a firm, whereas accountants measure only explicit costs. Therefore, economic profit is smaller than accounting profit.*

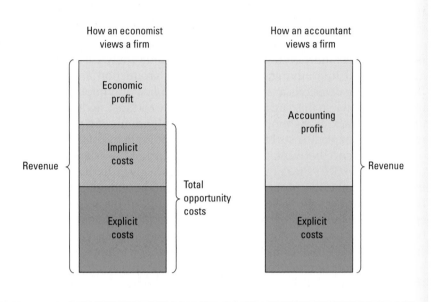

**economic profit**
total revenue minus total cost, including both explicit and implicit costs
**accounting profit**
total revenue minus total explicit cost

economist measures a firm's **economic profit** as the firm's total revenue minus all the opportunity costs (explicit and implicit) of producing the goods and services sold. An accountant measures the firm's **accounting profit** as the firm's total revenue minus only the firm's explicit costs.

Figure 13.1 summarizes this difference. Notice that because the accountant ignores the implicit costs, accounting profit is usually larger than economic profit. For a business to be profitable from an economist's standpoint, total revenue must cover all the opportunity costs, both explicit and implicit.

> **Quick Quiz** Farmer MacDonald gives bagpipe lessons for €20 an hour. One day, he spends 10 hours planting €100 worth of seeds on his farm. What opportunity cost has he incurred? What cost would his accountant measure? If these seeds will yield €200 worth of crops, does old MacDonald earn an accounting profit? Does he earn an economic profit?

## PRODUCTION AND COSTS

Firms incur costs when they buy inputs to produce the goods and services that they plan to sell. In this section we examine the link between a firm's production process and its total cost. Once again, we consider Hungry Horace's Pizza Factory.

In the analysis that follows, we make an important simplifying assumption: we assume that the size of Horace's factory is fixed and that Horace can vary the quantity of pizzas produced only by changing the number of workers. This assumption is realistic in the short run, but not in the long run. That is, Horace cannot build a larger factory overnight, but he can do so within a year or so. This analysis, therefore, should be viewed as describing the production decisions that

# IN THE NEWS

## True Profit Versus Fictitious Profit

*The analysis of firm behaviour begins with the measurement of revenue, costs and profits. In 2001 and 2002, this topic made the news when several major companies were revealed to have lied about these key measures of performance.*

### Flavours of Fraud
*By Paul Krugman*

So you're the manager of an ice cream parlour. It's not very profitable, so how can you get rich? Each of the big business scandals uncovered so far suggests a different strategy for executive self-dealing.

First there's the Enron strategy. You sign contracts to provide customers with an ice cream cone a day for the next 30 years. You deliberately underestimate the cost of providing each cone; then you book all the projected profits on those future ice cream sales as part of this year's bottom line. Suddenly you appear to have a highly profitable business, and you can sell shares in your store at inflated prices.

Then there's the Dynegy strategy. Ice cream sales aren't profitable, but you convince investors that they will be

profitable in the future. Then you enter into a quiet agreement with another ice cream parlor down the street: each of you will buy hundreds of cones from the other every day. Or rather, pretend to buy – no need to go to the trouble of actually moving all those cones back and forth. The result is that you appear to be a big player in a coming business, and can sell shares at inflated prices.
...

Finally, there's the WorldCom strategy. Here you don't create imaginary sales; you make real costs disappear, by pretending that operating expenses – cream, sugar, chocolate syrup – are part of the purchase price of a new refrigerator. So your unprofitable business seems, on paper, to be a highly profitable business that borrows money only to finance its purchases of new equipment. And you can sell shares at inflated prices. ...

Oh, I almost forgot: How do you enrich yourself personally? The easiest way is to give yourself lots of stock options, so that you benefit from those inflated prices. ...

I'm not saying that all US corporations are corrupt. But it's clear that executives who want to be corrupt have faced few obstacles. Auditors weren't interested in giving a hard time to companies that gave them lots of consulting income; bank executives weren't interested in giving a hard time to companies that, as we've learned in the Enron case, let them in on some of those lucrative side deals. And elected officials, kept compliant by campaign contributions and other inducements, kept the regulators from doing their job.

Source: *The New York Times,* 28 June 2002, p. A27. Copyright © 2002 by The New York Times Co. Reprinted by permission.

Horace faces in the short run. We examine the relationship between costs and time horizon more fully later in the chapter.

## The Production Function

Table 13.1 shows how the quantity of pizzas Horace's factory produces per hour depends on the number of workers. As you see in the first two columns, if there are no workers in the factory Horace produces no pizzas. When there is 1 worker he produces 50 pizzas. When there are 2 workers he produces 90 pizzas, and so on. Figure 13.2 presents a graph of these two columns of numbers. The number of workers is on the horizontal axis, and the number of pizzas produced is on the vertical axis. This relationship between the quantity of inputs (workers) and quantity of output (pizzas) is called the **production function.**

One of the *Ten Principles of Economics* introduced in Chapter 1 is that rational people think at the margin. As we will see in future chapters, this idea is the key

**production function**
the relationship between quantity of inputs used to make a good and the quantity of output of that good

**marginal product**
the increase in output that arises from an additional unit of input

**diminishing marginal product**
the property whereby the marginal product of an input declines as the quantity of the input increases

to understanding the decision a firm makes about how many workers to hire and how much output to produce. To take a step toward understanding these decisions, the third column in the table gives the marginal product of a worker. The **marginal product** of any input in the production process is the increase in the quantity of output obtained from one additional unit of that input. When the number of workers goes from 1 to 2, pizza production increases from 50 to 90, so the marginal product of the second worker is 40 pizzas. And when the number of workers goes from 2 to 3, pizza production increases from 90 to 120, so the marginal product of the third worker is 30 pizzas.

Notice that as the number of workers increases, the marginal product declines. The second worker has a marginal product of 40 pizzas, the third worker has a marginal product of 30 pizzas and the fourth worker has a marginal product of 20 pizzas. This property is called **diminishing marginal product.** At first, when only a few workers are hired, they have easy access to Horace's kitchen equipment. As the number of workers increases, additional workers have to share equipment and work in more crowded conditions. Hence, as more and more workers are hired, each additional worker contributes less to the production of pizzas.

Diminishing marginal product is also apparent in Figure 13.2. The production function's slope ('rise over run') tells us the change in Horace's output of pizzas ('rise') for each additional input of labour ('run'). That is, the slope of the

## FIGURE 13.2

**Hungry Horace's Production Function**

*A production function shows the relationship between the number of workers hired and the quantity of output produced. Here the number of workers hired (on the horizontal axis) is from the first column in Table 13.1, and the quantity of output produced (on the vertical axis) is from the second column. The production function gets flatter as the number of workers increases, which reflects diminishing marginal product.*

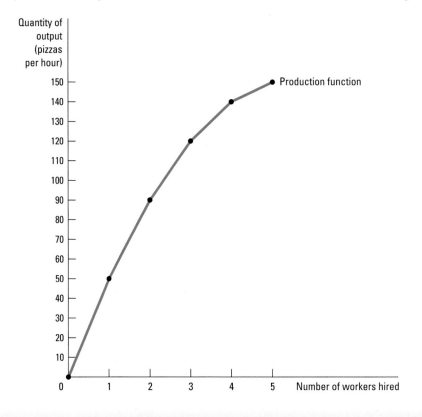

### TABLE 13.1

**A Production Function and Total Cost: Hungry Horace's Pizza Factory**

| Number of workers | Output (quantity of pizzas produced per hour) | Marginal product of labour | Cost of factory | Cost of workers | Total cost of inputs (cost of factory + cost of workers) |
|---|---|---|---|---|---|
| 0 | 0 | | €30 | €0 | €30 |
| | | 50 | | | |
| 1 | 50 | | 30 | 10 | 40 |
| | | 40 | | | |
| 2 | 90 | | 30 | 20 | 50 |
| | | 30 | | | |
| 3 | 120 | | 30 | 30 | 60 |
| | | 20 | | | |
| 4 | 140 | | 30 | 40 | 70 |
| | | 10 | | | |
| 5 | 150 | | 30 | 50 | 80 |

production function measures the marginal product of a worker. As the number of workers increases, the marginal product declines, and the production function becomes flatter.

## From the Production Function to the Total Cost Curve

The last three columns of Table 13.1 show Horace's cost of producing pizzas. In this example, the cost of Horace's factory is €30 per hour and the cost of a worker is €10 per hour. If he hires 1 worker, his total cost is €40. If he hires 2 workers, his total cost is €50, and so on. With this information, the table now shows how the number of workers Horace hires is related to the quantity of pizzas he produces and to his total cost of production.

Our goal in the next several chapters is to study firms' production and pricing decisions. For this purpose, the most important relationship in Table 13.1 is between quantity produced (in the second column) and total costs (in the sixth column). Figure 13.3 graphs these two columns of data with the quantity produced on the horizontal axis and total cost on the vertical axis. This graph is called the *total cost curve*.

Now compare the total cost curve in Figure 13.3 with the production function in Figure 13.2. These two curves are opposite sides of the same coin. The total cost curve gets steeper as the amount produced rises, whereas the production function gets flatter as production rises. These changes in slope occur for the same reason. High production of pizzas means that Horace's kitchen is crowded with many workers. Because the kitchen is crowded, each additional worker adds less to production, reflecting diminishing marginal product. Therefore, the production function is relatively flat. But now turn this logic around: when the kitchen is crowded, producing an additional pizza requires a lot of additional labour and is thus very costly. Therefore, when the quantity produced is large, the total cost curve is relatively steep.

**Quick Quiz** If Farmer Jones plants no seeds on his farm, he gets no harvest. If he plants 1 bag of seeds he gets 3 tonnes of wheat. If he plants 2 bags he gets 5 tonnes. If he plants 3 bags he gets 6 tonnes. A bag of seeds costs €100, and seeds are his only cost. Use these data to graph the farmer's production function and total cost curve. Explain their shapes.

**FIGURE 13.3**

## Hungry Horace's Total Cost Curve

*A total cost curve shows the relationship between the quantity of output produced and total cost of production. Here the quantity of output produced (on the horizontal axis) is from the second column in Table 13.1, and the total cost (on the vertical axis) is from the sixth column. The total cost curve gets steeper as the quantity of output increases because of diminishing marginal product.*

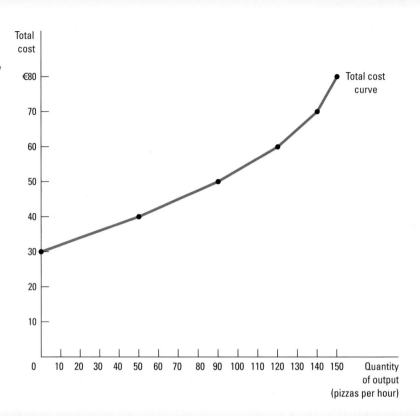

**TABLE 13.2**

### The Various Measures of Cost: Thirsty Virgil's Lemonade Stand

| Quantity of lemonade glasses (per hour) | Total cost | Fixed cost | Variable cost | Average fixed cost | Average variable cost | Average total cost | Marginal cost |
|---|---|---|---|---|---|---|---|
| 0 | €3.00 | €3.00 | €0.00 | – | – | – | |
| 1 | 3.30 | 3.00 | 0.30 | €3.00 | €0.30 | €3.30 | €0.30 |
| 2 | 3.80 | 3.00 | 0.80 | 1.50 | 0.40 | 1.90 | 0.50 |
| 3 | 4.50 | 3.00 | 1.50 | 1.00 | 0.50 | 1.50 | 0.70 |
| 4 | 5.40 | 3.00 | 2.40 | 0.75 | 0.60 | 1.35 | 0.90 |
| 5 | 6.50 | 3.00 | 3.50 | 0.60 | 0.70 | 1.30 | 1.10 |
| 6 | 7.80 | 3.00 | 4.80 | 0.50 | 0.80 | 1.30 | 1.30 |
| 7 | 9.30 | 3.00 | 6.30 | 0.43 | 0.90 | 1.33 | 1.50 |
| 8 | 11.00 | 3.00 | 8.00 | 0.38 | 1.00 | 1.38 | 1.70 |
| 9 | 12.90 | 3.00 | 9.90 | 0.33 | 1.10 | 1.43 | 1.90 |
| 10 | 15.00 | 3.00 | 12.00 | 0.30 | 1.20 | 1.50 | 2.10 |

# THE VARIOUS MEASURES OF COST

Our analysis of Hungry Horace's Pizza Factory demonstrated how a firm's total cost reflects its production function. From data on a firm's total cost we can derive several related measures of cost which will turn out to be useful when we analyse production and pricing decisions in future chapters. To see how these related measures are derived, we consider the example in Table 13.2. This table presents cost data on Horace's neighbour: Thirsty Virgil's Lemonade Stand.

The first column of the table shows the number of glasses of lemonade that Virgil might produce, ranging from 0 to 10 glasses per hour. The second column shows Virgil's total cost of producing glasses of lemonade. Figure 13.4 plots Virgil's total cost curve. The quantity of lemonade (from the first column) is on the horizontal axis, and total cost (from the second column) is on the vertical axis. Thirsty Virgil's total cost curve has a shape similar to Hungry Horace's. In particular, it becomes steeper as the quantity produced rises, which (as we have discussed) reflects diminishing marginal product.

## Fixed and Variable Costs

Virgil's total cost can be divided into two types. Some costs, called **fixed costs,** do not vary with the quantity of output produced. They are incurred even if the firm produces nothing at all. Virgil's fixed costs include any rent he pays because this cost is the same regardless of how much lemonade Virgil produces. Similarly, if Virgil needs to hire a barman to serve the drinks, regardless of the quantity of lemonade sold, the barman's salary is a fixed cost. The third column in Table 13.2 shows Virgil's fixed cost, which in this example is €3.00.

**fixed costs**
costs that do not vary with the quantity of output produced

## FIGURE 13.4

**Thirsty Virgil's Total Cost Curve**

*Here the quantity of output produced (on the horizontal axis) is from the first column in Table 13.2, and the total cost (on the vertical axis) is from the second column. As in Figure 13.3, the total cost curve gets steeper as the quantity of output increases because of diminishing marginal product.*

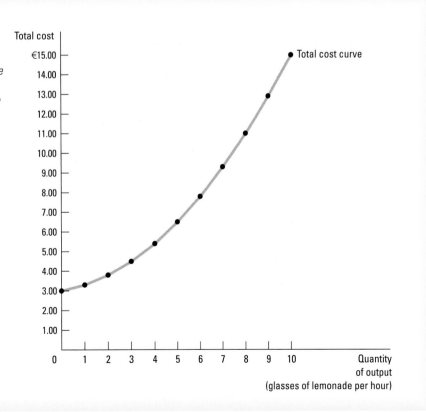

**variable costs**
costs that vary with the quantity of output produced

Some of the firm's costs, called **variable costs,** change as the firm alters the quantity of output produced. Virgil's variable costs include the cost of lemons, sugar, paper cups and straws: the more lemonade Virgil makes, the more of these items he needs to buy. Similarly, if Virgil has to hire more workers to make more lemonade, the salaries of these workers are variable costs. The fourth column of the table shows Virgil's variable cost. The variable cost is 0 if he produces nothing, €0.30 if he produces 1 glass of lemonade, €0.80 if he produces 2 glasses and so on.

A firm's total cost is the sum of fixed and variable costs. In Table 13.2, total cost in the second column equals fixed cost in the third column plus variable cost in the fourth column.

## Average and Marginal Cost

As the owner of his firm, Virgil has to decide how much to produce. A key part of this decision is how his costs will vary as he changes the level of production. In making this decision, Virgil might ask his production supervisor the following two questions about the cost of producing lemonade:

- How much does it cost to make the typical glass of lemonade?
- How much does it cost to increase production of lemonade by 1 glass?

Although at first these two questions might seem to have the same answer, they do not. Both answers will turn out to be important for understanding how firms make production decisions.

**average total cost**
total cost divided by the quantity of output
**average fixed cost**
fixed costs divided by the quantity of output
**average variable cost**
variable costs divided by the quantity of output

To find the cost of the typical unit produced, we would divide the firm's costs by the quantity of output it produces. For example, if the firm produces 2 glasses per hour, its total cost is €3.80, and the cost of the typical glass is €3.80/2, or €1.90. Total cost divided by the quantity of output is called **average total cost.** Because total cost is just the sum of fixed and variable costs, average total cost can be expressed as the sum of average fixed cost and average variable cost. **Average fixed cost** is the fixed cost divided by the quantity of output, and **average variable cost** is the variable cost divided by the quantity of output.

**marginal cost**
the increase in total cost that arises from an extra unit of production

Although average total cost tells us the cost of the typical unit, it does not tell us how much total cost will change as the firm alters its level of production. The last column in Table 13.2 shows the amount that total cost rises when the firm increases production by 1 unit of output. This number is called **marginal cost.** For example, if Virgil increases production from 2 to 3 glasses, total cost rises from €3.80 to €4.50, so the marginal cost of the third glass of lemonade is €4.50 minus €3.80, or €0.70.

It may be helpful to express these definitions mathematically:

$$\text{Average total cost} = \text{Total cost/Quantity}$$
$$ATC = TC/Q$$

and

$$\text{Marginal cost} = \text{Change in total cost/Change in quantity}$$
$$MC = \Delta TC/\Delta Q.$$

Here $\Delta$, the Greek letter delta, represents the change in a variable. These equations show how average total cost and marginal cost are derived from total cost. Average total cost tells us the cost of a typical unit of output if total cost is divided evenly over all the units produced. Marginal cost tells us the increase in total cost that arises from producing an additional unit of output. As we will see more fully in the next chapter, Virgil, our lemonade entrepreneur, will find the concepts of average total cost and marginal cost useful when deciding how much lemonade to produce.

## Cost Curves and Their Shapes

Just as in previous chapters we found graphs of supply and demand useful when analysing the behaviour of markets, we will find graphs of average and marginal cost useful when analysing the behaviour of firms. Figure 13.5 graphs Virgil's costs using the data from Table 13.2. The horizontal axis measures the quantity the firm produces, and the vertical axis measures marginal and average costs. The graph shows four curves: average total cost *(ATC)*, average fixed cost *(AFC)*, average variable cost *(AVC)*, and marginal cost *(MC)*.

The cost curves shown here for Thirsty Virgil's Lemonade Bar have some features that are common to the cost curves of many firms in the economy. Let's examine three features in particular: the shape of marginal cost, the shape of average total cost and the relationship between marginal and average total cost.

**Rising Marginal Cost** Thirsty Virgil's marginal cost rises with the quantity of output produced. This reflects the property of diminishing marginal product. When Virgil is producing a small quantity of lemonade he has few workers and much of his equipment is not being used. Because he can easily put these idle resources to use, the marginal product of an extra worker is large, and the marginal cost of an extra glass of lemonade is small. By contrast, when Virgil is producing a large quantity of lemonade his stand is crowded with workers and most of his

## FIGURE 13.5

**Thirsty Virgil's Average Cost and Marginal Cost Curves**

*This figure shows the average total cost (ATC), average fixed cost (AFC) average variable cost (AVC) and marginal cost (MC) for Thirsty Virgil's Lemonade Bar. All of these curves are obtained by graphing the data in Table 13.2. These cost curves show three features that are typical of many firms: (1) Marginal cost rises with the quantity of output. (2) The average total cost curve is U-shaped. (3) The marginal cost curve crosses the average total cost curve at the minimum of average total cost.*

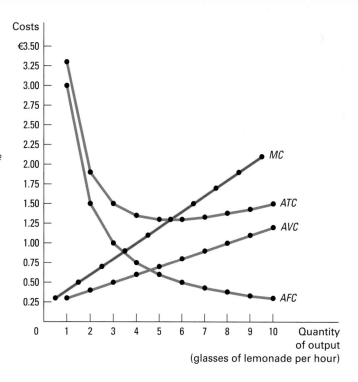

equipment is fully utilized. Virgil can produce more lemonade by adding workers, but these new workers have to work in crowded conditions and may have to wait to use the equipment. Therefore, when the quantity of lemonade being produced is already high, the marginal product of an extra worker is low, and the marginal cost of an extra glass of lemonade is large.

**U-Shaped Average Total Cost** Thirsty Virgil's average total cost curve is U-shaped. To understand why this is so, remember that average total cost is the sum of average fixed cost and average variable cost. Average fixed cost always declines as output rises because the fixed cost is getting spread over a larger number of units. Average variable cost typically rises as output increases because of diminishing marginal product. Average total cost reflects the shapes of both average fixed cost and average variable cost. As shown in Figure 13.5, at very low levels of output, such as 1 or 2 glasses per hour, average total cost is high because the fixed cost is spread over only a few units. Average total cost then declines as output increases until the firm's output reaches 5 glasses of lemonade per hour, when average total cost falls to €1.30 per glass. When the firm produces more than 6 glasses, average total cost starts rising again because average variable cost rises substantially.

The bottom of the U-shape occurs at the quantity that minimizes average total cost. This quantity is sometimes called the **efficient scale** of the firm. For Thirsty Virgil, the efficient scale is 5 or 6 glasses of lemonade. If he produces more or less than this amount, his average total cost rises above the minimum of €1.30.

**efficient scale**
the quantity of output that minimizes average total cost

**The Relationship between Marginal Cost and Average Total Cost** If you look at Figure 13.5 (or back at Table 13.2), you will see something that may be surprising at first. Whenever marginal cost is less than average total cost, average total cost is falling. Whenever marginal cost is greater than average total cost, average total cost is rising. This feature of Thirsty Virgil's cost curves is not a coincidence from the particular numbers used in the example: it is true for all firms.

To see why, consider what happens to average cost as output goes up by one unit. If the cost of the extra unit is above the average cost of units produced up to that point, then it will tend to pull up the new average cost of a unit. If the new unit actually costs less than the average cost of a unit up to that point, it will tend to drag the new average down. But the price of an extra unit is what economists call marginal cost, so what we have just asserted is tantamount to saying that if marginal cost is less than average cost, average cost will be falling; and if marginal cost is above average cost, average cost will be rising.

This relationship between average total cost and marginal cost has an important corollary: the marginal cost curve crosses the average total cost curve at its minimum. Why? At low levels of output, marginal cost is below average total cost, so average total cost is falling. But after the two curves cross, marginal cost rises above average total cost. For the reason we have just discussed, average total cost must start to rise at this level of output. Hence, this point of intersection is the minimum of average total cost. As you will see in the next chapter, this point of minimum average total cost plays a key role in the analysis of competitive firms.

## Typical Cost Curves

In the examples we have studied so far, the firms exhibit diminishing marginal product and, therefore, rising marginal cost at all levels of output. Yet actual firms are often a bit more complicated than this. In many firms, diminishing marginal product does not start to occur immediately after the first worker is hired. Depending on the production process, the second or third worker might have higher marginal product than the first because a team of workers can divide tasks and work more productively than a single worker. Such firms would first experience increasing marginal product for a while before diminishing marginal product sets in.

The table in Figure 13.6 shows the cost data for such a firm, called Big Bob's Bagel Bin. These data are used in the graphs. Panel (a) shows how total cost (*TC*)

## FIGURE 13.6

### Big Bob's Cost Curves

*Many firms, like Big Bob's Bagel Bin, experience increasing marginal product before diminishing marginal product and, therefore, have cost curves shaped like those in this figure. Panel (a) shows how total cost (TC) depends on the quantity produced. Panel (b) shows how average total cost (ATC), average fixed cost (AFC), average variable cost (AVC) and marginal cost (MC) depend on the quantity produced. These curves are derived by graphing the data from the table. Notice that marginal cost and average variable cost fall for a while before starting to rise.*

| Quantity of bagels (per hour) | Total cost | Fixed cost | Variable cost | Average fixed cost | Average variable cost | Average total cost | Marginal cost |
|---|---|---|---|---|---|---|---|
| $Q$ | $TC = FC + VC$ | $FC$ | $VC$ | $AFC = FC/Q$ | $AVC = VC/Q$ | $ATC = TC/Q$ | $MC = \Delta TC/\Delta Q$ |
| 0 | €2.00 | €2.00 | €0.00 | – | – | – | |
| 1 | 3.00 | 2.00 | 1.00 | €2.00 | €1.00 | €3.00 | €1.00 |
| 2 | 3.80 | 2.00 | 1.80 | 1.00 | 0.90 | 1.90 | 0.80 |
| 3 | 4.40 | 2.00 | 2.40 | 0.67 | 0.80 | 1.47 | 0.60 |
| 4 | 4.80 | 2.00 | 2.80 | 0.50 | 0.70 | 1.20 | 0.40 |
| 5 | 5.20 | 2.00 | 3.20 | 0.40 | 0.64 | 1.04 | 0.40 |
| 6 | 5.80 | 2.00 | 3.80 | 0.33 | 0.63 | 0.96 | 0.60 |
| 7 | 6.60 | 2.00 | 4.60 | 0.29 | 0.66 | 0.95 | 0.80 |
| 8 | 7.60 | 2.00 | 5.60 | 0.25 | 0.70 | 0.95 | 1.00 |
| 9 | 8.80 | 2.00 | 6.80 | 0.22 | 0.76 | 0.98 | 1.20 |
| 10 | 10.20 | 2.00 | 8.20 | 0.20 | 0.82 | 1.02 | 1.40 |
| 11 | 11.80 | 2.00 | 9.80 | 0.18 | 0.89 | 1.07 | 1.60 |
| 12 | 13.60 | 2.00 | 11.60 | 0.17 | 0.97 | 1.14 | 1.80 |
| 13 | 15.60 | 2.00 | 13.60 | 0.15 | 1.05 | 1.20 | 2.00 |
| 14 | 17.80 | 2.00 | 15.80 | 0.14 | 1.13 | 1.27 | 2.20 |

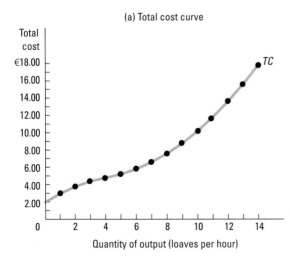

(a) Total cost curve

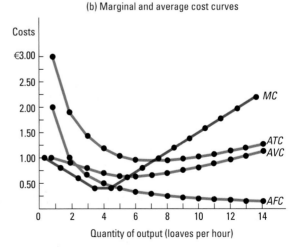

(b) Marginal and average cost curves

depends on the quantity produced, and panel (b) shows average total cost (*ATC*), average fixed cost (*AFC*), average variable cost (*AVC*) and marginal cost (*MC*). In the range of output from 0 to 4 bagels per hour, the firm experiences increasing marginal product, and the marginal cost curve falls. After 5 bagels per hour, the firm starts to experience diminishing marginal product, and the marginal cost curve starts to rise. This combination of increasing then diminishing marginal product also makes the average variable cost curve U-shaped.

Despite these differences from our previous example, Big Bob's cost curves share the three properties that are most important to remember:

- Marginal cost eventually rises with the quantity of output.
- The average total cost curve is U-shaped.
- The marginal cost curve crosses the average total cost curve at the minimum of average total cost.

**Quick Quiz** Suppose BMW's total cost of producing 4 cars is €225,000 and its total cost of producing 5 cars is €250,000. What is the average total cost of producing 5 cars? What is the marginal cost of the fifth car? • Draw the marginal cost curve and the average total cost curve for a typical firm, and explain why these curves cross where they do.

# COSTS IN THE SHORT RUN AND IN THE LONG RUN

We noted at the beginning of this chapter that a firm's costs might depend on the time horizon being examined. Let's discuss more precisely why this might be the case.

## The Relationship Between Short-Run and Long-Run Average Total Cost

For many firms, the division of total costs between fixed and variable costs depends on the time horizon. Consider, for instance, a car manufacturer, such as Renault. Over a period of only a few months, Renault cannot adjust the number or sizes of its car factories. The only way it can produce additional cars is to hire more workers at the factories it already has. The cost of these factories is, therefore, a fixed cost in the short run. By contrast, over a period of several years, Renault can expand the size of its factories, build new factories or close old ones. Thus, the cost of its factories is a variable cost in the long run.

Because many decisions are fixed in the short run but variable in the long run, a firm's long-run cost curves differ from its short-run cost curves. Figure 13.7 shows an example. The figure presents three short-run average total cost curves – for a small, medium and large factory. It also presents the long-run average total cost curve. As the firm moves along the long-run curve, it is adjusting the size of the factory to the quantity of production.

This graph shows how short-run and long-run costs are related. The long-run average total cost curve is a much flatter U-shape than the short-run average total cost curve. In addition, all the short-run curves lie on or above the long-run curve. These properties arise because firms have greater flexibility in the long run. In essence, in the long run, the firm chooses which short-run curve it wants to use. But in the short run, it has to use whatever short-run curve it chose in the past.

## FIGURE 13.7

**Average Total Cost in the Short and Long Runs**

*Because fixed costs are variable in the long run, the average total cost curve in the short run differs from the average-total-cost curve in the long run.*

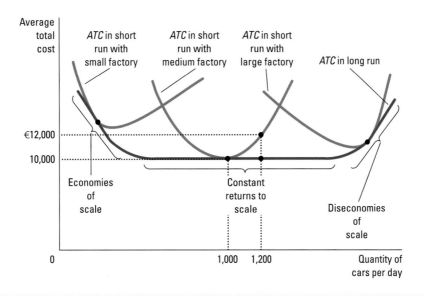

The figure shows an example of how a change in production alters costs over different time horizons. When Renault wants to increase production from 1,000 to 1,200 cars per day, it has no choice in the short run but to hire more workers at its existing medium-sized factory. Because of diminishing marginal product, average total cost rises from €10,000 to €12,000 per car. In the long run, however, Renault can expand both the size of the factory and its workforce, and average total cost returns to €10,000.

How long does it take for a firm to get to the long run? The answer depends on the firm. It can take a year or longer for a major manufacturing firm, such as a car company, to build a larger factory. By contrast, a person running a newspaper stand might be able to find new premises and expand sales in a matter of weeks or days. There is, therefore, no single answer about how long it takes a firm to adjust its production facilities.

## Economies and Diseconomies of Scale

The shape of the long-run average total cost curve conveys important information about the technology for producing a good. When long-run average total cost declines as output increases, there are said to be **economies of scale.** When long-run average total cost rises as output increases, there are said to be **diseconomies of scale.** When long-run average total cost does not vary with the level of output, there are said to be **constant returns to scale.** In this example, Renault has economies of scale at low levels of output, constant returns to scale at intermediate levels of output and diseconomies of scale at high levels of output.

What might cause economies or diseconomies of scale? Economies of scale often arise because higher production levels allow *specialization* among workers, which permits each worker to become better at his or her assigned tasks. For

**economies of scale**
the property whereby long-run average total cost falls as the quantity of output increases
**diseconomies of scale**
the property whereby long-run average total cost rises as the quantity of output increases
**constant returns to scale**
the property whereby long-run average total cost stays the same as the quantity of output changes

instance, modern assembly line production requires a large number of workers. If Renault were producing only a small quantity of cars, it could not take advantage of this approach and would have higher average total cost. Diseconomies of scale can arise because of *coordination problems* that are inherent in any large organization. The more cars Renault produces, the more stretched the management team becomes, and the less effective the managers become at keeping costs down.

This analysis shows why long-run average total cost curves are often U-shaped. At low levels of production, the firm benefits from increased size because it can take advantage of greater specialization. Coordination problems, meanwhile, are not yet acute. By contrast, at high levels of production, the benefits of specialization have already been realized, and coordination problems become more severe as the firm grows larger. Thus, long-run average total cost is falling at low levels of production because of increasing specialization and rising at high levels of production because of increasing coordination problems.

> **Quick Quiz** If Airbus produces 9 jets per month, its long-run total cost is €9.0 million per month. If it produces 10 jets per month, its long-run total cost is €9.5 million per month. Does Airbus exhibit economies or diseconomies of scale?

**FYI**

## Lessons From a Pin Factory

'Jack of all trades, master of none.' This well known adage helps explain why firms sometimes experience economies of scale. A person who tries to do everything usually ends up doing nothing very well. If a firm wants its workers to be as productive as they can be, it is often best to give each a limited task that he or she can master. But this is possible only if a firm employs many workers and produces a large quantity of output.

In his celebrated book *An Inquiry into the Nature and Causes of the Wealth of Nations*, Adam Smith described a visit he made to a pin factory. Smith was impressed by the specialization among the workers and the resulting economies of scale. He wrote:

One man draws out the wire, another straightens it, a third cuts it, a fourth points it, a fifth grinds it at the top for receiving the head; to make the head requires two or three distinct operations; to put it on is a peculiar business; to whiten it is another; it is even a trade by itself to put them into paper.

Smith reported that because of this specialization, the pin factory produced thousands of pins per worker every day. He conjectured that if the workers had chosen to work separately, rather than as a team of specialists, 'they certainly could not each of them make twenty, perhaps not one pin a day.' In other words, because of specialization, a large

pin factory could achieve higher output per worker and lower average cost per pin than a small pin factory.

The specialization that Smith observed in the pin factory is prevalent in the modern economy. If you want to build a house, for instance, you could try to do all the work yourself. But most people turn to a builder, who in turn hires carpenters, plumbers, electricians, painters and many other types of workers. These workers specialize in particular jobs, and this allows them to become better at their jobs than if they were generalists. Indeed, the use of specialization to achieve economies of scale is one reason modern societies are as prosperous as they are.

**TABLE 13.3**

**The Many Types of Cost: A Summary**

| Term | Definition | Mathematical description |
|------|-----------|--------------------------|
| Explicit costs | Costs that require an outlay of money by the firm | – |
| Implicit costs | Costs that do not require an outlay of money by the firm | – |
| Fixed costs | Costs that do not vary with the quantity of output produced | $FC$ |
| Variable costs | Costs that do vary with the quantity of output produced | $VC$ |
| Total cost | The market value of all the inputs that a firm uses in production | $TC = FC + VC$ |
| Average fixed cost | Fixed costs divided by the quantity of output | $AFC = FC/Q$ |
| Average variable cost | Variable costs divided by the quantity of output | $AVC = VC/Q$ |
| Average total cost | Total cost divided by the quantity of output | $ATC = TC/Q$ |
| Marginal cost | The increase in total cost that arises from an extra unit of production | $MC = \Delta TC/\Delta Q$ |

# CONCLUSION

The purpose of this chapter has been to develop some tools that we can use to study how firms make production and pricing decisions. You should now understand what economists mean by the term *costs* and how costs vary with the quantity of output a firm produces. To refresh your memory, Table 13.3 summarizes some of the definitions we have encountered.

By themselves, of course, a firm's cost curves do not tell us what decisions the firm will make. But they are an important component of that decision, as we will begin to see in the next chapter.

## SUMMARY

- The goal of firms is to maximize profit, which equals total revenue minus total cost.

- When analysing a firm's behaviour, it is important to include all the opportunity costs of production. Some of the opportunity costs, such as the wages a firm pays its workers, are explicit. Other opportunity costs, such as the wages the firm owner gives up by working in the firm rather than taking another job, are implicit.

- A firm's costs reflect its production process. A typical firm's production function gets flatter as the quantity of an input increases, displaying the property of diminishing marginal product. As a result, a firm's total cost curve gets steeper as the quantity produced rises.

- A firm's total costs can be divided between fixed costs and variable costs. Fixed costs are costs that do not change when the firm alters the quantity of output produced. Variable costs are costs that do change when the firm alters the quantity of output produced.

- From a firm's total cost, two related measures of cost are derived. Average total cost is total cost divided by the quantity of output. Marginal cost is the amount by which total cost rises if output increases by 1 unit.

- When analysing firm behaviour, it is often useful to graph average total cost and marginal cost. For a typical firm, marginal cost rises with the quantity of output. Average total cost first falls as output increases and then rises as output increases further. The marginal cost curve always crosses the average total cost curve at the minimum of average total cost.

- A firm's costs often depend on the time horizon being considered. In particular, many costs are fixed in the short run but variable in the long run. As a result, when the firm changes its level of production, average total cost may rise more in the short run than in the long run.

## KEY CONCEPTS

total revenue, p. 248
total cost, p. 248
profit, p. 248
explicit costs, p. 249
implicit costs, p. 249
economic profit, p. 250
accounting profit, p. 250

production function, p. 251
marginal product, p. 252
diminishing marginal product, p. 252
fixed costs, p. 255
variable costs, p. 256
average total cost, p. 256
average fixed cost, p. 256

average variable cost, p. 256
marginal cost, p. 256
efficient scale, p. 258
economies of scale, p. 261
diseconomies of scale, p. 216
constant returns to scale, p. 261

## QUESTIONS FOR REVIEW

1. What is the relationship between a firm's total revenue, profit and total cost?

2. Give an example of an opportunity cost that an accountant might not count as a cost. Why would the accountant ignore this cost?

3. What is marginal product, and what does it mean if it is diminishing?

4. Draw a production function that exhibits diminishing marginal product of labour. Draw the associated total cost curve. (In both cases, be sure to label the axes.) Explain the shapes of the two curves you have drawn.

5. Define total cost, average total cost and marginal cost. How are they related?

6. Draw the marginal cost and average total cost curves for a typical firm. Explain why the curves have the shapes that they do and why they cross where they do.

7. How and why does a firm's average total cost curve differ in the short run and in the long run?

8. Define *economies of scale* and explain why they might arise. Define *diseconomies of scale* and explain why they might arise.

## PROBLEMS AND APPLICATIONS

1. This chapter discusses many types of costs: opportunity cost, total cost, fixed cost, variable cost, average total cost and marginal cost. Fill in the type of cost that best completes each phrase below:
   a. The true cost of taking some action is its _____.
   b. _____ is falling when marginal cost is below it, and rising when marginal cost is above it.
   c. A cost that does not depend on the quantity produced is a _____ .
   d. In the ice cream industry in the short run, _____ includes the cost of cream and sugar, but not the cost of the factory.
   e. Profits equal total revenue minus _____ .
   f. The cost of producing an extra unit of output is the _____.

2. Your Aunt Imelda is thinking about opening a pub. She estimates that it would cost €500,000 per year to rent the premises, buy a licence to serve alcohol and to buy in enough Murphy's Irish Stout from the brewery. In addition, she would have to leave her €50,000 per year job as an accountant.
   a. Define opportunity cost.
   b. What is your aunt's opportunity cost of running the pub for a year? If your aunt thought she could sell €510,000 worth of Murphy's in a year, should she open the pub? Explain.

3. Suppose that your university charges you separately for tuition and for room and board.
   a. What is a cost of going to university that is not an opportunity cost?
   b. What is an explicit opportunity cost of going to university?
   c. What is an implicit opportunity cost of going to university?

4. A commercial fisherman notices the following relationship between hours spent fishing and the quantity of fish caught:

| Hours | Quantity of fish (in kilograms) |
| --- | --- |
| 0 | 0 |
| 1 | 10 |
| 2 | 18 |
| 3 | 24 |
| 4 | 28 |
| 5 | 30 |

   a. What is the marginal product of each hour spent fishing?
   b. Use these data to graph the fisherman's production function. Explain its shape.
   c. The fisherman has a fixed cost of €10 (his fishing rod). The opportunity cost of his time is €5 per hour. Graph the fisherman's total cost curve. Explain its shape.

5. Clean Sweep is a company that makes brooms and then sells them door-to-door. Here is the relationship between the number of workers and Clean Sweep's output in a given day:

| Workers | Output | Marginal product | Average total cost | Marginal cost |
| --- | --- | --- | --- | --- |
| 0 | 0 | | | |
| 1 | 20 | | | |
| 2 | 50 | | | |
| 3 | 90 | | | |
| 4 | 120 | | | |
| 5 | 140 | | | |
| 6 | 150 | | | |
| 7 | 155 | | | |

   a. Fill in the column of marginal products. What pattern do you see? How might you explain it?
   b. A worker costs €100 a day, and the firm has fixed costs of €200. Use this information to fill in the column for total cost.
   c. Fill in the column for average total cost. (Recall that $ATC = TC/Q$.) What pattern do you see?
   d. Now fill in the column for marginal cost. (Recall that $MC = \Delta TC/\Delta Q$.) What pattern do you see?
   e. Compare the column for marginal product and the column for marginal cost. Explain the relationship.
   f. Compare the column for average total cost and the column for marginal cost. Explain the relationship.

6. Suppose that you and your roommate have started a bagel delivery service on campus. List some of your fixed costs and describe why they are fixed. List some of your variable costs and describe why they are variable.

7. Consider the following cost information for a pizzeria:

| Q (dozens) | Total cost | Variable cost |
|---|---|---|
| 0 | €300 | €0 |
| 1 | 350 | 50 |
| 2 | 390 | 90 |
| 3 | 420 | 120 |
| 4 | 450 | 150 |
| 5 | 490 | 190 |
| 6 | 540 | 240 |

   a.  What is the pizzeria's fixed cost?
   b.  Construct a table in which you calculate the marginal cost per dozen pizzas using the information on total cost. Also calculate the marginal cost per dozen pizzas using the information on variable cost. What is the relationship between these sets of numbers? Comment.

8.  You are thinking about setting up a lemonade bar. The bar itself costs €200 a week to rent. The ingredients for each cup of lemonade cost €0.50.
   a.  What is your fixed cost of doing business? What is your variable cost per cup?
   b.  Construct a table showing your total cost, average total cost and marginal cost for output levels varying from 0 to 100 litres. (Hint: there are 4 cups in a litre.) Draw the three cost curves.

9.  Your cousin Vinnie owns a painting company with fixed costs of €200 and the following schedule for variable costs:

| Quantity of houses painted per month | 1 | 2 | 3 | 4 | 5 | 6 | 7 |
|---|---|---|---|---|---|---|---|
| Variable costs | €10 | €20 | €40 | €80 | €160 | €320 | €640 |

Calculate average fixed cost, average variable cost and average total cost for each quantity. What is the efficient scale of the painting company?

10. Healthy Harry's Juice Bar has the following cost schedules:

| Q (vats) | Variable cost | Total cost |
|---|---|---|
| 0 | €0 | €30 |
| 1 | 10 | 40 |
| 2 | 25 | 55 |
| 3 | 45 | 75 |
| 4 | 70 | 100 |
| 5 | 100 | 130 |
| 6 | 135 | 165 |

   a.  Calculate average variable cost, average total cost and marginal cost for each quantity.
   b.  Graph all three curves. What is the relationship between the marginal cost curve and the average total cost curve? Between the marginal cost curve and the average variable cost curve? Explain.

11. Consider the following table of long-run total cost for three different firms:

| Quantity | 1 | 2 | 3 | 4 | 5 | 6 | 7 |
|---|---|---|---|---|---|---|---|
| Firm A | €60 | €70 | €80 | €90 | €100 | €110 | €120 |
| Firm B | 11 | 24 | 39 | 56 | 75 | 96 | 119 |
| Firm C | 21 | 34 | 49 | 66 | 85 | 106 | 129 |

Does each of these firms experience economies of scale or diseconomies of scale?

For further resources, visit
http://www.thomsonlearning.co.uk/mankiw_taylor

# 14 FIRMS IN COMPETITIVE MARKETS

If your local petrol station raised the price it charges for petrol by 20 per cent, it would see a large drop in the amount of petrol it sold. Its customers would quickly switch to buying their petrol at other petrol stations. By contrast, if your regional water company raised the price of water by 20 per cent, it would see only a small decrease in the amount of water it sold. People might water their lawns less often and buy more water-efficient showers, but they would be hard pressed to reduce water consumption greatly and would be unlikely to find another supplier. The difference between the petrol market and the water market is obvious: there are many firms selling petrol in your area, but there is only one firm selling water. As you might expect, this difference in market structure shapes the pricing and production decisions of the firms that operate in these markets.

In this chapter we examine the behaviour of competitive firms, such as your local petrol station. You may recall that a market is competitive if each buyer and seller is small compared to the size of the market and, therefore, has little ability to influence market prices. By contrast, if a firm can influence the market price of the good it sells, it is said to have *market power*. Later in the book we examine the behaviour of firms with market power, such as your local water company.

Our analysis of competitive firms in this chapter will shed light on the decisions that lie behind the supply curve in a competitive market. Not surprisingly, we will find that a market supply curve is tightly linked to firms' costs of production. (Indeed, this general insight should be familiar to you from our analysis in Chapter 7.) But among a firm's various costs – fixed, variable, average and marginal – which ones are most relevant for its decision about the quantity to supply at any given price? We will see that all these measures of cost play important and interrelated roles.

# WHAT IS A COMPETITIVE MARKET?

Our goal in this chapter is to examine how firms make production decisions in competitive markets. As a background for this analysis, we begin by considering what a competitive market is.

## The Meaning of Competition

**competitive market**
a market with many buyers and sellers trading identical products so that each buyer and seller is a price taker

Although we already discussed the meaning of competition in Chapter 4, let's review the lesson briefly. A **competitive market,** sometimes called a *perfectly competitive market,* has two characteristics:

- There are many buyers and many sellers in the market.
- The goods offered by the various sellers are largely the same.

As a result of these conditions, the actions of any single buyer or seller in the market have a negligible impact on the market price. Each buyer and seller takes the market price as given.

An example is the market for milk. No single buyer of milk can influence the price of milk because each buyer purchases a small amount relative to the size of the market. Similarly, each seller of milk has limited control over the price because many other sellers are offering milk that is essentially identical. Because each seller can sell all he wants at the going price, he has little reason to charge less, and if he charges more, buyers will go elsewhere. Buyers and sellers in competitive markets must accept the price the market determines and, therefore, are said to be *price takers.*

In addition to the foregoing two conditions for competition, there is a third condition sometimes thought to characterize perfectly competitive markets:

- Firms can freely enter or exit the market.

If, for instance, anyone can decide to start a dairy farm, and if any existing dairy farmer can decide to leave the dairy business, then the dairy industry would satisfy this condition. It should be noted that much of the analysis of competitive firms does not rely on the assumption of free entry and exit because this condition is not necessary for firms to be price takers. But as we will see later in this chapter, entry and exit are often powerful forces shaping the long-run outcome in competitive markets.

## The Revenue of a Competitive Firm

A firm in a competitive market, like most other firms in the economy, tries to maximize profit, which equals total revenue minus total cost. To see how it does this, we first consider the revenue of a competitive firm. To keep matters concrete, let's consider a specific firm: the Grundy Family Dairy Farm.

The Grundy Farm produces a quantity of milk $Q$ and sells each unit at the market price $P$. The farm's total revenue is $P \times Q$. For example, if a litre of milk sells for €6 and the farm sells 1,000 litres, its total revenue is €6,000.

Because the Grundy Farm is small compared to the world market for milk, it takes the price as given by market conditions. This means, in particular, that the price of milk does not depend on the quantity of output that the Grundy Farm produces and sells. If the Grundys double the amount of milk they produce, the price of milk remains the same, and their total revenue doubles. As a result, total revenue is proportional to the amount of output.

**TABLE 14.1**

Total, Average and Marginal Revenue for a Competitive Firm

| Quantity | Price | Total revenue | Average revenue | Marginal revenue |
|---|---|---|---|---|
| (Q) | (P) | (TR = P × Q) | (AR = TR/Q) | (MR = ΔTR/ΔQ) |
| 1 litre | €6 | €6 | €6 | |
| | | | | €6 |
| 2 | 6 | 12 | 6 | |
| | | | | 6 |
| 3 | 6 | 18 | 6 | |
| | | | | 6 |
| 4 | 6 | 24 | 6 | |
| | | | | 6 |
| 5 | 6 | 30 | 6 | |
| | | | | 6 |
| 6 | 6 | 36 | 6 | |
| | | | | 6 |
| 7 | 6 | 42 | 6 | |
| | | | | 6 |
| 8 | 6 | 48 | 6 | |

Table 14.1 shows the revenue for the Grundy Family Dairy Farm. The first two columns show the amount of output the farm produces and the price at which it sells its output. The third column is the farm's total revenue. The table assumes that the price of milk is €6 a litre, so total revenue is simply €6 times the number of litres.

Just as the concepts of average and marginal were useful in the preceding chapter when analyzing costs, they are also useful when analysing revenue. To see what these concepts tell us, consider these two questions:

● How much revenue does the farm receive for the typical litre of milk?
● How much additional revenue does the farm receive if it increases production of milk by 1 litre?

The last two columns in Table 14.1 answer these questions.

The fourth column in the table shows **average revenue,** which is total revenue (from the third column) divided by the amount of output (from the first column). Average revenue tells us how much revenue a firm receives for the typical unit sold. In Table 14.1, you can see that average revenue equals €6, the price of a litre of milk. This illustrates a general lesson that applies not only to competitive firms but to other firms as well. Total revenue is the price times the quantity (P × Q), and average revenue is total revenue (P × Q) divided by the quantity (Q). Therefore, *for all firms, average revenue equals the price of the good.*

**average revenue**
total revenue divided by the quantity sold

The fifth column shows **marginal revenue,** which is the change in total revenue from the sale of each additional unit of output. In Table 14.1, marginal revenue equals €6, the price of a litre of milk. This result illustrates a lesson that applies only to competitive firms. Total revenue is P × Q, and P is fixed for a competitive firm. Therefore, when Q rises by 1 unit, total revenue rises by P euros. For competitive firms, marginal revenue equals the price of the good.

**marginal revenue**
the change in total revenue from an additional unit sold

**Quick Quiz** When a competitive firm doubles the amount it sells, what happens to the price of its output and its total revenue?

# PROFIT MAXIMIZATION AND THE COMPETITIVE FIRM'S SUPPLY CURVE

The goal of a competitive firm is to maximize profit, which equals total revenue minus total cost. We have just discussed the firm's revenue, and in the last chapter we discussed the firm's costs. We are now ready to examine how the firm maximizes profit and how that decision leads to its supply curve.

## A Simple Example of Profit Maximization

Let's begin our analysis of the firm's supply decision with the example in Table 14.2. In the first column of the table is the number of litres of milk the Grundy Family Dairy Farm produces. The second column shows the farm's total revenue, which is €6 times the number of litres. The third column shows the farm's total cost. Total cost includes fixed costs, which are €3 in this example, and variable costs, which depend on the quantity produced.

The fourth column shows the farm's profit, which is computed by subtracting total cost from total revenue. If the farm produces nothing, it has a loss of €3. If it produces 1 litre, it has a profit of €1. If it produces 2 litres, it has a profit of €4, and so on. To maximize profit, the Grundy Farm chooses the quantity that makes profit as large as possible. In this example, profit is maximized when the farm produces 4 or 5 litres of milk, when the profit is €7.

There is another way to look at the Grundy Farm's decision: the Grundys can find the profit-maximizing quantity by comparing the marginal revenue and marginal cost from each unit produced. The fifth and sixth columns in Table 14.2 compute marginal revenue and marginal cost from the changes in total revenue and total cost, and the last column shows the change in profit for each additional litre produced. The first litre of milk the farm produces has a marginal revenue of €6 and a marginal cost of €2; hence, producing that litre increases profit by €4 (from −€3 to €1). The second litre produced has a marginal revenue of €6 and a marginal cost of €3, so that litre increases profit by €3 (from €1 to €4). As long as marginal revenue exceeds marginal cost, increasing the quantity produced raises profit. Once the Grundy Farm has reached 5 litres of milk, however, the situation is very different. The sixth litre would have marginal revenue of €6 and marginal

**TABLE 14.2**

**Profit Maximization: A Numerical Example**

| Quantity | Total revenue | Total cost | Profit | Marginal revenue | Marginal cost | Change in profit |
|---|---|---|---|---|---|---|
| (Q) | (TR) | (TC) | (TR − TC) | (MR = ΔTR/ΔQ) | (MC = ΔTC/ΔQ) | (MR − MC) |
| 0 litres | €0 | €3 | −€3 | | | |
| | | | | €6 | €2 | €4 |
| 1 | 6 | 5 | 1 | | | |
| | | | | 6 | 3 | 3 |
| 2 | 12 | 8 | 4 | | | |
| | | | | 6 | 4 | 2 |
| 3 | 18 | 12 | 6 | | | |
| | | | | 6 | 5 | 1 |
| 4 | 24 | 17 | 7 | | | |
| | | | | 6 | 6 | 0 |
| 5 | 30 | 23 | 7 | | | |
| | | | | 6 | 7 | −1 |
| 6 | 36 | 30 | 6 | | | |
| | | | | 6 | 8 | −2 |
| 7 | 42 | 38 | 4 | | | |
| | | | | 6 | 9 | −3 |
| 8 | 48 | 47 | 1 | | | |

cost of €7, so producing it would reduce profit by €1 (from €7 to €6). As a result, the Grundys would not produce beyond 5 litres.

One of the *Ten Principles of Economics* in Chapter 1 is that rational people think at the margin. We now see how the Grundy Family Dairy Farm can apply this principle. If marginal revenue is greater than marginal cost – as it is at 1, 2 or 3 litres – the Grundys should increase the production of milk. If marginal revenue is less than marginal cost – as it is at 6, 7 or 8 litres – the Grundys should decrease production. If the Grundys think at the margin and make incremental adjustments to the level of production, they are naturally led to produce the profit-maximizing quantity.

## The Marginal Cost Curve and the Firm's Supply Decision

To extend this analysis of profit maximization, consider the cost curves in Figure 14.1. These cost curves have the three features that, as we discussed in the previous chapter, are thought to describe most firms: the marginal cost curve (*MC*) is upward sloping. The average total cost curve (*ATC*) is U-shaped. And the marginal cost curve crosses the average total cost curve at the minimum of average total cost. The figure also shows a horizontal line at the market price (*P*). The price line is horizontal because the firm is a price taker: The price of the firm's output is the same regardless of the quantity that the firm decides to produce. Keep in mind that, for a competitive firm, the firm's price equals both its average revenue (*AR*) and its marginal revenue (*MR*).

We can use Figure 14.1 to find the quantity of output that maximizes profit. Imagine that the firm is producing at $Q_1$. At this level of output, marginal revenue

### FIGURE 14.1

**Profit Maximization for a Competitive Firm**

*This figure shows the marginal cost curve (MC), the average total cost curve (ATC) and the average variable cost curve (AVC). It also shows the market price (P), which equals marginal revenue (MR) and average revenue (AR). At the quantity $Q_1$, marginal revenue $MR_1$ exceeds marginal cost $MC_1$, so raising production increases profit. At the quantity $Q_2$, marginal cost $MC_2$ is above marginal revenue $MR_2$, so reducing production increases profit. The profit maximizing quantity $Q_{MAX}$ is found where the horizontal price line intersects the marginal cost curve.*

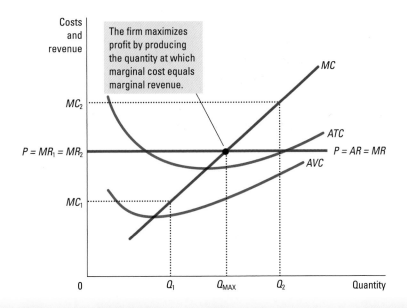

is greater than marginal cost. That is, if the firm raised its level of production and sales by 1 unit, the additional revenue ($MR_1$) would exceed the additional costs ($MC_1$). Profit, which equals total revenue minus total cost, would increase. Hence, if marginal revenue is greater than marginal cost, as it is at $Q_1$, the firm can increase profit by increasing production.

A similar argument applies when output is at $Q_2$. In this case, marginal cost is greater than marginal revenue. If the firm reduced production by 1 unit, the costs saved ($MC_2$) would exceed the revenue lost ($MR_2$). Therefore, if marginal revenue is less than marginal cost, as it is at $Q_2$, the firm can increase profit by reducing production.

Where do these marginal adjustments to level of production end? Regardless of whether the firm begins with production at a low level (such as $Q_1$) or at a high level (such as $Q_2$), the firm will eventually adjust production until the quantity produced reaches $Q_{MAX}$. This analysis shows a general rule for profit maximization: at the profit-maximizing level of output, marginal revenue and marginal cost are exactly equal.

We can now see how the competitive firm decides the quantity of its good to supply to the market. Because a competitive firm is a price taker, its marginal revenue equals the market price. For any given price, the competitive firm's profit-maximizing quantity of output is found by looking at the intersection of the price with the marginal cost curve. In Figure 14.1, that quantity of output is $Q_{MAX}$.

Figure 14.2 shows how a competitive firm responds to an increase in the price. When the price is $P_1$, the firm produces quantity $Q_1$, the quantity that equates marginal cost to the price. When the price rises to $P_2$, the firm finds that marginal revenue is now higher than marginal cost at the previous level of output, so the firm increases production. The new profit-maximizing quantity is $Q_2$, at which marginal cost equals the new higher price. In essence, because the firm's mar-

## FIGURE 14.2

### Marginal Cost as the Competitive Firm's Supply Curve

*An increase in the price from $P_1$ to $P_2$ leads to an increase in the firm's profit-maximizing quantity from $Q_1$ to $Q_2$. Because the marginal cost curve shows the quantity supplied by the firm at any given price, it is the firm's supply curve.*

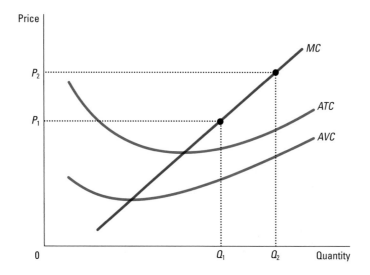

ginal-cost curve determines the quantity of the good the firm is willing to supply at any price, it is the competitive firm's supply curve.

## The Firm's Short-Run Decision to Shut Down

So far we have been analysing the question of how much a competitive firm will produce. In some circumstances, however, the firm will decide to shut down and not produce anything at all.

Here we should distinguish between a temporary shutdown of a firm and the permanent exit of a firm from the market. A *shutdown* refers to a short-run decision not to produce anything during a specific period of time because of current market conditions. *Exit* refers to a long-run decision to leave the market. The short-run and long-run decisions differ because most firms cannot avoid their fixed costs in the short run but can do so in the long run. That is, a firm that shuts down temporarily still has to pay its fixed costs, whereas a firm that exits the market saves both its fixed and its variable costs.

For example, consider the production decision that a farmer faces. The cost of the land is one of the farmer's fixed costs. If the farmer decides not to produce any crops one season, the land lies fallow, and he cannot recover this cost. When making the short-run decision whether to shut down for a season, the fixed cost of land is said to be a *sunk cost.* By contrast, if the farmer decides to leave farming altogether, he can sell the land. When making the long-run decision whether to exit the market, the cost of land is not sunk. (We return to the issue of sunk costs shortly.)

Now let's consider what determines a firm's shutdown decision. If the firm shuts down, it loses all revenue from the sale of its product. At the same time, it saves the variable costs of making its product (but must still pay the fixed costs). Thus, the firm shuts down if the revenue that it would get from producing is less than its variable costs of production.

A little bit of mathematics can make this shutdown criterion more useful. If *TR* stands for total revenue and *VC* stands for variable costs, then the firm's decision can be written as:

$$\text{Shut down if } TR < VC$$

The firm shuts down if total revenue is less than variable cost. By dividing both sides of this inequality by the quantity *Q*, we can write it as:

$$\text{Shut down if } TR/Q < VC/Q$$

Notice that this can be further simplified. *TR/Q* is total revenue divided by quantity, which is average revenue. As we discussed previously, average revenue for any firm is simply the good's price *P*. Similarly, *VC/Q* is average variable cost *AVC*. Therefore, the firm's shutdown criterion is:

$$\text{Shut down if } P < AVC.$$

That is, a firm chooses to shut down if the price of the good is less than the average variable cost of production. This criterion is intuitive: when choosing to produce, the firm compares the price it receives for the typical unit to the average variable cost that it must incur to produce the typical unit. If the price doesn't cover the average variable cost, the firm is better off stopping production altogether. The firm can reopen in the future if conditions change so that price exceeds average variable cost.

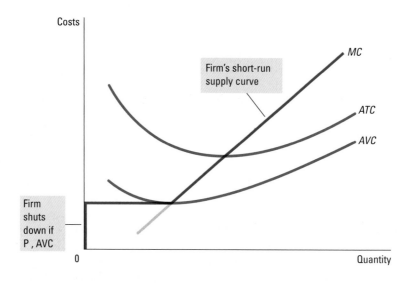

**FIGURE 14.3**

**The Competitive Firm's Short-Run Supply Curve**

*In the short run, the competitive firm's supply curve is its marginal cost curve (MC) above average variable cost (AVC). If the price falls below average variable cost, the firm is better off shutting down.*

We now have a full description of a competitive firm's profit-maximizing strategy. If the firm produces anything, it produces the quantity at which marginal cost equals the price of the good. Yet if the price is less than average variable cost at that quantity, the firm is better off shutting down and not producing anything. These results are illustrated in Figure 14.3. The competitive firm's short-run supply curve is the portion of its marginal cost curve that lies above average variable cost.

## Spilt Milk and Other Sunk Costs

Sometime in your life you have probably been told, 'Don't cry over spilt milk,' or 'Let bygones be bygones.' These adages hold a deep truth about rational decision making. Economists say that a cost is a **sunk cost** when it has already been committed and cannot be recovered. In a sense, a sunk cost is the opposite of an opportunity cost: an opportunity cost is what you have to give up if you choose to do one thing instead of another, whereas a sunk cost cannot be avoided, regardless of the choices you make. Because nothing can be done about sunk costs, you can ignore them when making decisions about various aspects of life, including business strategy.

Our analysis of the firm's shutdown decision is one example of the irrelevance of sunk costs. We assume that the firm cannot recover its fixed costs by temporarily stopping production. As a result, the firm's fixed costs are sunk in the short run, and the firm can safely ignore these costs when deciding how much to produce. The firm's short-run supply curve is the part of the marginal cost curve that lies above average variable cost, and the size of the fixed cost does not matter for this supply decision.

**sunk cost**
a cost that has already been committed and cannot be recovered

The irrelevance of sunk costs is also important for personal decisions. Imagine, for instance, that you place a €10 value on seeing a newly released film. You buy a ticket for €7, but before entering the cinema you lose the ticket. Should you buy another ticket? Or should you now go home and refuse to pay a total of €14 to see the film? The answer is that you should buy another ticket. The benefit of seeing the film (€10) still exceeds the opportunity cost (the €7 for the second ticket). The €7 you paid for the lost ticket is a sunk cost. As with spilt milk, there is no point in crying about it.

## CASE STUDY

### Near-Empty Restaurants and Off-Season Miniature Golf

Have you ever walked into a restaurant for lunch and found it almost empty? Why, you might have asked, does the restaurant even bother to stay open? It might seem that the revenue from the few customers could not possibly cover the cost of running the restaurant.

In making the decision whether to open for lunch, a restaurant owner must keep in mind the distinction between fixed and variable costs. Many of a restaurant's costs – the rent, kitchen equipment, tables, plates, cutlery and so on – are fixed. Shutting down during lunch would not reduce these costs. In other words, these costs are sunk in the short run. When the owner is deciding whether to serve lunch, only the variable costs – the price of the additional food and the wages of the extra staff – are relevant. The owner shuts down the restaurant at lunchtime only if the revenue from the few lunchtime customers fails to cover the restaurant's variable costs.

An operator of a miniature golf course in a seaside resort faces a similar decision. Because revenue varies substantially from season to season, the firm must decide when to open and when to close. Once again, the fixed costs – the costs of buying the land and building the course – are irrelevant. The miniature golf course should be open for business only during those times of year when its revenue exceeds its variable costs.

*Staying open can be profitable, even with many tables empty.*

## The Firm's Long-Run Decision to Exit or Enter a Market

The firm's long-run decision to exit the market is similar to its shutdown decision. If the firm exits, it again will lose all revenue from the sale of its product, but now it saves on both fixed and variable costs of production. Thus, the firm exits the market if the revenue it would get from producing is less than its total costs.

We can again make this criterion more useful by writing it mathematically. If $TR$ stands for total revenue and $TC$ stands for total cost, then the firm's criterion can be written as:

$$\text{Exit if } TR < TC$$

The firm exits if total revenue is less than total cost. By dividing both sides of this inequality by quantity $Q$, we can write it as:

$$\text{Exit if } TR/Q < TC/Q$$

We can simplify this further by noting that $TR/Q$ is average revenue, which equals the price $P$, and that $TC/Q$ is average total cost $ATC$. Therefore, the firm's exit criterion is:

**FIGURE 14.4**

### The Competitive Firm's Long-Run Supply Curve

*In the long run, the competitive firm's supply curve is its marginal cost curve (MC) above average total cost (ATC). If the price falls below average total cost, the firm is better off exiting the market.*

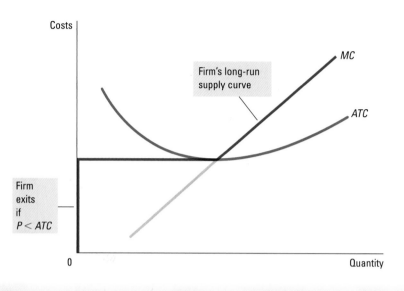

$$\text{Exit if } P < ATC$$

That is, a firm chooses to exit if the price of the good is less than the average total cost of production.

A parallel analysis applies to an entrepreneur who is considering starting a firm. The firm will enter the market if such an action would be profitable, which occurs if the price of the good exceeds the average total cost of production. The entry criterion is:

$$\text{Enter if } P > ATC$$

The criterion for entry is exactly the opposite of the criterion for exit.

We can now describe a competitive firm's long-run profit-maximizing strategy. If the firm is in the market, it produces the quantity at which marginal cost equals the price of the good. Yet if the price is less than average total cost at that quantity, the firm chooses to exit (or not enter) the market. These results are illustrated in Figure 14.4. The competitive firm's long-run supply curve is the portion of its marginal cost curve that lies above average total cost.

## Measuring Profit in Our Graph for the Competitive Firm

As we analyse exit and entry, it is useful to be able to analyse the firm's profit in more detail. Recall that profit equals total revenue (*TR*) minus total cost (*TC*):

$$\text{Profit} = TR - TC$$

We can rewrite this definition by multiplying and dividing the right-hand side by *Q*:

$$\text{Profit} = (TR/Q - TC/Q) \times Q$$

But note that $TR/Q$ is average revenue, which is the price $P$, and $TC/Q$ is average total cost $ATC$. Therefore:

$$\text{Profit} = (P - ATC) \times Q$$

This way of expressing the firm's profit allows us to measure profit in our graphs.

Panel (a) of Figure 14.5 shows a firm earning positive profit. As we have already discussed, the firm maximizes profit by producing the quantity at which price equals marginal cost. Now look at the shaded rectangle. The height of the rectangle is $P - ATC$, the difference between price and average total cost. The width of the rectangle is $Q$, the quantity produced. Therefore, the area of the rectangle is $(P - ATC) \times Q$, which is the firm's profit.

Similarly, panel (b) of this figure shows a firm with losses (negative profit). In this case, maximizing profit means minimizing losses, a task accomplished once again by producing the quantity at which price equals marginal cost. Now consider the shaded rectangle. The height of the rectangle is $ATC - P$, and the width is $Q$. The area is $(ATC - P) \times Q$, which is the firm's loss. Because a firm in this situation is not making enough revenue to cover its average total cost, the firm would choose to exit the market.

**Quick Quiz** How does the price faced by a profit-maximizing competitive firm compare to its marginal cost? Explain. • When does a profit-maximizing competitive firm decide to shut down? When does a profit-maximizing competitive firm decide to exit a market?

**FIGURE 14.5**

**Profit as the Area Between Price and Average Total Cost**

*The area of the shaded box between price and average total cost represents the firm's profit. The height of this box is price minus average total cost $(P - ATC)$, and the width of the box is the quantity of output $(Q)$. In panel (a), price is above average total cost, so the firm has positive profit. In panel (b), price is less than average total cost, so the firm has losses.*

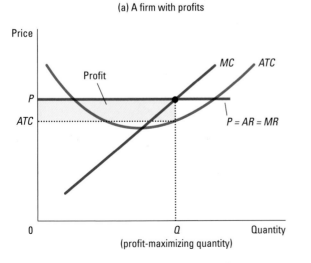

(a) A firm with profits

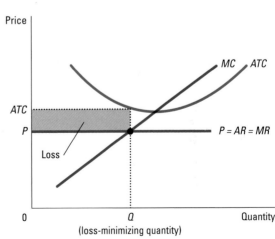

(b) A firm with losses

# THE SUPPLY CURVE IN A COMPETITIVE MARKET

Now that we have examined the supply decision of a single firm, we can discuss the supply curve for a market. There are two cases to consider. First, we examine a market with a fixed number of firms. Secondly, we examine a market in which the number of firms can change as old firms exit the market and new firms enter. Both cases are important, for each applies over a specific time horizon. Over short periods of time it is often difficult for firms to enter and exit, so the assumption of a fixed number of firms is appropriate. But over long periods of time, the number of firms can adjust to changing market conditions.

## The Short Run: Market Supply With a Fixed Number of Firms

Consider first a market with 1,000 identical firms. For any given price, each firm supplies a quantity of output so that its marginal cost equals the price, as shown in panel (a) of Figure 14.6. That is, as long as price is above average variable cost, each firm's marginal cost curve is its supply curve. The quantity of output supplied to the market equals the sum of the quantities supplied by each of the 1,000 individual firms. Thus, to derive the market supply curve, we add the quantity supplied by each firm in the market. As panel (b) of Figure 14.6 shows, because the firms are identical, the quantity supplied to the market is 1,000 times the quantity supplied by each firm.

## FIGURE 14.6

**Market Supply With a Fixed Number of Firms**

*When the number of firms in the market is fixed, the market supply curve, shown in panel (b), reflects the individual firms' marginal cost curves, shown in panel (a). Here, in a market of 1,000 firms, the quantity of output supplied to the market is 1,000 times the quantity supplied by each firm.*

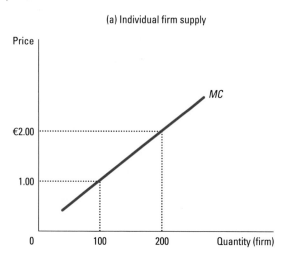

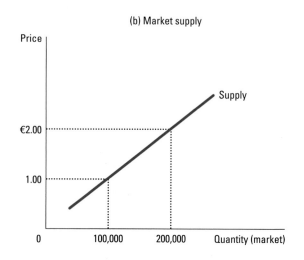

# The Long Run: Market Supply With Entry and Exit

Now consider what happens if firms are able to enter or exit the market. Let's suppose that everyone has access to the same technology for producing the good and access to the same markets to buy the inputs into production. Therefore, all firms and all potential firms have the same cost curves.

Decisions about entry and exit in a market of this type depend on the incentives facing the owners of existing firms and the entrepreneurs who could start new firms. If firms already in the market are profitable, then new firms will have an incentive to enter the market. This entry will expand the number of firms, increase the quantity of the good supplied, and drive down prices and profits. Conversely, if firms in the market are making losses, then some existing firms will exit the market. Their exit will reduce the number of firms, decrease the quantity of the good supplied, and drive up prices and profits. At the end of this process of entry and exit, firms that remain in the market must be making zero economic profit. Recall that we can write a firm's profits as:

$$\text{Profit} = (P - ATC) \times Q$$

This equation shows that an operating firm has zero profit if and only if the price of the good equals the average total cost of producing that good. If price is above average total cost, profit is positive, which encourages new firms to enter. If price is less than average total cost, profit is negative, which encourages some firms to exit. The process of entry and exit ends only when price and average total cost are driven to equality.

This analysis has a surprising implication. We noted earlier in the chapter that competitive firms produce so that price equals marginal cost. We just noted that free entry and exit forces price to equal average total cost. But if price is to equal both marginal cost and average total cost, these two measures of cost must equal

## FIGURE 14.7

### Market Supply With Entry and Exit

*Firms will enter or exit the market until profit is driven to zero. Thus, in the long run, price equals the minimum of average total cost, as shown in panel (a). The number of firms adjusts to ensure that all demand is satisfied at this price. The long-run market supply curve is horizontal at this price, as shown in panel (b).*

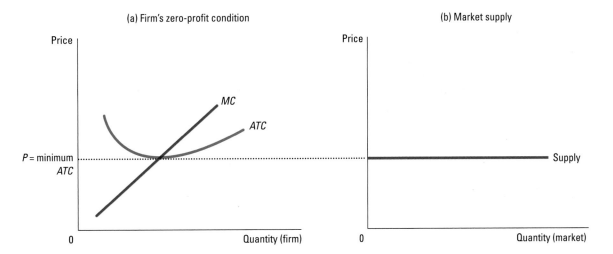

each other. Marginal cost and average total cost are equal, however, only when the firm is operating at the minimum of average total cost. Recall from the preceding chapter that the level of production with lowest average total cost is called the firm's efficient scale. Therefore, the long-run equilibrium of a competitive market with free entry and exit must have firms operating at their efficient scale.

Panel (a) of Figure 14.7 shows a firm in such a long-run equilibrium. In this figure, price $P$ equals marginal cost $MC$, so the firm is profit-maximizing. Price also equals average total cost $ATC$, so profits are zero. New firms have no incentive to enter the market, and existing firms have no incentive to leave the market.

From this analysis of firm behaviour, we can determine the long-run supply curve for the market. In a market with free entry and exit, there is only one price consistent with zero profit – the minimum of average total cost. As a result, the long-run market supply curve must be horizontal at this price, as in panel (b) of Figure 14.7. Any price above this level would generate profit, leading to entry and an increase in the total quantity supplied. Any price below this level would generate losses, leading to exit and a decrease in the total quantity supplied. Eventually, the number of firms in the market adjusts so that price equals the minimum of average total cost, and there are enough firms to satisfy all the demand at this price.

## Why Do Competitive Firms Stay in Business If They Make Zero Profit?

At first, it might seem odd that competitive firms earn zero profit in the long run. After all, people start businesses to make a profit. If entry eventually drives profit to zero, there might seem to be little reason to stay in business.

To understand the zero-profit condition more fully, recall that profit equals total revenue minus total cost, and that total cost includes all the opportunity costs of the firm. In particular, total cost includes the opportunity cost of the time and money that the firm owners devote to the business. In the zero-profit equilibrium, the firm's revenue must compensate the owners for the time and money that they expend to keep their business going.

Consider an example. Suppose that a farmer had to invest €1 million to open his farm, which otherwise he could have deposited in a bank to earn €50,000 a year in interest. In addition, he had to give up another job that would have paid him €30,000 a year. Then the farmer's opportunity cost of farming includes both the interest he could have earned and the forgone wages – a total of €80,000. Even if his profit is driven to zero, his revenue from farming compensates him for these opportunity costs.

Keep in mind that accountants and economists measure costs differently. As we discussed in the previous chapter, accountants keep track of explicit costs but usually miss implicit costs. That is, they measure costs that require an outflow of money from the firm, but they fail to include opportunity costs of production that do not involve an outflow of money. As a result, in the zero-profit equilibrium, economic profit is zero, but accounting profit is positive. Our farmer's accountant, for instance, would conclude that the farmer earned an accounting profit of €80,000, which is enough to keep the farmer in business.

*"We're a nonprofit organization – we don't intend to be, but we are!"*

## A Shift in Demand in the Short Run and Long Run

Because firms can enter and exit a market in the long run but not in the short run, the response of a market to a change in demand depends on the time horizon. To

# FIGURE 14.8

## An Increase in Demand in the Short Run and Long Run

*The market starts in a long-run equilibrium, shown as point A in panel (a). In this equilibrium, each firm makes zero profit, and the price equals the minimum average total cost. Panel (b) shows what happens in the short run when demand rises from $D_1$ to $D_2$. The equilibrium goes from point A to point B, price rises from $P_1$ to $P_2$, and the quantity sold in the market rises from $Q_1$ to $Q_2$. Because price now exceeds average total cost, firms make profits, which over time encourage new firms to enter the market. This entry shifts the short-run supply curve to the right from $S_1$ to $S_2$, as shown in panel (c). In the new long-run equilibrium, point C, price has returned to $P_1$ but the quantity sold has increased to $Q_3$. Profits are again zero, price is back to the minimum of average total cost, but the market has more firms to satisfy the greater demand.*

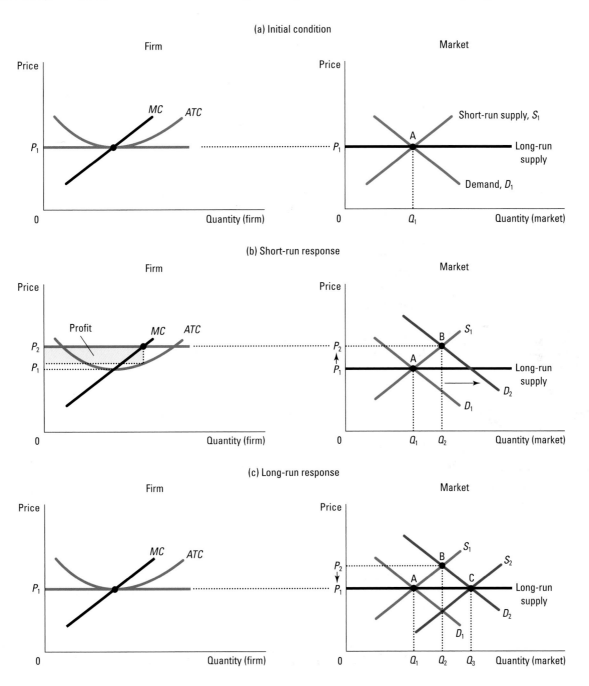

see this, let's trace the effects of a shift in demand. This analysis will show how a market responds over time, and it will show how entry and exit drive a market to its long-run equilibrium.

Suppose the market for milk begins in long-run equilibrium. Firms are earning zero profit, so price equals the minimum of average total cost. Panel (a) of Figure 14.8 shows the situation. The long-run equilibrium is point A, the quantity sold in the market is $Q_1$, and the price is $P_1$.

Now suppose scientists discover that milk has miraculous health benefits. As a result, the demand curve for milk shifts outward from $D_1$ to $D_2$, as in panel (b). The short-run equilibrium moves from point A to point B; as a result, the quantity rises from $Q_1$ to $Q_2$ and the price rises from $P_1$ to $P_2$. All of the existing firms respond to the higher price by raising the amount produced. Because each firm's supply curve reflects its marginal cost curve, how much they each increase production is determined by the marginal cost curve. In the new short-run equilibrium, the price of milk exceeds average total cost, so the firms are making positive profit.

Over time, the profit in this market encourages new firms to enter. Some farmers may switch to milk from other farm products, for example. As the number of firms grows, the short-run supply curve shifts to the right from $S_1$ to $S_2$, as in panel (c), and this shift causes the price of milk to fall. Eventually, the price is driven back down to the minimum of average total cost, profits are zero and firms stop entering. Thus, the market reaches a new long-run equilibrium, point C. The price of milk has returned to $P_1$, but the quantity produced has risen to $Q_3$. Each firm is again producing at its efficient scale, but because more firms are in the dairy business, the quantity of milk produced and sold is higher.

## Why the Long-Run Supply Curve Might Slope Upward

So far we have seen that entry and exit can cause the long-run market supply curve to be horizontal. The essence of our analysis is that there are a large number of potential entrants, each of which faces the same costs. As a result, the long-run market supply curve is horizontal at the minimum of average total cost. When the demand for the good increases, the long-run result is an increase in the number of firms and in the total quantity supplied, without any change in the price.

There are, however, two reasons that the long-run market supply curve might slope upward. The first is that some resource used in production may be available only in limited quantities. For example, consider the market for farm products. Anyone can choose to buy land and start a farm, but the quantity of land is limited. As more people become farmers, the price of farmland is bid up, which raises the costs of all farmers in the market. Thus, an increase in demand for farm products cannot induce an increase in quantity supplied without also inducing a rise in farmers' costs, which in turn means a rise in price. The result is a long-run market supply curve that is upward sloping, even with free entry into farming.

A second reason for an upward sloping supply curve is that firms may have different costs. For example, consider the market for painters. Anyone can enter the market for painting services, but not everyone has the same costs. Costs vary in part because some people work faster than others and in part because some people have better alternative uses of their time than others. For any given price, those with lower costs are more likely to enter than those with higher costs. To increase the quantity of painting services supplied, additional entrants must be encouraged to enter the market. Because these new entrants have higher costs, the price must rise to make entry profitable for them. Thus, the market supply curve for painting services slopes upward even with free entry into the market.

# IN THE NEWS

## The Invisible Hand at Work

*In competitive markets, strong demand leads to high prices and high profits, which then lead to increased entry and investment, falling prices and falling profits. To economists, these market forces are one reflection of the invisible hand at work, although that is little comfort to the business managers and owners in the industry concerned. Here's a recent example from the Australian wine industry.*

### Australian Wine Boom Ends With a Hangover
*By Nick Squires*

Australia's booming wine industry has become a victim of its own success with so many new vineyards that the country has a chronic over-supply of grapes.

Vineyards in some of the most famous wine regions, including the Hunter Valley, Margaret River and the Barossa Valley, are facing the miserable prospect of watching their grapes wither on the vine because of a lack of buyers.

The popularity of Australian wine, particularly in Britain and America, encouraged the planting of hundreds of vineyards from the late 1990s, with most growers opting for red grape varieties such as shiraz and cabernet sauvignon. Those vineyards are now starting to produce wine. ...

Australia now has 370,000 acres of vineyards, a three-fold increase compared with a decade ago. Demand for its wine overseas remains strong but the glut is so serious that thousands of tons of red grapes will go to waste

in the next few weeks. The problem has been made worse by plentiful harvests in 2002 and 2004, and predictions of another bumper crop this year, due to steady summer rain and prolonged autumn sunshine.

'It really hurts,' said Peter Lidgerwood, surveying the ripened bunches of shiraz grapes on his 23-acre vineyard in Loxton, South Australia. 'It means the last 12 months have been a total waste of time.' Despite telephoning every wine company he could think of, Mr Lidgerwood, 55, could not find a buyer. His entire crop of more than 150 tons of grapes, which he had hoped would fetch £40,000, will now be left to rot. 'You put in all this hard work and all of a sudden the buyers say they don't want the grapes. ... The next year will be very tight financially. If things don't improve there'll be a lot of for sale signs going up on the vineyards round here.'

Those vineyard owners who have managed to find willing buyers are being paid a pittance because prices have collapsed. In the Riverland region of South Australia growers received up to £340 a ton for their grapes last year; this year they are being offered £60.

'It's extremely distressing,' said Chris Byrne, of the Riverland Winegrape Growers' Association. 'If the downward spiral continues there's no way we'll be able to make a living. Already some growers are heading towards bankruptcy.' He said some wine companies were preying on the vulnerability of small vineyard owners to force down prices. 'It's a race to the bottom in terms of prices,' Mr Byrne said. 'It's a really grim situation – awful, really awful.'

Of the two million tons of grapes expected to be harvested this season, around five per cent will be left to rot. The glut is expected to last for another two years, after which reduced supply will begin to fall back into line with demand.

'The years of spectacular growth are over,' said Lawrie Stanford, of the Australian Wine and Brandy Corporation. 'There are a lot of people who came into the industry when it was on the up who are going to get burnt.'

Source: *Daily Telegraph, 23 April 2005.*

Notice that if firms have different costs, some firms earn profit even in the long run. In this case, the price in the market reflects the average total cost of the *marginal firm* – the firm that would exit the market if the price were any lower. This firm earns zero profit, but firms with lower costs earn positive profit. Entry does not eliminate this profit because would-be entrants have higher costs than firms already in the market. Higher-cost firms will enter only if the price rises, making the market profitable for them.

Thus, for these two reasons, the long-run supply curve in a market may be upward sloping rather than horizontal, indicating that a higher price is necessary to induce a larger quantity supplied. Nevertheless, the basic lesson about entry and exit remains true. Because firms can enter and exit more easily in the long run than in the short run, the long-run supply curve is typically more elastic than the short-run supply curve.

> **Quick Quiz** In the long run with free entry and exit, is the price in a market equal to marginal cost, average total cost, both, or neither? Explain with a diagram.

## CONCLUSION: BEHIND THE SUPPLY CURVE

We have been discussing the behaviour of competitive profit-maximizing firms. You may recall from Chapter 1 that one of the *Ten Principles of Economics* is that rational people think at the margin. This chapter has applied this idea to the competitive firm. Marginal analysis has given us a theory of the supply curve in a competitive market and, as a result, a deeper understanding of market outcomes.

We have learned that when you buy a good from a firm in a competitive market, you can be assured that the price you pay is close to the cost of producing that good. In particular, if firms are competitive and profit-maximizing, the price of a good equals the marginal cost of making that good. In addition, if firms can freely enter and exit the market, the price also equals the lowest possible average total cost of production.

Although we have assumed throughout this chapter that firms are price takers, many of the tools developed here are also useful for studying firms in less competitive markets. In the next chapter we will examine the behaviour of firms with market power. Marginal analysis will again be useful in analysing these firms, but it will have quite different implications.

## SUMMARY

- Because a competitive firm is a price taker, its revenue is proportional to the amount of output it produces. The price of the good equals both the firm's average revenue and its marginal revenue.

- To maximize profit, a firm chooses a quantity of output such that marginal revenue equals marginal cost. Because marginal revenue for a competitive firm equals the market price, the firm chooses quantity so that price equals marginal cost. Thus, the firm's marginal cost curve is its supply curve.

- In the short run when a firm cannot recover its fixed costs, the firm will choose to shut down temporarily if the price of the good is less than average variable cost. In the long run when the firm can recover both fixed and variable

costs, it will choose to exit if the price is less than average total cost.

- In a market with free entry and exit, profits are driven to zero in the long run. In this long-run equilibrium, all firms produce at the efficient scale, price equals the minimum of average total cost, and the number of firms adjusts to satisfy the quantity demanded at this price.

- Changes in demand have different effects over different time horizons. In the short run, an increase in demand raises prices and leads to profits, and a decrease in demand lowers prices and leads to losses. But if firms can freely enter and exit the market, then in the long run the number of firms adjusts to drive the market back to the zero-profit equilibrium.

# KEY CONCEPTS

competitive market, p. 268
average revenue, p. 269

marginal revenue, p. 269

sunk cost, p. 274

# QUESTIONS FOR REVIEW

1. What is meant by a competitive firm?
2. Draw the cost curves for a typical firm. For a given price, explain how the firm chooses the level of output that maximizes profit.
3. Under what conditions will a firm shut down temporarily? Explain.
4. Under what conditions will a firm exit a market? Explain.
5. Does a firm's price equal marginal cost in the short run, in the long run, or both? Explain.
6. Does a firm's price equal the minimum of average total cost in the short run, in the long run, or both? Explain.
7. Are market supply curves typically more elastic in the short run or in the long run? Explain.

# PROBLEMS AND APPLICATIONS

1. What are the characteristics of a competitive market? Which of the following drinks do you think is best described by these characteristics? Why aren't the others?
   a. tap water
   b. bottled water
   c. cola
   d. beer.
2. Your flatmate's long hours in the chemistry lab finally paid off – she discovered a secret formula that lets people do an hour's worth of studying in 5 minutes. So far, she's sold 200 doses, and faces the following average total cost schedule:

   | Q | Average total cost |
   | --- | --- |
   | 199 | €199 |
   | 200 | 200 |
   | 201 | 201 |

   If a new customer offers to pay your flatmate €300 for one dose, should she make one more? Explain.
3. The liquorice industry is competitive. Each firm produces 2 million liquorice bootlaces per year. The bootlaces have an average total cost of €0.20 each, and they sell for €0.30.

   a. What is the marginal cost of a liquorice bootlace?
   b. Is this industry in long-run equilibrium? Why or why not?
4. You go out to the best restaurant in town and order a steak tartar dinner for €40. After eating half of the steak tartar, you realize that you are quite full. Your date wants you to finish your dinner, because you can't take it home and because 'you've already paid for it.' What should you do? Relate your answer to the material in this chapter.
5. Alejandro's lawn-mowing service is a profit-maximizing, competitive firm. Alejandro mows lawns for €27 each. His total cost each day is €280, of which €30 is a fixed cost. He mows 10 lawns a day. What can you say about Alejandro's short-run decision regarding shutdown and his long-run decision regarding exit?
6. Consider total cost and total revenue given in the table below:

   | Quantity | 0 | 1 | 2 | 3 | 4 | 5 | 6 | 7 |
   | --- | --- | --- | --- | --- | --- | --- | --- | --- |
   | Total cost | €8 | €9 | €10 | €11 | €13 | €19 | €27 | €37 |
   | Total revenue | 0 | 8 | 16 | 24 | 32 | 40 | 48 | 56 |

   a. Calculate profit for each quantity. How much should the firm produce to maximize profit?

b. Calculate marginal revenue and marginal cost for each quantity. Graph them. (Hint: put the points between whole numbers. For example, the marginal cost between 2 and 3 should be graphed at 2 ½.) At what quantity do these curves cross? How does this relate to your answer to part (a)?

c. Can you tell whether this firm is in a competitive industry? If so, can you tell whether the industry is in long-run equilibrium?

7. 'High prices traditionally cause expansion in an industry, eventually bringing an end to high prices and manufacturers' prosperity.' Explain, using appropriate diagrams

8. Suppose the book-printing industry is competitive and begins in long-run equilibrium.

a. Draw a diagram describing the typical firm in the industry.

b. Hi-Tech Printing Company invents a new process that sharply reduces the cost of printing books. What happens to Hi-Tech's profits and the price of books in the short run when Hi-Tech's patent prevents other firms from using the new technology?

c. What happens in the long run when the patent expires and other firms are free to use the technology?

9. Many small boats are made of fibreglass, which is derived from crude oil. Suppose that the price of oil rises.

a. Using diagrams, show what happens to the cost curves of an individual boat-making firm and to the market supply curve.

b. What happens to the profits of boat makers in the short run? What happens to the number of boat makers in the long run?

10. Suppose that the European Union textile industry is competitive, and there is no international trade in textiles. In long-run equilibrium, the price per unit of cloth is €30.

a. Describe the equilibrium using graphs for the entire market and for an individual producer.

Now suppose that textile producers in non-EU countries are willing to sell large quantities of cloth in the EU for only €25 per unit.

b. Assuming that EU textile producers have large fixed costs, what is the short-run effect of these imports on the quantity produced by an individual producer? What is the short-run effect on profits? Illustrate your answer with a graph.

c. What is the long-run effect on the number of EU firms in the industry?

11. Assume that the gold-mining industry is competitive.

a. Illustrate a long-run equilibrium using diagrams for the gold market and for a representative gold mine.

b. Suppose that an increase in jewellery demand induces a surge in the demand for gold. Using your diagrams from part (a), show what happens in the short run to the gold market and to each existing gold mine.

c. If the demand for gold remains high, what would happen to the price over time? Specifically, would the new long-run equilibrium price be above, below or equal to the short-run equilibrium price in part (b)? Is it possible for the new long-run equilibrium price to be above the original long-run equilibrium price? Explain.

For further resources, visit
http://www.thomsonlearning.co.uk/mankiw_taylor

# 15 MONOPOLY

I f you own a personal computer, it probably uses some version of Windows, the operating system sold by the US company, Microsoft Corporation. When Microsoft first designed Windows many years ago, it applied for and received a copyright, first from the US government and then from many of the governments of the world. The copyright gives Microsoft the exclusive right to make and sell copies of the Windows operating system. So if a person wants to buy a copy of Windows, he or she has little choice but to give Microsoft the price that the firm has decided to charge for its product. Microsoft is said to have a *monopoly* in the market for Windows.

Microsoft's business decisions are not well described by the model of firm behaviour we developed in the previous chapter. In that chapter we analysed competitive markets in which there are many firms offering essentially identical products, so each firm has little influence over the price it receives. By contrast, a monopoly such as Microsoft has no close competitors and, therefore, can influence the market price of its product. While a competitive firm is a *price taker,* a monopoly firm is a *price maker.*

In this chapter we examine the implications of this market power. We will see that market power alters the relationship between a firm's costs and the price at which it sells its product to the market. A competitive firm takes the price of its output as given by the market and then chooses the quantity it will supply so that price equals marginal cost. By contrast, the price charged by a monopoly exceeds marginal cost. This result is clearly true in the case of Microsoft's Windows. The marginal cost of Windows – the extra cost that Microsoft would incur by printing one more copy of the program onto a CD – is only a few euros. The market price of Windows is many times marginal cost.

It is perhaps not surprising that monopolies charge high prices for their products. Customers of monopolies might seem to have little choice but to pay whatever the monopoly charges. But, if so, why does a copy of Windows cost about €50 and not €500? Or €5,000? The reason, of course, is that if Microsoft set the price that high, fewer people would buy the product. People would buy fewer computers, switch to other operating systems, or make illegal copies. Monopolies cannot achieve any level of profit they want because high prices reduce the amount that their customers buy. Although monopolies can control the prices of their goods, their profits are not unlimited.

As we examine the production and pricing decisions of monopolies, we also consider the implications of monopoly for society as a whole. Monopoly firms, like competitive firms, aim to maximize profit. But this goal has very different ramifications for competitive and monopoly firms. As we first saw in Chapter 7, self-interested buyers and sellers in competitive markets are unwittingly led by an invisible hand to promote general economic well-being. By contrast, because monopoly firms are unchecked by competition, the outcome in a market with a monopoly is often not in the best interest of society.

One of the *Ten Principles of Economics* in Chapter 1 is that governments can sometimes improve market outcomes. The analysis in this chapter will shed more light on this principle. As we examine the problems that monopolies raise for society, we will also discuss the various ways in which government policy makers might respond to these problems. The US government, for example, keeps a close eye on Microsoft's business decisions. In 1994, it prevented Microsoft from buying Intuit, a software firm that sells the leading program for personal finance, on the grounds that the combination of Microsoft and Intuit would concentrate too much market power in one firm. Similarly, in 1998 the US Justice Department objected when Microsoft started integrating its internet browser into its Windows operating system, claiming that this would impede competition from other companies, such as Netscape. This concern led the Justice Department to file a lawsuit against Microsoft. When the suit was finally settled in 2002, Microsoft agreed to some restrictions on its business practices, but it was allowed to keep the browser as part of Windows.

## WHY MONOPOLIES ARISE

**monopoly**
a firm that is the sole seller of a product without close substitutes

A firm is a **monopoly** if it is the sole seller of its product and if its product does not have close substitutes. The fundamental cause of monopoly is *barriers to entry*: a monopoly remains the only seller in its market because other firms cannot enter the market and compete with it. Barriers to entry, in turn, have three main sources:

● A key resource is owned by a single firm.
● The government gives a single firm the exclusive right to produce some good or service.
● The costs of production make a single producer more efficient than a large number of producers.
  Let's briefly discuss each of these.

## Monopoly Resources

The simplest way for a monopoly to arise is for a single firm to own a key resource. For example, consider the market for water in a small town on a remote Scottish island not served by the water company from the mainland. If dozens of town residents on the island have working wells, the competitive model discussed in the preceding chapter describes the behaviour of sellers. As a result, the price of a litre of water is driven to equal the marginal cost of pumping an extra litre. But if there is only one well in town and it is impossible to get water from anywhere else, then the owner of the well has a monopoly on water. Not surprisingly, the monopolist has much greater market power than any single firm in a competitive market. In the case of a necessity like water, the monopolist could command quite a high price, even if the marginal cost is low.

Although exclusive ownership of a key resource is a potential cause of monopoly, in practice monopolies rarely arise for this reason. Actual economies are large, and resources are owned by many people. Indeed, because many goods are traded internationally, the natural scope of their markets is often worldwide. There are, therefore, few examples of firms that own a resource for which there are no close substitutes.

"Excellent. I'll buy the lot."

## CASE STUDY

### The DeBeers Diamond Monopoly

A classic example of a monopoly that arises from the ownership of a key resource is DeBeers, the South African diamond company. DeBeers controls about 80 per cent of the world's production of diamonds. Although the firm's share of the market is not 100 per cent, it is large enough to exert substantial influence over the market price of diamonds.

How much market power does DeBeers have? The answer depends in part on whether there are close substitutes for its product. If people view emeralds, rubies and sapphires as good substitutes for diamonds, then DeBeers has relatively little market power. In this case, any attempt by DeBeers to raise the price of diamonds would cause people to switch to other gemstones. But if people view these other stones as very different from diamonds, then DeBeers can exert substantial influence over the price of its product.

DeBeers pays for large amounts of advertising. At first, this decision might seem surprising. If a monopoly is the sole seller of its product, why does it need to advertise? One goal of the DeBeers ads is to differentiate diamonds from other gems in the minds of consumers. When their slogan tells you that 'a diamond is forever,' you are meant to think that the same is not true of emeralds, rubies and sapphires. (And notice that the slogan is applied to all diamonds, not just DeBeers diamonds – a sign of DeBeers' monopoly position.) If the ads are successful, consumers will view diamonds as unique, rather than as one among many gemstones, and this perception will give DeBeers greater market power.

## Government-Created Monopolies

In many cases, monopolies arise because the government has given one person or firm the exclusive right to sell some good or service. Sometimes the monopoly arises from the sheer political clout of the would-be monopolist. European kings, for example, once granted exclusive business licences to their friends and allies in order to raise money – a highly prized monopoly being the exclusive right to sell and distribute salt in a particular region of Europe. Even today, governments sometimes grants a monopoly (perhaps even to itself) because doing so is viewed to be in the public interest. In Sweden, for example, the retailing of alcoholic beverages is carried out under a state-owned monopoly known as the Systembolaget, because the Swedish government deems it to be in the interests of public health to be able to control directly the sale of alcohol.

The patent and copyright laws are two important examples of how the government creates a monopoly to serve the public interest. When a pharmaceutical company discovers a new drug, it can apply to the government for a patent. If the government deems the drug to be truly original, it approves the patent, which gives the company the exclusive right to manufacture and sell the drug for a fixed number of years – often 20 years. Similarly, when a novelist finishes a book, he can copyright it. The copyright is a government guarantee that no one can print and sell the work without the author's permission. The copyright makes the novelist a monopolist in the sale of his novel.

The effects of patent and copyright laws are easy to see. Because these laws give one producer a monopoly, they lead to higher prices than would occur under competition. But by allowing these monopoly producers to charge higher prices and earn higher profits, the laws also encourage some desirable behaviour. Drug companies are allowed to be monopolists in the drugs they discover in order to encourage research. Authors are allowed to be monopolists in the sale of their books to encourage them to write more and better books.

Thus, the laws governing patents and copyrights have benefits and costs. The benefits of the patent and copyright laws are the increased incentive for creative activity. These benefits are offset, to some extent, by the costs of monopoly pricing, which we examine fully later in this chapter.

## Natural Monopolies

**natural monopoly**
a monopoly that arises because a single firm can supply a good or service to an entire market at a smaller cost than could two or more firms

An industry is a **natural monopoly** when a single firm can supply a good or service to an entire market at a lower cost than could two or more firms. A natural monopoly arises when there are economies of scale over the relevant range of output. Figure 15.1 shows the average total costs of a firm with economies of scale. In this case, a single firm can produce any amount of output at least cost. That is, for any given amount of output, a larger number of firms leads to less output per firm and higher average total cost.

An example of a natural monopoly is the distribution of water. To provide water to residents of a town, a firm must build a network of pipes throughout the town. If two or more firms were to compete in the provision of this service, each firm would have to pay the fixed cost of building a network. Thus, the average total cost of water is lowest if a single firm serves the entire market.

We saw other examples of natural monopolies when we discussed public goods and common resources in Chapter 11. We noted in passing that some goods in the economy are excludable but not rival. An example is a bridge used so infrequently that it is never congested. The bridge is excludable because a toll collector can prevent someone from using it. The bridge is not rival because use of the bridge by one person does not diminish the ability of others to use it. Because there is a fixed cost of building the bridge and a negligible marginal cost of additional users, the average total cost of a trip across the bridge (the total cost divided by the number of trips) falls as the number of trips rises. Hence, the bridge is a natural monopoly.

**FIGURE 15.1**

**Economies of Scale as a Cause of Monopoly**

*When a firm's average total cost curve continually declines, the firm has what is called a natural monopoly. In this case, when production is divided among more firms, each firm produces less, and average total cost rises. As a result, a single firm can produce any given amount at the smallest cost.*

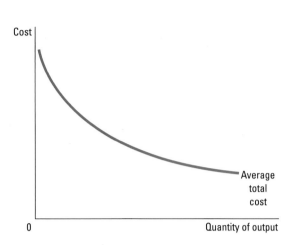

When a firm is a natural monopoly, it is less concerned about new entrants eroding its monopoly power. Normally, a firm has trouble maintaining a monopoly position without ownership of a key resource or protection from the government. The monopolist's profit attracts entrants into the market, and these entrants make the market more competitive. By contrast, entering a market in which another firm has a natural monopoly is unattractive. Would-be entrants know that they cannot achieve the same low costs that the monopolist enjoys because, after entry, each firm would have a smaller piece of the market.

In some cases, the size of the market is one determinant of whether an industry is a natural monopoly. Again, consider a bridge across a river. When the population is small, the bridge may be a natural monopoly. A single bridge can satisfy the entire demand for trips across the river at lowest cost. Yet as the population grows and the bridge becomes congested, satisfying the entire demand may require two or more bridges across the same river. Thus, as a market expands, a natural monopoly can evolve into a competitive market.

**Quick Quiz** What are the three reasons that a market might have a monopoly? • Give two examples of monopolies, and explain the reason for each.

## HOW MONOPOLIES MAKE PRODUCTION AND PRICING DECISIONS

Now that we know how monopolies arise, we can consider how a monopoly firm decides how much of its product to make and what price to charge for it. The analysis of monopoly behaviour in this section is the starting point for evaluating whether monopolies are desirable and what policies the government might pursue in monopoly markets.

## Monopoly Versus Competition

The key difference between a competitive firm and a monopoly is the monopoly's ability to influence the price of its output. A competitive firm is small relative to the market in which it operates and, therefore, takes the price of its output as given by market conditions. By contrast, because a monopoly is the sole producer in its market, it can alter the price of its good by adjusting the quantity it supplies to the market.

One way to view this difference between a competitive firm and a monopoly is to consider the demand curve that each firm faces. When we analysed profit maximization by competitive firms in the preceding chapter, we drew the market price as a horizontal line. Because a competitive firm can sell as much or as little as it wants at this price, the competitive firm faces a horizontal demand curve, as in panel (a) of Figure 15.2. In effect, because the competitive firm sells a product with many perfect substitutes (the products of all the other firms in its market), the demand curve that any one firm faces is perfectly elastic.

By contrast, because a monopoly is the sole producer in its market, its demand curve is the market demand curve. Thus, the monopolist's demand curve slopes downward for all the usual reasons, as in panel (b) of Figure 15.2. If the monopolist raises the price of its good, consumers buy less of it. Looked at another way, if the monopolist reduces the quantity of output it sells, the price of its output increases.

The market demand curve provides a constraint on a monopoly's ability to profit from its market power. A monopolist would prefer, if it were possible, to charge a high price and sell a large quantity at that high price. The market demand curve makes that outcome impossible. In particular, the market demand curve describes the combinations of price and quantity that are available to a monopoly firm. By adjusting the quantity produced (or, equivalently, the price

### FIGURE 15.2

**Demand Curves for Competitive and Monopoly Firms**

*Because competitive firms are price takers, they in effect face horizontal demand curves, as in panel (a). Because a monopoly firm is the sole producer in its market, it faces the downward sloping market demand curve, as in panel (b). As a result, the monopoly has to accept a lower price if it wants to sell more output.*

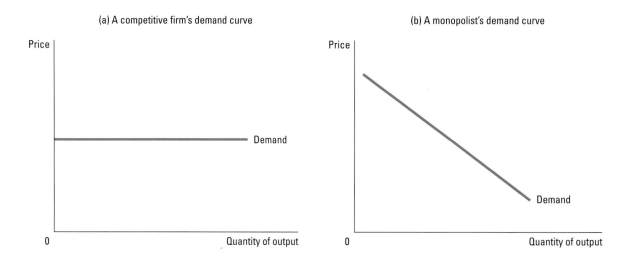

charged), the monopolist can choose any point on the demand curve, but it cannot choose a point off the demand curve.

What point on the demand curve will the monopolist choose? As with competitive firms, we assume that the monopolist's goal is to maximize profit. Because the firm's profit is total revenue minus total costs, our next task in explaining monopoly behaviour is to examine a monopolist's revenue.

## A Monopoly's Revenue

Consider a town with a single producer of water. Table 15.1 shows how the monopoly's revenue might depend on the amount of water produced.

The first two columns show the monopolist's demand schedule. If the monopolist produces just 1 litre of water, it can sell that litre for €1. If it produces 2 litres, it must lower the price to €0.90 in order to sell both litres. And if it produces 3 litres, it must lower the price to €0.80, and so on. If you graphed these two columns of numbers, you would get a typical downward sloping demand curve.

The third column of the table presents the monopolist's *total revenue*. It equals the quantity sold (from the first column) times the price (from the second column). The fourth column computes the firm's *average revenue*, the amount of revenue the firm receives per unit sold. We compute average revenue by taking the number for total revenue in the third column and dividing it by the quantity of output in the first column. As we discussed in the previous chapter, average revenue always equals the price of the good. This is true for monopolists as well as for competitive firms.

The last column of Table 15.1 computes the firm's *marginal revenue*, the amount of revenue that the firm receives for each additional unit of output. We compute marginal revenue by taking the change in total revenue when output increases by 1 unit. For example, when the firm is producing 3 litres of water it receives total revenue of €2.40. Raising production to 4 litres increases total revenue to €2.80. Thus, marginal revenue is €2.80 minus €2.40, or €0.40.

Table 15.1 shows a result that is important for understanding monopoly behaviour: a monopolist's marginal revenue is always less than the price of its good. For example, if the firm raises production of water from 3 to 4 litres, it will increase total revenue by only €0.40, even though it will be able to sell each litre for €0.70. For a monopoly, marginal revenue is lower than price because a monopoly faces a downward sloping demand curve. To increase the amount sold, a monopoly

### TABLE 15.1

A Monopoly's Total, Average and Marginal Revenue

| Quantity of water | Price | Total revenue | Average revenue | Marginal revenue |
|---|---|---|---|---|
| (Q) | (P) | (TR = P × Q) | (AR = TR/Q) | (MR = ΔTR/ΔQ) |
| 0 litres | €1.1 | €0 | – | |
| | | | | €1 |
| 1 | 1.0 | 1.0 | €1 | |
| | | | | 0.8 |
| 2 | 0.9 | 1.8 | 0.9 | |
| | | | | 0.6 |
| 3 | 0.8 | 2.4 | 0.8 | |
| | | | | 0.4 |
| 4 | 0.7 | 2.8 | 0.7 | |
| | | | | 0.2 |
| 5 | 0.6 | 3.0 | 0.6 | |
| | | | | 0 |
| 6 | 0.5 | 3.0 | 0.5 | |
| | | | | –0.2 |
| 7 | 0.4 | 2.8 | 0.4 | |
| | | | | –0.4 |
| 8 | 0.3 | 2.4 | 0.3 | |

firm must lower the price of its good. Hence, to sell the fourth litre of water, the monopolist must get less revenue for each of the first three litres.

Marginal revenue for monopolies is very different from marginal revenue for competitive firms. When a monopoly increases the amount it sells, it has two effects on total revenue ($P \times Q$):

- *The output effect.* More output is sold, so $Q$ is higher.
- *The price effect.* The price falls, so $P$ is lower.

Because a competitive firm can sell all it wants at the market price, there is no price effect. When it increases production by 1 unit, it receives the market price for that unit, and it does not receive any less for the units it was already selling. That is, because the competitive firm is a price taker, its marginal revenue equals the price of its good. By contrast, when a monopoly increases production by 1 unit, it must reduce the price it charges for every unit it sells, and this cut in price reduces revenue on the units it was already selling. As a result, a monopoly's marginal revenue is less than its price.

Figure 15.3 graphs the demand curve and the marginal revenue curve for a monopoly firm. (Because the firm's price equals its average revenue, the demand curve is also the average-revenue curve.) These two curves always start at the same point on the vertical axis because the marginal revenue of the first unit sold equals the price of the good. But thereafter, for the reason we just discussed, the monopolist's marginal revenue is less than the price of the good. Thus, a monopoly's marginal revenue curve lies below its demand curve.

You can see in the figure (as well as in Table 15.1) that marginal revenue can even become negative. Marginal revenue is negative when the price effect on revenue is greater than the output effect. In this case, when the firm produces an extra unit of output, the price falls by enough to cause the firm's total revenue to decline, even though the firm is selling more units.

## FIGURE 15.3

### Demand and Marginal Revenue Curves For a Monopoly

*The demand curve shows how the quantity affects the price of the good. The marginal revenue curve shows how the firm's revenue changes when the quantity increases by 1 unit. Because the price on all units sold must fall if the monopoly increases production, marginal revenue is always less than the price.*

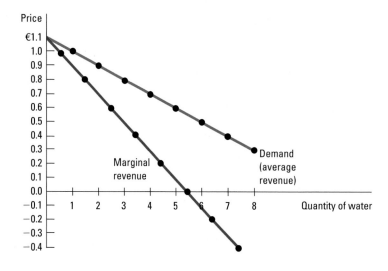

# Profit Maximization

Now that we have considered the revenue of a monopoly firm, we are ready to examine how such a firm maximizes profit. Recall from Chapter 1 that one of the *Ten Principles of Economics* is that rational people think at the margin. This lesson is as true for monopolists as it is for competitive firms. Here we apply the logic of marginal analysis to the monopolist's decision about how much to produce.

Figure 15.4 graphs the demand curve, the marginal revenue curve and the cost curves for a monopoly firm. All these curves should seem familiar: the demand and marginal revenue curves are like those in Figure 15.3, and the cost curves are like those we encountered in the last two chapters. These curves contain all the information we need to determine the level of output that a profit-maximizing monopolist will choose.

Suppose, first, that the firm is producing at a low level of output, such as $Q_1$. In this case, marginal cost is less than marginal revenue. If the firm increased production by 1 unit, the additional revenue would exceed the additional costs, and profit would rise. Thus, when marginal cost is less than marginal revenue, the firm can increase profit by producing more units.

A similar argument applies at high levels of output, such as $Q_2$. In this case, marginal cost is greater than marginal revenue. If the firm reduced production by 1 unit, the costs saved would exceed the revenue lost. Thus, if marginal cost is greater than marginal revenue, the firm can raise profit by reducing production.

In the end, the firm adjusts its level of production until the quantity reaches $Q_{MAX}$, at which marginal revenue equals marginal cost. Thus, the monopolist's profit-maximizing quantity of output is determined by the intersection of the marginal revenue curve and the marginal cost curve. In Figure 15.4, this intersection occurs at point A.

## FIGURE 15.4

### Profit Maximization For a Monopoly

*A monopoly maximizes profit by choosing the quantity at which marginal revenue equals marginal cost (point A). It then uses the demand curve to find the price that will induce consumers to buy that quantity (point B).*

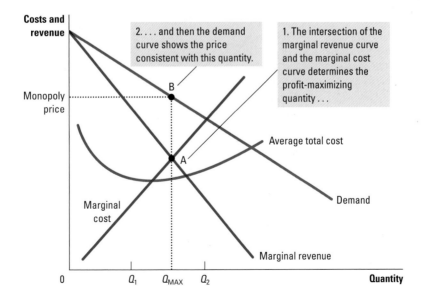

You might recall from the last chapter that competitive firms also choose the quantity of output at which marginal revenue equals marginal cost. In following this rule for profit maximization, competitive firms and monopolies are alike. But there is also an important difference between these types of firm: the marginal revenue of a competitive firm equals its price, whereas the marginal revenue of a monopoly is less than its price. That is:

For a competitive firm:   $P = MR = MC$
For a monopoly firm:   $P > MR = MC$

The equality of marginal revenue and marginal cost at the profit-maximizing quantity is the same for both types of firm. What differs is the relationship of the price to marginal revenue and marginal cost.

How does the monopoly find the profit-maximizing price for its product? The demand curve answers this question because the demand curve relates the amount that customers are willing to pay to the quantity sold. Thus, after the monopoly firm chooses the quantity of output that equates marginal revenue and marginal cost, it uses the demand curve to find the price consistent with that quantity. In Figure 15.4, the profit-maximizing price is found at point B.

We can now see a key difference between markets with competitive firms and markets with a monopoly firm: in competitive markets, price equals marginal cost. In monopolized markets, price exceeds marginal cost. As we will see in a moment, this finding is crucial to understanding the social cost of monopoly.

## A Monopoly's Profit

How much profit does the monopoly make? To see the monopoly's profit, recall that profit equals total revenue ($TR$) minus total costs ($TC$):

$$\text{Profit} = TR - TC$$

### FIGURE 15.5

**The Monopolist's Profit**

*The area of the box BCDE equals the profit of the monopoly firm. The height of the box (BC) is price minus average total cost, which equals profit per unit sold. The width of the box (DC) is the number of units sold.*

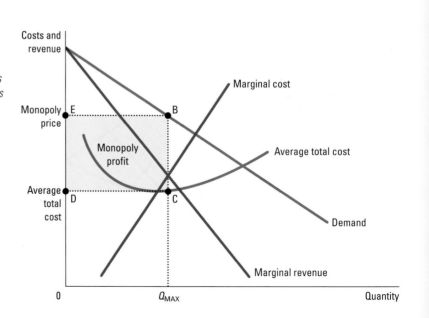

## F Y I

### Why a Monopoly Does Not Have a Supply Curve

You may have noticed that we have analysed the price in a monopoly market using the market demand curve and the firm's cost curves. We have not made any mention of the market supply curve. By contrast, when we analysed prices in competitive markets beginning in Chapter 4, the two most important words were always *supply* and *demand*.

What happened to the supply curve? Although monopoly firms make decisions about what quantity to supply (in the way described in this chapter), a monopoly does not have a supply curve. A supply curve tells us the quantity that firms choose to supply at any given price. This concept makes sense when we are analysing competitive firms, which are price takers. But a monopoly firm is a price maker, not a price taker. It is not meaningful to ask what such a firm would produce at any price because the firm sets the price at the same time it chooses the quantity to supply.

Indeed, the monopolist's decision about how much to supply is impossible to separate from the demand curve it faces. The shape of the demand curve determines the shape of the marginal revenue curve, which in turn determines the monopolist's profit-maximizing quantity. In a competitive market, supply decisions can be analysed without knowing the demand curve, but that is not true in a monopoly market. Therefore, we never talk about a monopoly's supply curve.

We can rewrite this as:

$$\text{Profit} = (TR/Q - TC/Q) \times Q$$

$TR/Q$ is average revenue, which equals the price $P$, and $TC/Q$ is average total cost $ATC$. Therefore:

$$\text{Profit} = (P - ATC) \times Q$$

This equation for profit (which is the same as the profit equation for competitive firms) allows us to measure the monopolist's profit in our graph.

Consider the shaded box in Figure 15.5. The height of the box (the segment BC) is price minus average total cost, $P - ATC$, which is the profit on the typical unit sold. The width of the box (the segment DC) is the quantity sold $Q_{MAX}$. Therefore, the area of this box is the monopoly firm's total profit.

## CASE STUDY

### Monopoly Drugs Versus Generic Drugs

According to our analysis, prices are determined quite differently in monopolized markets from the way they are in competitive markets. A natural place to test this theory is the market for pharmaceutical drugs, because this market takes on both market structures. When a firm discovers a new drug, patent laws give the firm a monopoly on the sale of that drug. But eventually the firm's patent runs out, and any company can make and sell the drug. At that time, the market switches from being monopolistic to being competitive.

What should happen to the price of a drug when the patent runs out? Figure 15.6 shows the market for a typical drug. In this figure, the marginal cost of producing the drug is constant. (This is approximately true for many drugs.)

**FIGURE 15.6**

**The Market for Drugs**

*When a patent gives a firm a monopoly over the sale of a drug, the firm charges the monopoly price, which is well above the marginal cost of making the drug. When the patent on a drug runs out, new firms enter the market, making it more competitive. As a result, the price falls from the monopoly price to marginal cost.*

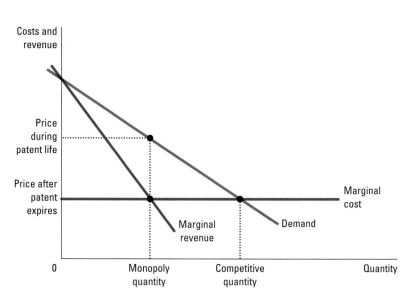

During the life of the patent, the monopoly firm maximizes profit by producing the quantity at which marginal revenue equals marginal cost and charging a price well above marginal cost. But when the patent runs out, the profit from making the drug should encourage new firms to enter the market. As the market becomes more competitive, the price should fall to equal marginal cost.

Experience is, in fact, consistent with our theory. When the patent on a drug expires, other companies quickly enter and begin selling so-called generic products that are chemically identical to the former monopolist's brand-name product. And just as our analysis predicts, the price of the competitively produced generic drug is well below the price that the monopolist was charging.

The expiration of a patent, however, does not cause the monopolist to lose all its market power. Some consumers remain loyal to the brand-name drug, perhaps out of fear that the new generic drugs are not actually the same as the drug they have been using for years. As a result, the former monopolist can continue to charge a price somewhat above the price charged by its new competitors.

**Quick Quiz** Explain how a monopolist chooses the quantity of output to produce and the price to charge.

## THE WELFARE COST OF MONOPOLY

Is monopoly a good way to organize a market? We have seen that a monopoly, in contrast to a competitive firm, charges a price above marginal cost. From the standpoint of consumers, this high price makes monopoly undesirable. At the same time, however, the monopoly is earning profit from charging this high price. From the standpoint of the owners of the firm, the high price makes monopoly very desirable. Is it possible that the benefits to the firm's owners exceed the costs imposed on consumers, making monopoly desirable from the standpoint of society as a whole?

We can answer this question using the type of analysis we first saw in Chapter 7. As in that chapter, we use total surplus as our measure of economic well-being. Recall that total surplus is the sum of consumer surplus and producer surplus. Consumer surplus is consumers' willingness to pay for a good minus the amount they actually pay for it. Producer surplus is the amount producers receive for a good minus their costs of producing it. In this case, there is a single producer – the monopolist.

You might already be able to guess the result of this analysis. In Chapter 7 we concluded that the equilibrium of supply and demand in a competitive market is not only a natural outcome but a desirable one. In particular, the invisible hand of the market leads to an allocation of resources that makes total surplus as large as it can be. Because a monopoly leads to an allocation of resources different from that in a competitive market, the outcome must, in some way, fail to maximize total economic well-being.

## The Deadweight Loss

We begin by considering what the monopoly firm would do if it were run by a benevolent social planner. The social planner cares not only about the profit earned by the firm's owners but also about the benefits received by the firm's consumers. The planner tries to maximize total surplus, which equals producer surplus (profit) plus consumer surplus. Keep in mind that total surplus equals the value of the good to consumers minus the costs of making the good incurred by the monopoly producer.

**FIGURE 15.7**

### The Efficient Level of Output

*A benevolent social planner who wanted to maximize total surplus in the market would choose the level of output where the demand curve and marginal cost curve intersect. Below this level, the value of the good to the marginal buyer (as reflected in the demand curve) exceeds the marginal cost of making the good. Above this level, the value to the marginal buyer is less than marginal cost.*

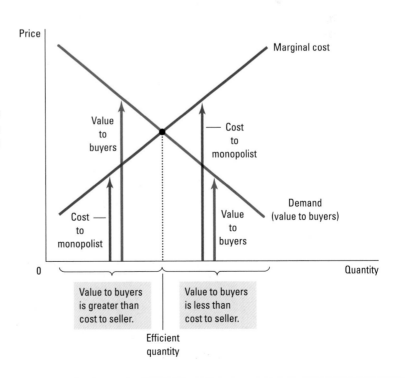

Figure 15.7 analyses what level of output a benevolent social planner would choose. The demand curve reflects the value of the good to consumers, as measured by their willingness to pay for it. The marginal cost curve reflects the costs of the monopolist. Thus, the socially efficient quantity is found where the demand curve and the marginal cost curve intersect. Below this quantity, the value to consumers exceeds the marginal cost of providing the good, so increasing output would raise total surplus. Above this quantity, the marginal cost exceeds the value to consumers, so decreasing output would raise total surplus.

If the social planner were running the monopoly, the firm could achieve this efficient outcome by charging the price found at the intersection of the demand and marginal cost curves. Thus, like a competitive firm and unlike a profit-maximizing monopoly, a social planner would charge a price equal to marginal cost. Because this price would give consumers an accurate signal about the cost of producing the good, consumers would buy the efficient quantity.

We can evaluate the welfare effects of monopoly by comparing the level of output that the monopolist chooses to the level of output that a social planner would choose. As we have seen, the monopolist chooses to produce and sell the quantity of output at which the marginal revenue and marginal cost curves intersect; the social planner would choose the quantity at which the demand and marginal cost curves intersect. Figure 15.8 shows the comparison. The monopolist produces less than the socially efficient quantity of output.

We can also view the inefficiency of monopoly in terms of the monopolist's price. Because the market demand curve describes a negative relationship between the price and quantity of the good, a quantity that is inefficiently low is equivalent to a price that is inefficiently high. When a monopolist charges a price above marginal cost, some potential consumers value the good at more than its marginal cost but less than the monopolist's price. These consumers do not end up

**FIGURE 15.8**

### The Inefficiency of Monopoly

*Because a monopoly charges a price above marginal cost, not all consumers who value the good at more than its cost buy it. Thus, the quantity produced and sold by a monopoly is below the socially efficient level. The deadweight loss is represented by the area of the triangle between the demand curve (which reflects the value of the good to consumers) and the marginal cost curve (which reflects the costs of the monopoly producer).*

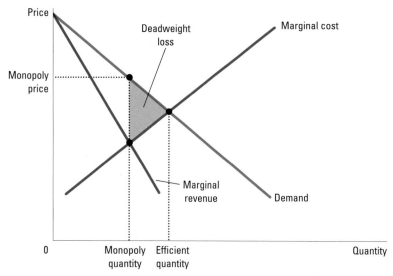

buying the good. Because the value these consumers place on the good is greater than the cost of providing it to them, this result is inefficient. Thus, monopoly pricing prevents some mutually beneficial trades from taking place.

Just as we measured the inefficiency of taxes with the deadweight loss triangle in Chapter 8, we can similarly measure the inefficiency of monopoly. Figure 15.8 shows the deadweight loss. Recall that the demand curve reflects the value to consumers and the marginal cost curve reflects the costs to the monopoly producer. Thus, the area of the deadweight loss triangle between the demand curve and the marginal cost curve equals the total surplus lost because of monopoly pricing.

The deadweight loss caused by monopoly is similar to the deadweight loss caused by a tax. Indeed, a monopolist is like a private tax collector. As we saw in Chapter 8, a tax on a good places a wedge between consumers' willingness to pay (as reflected in the demand curve) and producers' costs (as reflected in the supply curve). Because a monopoly exerts its market power by charging a price above marginal cost, it places a similar wedge. In both cases, the wedge causes the quantity sold to fall short of the social optimum. The difference between the two cases is that the government gets the revenue from a tax, whereas a private firm gets the monopoly profit.

## The Monopoly's Profit: A Social Cost?

It is tempting to decry monopolies for 'profiteering' at the expense of the public. And, indeed, a monopoly firm does earn a higher profit by virtue of its market power. According to the economic analysis of monopoly, however, the firm's profit is not in itself necessarily a problem for society.

Welfare in a monopolized market, like all markets, includes the welfare of both consumers and producers. Whenever a consumer pays an extra euro to a producer because of a monopoly price, the consumer is worse off by a euro, and the producer is better off by the same amount. This transfer from the consumers of the good to the owners of the monopoly does not affect the market's total surplus – the sum of consumer and producer surplus. In other words, the monopoly profit itself does not represent a shrinkage in the size of the economic pie; it merely represents a bigger slice for producers and a smaller slice for consumers. Unless consumers are for some reason more deserving than producers – a judgement that goes beyond the realm of economic efficiency – the monopoly profit is not a social problem.

The problem in a monopolized market arises because the firm produces and sells a quantity of output below the level that maximizes total surplus. The deadweight loss measures how much the economic pie shrinks as a result. This inefficiency is connected to the monopoly's high price: consumers buy fewer units when the firm raises its price above marginal cost. But keep in mind that the profit earned on the units that continue to be sold is not the problem. The problem stems from the inefficiently low quantity of output. Put differently, if the high monopoly price did not discourage some consumers from buying the good, it would raise producer surplus by exactly the amount it reduced consumer surplus, leaving total surplus the same as could be achieved by a benevolent social planner.

There is, however, a possible exception to this conclusion. Suppose that a monopoly firm has to incur additional costs to maintain its monopoly position. For example, a firm with a government-created monopoly might need to hire lobbyists to convince lawmakers to continue its monopoly. In this case, the monopoly may use up some of its monopoly profits paying for these additional costs. If so, the social loss from monopoly includes both these costs and the deadweight loss resulting from a price above marginal cost.

**Quick Quiz** How does a monopolist's quantity of output compare to the quantity of output that maximizes total surplus?

# PUBLIC POLICY TOWARDS MONOPOLIES

We have seen that monopolies, in contrast to competitive markets, fail to allocate resources efficiently. Monopolies produce less than the socially desirable quantity of output and, as a result, charge prices above marginal cost. Policy makers in the government can respond to the problem of monopoly in one of four ways:

- By trying to make monopolized industries more competitive.
- By regulating the behaviour of the monopolies.
- By turning some private monopolies into public enterprises.
- By doing nothing at all.

## Increasing Competition

All industrialized countries have some sort of process for legally prohibiting mergers that are against the public interest.

The earliest moves towards using legal remedies to monopoly power were taken in the US in the late 19th and early 20th centuries, forming the basis of legislation that has become known in the US as the anti-trust laws (in the UK and the rest of Europe, anti-trust law and anti-trust policy are more commonly referred to as competition law and competition policy, although usage of both terms is becoming widespread). The first and most important of the US anti-trust laws was the Sherman Anti-trust Act, which the US Congress passed in 1890 to reduce the market power of the large and powerful 'trusts' or companies that were viewed as dominating the economy at the time. The anti-trust laws give the government various ways to promote competition. For example, a proposed merger between two companies which already have substantial market share would be closely examined by the lawyers and economists in the US Department of Justice, who might well decide that the merger would make the industry in question substantially less competitive and, as a result, would reduce the economic well-being of the country as a whole. If so, the Justice Department would challenge the merger in court, and if the judge agreed, the two companies would not be allowed to merge. It is precisely this kind of challenge that prevented software giant Microsoft from buying Intuit in 1994. The anti-trust laws also allow the US government to break up companies. For example, in 1984 the government split up AT&T, the large telecommunications company, into eight smaller companies. Finally, the anti-trust laws prevent companies from coordinating their activities in ways that make markets less competitive. Traditionally, however, the US anti-trust laws start from the twin suppositions that large companies will abuse their market power and that mergers will lead to increased market power which will be abused. These suppositions are, perhaps, not unreasonable. The executives of large corporations have a duty to make as much profit as possible for their shareholders, not to raise public welfare.

Nevertheless, while other industrialized countries all to some extent follow the early lead given by the Unitied States in increasing competition through legislation, they often differ in emphasis. In the UK, for example, the approach to competition law has always been much more pragmatic than that traditionally taken in the USA, especially with respect to proposed mergers. This is in recognition of the fact that companies sometimes merge not to reduce competition but to lower costs through more efficient joint production. These benefits from mergers are often called *synergies*.

Clearly, the government must be able to determine which mergers are desirable and which are not. That is, it must be able to measure and compare the social benefit from synergies to the social costs of reduced competition. In the UK, the Director-General of Fair Trading advises the Secretary of State for Trade and Industry (a government minister) on whether or not a particular merger should be referred for investigation by the Competition Commission – an independent body with members from private industry as well as some academic economists – which then reports its conclusions as to whether the proposed merger is in 'the public interest', so that the minister can then rule on whether to allow or prohibit the merger (although the Secretary of State has the power to – and occasionally does – overrule the recommendations of the Competition Commission).

In 1998, the German popular car manufacturer Volkswagen (the name 'Volkswagen' actually means 'people's car') bought the British luxury car producer Rolls Royce, ostensibly with the aim of obtaining scale economies that would allow the resulting European firm to compete more effectively with Far-Eastern car producers and at the same time produce a company whose output was diversified across both popular and luxury cars. Many economists agreed that the potential social benefits of the merger would outweigh the costs, so that the merger was, overall, 'in the public interest'. Nevertheless, the Volkswagen-Rolls Royce merger highlights an important issue: to which legislation should such a proposed merger be subject? Legislation in the home country of one of the firms' (in this case, Germany or the UK) or legislation pertaining to *all* companies operating within the European Union? In fact, there are now well defined criteria for deciding whether a proposed merger of companies belonging to more than one European Union country is subject to reference exclusively to the European Commission rather than to national authorities, such as the size of the worldwide or European turnover of the companies in question.

"But if we do merge with Amalgamated, we'll have enough resources to fight the anti-trust violation caused by the merger."

## Regulation

Another way in which the government deals with the problem of monopoly is by regulating the behaviour of monopolists. This solution is common in the case of natural monopolies, such as utility companies like water, gas and electricity companies. These companies are not allowed to charge any price they want. Instead, government agencies regulate their prices.

What price should the government set for a natural monopoly? This question is not as easy as it might at first appear. One might conclude that the price should equal the monopolist's marginal cost. If price equals marginal cost, customers will buy the quantity of the monopolist's output that maximizes total surplus, and the allocation of resources will be efficient.

There are, however, two practical problems with marginal-cost pricing as a regulatory system. The first is illustrated in Figure 15.9. Natural monopolies, by definition, have declining average total cost. As we discussed in Chapter 13, when average total cost is declining, marginal cost is less than average total cost. If regulators are to set price equal to marginal cost, that price will be less than the firm's average total cost, and the firm will lose money. Instead of charging such a low price, the monopoly firm would just exit the industry.

*FIGURE 15.9*

**Marginal Cost Pricing For a Natural Monopoly**

*Because a natural monopoly has declining average total cost, marginal cost is less than average total cost. Therefore, if regulators require a natural monopoly to charge a price equal to marginal cost, price will be below average total cost, and the monopoly will lose money.*

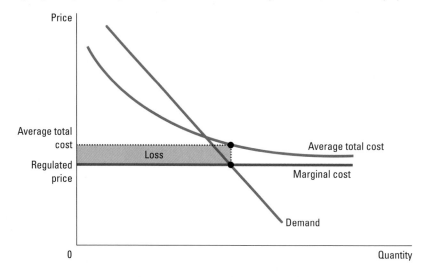

Regulators can respond to this problem in various ways, none of which is perfect. One way is to subsidize the monopolist. In essence, the government picks up the losses inherent in marginal-cost pricing. Yet to pay for the subsidy, the government needs to raise money through taxation, which involves its own deadweight losses. Alternatively, the regulators can allow the monopolist to charge a price higher than marginal cost. If the regulated price equals average total cost, the monopolist earns exactly zero economic profit. Yet average-cost pricing leads to deadweight losses, because the monopolist's price no longer reflects the marginal cost of producing the good. In essence, average-cost pricing is like a tax on the good the monopolist is selling.

The second problem with marginal-cost pricing as a regulatory system (and with average-cost pricing as well) is that it gives the monopolist no incentive to reduce costs. Each firm in a competitive market tries to reduce its costs because lower costs mean higher profits. But if a regulated monopolist knows that regulators will reduce prices whenever costs fall, the monopolist will not benefit from lower costs. In practice, regulators deal with this problem by allowing monopolists to keep some of the benefits from lower costs in the form of higher profit, a practice that requires some departure from marginal-cost pricing. For example, in the UK, utility companies have often been subject to price caps whereby the regulator determines that the real price of the company's product – a kilowatt hour of electricity, for example – should fall by a given number of percentage points each year, reflecting productivity rises. Say, for example, this is 2 per cent. The company would then be allowed to raise its prices each year by the inflation rate *minus* 2 per cent. If the company increases its productivity by, say 4 per cent each year, however (in other words it can produce the same amount of output with 4 per cent less inputs), then in real terms its profits will go up each year. In this way, the system of price caps aims to give natural monopolies the motivation to improve efficiency and productivity that would be supplied by the invisible hand in a competitive market.

# IN THE NEWS

## Mail Domination

*The postal service in many countries is dominated by a single, often state-owned or largely state-owned operator. The European Commission is trying to introduce more competition into these industries, as this article discusses.*

### Europe's Last Post: A Battle to Break the Monopolies in Europe's Postal Industry is About to Begin. Can the European Commission Create a Single Market?

When the Council of Ministers met in Lisbon a few weeks ago, Europe's political leaders set out an ambitious goal for this decade: Europe, they proclaimed, should become a dynamic and competitive knowledge-based economy. To speed that, the council called for faster progress on liberalising important economic sectors such as gas, electricity, transport and postal services.

Postal services? Surely the ministers were joking? To date, the European Commission has utterly failed to tackle the powerful state monopolies that dominate the industry. ...

Postal services, for all their lack of glamour, represent a surprisingly large sector of the European economy: the annual turnover, of €80 billion ($72 billion), is equivalent to 1.4% of the European Union's GDP, and the public-sector operators employ 1.4m people. They also represent one of the more egregious cases where crude national interests have ridden roughshod over wider European goals. ...

Today's postal firms face a greater threat than mere deregulation. The way people and companies communicate is changing. Electronic messages are substituting for 'snail mail'. Specialists in logistics are threatening to grab big chunks of the market for moving the

goods required by business. As the head of one big European post office admits, in a decade's time, national postal systems may no longer be the basis of Europe's post.

To bring home these dangers to Europe's politicians will be difficult. In Brussels, the commission is about to try to do so. It has been quietly drafting a revised directive that will determine the next phase of market opening in 2003. Officials say the aim is modernisation, rather than liberalisation. But the idea of an open market appals public-sector giants such as Britain's Post Office and La Poste of France. They argue that they must be protected in order to ensure that they can fulfil an essential public duty: guaranteeing customers a universal standard of service at a single price, regardless of where they live.

In fact, this so-called Universal Service Obligation (USO) is accepted by almost everyone in the industry as a legitimate concern. The disagreements are over how much of a monopoly is required to finance it, and in which areas. In Sweden, which fully opened its postal market to competition in 1994, simple rules protect the USO. Most observers agree that the market has become more efficient since it was liberalised. ...

Arguably the USO is less important than it appears. Much of the row turns on private letters sent between individuals. In fact, these account for only 8% of total mail volume, and Christmas cards account for half of this. In addition, state operators already use their

unique delivery networks as a competitive weapon in the market for bulk business mailings. No commercial operator can rival the reach and distribution of the incumbent post offices, which is therefore just as likely to be a marketing strength to incumbents as an expensive handicap. ...

Opposition to liberalisation runs extraordinarily deep. This became clear after the passing of the first, flawed directive. As usual with European rules, governments were given some time to implement it in national laws. Instead, several countries grabbed the chance to extend the markets reserved for their state postal monopolies.

The EC is currently investigating Italy, France and Spain for these flagrant breaches of competition law. Meanwhile, the commission is caught between governments, postal operators and their privately owned would-be competitors.

Several big European governments, for all their fine words about the future, are implacably opposed to radical liberalisation. Not only do they worry about the social (and electoral) costs. In addition, they tend to see domestic postal operators as national assets, to be protected from the marketplace. If forced to liberalise, they want to coddle their incumbent operators for as long as possible. ...

Perhaps the most vociferous advocate of open competition has been UPS, which raised $5.5 billion in a partial flotation of its own last year. It has consistently battled against incumbent operators from Europe to Canada, taking them to court where it can. Critics say that it uses its own dominant position in the domestic American parcels market to throw its weight around in international markets, although to date UPS has not been sued for any alleged

abuse. Not surprisingly, UPS wants full liberalisation of Europe's postal market, but knows it will get something short of this.

The question is how far short. The current draft directive, released for consultation within the EU in the first week of May, is surprisingly radical. Frits Bolkestein, the commissioner for the internal market whose cabinet is responsible for the directive, wants to:

- reduce the letters monopoly to 50 grams
- liberalise direct mail; and
- liberalise outbound, but not incoming, cross-border mail.

The cumulative effect, were these measures to be implemented in 2003 as planned, would be to open 27% of incumbent operators' revenues to free competition. By far the biggest impact would come from the reduction of the letter monopoly to 50 grams (16% of revenues), and direct mail (8%).

For comparison, were the letter monopoly to be reduced to 100 grams, the directive would open 20% of incumbents' revenues to competition; at 150 grams, a mere 17%. It is important to

grasp that incumbents do not stand to lose 27% of their revenues: rather, they will now have to defend this portion against competitors. Studies suggest that most incumbents should hang on to around 80% of the affected amount ....

Once the first step of liberalisation is taken at the start of 2003, there will be at least two years during which the impact on the USO will be assessed. Depending on the outcome, a further step might take effect in 2007, but it will be left open as to whether this will be to full liberalisation. This is shrewd because a big objection from incumbents has been that the effects of market opening are unknowable and could be disastrous. ...

The danger for Europe is that its postal system is left behind as e-commerce grows. ... If Europe's postal system is to flourish in the future, its operators cannot afford to hide behind a lethargic liberalisation. Otherwise, like so many parcels and letters, they will simply get lost.

Source: *The Economist*, 11 May 2000.
Copyright © The Economist Newspaper Limted, London.

## Public Ownership

The third policy used by the government to deal with monopoly is public ownership. That is, rather than regulating a natural monopoly that is run by a private firm, the government can run the monopoly itself. An industry owned by the government is called a nationalized industry. This solution is common in many European countries, where the government owns and operates utilities such as the telephone, water and electric companies.

Economists usually prefer private to public ownership of natural monopolies. The key issue is how the ownership of the firm affects the costs of production. Private owners have an incentive to minimize costs as long as they reap part of the benefit in the form of higher profit. If the firm's managers are doing a bad job of keeping costs down, the firm's owners will fire them. By contrast, if the government bureaucrats who run a monopoly do a bad job, the losers are the customers and taxpayers, whose only recourse is the political system. The bureaucrats may become a special interest group and attempt to block cost reducing reforms. Put simply, as a way of ensuring that firms are well run, the voting booth is less reliable than the profit motive.

This is why, since the 1980s, the trend has been the other way in several European countries – i.e. towards privatization of former nationalized industries.

This trend has been especially marked in the United Kingdom, where all of the utility companies are now private companies.

## Doing Nothing

Each of the foregoing policies aimed at reducing the problem of monopoly has drawbacks. As a result, some economists argue that it is often best for the government not to try to remedy the inefficiencies of monopoly pricing. Here is the assessment of economist George Stigler, who won the Nobel Prize for his work in industrial organization, writing in the *Fortune Encyclopedia of Economics*:

> A famous theorem in economics states that a competitive enterprise economy will produce the largest possible income from a given stock of resources. No real economy meets the exact conditions of the theorem, and all real economies will fall short of the ideal economy – a difference called 'market failure.' In my view, however, the degree of 'market failure' for the American economy is much smaller than the 'political failure' arising from the imperfections of economic policies found in real political systems.

As this quotation makes clear, determining the proper role of the government in the economy requires judgements about politics as well as economics.

**Quick Quiz** Describe the ways policy makers can respond to the inefficiencies caused by monopolies. List a potential problem with each of these policy responses.

# PRICE DISCRIMINATION

So far we have been assuming that the monopoly firm charges the same price to all customers. Yet in many cases firms try to sell the same good to different customers for different prices, even though the costs of producing for the two customers are the same. This practice is called **price discrimination.**

Before discussing the behaviour of a price-discriminating monopolist, we should note that price discrimination is not possible when a good is sold in a competitive market. In a competitive market, there are many firms selling the same good at the market price. No firm is willing to charge a lower price to any customer because the firm can sell all it wants at the market price. And if any firm tried to charge a higher price to a customer, that customer would buy from another firm. For a firm to price discriminate, it must have some market power.

**price discrimination**
the business practice of selling the same good at different prices to different customers

## A Parable about Pricing

To understand why a monopolist would want to price discriminate, let's consider a simple example. Imagine that you are the chief executive officer of Readalot Publishing Company. Readalot's best-selling author has just written her latest novel. To keep things simple, let's imagine that you pay the author a flat €2 million for the exclusive rights to publish the book. Let's also assume – for simplicity – that the cost of printing the book is zero. Readalot's profit, therefore, is the revenue it gets from selling the book minus the €2 million it has paid to the author. Given these assumptions, how would you, as Readalot's CEO, decide what price to charge for the book?

Your first step in setting the price is to estimate what the demand for the book is likely to be. Readalot's marketing department tells you that the book will attract two types of readers. The book will appeal to the author's 100,000 die-hard fans. These fans will be willing to pay as much as €30 for the book. In addition, the book will appeal to about 400,000 less enthusiastic readers who will be willing to pay up to €5 for the book.

What price maximizes Readalot's profit? There are two natural prices to consider: €30 is the highest price Readalot can charge and still get the 100,000 die-hard fans, and €5 is the highest price it can charge and still get the entire market of 500,000 potential readers. It is a matter of simple arithmetic to solve Readalot's problem. At a price of €30, Readalot sells 100,000 copies, has revenue of €3 million, and makes profit of €1 million. At a price of €5, it sells 500,000 copies, has revenue of €2.5 million, and makes profit of €500,000. Thus, Readalot maximizes profit by charging €30 and forgoing the opportunity to sell to the 400,000 less enthusiastic readers.

Notice that Readalot's decision causes a deadweight loss. There are 400,000 readers willing to pay €5 for the book, and the marginal cost of providing it to them is zero. Thus, €2 million of total surplus is lost when Readalot charges the higher price. This deadweight loss is the usual inefficiency that arises whenever a monopolist charges a price above marginal cost.

Now suppose that Readalot's marketing department makes an important discovery: these two groups of readers are in separate markets. All the die-hard fans live in the United Kingdom and all the other readers live in the United States. Moreover, it is difficult for readers in one country to buy books in the other. How does this discovery affect Readalot's marketing strategy?

In this case, the company can make even more profit. To the 100,000 UK readers, it can charge €30 (or the sterling equivalent of €30) for the book. To the 400,000 American readers, it can charge €5 (or the dollar equivalent) for the book. In this case, revenue is €3 million in the UK and €2 million in the US, for a total of €5 million. Profit is then €3 million, which is substantially greater than the €1 million the company could earn charging the same €30 price to all customers. Not surprisingly, Readalot chooses to follow this strategy of price discrimination.

Although the story of Readalot Publishing is hypothetical, it describes accurately the business practice of many publishing companies. Textbooks, for example, are often sold at a lower price in Europe than in the United States. Even more important is the price differential between hardcover books and paperbacks. When a publisher has a new novel, it initially releases an expensive hardcover edition and later releases a cheaper paperback edition. The difference in price between these two editions far exceeds the difference in printing costs. The publisher's goal is just as in our example. By selling the hardcover to die-hard fans (and libraries) who must have the book as soon as it is published and the paperback to less enthusiastic readers who don't mind waiting, the publisher price discriminates and raises its profit.

## The Moral of the Story

Like any parable, the story of Readalot Publishing is stylized. Yet, also like any parable, it teaches some important and general lessons. In this case, there are three lessons to be learned about price discrimination.

The first and most obvious lesson is that price discrimination is a rational strategy for a profit-maximizing monopolist. In other words, by charging different prices to different customers, a monopolist can increase its profit. In essence, a price-discriminating monopolist charges each customer a price closer to his or her willingness to pay than is possible with a single price.

The second lesson is that price discrimination requires the ability to separate customers according to their willingness to pay. In our example, customers were separated geographically. But sometimes monopolists choose other differences, such as age or income, to distinguish among customers.

A corollary to this second lesson is that certain market forces can prevent firms from price discriminating. In particular, one such force is *arbitrage*, the process of buying a good in one market at a low price and selling it in another market at a higher price in order to profit from the price difference. In our example, suppose that UK bookshops could buy the book in the United States and resell it to UK readers. This arbitrage would prevent Readalot from price discriminating because no UK resident would buy the book at the higher price. In fact, the increased use of the internet for buying books and other goods through companies like Amazon is likely to affect the ability of companies to price discriminate internationally.

The third lesson from our parable is perhaps the most surprising: price discrimination can raise economic welfare. Recall that a deadweight loss arises when Readalot charges a single €30 price, because the 400,000 less enthusiastic readers do not end up with the book, even though they value it at more than its marginal cost of production. By contrast, when Readalot price discriminates, all readers end up with the book, and the outcome is efficient. Thus, price discrimination can eliminate the inefficiency inherent in monopoly pricing.

Note that the increase in welfare from price discrimination shows up as higher producer surplus rather than higher consumer surplus. In our example, consumers are no better off for having bought the book: the price they pay exactly equals the value they place on the book, so they receive no consumer surplus. The entire increase in total surplus from price discrimination accrues to Readalot Publishing in the form of higher profit.

## The Analytics of Price Discrimination

Let's consider a little more formally how price discrimination affects economic welfare. We begin by assuming that the monopolist can price discriminate perfectly. *Perfect price discrimination* describes a situation in which the monopolist knows exactly the willingness to pay of each customer and can charge each customer a different price. In this case, the monopolist charges each customer exactly his willingness to pay, and the monopolist gets the entire surplus in every transaction.

Figure 15.10 shows producer and consumer surplus with and without price discrimination. Without price discrimination, the firm charges a single price above marginal cost, as shown in panel (a). Because some potential customers who value the good at more than marginal cost do not buy it at this high price, the monopoly causes a deadweight loss. Yet when a firm can perfectly price discriminate, as shown in panel (b), each customer who values the good at more than marginal cost buys the good and is charged his willingness to pay. All mutually beneficial trades take place, there is no deadweight loss, and the entire surplus derived from the market goes to the monopoly producer in the form of profit.

In reality, of course, price discrimination is not perfect. Customers do not walk into shops with signs displaying their willingness to pay. Instead, firms price discriminate by dividing customers into groups: young versus old, weekday versus weekend shoppers, Americans versus British, and so on. Unlike those in our parable of Readalot Publishing, customers within each group differ in their willingness to pay for the product, making perfect price discrimination impossible.

How does this imperfect price discrimination affect welfare? The analysis of these pricing schemes is quite complicated, and it turns out that there is no

**FIGURE 15.10**

## Welfare With and Without Price Discrimination

*Panel (a) shows a monopolist that charges the same price to all customers. Total surplus in this market equals the sum of profit (producer surplus) and consumer surplus. Panel (b) shows a monopolist that can perfectly price discriminate. Because consumer surplus equals zero, total surplus now equals the firm's profit. Comparing these two panels, you can see that perfect price discrimination raises profit, raises total surplus and lowers consumer surplus.*

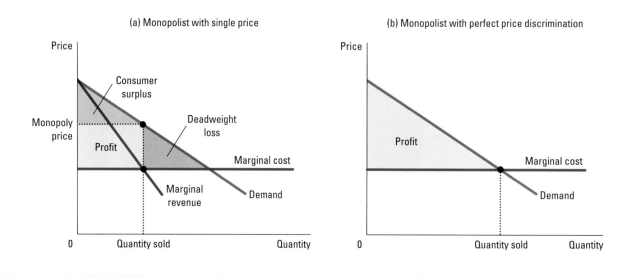

general answer to this question. Compared to the monopoly outcome with a single price, imperfect price discrimination can raise, lower or leave unchanged total surplus in a market. The only certain conclusion is that price discrimination raises the monopoly's profit – otherwise the firm would choose to charge all customers the same price.

## Examples of Price Discrimination

Firms use various business strategies aimed at charging different prices to different customers. Now that we understand the economics of price discrimination, let's consider some examples.

**Cinema Tickets**   Many cinemas charge a lower price for children and senior citizens than for other patrons. This fact is hard to explain in a competitive market. In a competitive market, price equals marginal cost, and the marginal cost of providing a seat for a child or senior citizen is the same as the marginal cost of providing a seat for anyone else. Yet this fact is easily explained if cinemas have some local monopoly power and if children and senior citizens have a lower willingness to pay for a ticket. In this case, cinemas raise their profit by price discriminating.

**Airline Prices**   Seats on aeroplanes are sold at many different prices. Most airlines charge a lower price for a round-trip ticket between two cities if the traveller stays over a Saturday night. At first this seems odd. Why should it matter to the airline whether a passenger stays over a Saturday night? The reason is that this rule provides a way to separate business travellers and personal travellers. A passenger on a business trip has a high willingness to pay and, most likely, does not want to stay over a Saturday night. By contrast, a passenger travelling for personal reasons has a lower willingness to pay and is more likely to be willing to stay over a Saturday night. Thus, the airlines can successfully price discriminate by charging a lower price for passengers who stay over a Saturday night.

**Discount Coupons** Many companies offer discount coupons to the public in newspapers and magazines. A buyer simply has to cut out the coupon in order to get €0.50 off his next purchase. Why do companies offer these coupons? Why don't they just cut the price of the product by €0.50?

The answer is that coupons allow companies to price discriminate. Companies know that not all customers are willing to spend the time to cut out coupons. Moreover, the willingness to clip coupons is related to the customer's willingness to pay for the good. A rich and busy executive is unlikely to spend her time cutting discount coupons out of the newspaper, and she is probably willing to pay a higher price for many goods. A person who is unemployed is more likely to clip coupons and has a lower willingness to pay. Thus, by charging a lower price only to those customers who cut out coupons, firms can successfully price discriminate.

**Quantity Discounts** So far in our examples of price discrimination, the monopolist charges different prices to different customers. Sometimes, however, monopolists price discriminate by charging different prices to the same customer for different units that the customer buys. Traditionally, English bakers would give you an extra cake for nothing if you bought 12. While the quaint custom of the 'baker's dozen' (i.e. 13 for the price of 12) is largely a thing of the past, many firms offer lower prices to customers who buy large quantities. This is a form of price discrimination because the customer effectively pays a higher price for the first unit bought than for last. Quantity discounts are often a successful way of price discriminating because a customer's willingness to pay for an additional unit declines as the customer buys more units.

*"Would it bother you to hear how little I paid for this flight?"*

> **Quick Quiz** Give two examples of price discrimination. • How does perfect price discrimination affect consumer surplus, producer surplus and total surplus?

## CONCLUSION: THE PREVALENCE OF MONOPOLY

This chapter has discussed the behaviour of firms that have control over the prices they charge. We have seen that these firms behave very differently from the competitive firms studied in the previous chapter. Table 15.2 summarizes some of the key similarities and differences between competitive and monopoly markets.

From the standpoint of public policy, a crucial result is that monopolists produce less than the socially efficient quantity and charge prices above marginal cost. As a result, they cause deadweight losses. In some cases, these inefficiencies can be mitigated through price discrimination by the monopolist, but at other times they call for policy makers to take an active role.

How prevalent are the problems of monopoly? There are two answers to this question.

In one sense, monopolies are common. Most firms have some control over the prices they charge. They are not forced to charge the market price for their goods,

# IN THE NEWS

## Big Brother is Discriminating Against You

*The growth of internet shopping increases the amount of information at the consumer's disposal, allowing them to make more informed choices. At the same time, however, it also gives sellers more information about the consumer, making price discrimination easier, as this article from* The Economist *discusses.*

### They're Watching You: The Internet is Eroding Privacy. It Also Allows Unprecedented Price Discrimination. Are the Two Related?

'On the internet, nobody knows you're a dog,' ran the caption of a cartoon in the *New Yorker* in 1993, showing one grinning pooch at the keyboard and another looking on. In fact, plenty of people know not only that you're a dog, but lots of other things about you, including your favourite brand of dogfood. The internet and associated technologies have had a devastating impact on privacy. The effect, argues Andrew Odlyzko of the University of Minnesota in a new paper, will be to usher in an unprecedented level of price discrimination.

That is not what most people expect. Because the internet makes it easier to compare prices, the consensus has been that sellers' ability to charge different amounts to different buyers will be eroded. Not so, argues Mr Odlyzko. Thanks to the internet, lots more opportunities for price discrimination are emerging. The most obvious example is airlines. Airline websites now discriminate in extraordinarily refined ways, setting fares that may vary not just by class but by the date of booking and the time of the flight. Some manufacturers are starting to do the same: Dell Computer, Mr Odlyzko notices, charges different prices for the same computer on its web pages, depending on

whether the buyer is a state or local government, or a small business. And such discrimination is being extended to other parts of the economy. JSTOR, a non-profit organisation that makes available online back numbers of scholarly journals, analyses the electronic data it thus accumulates to charge libraries and academic institutions different fees, depending on their use and circumstances.

Of course, not all products and services can be priced in such ways. Price discrimination will be undermined if secondary markets develop in which people who can buy at low prices resell to those who would otherwise have to pay higher prices. In the case of airlines, that cannot happen: government security requires that a passenger's name must match the one on the ticket. The result is that the ticket cannot be sold to somebody who might otherwise have to pay more for it. It is harder to discriminate in sophisticated ways among train passengers, say, because there are fewer identity checks to prevent tickets being resold.

Generally speaking, goods are easier to sell on than services. That is why American private universities are extremely good at charging students who can afford high fees and giving rebates to those who can't; and also why drug companies have been so unwilling to set prices for AIDS drugs that discriminate in favour of poor countries. The electronic collection of data,

which is the consequence (and cause) of the erosion of privacy online, provides new ways to see who is likely to pay what and to monitor whether secondary markets are developing.

Price discrimination, points out Mr Odlyzko, makes economic sense. Customers are willing to pay different amounts for the same product or service, depending on how well off they are and how much they need it. A company will maximise its revenues if it can extract from each customer the maximum amount that person is willing to pay. In primitive street markets, plenty of price discrimination goes on, through a mix of haggling and local knowledge. But in supermarkets and restaurants, the goods generally have a single, published price tag.

And that is how customers prefer it. People generally resent the idea that somebody else should pay less than they have had to do. In the 19th century, railways charged more for some freight routes than others. But customers bitterly resented that. In America, they eventually won government intervention, in the form of the Interstate Commerce Act of 1887 – 'the first serious federal regulation of private business,' Mr Odlyzko observes.

Today's customers will also hate the trend towards price discrimination on and through internet-associated technology, even if some of them enjoy lower prices and are better off as a result. Companies will therefore have to find increasingly clever ways of hiding it. They already discriminate in the non-electronic world: petrol stations, for example, charge more in some parts of town than in others. But two techniques look likely to flourish: loyalty clubs, which extract additional information from members and give them discounts; and 'bundling', or the offering of packages of services, partly in order to make it harder for consumers to compare the prices of individual components.

The world of electronic communications is full of examples of bundling, such as the charging arrangements offered by telecoms companies and by internet-service providers. Curiously, individual customers turn out greatly to prefer paying a single fee for, say, unlimited text-messaging or 90 hours of telephone talk-time, rather than paying for each item, one at a time – even though that might be a cheaper option. Many bundling arrangements take the form of site-licensing agreements, under which companies or other organisations pay a single fee for unlimited online access to a database, say, or a software package. A company may feel it has a bargain if it pays a single fee that gives all its employees access – even though it might cost less to charge only the employees who are likely to make use of the package. Mr Odlyzko's explanation is that at least with such 'bundles' both individuals and companies can be sure of the total bill. With charging by item, they cannot.

Such devices offer the best way to square the circle. As electronic media elicit more personal information, discrimination will increase. Most consumers are likely to resent it. Only by disguising what is happening can sellers discriminate, yet keep buyers happy.

Source: *The Economist*, 16 October 2003. Copyright © The Economist Newspaper Limited, London.

---

because their goods are not exactly the same as those offered by other firms. A Honda Accord is not the same as a Volkswagen Passat. Ben and Jerry's ice cream is not the same as Wall's. Each of these goods has a downward sloping demand curve, which gives each producer some degree of monopoly power.

Yet firms with substantial monopoly power are quite rare. Few goods are truly unique. Most have substitutes that, even if not exactly the same, are very similar. Ben and Jerry can raise the price of their ice cream a little without losing all their sales; but if they raise it very much, sales will fall substantially.

In the end, monopoly power is a matter of degree. It is true that many firms have some monopoly power. It is also true that their monopoly power is usually limited. In these cases, we will not go far wrong assuming that firms operate in competitive markets, even if that is not precisely the case.

---

### TABLE 15.2

**Competition Versus Monopoly: A Summary Comparison**

|  | Competition | Monopoly |
|---|---|---|
| **Similarities** | | |
| Goal of firms | Maximize profits | Maximize profits |
| Rule for maximizing | $MR = MC$ | $MR = MC$ |
| Can earn economic profits in the short run? | Yes | Yes |
| **Differences** | | |
| Number of firms | Many | One |
| Marginal revenue | $MR = P$ | $MR < P$ |
| Price | $P = MC$ | $P > MC$ |
| Produces welfare-maximizing level of output? | Yes | No |
| Entry in long run? | Yes | No |
| Can earn economic profits in long run? | No | Yes |
| Price discrimination possible? | No | Yes |

## SUMMARY

- A monopoly is a firm that is the sole seller in its market. A monopoly arises when a single firm owns a key resource, when the government gives a firm the exclusive right to produce a good, or when a single firm can supply the entire market at a smaller cost than many firms could.

- Because a monopoly is the sole producer in its market, it faces a downward sloping demand curve for its product. When a monopoly increases production by 1 unit, it causes the price of its good to fall, which reduces the amount of revenue earned on all units produced. As a result, a monopoly's marginal revenue is always below the price of its good.

- Like a competitive firm, a monopoly firm maximizes profit by producing the quantity at which marginal revenue equals marginal cost. The monopoly then chooses the price at which that quantity is demanded. Unlike a competitive firm, a monopoly firm's price exceeds its marginal revenue, so its price exceeds marginal cost.

- A monopolist's profit-maximizing level of output is below the level that maximizes the sum of consumer and producer surplus. That is, when the monopoly charges a price above marginal cost, some consumers who value the good more than its cost of production do not buy it. As a result, monopoly causes deadweight losses similar to the deadweight losses caused by taxes.

- Policy makers can respond to the inefficiency of monopoly behaviour in four ways. They can use competition law to try to make the industry more competitive. They can regulate the prices that the monopoly charges. They can turn the monopolist into a government-run enterprise. Or, if the market failure is deemed small compared to the inevitable imperfections of policies, they can do nothing at all.

- Monopolists often can raise their profits by charging different prices for the same good based on a buyer's willingness to pay. This practice of price discrimination can raise economic welfare by getting the good to some consumers who otherwise would not buy it. In the extreme case of perfect price discrimination, the deadweight losses of monopoly are completely eliminated. More generally, when price discrimination is imperfect, it can either raise or lower welfare compared to the outcome with a single monopoly price.

## KEY CONCEPTS

## QUESTIONS FOR REVIEW

1. Give an example of a government-created monopoly. Is creating this monopoly necessarily bad public policy? Explain.

2. Define natural monopoly. What does the size of a market have to do with whether an industry is a natural monopoly?

3. Why is a monopolist's marginal revenue less than the price of its good? Can marginal revenue ever be negative? Explain.

4. Draw the demand, marginal revenue and marginal cost curves for a monopolist. Show the profit-maximizing level of output. Show the profit-maximizing price.

5. In your diagram from the previous question, show the level of output that maximizes total surplus. Show the deadweight loss from the monopoly. Explain your answer.

6. What gives the government the power to regulate mergers between firms? From the standpoint of the welfare of society, give a good reason and a bad reason that two firms might want to merge.

7. Describe the two problems that arise when regulators tell a natural monopoly that it must set a price equal to marginal cost.

8. Give two examples of price discrimination. In each case, explain why the monopolist chooses to follow this business strategy.

# PROBLEMS AND APPLICATIONS

1. A publisher faces the following demand schedule for the next novel of one of its popular authors:

| Price | Quantity demanded |
| --- | --- |
| €100 | 0 |
| 90 | 100,000 |
| 80 | 200,000 |
| 70 | 300,000 |
| 60 | 400,000 |
| 50 | 500,000 |
| 40 | 600,000 |
| 30 | 700,000 |
| 20 | 800,000 |
| 10 | 900,000 |
| 0 | 1,000,000 |

The author is paid €2 million to write the book, and the marginal cost of publishing the book is a constant €10 per book.

a. Compute total revenue, total cost and profit at each quantity. What quantity would a profit-maximizing publisher choose? What price would it charge?

b. Compute marginal revenue. (Recall that $MR = \Delta TR/\Delta Q$.) How does marginal revenue compare to the price? Explain.

c. Graph the marginal revenue, marginal cost and demand curves. At what quantity do the marginal revenue and marginal cost curves cross? What does this signify?

d. In your graph, shade in the deadweight loss. Explain in words what this means.

e. If the author were paid €3 million instead of €2 million to write the book, how would this affect the publisher's decision regarding the price to charge? Explain.

f. Suppose the publisher was not profit-maximizing but was concerned with maximizing economic efficiency. What price would it charge for the book? How much profit would it make at this price?

2. Suppose that a natural monopolist was required by law to charge average total cost. On a diagram, label the price charged and the deadweight loss to society relative to marginal-cost pricing.

3. Consider the delivery of mail. In general, what is the shape of the average total cost curve? How might the shape differ between isolated rural areas and densely populated urban areas? How might the shape have changed over time? Explain.

4. Suppose the Eau de Jeunesse Water Company has a monopoly on bottled water sales in France. If the price of tap water increases, what is the change in Eau de Jeunesse's profit-maximizing levels of output, price and profit? Explain in words and with a graph.

5. A small town is served by many competing supermarkets, which have constant marginal cost.

a. Using a diagram of the market for groceries, show the consumer surplus, producer surplus and total surplus.

b. Now suppose that the independent supermarkets combine into one chain. Using a new diagram, show the new consumer surplus, producer surplus and total surplus. Relative to the competitive market, what is the transfer from consumers to producers? What is the deadweight loss?

6. Guy Rope and his backing group, the Tent Pegs, have just finished recording their latest music CD. Their record company's marketing department determines that the demand for the CD is as follows:

| Price | Number of CDs |
| --- | --- |
| €24 | 10,000 |
| 22 | 20,000 |
| 20 | 30,000 |
| 18 | 40,000 |
| 16 | 50,000 |
| 14 | 60,000 |

The company can produce the CD with no fixed cost and a variable cost of €5 per CD.

a. Find total revenue for quantity equal to 10,000, 20,000 and so on. What is the marginal revenue for each 10,000 increase in the quantity sold?

b. What quantity of CDs would maximize profit? What would the price be? What would the profit be?

c. If you were Guy Rope's agent, what recording fee would you advise Guy to demand from the record company? Why?

7. In 1969 the US government charged IBM with monopolizing the computer market. The government argued (correctly) that a large share of all mainframe computers sold in the United States were produced by IBM. IBM argued (correctly) that a much smaller share of the market for *all* types of computers consisted of IBM products. Based on these facts, do you think that the government should have brought a lawsuit against IBM for violating the US anti-trust laws? Explain.

8. A company is considering building a bridge across a river. The bridge would cost €2 million to build and nothing to maintain. The following table shows the company's anticipated demand over the lifetime of the bridge:

| Price per crossing | Number of crossings (in thousands) |
| --- | --- |
| €8 | 0 |
| 7 | 100 |
| 6 | 200 |
| 5 | 300 |
| 4 | 400 |
| 3 | 500 |
| 2 | 600 |
| 1 | 700 |
| 0 | 800 |

   a. If the company were to build the bridge, what would be its profit-maximizing price? Would that be the efficient level of output? Why or why not?
   b. If the company is interested in maximizing profit, should it build the bridge? What would be its profit or loss?
   c. If the government were to build the bridge, what price should it charge?
   d. Should the government build the bridge? Explain.

9. The Placebo Drug Company holds a patent on one of its discoveries.
   a. Assuming that the production of the drug involves rising marginal cost, draw a diagram to illustrate Placebo's profit-maximizing price and quantity. Also show Placebo's profits.
   b. Now suppose that the government imposes a tax on each bottle of the drug produced. On a new diagram, illustrate Placebo's new price and quantity. How does each compare to your answer in part (a)?
   c. Although it is not easy to see in your diagrams, the tax reduces Placebo's profit. Explain why this must be true.
   d. Instead of the tax per bottle, suppose that the government imposes a tax on Placebo of €10,000 regardless of how many bottles are produced. How does this tax affect Placebo's price, quantity and profits? Explain.

10. Tom, Dick and Harry run the only saloon in town. Tom wants to sell as many drinks as possible without losing money. Dick wants the saloon to bring in as much revenue as possible. Harry wants to make the largest possible profits. Using a single diagram of the saloon's demand curve and its cost curves, show the price and quantity combinations favoured by each of the three partners. Explain.

11. The Best Computer Company just developed a new computer chip, on which it immediately acquires a patent.
   a. Draw a diagram that shows the consumer surplus, producer surplus and total surplus in the market for this new chip.
   b. What happens to these three measures of surplus if the firm can perfectly price discriminate? What is the change in deadweight loss? What transfers occur?

12. Explain why a monopolist will always produce a quantity at which the demand curve is elastic. (Hint: if demand is inelastic and the firm raises its price, what happens to total revenue and total costs?)

13. Singer Britney Spears has a monopoly over a scarce resource: herself. She is the only person who can produce a Britney Spears concert. Does this fact imply that the government should regulate the prices of her concerts? Why or why not?

14. Napster, the on-line file-swapping service, allowed people to use the internet to download copies of their favourite songs from other people's computers without cost. In what sense did Napster enhance economic efficiency in the short run? In what sense might Napster have reduced economic efficiency in the long run? Why do you think the courts eventually shut Napster down? Do you think this was the right policy?

15. Many schemes for price discriminating involve some cost. For example, discount coupons take up time and resources from both the buyer and the seller. This question considers the implications of costly price discrimination. To keep things simple, let's assume that our monopolist's production costs are simply proportional to output, so that average total cost and marginal cost are constant and equal to each other.
   a. Draw the cost, demand and marginal revenue curves for the monopolist. Show the price the monopolist would charge without price discrimination.
   b. In your diagram, mark the area equal to the monopolist's profit and call it X. Mark the area equal to consumer surplus and call it Y. Mark the area equal to the deadweight loss and call it Z.
   c. Now suppose that the monopolist can perfectly price discriminate. What is the monopolist's profit? (Give your answer in terms of X, Y and Z.)
   d. What is the change in the monopolist's profit from price discrimination? What is the change in total surplus from price discrimination? Which change is larger? Explain. (Give your answer in terms of X, Y and Z.)
   e. Now suppose that there is some cost of price discrimination. To model this cost, let's assume that

the monopolist has to pay a fixed cost *C* in order to price discriminate. How would a monopolist make the decision whether to pay this fixed cost? (Give your answer in terms of X, Y, Z and *C*.)

f.  How would a benevolent social planner, who cares about total surplus, decide whether the monopolist should price discriminate? (Give your answer in terms of X, Y, Z and *C*.)

g.  Compare your answers to parts (e) and (f). How does the monopolist's incentive to price discriminate differ from the social planner's? Is it possible that the monopolist will price discriminate even though it is not socially desirable?

For further resources, visit
http://www.thomsonlearning.co.uk/mankiw_taylor

# 16 OLIGOPOLY

The British love chocolate. The average Brit eats about 200 bars of chocolate a year. Out of all the nations in the world, only the Swiss eat more. But if you buy a bar of chocolate in the UK, it will most likely be made by one of three companies: Cadbury Schweppes, Mars or Nestlé. These three firms make almost all of the chocolate bars sold in the United Kingdom. Together, they determine the quantity of chocolate bars produced and, given the market demand curve, the price at which chocolate bars are sold.

How can we describe the UK market for chocolate bars? The previous two chapters discussed two types of market structure. In a competitive market, each firm is so small compared to the market that it cannot influence the price of its product and, therefore, takes the price as given by market conditions. In a monopolized market, a single firm supplies the entire market for a good, and that firm can choose any price and quantity on the market demand curve.

The British market for chocolate bars fits neither the competitive nor the monopoly model. Competition and monopoly are extreme forms of market structure. Competition occurs when there are many firms in a market offering essentially identical products; monopoly occurs when there is only one firm in a market. It is natural to start the study of industrial organization with these polar cases, for they are the easiest cases to understand. Yet many industries, including the chocolate industry, fall somewhere between these two extremes. Firms in these industries have competitors but, at the same time, do not face so much competition that they are price takers. Economists call this situation *imperfect competition*.

In this chapter we discuss the types of imperfect competition and examine a particular type called *oligopoly*. The essence of an oligopolistic market is that there are only a few sellers. As a result, the actions of any one seller in the market can have a large impact on the profits of all the other sellers. That is, oligopolistic firms are interdependent in a way that competitive firms are not. Our goal in this chapter is to see how this interdependence shapes the firms' behaviour and what problems it raises for public policy.

## BETWEEN MONOPOLY AND PERFECT COMPETITION

The previous two chapters analysed markets with many competitive firms and markets with a single monopoly firm. In Chapter 14 we saw that the price in a perfectly competitive market always equals the marginal cost of production. We also saw that, in the long run, entry and exit drive economic profit to zero, so the price also equals average total cost. In Chapter 15 we saw how firms with market power can use that power to keep prices above marginal cost, leading to a positive economic profit for the firm and a deadweight loss for society.

The cases of perfect competition and monopoly illustrate some important ideas about how markets work. Most markets in the economy, however, include elements of both these cases and, therefore, are not completely described by either of them. The typical firm in the economy faces competition, but the competition is not so rigorous as to make the firm exactly described by the price-taking firm analysed in Chapter 14. The typical firm also has some degree of market power, but its market power is not so great that the firm can be exactly described by the monopoly firm analysed in Chapter 15. In other words, the typical firm in our economy is imperfectly competitive.

**oligopoly**
a market structure in which only a few sellers offer similar or identical products

**monopolistic competition**
a market structure in which many firms sell products that are similar but not identical

There are two types of imperfectly competitive markets. An **oligopoly** is a market with only a few sellers, each offering a product similar or identical to the others. One example is the market for chocolate bars. Another is the world market for crude oil: a few countries in the Middle East control much of the world's oil reserves. **Monopolistic competition** describes a market structure in which there are many firms selling products that are similar but not identical. Examples include the markets for novels, films, CDs and computer games. In a monopolistically competitive market, each firm has a monopoly over the product it makes, but many other firms make similar products that compete for the same customers.

Figure 16.1 summarizes the four types of market structure. The first question to ask about any market is how many firms there are. If there is only one firm, the market is a monopoly. If there are only a few firms, the market is an oligopoly. If there are many firms, we need to ask another question: do the firms sell identical or differentiated products? If the many firms sell differentiated products, the market is monopolistically competitive. If the many firms sell identical products, the market is perfectly competitive.

Reality, of course, is never as clear-cut as theory. In some cases you may find it hard to decide what structure best describes a market. There is, for instance, no magic number that separates 'few' from 'many' when counting the number of firms. (Do the approximately dozen companies that now sell cars in Europe make this market an oligopoly or more competitive? The answer is open to debate.) Similarly, there is no sure way to determine when products are differentiated and when they are identical. (Are different brands of milk really the same? Again, the answer is debatable.) When analysing actual markets, economists have to keep in mind the lessons learned from studying all types of market structure and then apply each lesson as it seems appropriate.

Now that we understand how economists define the various types of market structure, we can continue our analysis of them. In the next chapter we analyse monopolistic competition. In this chapter we examine oligopoly.

### FIGURE 16.1

**The Four Types of Market Structure**

*Economists who study industrial organization divide markets into four types – monopoly, oligopoly, monopolistic competition and perfect competition.*

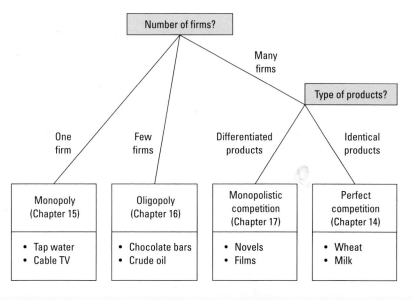

**Quick Quiz** Define oligopoly and monopolistic competition and give an example of each.

# MARKETS WITH ONLY A FEW SELLERS

Because an oligopolistic market has only a small group of sellers, a key feature of oligopoly is the tension between cooperation and self-interest. The group of oligopolists is best off cooperating and acting like a monopolist – producing a small quantity of output and charging a price above marginal cost. Yet because each oligopolist cares about only its own profit, there are powerful incentives at work that hinder a group of firms from maintaining the monopoly outcome.

## A Duopoly Example

To understand the behaviour of oligopolies, let's consider an oligopoly with only two members, called a *duopoly*. Duopoly is the simplest type of oligopoly. Oligopolies with three or more members face the same problems as oligopolies with only two members, so we do not lose much by starting with the case of duopoly.

Imagine a town in which only two residents – Jack and Jill – own wells that produce water safe for drinking. Each Saturday, Jack and Jill decide how many litres of water to pump, bring the water to town, and sell it for whatever price the market will bear. To keep things simple, suppose that Jack and Jill can pump as

## TABLE 16.1

**The Demand Schedule for Water**

| Quantity (in litres) | Price | Total revenue (and total profit) |
|---|---|---|
| 0 | €120 | €0 |
| 10 | 110 | 1,100 |
| 20 | 100 | 2,000 |
| 30 | 90 | 2,700 |
| 40 | 80 | 3,200 |
| 50 | 70 | 3,500 |
| 60 | 60 | 3,600 |
| 70 | 50 | 3,500 |
| 80 | 40 | 3,200 |
| 90 | 30 | 2,700 |
| 100 | 20 | 2,000 |
| 110 | 10 | 1,100 |
| 120 | 0 | 0 |

much water as they want without cost. That is, the marginal cost of water equals zero.

Table 16.1 shows the town's demand schedule for water. The first column shows the total quantity demanded, and the second column shows the price. If the two well owners sell a total of 10 litres of water, water goes for €110 a litre. If they sell a total of 20 litres, the price falls to €100 a litre. And so on. If you graphed these two columns of numbers, you would get a standard downward sloping demand curve.

The last column in Table 16.1 shows the total revenue from the sale of water. It equals the quantity sold times the price. Because there is no cost to pumping water, the total revenue of the two producers equals their total profit.

Let's now consider how the organization of the town's water industry affects the price of water and the quantity of water sold.

## Competition, Monopolies and Cartels

Before considering the price and quantity of water that would result from the duopoly of Jack and Jill, let's discuss briefly the two market structures we already understand: competition and monopoly.

Consider first what would happen if the market for water were perfectly competitive. In a competitive market, the production decisions of each firm drive price equal to marginal cost. In the market for water, marginal cost is zero. Thus, under competition, the equilibrium price of water would be zero, and the equilibrium quantity would be 120 litres. The price of water would reflect the cost of producing it, and the efficient quantity of water would be produced and consumed.

Now consider how a monopoly would behave. Table 16.1 shows that total profit is maximized at a quantity of 60 litres and a price of €60 a litre. A profit-maximizing monopolist, therefore, would produce this quantity and charge this price. As is standard for monopolies, price would exceed marginal cost. The result would be inefficient, for the quantity of water produced and consumed would fall short of the socially efficient level of 120 litres.

What outcome should we expect from our duopolists? One possibility is that Jack and Jill get together and agree on the quantity of water to produce and the price to charge for it. Such an agreement among firms over production and price is called **collusion,** and the group of firms acting in unison is called a **cartel.** Once a cartel is formed, the market is in effect served by a monopoly, and we can apply our analysis from Chapter 15. That is, if Jack and Jill were to collude, they would agree on the monopoly outcome because that outcome maximizes the total profit that the producers can get from the market. Our two producers would produce a total of 60 litres, which would be sold at a price of €60 a litre. Once again, price exceeds marginal cost, and the outcome is socially inefficient.

A cartel must agree not only on the total level of production but also on the amount produced by each member. In our case, Jack and Jill must agree how to split between themselves the monopoly production of 60 litres. Each member of the cartel will want a larger share of the market because a larger market share means larger profit. If Jack and Jill agreed to split the market equally, each would produce 30 litres, the price would be €60 a litre and each would get a profit of €1,800.

**collusion**
an agreement among firms in a market about quantities to produce or prices to charge
**cartel**
a group of firms acting in unison

## The Equilibrium For an Oligopoly

Although oligopolists would like to form cartels and earn monopoly profits, often that is not possible. As we discuss later in this chapter, competition laws prohibit explicit agreements among oligopolists as a matter of public policy. In addition, squabbling among cartel members over how to divide the profit in the market sometimes makes agreement among them impossible. Let's therefore consider what happens if Jack and Jill decide separately how much water to produce.

At first, one might expect Jack and Jill to reach the monopoly outcome on their own, for this outcome maximizes their joint profit. In the absence of a binding agreement, however, the monopoly outcome is unlikely. To see why, imagine that Jack expects Jill to produce only 30 litres (half of the monopoly quantity). Jack would reason as follows:

> I could produce 30 litres as well. In this case, a total of 60 litres of water would be sold at a price of €60 a litre. My profit would be €1,800 (30 litres × €60 a litre). Alternatively, I could produce 40 litres. In this case, a total of 70 litres of water would be sold at a price of €50 a litre. My profit would be €2,000 (40 litres × €50 a litre). Even though total profit in the market would fall, my profit would be higher, because I would have a larger share of the market.

Of course, Jill might reason the same way. If so, Jack and Jill would each bring 40 litres to town. Total sales would be 80 litres, and the price would fall to €40. Thus, if the duopolists individually pursue their own self-interest when deciding how much to produce, they produce a total quantity greater than the monopoly quantity, charge a price lower than the monopoly price and earn total profit less than the monopoly profit.

Although the logic of self-interest increases the duopoly's output above the monopoly level, it does not push the duopolists to reach the competitive allocation. Consider what happens when each duopolist is producing 40 litres. The price is €40, and each duopolist makes a profit of €1,600. In this case, Jack's self-interested logic leads to a different conclusion:

> Right now my profit is €1,600. Suppose I increase my production to 50 litres. In this case, a total of 90 litres of water would be sold, and the price would be €30 a litre. Then my profit would be only €1,500. Rather than increasing production and driving down the price, I am better off keeping my production at 40 litres.

**Nash equilibrium**
a situation in which economic actors interacting with one another each choose their best strategy given the strategies that all the other actors have chosen

The outcome in which Jack and Jill each produce 40 litres looks like some sort of equilibrium. In fact, this outcome is called a **Nash equilibrium**. (named after economic theorist John Nash, whose life was portrayed in the book, *A Beautiful Mind*, and the film of the same name). A Nash equilibrium is a situation in which economic actors interacting with one another each choose their best strategy given the strategies the others have chosen. In this case, given that Jill is producing 40 litres, the best strategy for Jack is to produce 40 litres. Similarly, given that Jack is producing 40 litres, the best strategy for Jill is to produce 40 litres. Once they reach this Nash equilibrium, neither Jack nor Jill has an incentive to make a different decision.

This example illustrates the tension between cooperation and self-interest. Oligopolists would be better off cooperating and reaching the monopoly outcome. Yet because they pursue their own self-interest, they do not end up reaching the monopoly outcome and maximizing their joint profit. Each oligopolist is tempted to raise production and capture a larger share of the market. As each of them tries to do this, total production rises, and the price falls.

At the same time, self-interest does not drive the market all the way to the competitive outcome. Like monopolists, oligopolists are aware that increases in the amount they produce reduce the price of their product. Therefore, they stop short of following the competitive firm's rule of producing up to the point where price equals marginal cost.

In summary, when firms in an oligopoly individually choose production to maximize profit, they produce a quantity of output greater than the level produced by monopoly and less than the level produced by competition. The oligopoly price is less than the monopoly price but greater than the competitive price (which equals marginal cost).

# IN THE NEWS

## Cartels Under the Hammer

*Competition regulators around the world are becoming increasingly sharp-eyed with respect to price-fixing cartels and have widened their field of examination to look for cosy deals in areas such as art auctioneering and banking, as this article discusses.*

**Fixing For a Fight: Bosses Beware: Price-Fixing and Other Dodgy Dealings are Under Fire from Governments Everywhere, as Regulators Cast a Wider Net for Culprits**

Until recently, the world of art seemed an unlikely place to find a cartel. For a long time, shady price-fixing deals were the province of the decidedly less chic: industries such as steel tubes, animal feed, graphite electrodes and construction are just a few recent examples. So it must be particularly galling for Alfred Taubman, a former chairman of Sotheby's, an auctioneer, to have been convicted last December in America of fixing prices with his ostensible arch-rival, Christie's. But Mr Taubman, who faces a probable prison term when he is sentenced on April 22nd, will not be the last colluding boss to come in for a nasty surprise. Many see his case as a sign of things to come.

To see why, consider Mr Taubman's alleged co-conspirator in the case, Christie's former chief, Sir Anthony Tennant, who remains safely at home in Britain. Price-fixing in Britain, as in most countries, is not yet treated as a crime. But that is changing across the world, as a wave of new rules and stronger enforcement seeks to stamp out anti-competitive practices.

Just a few years ago, America seemed uniquely obsessed with price-fixing. Today, new measures against cartel behaviour (which includes bid-rigging and deals to carve up market share, as well as price-fixing) are being taken from Sweden to South Korea, where the competition body levied its first fine against a foreign firm earlier this year. In Britain, a planned law will introduce jail sentences for cartel conspirators. In the past few years, the European Commission has crusaded with new fervour against cartels, levying the biggest fines in its history, totalling €1.8 billion ($1.6 billion) in 2001 alone.

Moreover, these days it is not only manufacturers and commodity-mongers who can expect a visit from the competition cops. Recent inquiries have led them to brewers, banks and even bus operators. The current attack on cartels comes at a time when the temptation to strike cosy deals with competitors is stronger than ever, as pricing power remains weak and excess capacity abounds in the wake of the global economic slowdown.

The costs of collusion should make any boss think twice, though. The European Commission can levy fines of up to 10% of a company's turnover for cartel offences. Dawn raids are running at about one a month in the European Union. In America, fines are based on the size of the market affected, but private lawsuits can be far more costly: Sotheby's was hit by a $45m fine by the American government, but its customers' lawsuits have cost it hundreds of millions more. Such private lawsuits are on the rise in Europe, says Elizabeth Morony of Clifford Chance, a law firm.

International cartels – those in which member firms are headquartered all over the world – face new attack too. Last year, eight vitamin makers from France, Germany, Japan and Switzerland, including Aventis, BASF and Roche, were fined €855m by the European Commission for fixing prices

and setting sales quotas. The cartel had earlier been fined in America, and several executives have served time in American prisons. America's Department of Justice estimates that 70% of its cartel targets last year were foreign-based, compared with none in 1990.

Global telecoms companies may soon receive similar treatment. Last summer, European enforcers raided the offices of mobile-phone companies, including Britain's Vodafone and a division of Deutsche Telekom, seeking evidence of price-fixing in international roaming charges. Mario Monti, Europe's competition commissioner, now plans to go after the industry over connection fees for fixed-line calls. Pharmaceutical companies, already humbled by the fines for the vitamin cartel, became the target of yet another investigation in Britain, earlier this month, into the alleged price-fixing of generic drugs.

Several things are driving the anti-cartel push. One is the desire to create a genuine single market in Europe, where geographic 'market sharing' is seen as particularly damaging, according to Alec Burnside of Linklaters, a law firm. Last month, for example, the commission accused Carlsberg, a Danish brewer, and Heineken, a Dutch rival, of plotting not to compete on each other's home turf.

Secondly, regulators have become more sympathetic to consumer lobbies, and have turned their attention to retail goods. Britain's Office of Fair Trading claims to be running 25 cartel probes, with a shift towards recognisable household names.

Another snag for would-be price-fixers is legislation to make whistle-blowing more attractive. Many countries have now followed America in encouraging guilty parties to spill the beans: the first member of a cartel to

come forward now wins leniency, a concession taken advantage of in both the vitamin and auctioneering cases.

The smoke-filled room is the fabled venue for hatching cartels, but new technologies such as the Internet, once seen as sources of price transparency, have ironically created new concerns about collusion. Covisint, the car industry's online parts exchange, was scrutinised by America's Federal Trade Commission last year, with these fears in mind. One way to avoid problems with such exchanges is to ensure anonymity and to stop competing firms from seeing each other's bids. E-mail should also worry company bosses, as it may create an appearance of collusion if salesmen from competing firms casually correspond about, say, pricing patterns – and e-mails are hard to delete.

Given regulators' aggressive new approach to cartels, companies are having to educate themselves. Roche, a member of the vitamin cartel, has put thousands of its managers in training to teach them to follow the law. In truth, avoiding cartels such as the one for vitamins should not be so difficult. The best advice, as one lawyer puts it, is: 'Don't talk to the competition.'

But there are shades of grey. Trade associations and annual conventions are one source of problems; sugar companies once came under scrutiny after such a meeting. Bosses are often keen to hear about the state of demand in their industry, but comments about price and volume targets can be taken as a tacit attempt at collusion. Joint ventures and merger negotiations are another possible minefield. When, as Adam Smith once put it, talk turns to 'some contrivance to raise prices', the best policy these days is just to say no.

Source: *The Economist*, 18 April 2002.
Copyright © The Economist Newspaper Limited, London.

## How the Size of an Oligopoly Affects the Market Outcome

We can use the insights from this analysis of duopoly to discuss how the size of an oligopoly is likely to affect the outcome in a market. Suppose, for instance, that Darby and Joan suddenly discover water sources on their property and join Jack and Jill in the water oligopoly. The demand schedule in Table 16.1 remains the same, but now more producers are available to satisfy this demand. How would an increase in the number of sellers from two to four affect the price and quantity of water in the town?

If the sellers of water could form a cartel, they would once again try to maximize total profit by producing the monopoly quantity and charging the monopoly price. Just as when there were only two sellers, the members of the cartel would need to agree on production levels for each member and find some way to enforce the agreement. As the cartel grows larger, however, this outcome is less likely. Reaching and enforcing an agreement becomes more difficult as the size of the group increases.

If the oligopolists do not form a cartel – perhaps because competition laws prohibit it – they must each decide on their own how much water to produce. To see how the increase in the number of sellers affects the outcome, consider the decision facing each seller. At any time, each well owner has the option to raise production by 1 litre. In making this decision, the well owner weighs two effects:

● *The output effect*. Because price is above marginal cost, selling one more litre of water at the going price will raise profit.
● *The price effect*. Raising production will increase the total amount sold, which will lower the price of water and lower the profit on all the other litres sold.

If the output effect is larger than the price effect, the well owner will increase production. If the price effect is larger than the output effect, the owner will not raise production. (In fact, in this case, it is profitable to reduce production.) Each oligopolist continues to increase production until these two marginal effects exactly balance, taking the other firms' production as given.

Now consider how the number of firms in the industry affects the marginal analysis of each oligopolist. The larger the number of sellers, the less concerned each seller is about its own impact on the market price. That is, as the oligopoly grows in size, the magnitude of the price effect falls. When the oligopoly grows very large, the price effect disappears altogether, leaving only the output effect. In this extreme case, each firm in the oligopoly increases production as long as price is above marginal cost.

We can now see that a large oligopoly is essentially a group of competitive firms. A competitive firm considers only the output effect when deciding how much to produce: because a competitive firm is a price taker, the price effect is absent. Thus, as the number of sellers in an oligopoly grows larger, an oligopolistic market looks more and more like a competitive market. The price approaches marginal cost, and the quantity produced approaches the socially efficient level.

This analysis of oligopoly offers a new perspective on the effects of international trade. Imagine that Toyota and Honda are the only car manufacturers in Japan, Volkswagen and BMW are the only car manufacturers in Germany, and Citroën and Peugeot are the only car manufacturers in France. If these nations prohibited international trade in cars, each would have a motorcar oligopoly with only two members, and the market outcome would likely depart substantially from the competitive ideal. With international trade, however, the car market is a world market, and the oligopoly in this example has six members. Allowing free trade increases the number of producers from which each consumer can choose, and this increased competition keeps prices closer to marginal cost. Thus, the theory of oligopoly provides another reason, in addition to the theory of comparative advantage discussed in Chapter 3, why all countries can benefit from free trade.

## CASE STUDY

### OPEC and the World Oil Market

Our story about the town's market for water is fictional, but if we change water to crude oil, and Jack and Jill to Iran and Saudi Arabia, the story is quite close to being true. Much of the world's oil is produced by a few countries, mostly in the Middle East. These countries together make up an oligopoly. Their decisions about how much oil to pump are much the same as Jack and Jill's decisions about how much water to pump.

The countries that produce most of the world's oil have formed a cartel, called the Organization of Petroleum Exporting Countries (OPEC). As originally formed in 1960, OPEC included Iran, Saudi Arabia, Kuwait, Iraq and Venezuela. By 1973, eight other nations had joined: Qatar, Indonesia, Libya, the United Arab Emirates, Algeria, Nigeria, Ecuador and Gabon. These countries control about three-quarters of the world's oil reserves. Like any cartel, OPEC tries to raise the price of its product through a coordinated reduction in quantity produced. OPEC tries to set production levels for each of the member countries.

The problem that OPEC faces is much the same as the problem that Jack and Jill face in our story. The OPEC countries would like to maintain a high price of oil. But each member of the cartel is tempted to increase its production in order to get a larger share of the total profit. OPEC members frequently agree to reduce production but then cheat on their agreements.

OPEC was most successful at maintaining cooperation and high prices in the period from 1973 to 1985. The price of crude oil rose from $2.64 a barrel in 1972 to $11.17 in 1974 and then to $35.10 in 1981. But in the early 1980s member countries began arguing about production levels, and OPEC became ineffective at maintaining cooperation. By 1986 the price of crude oil had fallen back to $12.52 a barrel.

In recent years, the members of OPEC have continued to meet regularly, but the cartel has been far less successful at reaching and enforcing agreements. The price of crude oil, adjusted for overall inflation, has remained far below the level OPEC achieved in 1981. While this lack of cooperation has hurt the profits of the oil-producing nations, it has benefited consumers around the world.

**Quick Quiz** If the members of an oligopoly could agree on a total quantity to produce, what quantity would they choose? • If the oligopolists do not act together but instead make production decisions individually, do they produce a total quantity more or less than in your answer to the previous question? Why?

# IN THE NEWS

## Reputation: The Ultimate Barrier to Entry

*One of the characteristics of an oligopolistic market is the presence of barriers to entry. One of the toughest barriers to entry is the need to have already entered. Sound weird? Read on.*

### Too Few Accountants: Two Proposed Mergers Among Accountancy Firms Add Up to Serious Restraints on Competition

Who in the business world has not grumbled about all those bean-counters who stifle initiative and crimp innovation? Yet now those self-same businessmen are voicing precisely the opposite complaint: too few bean-counters, not too many. Of the six large firms that dominate the accountancy business worldwide, four are proposing mergers – KPMG with Ernst & Young and Price Waterhouse with Coopers & Lybrand. Competition authorities in America and Europe are investigating these proposed transactions. They have ample cause to block both deals.

Accountancy, it must be said, is a unique business. It is not all that hard to enter; in most countries, if you sit through a few classes and pass some sort of exam, you can call yourself an accountant. A consumer looking for help with filing his tax return or a small business needing to give the bank a financial statement has no shortage of accountancy firms to call upon. In the corporate world, however, things are dramatically different. A company that seeks to entice investors to buy its bonds or shares had best provide a financial statement certified by one of the Big Six – Arthur Andersen, Ernst & Young, KPMG, Deloitte Touche Tohmatsu, Coopers & Lybrand and Price Waterhouse. An equally good company whose books are certified by an obscure accountancy firm will have a tough time in the capital markets.

Reputation has thus become a barrier to entry. No matter how skilled or willing other accountancy firms may be, they will have an almost impossible time marketing their services to large or medium-sized companies that issue publicly traded securities. These clients would gain by offering work to smaller firms in order to boost competition, but any company that does so is likely to be punished by lower share or bond prices. Would-be challengers have difficulty reaching even the lowest rungs of the competitive ladder, and have no chance of building the global networks clients want.

The Big Six thus have an unassailable oligopoly in many fields. Their imprimatur is a prerequisite for a Russian municipality or a Mexican industrial group to raise funds internationally. They audit all but the tiniest of Britain's banks. Search the pages of 'Hoover's Handbook', a standard reference to American companies, and you'll be hard-pressed to find one audited by anyone else. Not long ago, the Big Six were the Big Eight. If they were now to become the Big Four, the choices would be even fewer, and not just when it comes to auditing. A bank wishing to investigate losses by its bond traders would have only three accountancies among which to choose (as it would be unlikely to select its customary auditor). Two companies wishing to merge might well need to employ all four firms in order to complete the transaction. How this will affect the accountants' ability to extract higher fees from their customers – the fundamental test of whether they are exercising undue market power – is easy to imagine.

Would not the survival of four international accountancy firms be enough to assure vibrant competition? A fair enough question, given that in some activities, notably auditing, competition amongst the Big Six has kept prices in check. But in a four-firm industry, companies will face a worryingly restricted choice, especially since competitors prefer to be audited by different accountancy firms. The consequence risks being not only higher costs for business, but also conflicts of interest if, as is likely, accountancies find their clients involved in the same bid or tendering for the same business.

Barriers to entry are not an uncommon problem in judging mergers. Often, they are easy enough to surmount. By selling a factory or a few airport gates, altering distribution arrangements, or agreeing to license a technology, merger partners can often make it feasible for others to enter the market and thus forestall worries about potential anti-competitive behaviour. If the accountancy firms could do likewise, the two pending mergers would offer little cause for concern. But it is precisely the peculiar nature of the barrier to entry in accountancy that makes these mergers so problematic. This is freely acknowledged by the big accountancy firms themselves. Unlike the participants in other big mergers, the accountancy firms have offered no concessions to ease concerns about diminished competition. This is because no concessions they might offer could address the problem. That leaves competition authorities with no choice but to say no.

# GAME THEORY AND THE ECONOMICS OF COOPERATION

As we have seen, oligopolies would like to reach the monopoly outcome, but doing so requires cooperation, which at times is difficult to maintain. In this section we look more closely at the problems people face when cooperation is desirable but difficult. To analyse the economics of cooperation, we need to learn a little about game theory.

**Game theory** is the study of how people behave in strategic situations. By 'strategic' we mean a situation in which each person, when deciding what actions to take, must consider how others might respond to that action. Because the number of firms in an oligopolistic market is small, each firm must act strategically. Each firm knows that its profit depends not only on how much it produces but also on how much the other firms produce. In making its production decision, each firm in an oligopoly should consider how its decision might affect the production decisions of all the other firms.

Game theory is not necessary for understanding competitive or monopoly markets. In a competitive market, each firm is so small compared to the market that strategic interactions with other firms are not important. In a monopolized market, strategic interactions are absent because the market has only one firm. But, as we will see, game theory is quite useful for understanding the behaviour of oligopolies.

A particularly important 'game' is called the **prisoners' dilemma.** This game provides insight into the difficulty of maintaining cooperation. Many times in life, people fail to cooperate with one another even when cooperation would make them all better off. An oligopoly is just one example. The story of the prisoners' dilemma contains a general lesson that applies to any group trying to maintain cooperation among its members.

**game theory**
the study of how people behave in strategic situations

**prisoners' dilemma**
a particular 'game' between two captured prisoners that illustrates why cooperation is difficult to maintain even when it is mutually beneficial

## The Prisoners' Dilemma

The prisoners' dilemma is a story about two criminals who have been captured by the police. Let's call them Mr Black and Mr Pink. The police have enough evidence to convict Mr Black and Mr Pink of a relatively minor crime, illegal possession of a handgun, so that each would spend a year in jail. The police also suspect that the two criminals have committed a jewellery robbery together, but they lack hard evidence to convict them of this major crime. The police question Mr Black and Mr Pink in separate rooms, and they offer each of them the following deal:

> Right now we can lock you up for 1 year. If you confess to the jewellery robbery and implicate your partner, however, we'll give you immunity and you can go free. Your partner will get 20 years in jail. But if you both confess to the crime, we won't need your testimony and we can avoid the cost of a trial, so you will each get an intermediate sentence of 8 years.

If Mr Black and Mr Pink, heartless criminals that they are, care only about their own sentences, what would you expect them to do? Would they confess or remain silent? Figure 16.2 shows their choices. Each prisoner has two strategies: confess or remain silent. The sentence each prisoner gets depends on the strategy he or she chooses and the strategy chosen by his or her partner in crime.

Consider first Mr Black's decision. He reasons as follows:

> I don't know what Mr Pink is going to do. If he remains silent, my best strategy is to confess, since then I'll go free rather than spending a year in jail. If he confesses, my best strategy is still to confess, since then I'll spend 8

**FIGURE 16.2**

**The Prisoners' Dilemma**

*In this game between two criminals suspected of committing a crime, the sentence that each receives depends both on his decision whether to confess or remain silent and on the decision made by the other.*

|  | Mr Black's decision | |
|---|---|---|
|  | Confess | Remain silent |
| **Mr Pink's decision — Confess** | Mr Black gets 8 years / Mr Pink gets 8 years | Mr Black gets 20 years / Mr Pink goes free |
| **Mr Pink's decision — Remain silent** | Mr Black goes free / Mr Pink gets 20 years | Mr Black gets 1 year / Mr Pink gets 1 year |

**dominant strategy**

a strategy that is best for a player in a game regardless of the strategies chosen by the other players

years in jail rather than 20. So, regardless of what Mr Pink does, I am better off confessing.

In the language of game theory, a strategy is called a **dominant strategy** if it is the best strategy for a player to follow regardless of the strategies pursued by other players. In this case, confessing is a dominant strategy for Mr Black. He spends less time in jail if he confesses, regardless of whether Mr Pink confesses or remains silent.

Now consider Mr Pink's decision. He faces exactly the same choices as Mr Black, and he reasons in much the same way. Regardless of what Mr Black does, Mr Pink can reduce his time in jail by confessing. In other words, confessing is also a dominant strategy for Mr Pink.

In the end, both Mr Black and Mr Pink confess, and both spend 8 years in jail. Yet, from their standpoint, this is a terrible outcome. If they had *both* remained silent, both of them would have been better off, spending only 1 year in jail on the gun charge. By each pursuing his own interests, the two prisoners together reach an outcome that is worse for each of them.

To see how difficult it is to maintain cooperation, imagine that, before the police captured Mr Black and Mr Pink, the two criminals had made a pact not to confess. Clearly, this agreement would make them both better off *if* they both live up to it, because they would each spend only 1 year in jail. But would the two criminals in fact remain silent, simply because they had agreed to? Once they are being questioned separately, the logic of self-interest takes over and leads them to confess. Cooperation between the two prisoners is difficult to maintain, because cooperation is individually irrational.

## Oligopolies as a Prisoner's Dilemma

What does the prisoners' dilemma have to do with markets and imperfect competition? It turns out that the game oligopolists play in trying to reach the monopoly outcome is similar to the game that the two prisoners play in the prisoners' dilemma.

Consider an oligopoly with two members, called Iran and Saudi Arabia. Both countries sell crude oil. After prolonged negotiation, the countries agree to keep oil production low in order to keep the world price of oil high. After they agree on production levels, each country must decide whether to cooperate and live up to this agreement or to ignore it and produce at a higher level. Figure 16.3 shows how the profits of the two countries depend on the strategies they choose.

Suppose you are the leader of Saudi Arabia. You might reason as follows:

I could keep production low as we agreed, or I could raise my production and sell more oil on world markets. If Iran lives up to the agreement and keeps its production low, then my country earns profit of $60 billion with high production and $50 billion with low production. In this case, Saudi Arabia is better off with high production. If Iran fails to live up to the agreement and produces at a high level, then my country earns $40 billion with high production and $30 billion with low production. Once again, Saudi Arabia is better off with high production. So, regardless of what Iran chooses to do, my country is better off reneging on our agreement and producing at a high level.

Producing at a high level is a dominant strategy for Saudi Arabia. Of course, Iran reasons in exactly the same way, and so both countries produce at a high level. The result is the inferior outcome (from Iran and Saudi Arabia's standpoint) with low profits for each country.

This example illustrates why oligopolies have trouble maintaining monopoly profits. The monopoly outcome is jointly rational for the oligopoly, but each oligopolist has an incentive to cheat. Just as self-interest drives the prisoners in the prisoners' dilemma to confess, self-interest makes it difficult for the oligopoly to maintain the cooperative outcome with low production, high prices and monopoly profits.

**FIGURE 16.3**

**An Oligopoly Game**

*In this game between members of an oligopoly, the profit that each earns depends on both its production decision and the production decision of the other oligopolist.*

|  | | Saudi Arabia's decision | |
|---|---|---|---|
|  | | High production | Low production |
| **Iran's decision** | High production | Saudi Arabia gets $40 billion — Iran gets $40 billion | Saudi Arabia gets $30 billion — Iran gets $60 billion |
|  | Low production | Saudi Arabia gets $60 billion — Iran gets $30 billion | Saudi Arabia gets $50 billion — Iran gets $50 billion |

## Other Examples of the Prisoners' Dilemma

We have seen how the prisoners' dilemma can be used to understand the problem facing oligopolies. The same logic applies to many other situations as well. Here we consider three examples in which self-interest prevents cooperation and leads to an inferior outcome for the parties involved.

**Arms Races** An arms race is much like the prisoners' dilemma. To see this, consider the decisions of two countries – the United States and the Soviet Union – about whether to build new weapons or to disarm. Each country prefers to have more arms than the other because a larger arsenal would give it more influence in world affairs. But each country also prefers to live in a world safe from the other country's weapons.

Figure 16.4 shows the deadly game. If the Soviet Union chooses to arm, the United States is better off doing the same to prevent the loss of power. If the Soviet Union chooses to disarm, the United States is better off arming because doing so would make it more powerful. For each country, arming is a dominant strategy. Thus, each country chooses to continue the arms race, resulting in the inferior outcome in which both countries are at risk.

Throughout the era of the Cold War, the United States and the Soviet Union attempted to solve this problem through negotiation and agreements over arms control. The problems that the two countries faced were similar to those that oligopolists encounter in trying to maintain a cartel. Just as oligopolists argue over production levels, the United States and the Soviet Union argued over the amount of arms that each country would be allowed. And just as cartels have trouble enforcing production levels, the United States and the Soviet Union each feared that the other country would cheat on any agreement. In both arms races and oligopolies, the relentless logic of self-interest drives the participants toward a non-cooperative outcome that is worse for each party. In fact, the soaring cost of remaining in the arms race with the United States was a key factor in the fall of communism and the break-up of the Soviet Union. While some people have

**FIGURE 16.4**

**An Arms Race Game**

*In this game between two countries, the safety and power of each country depends on both its decision whether to arm and the decision made by the other country.*

| Decision of the USSR \ Decision of the USA | Arm | Disarm |
|---|---|---|
| Arm | USA at risk / USSR at risk | USA at risk and weak / USSR safe and powerful |
| Disarm | USA safe and powerful / USSR at risk and weak | USA safe / USSR safe |

argued that this was the ultimate aim of US policy – to bankrupt the Soviet Union – this is in fact not at all clear, since it is only with the benefit of hindsight that it became apparent that the Soviet Union could not sustain the arms race.

**Advertising** When two firms advertise to attract the same customers, they face a problem similar to the prisoners' dilemma. For example, consider the decisions facing two cigarette companies, Marlboro and Camel. If neither company advertises, the two companies split the market. If both advertise, they again split the market, but profits are lower, since each company must bear the cost of advertising. Yet if one company advertises while the other does not, the one that advertises attracts customers from the other.

Figure 16.5 shows how the profits of the two companies depend on their actions. You can see that advertising is a dominant strategy for each firm. Thus, both firms choose to advertise, even though both firms would be better off if neither firm advertised.

A test of this theory of advertising occurred in many countries during the 1970s and 1980s, when laws were passed in Europe and North America banning cigarette advertisements on television. To the surprise of many observers, cigarette companies did not use their considerable political clout to oppose these bans. When the laws went into effect, cigarette advertising fell and the profits of cigarette companies rose. The television advertising bans did for the cigarette companies what they could not do on their own: they solved the prisoners' dilemma by enforcing the cooperative outcome with low advertising and high profit.

**Common Resources** In Chapter 11 we saw that people tend to overuse common resources. One can view this problem as an example of the prisoners' dilemma.

Imagine that two oil companies – Shell and BP – own adjacent oil fields. Under the fields is a common pool of oil worth €12 million. Drilling a well to recover the oil costs €1 million. If each company drills one well, each will get half of the oil and earn a €5 million profit (€6 million in revenue minus €1 million in costs).

**FIGURE 16.5**

**An Advertising Game**

*In this game between firms selling similar products, the profit that each earns depends on both its own advertising decision and the advertising decision of the other firm.*

| Camel's decision | Marlboro's decision: Advertise | Marlboro's decision: Don't advertise |
|---|---|---|
| Advertise | Marlboro gets $3 billion profit<br>Camel gets $3 billion profit | Marlboro gets $2 billion profit<br>Camel gets $5 billion profit |
| Don't advertise | Marlboro gets $5 billion profit<br>Camel gets $2 billion profit | Marlboro gets $4 billion profit<br>Camel gets $4 billion profit |

**FIGURE 16.6**

**A Common Resources Game**

*In this game between firms pumping oil from a common pool, the profit that each earns depends on both the number of wells it drills and the number of wells drilled by the other firm.*

| BP's decision \ Shell's decision | Drill two wells | Drill one well |
|---|---|---|
| Drill two wells | Shell gets €4 million profit; BP gets €4 million profit | Shell gets €3 million profit; BP gets €6 million profit |
| Drill one well | Shell gets €6 million profit; BP gets €3 million profit | Shell gets €5 million profit; BP gets €5 million profit |

Because the pool of oil is a common resource, the companies will not use it efficiently. Suppose that either company could drill a second well. If one company has two of the three wells, that company gets two-thirds of the oil, which yields a profit of €6 million. The other company gets one-third of the oil, for a profit of €3 million. Yet if each company drills a second well, the two companies again split the oil. In this case, each bears the cost of a second well, so profit is only €4 million for each company.

Figure 16.6 shows the game. Drilling two wells is a dominant strategy for each company. Once again, the self-interest of the two players leads them to an inferior outcome.

## The Prisoners' Dilemma and the Welfare of Society

The prisoners' dilemma describes many of life's situations, and it shows that cooperation can be difficult to maintain, even when cooperation would make both players in the game better off. Clearly, this lack of cooperation is a problem for those involved in these situations. But is lack of cooperation a problem from the standpoint of society as a whole? The answer depends on the circumstances.

In some cases, the non-cooperative equilibrium is bad for society as well as the players. In the arms race game in Figure 16.4, both the United States and the Soviet Union end up at risk. In the common resources game in Figure 16.6, the extra wells dug by Shell and BP are pure waste. In both cases, society would be better off if the two players could reach the cooperative outcome.

By contrast, in the case of oligopolists trying to maintain monopoly profits, lack of cooperation is desirable from the standpoint of society as a whole. The monopoly outcome is good for the oligopolists, but it is bad for the consumers of the product. As we first saw in Chapter 7, the competitive outcome is best for society because it maximizes total surplus. When oligopolists fail to cooperate, the quantity they produce is closer to this optimal level. Put differently, the invisible hand guides markets to allocate resources efficiently only when markets are competitive, and markets are competitive only when firms in the market fail to cooperate with one another.

Similarly, consider the case of the police questioning two suspects. Lack of cooperation between the suspects is desirable, for it allows the police to convict more criminals. The prisoners' dilemma is a dilemma for the prisoners, but it can be a boon to everyone else.

## Why People Sometimes Cooperate

The prisoners' dilemma shows that cooperation is difficult. But is it impossible? Not all prisoners, when questioned by the police, decide to turn in their partners in crime. Cartels sometimes do manage to maintain collusive arrangements, despite the incentive for individual members to defect. Very often, the reason that players can solve the prisoners' dilemma is that they play the game not once but many times.

To see why cooperation is easier to enforce in repeated games, let's return to our duopolists, Jack and Jill. Recall that Jack and Jill would like to maintain the monopoly outcome in which each produces 30 litres, but self-interest drives them to an equilibrium in which each produces 40 litres. Figure 16.7 shows the game they play. Producing 40 litres is a dominant strategy for each player in this game.

Imagine that Jack and Jill try to form a cartel. To maximize total profit they would agree to the cooperative outcome in which each produces 30 litres. Yet, if Jack and Jill are to play this game only once, neither has any incentive to live up to this agreement. Self-interest drives each of them to renege and produce 40 litres.

Now suppose that Jack and Jill know that they will play the same game every week. When they make their initial agreement to keep production low, they can also specify what happens if one party reneges. They might agree, for instance, that once one of them reneges and produces 40 litres, both of them will produce

### FIGURE 16.7

**Jack and Jill's Oligopoly Game**

*In this game between Jack and Jill, the profit that each earns from selling water depends on both the quantity he or she chooses to sell and the quantity the other chooses to sell.*

| | | Jack's decision | |
| --- | --- | --- | --- |
| | | Sell 40 litres | Sell 30 litres |
| **Jill's decision** | **Sell 40 litres** | Jack gets €1,600 profit / Jill gets €1,600 profit | Jack gets €1,500 profit / Jill gets €2,000 profit |
| | **Sell 30 litres** | Jack gets €2,000 profit / Jill gets €1,500 profit | Jack gets €1,800 profit / Jill gets €1,800 profit |

40 litres forever after. This penalty is easy to enforce, for if one party is producing at a high level, the other has every reason to do the same.

The threat of this penalty may be all that is needed to maintain cooperation. Each person knows that defecting would raise his or her profit from €1,800 to €2,000. But this benefit would last for only one week. Thereafter, profit would fall to €1,600 and stay there. As long as the players care enough about future profits, they will choose to forgo the one-time gain from defection. Thus, in a game of repeated prisoners' dilemma, the two players may well be able to reach the cooperative outcome.

# CASE STUDY

## The Prisoners' Dilemma Tournament

Imagine that you are playing a game of prisoners' dilemma with a person being 'questioned' in a separate room. Moreover, imagine that you are going to play not once but many times. Your score at the end of the game is the total number of years in jail. You would like to make this score as small as possible. What strategy would you play? Would you begin by confessing or remaining silent? How would the other player's actions affect your subsequent decisions about confessing?

Repeated prisoners' dilemma is quite a complicated game. To encourage cooperation, players must penalize each other for not cooperating. Yet the strategy described earlier for Jack and Jill's water cartel – defect forever as soon as the other player defects – is not very forgiving. In a game repeated many times, a strategy that allows players to return to the cooperative outcome after a period of non-cooperation may be preferable.

To see what strategies work best, political scientist Robert Axelrod held a tournament. People entered by sending computer programs designed to play repeated prisoners' dilemma. Each program then played the game against all the other programs. The 'winner' was the program that received the fewest total years in jail.

The winner turned out to be a simple strategy called *tit-for-tat*. According to tit-for-tat, a player should start by cooperating and then do whatever the other player did last time. Thus, a tit-for-tat player cooperates until the other player defects; he then defects until the other player cooperates again. In other words, this strategy starts out friendly, penalizes unfriendly players, and forgives them if warranted. To Axelrod's surprise, this simple strategy did better than all the more complicated strategies that people had sent in.

The tit-for-tat strategy has a long history. It is essentially the biblical strategy of 'an eye for an eye, a tooth for a tooth.' The prisoners' dilemma tournament suggests that this may be a good rule of thumb for playing some of the games of life.

**Quick Quiz** Tell the story of the prisoners' dilemma. Write down a table showing the prisoners' choices and explain what outcome is likely. • What does the prisoners' dilemma teach us about oligopolies?

# PUBLIC POLICY TOWARD OLIGOPOLIES

One of the *Ten Principles of Economics* in Chapter 1 is that governments can sometimes improve market outcomes. The application of this principle to oligopolistic markets is, as a general matter, straightforward. As we have seen, cooperation among oligopolists is undesirable from the standpoint of society as a whole, because it leads to production that is too low and prices that are too high. To move the allocation of resources closer to the social optimum, policy makers should try to induce firms in an oligopoly to compete rather than cooperate. Let's consider how policy makers do this and then examine the controversies that arise in this area of public policy.

## Restraint of Trade and Competition Law

One way that policy discourages cooperation is through the common law. Normally, freedom of contract is an essential part of a market economy. Businesses and households use contracts to arrange mutually advantageous trades. In doing this, they rely on the court system to enforce contracts. Yet, for many centuries, courts in Europe and North America have deemed agreements among competitors to reduce quantities and raise prices to be contrary to the public interest. They have therefore refused to enforce such agreements.

In the UK, for example, the Office of Fair Trading (OFT) plays a key role in enforcing anti-cartel competition law such as the 1998 Competition Act: under that Act of Parliament, any firm or business involved in a price-fixing cartel risks being fined up to 10 per cent of its UK turnover for up to three years. The Enterprise Act 2002 introduced a new criminal offence for individual company directors who dishonestly engage in cartel agreements. Where there is evidence of more widespread collusive behaviour in a market, the OFT may refer the matter to the Competition Commission for them to make a full investigation and suggest appropriate remedies.

Given the long experience of many European countries in tackling abuses of market power, it is perhaps not surprising that competition law is one of the few areas in which the European Union has been able to agree on a common policy. The European Commission can refer directly to the Treaty of Rome to prohibit price-fixing and other restrictive practices such as production limitation, and is especially likely to do so where a restrictive practice affects trade between EU member countries.

## *CASE STUDY*

### An Illegal Phone Call

Firms in oligopolies have a strong incentive to collude in order to reduce production, raise price and increase profit. The great 18th century British economist Adam Smith was well aware of this potential market failure. In *The Wealth of Nations* he wrote, 'People of the same trade seldom meet together, but the conversation ends in a conspiracy against the public, or in some diversion to raise prices.'

To see a modern example of Smith's observation, consider the following excerpt of a phone conversation between two US airline executives in the early 1980s. The call was reported in *The New York Times* on 24 February 1983. Robert

Crandall was president of American Airlines, and Howard Putnam was president of Braniff Airways.

CRANDALL: I think it's dumb as hell … to sit here and pound the @#!% out of each other and neither one of us making a #!%& dime.
PUTNAM: Do you have a suggestion for me?
CRANDALL: Yes, I have a suggestion for you. Raise your !%*& fares 20 per cent. I'll raise mine the next morning.
PUTNAM: Robert, we …
CRANDALL: You'll make more money, and I will, too.
PUTNAM: We can't talk about pricing!
CRANDALL: Oh @#!%, Howard. We can talk about any &*#@ thing we want to talk about.

Putnam was right: US competition law (the Sherman Anti-trust Act of 1890) prohibits competing executives from even talking about fixing prices. When Putnam gave a tape of this conversation to the US Justice Department, the Justice Department filed a lawsuit against Crandall.

Two years later, Crandall and the Justice Department reached a settlement in which Crandall agreed to various restrictions on his business activities, including his contacts with officials at other airlines. The Justice Department said that the terms of settlement would 'protect competition in the airline industry, by preventing American and Crandall from any further attempts to monopolize passenger airline service on any route through discussions with competitors about the prices of airline services.'

## Controversies over Competition Policy

Over time, much controversy has centred on the question of what kinds of behaviour competition law should prohibit. Most commentators agree that price-fixing agreements among competing firms should be illegal. Yet competition law has been used to condemn some business practices whose effects are not obvious. Here we consider three examples.

**Resale Price Maintenance** One example of a controversial business practice is *resale price maintenance*, also called *fair trade*. Imagine that Superduper Electronics sells DVD players to retail stores for €300. If Superduper requires the retailers to charge customers €350, it is said to engage in resale price maintenance. Any retailer that charged less than €350 would have violated its contract with Superduper.

At first, resale price maintenance might seem anti-competitive and, therefore, detrimental to society. Like an agreement among members of a cartel, it prevents the retailers from competing on price. For this reason, the courts have often viewed resale price maintenance as a violation of competition law.

Yet some economists defend resale price maintenance on two grounds. First, they deny that it is aimed at reducing competition. To the extent that Superduper Electronics has any market power, it can exert that power through the wholesale price, rather than through resale price maintenance. Moreover, Superduper has no incentive to discourage competition among its retailers. Indeed, because a cartel of retailers sells less than a group of competitive retailers, Superduper would be worse off if its retailers were a cartel.

Secondly, economists believe that resale price maintenance has a legitimate goal. Superduper may want its retailers to provide customers with a pleasant showroom and a knowledgeable salesforce. Yet, without resale price maintenance, some customers would take advantage of one store's service to learn about the DVD player's special features and then buy the item at a discount retailer that does not provide this service. To some extent, good service is a public good among the retailers that sell Superduper products. As we discussed in Chapter 11, when one person provides a public good, others are able to enjoy it without paying for it. In this case, discount retailers would free ride on the service provided by other retailers, leading to less service than is desirable. Resale price maintenance is one way for Superduper to solve this free-rider problem.

The example of resale price maintenance illustrates an important principle: business practices that appear to reduce competition may in fact have legitimate purposes. This principle makes the application of competition law all the more difficult. The bodies in charge of enforcing these laws such as the UK Competition Commission or the European Commission must determine what kinds of behaviour public policy should prohibit as impeding competition and reducing economic well-being. Often that job is not easy.

**Predatory Pricing** Firms with market power normally use that power to raise prices above the competitive level. But should policy makers ever be concerned that firms with market power might charge prices that are too low? This question is at the heart of a second debate over competition policy.

Imagine that a large airline, call it Tom Airlines, has a monopoly on some route. Then Jerry Express enters and takes 20 per cent of the market, leaving Tom with 80 per cent. In response to this competition, Tom starts slashing its fares. Some anti-trust analysts argue that Tom's move could be anti-competitive: the price cuts may be intended to drive Jerry out of the market so Tom can recapture its monopoly and raise prices again. Such behaviour is called *predatory pricing*.

Although it is common for companies to complain to the relevant authorities that a competitor is pursuing predatory pricing, some economists are sceptical of this argument and believe that predatory pricing is rarely, and perhaps never, a profitable business strategy. Why? For a price war to drive out a rival, prices have to be driven below cost. Yet if Tom starts selling cheap tickets at a loss, it had better be ready to fly more planes, because low fares will attract more customers. Jerry, meanwhile, can respond to Tom's predatory move by cutting back on flights. As a result, Tom ends up bearing more than 80 per cent of the losses, putting Jerry in a good position to survive the price war. As in the old Tom and Jerry cartoons, the predator suffers more than the prey.

Economists continue to debate whether predatory pricing should be a concern for competition policy makers. Various questions remain unresolved. Is predatory pricing ever a profitable business strategy? If so, when? Are the authorities capable of telling which price cuts are competitive and thus good for consumers and which are predatory? There are no simple answers.

**Tying** A third example of a controversial business practice is *tying*. Suppose that Makemoney Movies produces two new films – *Spiderman* and *Hamlet*. If Makemoney offers cinemas the two films together at a single price, rather than separately, the studio is said to be tying its two products.

Some economists have argued that the practice of tying should be banned. Their reasoning is as follows: imagine that *Spiderman* is a blockbuster, whereas *Hamlet* is an unprofitable art film. Then the studio could use the high demand for *Spiderman* to force cinemas to buy *Hamlet*. It seemed that the studio could use tying as a mechanism for expanding its market power.

Other economists are sceptical of this argument. Imagine that cinemas are willing to pay €20,000 for *Spiderman* and nothing for *Hamlet*. Then the most that a cinema would pay for the two films together is €20,000 – the same as it would pay for *Spiderman* by itself. Forcing the cinema to accept a worthless film as part of the deal does not increase the cinema's willingness to pay. Makemoney cannot increase its market power simply by bundling the two films together.

Why, then, does tying exist? One possibility is that it is a form of price discrimination. Suppose there are two cinemas. City Cinema is willing to pay €15,000 for *Spiderman* and €5,000 for *Hamlet*. Country Cinema is just the opposite: it is willing to pay €5,000 for *Spiderman* and €15,000 for *Hamlet*. If Makemoney charges separate prices for the two films, its best strategy is to charge €15,000 for each film, and each cinema chooses to show only one film. Yet if Makemoney offers the two films as a bundle, it can charge each cinema €20,000 for the films. Thus, if different cinemas value the films differently, tying may allow the studio to increase profit by charging a combined price closer to the buyers' total willingness to pay.

Tying remains a controversial business practice. The argument that tying allows a firm to extend its market power to other goods is not well founded, at least in its simplest form. Yet economists have proposed more elaborate theories for how tying can impede competition. Given our current economic knowledge, it is unclear whether tying has adverse effects for society as a whole.

## CASE STUDY

### The Microsoft Case

One of the most important and controversial anti-trust cases in recent years has been the US government's suit against the Microsoft Corporation, filed in 1998. Certainly, the case did not lack drama. It pitted one of the world's richest men (Bill Gates) against one of the world's most powerful regulatory agencies (the US Justice Department). Testifying for the US government was a prominent economist (MIT professor Franklin Fisher). Testifying for Microsoft was an equally prominent economist (MIT professor Richard Schmalensee). At stake was the future of one of the world's most valuable companies (Microsoft) in one of the economy's fastest growing industries (computer software).

A central issue in the Microsoft case involved tying – in particular, whether Microsoft should be allowed to integrate its internet browser into its Windows operating system. The US government claimed that Microsoft was bundling these two products together to expand the market power it had in the market for computer operating systems into an unrelated market (for internet browsers). Allowing Microsoft to incorporate such products into its operating system, the US government argued, would deter other software companies such as Netscape from entering the market and offering new products.

Microsoft responded by pointing out that putting new features into old products is a natural part of technological progress. Cars today include stereos and air conditioners, which were once sold separately, and cameras come with built-in flashes. The same is true with operating systems. Over time, Microsoft has added many features to Windows that were previously stand-alone products. This has made computers more reliable and easier to use because consumers can be confident that the pieces work together. The integration of internet technology, Microsoft argued, was the natural next step.

One point of disagreement concerned the extent of Microsoft's market power. Noting that more than 80 per cent of new personal computers use a Microsoft operating system, the US government argued that the company had substantial monopoly power, which it was trying to expand. Microsoft replied that the software market is always changing and that Microsoft's Windows was constantly being challenged by competitors, such as the Apple Mac and Linux operating systems. It also argued that the low price it charged for Windows

*"Me? A monopolist? Now just wait a minute ..."*

– about €50, or only 3 per cent of the price of a typical computer – was evidence that its market power was severely limited.

Like many large anti-trust lawsuits, the Microsoft case became a legal morass. In November 1999, after a long trial, Judge Penfield Jackson ruled that Microsoft had great monopoly power and that it had illegally abused that power. In June 2000, after hearings about possible remedies, he ordered that Microsoft be broken up into two companies – one that sold the operating system and one that sold applications software. A year later, an appeals court overturned Jackson's break-up order and handed the case to a new judge. In September 2001, the US Justice Department announced that it no longer sought a break-up of the company and wanted to settle the case quickly.

A settlement was finally reached in November 2002. Microsoft accepted some restrictions on its business practices. The US government accepted that a browser would remain part of the Windows operating system.

**Quick Quiz** What kind of agreement is illegal for businesses to make? • Why is competition law controversial?

# IN THE NEWS

## Running Fast to Stand Still

*Big firms that dominate an industry and have considerable monopoly power often turn out to spend huge amounts on research and development and are key innovators. Why do they spend their profits on research if the competition is not up to much?*

### Slackers or Pace-Setters? Monopolies May Have More Incentive to Innovate Than Economists Have Thought

A LOT of attention has been paid to the ill effects of monopoly. Economists long ago pointed out why it is bad for a single firm to dominate a market. In essence, the trouble with monopolists is that they can set prices almost as they please. Unlike in competitive industries, a monopolist's price, in the jargon, can be way above the marginal cost of production. Worse, immunity to competition makes a monopolist fat and lazy. It needn't worry too much about keeping customers happy. Worse still, if a company has no fear of competition, why should it bother creating new and better products?

By and large, officialdom these days continues to take a dim view of monopoly. Antitrust authorities in many countries do not shrink from picking fights with companies that they believe are too powerful. The biggest target in recent years, first in America and now in Europe, has been Microsoft, creator of the operating system that runs on some 95% of the world's personal computers. One of the arguments against Microsoft is that its dominance of the desktop allows it to squeeze out smaller and (say the company's critics) more innovative rivals.

Despite this, compelling evidence that monopolists stifle innovation is harder to come by than simple theory suggests. Joseph Schumpeter, an Austrian economist, pointed out many

years ago that established firms play a big role in innovation. In modern times, it appears that many product innovations, in industries from razor blades to software, are made by companies that have a dominant share of the market. Most mainstream economists, however, have had difficulty explaining why this might be so. Kenneth Arrow, a Nobel prize-winner, once posed the issue as a paradox. Economic theory says that a monopolist should have far less incentive to invest in creating innovations than a firm in a competitive environment: experience suggests otherwise. How can this be so?

One possibility might be that the empirical connection between market share and innovation is spurious: might big firms innovate more simply because

▶

they are big, not because they are dominant? A paper published a few years ago by Richard Blundell, Rachel Griffith and John Van Reenen, of Britain's Institute for Fiscal Studies, did much to resolve this empirical question. In a detailed analysis of British manufacturing firms, it found that higher market shares do go with higher investment in research and development, which in turn is likely to lead to greater innovation. Still, the question remains: why does it happen?

A new paper by Federico Etro, of the University of Milan, aims to resolve Mr Arrow's paradox. He sets out a model in which a market leader has a greater incentive than any other firm to keep innovating and thus stay on top. Blessed with scale and market knowledge, it is better placed than potential rivals to commit itself to financing innovations. Oddly – paradoxically, if you like – in fighting to maintain its monopoly it acts more competitively than firms in markets in which there is no obviously dominant player.

The most important requirement for this result is a lack of barriers to entry: these might include, for example, big capital outlays to fund the building of new laboratories, or regulatory or licensing restrictions that make it hard for new firms to threaten an incumbent.

If there are no such barriers, a monopolist will have an excellent reason to innovate before any potential competitor comes up with the next new thing. It stands to lose its current, bloated profits if it does not; it stands to gain plenty from continued market dominance if it does.

If the world works in the way Mr Etro supposes, the fact that a dominant firm remains on top might actually be strong evidence of vigorous competition. However, observers (including antitrust authorities) may well find it difficult to work out whether a durable monopoly is the product of brilliant innovation or the deliberate strangulation of competitors. More confusing still, any half-awake monopolist will engage in some of the former in order to help bring about plenty of the latter. The very ease of entry, and the aggressiveness of the competitive environment, are what spur monopolists to innovate so fiercely.

But what if there are barriers to entry? These tend to make the dominant firm less aggressive in investing in new technologies – in essence, because its monopoly with the existing technology is less likely to be challenged. Over time, however, other companies can innovate and gradually overcome the barriers – 'leapfrogging', as Mr Etro

calls it. Meanwhile, the monopolist lives on marked time, burning off the fat of its past innovations.

So much for theorising. What might the practical implications be? One is that antitrust authorities should be especially careful when trying to stamp out monopoly power in markets that are marked by technical innovation. It could still be that firms like Microsoft are capable of using their girth to squish their rivals; the point is that continued monopoly is not cast-iron evidence of bad behaviour.

There might be a further implication for patent policy. Patents, after all, are government-endorsed monopolies for a given technology for a specified period. Mr Blundell and his colleagues found that the pharmaceutical industry provided the strongest evidence of correlation between market share and innovation. Thus strong patents, despite their recent bad press, can be a source of innovation. Generally, though, when one company dominates a market, people should be careful in assuming that it is guilty of sloth. It may be fighting for its life.

Source: *The Economist*, 20 May 2004.

## CONCLUSION

Oligopolies would like to act like monopolies, but self-interest drives them closer to competition. Thus, oligopolies can end up looking either more like monopolies or more like competitive markets, depending on the number of firms in the oligopoly and how cooperative the firms are. The story of the prisoners' dilemma shows why oligopolies can fail to maintain cooperation, even when cooperation is in their best interest.

Policy makers regulate the behaviour of oligopolists through competition law. The proper scope of these laws is the subject of ongoing controversy. Although price fixing among competing firms clearly reduces economic welfare and should be illegal, some business practices that appear to reduce competition may have legitimate if subtle purposes. As a result, policy makers need to be careful when they use the substantial powers of competition law to place limits on firm behaviour.

## SUMMARY

- Oligopolists maximize their total profits by forming a cartel and acting like a monopolist. Yet, if oligopolists make decisions about production levels individually, the result is a greater quantity and a lower price than under the monopoly outcome. The larger the number of firms in the oligopoly, the closer the quantity and price will be to the levels that would prevail under competition.

- The prisoners' dilemma shows that self-interest can prevent people from maintaining cooperation, even when cooperation is in their mutual interest. The logic of the prisoners' dilemma applies in many situations, including arms races, advertising, common-resource problems and oligopolies.

- Policy makers use competition law to prevent oligopolies from engaging in behaviour that reduces competition. The application of these laws can be controversial, because some behaviour that may seem to reduce competition may in fact have legitimate business purposes.

## KEY CONCEPTS

oligopoly, p. 320
monopolistic competition, p. 320
collusion, p. 323

cartel, p. 323
Nash equilibrium, p. 324
game theory, p. 329

prisoners' dilemma, p. 329
dominant strategy, p. 330

## QUESTIONS FOR REVIEW

1. If a group of sellers could form a cartel, what quantity and price would they try to set?

2. Compare the quantity and price of an oligopoly to those of a monopoly.

3. Compare the quantity and price of an oligopoly to those of a competitive market.

4. How does the number of firms in an oligopoly affect the outcome in its market?

5. What is the prisoners' dilemma, and what does it have to do with oligopoly?

6. Give two examples other than oligopoly to show how the prisoners' dilemma helps to explain behaviour.

7. What kinds of behaviour do the competition laws prohibit?

8. What is resale price maintenance, and why is it controversial?

# PROBLEMS AND APPLICATIONS

1. *The Economist* (15 November, 2001) reported that 'OPEC has failed to agree immediate production cuts to shore up oil prices. Afraid of losing market share, it wants non-members, who would also benefit from any price support, to cut output as well. So far, they have refused to agree. If oil prices continue to fall, that would provide relief to the beleaguered world economy, but it might wreak havoc on the finances of OPEC members.'

   a. Why do you suppose OPEC was unable to agree on cutting production?

   b. Why do you think oil-producing non-members refused to cut output?

2. A large share of the world supply of diamonds comes from Russia and South Africa. Suppose that the marginal cost of mining diamonds is constant at €1,000 per diamond, and the demand for diamonds is described by the following schedule:

   | Price | Quantity |
   | --- | --- |
   | €8,000 | 5,000 |
   | 7,000 | 6,000 |
   | 6,000 | 7,000 |
   | 5,000 | 8,000 |
   | 4,000 | 9,000 |
   | 3,000 | 10,000 |
   | 2,000 | 11,000 |
   | 1,000 | 12,000 |

   a. If there were many suppliers of diamonds, what would be the price and quantity?

   b. If there were only one supplier of diamonds, what would be the price and quantity?

   c. If Russia and South Africa formed a cartel, what would be the price and quantity? If the countries split the market evenly, what would be South Africa's production and profit? What would happen to South Africa's profit if it increased its production by 1,000 while Russia stuck to the cartel agreement?

   d. Use your answer to part (c) to explain why cartel agreements are often not successful.

3. This chapter discusses companies that are oligopolists in the market for the goods they sell. Many of the same ideas apply to companies that are oligopolists in the market for the inputs they buy. If sellers who are oligopolists try to increase the price of goods they sell, what is the goal of buyers who are oligopolists?

4. Describe several activities in your life in which game theory could be useful. What is the common link among these activities?

5. Suppose that you and a fellow student are assigned a project on which you will receive one combined grade. You each want to receive a good grade, but you also want to do as little work as possible. The decision box and pay-offs are as follows:

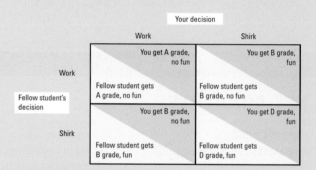

   Assume that having fun is your normal state, but having no fun is as unpleasant as receiving a grade that is two letters lower.

   a. Write out the decision box that combines the letter grade and the amount of fun you have into a single pay-off for each outcome.

   b. If neither you nor your fellow student knows how much work the other person is doing, what is the likely outcome? Does it matter whether you are likely to work with this person again? Explain your answer.

6. The chapter states that the ban on cigarette advertising on television which many countries imposed in the 1970s increased the profits of cigarette companies. Could the ban still be good public policy? Explain your answer.

7. A case study in the chapter describes a telephone conversation between the presidents of two airline companies. Let's analyse the game between two such companies. Suppose that each company can charge either a high price for tickets or a low price. If one company charges €100, it earns low profits if the other company charges €100 also, and high profits if the other company charges €200. On the other hand, if the company charges €200, it earns very low profits if the other company charges €100, and medium profits if the other company charges €200 also.

   a. Draw the decision box for this game.

   b. What is the Nash equilibrium in this game? Explain.

c.  Is there an outcome that would be better than the Nash equilibrium for both airlines? How could it be achieved? Who would lose if it were achieved?

8.  Farmer Jones and Farmer MacDonald graze their cattle on the same field. If there are 20 cows grazing in the field, each cow produces €4,000 of milk over its lifetime. If there are more cows in the field, then each cow can eat less grass, and its milk production falls. With 30 cows on the field, each produces €3,000 of milk; with 40 cows, each produces €2,000 of milk. Cows cost €1,000 apiece.

a.  Assume that Farmer Jones and Farmer MacDonald can each purchase either 10 or 20 cows, but that neither knows how many the other is buying when she makes her purchase. Calculate the pay-offs of each outcome.

b.  What is the likely outcome of this game? What would be the best outcome? Explain.

c.  There used to be more common fields than there are today. Why? (For more discussion of this topic, reread Chapter 11.)

9.  Little Kona is a small coffee company that is considering entering a market dominated by Big Brew. Each company's profit depends on whether Little Kona enters and whether Big Brew sets a high price or a low price:

|  |  | **Big Brew** | |
| --- | --- | --- | --- |
|  |  | High price | Low price |
| **Little Kona** | **Enter** | Brew makes €3 million / Kona makes €2 million | Brew makes €1 million / Kona loses €1 million |
|  | **Don't enter** | Brew makes €7 million / Kona makes zero | Brew makes €2 million / Kona makes zero |

Big Brew threatens Little Kona by saying, 'If you enter, we're going to set a low price, so you had better stay out.' Do you think Little Kona should believe the threat? Why or why not? What do you think Little Kona should do?

10. Tim and Greg are playing tennis. Every point comes down to whether Greg guesses correctly whether Tim will hit the ball to Greg's left or right. The outcomes are:

|  |  | **Greg guesses** | |
| --- | --- | --- | --- |
|  |  | Left | Right |
| **Tim hits** | **Left** | Greg wins point / Tim loses point | Greg loses point / Tim wins point |
|  | **Right** | Greg loses point / Tim wins point | Greg wins point / Tim loses point |

Does either player have a dominant strategy? If Tim chooses a particular strategy (Left or Right) and sticks with it, what will Greg do? So, can you think of a better strategy for Tim to follow?

For further resources, visit
http://www.thomsonlearning.co.uk/mankiw_taylor

# 17 MONOPOLISTIC COMPETITION

You walk into a bookshop to buy a book to read during your next summer holiday. On the shop's shelves you find the latest *Harry Potter* novel, an interesting looking political novel by a new author, a crime novel by that author who used to be a lawyer, an intellectual literary novel by a French female author, the autobiography of a former prime minister and many other choices. When you pick out a book and buy it, what kind of market are you participating in?

On the one hand, the market for books seems competitive. As you look over the shelves at your bookshop, you find many authors and many publishers vying for your attention. A buyer in this market has thousands of competing products from which to choose. And because many people are willing to put the time and effort into becoming a writer, there are a lot of people wanting to enter the market. Because of this, the book business is not very profitable. For every highly paid novelist, there are hundreds of struggling ones.

On the other hand, the market for books seems monopolistic. Because each book is unique, publishers have some latitude in choosing what price to charge. The sellers in this market are price makers rather than price takers. And, indeed, the price of books greatly exceeds marginal cost. The price of a typical hardcover novel in the UK, for instance, is about £15, whereas the cost of printing one additional copy of the novel is only a few pounds.

In this chapter we examine markets that have some features of competition and some features of monopoly. This market structure is called **monopolistic competition.** Monopolistic competition describes a market with the following attributes:

**monopolistic competition**
a market structure in which many firms sell products that are similar but not identical

- *Many sellers.* There are many firms competing for the same group of customers.
- *Product differentiation.* Each firm produces a product that is at least slightly different from those of other firms. Thus, rather than being a price taker, each firm faces a downward sloping demand curve.
- *Free entry.* Firms can enter (or exit) the market without restriction. Thus, the number of firms in the market adjusts until economic profits are driven to zero.

A moment's thought reveals a long list of markets with these attributes: books, CDs, films, computer games, restaurants, piano lessons, pizza, furniture and so on.

Monopolistic competition, like oligopoly, is a market structure that lies between the extreme cases of competition and monopoly. But oligopoly and monopolistic competition are quite different. Oligopoly departs from the perfectly competitive ideal of Chapter 14 because there are only a few sellers in the market. The small number of sellers makes rigorous competition less likely, and it makes strategic interactions among them vitally important. By contrast, under monopolistic competition, there are many sellers, each of which is small compared to the market. A monopolistically competitive market departs from the perfectly competitive ideal because each of the sellers offers a somewhat different product.

## COMPETITION WITH DIFFERENTIATED PRODUCTS

To understand monopolistically competitive markets, we first consider the decisions facing an individual firm. We then examine what happens in the long run as firms enter and exit the industry. Next, we compare the equilibrium under monopolistic competition to the equilibrium under perfect competition that we examined in Chapter 14. Finally, we consider whether the outcome in a monopolistically competitive market is desirable from the standpoint of society as a whole.

### The Monopolistically Competitive Firm in the Short Run

Each firm in a monopolistically competitive market is, in many ways, like a monopoly. Because its product is different from those offered by other firms, it faces a downward sloping demand curve. (By contrast, a perfectly competitive firm faces a horizontal demand curve at the market price.) Thus, the monopolistically competitive firm follows a monopolist's rule for profit maximization: it chooses the quantity at which marginal revenue equals marginal cost and then uses its demand curve to find the price consistent with that quantity.

Figure 17.1 shows the cost, demand and marginal revenue curves for two typical firms, each in a different monopolistically competitive industry. In both panels of this figure, the profit-maximizing quantity is found at the intersection of the marginal revenue and marginal cost curves. The two panels in this figure show different outcomes for the firm's profit. In panel (a), price exceeds average total cost, so the firm makes a profit. In panel (b), price is below average total cost. In this case, the firm is unable to make a positive profit, so the best the firm can do is to minimize its losses.

All this should seem familiar. A monopolistically competitive firm chooses its quantity and price just as a monopoly does. In the short run, these two types of market structure are similar.

**FIGURE 17.1**

**Monopolistic Competitors in the Short Run**

*Monopolistic competitors, like monopolists, maximize profit by producing the quantity at which marginal revenue equals marginal cost. The firm in panel (a) makes a profit because, at this quantity, price is above average total cost. The firm in panel (b) makes losses because, at this quantity, price is less than average total cost.*

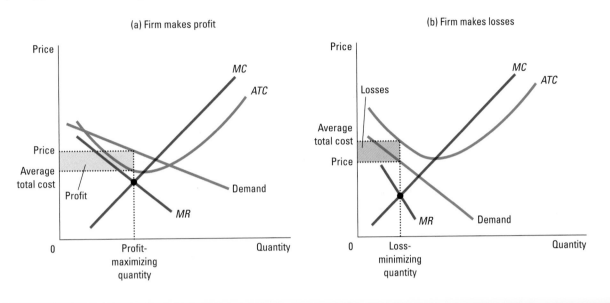

## The Long-Run Equilibrium

The situations depicted in Figure 17.1 do not last long. When firms are making profits, as in panel (a), new firms have an incentive to enter the market. This entry increases the number of products from which customers can choose and, therefore, reduces the demand faced by each firm already in the market. In other words, profit encourages entry, and entry shifts the demand curves faced by the incumbent firms to the left. As the demand for incumbent firms' products falls, these firms experience declining profit.

Conversely, when firms are making losses, as in panel (b), firms in the market have an incentive to exit. As firms exit, customers have fewer products from which to choose. This decrease in the number of firms expands the demand faced by those firms that stay in the market. In other words, losses encourage exit, and exit shifts the demand curves of the remaining firms to the right. As the demand for the remaining firms' products rises, these firms experience rising profit (that is, declining losses).

This process of entry and exit continues until the firms in the market are making exactly zero economic profit. Figure 17.2 depicts the long-run equilibrium. Once the market reaches this equilibrium, new firms have no incentive to enter, and existing firms have no incentive to exit.

Notice that the demand curve in this figure just barely touches the average total cost curve. Mathematically, we say the two curves are *tangent* to each other. These two curves must be tangent once entry and exit have driven profit to zero. Because profit per unit sold is the difference between price (found on the demand curve) and average total cost, the maximum profit is zero only if these two curves touch each other without crossing.

**FIGURE 17.2**

### A Monopolistic Competitor in the Long Run

*In a monopolistically competitive market, if firms are making profit, new firms enter and the demand curves for the incumbent firms shift to the left. Similarly, if firms are making losses, old firms exit and the demand curves of the remaining firms shift to the right. Because of these shifts in demand, a monopolistically competitive firm eventually finds itself in the long-run equilibrium shown here. In this long-run equilibrium, price equals average total cost, and the firm earns zero profit.*

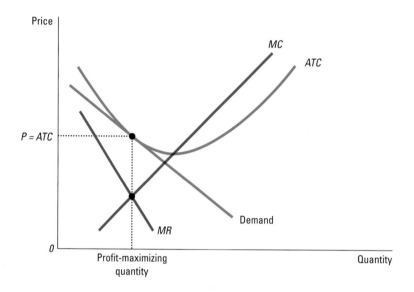

"GIVEN THE DOWNWARD SLOPE OF OUR DEMAND CURVE, AND THE EASE WITH WHICH OTHER FIRMS CAN ENTER THE INDUSTRY, WE CAN STRENGTHEN OUR PROFIT POSITION ONLY BY EQUATING MARGINAL COST AND MARGINAL REVENUE. ORDER MORE JELLY BEANS."

To sum up, two characteristics describe the long-run equilibrium in a monopolistically competitive market:

- As in a monopoly market, price exceeds marginal cost. This conclusion arises because profit maximization requires marginal revenue to equal marginal cost and because the downward sloping demand curve makes marginal revenue less than the price.
- As in a competitive market, price equals average total cost. This conclusion arises because free entry and exit drive economic profit to zero.

The second characteristic shows how monopolistic competition differs from monopoly. Because a monopoly is the sole seller of a product without close substitutes, it can earn positive economic profit, even in the long run. By contrast, because there is free entry into a monopolistically competitive market, the economic profit of a firm in this type of market is driven to zero.

## Monopolistic Versus Perfect Competition

Figure 17.3 compares the long-run equilibrium under monopolistic competition to the long-run equilibrium under perfect competition. (Chapter 14 discussed the equilibrium with perfect competition.) There are two noteworthy differences between monopolistic and perfect competition – excess capacity and the mark-up.

**Excess Capacity** As we have just seen, entry and exit drive each firm in a monopolistically competitive market to a point of tangency between its demand

### FIGURE 17.3

**Monopolistic Versus Perfect Competition**

*Panel (a) shows the long-run equilibrium in a monopolistically competitive market, and panel (b) shows the long-run equilibrium in a perfectly competitive market. Two differences are notable. (1) The perfectly competitive firm produces at the efficient scale, where average total cost is minimized. By contrast, the monopolistically competitive firm produces at less than the efficient scale. (2) Price equals marginal cost under perfect competition, but price is above marginal cost under monopolistic competition.*

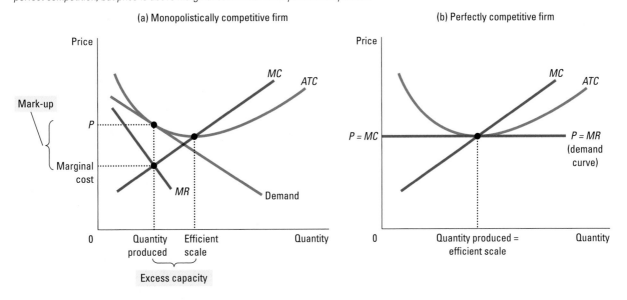

and average total cost curves. Panel (a) of Figure 17.3 shows that the quantity of output at this point is smaller than the quantity that minimizes average total cost. Thus, under monopolistic competition, firms produce on the downward sloping portion of their average total cost curves. In this way, monopolistic competition contrasts starkly with perfect competition. As panel (b) of Figure 17.3 shows, free entry in competitive markets drives firms to produce at the minimum of average total cost.

The quantity that minimizes average total cost is called the *efficient scale* of the firm. In the long run, perfectly competitive firms produce at the efficient scale, whereas monopolistically competitive firms produce below this level. Firms are said to have *excess capacity* under monopolistic competition. In other words, a monopolistically competitive firm, unlike a perfectly competitive firm, could increase the quantity it produces and lower the average total cost of production.

**Mark-up over Marginal Cost** A second difference between perfect competition and monopolistic competition is the relationship between price and marginal cost. For a competitive firm, such as that shown in panel (b) of Figure 17.3, price equals marginal cost. For a monopolistically competitive firm, such as that shown in panel (a), price exceeds marginal cost, because the firm always has some market power.

How is this mark-up over marginal cost consistent with free entry and zero profit? The zero-profit condition ensures only that price equals average total cost. It does *not* ensure that price equals marginal cost. Indeed, in the long-run equilibrium, monopolistically competitive firms operate on the declining portion of their average total cost curves, so marginal cost is below average total cost. Thus, for price to equal average total cost, price must be above marginal cost.

In this relationship between price and marginal cost, we see a key behavioural difference between perfect competitors and monopolistic competitors. Imagine that you were to ask a firm the following question: 'Would you like to see another customer come through your door ready to buy from you at your current price?' A perfectly competitive firm would answer that it didn't care. Because price exactly equals marginal cost, the profit from an extra unit sold is zero. By contrast, a monopolistically competitive firm is always eager to get another customer. Because its price exceeds marginal cost, an extra unit sold at the posted price means more profit. According to an old quip, monopolistically competitive markets are those in which sellers send Christmas cards to the buyers.

## Monopolistic Competition and the Welfare of Society

Is the outcome in a monopolistically competitive market desirable from the standpoint of society as a whole? Can policy makers improve on the market outcome? There are no simple answers to these questions.

One source of inefficiency is the mark-up of price over marginal cost. Because of the mark-up, some consumers who value the good at more than the marginal cost of production (but less than the price) will be deterred from buying it. Thus, a monopolistically competitive market has the normal deadweight loss of monopoly pricing. We first saw this type of inefficiency when we discussed monopoly in Chapter 15.

Although this outcome is clearly undesirable compared to the first-best outcome of price equal to marginal cost, there is no easy way for policymakers to fix the problem. To enforce marginal-cost pricing, policymakers would need to regulate all firms that produce differentiated products. Because such products are so common in the economy, the administrative burden of such regulation would be overwhelming.

Moreover, regulating monopolistic competitors would entail all the problems of regulating natural monopolies. In particular, because monopolistic competitors are making zero profits already, requiring them to lower their prices to equal marginal cost would cause them to make losses. To keep these firms in business, the government would need to help them cover these losses. Rather than raising taxes to pay for these subsidies, policymakers may decide it is better to live with the inefficiency of monopolistic pricing.

Another way in which monopolistic competition may be socially inefficient is that the number of firms in the market may not be the 'ideal' one. That is, there may be too much or too little entry. One way to think about this problem is in terms of the externalities associated with entry. Whenever a new firm considers entering the market with a new product, it considers only the profit it would make. Yet its entry would also have two external effects:

- *The product-variety externality.* Because consumers get some consumer surplus from the introduction of a new product, entry of a new firm conveys a positive externality on consumers.
- *The business-stealing externality.* Because other firms lose customers and profits from the entry of a new competitor, entry of a new firm imposes a negative externality on existing firms.

Thus, in a monopolistically competitive market, there are both positive and negative externalities associated with the entry of new firms. Depending on which externality is larger, a monopolistically competitive market could have either too few or too many products.

Both of these externalities are closely related to the conditions for monopolistic competition. The product-variety externality arises because a new firm would offer a product different from those of the existing firms. The business-stealing externality arises because firms post a price above marginal cost and, therefore, are always eager to sell additional units. Conversely, because perfectly competitive firms produce identical goods and charge a price equal to marginal cost, neither of these externalities exists under perfect competition.

**FYI**

## Is Excess Capacity a Social Problem?

As we have seen, monopolistically competitive firms produce a quantity of output below the level that minimizes average total cost. By contrast, firms in perfectly competitive markets are driven to produce at the quantity that minimizes average total cost. This comparison between perfect and monopolistic competition led some economists in the past to argue that the excess capacity of monopolistic competitors was a source of inefficiency.

Today economists understand that the excess capacity of monopolistic competitors is not directly relevant for evaluating economic welfare. There is no reason that society should want all firms to produce at the minimum of average total cost. For example, consider a publishing firm. Producing a novel might take a fixed cost of €50,000 (the author's time) and variable costs of €5 per book (the cost of printing). In this case, the average total cost of a book declines as the number of books increases because the fixed cost gets spread over more and more units. The average total cost is minimized by printing an infinite number of books. But in no sense is infinity the right number of books for society to produce.

In short, monopolistic competitors do have excess capacity, but this fact tells us little about the desirability of the market outcome.

In the end, we can conclude only that monopolistically competitive markets do not have all the desirable welfare properties of perfectly competitive markets. That is, the invisible hand does not ensure that total surplus is maximized under monopolistic competition. Yet because the inefficiencies are subtle, hard to measure and hard to fix, there is no easy way for public policy to improve the market outcome.

**Quick Quiz** List the three key attributes of monopolistic competition. • Draw and explain a diagram to show the long-run equilibrium in a monopolistically competitive market. How does this equilibrium differ from that in a perfectly competitive market?

# ADVERTISING

It is nearly impossible to go through a typical day in a modern economy without being bombarded with advertising. Whether you are reading a newspaper, watching television or driving down the motorway, some firm will try to convince you to buy its product. Such behaviour is a natural feature of monopolistic competition. When firms sell differentiated products and charge prices above marginal cost, each firm has an incentive to advertise in order to attract more buyers to its particular product.

The amount of advertising varies substantially across products. Firms that sell highly differentiated consumer goods, such as over-the-counter drugs, perfumes, soft drinks, razor blades, breakfast cereals and dog food, typically spend between 10 and 20 per cent of revenue for advertising. Firms that sell industrial products, such as drill presses and communications satellites, typically spend very little on advertising. And firms that sell homogeneous products, such as wheat, peanuts or crude oil, spend nothing at all. In the UK in 2002, spending on advertising was about £17 billion. Put another way, about 2.5 pence out of every pound of UK household expenditure pays for advertising.

Advertising takes many forms. Most advertising expenditure in the UK pays for space in newspapers and magazines (44 per cent of the total in 2002), television and radio advertisements (29 per cent), direct mail (14 per cent), the yellow pages and other telephone directories (6 per cent). About 1 per cent of total advertising spending goes on the internet and the remainder (6 per cent) is for miscellaneous other ways of reaching customers, such as roadside hoardings, advertisements on buses, taxis and the London Underground, cinema advertising and blimps.

## The Debate Over Advertising

Is society wasting the resources it devotes to advertising? Or does advertising serve a valuable purpose? Assessing the social value of advertising is difficult and often generates heated argument among economists. Let's consider both sides of the debate.

**The Critique of Advertising** Critics of advertising argue that firms advertise in order to manipulate people's tastes. Much advertising is psychological rather than informational. Consider, for example, the typical television advert for some brand of soft drink. The advert most likely does not tell the viewer about the product's price or quality. Instead, it might show a group of happy people at a party on a beach on a beautiful sunny day. In their hands are cans of the soft drink. The goal of the advert is to convey a subconscious (if not subtle) message: 'You too can have many friends and be happy and beautiful, if only you drink our product.' Critics of advertising argue that such an advert creates a desire that otherwise might not exist.

Critics also argue that advertising impedes competition. Advertising often tries to convince consumers that products are more different than they truly are. By increasing the perception of product differentiation and fostering brand loyalty, advertising makes buyers less concerned with price differences among similar goods. With a less elastic demand curve, each firm charges a larger mark-up over marginal cost.

**The Defence of Advertising** Defenders of advertising argue that firms use advertising to provide information to customers. Advertising conveys the prices of the goods being offered for sale, the existence of new products and the locations of retail outlets. This information allows customers to make better choices about what to buy and, thus, enhances the ability of markets to allocate resources efficiently.

Defenders also argue that advertising fosters competition. Because advertising allows customers to be more fully informed about all the firms in the market, customers can more easily take advantage of price differences. Thus, each firm has less market power. In addition, advertising allows new firms to enter more easily, because it gives entrants a means to attract customers from existing firms.

Over time, policymakers have come to accept the view that advertising can make markets more competitive. One important example is the regulation of advertising for certain professions, such as lawyers, doctors and pharmacists. In the past, these groups succeeded in getting state governments to prohibit advertising in their fields on the grounds that advertising was 'unprofessional'. In recent years, however, the courts have concluded that the primary effect of these restrictions on advertising was to curtail competition. They have, therefore, overturned many of the laws that prohibit advertising by members of these professions.

## CASE STUDY

### Advertising and the Price of Spectacles

What effect does advertising have on the price of a good? On the one hand, advertising might make consumers view products as being more different than they otherwise would. If so, it would make markets less competitive and firms' demand curves less elastic, and this would lead firms to charge higher prices. On the other hand, advertising might make it easier for consumers to find the firms offering the best prices. In this case, it would make markets more competitive and firms' demand curves more elastic, and this would lead to lower prices.

In an article published in the *Journal of Law and Economics* in 1972, economist Lee Benham tested these two views of advertising. In the United States during the 1960s, the various state governments had vastly different rules about advertising by opticians. Some states allowed advertising for spectacles and eye examinations. Many states, however, prohibited it. For example, the law in the state of Florida read as follows:

> It is unlawful for any person, firm, or corporation to … advertise either directly or indirectly by any means whatsoever any definite or indefinite price or credit terms on prescriptive or corrective lens, frames, complete

> prescriptive or corrective glasses, or any optometric service. … This
> section is passed in the interest of public health, safety, and welfare, and
> its provisions shall be liberally construed to carry out its objects and
> purposes.

Professional opticians enthusiastically endorsed these restrictions on advertising.

Benham used the differences in state law as a natural experiment to test the two views of advertising. The results were striking. In those states that prohibited advertising, the average price paid for a pair of glasses was $33 (the equivalent of about $170 today, after allowing for inflation since 1963). In those states that did not restrict advertising, the average price was $26. Thus, advertising reduced average prices by more than 20 per cent. In the market for glasses, and probably in many other markets as well, advertising fosters competition and leads to lower prices for consumers.

## Advertising as a Signal of Quality

Many types of advertising contain little apparent information about the product being advertised. Consider a firm introducing a new breakfast cereal. A typical advertisement might have some highly paid actor eating the cereal and exclaiming how wonderful it tastes. How much information does the advertisement really provide?

The answer is: more than you might think. Defenders of advertising argue that even advertising that appears to contain little hard information may in fact tell consumers something about product quality. The willingness of the firm to spend a large amount of money on advertising can itself be a *signal* to consumers about the quality of the product being offered.

Consider the problem facing two firms – Nestlé and Kellogg. Each company has just come up with a recipe for a new breakfast cereal, which it would sell for €3 a box. To keep things simple, let's assume that the marginal cost of making cereal is zero, so the €3 is all profit. Each company knows that if it spends €10 million on advertising, it will get 1 million consumers to try its new cereal. And each company knows that if consumers like the cereal, they will buy it not once but many times.

First consider Nestlé's decision. Based on market research, Nestlé knows that its cereal is only mediocre. Although advertising would sell one box to each of 1 million consumers, the consumers would quickly learn that the cereal is not very good and stop buying it. Nestlé decides it is not worth paying €10 million in advertising to get only €3 million in sales. So it does not bother to advertise. It sends its cooks back to the drawing board to find another recipe.

Kellogg, on the other hand, knows that its cereal is great. Each person who tries it will buy a box a month for the next year. Thus, the €10 million in advertising will bring in €36 million in sales. Advertising is profitable here because Kellogg has a good product that consumers will buy repeatedly. Thus, Kellogg chooses to advertise.

Now that we have considered the behaviour of the two firms, let's consider the behaviour of consumers. We began by asserting that consumers are inclined to try a new cereal that they see advertised. But is this behaviour rational? Should a consumer try a new cereal just because the seller has chosen to advertise it?

In fact, it may be completely rational for consumers to try new products that they see advertised. In our story, consumers decide to try Kellogg's new cereal because Kellogg advertises. Kellogg chooses to advertise because it knows that its cereal is quite good, while Nestlé chooses not to advertise because it knows that its cereal is only mediocre. By its willingness to spend money on advertising, Kellogg signals to consumers the quality of its cereal. Each consumer thinks, quite sensibly, 'Crikey, if the Kellogg Company is willing to spend so much money advertising this new cereal, it must be really good.'

What is most surprising about this theory of advertising is that the content of the advertisement is irrelevant. Kellogg signals the quality of its product by its willingness to spend money on advertising. What the advertisements say is not as important as the fact that consumers know ads are expensive. By contrast, cheap advertising cannot be effective at signalling quality to consumers. In our example, if an advertising campaign cost less than €3 million, both Nestlé and Kellogg would use it to market their new cereals. Because both good and mediocre cereals would be advertised, consumers could not infer the quality of a new cereal from the fact that it is advertised. Over time, consumers would learn to ignore such cheap advertising.

This theory can explain why firms pay famous actors large amounts of money to make advertisements that, on the surface, appear to convey no information at all. The information is not in the advertisement's content, but simply in its existence and expense.

## Brand Names

Advertising is closely related to the existence of brand names. In many markets, there are two types of firms. Some firms sell products with widely recognized brand names, while other firms sell generic substitutes. For example, in a typical supermarket, you can find Pepsi next to less familiar colas, or Kellogg's cornflakes next to the supermarket's own brand of cornflakes, made for it by an unknown firm. Most often, the firm with the famous brand name spends more on advertising and charges a higher price for its product.

Just as there is disagreement about the economics of advertising, there is disagreement about the economics of brand names. Let's consider both sides of the debate.

Critics of brand names argue that brand names cause consumers to perceive differences that do not really exist. In many cases, the generic good is almost indistinguishable from the brand-name good. Consumers' willingness to pay more for the brand-name good, these critics assert, is a form of irrationality fostered by advertising. Economist Edward Chamberlin, one of the early developers of the theory of monopolistic competition, concluded from this argument that brand names were bad for the economy. He proposed that the government discourage their use by refusing to enforce the exclusive trademarks that companies use to identify their products.

More recently, economists have defended brand names as a useful way for consumers to ensure that the goods they buy are of high quality. There are two related arguments. First, brand names provide consumers with *information* about quality when quality cannot be easily judged in advance of purchase. Second, brand names give firms an *incentive* to maintain high quality, because firms have a financial stake in maintaining the reputation of their brand names.

To see how these arguments work in practice, consider a famous brand name: Ibis hotels. Imagine that you are driving through an unfamiliar town and you need somewhere to stay for the night. You see a Hotel Ibis and a local hotel next door to it. Which do you choose? The local hotel may in fact offer better accommodation at lower prices, but you have no way of knowing that. In contrast, Hotel Ibis offers a consistent product across many European cities. Its brand name is useful to you as a way of judging the quality of what you are about to buy.

The Ibis brand name also ensures that the company has an incentive to maintain quality. For example, if some customers were to become very ill from bad food served at breakfast at a Hotel Ibis, the news would be disastrous for the company. Ibis would lose much of the valuable reputation that it has built up over the years and, as a result, it would lose sales and profit not just in the hotel that served the bad food but in its many hotels across Europe. By contrast, if some customers were to become ill from bad food served at breakfast in a local hotel, that restaurant might have to close down, but the lost profits would be much smaller. Hence, Ibis has a greater incentive to ensure that its breakfast food is safe.

The debate over brand names thus centres on the question of whether consumers are rational in preferring brand names over generic substitutes. Critics of brand names argue that brand names are the result of an irrational consumer response to advertising. Defenders of brand names argue that consumers have good reason to pay more for brand-name products because they can be more confident in the quality of these products.

> **Quick Quiz** How might advertising make markets less competitive? How might it make markets more competitive? • Give the arguments for and against brand names.

## CONCLUSION

Monopolistic competition is true to its name: it is a hybrid of monopoly and competition. Like a monopoly, each monopolistic competitor faces a downward sloping demand curve and, as a result, charges a price above marginal cost. As in a perfectly competitive market, there are many firms, and entry and exit drive

### TABLE 17.1

**Monopolistic Competition: Between Perfect Competition and Monopoly**

| | Market structure | | |
| --- | --- | --- | --- |
| | **Perfect competition** | **Monopolistic competition** | **Monopoly** |
| **Features that all three market structures share** | | | |
| Goal of firms | Maximize profits | Maximize profits | Maximize profits |
| Rule for maximizing | MR = MC | MR = MC | MR = MC |
| Can earn economic profits in the short run? | Yes | Yes | Yes |
| **Features that monopoly and monopolistic competition share** | | | |
| Price taker? | Yes | No | No |
| Price | P = MC | P > MC | P > MC |
| Produces welfare-maximizing level of output? | Yes | No | No |
| **Features that perfect competition and monopolistic competition share** | | | |
| Number of firms | Many | Many | One |
| Entry in long run? | Yes | Yes | No |
| Can earn economic profits in long run? | No | No | Yes |

the profit of each monopolistic competitor toward zero. Table 17.1 summarizes these lessons.

Because monopolistically competitive firms produce differentiated products, each firm advertises in order to attract customers to its own brand. To some extent, advertising manipulates consumers' tastes, promotes irrational brand loyalty and impedes competition. To a larger extent, advertising provides information, establishes brand names of reliable quality and fosters competition.

The theory of monopolistic competition seems to describe many markets in the economy. It is somewhat disappointing, therefore, that the theory does not yield simple and compelling advice for public policy. From the standpoint of the economic theorist, the allocation of resources in monopolistically competitive markets is not perfect. Yet, from the standpoint of a practical policymaker, there may be little that can be done to improve it.

## SUMMARY

- A monopolistically competitive market is characterized by three attributes: many firms, differentiated products and free entry.

- The equilibrium in a monopolistically competitive market differs from that in a perfectly competitive market in two related ways. First, each firm in a monopolistically competitive market has excess capacity. That is, it operates on the downward sloping portion of the average total cost curve. Secondly, each firm charges a price above marginal cost.

- Monopolistic competition does not have all the desirable properties of perfect competition. There is the standard deadweight loss of monopoly caused by the mark-up of price over marginal cost. In addition, the number of firms (and thus the variety of products) can be too large or too small. In practice, the ability of policymakers to correct these inefficiencies is limited.

- The product differentiation inherent in monopolistic competition leads to the use of advertising and brand names. Critics of advertising and brand names argue that firms use them to take advantage of consumer irrationality and to reduce competition. Defenders of advertising and brand names argue that firms use them to inform consumers and to compete more vigorously on price and product quality.

## KEY CONCEPT

monopolistic competition, p. 347

## QUESTIONS FOR REVIEW

1. Describe the three attributes of monopolistic competition. How is monopolistic competition like monopoly? How is it like perfect competition?

2. Draw a diagram depicting a firm in a monopolistically competitive market that is making profits. Now show what happens to this firm as new firms enter the industry.

3. Draw a diagram of the long-run equilibrium in a monopolistically competitive market. How is price related to average total cost? How is price related to marginal cost?

4. Does a monopolistic competitor produce too much or too little output compared to the most efficient level? What practical considerations make it difficult for policymakers to solve this problem?

5. How might advertising reduce economic well-being? How might advertising increase economic well-being?

6. How might advertising with no apparent informational content in fact convey information to consumers?

7. Explain two benefits that might arise from the existence of brand names.

## PROBLEMS AND APPLICATIONS

1. Classify the following markets as perfectly competitive, monopolistic or monopolistically competitive, and explain your answers.
   a. wooden HB pencils
   b. bottled water
   c. copper
   d. local telephone service
   e. strawberry jam
   f. lipstick.

2. What feature of the product being sold distinguishes a monopolistically competitive firm from a monopolistic firm?

3. The chapter states that monopolistically competitive firms could increase the quantity they produce and lower the average total cost of production. Why don't they do so?

4. Sparkle is one firm of many in the market for toothpaste, which is in long-run equilibrium.
   a. Draw a diagram showing Sparkle's demand curve, marginal revenue curve, average total cost curve, and marginal cost curve. Label Sparkle's profit-maximizing output and price.
   b. What is Sparkle's profit? Explain.
   c. On your diagram, show the consumer surplus derived from the purchase of Sparkle toothpaste. Also show the deadweight loss relative to the efficient level of output.
   d. If the government forced Sparkle to produce the efficient level of output, what would happen to the firm? What would happen to Sparkle's customers?

5. Do monopolistically competitive markets typically have the optimal number of products? Explain.

6. The chapter says that monopolistically competitive firms may send Christmas cards to their customers. What do they accomplish by this? Explain in words and with a diagram.

7. If you were thinking of entering the ice cream business, would you try to make ice cream that is just like one of the existing brands? Explain your decision using the ideas of this chapter.

8. Describe three adverts that you have seen on TV. In what ways, if any, were each of these adverts socially useful? In what ways were they socially wasteful? Did the adverts affect the likelihood of your buying the product? Why or why not?

9. For each of the following pairs of firms, explain which firm would be more likely to engage in advertising:
   a. A family-owned farm or a family-owned restaurant.
   b. A manufacturer of forklift trucks or a manufacturer of cars.
   c. A company that invented a very reliable watch or a company that invented a less reliable watch that costs the same amount to make.

10. The makers of Panadol pain reliever do a lot of advertising and have very loyal customers. In contrast, the makers of generic paracetamol do no advertising, and their customers shop only for the lowest price. Assume that the marginal costs of Panadol and generic paracetamol are the same and constant.

a.  Draw a diagram showing Panadol's demand, marginal revenue and marginal cost curves. Label Panadol's price and mark-up over marginal cost.

b.  Repeat part (a) for a producer of generic paracetamol. How do the diagrams differ? Which company has the bigger mark-up? Explain.

c.  Which company has the bigger incentive for careful quality control? Why?

For further resources, visit
http://www.thomsonlearning.co.uk/mankiw_taylor

# 6

# THE ECONOMICS
# OF LABOUR MARKETS

# 18 THE MARKETS FOR THE FACTORS OF PRODUCTION

When you finish university, your income will be determined largely by what kind of job you take. If you become a professional economist, you will earn more than if you become a petrol station attendant. This fact is not surprising, but it is not obvious why it is true. No law requires that economists be paid more than petrol station attendants. No ethical principle says that economists are more deserving. If you become an academic economist in a university, you will probably earn less than if you become a banker. What then determines which job will pay you the higher wage?

Your income, of course, is a small piece of a larger economic picture. In 2003 the total income of all UK residents was about £1.1 trillion. People earned this income in various ways. Workers earned about two-thirds of it in the form of wages and fringe benefits and about ten per cent of it is income from self-employment. The rest went to landowners and to the owners of *capital* – the economy's stock of equipment and structures – in the form of rent, profit and interest. What determines how much goes to workers? To landowners? To the owners of capital? Why do some workers earn higher wages than others, some landowners higher rental income than others and some capital owners greater profit than others? Why, in particular, do computer programmers earn more than petrol station attendants?

The answers to these questions, like most in economics, hinge on supply and demand. The supply and demand for labour, land and capital determine the prices paid to workers, landowners and capital owners. To understand why some people have higher incomes than others, therefore, we need to look more deeply at the markets for the services they provide. That is our job in this and the next two chapters.

**factors of production**
the inputs used to produce goods and services

This chapter provides the basic theory for the analysis of factor markets. As you may recall from Chapter 2, the **factors of production** are the inputs used to produce goods and services. Labour, land and capital are the three most important factors of production. When a computer firm produces a new software program, it uses programmers' time (labour), the physical space on which its offices sit (land), and an office building and computer equipment (capital). Similarly, when a petrol station sells petrol, it uses attendants' time (labour), the physical space (land), and the petrol tanks and pumps (capital).

Although in many ways factor markets resemble the goods markets we have analysed in previous chapters, they are different in one important way: the demand for a factor of production is a *derived demand*. That is, a firm's demand for a factor of production is derived from its decision to supply a good in another market. The demand for computer programmers is inextricably tied to the supply of computer software, and the demand for petrol station attendants is inextricably tied to the supply of petrol.

In this chapter we analyse factor demand by considering how a competitive, profit-maximizing firm decides how much of any factor to buy. We begin our analysis by examining the demand for labour. Labour is the most important factor of production, for workers receive most of the total income earned in all of the economies of Europe and North America. Later in the chapter, we see that the lessons we learn about the labour market apply directly to the markets for the other factors of production.

The basic theory of factor markets developed in this chapter takes a large step towards explaining how the income of a large industrialized economy is distributed among workers, landowners and owners of capital. Chapter 19 will build on this analysis to examine in more detail why some workers earn more than others. Chapter 20 will examine how much inequality results from this process and then consider what role the government should and does play in altering the distribution of income.

## THE DEMAND FOR LABOUR

Labour markets, like other markets in the economy, are governed by the forces of supply and demand. This is illustrated in Figure 18.1. In panel (a) the supply and demand for apples determine the price of apples. In panel (b) the supply and demand for apple pickers determine the price, or wage, of apple pickers.

As we have already noted, labour markets are different from most other markets because labour demand is a derived demand. Most labour services, rather than being final goods ready to be enjoyed by consumers, are inputs into the production of other goods. To understand labour demand, we need to focus on the firms that hire the labour and use it to produce goods for sale. By examining the link between the production of goods and the demand for labour, we gain insight into the determination of equilibrium wages.

### The Competitive Profit-Maximizing Firm

Let's look at how a typical firm, such as an apple producer, decides the quantity of labour to demand. The firm owns an apple orchard and each week must decide how many apple pickers to hire to harvest its crop. After the firm makes its hiring decision, the workers pick as many apples as they can. The firm then sells the apples, pays the workers, and keeps what is left as profit.

### FIGURE 18.1

**The Versatility of Supply and Demand**

*The basic tools of supply and demand apply to goods and to labour services. Panel (a) shows how the supply and demand for apples determine the price of apples. Panel (b) shows how the supply and demand for apple pickers determine the wage of apple pickers.*

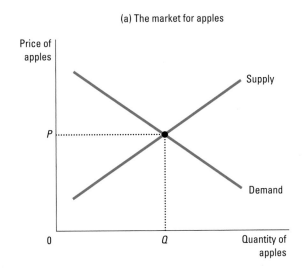

(a) The market for apples

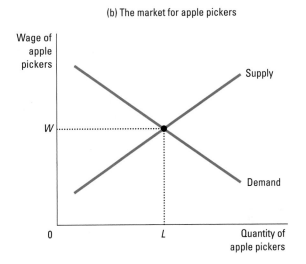

(b) The market for apple pickers

We make two assumptions about our firm. First, we assume that our firm is *competitive* both in the market for apples (where the firm is a seller) and in the market for apple pickers (where the firm is a buyer). Recall from Chapter 14 that a competitive firm is a price taker. Because there are many other firms selling apples and hiring apple pickers, a single firm has little influence over the price it gets for apples or the wage it pays apple pickers. The firm takes the price and the wage as given by market conditions. It only has to decide how many workers to hire and how many apples to sell.

Secondly, we assume that the firm is *profit-maximizing*. Thus, the firm does not directly care about the number of workers it has or the number of apples it produces. It cares only about profit, which equals the total revenue from the sale of apples minus the total cost of producing them. The firm's supply of apples and its demand for workers are derived from its primary goal of maximizing profit.

## The Production Function and the Marginal Product of Labour

To make its hiring decision, the firm must consider how the size of its workforce affects the amount of output produced. In other words, it must consider how the number of apple pickers affects the quantity of apples it can harvest and sell. Table 18.1 gives a numerical example. In the first column is the number of workers. In the second column is the quantity of apples the workers harvest each week.

These two columns of numbers describe the firm's ability to produce. As we noted in Chapter 13, economists use the term **production function** to describe the relationship between the quantity of the inputs used in production and the quantity of output from production. Here the 'input' is the apple pickers and the

**production function**
the relationship between the quantity of inputs used to make a good and the quantity of output of that good

**TABLE 18.1**

How the Competitive Firm Decides How Much Labour to Hire

| Labour | Output | Marginal product of labour | Value of the marginal product of labour | Wage | Marginal profit |
|---|---|---|---|---|---|
| $L$ (number of workers) | $Q$ (kilos per week) | $MPL = \Delta Q/\Delta L$ (kilos per week) | $VMPL = P \times MPL$ | $W$ | $\Delta Profit = VMPL - W$ |
| 0 | 0 | | | | |
| | | 1,000 | €1,000 | €500 | €500 |
| 1 | 1,000 | | | | |
| | | 800 | 800 | 500 | 300 |
| 2 | 1,800 | | | | |
| | | 600 | 600 | 500 | 100 |
| 3 | 2,400 | | | | |
| | | 400 | 400 | 500 | −100 |
| 4 | 2,800 | | | | |
| | | 200 | 200 | 500 | −300 |
| 5 | 3,000 | | | | |

**FIGURE 18.2**

**The Production Function**

*The production function is the relationship between the inputs into production (apple pickers) and the output from production (apples). As the quantity of the input increases, the production function gets flatter, reflecting the property of diminishing marginal product.*

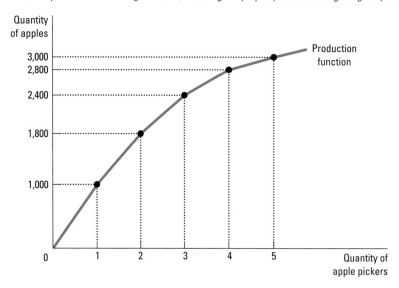

'output' is the apples. The other inputs – the trees themselves, the land, the firm's trucks and tractors, and so on – are held fixed for now. This firm's production function shows that if the firm hires 1 worker, that worker will pick 1,000 kilos of apples per week. If the firm hires 2 workers, the two workers together will pick 1,800 kilos per week, and so on.

Figure 18.2 graphs the data on labour and output presented in Table 18.1. The number of workers is on the horizontal axis, and the amount of output is on the vertical axis. This figure illustrates the production function.

One of the *Ten Principles of Economics* introduced in Chapter 1 is that rational people think at the margin. This idea is the key to understanding how firms decide what quantity of labour to hire. To take a step towards this decision, the third column in Table 18.1 gives the **marginal product of labour**, the increase in the amount of output from an additional unit of labour. When the firm increases the number of workers from 1 to 2, for example, the amount of apples produced rises from 1,000 to 1,800 kilos. Therefore, the marginal product of the second worker is 800 kilos.

Notice that as the number of workers increases, the marginal product of labour declines. As you may recall from Chapter 13, this property is called **diminishing marginal product.** At first, when only a few workers are hired, they pick apples from the best trees in the orchard. As the number of workers increases, additional workers have to pick from the trees with fewer apples. Hence, as more and more workers are hired, each additional worker contributes less to the production of apples. For this reason, the production function in Figure 18.2 becomes flatter as the number of workers rises.

**marginal product of labour**
the increase in the amount of output from an additional unit of labour

**diminishing marginal product**
the property whereby the marginal product of an input declines as the quantity of the input increases

## The Value of the Marginal Product and the Demand for Labour

Our profit-maximizing firm is concerned more with money than with apples. As a result, when deciding how many workers to hire, the firm considers how much profit each worker would bring in. Because profit is total revenue minus total cost, the profit from an additional worker is the worker's contribution to revenue minus the worker's wage.

To find the worker's contribution to revenue, we must convert the marginal product of labour (which is measured in kilos of apples) into the *value* of the marginal product (which is measured in euros). We do this using the price of apples. To continue our example, if a kilo of apples sells for €1 and if an additional worker produces 800 kilos of apples, then the worker produces €800 of revenue.

The **value of the marginal product** of any input is the marginal product of that input multiplied by the market price of the output. The fourth column in Table 18.1 shows the value of the marginal product of labour in our example, assuming the price of apples is €1 per kilo. Because the market price is constant for a competitive firm, the value of the marginal product (like the marginal product itself) diminishes as the number of workers rises. Economists sometimes call this column of numbers the firm's *marginal revenue product*: it is the extra revenue the firm gets from hiring an additional unit of a factor of production.

**value of the marginal product**
the marginal product of an input times the price of the output

Now consider how many workers the firm will hire. Suppose that the market wage for apple pickers is €500 per week. In this case, as you see in Table 18.1, the first worker that the firm hires is profitable: the first worker yields €1,000 in revenue, or €500 in profit. Similarly, the second worker yields €800 in additional revenue, or €300 in profit. The third worker produces €600 in additional revenue, or €100 in profit. After the third worker, however, hiring workers is unprofitable. The fourth worker would yield only €400 of additional revenue. Because the worker's wage is €500, hiring the fourth worker would mean a €100 reduction in profit. Thus, the firm hires only three workers.

It is instructive to consider the firm's decision graphically. Figure 18.3 graphs the value of the marginal product. This curve slopes downward because the marginal product of labour diminishes as the number of workers rises. The figure also includes a horizontal line at the market wage. To maximize profit, the firm hires workers up to the point where these two curves cross. Below this level of employment, the value of the marginal product exceeds the wage, so hiring another worker would increase profit. Above this level of employment, the value of the marginal product is less than the wage, so the marginal worker is unprofitable.

**FIGURE 18.3**

**The Value of the Marginal Product of Labour**

*This figure shows how the value of the marginal product (the marginal product times the price of the output) depends on the number of workers. The curve slopes downward because of diminishing marginal product. For a competitive, profit-maximizing firm, this value of marginal product curve is also the firm's labour demand curve.*

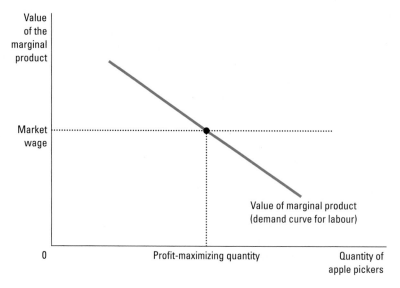

Thus, a competitive, profit-maximizing firm hires workers up to the point where the value of the marginal product of labour equals the wage.

Having explained the profit-maximizing hiring strategy for a competitive firm, we can now offer a theory of labour demand. Recall that a firm's labour demand curve tells us the quantity of labour that a firm demands at any given wage. We have just seen in Figure 18.3 that the firm makes that decision by choosing the quantity of labour at which the value of the marginal product equals the wage. As a result, the value of marginal product curve is the labour demand curve for a competitive, profit-maximizing firm.

## What Causes the Labour Demand Curve to Shift?

We now understand the labour demand curve: it reflects the value of the marginal product of labour. With this insight in mind, let's consider a few of the things that might cause the labour demand curve to shift.

**The Output Price** The value of the marginal product is marginal product times the price of the firm's output. Thus, when the output price changes, the value of the marginal product changes, and the labour demand curve shifts. An increase in the price of apples, for instance, raises the value of the marginal product of each worker who picks apples and, therefore, increases labour demand from the firms that supply apples. Conversely, a decrease in the price of apples reduces the value of the marginal product and decreases labour demand.

**Technological Change** Between 1960 and 2003, the amount of output a typical UK worker produced in an hour rose by 145 per cent. Why? The most important

## Input Demand and Output Supply: Two Sides of the Same Coin

In Chapter 14 we saw how a competitive, profit-maximizing firm decides how much of its output to sell: it chooses the quantity of output at which the price of the good equals the marginal cost of production. We have just seen how such a firm decides how much labour to hire: it chooses the quantity of labour at which the wage equals the value of the marginal product. Because the production function links the quantity of inputs to the quantity of output, you should not be surprised to learn that the firm's decision about input demand is closely linked to its decision about output supply. In fact, these two decisions are two sides of the same coin.

To see this relationship more fully, let's consider how the marginal product of labour (*MPL*) and marginal cost (*MC*) are related. Suppose an additional worker costs €500 and has a marginal product of 50 kilos of apples. In this case,

producing 50 more kilos costs €500; the marginal cost of a kilo is €500/50, or €10. More generally, if *W* is the wage, and an extra unit of labour produces *MPL* units of output, then the marginal cost of a unit of output is $MC = W/MPL$.

This analysis shows that diminishing marginal product is closely related to increasing marginal cost. When our apple orchard grows crowded with workers, each additional worker adds less to the production of apples (*MPL* falls). Similarly, when the apple firm is producing a large quantity of apples, the orchard is already crowded with workers, so it is more costly to produce an additional kilo of apples (*MC* rises).

Now consider our criterion for profit maximization. We determined earlier that a profit-maximizing firm chooses the quantity of labour so that the value of the marginal product ($P \times MPL$) equals the wage (*W*). We can write this mathematically as:

$$P \times MPL = W$$

If we divide both sides of this equation by *MPL*, we obtain:

$$P = W/MPL$$

We just noted that $W/MPL$ equals marginal cost *MC*. Therefore, we can substitute to obtain:

$$P = MC$$

This equation states that the price of the firm's output is equal to the marginal cost of producing a unit of output. *Thus, when a competitive firm hires labour up to the point at which the value of the marginal product equals the wage, it also produces up to the point at which the price equals marginal cost.* Our analysis of labour demand in this chapter is just another way of looking at the production decision we first saw in Chapter 14.

reason is technological progress: scientists and engineers are constantly figuring out new and better ways of doing things. This has profound implications for the labour market. Technological advance raises the marginal product of labour, which in turn increases the demand for labour. Such technological advance explains persistently rising employment in the face of rising wages: even though UK wages (adjusted for inflation) increased by 120 per cent over these four decades, firms nevertheless increased by 17 per cent the amount of labour they employed.

**The Supply of Other Factors** The quantity available of one factor of production can affect the marginal product of other factors. A fall in the supply of ladders, for instance, will reduce the marginal product of apple pickers and thus the demand for apple pickers. We consider this linkage among the factors of production more fully later in the chapter.

**Quick Quiz** Define *marginal product of labour* and *value of the marginal product of labour*. • Describe how a competitive, profit-maximizing firm decides how many workers to hire.

# THE SUPPLY OF LABOUR

Having analysed labour demand in detail, let's turn to the other side of the market and consider labour supply. A formal model of labour supply is included in Chapter 21, where we develop the theory of household decision making. Here we discuss briefly and informally the decisions that lie behind the labour supply curve.

## The Trade-Off between Work and Leisure

One of the *Ten Principles of Economics* in Chapter 1 is that people face trade-offs. Probably no trade-off is more obvious or more important in a person's life than the trade-off between work and leisure. The more hours you spend working, the fewer hours you have to watch TV, have dinner with friends or pursue your favourite hobby. The trade-off between labour and leisure lies behind the labour supply curve.

Another of the *Ten Principles of Economics* is that the cost of something is what you give up to get it. What do you give up to get an hour of leisure? You give up an hour of work, which in turn means an hour of wages. Thus, if your wage is €15 per hour, the opportunity cost of an hour of leisure is €15. And when you get a pay rise to €20 per hour, the opportunity cost of enjoying leisure goes up.

The labour supply curve reflects how workers' decisions about the labour–leisure trade-off respond to a change in that opportunity cost. An upward sloping labour supply curve means that an increase in the wage induces workers to increase the quantity of labour they supply. Because time is limited, more hours of work means that workers are enjoying less leisure. That is, workers respond to the increase in the opportunity cost of leisure by taking less of it.

It is worth noting that the labour supply curve need not be upward sloping. Imagine you got that raise from €15 to €20 per hour. The opportunity cost of leisure is now greater, but you are also richer than you were before. You might decide that with your extra wealth you can now afford to enjoy more leisure. That is, at the higher wage, you might choose to work fewer hours. If so, your labour supply curve would slope backwards. In Chapter 21, we discuss this possibility in terms of conflicting effects on your labour supply decision (called the income and substitution effects). For now, we ignore the possibility of backward sloping labour supply and assume that the labour supply curve is upward sloping.

## What Causes the Labour Supply Curve to Shift?

The labour supply curve shifts whenever people change the amount they want to work at a given wage. Let's now consider some of the events that might cause such a shift.

**Changes in Tastes** In 1960, 48.7 per cent of women in the UK were employed at paid jobs or looking for work. By 2000, the proportion had risen to 69.5 per cent. There are, of course, many explanations for this development, but one of them is changing tastes, or attitudes toward work. A generation or two ago, it was the norm for women to stay at home while raising children. Today, family sizes are smaller and more mothers choose to work. The result is an increase in the supply of labour.

**Changes in Alternative Opportunities** The supply of labour in any one labour market depends on the opportunities available in other labour markets. If the wage earned by pear pickers suddenly rises, some apple pickers may choose to switch occupations. The supply of labour in the market for apple pickers falls.

**Immigration**  Movement of workers from region to region, or country to country, is an obvious and often important source of shifts in labour supply. When immigrants move from one European country to another – from Poland to the UK, for instance – the supply of labour in the United Kingdom increases and the supply of labour in Poland contracts. In fact, much of the policy debate about immigration centres on its effect on labour supply and, thereby, equilibrium in the labour market.

> **Quick Quiz** Who has a greater opportunity cost of enjoying leisure – a petrol station attendant or a brain surgeon? Explain. Can this help explain why doctors work such long hours?

## EQUILIBRIUM IN THE LABOUR MARKET

So far we have established two facts about how wages are determined in competitive labour markets:

- The wage adjusts to balance the supply and demand for labour.
- The wage equals the value of the marginal product of labour.

At first, it might seem surprising that the wage can do both these things at once. In fact, there is no real puzzle here, but understanding why there is no puzzle is an important step to understanding wage determination.

Figure 18.4 shows the labour market in equilibrium. The wage and the quantity of labour have adjusted to balance supply and demand. When the market is in this equilibrium, each firm has bought as much labour as it finds profitable at the

### FIGURE 18.4

**Equilibrium in a Labour Market**

*Like all prices, the price of labour (the wage) depends on supply and demand. Because the demand curve reflects the value of the marginal product of labour, in equilibrium workers receive the value of their marginal contribution to the production of goods and services.*

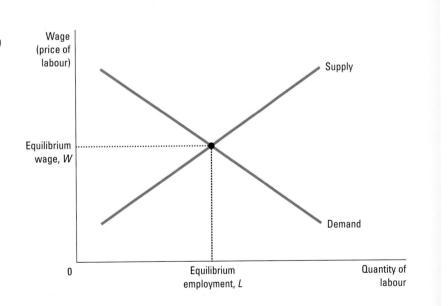

equilibrium wage. That is, each firm has followed the rule for profit maximization: it has hired workers until the value of the marginal product equals the wage. Hence, the wage must equal the value of the marginal product of labour once it has brought supply and demand into equilibrium.

This brings us to an important lesson: any event that changes the supply or demand for labour must change the equilibrium wage and the value of the marginal product by the same amount, because these must always be equal. To see how this works, let's consider some events that shift these curves.

## Shifts in Labour Supply

Suppose that immigration increases the number of workers willing to pick apples. As Figure 18.5 shows, the supply of labour shifts to the right from $S_1$ to $S_2$. At the initial wage $W_1$, the quantity of labour supplied now exceeds the quantity demanded. This surplus of labour puts downward pressure on the wage of apple pickers, and the fall in the wage from $W_1$ to $W_2$ in turn makes it profitable for firms to hire more workers. As the number of workers employed in each apple orchard rises, the marginal product of a worker falls, and so does the value of the marginal product. In the new equilibrium, both the wage and the value of the marginal product of labour are lower than they were before the influx of new workers.

An episode from Israel illustrates how a shift in labour supply can alter the equilibrium in a labour market. During most of the 1980s, many thousands of Palestinians regularly commuted from their homes in the Israeli-occupied West Bank and Gaza Strip to jobs in Israel, primarily in the construction and agriculture industries. In 1988, however, political unrest in these occupied areas induced

### FIGURE 18.5

**A Shift in Labour Supply**

*When labour supply increases from $S_1$ to $S_2$, perhaps because of immigration of new workers, the equilibrium wage falls from $W_1$ to $W_2$. At this lower wage, firms hire more labour, so employment rises from $L_1$ to $L_2$. The change in the wage reflects a change in the value of the marginal product of labour: with more workers, the added output from an extra worker is smaller.*

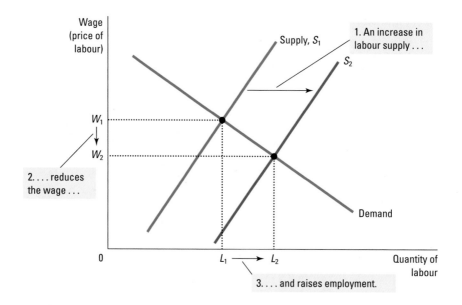

the Israeli government to take steps that, as a by-product, reduced this supply of workers. Curfews were imposed, work permits were checked more thoroughly, and a ban on overnight stays of Palestinians in Israel was enforced more rigorously. The economic impact of these steps was exactly as theory predicts: the number of Palestinians with jobs in Israel fell by half, while those who continued to work in Israel enjoyed wage increases of about 50 per cent. With a reduced number of Palestinian workers in Israel, the value of the marginal product of the remaining workers was much higher.

## Shifts in Labour Demand

Now suppose that an increase in the popularity of apples causes their price to rise. This price increase does not change the marginal product of labour for any given number of workers, but it does raise the *value* of the marginal product. With a higher price of apples, hiring more apple pickers is now profitable. As Figure 18.6 shows, when the demand for labour shifts to the right from $D_1$ to $D_2$, the equilibrium wage rises from $W_1$ to $W_2$, and equilibrium employment rises from $L_1$ to $L_2$. Once again, the wage and the value of the marginal product of labour move together.

This analysis shows that prosperity for firms in an industry is often linked to prosperity for workers in that industry. When the price of apples rises, apple producers make greater profit and apple pickers earn higher wages. When the price of apples falls, apple producers earn smaller profit and apple pickers earn lower wages. This lesson is well known to workers in industries with highly volatile prices. Workers in oil fields, for instance, know from experience that their earnings are closely linked to the world price of crude oil.

### FIGURE 18.6

**A Shift in Labour Demand**

*When labour demand increases from $D_1$ to $D_2$, perhaps because of an increase in the price of the firms' output, the equilibrium wage rises from $W_1$ to $W_2$, and employment rises from $L_1$ to $L_2$. Again, the change in the wage reflects a change in the value of the marginal product of labour: with a higher output price, the added output from an extra worker is more valuable.*

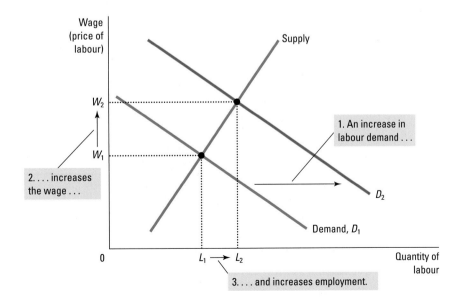

From these examples, you should now have a good understanding of how wages are set in competitive labour markets. Labour supply and labour demand together determine the equilibrium wage, and shifts in the supply or demand curve for labour cause the equilibrium wage to change. At the same time, profit maximization by the firms that demand labour ensures that the equilibrium wage always equals the value of the marginal product of labour.

## CASE STUDY

### Productivity and Wages

One of the *Ten Principles of Economics* in Chapter 1 is that our standard of living depends on our ability to produce goods and services. We can now see how this principle works in the market for labour. In particular, our analysis of labour demand shows that wages equal productivity as measured by the value of the marginal product of labour. Put simply, highly productive workers are highly paid, and less productive workers are less highly paid.

This lesson is key to understanding why workers today are better off than workers in previous generations. Table 18.2 presents some data on growth in productivity and growth in real wages (that is, wages adjusted for inflation) in the United Kingdom. From 1963 to 2003, productivity as measured by output per hour of work grew about 2.1 per cent per year. Real wages grew at almost the same rate: 2.0 per cent per year. With a growth rate of close to 2.0 per cent per year, productivity and real wages double about every 35 years.

Table 18.2 also shows the rates of growth for three shorter periods of time. Notice that from 1973 to 1995 growth in productivity, at 1.75 per cent per year, was slow compared to the period before 1973. Over the period 1995–2003, productivity growth slowed down even more, to about 1.6 per cent per year. The cause of the productivity slowdown in 1973 is not well understood, but the link between productivity and real wages that we find in the data is exactly as standard theory predicts. The slowdown in productivity growth from 2.8 to 1.75 per cent per year coincided with a slowdown in real wage growth from 3.1 to 1.5 per cent per year over the period 1973–95, and the growth in productivity over the more recent period of about 1.6 per cent was also reflected in a similar growth rate of real wages of 1.7 per cent per annum. Both theory and history confirm the close connection between productivity and real wages.

### TABLE 18.2

**Productivity and Wage Growth (%) in the United Kingdom**

| Time period | Growth rate of productivity | Growth rate of real wages |
|---|---|---|
| 1963–2003 | 2.10 | 2.00 |
| 1963–1973 | 2.80 | 3.10 |
| 1973–1995 | 1.75 | 1.50 |
| 1995–2003 | 1.60 | 1.70 |

Source: UK Office for National Statistics. Growth in productivity is measured here as the annualized rate of change in output per worker. Growth in real wages is measured as the annualized change in average wages deflated by the Retail Price Index. These productivity data measure average productivity – the quantity of output divided by the quantity of labour – rather than marginal productivity, but average and marginal productivity are thought to move closely together.

**Quick Quiz** How does immigration of workers affect labour supply, labour demand, the marginal product of labour and the equilibrium wage?

---

## FYI

### Monopsony

On the preceding pages, we built our analysis of the labour market with the tools of supply and demand. In doing so, we assumed that the labour market was competitive. That is, we assumed that there were many buyers of labour and many sellers of labour, so each buyer or seller had a negligible effect on the wage.

Yet imagine the labour market in a small town dominated by a single large employer. That employer can exert a large influence on the going wage, and it may well use that market power to alter the outcome. Such a market in which there is a single buyer is called a *monopsony*.

A monopsony (a market with one buyer) is in many ways similar to a monopoly (a market with one seller). Recall from Chapter 15 that a monopoly firm produces less of the good than would a competitive firm: by reducing the quantity offered for sale, the monopoly firm moves along the product's demand curve, raising the price and also its profits. Similarly, a monopsony firm in a labour market hires fewer workers than would a competitive firm: by reducing the number of jobs available, the monopsony firm moves along the labour supply curve, reducing the wage it pays and raising its profits. Thus, both monopolists and

monopsonists reduce economic activity in a market below the socially optimal level. In both cases, the existence of market power distorts the outcome and causes deadweight losses.

This book does not present the formal model of monopsony because, in the real world, monopsonies are rare. In most labour markets, workers have many possible employers, and firms compete with one another to attract workers. In this case, the model of supply and demand is the best one to use.

---

## THE OTHER FACTORS OF PRODUCTION: LAND AND CAPITAL

We have seen how firms decide how much labour to hire and how these decisions determine workers' wages. At the same time that firms are hiring workers, they are also deciding about other inputs to production. For example, our apple-producing firm might have to choose the size of its apple orchard and the number of ladders to make available to its apple pickers. We can think of the firm's factors of production as falling into three categories: labour, land and capital.

The meaning of the terms *labour* and *land* is clear, but the definition of *capital* is somewhat tricky. Economists use the term **capital** to refer to the stock of equipment and structures used for production. That is, the economy's capital represents the accumulation of goods produced in the past that are being used in the present to produce new goods and services. For our apple firm, the capital stock includes the ladders used to climb the trees, the trucks used to transport the apples, the buildings used to store the apples, and even the trees themselves.

**capital**
the equipment and structures used to produce goods and services

## Equilibrium in the Markets for Land and Capital

What determines how much the owners of land and capital earn for their contribution to the production process? Before answering this question, we need to distinguish between two prices: the purchase price and the rental price. The *purchase price* of land or capital is the price a person pays to own that factor of production indefinitely. The *rental price* is the price a person pays to use that factor for a limited period of time. It is important to keep this distinction in mind because, as we will see, these prices are determined by somewhat different economic forces.

Having defined these terms, we can now apply the theory of factor demand that we developed for the labour market to the markets for land and capital. The wage is, after all, simply the rental price of labour. Therefore, much of what we have learned about wage determination applies also to the rental prices of land and capital. As Figure 18.7 illustrates, the rental price of land, shown in panel (a), and the rental price of capital, shown in panel (b), are determined by supply and demand. Moreover, the demand for land and capital is determined just like the demand for labour. That is, when our apple-producing firm is deciding how much land and how many ladders to rent, it follows the same logic as when deciding how many workers to hire. For both land and capital, the firm increases the quantity hired until the value of the factor's marginal product equals the factor's price. Thus, the demand curve for each factor reflects the marginal productivity of that factor.

We can now explain how much income goes to labour, how much goes to landowners and how much goes to the owners of capital. As long as the firms using the factors of production are competitive and profit-maximizing, each factor's rental price must equal the value of the marginal product for that factor: labour, land and capital each earn the value of their marginal contribution to the production process.

### FIGURE 18.7

**The Markets for Land and Capital**

*Supply and demand determine the compensation paid to the owners of land, as shown in panel (a), and the compensation paid to the owners of capital, as shown in panel (b). The demand for each factor, in turn, depends on the value of the marginal product of that factor.*

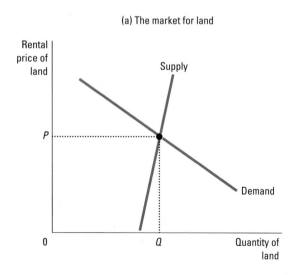

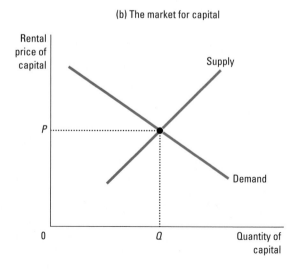

Now consider the purchase price of land and capital. The rental price and the purchase price are obviously related: buyers are willing to pay more for a piece of land or capital if it produces a valuable stream of rental income. And, as we have just seen, the equilibrium rental income at any point in time equals the value of that factor's marginal product. Therefore, the equilibrium purchase price of a piece of land or capital depends on both the current value of the marginal product and the value of the marginal product expected to prevail in the future.

## Linkages Among the Factors of Production

We have seen that the price paid to any factor of production – labour, land, or capital – equals the value of the marginal product of that factor. The marginal product of any factor, in turn, depends on the quantity of that factor that is available. Because of diminishing marginal product, a factor in abundant supply has a low marginal product and thus a low price, and a factor in scarce supply has a high marginal product and a high price. As a result, when the supply of a factor falls, its equilibrium factor price rises.

When the supply of any factor changes, however, the effects are not limited to the market for that factor. In most situations, factors of production are used together in a way that makes the productivity of each factor dependent on the quantities of the other factors available to be used in the production process. As a result, a change in the supply of any one factor alters the earnings of all the factors.

**FYI**

## What Is Capital Income?

Labour income is an easy concept to understand: it is the wages and salaries that workers get from their employers. The income earned by capital, however, is less obvious.

In our analysis, we have been implicitly assuming that households own the economy's stock of capital – ladders, drill presses, warehouses and so forth – and rent it to the firms that use it. Capital income, in this case, is the rent that households receive for the use of their capital. This assumption simplified our analysis of how capital owners are compensated, but it is not entirely realistic. In fact, firms usually own the capital they use and, therefore, they receive the earnings from this capital.

These earnings from capital, however, eventually get paid to households. Some of the earnings are paid in the form of interest to those households who have lent money to firms. Bondholders and bank depositors are two examples of recipients of interest. Thus, when you receive interest on your bank account, that income is part of the economy's capital income.

In addition, some of the earnings from capital are paid to households in the form of dividends. Dividends are payments by a firm to the firm's shareholders. A shareholder is a person who has bought a share in the ownership of the firm and, therefore, is entitled to share in the firm's profits. (This is usually called an equity or, quite simply, a share.)

A firm does not have to pay out all of its earnings to households in the form of interest and dividends. Instead, it can retain some earnings within the firm and use these earnings to buy additional capital. Although these retained earnings do not get paid to the firm's shareholders, the shareholders benefit from them nonetheless. Because retained earnings increase the amount of capital the firm owns, they tend to increase future earnings and, thereby, the value of the firm's equities.

These institutional details are interesting and important, but they do not alter our conclusion about the income earned by the owners of capital. Capital is paid according to the value of its marginal product, regardless of whether this income gets transmitted to households in the form of interest or dividends or whether it is kept within firms as retained earnings.

For example, suppose one night lightning strikes the storehouse in which is kept the ladders that the apple pickers use to pick apples from the orchards, and many of the ladders are destroyed in the ensuing fire. What happens to the earnings of the various factors of production? Most obviously, the supply of ladders falls and, therefore, the equilibrium rental price of ladders rises. Those owners who were lucky enough to avoid damage to their ladders now earn a higher return when they rent out their ladders to the firms that produce apples.

Yet the effects of this event do not stop at the ladder market. Because there are fewer ladders with which to work, the workers who pick apples have a smaller marginal product. Thus, the reduction in the supply of ladders reduces the demand for the labour of apple pickers, and this causes the equilibrium wage to fall.

This story shows a general lesson: an event that changes the supply of any factor of production can alter the earnings of all the factors. The change in earnings of any factor can be found by analysing the impact of the event on the value of the marginal product of that factor.

## CASE STUDY

### The Economics of the Black Death

In 14th-century Europe, the bubonic plague wiped out about one-third of the population within a few years. This event, called the *Black Death*, provides a grisly natural experiment to test the theory of factor markets that we have just developed. Consider the effects of the Black Death on those who were lucky enough to survive. What do you think happened to the wages earned by workers and the rents earned by landowners?

To answer this question, let's examine the effects of a reduced population on the marginal product of labour and the marginal product of land. With a smaller supply of workers, the marginal product of labour rises. (This is simply diminishing marginal product working in reverse.) Thus, we would expect the Black Death to raise wages.

Because land and labour are used together in production, a smaller supply of workers also affects the market for land, the other major factor of production in medieval Europe. With fewer workers available to farm the land, an additional unit of land produced less additional output. In other words, the marginal product of land fell. Thus, we would expect the Black Death to lower rents.

In fact, both predictions are consistent with the historical evidence. Wages approximately doubled during this period, and rents declined 50 per cent or more. The Black Death led to economic prosperity for the peasant classes and reduced incomes for the landed classes.

*Workers who survived the plague were lucky in more ways than one.*

PHOTO: COPYRIGHT © BETTMAN/CORBIS

**Quick Quiz** What determines the income of the owners of land and capital? • How would an increase in the quantity of capital affect the incomes of those who already own capital? How would it affect the incomes of workers?

# CONCLUSION

This chapter explained how labour, land and capital are compensated for the roles they play in the production process. The theory developed here is called the *neo-classical theory of distribution*. According to the neoclassical theory, the amount paid to each factor of production depends on the supply and demand for that factor. The demand, in turn, depends on that particular factor's marginal productivity. In equilibrium, each factor of production earns the value of its marginal contribution to the production of goods and services.

The neoclassical theory of distribution is widely accepted. Most economists begin with the neoclassical theory when trying to explain how an economy's income is distributed among the economy's various members. In the following two chapters, we consider the distribution of income in more detail. As you will see, the neoclassical theory provides the framework for this discussion.

Even at this point you can use the theory to answer the question that began this chapter: why are computer programmers paid more than petrol station attendants? It is because programmers can produce a good of greater market value than can a petrol station attendant. People are willing to pay dearly for a good computer game, but they are willing to pay little to have their petrol pumped and their windscreen washed. The wages of these workers reflect the market prices of the goods they produce. If people suddenly got tired of using computers and decided to spend more time driving, the prices of these goods would change, and so would the equilibrium wages of these two groups of workers.

## SUMMARY

- The economy's income is distributed in the markets for the factors of production. The three most important factors of production are labour, land and capital.

- The demand for factors, such as labour, is a derived demand that comes from firms that use the factors to produce goods and services. Competitive, profit-maximizing firms hire each factor up to the point at which the value of the marginal product of the factor equals its price.

- The supply of labour arises from individuals' trade-off between work and leisure. An upward sloping labour supply curve means that people respond to an increase in the wage by enjoying less leisure and working more hours.

- The price paid to each factor adjusts to balance the supply and demand for that factor. Because factor demand reflects the value of the marginal product of that factor, in equilibrium each factor is compensated according to its marginal contribution to the production of goods and services.

- Because factors of production are used together, the marginal product of any one factor depends on the quantities of all factors that are available. As a result, a change in the supply of one factor alters the equilibrium earnings of all the factors.

## KEY CONCEPTS

factors of production, p. 366
production function, p. 367

marginal product of labour, p. 369
diminishing marginal product, p. 369

value of the marginal product, p. 369
capital, p. 377

## QUESTIONS FOR REVIEW

1. Explain how a firm's production function is related to its marginal product of labour, how a firm's marginal product of labour is related to the value of its marginal product and how a firm's value of marginal product is related to its demand for labour.

2. Give two examples of events that could shift the demand for labour.

3. Give two examples of events that could shift the supply of labour.

4. Explain how the wage can adjust to balance the supply and demand for labour while simultaneously equalling the value of the marginal product of labour.

5. If the population of Norway suddenly grew because of a large immigration, what would happen to wages? What would happen to the rents earned by the owners of land and capital?

## PROBLEMS AND APPLICATIONS

1. Suppose that the government proposes a new law aimed at reducing heath care costs: all citizens are to be required to eat one apple daily.
   a. How would this apple-a-day law affect the demand and equilibrium price of apples?
   b. How would the law affect the marginal product and the value of the marginal product of apple pickers?
   c. How would the law affect the demand and equilibrium wage for apple pickers?

2. Show the effect of each of the following events on the market for labour in the computer manufacturing industry.
   a. The government buys personal computers for all university students.
   b. More university students graduate in engineering and computer science.
   c. Computer firms build new manufacturing factories.

3. Your enterprising uncle opens a sandwich shop that employs 7 people. The employees are paid €6 per hour and a sandwich sells for €3. If your uncle is maximizing his profit, what is the value of the marginal product of the last worker he hired? What is that worker's marginal product?

4. Imagine a firm that hires two types of workers – some with computer skills and some without. If technology advances so that computers become more useful to the firm, what happens to the marginal product of the two types? What happens to equilibrium wages? Explain, using appropriate diagrams.

5. Suppose a harsh winter in Normandy destroys part of the French apple crop.
   a. Explain what happens to the price of apples and the marginal product of apple pickers as a result of the freeze. Can you say what happens to the demand for apple pickers? Why or why not?
   b. Suppose the price of apples doubles and the marginal product falls by 30 per cent. What happens to the equilibrium wage of apple pickers?
   c. Suppose the price of apples rises by 30 per cent and the marginal product falls by 50 per cent. What happens to the equilibrium wage of apple pickers?

6. In recent years, the United Kingdom has experienced a significant inflow of capital in the form of direct investment, especially from the Far East. For example, both Honda and Nissan have built car plants in the United Kingdom.
   a. Using a diagram of the UK capital market, show the effect of this inflow on the rental price of capital in the United Kingdom and on the quantity of capital in use.
   b. Using a diagram of the UK labour market, show the effect of the capital inflow on the average wage paid to UK workers.

7. Suppose that labour is the only input used by a perfectly competitive firm that can hire workers for €50 per day. The firm's production function is as follows:

| Days of labour | Units of output |
| --- | --- |
| 0 | 0 |
| 1 | 7 |
| 2 | 13 |
| 3 | 19 |
| 4 | 25 |
| 5 | 28 |
| 6 | 29 |

Each unit of output sells for €10. Plot the firm's demand for labour. How many days of labour should the firm hire? Show this point on your graph.

8. (This question is challenging.) This chapter has assumed that labour is supplied by individual workers acting competitively. In some markets, however, the supply of labour is determined by a union of workers.
   a. Explain why the situation faced by a labour union may resemble the situation faced by a monopoly firm.
   b. The goal of a monopoly firm is to maximize profits. Is there an analogous goal for labour unions?
   c. Now extend the analogy between monopoly firms and unions. How do you suppose that the wage set by a union compares to the wage in a competitive market? How do you suppose employment differs in the two cases?
   d. What other goals might unions have that make unions different from monopoly firms?

For further resources, visit
http://www.thomsonlearning.co.uk/mankiw_taylor

# 19 EARNINGS AND DISCRIMINATION

In the United Kingdom today, a successful barrister will earn in excess of £150,000 a year, a typical physician in general practice about £66,000, an experienced secondary school teacher around £30,000 and the typical bus driver around £17,000. These examples illustrate the large differences in earnings that are so common in a modern economy. These differences explain why some people live in large houses, drive expensive cars and go on holiday to exotic places, while other people live in small houses or apartments, take the bus and seldom go abroad for a holiday.

Why do earnings vary so much from person to person? Chapter 18, which developed the basic neoclassical theory of the labour market, offers an answer to this question. There we saw that wages are governed by labour supply and labour demand. Labour demand, in turn, reflects the marginal productivity of labour. In equilibrium, each worker is paid the value of his or her marginal contribution to the economy's production of goods and services.

This theory of the labour market, though widely accepted by economists, is only the beginning of the story. To understand the wide variation in earnings that we observe, we must go beyond this general framework and examine more precisely what determines the supply and demand for different types of labour. That is our goal in this chapter.

## SOME DETERMINANTS OF EQUILIBRIUM WAGES

Workers differ from one another in many ways. Jobs also have differing characteristics – both in terms of the wage they pay and in terms of their non-monetary attributes. In this section we consider how the characteristics of workers and jobs affect labour supply, labour demand and equilibrium wages.

## Compensating Differentials

When a worker is deciding whether to take a job, the wage is only one of many job attributes that the worker takes into account. Some jobs are easy, fun and safe; others are hard, dull and dangerous. The better the job as gauged by these non-monetary characteristics, the more people there are who are willing to do the job at any given wage. In other words, the supply of labour for easy, fun and safe jobs is greater than the supply of labour for hard, dull and dangerous jobs. As a result, 'good' jobs will tend to have lower equilibrium wages than 'bad' jobs.

For example, imagine you are looking for a summer job at a seaside holiday resort. Two kinds of jobs are available. You can take a job hiring out deckchairs on the beach, or you can take one as a refuse collector. The deckchair attendants take leisurely strolls along the beach during the day and check to make sure the holidaymakers have paid for the hire of their deckchairs. The refuse collectors wake up before dawn to drive dirty, noisy lorries around town to pick up rubbish from households and firms. Which job would you want? Most people would prefer the beach job if the wages were the same. To induce people to become refuse collectors, the town has to offer higher wages to refuse collectors than to deckchair attendants.

Economists use the term **compensating differential** to refer to a difference in wages that arises from non-monetary characteristics of different jobs. Compensating differentials are prevalent in the economy. Here are some examples:

- Coal miners are paid more than other workers with similar levels of education. Their higher wage compensates them for the dirty and dangerous nature of coal mining, as well as the long-term health problems that coal miners experience.
- Workers who work night shifts at factories are paid more than similar workers who work day shifts. The higher wage compensates them for having to work at night and sleep during the day, a lifestyle that most people find undesirable.
- University lecturers and professors are on average paid less than lawyers and doctors, who have similar amounts of education. Lecturers' lower wages compensate them for the great intellectual and personal satisfaction that their jobs offer. (Indeed, teaching economics is so much fun that it is surprising that economics professors get paid anything at all!)

## Human Capital

As we discussed in the previous chapter, the word *capital* usually refers to the economy's stock of equipment and structures. The capital stock includes the farmer's tractor, the manufacturer's factory and the teacher's blackboard. The essence of capital is that it is a factor of production that itself has been produced.

There is another type of capital that, while less tangible than physical capital, is just as important to the economy's production. **Human capital** is the accumulation of investments in people. The most important type of human capital is education. Like all forms of capital, education represents an expenditure of resources at one point in time to raise productivity in the future. But, unlike an investment in other forms of capital, an investment in education is tied to a specific person, and this linkage is what makes it human capital.

*"On the one hand, I know I could make more money if I left public service for the private sector but, on the other hand, I couldn't chop off heads."*

**compensating differential**
a difference in wages that arises to offset the non-monetary characteristics of different jobs

**human capital**
the accumulation of investments in people, such as education and on-the-job training

Not surprisingly, workers with more human capital on average earn more than those with less human capital. University graduates in Europe and North America, for example, earn almost twice as much as those workers who end their education after secondary school. This large difference tends to be even larger in less developed countries, where educated workers are in scarce supply.

It is easy to see why education raises wages from the perspective of supply and demand. Firms – the demanders of labour – are willing to pay more for the highly educated because highly educated workers have higher marginal products. Workers – the suppliers of labour – are willing to pay the cost of becoming educated only if there is a reward for doing so. In essence, the difference in wages between highly educated workers and less educated workers may be considered a compensating differential for the cost of becoming educated.

## CASE STUDY

### The Increasing Value of Skills

'The rich get richer, and the poor get poorer.' Like many adages, this one is not always true, but recently it has been. Many studies have documented that the earnings gap between workers with high skills and workers with low skills has increased over the past two decades. In 1979 people with university degrees in the UK would earn on average 38 per cent more than people who had not been to university. This figure has risen, and in 2003 people with degrees earned nearly 50 per cent more than people without degrees. In the UK in 2003 men aged between 21 and 25 with degrees earned 23.2 per cent more than people who had only a secondary school education, and for women this figure was as high as 33 per cent. The incentive to go to university is as big as it's ever been!

Why has the gap in earnings between skilled and unskilled workers widened in recent years? No one knows for sure, but economists have proposed two hypotheses to explain this trend. Both hypotheses suggest that the demand for skilled labour has risen over time relative to the demand for unskilled labour. The shift in demand has led to a corresponding change in wages, which in turn has led to greater inequality.

The first hypothesis is that international trade has altered the relative demand for skilled and unskilled labour. In recent years, the amount of trade with other countries has increased. As a percentage of total UK expenditure, imports have risen from 22 per cent in 1970 to 25 per cent in 2000, and exports have risen from 22 per cent in 1970 to 27 per cent in 2000. Because unskilled labour is plentiful and cheap in many foreign countries, the United Kingdom tends to import goods produced with unskilled labour and export goods produced with skilled labour. Thus, when international trade expands, the domestic demand for skilled labour rises, and the domestic demand for unskilled labour falls.

The second hypothesis is that changes in technology have altered the relative demand for skilled and unskilled labour. Consider, for instance, the introduction of computers. Computers raise the demand for skilled workers who can use the new machines and reduce the demand for the unskilled workers whose jobs are replaced by the computers. For example, many companies now rely more on computer databases, and less on filing cabinets, to keep business records. This change raises the demand for computer programmers and reduces the demand for filing clerks. Thus, as more firms use computers, the demand for skilled labour rises, and the demand for unskilled labour falls.

Economists have found it difficult to gauge the validity of these two hypotheses. It is possible, of course, that both are true: increasing international trade and technological change may share responsibility for the increasing inequality we have observed in recent decades.

### Ability, Effort and Chance

Why do football players in the top European leagues such as the English Premiership or the Spanish La Liga get paid more than those in the minor leagues? Certainly, the higher wage is not a compensating differential. Playing in the major leagues is not a less pleasant task than playing in the minor leagues; in fact, the opposite is true. The major leagues do not require more years of schooling or more experience. To a large extent, players in the major leagues earn more just because they have greater natural ability.

Natural ability is important for workers in all occupations. Because of heredity and upbringing, people differ in their physical and mental attributes. Some people are strong, others weak. Some people are intelligent, others less so. Some people are outgoing, others awkward in social situations. These and many other personal characteristics determine how productive workers are and, therefore, play a role in determining the wages they earn.

Closely related to ability is effort. Some people work hard, others are lazy. We should not be surprised to find that those who work hard are more productive and earn higher wages. To some extent, firms reward workers directly by paying people on the basis of what they produce. Salespeople, for instance, are often paid as a percentage of the sales they make. At other times, hard work is rewarded less directly in the form of a higher annual salary or a bonus.

Chance also plays a role in determining wages. If a person attended college to learn how to repair televisions with vacuum tubes and then found this skill made obsolete by the invention of solid-state electronics, he or she would end up earning a low wage compared to others with similar years of training. The low wage of this worker is due to chance – a phenomenon that economists recognize but do not shed much light on.

How important are ability, effort and chance in determining wages? It is hard to say, because ability, effort and chance are hard to measure. But indirect evidence suggests that they are very important. When labour economists study wages, they relate a worker's wage to those variables that can be measured – years of schooling, years of experience, age and job characteristics. Although all of these measured variables affect a worker's wage as theory predicts, they account for less than half of the variation in wages in our economy. Because so much of the variation in wages is left unexplained, omitted variables, including ability, effort and chance, must play an important role.

## CASE STUDY

### The Benefits of Beauty

People differ in many ways. One difference is in how attractive they are. The actor Brad Pitt, for instance, is a handsome man. In part for this reason, his films attract large audiences. Not surprisingly, the large audiences mean a large income for Mr Pitt.

How prevalent are the economic benefits of beauty? Labour economists Daniel Hamermesh and Jeff Biddle tried to answer this question in a study published in the December 1994 issue of the *American Economic Review*. Hamermesh and Biddle examined data from surveys of individuals in the United States and Canada. The interviewers who conducted the survey were asked to rate each respondent's physical appearance. Hamermesh and Biddle then examined how much the wages of the respondents depended on the standard determinants – education, experience and so on – and how much they depended on physical appearance.

The researchers found that beauty pays. People who are deemed to be more attractive than average earn 5 per cent more than people of average looks. People of average looks earn 5 to 10 per cent more than people considered less attractive than average. Similar results were found for men and women.

What explains these differences in wages? There are several ways to interpret the 'beauty premium.'

One interpretation is that good looks are themselves a type of innate ability determining productivity and wages. Some people are born with the attributes of a film star; other people are not. Good looks are useful in any job in which workers present themselves to the public – such as acting, sales and waiting on tables. In this case, an attractive worker is more valuable to the firm than an unattractive worker. The firm's willingness to pay more to attractive workers reflects its customers' preferences.

A second interpretation is that reported beauty is an indirect measure of other types of ability. How attractive a person appears depends on more than just heredity. It also depends on dress, hairstyle, personal demeanour and other attributes that a person can control. Perhaps a person who successfully projects an attractive image in a survey interview is more likely to be an intelligent person who succeeds at other tasks as well.

A third interpretation is that the beauty premium is a type of discrimination, a topic to which we return later.

PHOTO: COPYRIGHT © ALLSTAR PICTURE LIBRARY/ALAMY

*Brad Pitt: good looks pay.*

## An Alternative View of Education: Signalling

Earlier we discussed the human capital view of education, according to which schooling raises workers' wages because it makes them more productive. Although this view is widely accepted, some economists have proposed an alternative theory, which emphasizes that firms use educational attainment as a way of sorting between high-ability and low-ability workers. According to this alternative view, when people earn a university degree, for instance, they do not become more productive, but they do *signal* their high ability to prospective employers. Because it is easier for high-ability people to earn a university degree than it is for low-ability people, more high-ability people get college degrees. As a result, it is rational for firms to interpret a college degree as a signal of ability.

The signalling theory of education is similar to the signalling theory of advertising discussed in Chapter 17. In the signalling theory of advertising, the advertisement itself contains no real information, but the firm signals the quality of its product to consumers by its willingness to spend money on advertising. In the signalling theory of education, schooling has no real productivity benefit, but the worker signals his innate productivity to employers by his willingness to spend years at school. In both cases, an action is being taken not for its intrinsic benefit but because the willingness to take that action conveys private information to someone observing it.

Thus, we now have two views of education: the human capital theory and the signalling theory. Both views can explain why more educated workers tend to earn more than less educated workers. According to the human capital view, education makes workers more productive; according to the signalling view, education is correlated with natural ability. But the two views have radically different predictions for the effects of policies that aim to increase educational attainment. According to the human capital view, increasing educational levels for all workers would raise all workers' productivity and thereby their wages. According to the signalling view, education does not enhance productivity, so raising all workers' educational levels would not affect wages.

Most likely, the truth lies somewhere between these two extremes. The benefits to education are probably a combination of the productivity enhancing effects of human capital and the productivity revealing effects of signalling. The open question is the relative size of these two effects.

## The Superstar Phenomenon

Although most actors earn little and often take jobs as waiters to support themselves, Catherine Zeta Jones earns millions of pounds for each film she makes. Similarly, while most people who play tennis do it for free as a hobby, Venus Williams earns millions on the professional circuit. Catherine Zeta Jones and Venus Williams are superstars in their fields, and their great public appeal is reflected in astronomical incomes.

Why do Catherine Zeta Jones and Venus Williams earn so much? It is not surprising that there are differences in incomes within occupations. Good carpenters earn more than mediocre carpenters, and good plumbers earn more than mediocre plumbers. People vary in ability and effort, and these differences lead to differences in income. Yet the best carpenters and plumbers do not earn the many millions that are common among the best actors and athletes. What explains the difference? To understand the tremendous incomes of Catherine Zeta Jones and Venus Williams, we must examine the special features of the markets in which they sell their services. Superstars arise in markets that have two characteristics:

- Every customer in the market wants to enjoy the good supplied by the best producer.
- The good is produced with a technology that makes it possible for the best producer to supply every customer at low cost.

If Catherine Zeta Jones is the best actor around, then everyone will want to see her next film; seeing twice as many films by an actor half as good is not a good substitute. Moreover, it is *possible* for everyone to enjoy Catherine Zeta Jones's acting skills. Because it is easy to make multiple copies of a film, Catherine Zeta Jones can provide her service to millions of people simultaneously. Similarly, because tennis games are broadcast on television, millions of fans can enjoy the extraordinary athletic skills of Venus Williams.

We can now see why there are no superstar carpenters and plumbers. Other things equal, everyone prefers to employ the best carpenter, but a carpenter, unlike a film actor, can provide his services to only a limited number of customers. Although the best carpenter will be able to command a somewhat higher wage than the average carpenter, the average carpenter will still be able to earn a good living.

*Catherine Zeta Jones: popularity + technology = superstar.*

# IN THE NEWS

## Education, Education, Education

*Should governments subsidize higher education? If it builds human capital and enhances the productive capacity of the economy, a case can be made. If it simply acts as a signal – 'sieves out' the higher ability people so that employers find it easier to identify them, the case is less compelling. This article discusses the pros and cons of government spending on higher education.*

---

### A little learning: In the OECD Countries, One in Five Youngsters Pursues Higher Education, Mostly at the Taxpayer's Expense. What Do Their Fellow Citizens Get in Return?

Once, going to university was strictly for the elite – a matter of ivy-clad halls and cucumber sandwiches on manicured lawns. Now, higher education has become a mass-market business. Across 17 OECD countries, the average proportion of those aged 18–21 in higher education has risen from 14.4% in 1985 to 22.4% in 1995. The cost has risen too: finance for higher education accounts for 1.6% of GDP. In most OECD countries, by far the largest share of the cost of university is met by taxpayers.

Economists take two contrasting views of all this. On the one hand, they regard higher education as a sort of intellectual sieve, designed merely to identify the brightest future employees, rather than to equip them with productive skills. On the other hand, economists regard education as an investment which builds 'human capital', making individuals more productive and thus benefiting society as a whole. The OECD hopes to weigh up these two views in a report for finance ministers, due to be published in May. This week it published two reports which make clear that it is much harder

to measure the benefits that accrue to society than those that go to individuals.

The sieving theory clearly makes some sense. Job advertisements specify 'graduate wanted'; companies trawl campuses to recruit future executives; many countries have rigid academic requirements for particular professions. All this helps to explain two striking facts: everywhere, graduates earn more than non-graduates; and everywhere, they are much less likely to be unemployed.

The OECD reckons, for instance, that British women graduates earn 95% more than women with only secondary education. And the mean rate of unemployment in OECD countries in 1995 for people aged 25–64 was 7% for people who had finished secondary school but a mere 4% for graduates.

If sieving were all that higher education achieved, there would be little reason for governments to subsidise it. For one thing, many people would willingly pay to study if that brought financial gain (although there might be a case for government loans for those unable to pay their own way). For another, to the extent that the sieving process benefits society as a whole, there are surely cheaper ways to sieve than through universities. Thirdly, the more people complete higher education, the less a university degree will provide an indicator of special merit.

Some supporting evidence for the sieving thesis comes from a study for a British committee that reported on higher education earlier this year. It noted that the graduate pay premium declined in the 1970s following a large expansion of higher education in the late 1960s. But other factors were also squeezing earnings differentials during that decade. Besides, even in OECD countries with high proportions of university graduates, graduates still earn much more than less educated folk. In the United States, which has the world's highest proportion of university graduates, in 1995 they earned on average 74% more than high-school graduates and had half the unemployment rate.

In fact, few students leave higher education without learning something, and what they learn probably makes them better and more skilful workers. The most direct payback, in the form of higher earnings and better employment prospects, benefits individual graduates. Individuals weigh this benefit against the costs, including both tuition fees and the earnings they lose by studying rather than taking full-time work. Society also benefits from those higher earnings, which result in higher tax revenues and lower payments for unemployment benefits and income support. But the gains are much smaller than those to individual students.

▶

What else could justify society's investing in higher education? The common answer is that society as a whole also earns benefits in the form of faster economic growth. Recent economic research has supported the existence of a link by emphasising the role of human capital in promoting growth and innovation. Societies which invest more in education, the argument goes, reap long-term rewards.

Plenty of evidence suggests that economies which invest little in education generally perform poorly. But it is harder to quantify the relationship between growth on the one hand and investment in education, specifically higher education, on the other. If, because a country spends more on higher education, university attendance rises from 20% to 22% of the 18–21 age group, will the economy grow faster as a result? No one knows.

Two conclusions can be drawn from the OECD studies. First, more of the cost of higher education should be borne by individual students. This has been happening in America, where tuition fees have been rising much faster than consumer prices in general, and in Britain, where, starting next September, most students will have to pay £1,000 ($1,651) a year in order to study. Despite much concern in Europe that fees will deter young people from going to university, the OECD finds little evidence that requiring students to share the cost reduces enrolment rates. In America, where students typically pay almost half the cost of a degree, enrolment rates are the world's highest.

Second, some governments can readily cut the cost of university education without harming quality. German universities, which educate young people at an average cost of $8,400 a year, appear far cheaper than Canada's, which cost an average of $11,300. Yet, because young Germans often spend six years at university while young Canadians can choose flexible, high-speed courses, Canada's total cost per qualified graduate is less than half of Germany's. Society should invest in academia, but it should invest wisely.

Source: *The Economist*, 11 December 1997. Copyright © The Economist Newspaper Limited, London.

## Above-Equilibrium Wages: Minimum Wage Laws, Unions and Efficiency Wages

Most analyses of wage differences among workers are based on the equilibrium model of the labour market – that is, wages are assumed to adjust to balance labour supply and labour demand. But this assumption does not always apply. For some workers, wages are set above the level that brings supply and demand into equilibrium. Let's consider three reasons why this might be so.

One reason for above-equilibrium wages is minimum wage laws, as we first saw in Chapter 6. Most workers in the economy are not affected by these laws because their equilibrium wages are well above the legal minimum. But for some workers, especially the least skilled and experienced, minimum wage laws raise wages above the level they would earn in an unregulated labour market.

A second reason that wages might rise above their equilibrium level is the market power of labour unions. A **union** is a worker association that bargains with employers over wages and working conditions. Unions often raise wages above the level that would prevail without a union, perhaps because they can threaten to withhold labour from the firm by calling a **strike.** Studies suggest that union workers earn about 10 to 20 per cent more than similar non-union workers.

A third reason for above-equilibrium wages is suggested by the theory of **efficiency wages.** This theory holds that a firm can find it profitable to pay high wages because doing so increases the productivity of its workers. In particular, high wages may reduce worker turnover, increase worker effort, and raise the quality of workers who apply for jobs at the firm. If this theory is correct, then some firms may choose to pay their workers more than they would normally earn.

Above-equilibrium wages, whether caused by minimum wage laws, unions or efficiency wages, have similar effects on the labour market. In particular, pushing a wage above the equilibrium level raises the quantity of labour supplied and reduces the quantity of labour demanded. The result is a surplus of

**union**
a worker association that bargains with employers over wages and working conditions

**strike**
the organized withdrawal of labour from a firm by a union

**efficiency wages**
above-equilibrium wages paid by firms in order to increase worker productivity

labour, or unemployment. The study of unemployment and the public policies aimed to deal with it is usually considered a topic within macroeconomics, so it goes beyond the scope of this chapter. But it would be a mistake to ignore these issues completely when analysing earnings. Although most wage differences can be understood while maintaining the assumption of equilibrium in the labour market, above-equilibrium wages play a role in some cases.

**Quick Quiz** Define *compensating differential* and give an example. • Give two reasons why more educated workers earn more than less educated workers.

# THE ECONOMICS OF DISCRIMINATION

Another source of differences in wages is discrimination. **Discrimination** occurs when the marketplace offers different opportunities to similar individuals who differ only by race, ethnic group, sex, age or other personal characteristics. Discrimination reflects some people's prejudice against certain groups in society. Although discrimination is an emotionally charged topic that often generates heated debate, economists try to study the topic objectively in order to separate myth from reality.

**discrimination**
the offering of different opportunities to similar individuals who differ only by race, ethnic group, sex, age or other personal characteristics

## Measuring Labour Market Discrimination

How much does discrimination in labour markets affect the earnings of different groups of workers? This question is important, but answering it is not easy.

There is no doubt that different groups of workers earn substantially different wages. An interesting and particularly striking example of this is in the average amount of money earned by people belonging to different ethnic groups in the United States, as Table 19.1 demonstrates. The median black man in the United States is paid 22 per cent less than the median white man, and the median black woman is paid 11 per cent less than the median white woman. The differences by sex show even larger differences. The median white woman in the USA is paid 28 per cent less than the median white man, and the median black woman is paid 17 per cent less than the median black man. Taken at face value, these differentials look like evidence that US employers discriminate against black people and women.

### TABLE 19.1

**US Median Annual Earnings by Race and Sex**

| | White | Black | Percentage by which earnings are lower for black workers |
|---|---|---|---|
| Men | $38,870 | $30,403 | 22% |
| Women | 28,080 | 25,107 | 11% |
| Percentage earnings are lower for women workers | 28% | 17% | |

Note: Earnings data are for the year 2000 and apply to full-time, year-round workers aged 14 and over.
Source: US Bureau of the Census.

Yet there is a potential problem with this inference. Even in a labour market free of discrimination, different people have different wages. People differ in the amount of human capital they have and in the kinds of work they are able and willing to do. The wage differences we observe in the economy are, to some extent, attributable to the determinants of equilibrium wages we discussed in the preceding section. Simply observing differences in wages among broad groups – whites and blacks, men and women – does not prove that employers discriminate.

Consider, for example, the role of human capital. Among male workers, in the United States whites are about 75 per cent more likely to have a university degree than blacks. Thus, at least some of the difference between the wages of American whites and the wages of American blacks can be traced to differences in educational attainment. Among white workers, American men and women are now about equally likely to have a university degree, but men are about 11 per cent more likely to earn a graduate or professional degree after university, indicating that some of the wage differential between men and women is attributable to educational attainment.

Moreover, human capital may be more important in explaining wage differentials than measures of years of schooling suggest. Historically, state schools in predominantly black areas of the United States have been of lower quality – as measured by expenditure, class size and so on – than state schools in predominantly white areas. Similarly, for many years, American schools – in common with European schools – directed girls away from science and mathematics courses, even though these subjects may have had greater value in the marketplace than some of the alternatives. If we could measure the quality as well as the quantity of education, the differences in human capital among these groups would seem even larger.

Human capital acquired in the form of job experience can also help explain wage differences. In particular, women tend to have less job experience on average than men. One reason is that female labour-force participation has increased in industrialized economies over the past several decades. Because of this historic change, in both Europe and North America, the average female worker today is younger than the average male worker. In addition, women are more likely to interrupt their careers to raise children. For both reasons, the experience of the average female worker is less than the experience of the average male worker.

Yet another source of wage differences is compensating differentials. Men and women do not always choose the same type of work, and this fact may help explain some of the earnings differential between men and women. For example, women are more likely to be secretaries, and men are more likely to be lorry drivers. The relative wages of secretaries and lorry drivers depend in part on the working conditions of each job. Because these non-monetary aspects are hard to measure, it is difficult to gauge the practical importance of compensating differentials in explaining the wage differences that we observe.

In the end, the study of wage differences among groups does not establish any clear conclusion about the prevalence of discrimination in US labour markets. Most economists believe that some of the observed wage differentials are attributable to discrimination, but there is no consensus about how much. The only conclusion about which economists are in consensus is a negative one: because the differences in average wages among groups in part reflect differences in human capital and job characteristics, they do not by themselves say anything about how much discrimination there is in the labour market.

Of course, differences in human capital among groups of workers may themselves reflect discrimination. The less rigorous curriculums historically offered to female students, for instance, can be considered a discriminatory practice.

Similarly, the inferior schools historically available to black American students may be traced to prejudice on the part of city councils and school boards. But this kind of discrimination occurs long before the worker enters the labour market. In this case, the disease is political, even if the symptom is economic.

## Discrimination by Employers

Let's now turn from measurement to the economic forces that lie behind discrimination in labour markets. If one group in society receives a lower wage than another group, even after controlling for human capital and job characteristics, who is to blame for this differential?

The answer is not obvious. It might seem natural to blame employers for discriminatory wage differences. After all, employers make the hiring decisions that determine labour demand and wages. If some groups of workers earn lower wages than they should, then it seems that employers are responsible. Yet many economists are sceptical of this easy answer. They believe that competitive, market economies provide a natural antidote to employer discrimination. That antidote is called the profit motive.

Imagine an economy in which workers are differentiated by their hair colour. Blondes and brunettes have the same skills, experience and work ethic. Yet, because of discrimination, employers prefer not to hire workers with blonde hair. Thus, the demand for blondes is lower than it otherwise would be. As a result, blondes earn a lower wage than brunettes.

How long can this wage differential persist? In this economy, there is an easy way for a firm to beat out its competitors: it can hire blonde workers. By hiring blondes, a firm pays lower wages and thus has lower costs than firms that hire brunettes. Over time, more and more 'blonde' firms enter the market to take advantage of this cost advantage. The existing 'brunette' firms have higher costs and, therefore, begin to lose money when faced with the new competitors. These losses induce the brunette firms to go out of business. Eventually, the entry of blonde firms and the exit of brunette firms cause the demand for blonde workers to rise and the demand for brunette workers to fall. This process continues until the wage differential disappears.

Put simply, business owners who care only about making money are at an advantage when competing against those who also care about discriminating. As a result, firms that do not discriminate tend to replace those that do. In this way, competitive markets have a natural remedy for employer discrimination.

# CASE STUDY

## Segregated Buses and the Profit Motive

In the early 20th century, buses in many southern cities of the United States were segregated by race. White passengers sat in the front of the buses and black passengers sat in the back. What do you suppose caused and maintained this discriminatory practice? And how was this practice viewed by the firms that ran the buses?

In a 1986 article in the *Journal of Economic History*, economic historian Jennifer Roback looked at these questions. Roback found that the segregation of races on buses was the result of laws that required such segregation. Before these laws were passed, racial discrimination in seating was rare. It was far more common to segregate smokers and non-smokers.

Moreover, the firms that ran the buses often opposed the laws requiring racial segregation. Providing separate seating for different races raised the firms' costs and reduced their profit. One railway company manager complained to the city council that, under the segregation laws, 'the company has to haul around a good deal of empty space.'

Here is how Roback describes the situation in one southern city:

> The railroad company did not initiate the segregation policy and was not at all eager to abide by it. State legislation, public agitation, and a threat to arrest the president of the railroad were all required to induce them to separate the races on their cars. ... There is no indication that the management was motivated by belief in civil rights or racial equality. The evidence indicates their primary motives were economic; separation was costly. ... Officials of the company may or may not have disliked blacks, but they were not willing to forgo the profits necessary to indulge such prejudice.

The story of buses in the American south illustrates a general lesson: business owners are usually more interested in making profit than in discriminating against a particular group. When firms engage in discriminatory practices, the ultimate source of the discrimination often lies not with the firms themselves but elsewhere. In this particular case, the bus companies segregated whites and blacks because discriminatory laws, which the companies opposed, required them to do so.

## Discrimination by Customers and Governments

Although the profit motive is a strong force acting to eliminate discriminatory wage differentials, there are limits to its corrective abilities. Here we consider two of the most important limits: *customer preferences* and *government policies.*

To see how customer preferences for discrimination can affect wages, consider again our imaginary economy with blondes and brunettes. Suppose that restaurant owners discriminate against blondes when hiring waiters. As a result, blonde waiters earn lower wages than brunette waiters. In this case, a restaurant could open up with blonde waiters and charge lower prices. If customers only cared about the quality and price of their meals, the discriminatory firms would be driven out of business, and the wage differential would disappear.

On the other hand, it is possible that customers prefer being served by brunette waiters. If this preference for discrimination is strong, the entry of blonde restaurants need not succeed in eliminating the wage differential between brunettes and blondes. That is, if customers have discriminatory preferences, a competitive market is consistent with a discriminatory wage differential. An economy with such discrimination would contain two types of restaurants. Blonde restaurants hire blondes, have lower costs and charge lower prices. Brunette restaurants hire brunettes, have higher costs and charge higher prices. Customers who did not care about the hair colour of their waiters would be attracted to the lower prices at the blonde restaurants. Bigoted customers would go to the brunette restaurants. They would pay for their discriminatory preference in the form of higher prices.

Another way for discrimination to persist in competitive markets is for the government to mandate discriminatory practices. If, for instance, the government passed a law stating that blondes could wash dishes in restaurants but could not work as waiters, then a wage differential could persist in a competitive market. The example of segregated buses in the case study is one example of government-mandated discrimination. More recently, before South Africa abandoned its system of apartheid, blacks were prohibited from working in some jobs. Discriminatory governments pass such laws to suppress the normal equalizing force of free and competitive markets.

To sum up: competitive markets contain a natural remedy for employer discrimination. The entry into the market of firms that care only about profit tends to eliminate discriminatory wage differentials. These wage differentials persist in competitive markets only when customers are willing to pay to maintain the discriminatory practice or when the government mandates it.

## CASE STUDY

### Discrimination in Sports: US Basketball and English Professional Football

A lot of research exists which suggests that racial discrimination is common in professional team sports in the United States and that much of the blame lies with the fans. One study, published in the *Journal of Labour Economics* in 1988, examined the salaries of American basketball players. It found that black players earned 20 per cent less than white players of comparable ability. The study also found that attendance at basketball games was larger for teams with a greater proportion of white players. One interpretation of these facts is that, at least at the time of the study, customer discrimination made black players less profitable than white players for team owners. In the presence of such customer discrimination, a discriminatory wage gap can persist, even if team owners care only about profit.

While there has been less work done by economists on the effects of discrimination in professional sports in Europe, a study by the economist Stefan Szymanski, published in the *Journal of Political Economy* in 2000, examined the effects of discrimination in 39 professional English soccer clubs over the period 1978–93. Although data on individual players' salaries was not available, the study cleverly applied some basic principles of economics to test for discrimination. We argued earlier in this chapter that discrimination can only exist in a competitive market if someone is willing to pay for it. We gave an example where bigoted restaurant customers were willing to pay more to be served by brunettes. But the same would be true if *owners* were willing – and able – to pay for discrimination: by paying more for workers from a particular group and accepting lower profits. If the market concerned was competitive, the discriminating firms would still eventually be driven out of business. But if the market was imperfectly competitive so that normal profits were not always driven to zero, and if firms were owned by very rich people, then some of the owners might be happy to accept lower profits in order to indulge a 'taste for discrimination'. If this was the case in English football, and there was discrimination against black players, then football teams with a relatively lower proportion of black players would have to pay a higher overall wage bill for its players for any given level of overall team performance (in terms of position in the league) than football teams with an average or relatively high proportion of black players. This is exactly what the study found. Also, the study found no evidence of any systematic relationship between the proportion of black players and ticket revenues and attendance, so it was probably not bigoted fans that led to the discrimination. The conclusion of the study, therefore, was that there was indeed evidence of discrimination in English professional football over the period 1978–93 and that football club owners were willing to pay for it.

One way one might expect this discrimination effect to decrease is if clubs were owned by a large number of shareholders rather than just a small number of rich individuals: shareholders – particularly professional investors – are much more likely to have a 'taste for profit' than a 'taste for discrimination'.

Another way would be if the market for players became more competitive, so that 'underpriced' black players could be snapped up by clubs with less of a taste for discrimination, driving up their wages. Both of these effects occurred during the 1990s. About 20 English football clubs are now listed or in some way have raised money on the stock exchange. In addition, in 1995, the European Court of Justice ruled that European football clubs in general were exercising too much control over the free movement of players between clubs: clubs owned the registration of players and could demand a high fee if a player wanted to move club, even if the player's contract with the club had expired. The Court of Justice – in a judgment known as the 'Bosman Ruling' after the player who brought the law case after being blocked in a move from a Belgian club – decided that this was contrary to European law, and the movement of players between clubs both nationally and across Europe is now very much easier. As a result – and also as a result of the greater number of English clubs raising money on the stock market – it seems highly likely that discrimination in English professional football has now diminished greatly.

**Quick Quiz** Why is it hard to establish whether a group of workers is being discriminated against? • Explain how profit-maximizing firms tend to eliminate discriminatory wage differentials. • How might a discriminatory wage differential persist?

## CONCLUSION

In competitive markets, workers earn a wage equal to the value of their marginal contribution to the production of goods and services. There are, however, many things that affect the value of the marginal product. Firms pay more for workers who are more talented, more diligent, more experienced and more educated because these workers are more productive. Firms pay less to those workers against whom customers discriminate because these workers contribute less to revenue.

The theory of the labour market we have developed in the last two chapters explains why some workers earn higher wages than other workers. The theory does not say that the resulting distribution of income is equal, fair or desirable in any way. That is the topic we take up in Chapter 20.

## SUMMARY

● Workers earn different wages for many reasons. To some extent, wage differentials compensate workers for job attributes. Other things equal, workers in hard, unpleasant jobs get paid more than workers in easy, pleasant jobs.

● Workers with more human capital get paid more than workers with less human capital. The return to accumulating human capital is high and has increased over the past two decades.

● Although years of education, experience and job characteristics affect earnings as theory predicts, there is much variation in earnings that cannot be explained by things that economists can measure. The unexplained variation in earnings is largely attributable to natural ability, effort and chance.

● Some economists have suggested that more educated workers earn higher wages not because education raises productivity but because workers with high natural ability use education as a way to signal their high ability to employers. If this signalling theory is correct, then increasing the educational attainment of all workers would not raise the overall level of wages.

● Wages are sometimes pushed above the level that brings supply and demand into balance. Three reasons for above-equilibrium wages are minimum-wage laws, unions and efficiency wages.

● Some differences in earnings are attributable to discrimination on the basis of race, sex or other factors. Measuring the amount of discrimination is difficult,

however, because one must correct for differences in human capital and job characteristics.

● Competitive markets tend to limit the impact of discrimination on wages. If the wages of a group of workers are lower than those of another group for reasons not related to marginal productivity, then non-discriminatory firms will be more profitable than discriminatory firms. Profit-maximizing behaviour, therefore, can reduce discriminatory wage differentials. Discrimination persists in competitive markets, however, if customers are willing to pay more to discriminatory firms or if the government passes laws requiring firms to discriminate.

## KEY CONCEPTS

| | | |
|---|---|---|
| compensating differential, p. 386 | union, p. 392 | efficiency wages, p. 392 |
| human capital, p. 386 | strike, p. 392 | discrimination, p. 393 |

## QUESTIONS FOR REVIEW

1. Why do coal miners get paid more than other workers with similar amounts of education?

2. In what sense is education a type of capital?

3. How might education raise a worker's wage without raising the worker's productivity?

4. What conditions lead to economic superstars? Would you expect to see superstars in dentistry? In music? Explain.

5. Give three reasons why a worker's wage might be above the level that balances supply and demand.

6. What difficulties arise in deciding whether a group of workers has a lower wage because of discrimination?

7. Do the forces of economic competition tend to exacerbate or ameliorate discrimination on the basis of race?

8. Give an example of how discrimination might persist in a competitive market.

## PROBLEMS AND APPLICATIONS

1. University students sometimes work as summer interns for private firms or the government. Many of these positions pay little or nothing.
   a. What is the opportunity cost of taking such a job?
   b. Explain why students are willing to take these jobs.
   c. If you were to compare the earnings later in life of workers who had worked as interns and those who

   had taken summer jobs that paid more, what would you expect to find?

2. As explained in Chapter 6, a minimum wage law distorts the market for low-wage labour. To reduce this distortion, some economists advocate a two-tiered minimum wage system, with a regular minimum wage for adult workers and a lower, 'sub-minimum' wage for teenage workers.

Give two reasons why a single minimum wage might distort the labour market for teenage workers more than it would the market for adult workers.

3. A basic finding of labour economics is that workers who have more experience in the labour force are paid more than workers who have less experience (holding constant the amount of formal education). Why might this be so? Some studies have also found that experience at the same job (called 'job tenure') has an extra positive influence on wages. Explain.

4. At some universities, economics professors receive higher salaries than professors in some other fields.
   a. Why might this be true?
   b. Some other universities have a policy of paying equal salaries to professors in all fields. At some of these, economics professors have lighter teaching loads than professors in some other fields. What role do the differences in teaching loads play?

5. Sarah works for Jeremy, whom she hates because of his snobbish attitude. Yet when she looks for other jobs, the best she can do is find a job paying €5,000 less than her current salary. Should she take the job? Analyse Sarah's situation from an economic point of view.

6. Imagine that someone were to offer you a choice: you could spend four years studying at the world's best university, but you would have to keep your attendance there a secret. Or you could be awarded an official degree from the world's best university, but you couldn't actually attend (although no one need ever know this). Which choice do you think would enhance your future earnings more? What does your answer say about the debate over signalling versus human capital in the role of education?

7. When recording devices were first invented almost 100 years ago, musicians could suddenly supply their music to large audiences at low cost. How do you suppose this development affected the income of the best musicians? How do you suppose it affected the income of average musicians?

8. When Alan Greenspan (chairman of the US Federal Reserve) ran an economic consulting firm in the 1960s, he hired primarily female economists. He once told

*The New York Times,* 'I always valued men and women equally, and I found that because others did not, good women economists were cheaper than men.' Is Greenspan's behaviour profit-maximizing? Is it admirable or despicable? If more employers were like Greenspan, what would happen to the wage differential between men and women? Why might other economic consulting firms at the time not have followed Greenspan's business strategy?

9. A case study in this chapter described how customer discrimination in sports seems to have an important effect on players' earnings. Note that this is possible because sports fans know the players' characteristics, including their race. Why is this knowledge important for the existence of discrimination? Give some specific examples of industries where customer discrimination is and is not likely to influence wages.

10. Suppose that all young women were channelled into careers as secretaries, nurses and teachers; at the same time, young men were encouraged to consider these three careers and many others as well.
    a. Draw a diagram showing the combined labour market for secretaries, nurses and teachers. Draw a diagram showing the combined labour market for all other fields. In which market is the wage higher? Do men or women receive higher wages on average?
    b. Now suppose that society changed and encouraged both young women and young men to consider a wide range of careers. Over time, what effect would this change have on the wages in the two markets you illustrated in part (a)? What effect would the change have on the average wages of men and women?

11. This chapter considers the economics of discrimination by employers, customers and governments. Now consider discrimination by workers. Suppose that some brunette workers did not like working with blonde workers. Do you think this worker discrimination could explain lower wages for blonde workers? If such a wage differential existed, what would a profit-maximizing entrepreneur do? If there were many such entrepreneurs, what would happen over time?

For further resources, visit
http://www.thomsonlearning.co.uk/mankiw_taylor

# 20 INCOME INEQUALITY AND POVERTY

F Scott Fitzgerald once wrote in one of his novels: 'Let me tell you about the very rich. They are different from you and me.' Fitzgerald's friend, Ernest Hemingway, later incorporated this line into a short story, adding the reply: 'Yes, they have more money.' Hemingway was, of course, right, but this statement leaves many questions unanswered. The gap between rich and poor is a fascinating and important topic of study – for the very rich, the comfortably rich, for the struggling poor, and indeed for all members of a modern economy. If Hemingway had studied economics, he might have used this reply instead: 'Yes, but why are they so rich while others are not so rich?'

From the previous two chapters you should have some understanding about why different people have different incomes. A person's earnings depend on the supply and demand for that person's labour, which in turn depend on natural ability, human capital, compensating differentials, discrimination and so on. Because labour earnings make up about 60 per cent of total income in the UK economy, the factors that determine wages are also largely responsible for determining how the economy's total income is distributed among the various members of society. In other words, they determine who is rich and who is poor.

In this chapter we discuss the distribution of income – a topic that raises some fundamental questions about the role of economic policy. One of the *Ten Principles of Economics* in Chapter 1 is that governments can sometimes improve market outcomes. This possibility is particularly important when considering the distribution of income. The invisible hand of the marketplace acts to allocate resources efficiently, but it does not necessarily ensure that resources are allocated fairly. As a result, many economists – though not all – believe that the government should redistribute income to achieve greater equality. In doing so, however, the government runs into another of the *Ten Principles of Economics*: people face trade-offs. When the government enacts policies to make the distribution of income more equitable, it distorts incentives, alters behaviour and makes the allocation of resources less efficient.

Our discussion of the distribution of income proceeds in three steps. First, we assess how much inequality there is in our society. Secondly, we consider some different views about what role the government should play in altering the distribution of income. Thirdly, we discuss various public policies aimed at helping society's poorest members.

## THE MEASUREMENT OF INEQUALITY

We begin our study of the distribution of income by addressing four questions of measurement:

- How much inequality is there in our society?
- How many people live in poverty?
- What problems arise in measuring the amount of inequality?
- How often do people move among income classes?

These measurement questions are the natural starting point from which to discuss public policies aimed at changing the distribution of income.

### UK Income Inequality

Imagine that you lined up all the families in the economy according to their annual income. Then you divided the families into four groups: the bottom quarter, the next quarter, the third quarter and the top quarter. Table 20.1 shows the income ranges for each of these groups in the United Kingdom in 2002. It also shows the cut-off for the bottom 10 per cent and the top 10 per cent. You can use this table to find where your family lies in the income distribution.

For examining differences in the income distribution over time, economists find it useful to present the income data as in Table 20.2. This table shows the share of total income that each group of families received. In 2002 the bottom fifth of all families received 7.5 per cent of all income, and the top fifth of all families received 42.0 per cent of all income. In other words, even though the top and bottom fifths include the same number of families, the top fifth has nearly six times as much income as the bottom fifth.

Table 20.2 also shows the distribution of income in 1979 and in 1990. Clearly, the distribution was quite stable over the period 1990–2002. But comparing the distributions in these years with the distribution in 1979, we can see that UK income inequality increased over the 1980s: the top fifth increased its share by about 7 per cent over that decade and every other fifth decreased its share of total disposable income. In fact, the poorer a group was in relative terms, the more they contributed to the richest group's increased share, with the bottom fifth reducing its share of the total from 10 per cent to 7.5 per cent and the next fifth from 14 to 12 per cent.

In Chapter 19 we discussed some explanations for this recent rise in inequality. Increases in international trade with low-wage countries and changes in technology have tended to reduce the demand for unskilled labour and raise the demand for skilled labour. As a result, the wages of unskilled workers have fallen relative to the wages of skilled workers, and this change in relative wages has increased inequality in family incomes.

*"As far as I'm concerned, they can do what they want with the minimum wage, just as long as they keep their hands off the maximum wage."*

**TABLE 20.1**

The Distribution of Annual Family Income in the United Kingdom, 2002

| | |
|---|---|
| 10% have income less than: | £8,277 |
| 25% have income less than: | £11,167 |
| 50% have income less than: | £16,176 |
| 75% have income less than: | £22,788 |
| 90% have income less than: | £33,067 |

Source: Institute for Fiscal Studies.

**TABLE 20.2**

Income Inequality in the United Kingdom

| Year | Bottom fifth | Second fifth | Middle fifth | Fourth fifth | Top fifth |
|---|---|---|---|---|---|
| 2002 | 7.5% | 12.0% | 16.0% | 22.% | 42.0% |
| 1990 | 7.5 | 12.0 | 16.5 | 22.5 | 41.5 |
| 1979 | 10.0 | 14.0 | 18.0 | 23.0 | 35.0 |

Source: UK Department for Work and Pensions and Department of Social Security.

# CASE STUDY

## The Role of Women in the Economy and Income Distribution

Over the past several decades, there has been a dramatic change in women's role in the economies of industrialized countries of Europe and North America. The average percentage of women who hold jobs in European countries rose from about a third in the 1950s to more than 50 per cent in the 1990s. As full-time homemakers have become less common, a woman's earnings have become a more important determinant of the total income of a typical family.

While this development has led to more equality between men and women in access to education and jobs, it has also led to less equality in family incomes. The reason is that the rise in women's labour-force participation has not been the same across all income groups. In particular, the women's movement has had its greatest impact on women from high-income households. Women from low-income households have long had high rates of participation in the labour force, even in the 1950s, and their behaviour has changed much less.

In essence, the increased role played by women in the economy has changed the behaviour of the wives of high-income men. In the 1950s, a male executive or physician in Europe or North America was likely to marry a woman who would stay at home and raise their children. Today, the wife of a male executive or physician in these countries is more likely to be an executive or physician herself. The result is that rich households have become even richer, a pattern that increases the inequality in family incomes.

As this example shows, there are social as well as economic determinants of the distribution of income. Moreover, the simplistic view that 'income inequality is bad' can be misleading. Increasing the opportunities available to women

*Anita Roddick, founder of The Body Shop – business tycoon.*

PHOTO: COPYRIGHT © ROGER BAMBER/ALAMY

was surely a good change for society, even if one effect was greater inequality in family incomes. When evaluating any change in the distribution of income, policy makers must look at the reasons for that change before deciding whether it presents a problem for society.

# CASE STUDY

## Inequality Around the World

How does the amount of inequality in the United Kingdom compare to that in other countries? This question is interesting, but answering it is problematic. For some countries, data are not available. Even when they are, not every country collects data in the same way; for example, some countries collect data on individual incomes, whereas other countries collect data on family incomes, and still others collect data on expenditure rather than income. As a result, whenever we find a difference between two countries, we can never be sure whether it reflects a true difference in the economies or merely a difference in the way data are collected.

With this warning in mind, consider Table 20.3, which compares inequality in 12 countries. The countries are ranked from the most equal to the most unequal. At the top of the list is Japan, where the richest tenth of the population has income only 4.5 times that of the poorest tenth. At the bottom of the list is Brazil, where the richest tenth has income of 46.7 times that of the poorest tenth. Germany, where the top 10 per cent have 7.2 times the income of the poorest tenth, is more equal in its income distribution than is the United Kingdom, where the corresponding ratio is 10.5. But the UK distribution is markedly more equal than the distribution in the USA, where the richest 10 per cent have an income nearly 17 times that of the poorest 10 per cent. In turn, the USA has a more equal income distribution than many developing countries, such as Mexico, South Africa and Brazil.

### TABLE 20.3

**Inequality Around the World**

*This table shows the percentage of income or expenditure of the lowest and highest 10 per cent of the population. The ratio of these two numbers measures the gap between rich and poor.*

| Country | Lowest 10% | Highest 10% | Ratio |
|---|---|---|---|
| Japan | 4.8% | 21.7% | 4.5 |
| Germany | 3.3 | 23.7 | 7.2 |
| Canada | 2.8 | 23.8 | 8.5 |
| India | 3.5 | 33.5 | 9.6 |
| United Kingdom | 2.6 | 27.3 | 10.5 |
| China | 2.4 | 30.4 | 12.7 |
| United States | 1.8 | 30.5 | 16.9 |
| Russia | 1.7 | 38.7 | 22.8 |
| Nigeria | 1.6 | 40.8 | 25.5 |
| Mexico | 1.6 | 41.1 | 25.7 |
| South Africa | 1.1 | 45.9 | 41.7 |
| Brazil | 1.0 | 46.7 | 46.7 |

Source: World Development Report: 2002, pp. 234–235. Copyright 2002 World Bank. Reproduced with permission of World Bank in the format Textbook via Copyright Clearance Center.

# Problems in Measuring Inequality

Although data on the income distribution give us some idea about the degree of inequality in our society, interpreting these data is not as straightforward as it might first appear. The data are based on households' annual incomes. What people care about, however, is not their incomes but their ability to maintain a good standard of living. For various reasons, data on the income distribution give an incomplete picture of inequality in living standards. We examine these reasons below.

**The Economic Life Cycle** Incomes vary predictably over people's lives. A young worker, especially one still engaged in full-time study, has a low income. Income rises as the worker gains maturity and experience, peaks at around age 50, and then falls sharply when the worker retires at around age 65. This regular pattern of income variation is called the **life cycle.**

**life cycle**
the regular pattern of income variation over a person's life

Because people can borrow and save to smooth out life cycle changes in income, their standard of living in any year depends more on lifetime income than on that year's income. The young often borrow, perhaps to go to university or to buy a house, and then repay these loans later when their incomes rise. People have their highest saving rates when they are middle-aged. Because people can save in anticipation of retirement, the large declines in incomes at retirement need not lead to similar declines in standard of living.

This normal life cycle pattern causes inequality in the distribution of annual income, but it does not represent true inequality in living standards. To gauge the inequality of living standards in our society, the distribution of lifetime incomes is more relevant than the distribution of annual incomes. Unfortunately, data on lifetime incomes are not readily available. When looking at any data on inequality, however, it is important to keep the life cycle in mind. Because a person's lifetime income smooths out the highs and lows of the life cycle, lifetime incomes are surely more equally distributed across the population than are annual incomes.

**Transitory Versus Permanent Income** Incomes vary over people's lives not only because of predictable life cycle variation but also because of random and transitory forces. One year a frost kills off the Normandy apple crop and Normandy apple growers see their incomes fall temporarily. At the same time, the Normandy frost drives up the price of apples and English apple growers see their incomes temporarily rise. The next year the reverse might happen.

Just as people can borrow and lend to smooth out life cycle variation in income, they can also borrow and lend to smooth out transitory variation in income. When English apple growers experience a good year, they would be foolish to spend all of their additional income. Instead, they save some of it, knowing that their good fortune is unlikely to persist. Similarly, the Normandy apple growers respond to their temporarily low incomes by drawing down their savings or by borrowing. To the extent that a family saves and borrows to buffer itself from transitory changes in income, these changes do not affect its standard of living. A family's ability to buy goods and services depends largely on its **permanent income,** which is its normal, or average, income.

**permanent income**
a person's normal income

To gauge inequality of living standards, the distribution of permanent income is more relevant than the distribution of annual income. Although permanent income is hard to measure, it is an important concept. Because permanent income excludes transitory changes in income, permanent income is more equally distributed than is current income.

## Economic Mobility

People sometimes speak of 'the rich' and 'the poor' as if these groups consisted of the same families year after year. In fact, this is not at all the case. Economic mobility, the movement of people among income classes, is quite substantial in European and North American economies. Movements up the income ladder can be due to good luck or hard work, and movements down the ladder can be due to bad luck or laziness. Some of this mobility reflects transitory variation in income, while some reflects more persistent changes in income.

Because economic mobility is so great, poverty is a long-term problem for relatively few families. Because it is likely that the temporarily poor and the persistently poor face different problems, policies that aim to combat poverty need to distinguish between these groups.

Another way to gauge economic mobility is the persistence of economic success from generation to generation. Economists who have studied this topic find substantial mobility. If a father earns 20 per cent above his generation's average income, his son will most likely earn 8 per cent above his generation's average income. There is almost no correlation between the income of a grandfather and the income of a grandson. There is much truth to the old saying, 'From shirt-sleeves to shirtsleeves in three generations.'

# THE POLITICAL PHILOSOPHY OF REDISTRIBUTING INCOME

We have just seen how the economy's income is distributed and have considered some of the problems in interpreting measured inequality. This discussion was *positive* in the sense that it merely described the world as it is. We now turn to the *normative* question facing policymakers: What should the government do about economic inequality?

This question is not just about economics. Economic analysis alone cannot tell us whether policymakers should try to make our society more egalitarian. Our views on this question are, to a large extent, a matter of political philosophy. Yet because the government's role in redistributing income is central to so many debates over economic policy, here we digress from economic science to consider a bit of political philosophy.

## Utilitarianism

**utilitarianism**
the political philosophy according to which the government should choose policies to maximize the total utility of everyone in society
**utility**
a measure of happiness or satisfaction

A prominent school of thought in political philosophy is **utilitarianism.** The founders of utilitarianism were the British philosophers Jeremy Bentham (1748–1832) and John Stuart Mill (1806–73). To a large extent, the goal of utilitarians is to apply the logic of individual decision making to questions concerning morality and public policy.

The starting point of utilitarianism is the notion of **utility** – the level of happiness or satisfaction that a person receives from his or her circumstances. Utility is a measure of well-being and, according to utilitarians, is the ultimate objective of all public and private actions. The proper goal of the government, they claim, is to maximize the sum of utility of everyone in society.

The utilitarian case for redistributing income is based on the assumption of *diminishing marginal utility.* It seems reasonable that an extra euro of income to a poor person provides that person with more additional utility than does an extra euro to a rich person. In other words, as a person's income rises, the extra well-being derived from an additional euro of income falls. This plausible assumption, together with the utilitarian goal of maximizing total utility, implies that the government should try to achieve a more equal distribution of income.

The argument is simple. Imagine that Peter and Paul are the same, except that Peter earns €80,000 and Paul earns €20,000. In this case, taking a euro from Peter to pay Paul will reduce Peter's utility and raise Paul's utility. But, because of diminishing marginal utility, Peter's utility falls by less than Paul's utility rises. Thus, this redistribution of income raises total utility, which is the utilitarian's objective.

At first, this utilitarian argument might seem to imply that the government should continue to redistribute income until everyone in society has exactly the same income. Indeed, that would be the case if the total amount of income – €100,000 in our example – were fixed. But, in fact, it is not. Utilitarians reject complete equalization of incomes because they accept one of the *Ten Principles of Economics* presented in Chapter 1: people respond to incentives.

To take from Peter to pay Paul, the government must pursue policies that redistribute income, such as the income tax and welfare systems that operate in all industrialized countries. Under these policies, people with high incomes pay high taxes, and people with low incomes receive income transfers. Yet, as we saw in Chapter 8, taxes distort incentives and cause deadweight losses. If the government takes away additional income a person might earn through higher income taxes or reduced transfers, both Peter and Paul have less incentive to work hard. As they work less, society's income falls, and so does total utility. The utilitarian government has to balance the gains from greater equality against the losses from distorted incentives. To maximize total utility, therefore, the government stops short of making society fully egalitarian.

A famous parable sheds light on the utilitarian's logic. Imagine that Peter and Paul are thirsty travellers trapped at different places in the desert. Peter's oasis has much water; Paul's has little. If the government could transfer water from one oasis to the other without cost, it would maximize total utility from water by equalizing the amount in the two places. But suppose that the government has only a leaky bucket. As it tries to move water from one place to the other, some of the water is lost in transit. In this case, a utilitarian government might still try to move some water from Peter to Paul, depending on how thirsty Paul is and how leaky the bucket is. But, with only a leaky bucket at its disposal, a utilitarian government will not try to reach complete equality.

## Liberalism

A second way of thinking about inequality might be called **liberalism.** Philosopher John Rawls develops this view in his book *A Theory of Justice*. This book was first published in 1971, and it quickly became a classic in political philosophy.

Rawls begins with the premise that a society's institutions, laws and policies should be just. He then takes up the natural question: how can we, the members of society, ever agree on what justice means? It might seem that every person's point of view is inevitably based on his or her particular circumstances – whether he or she is talented or less talented, diligent or lazy, educated or less educated, born to a wealthy family or a poor one. Could we ever *objectively* determine what a just society would be?

To answer this question, Rawls proposes the following thought experiment. Imagine that before any of us is born, we all get together for a meeting to design the rules that govern society. At this point, we are all ignorant about the station in life each of us will end up filling. In Rawls's words, we are sitting in an 'original position' behind a 'veil of ignorance'. In this original position, Rawls argues,

**liberalism**
the political philosophy according to which the government should choose policies deemed to be just, as evaluated by an impartial observer behind a 'veil of ignorance'

we can choose a just set of rules for society because we must consider how those rules will affect every person. As Rawls puts it, 'Since all are similarly situated and no one is able to design principles to favour his particular conditions, the principles of justice are the result of fair agreement or bargain.' Designing public policies and institutions in this way allows us to be objective about what policies are just.

Rawls then considers what public policy designed behind this veil of ignorance would try to achieve. In particular, he considers what income distribution a person would consider fair if that person did not know whether he or she would end up at the top, bottom or middle of the distribution. Rawls argues that a person in the original position would be especially concerned about the possibility of being at the *bottom* of the income distribution. In designing public policies, therefore, we should aim to raise the welfare of the worst-off person in society. That is, rather than maximizing the sum of everyone's utility, as a utilitarian would do, Rawls would maximize the minimum utility. Rawls's rule is called the **maximin criterion.**

**maximin criterion**
the claim that the government should aim to maximize the well-being of the worst-off person in society

Because the maximin criterion emphasizes the least fortunate person in society, it justifies public policies aimed at equalizing the distribution of income. By transferring income from the rich to the poor, society raises the well-being of the least fortunate. The maximin criterion would not, however, lead to a completely egalitarian society. If the government promised to equalize incomes completely, people would have no incentive to work hard, society's total income would fall substantially and the least fortunate person would be worse off. Thus, the maximin criterion still allows disparities in income, because such disparities can improve incentives and thereby raise society's ability to help the poor. Nonetheless, because Rawls's philosophy puts weight on only the least fortunate members of society, it calls for more income redistribution than does utilitarianism.

Rawls's views are controversial, but the thought experiment he proposes has much appeal. In particular, this thought experiment allows us to consider the redistribution of income as a form of *social insurance*. That is, from the perspective of the original position behind the veil of ignorance, income redistribution is like an insurance policy. Homeowners buy fire insurance to protect themselves from the risk of their housing burning down. Similarly, when we as a society choose policies that tax the rich to supplement the incomes of the poor, we are all insuring ourselves against the possibility that we might have been a member of a poor family. Because people dislike risk, we should be happy to have been born into a society that provides us this insurance.

It is not at all clear, however, that rational people behind the veil of ignorance would truly be so averse to risk as to follow the maximin criterion. Indeed, because a person in the original position might end up anywhere in the distribution of outcomes, he or she might treat all possible outcomes equally when designing public policies. In this case, the best policy behind the veil of ignorance would be to maximize the average utility of members of society, and the resulting notion of justice would be more utilitarian than Rawlsian.

## Libertarianism

**libertarianism**
the political philosophy according to which the government should punish crimes and enforce voluntary agreements but not redistribute income

A third view of inequality is called **libertarianism.** The two views we have considered so far – utilitarianism and liberalism – both view the total income of society as a shared resource that a social planner can freely redistribute to achieve some social goal. By contrast, libertarians argue that society itself earns no income – only individual members of society earn income. According to libertarians, the government should not take from some individuals and give to others in order to achieve any particular distribution of income.

For instance, philosopher Robert Nozick writes the following in his famous 1974 book *Anarchy, State, and Utopia*:

> We are not in the position of children who have been given portions of pie by someone who now makes last minute adjustments to rectify careless cutting. There is no *central* distribution, no person or group entitled to control all the resources, jointly deciding how they are to be doled out. What each person gets, he gets from others who give to him in exchange for something, or as a gift. In a free society, diverse persons control different resources, and new holdings arise out of the voluntary exchanges and actions of persons.

Whereas utilitarians and liberals try to judge what amount of inequality is desirable in a society, Nozick denies the validity of this very question.

The libertarian alternative to evaluating economic *outcomes* is to evaluate the *process* by which these outcomes arise. When the distribution of income is achieved unfairly – for instance, when one person steals from another – the government has the right and duty to remedy the problem. But, as long as the process determining the distribution of income is just, the resulting distribution is fair, no matter how unequal.

Nozick criticizes Rawls's liberalism by drawing an analogy between the distribution of income in society and the distribution of marks awarded to students taking a course of study. Suppose you were asked to judge the fairness of the marks awarded in the economics course you are now taking. Would you imagine yourself behind a veil of ignorance and choose a marks distribution without knowing the talents and efforts of each student? Or would you ensure that the process of assigning marks to students is fair without regard for whether the resulting distribution is equal or unequal? For the case of course marks at least, the libertarian emphasis on process over outcomes is compelling.

Libertarians conclude that equality of opportunities is more important than equality of incomes. They believe that the government should enforce individual rights to ensure that everyone has the same opportunity to use his or her talents and achieve success. Once these rules of the game are established, the government has no reason to alter the resulting distribution of income.

> **Quick Quiz** Rachel earns more than Phoebe. Someone proposes taxing Rachel in order to supplement Phoebe's income. How would a utilitarian, a liberal and a libertarian evaluate this proposal?

## POLICIES TO REDUCE POVERTY

As we have just seen, political philosophers hold various views about what role the government should take in altering the distribution of income. Political debate among the larger population of voters reflects a similar disagreement. Despite these continuing debates, however, most people believe that, at the very least, the government should try to help those most in need. According to a popular metaphor, the government should provide a 'safety net' to prevent any citizen from falling too far.

Poverty is one of the most difficult problems that policymakers face. Poor families are more likely than the overall population to experience homelessness, drug dependency, domestic violence, health problems, teenage pregnancy, illiteracy, unemployment and low educational attainment. Members of poor families are both more likely to commit crimes and more likely to be victims of crimes. Although it is hard to separate the causes of poverty from the effects, there is no doubt that poverty is associated with various economic and social ills.

Suppose that you were a policy maker in the government, and your goal was to reduce the number of people living in poverty. How would you achieve this goal? Here we consider some of the policy options that you might consider. Although each of these options does help some people escape poverty, none of them is perfect, and deciding which is best is not easy.

## Minimum Wage Laws

Laws setting a minimum wage that employers can pay workers are a perennial source of debate. Advocates view the minimum wage as a way of helping the working poor without any cost to the government. Critics view it as hurting those it is intended to help.

The minimum wage is easily understood using the tools of supply and demand, as we first saw in Chapter 6. For workers with low levels of skill and experience, a high minimum wage forces the wage above the level that balances supply and demand. It therefore raises the cost of labour to firms and reduces the quantity of labour that those firms demand. The result is higher unemployment among those groups of workers affected by the minimum wage. Although those workers who remain employed benefit from a higher wage, those who might have been employed at a lower wage are worse off.

The magnitude of these effects depends crucially on the elasticity of demand. Advocates of a high minimum wage argue that the demand for unskilled labour is relatively inelastic, so that a high minimum wage depresses employment only slightly. Critics of the minimum wage argue that labour demand is more elastic, especially in the long run when firms can adjust employment and production more fully. They also note that many minimum wage workers are teenagers from middle-class families, so that a high minimum wage is imperfectly targeted as a policy for helping the poor.

## Social Security

**social security**
government benefits that supplement the incomes of the needy

One way to raise the living standards of the poor is for the government of a country to supplement their incomes. The primary way in which the government does this is through **social security.** This is a broad term that generally encompasses various government benefits. In the UK, for example, Income Support is paid mainly to poor people who are either lone parents and carers, or incapable of work, or else disabled, while Jobseeker's Allowance is paid to unemployed people who are able and willing to work but temporarily cannot find a job.

A common criticism of the social security system is that it may create bad incentives. For example, since a single mother may lose Income Support if she were married to a man who was in work, the Income Support programme may encourage families to break up or encourage illegitimate births.

How severe are these potential problems with the benefit system? No one knows for sure. Proponents of the benefit system point out that being a poor, single mother is a difficult existence at best, and they are sceptical that many people would be encouraged to pursue such a life if it were not thrust upon them. Moreover, if it can be proved that a person is incapable of work or is disabled, it seems cruel and ridiculous to argue that this is because of the benefits they are receiving.

## Negative Income Tax

Whenever the government chooses a system to collect taxes, it affects the distribution of income. This is clearly true in the case of a progressive income tax, whereby high-income families pay a larger percentage of their income in taxes than do low-income families. Many economists have advocated supplementing the income of the poor using a **negative income tax.** According to this policy, every family would report its income to the government. High-income families would pay a tax based on their incomes. Low-income families would receive a subsidy. In other words, they would 'pay' a 'negative tax'.

For example, suppose the government used the following formula to compute a family's tax liability:

$$\text{Taxes due} = (1/3 \text{ of income}) - €10,000$$

In this case, a family that earned €60,000 would pay €10,000 in taxes, and a family that earned €90,000 would pay €20,000 in taxes. A family that earned €30,000 would owe nothing. And a family that earned €15,000 would 'owe' −€5,000. In other words, the government would send this family a cheque for €5,000.

Under a negative income tax, poor families would receive financial assistance without having to demonstrate need. The only qualification required to receive assistance would be a low income. Depending on one's point of view, this feature can be either an advantage or a disadvantage. On the one hand, a negative income tax does not encourage illegitimate births and the break-up of families, as critics of the welfare system believe current policy does. On the other hand, a negative income tax would subsidize those who are simply lazy and, in some people's eyes, undeserving of government support.

**negative income tax**
a tax system that collects revenue from high-income households and gives transfers to low-income households

## In-Kind Transfers

Another way to help the poor is to provide them directly with some of the goods and services they need to raise their living standards. For example, charities provide the needy with food, shelter and toys at Christmas. Governments in some countries give poor families vouchers that can be used to buy food in shops; the shops then redeem the vouchers for money. In the UK, poor people may qualify for free school meals for their children and medical benefits such as free prescriptions, dental treatment and eyesight tests.

Is it better to help the poor with these **in-kind transfers** or with direct cash payments? There is no clear answer.

Advocates of in-kind transfers argue that such transfers ensure that the poor get what they need most. Among the poorest members of society, alcohol and drug addiction is more common than it is in society as a whole. By providing the poor with food and shelter, society can be more confident that it is not helping to support such addictions.

**in-kind transfers**
transfers to the poor given in the form of goods and services rather than cash

Advocates of cash payments, on the other hand, argue that in-kind transfers are inefficient and disrespectful. The government does not know what goods and services the poor need most. Many of the poor are ordinary people down on their luck. Despite their misfortune, they are in the best position to decide how to raise their own living standards. Rather than giving the poor in-kind transfers of goods and services that they may not want, it may be better to give them cash and allow them to buy what they think they need most.

## Anti-Poverty Policies and Work Incentives

Many policies aimed at helping the poor can have the unintended effect of discouraging the poor from escaping poverty on their own. To see why, consider the following example. Suppose that a family needs an income of €10,000 to maintain a reasonable standard of living. And suppose that, out of concern for the poor, the government promises to guarantee every family that income. Whatever a family earns, the government makes up the difference between that income and €10,000. What effect would you expect this policy to have?

The incentive effects of this policy are obvious: any person who would earn under €10,000 by working has no incentive to find and keep a job. For every euro that the person would earn, the government would reduce the income supplement by one euro. In effect, the government taxes 100 per cent of additional earnings. An effective marginal tax rate of 100 per cent is surely a policy with a large deadweight loss.

The adverse effects of this high effective tax rate can persist over time. A person discouraged from working loses the on-the-job training that a job might offer. In addition, his or her children miss the lessons learned by observing a parent with a full-time job, and this may adversely affect their own ability to find and hold a job.

Although the anti-poverty policy we have been discussing is hypothetical, it is not as unrealistic as it might first appear. In the UK, for example, Income Support and Housing Benefit (a subsidy to a poor family's rent or mortgage interest payments) are benefits aimed at helping the poor and are tied to family income. As a family's income rises, the family becomes ineligible for these benefits. When all benefits being received are taken together, it is common for families to face effective marginal tax rates that are very high. Sometimes the effective marginal tax rates even exceed 100 per cent, so that poor families are worse off when they earn more: they are caught in a 'poverty trap'. By trying to help the poor, the government discourages those families from working. According to critics of anti-poverty policies, these social security benefits alter work attitudes and create a 'culture of poverty'.

It might seem that there is an easy solution to this problem: reduce benefits to poor families more gradually as their incomes rise. For example, if a poor family loses €0.30 of benefits for every extra €1 it earns, then it faces an effective marginal tax rate of 30 per cent. Although this effective tax reduces work effort to some extent, it does not eliminate the incentive to work completely.

The problem with this solution is that it greatly increases the cost of the social security system. The more gradual the phase-out, the more families are eligible for some level of benefits – and the more the social security system costs. Thus, policy makers face a trade-off between burdening the poor with high effective marginal tax rates and burdening taxpayers with a costly anti-poverty programme.

There are various other ways to try to reduce the work disincentive of anti-poverty programmes, such as stopping or reducing benefits to people who have not found a job within a reasonable period of time or who have turned down job offers for no good reason. In the UK, this kind of reasoning underpins the structure of the benefits paid to the unemployed: unemployed people may be eligible to receive a benefit called Jobseeker's Allowance. To receive the allowance, however, the claimant must be capable of starting work immediately and of actively taking steps to find a job such as attending interviews, writing applications or seeking job information. They must also have a current 'jobseeker's agreement' with the Employment Service, which includes such information as hours available for work, the desired job and any steps that the claimant is willing to take to find work (such as moving to a different town). They must be prepared to work up to 40 hours a week and have a reasonable prospect of finding work (i.e. not place too many restrictions on the type of work they are willing to undertake). If a claimant refuses to take up a job offer without good reason, they may be denied further payments of Jobseeker's Allowance. People aged 18–24 who have been unemployed and claiming Jobseeker's Allowance for six months or more are required to participate in a government scheme designed to get them into work (which includes, for example, a personal advisor on suitable job opportunities) called the New Deal for Young Persons. Those aged 25 or over must participate in a similar programme, called the New Deal 25-Plus programme, if they have been unemployed and claiming Jobseeker's Allowance for 18 months.

**Quick Quiz** List three policies aimed at helping the poor, and discuss the pros and cons of each.

# IN THE NEWS

## Reducing Inequality: Does the End Justify the Means?

*One way of making sure that benefits aimed at reducing inequality and poverty go to the people that really need them is to apply 'means testing' – a check on people's income to make sure that they really need the benefit. As this article discusses, this can be both costly and have a negative effect on incentives to work and save.*

**The Tender Trap: Gordon Brown Means Well With His Expansion of Means-Tested Benefits. But They Will Catch Too Many People in a System That Blunts Incentives to Work and Save**

AFTER the budget, which poured money into health care, and last month's spending review, which did the same for education, no one is in any doubt about the government's commitment to spend more on the public services. That has distracted attention from another of its priorities: the extra support for families, low-earners without children and pensioners that starts next year. Altogether, the full-year additional cost of the new credits – Labour's term for this welfare spending – will be £4.6 billion ($7.2 billion), close to next year's increase in the education budget.

Not only are these credits costly, they also mark a major extension of means-testing, the payment of benefits according to income rather than on a universal or contribution-linked basis. Unlike child benefit, which goes to every mother regardless of her family income, the new child tax credit will not be paid to richer families. Unlike the basic state pension, which goes to everyone who has contributed through their working lives to the national insurance system, the pension credit will be paid only to poorer pensioners.

In 1997, 14m people – 25% of the population – were on means-tested benefits. But according to an analysis by the impartial House of Commons Library carried out for the Liberal Democrats, the number of people on means-tested benefits next year will be 25m – 43% of the population. The impact will be especially pronounced among Britain's

11m pensioners, half of whom will be on means-tested benefits. ...

The advantage of means-testing benefits is that you get more bangs for your buck. The Labour government has ambitious targets to reduce child poverty, and it also wants to alleviate poverty among pensioners. But it does not want to push up tax bills too much. Means-testing allows it to concentrate benefits on the neediest while minimising overall spending.

But means-testing comes at a price. For one thing, such benefits are often regarded as stigmatising, so people are reluctant to claim them. They are also complicated to understand, which can affect take-up. The upshot is that in practice such benefits are less effective in reducing poverty than they look on paper.

As means-testing stretches out to embrace so many more people, stigma

▶

is unlikely to be the problem it once used to be, however. The government is also trying hard to tackle complexity by making forms simpler and claims less frequent. Even so, 'trying to work out how the pension credit works is beyond most of us,' says Steve Webb, the pensions spokesman for the Liberal Democrats. As he points out, the government's own target of paying the credit to at least 3m pensioner households by 2006 means that they will miss a million of the 4m eligible.

But the main price of means-tested benefits is the harm they do to incentives to work and to save. Unlike universal benefits, they are withdrawn as income rises. So people receiving them have less of an incentive to find work in the first place or to work long hours

when they get a job. And if working people know that they can expect to receive means-tested pension support, they have less of an incentive to save for their retirement.

However, each of these strategies has its limits. Mr Brown's scope for creating a clear gap between the rewards from working and not working is constrained by the commitment to cut child poverty. This means that the new child tax credit is delivering a lot more money to low-income families who are not working, as well as to those who are – a marked contrast with America's welfare-to-work strategy. More gradual taper rates mean that fewer people face effective marginal tax rates – taxes and benefit deductions on an extra pound of income – at penal levels of up to

100%. But they drag more people into a system where such marginal tax rates can still be higher than the 40% top rate of income tax. ...

There are alternatives. Since older pensioners are generally the poorest, those over 75 or 80 could be paid a much higher basic state pension, thus reducing poverty without creating disincentives to save for retirement. This could be combined with targeting means-tested benefits more tightly on low-income families. Some of these might be discouraged from working, but if fewer people overall faced higher marginal tax rates, it might well be preferable to ever more means-testing.

Source: *The Economist*, 1 August 2002. Copyright © The Economist Newspaper Limited, London.

## CONCLUSION

People have long reflected on the distribution of income in society. Plato, the ancient Greek philosopher, concluded that in an ideal society the income of the richest person would be no more than four times the income of the poorest person. Although the measurement of inequality is difficult, it is clear that our society has much more inequality than Plato recommended.

One of the *Ten Principles of Economics* discussed in Chapter 1 is that governments can sometimes improve market outcomes. There is little consensus, however, about how this principle should be applied to the distribution of income. Philosophers and policy makers today do not agree on how much income inequality is desirable, or even whether public policy should aim to alter the distribution of income. Much of public debate reflects this disagreement. Whenever taxes are raised, for instance, politicians argue over how much of the tax hike should fall on the rich, people from the middle-income group, and the poor.

Another of the *Ten Principles of Economics* is that people face trade-offs. This principle is important to keep in mind when thinking about economic inequality. Policies that penalize the successful and reward the unsuccessful reduce the incentive to succeed. Thus, policy makers face a trade-off between equality and efficiency. The more equally the pie is divided, the smaller the pie becomes. This is the one lesson concerning the distribution of income about which almost everyone agrees.

## SUMMARY

- Data on the distribution of income show wide disparity in industrialized economies.

- Because in-kind transfers, the economic life cycle, transitory income and economic mobility are so important for understanding variation in income, it is difficult to gauge the degree of inequality in our society using data on the distribution of income in a single year. When these other factors are taken into account, they tend to suggest that economic well-being is more equally distributed than is annual income.

- Political philosophers differ in their views about the role of government in altering the distribution of income. Utilitarians (such as John Stuart Mill) would choose the distribution of income to maximize the sum of utility of everyone in society. Liberals (such as John Rawls) would

determine the distribution of income as if we were behind a 'veil of ignorance' that prevented us from knowing our own stations in life. Libertarians (such as Robert Nozick) would have the government enforce individual rights to ensure a fair process but then not be concerned about inequality in the resulting distribution of income.

- Various policies aim to help the poor – minimum wage laws, social security, negative income taxes and in-kind transfers. Although each of these policies helps some families escape poverty, they also have unintended side effects. Because financial assistance declines as income rises, the poor often face effective marginal tax rates that are very high. Such high effective tax rates discourage poor families from escaping poverty on their own.

## KEY CONCEPTS

life cycle, p. 405
permanent income, p. 405
utilitarianism, p. 406
utility, p. 406

liberalism, p. 407
maximin criterion, p. 408
libertarianism, p. 408
social security, p. 410

negative income tax, p. 411
in-kind transfers, p. 411

## QUESTIONS FOR REVIEW

1. How does the extent of income inequality in your country compare to that of other nations around the world?

2. What groups in the population are most likely to live in poverty?

3. When gauging the amount of inequality, why do transitory and life cycle variations in income cause difficulties?

4. How would a utilitarian, a liberal and a libertarian determine how much income inequality is permissible?

5. What are the pros and cons of in-kind (rather than cash) transfers to the poor?

6. Describe how anti-poverty programmes can discourage the poor from working. How might you reduce this disincentive? What are the disadvantages with your proposed policy?

# PROBLEMS AND APPLICATIONS

1. Table 20.2 shows that income inequality in the United Kingdom has increased during the past 20 years. Some factors contributing to this increase were discussed in Chapter 19. What are they?

2. Economists often view life cycle variation in income as one form of transitory variation in income around people's lifetime, or permanent, income. In this sense, how does your current income compare to your permanent income? Do you think your current income accurately reflects your standard of living?

3. The chapter discusses the importance of economic mobility.
   a. What policies might the government pursue to increase economic mobility *within* a generation?
   b. What policies might the government pursue to increase economic mobility *across* generations?
   c. Do you think we should reduce spending on social security benefits in order to increase spending on government programmes that enhance economic mobility? What are some of the advantages and disadvantages of doing so?

4. Consider two communities. In one community, ten families have incomes of €100 each and ten families have incomes of €20 each. In the other community, ten families have incomes of €200 each and ten families have incomes of €22 each.
   a. In which community is the distribution of income more unequal? In which community is the problem of poverty likely to be worse?
   b. Which distribution of income would Rawls prefer? Explain.
   c. Which distribution of income do you prefer? Explain.

5. The chapter uses the analogy of a 'leaky bucket' to explain one constraint on the redistribution of income.
   a. What elements of your country's system for redistributing income create the leaks in the bucket? Be specific.
   b. Do you think that people with left-wing political views believe that the bucket used for redistributing income is more or less leaky than it is believed to be by people with more right-wing political views? How does that belief affect their views about the amount of income redistribution that the government should undertake?

6. Suppose there are two possible income distributions in a society of ten people. In the first distribution, nine people would have incomes of €30,000 and one person would have an income of €10,000. In the second distribution, all ten people would have incomes of €25,000.
   a. If the society had the first income distribution, what would be the utilitarian argument for redistributing income?
   b. Which income distribution would Rawls consider more equitable? Explain.
   c. Which income distribution would Nozick consider more equitable? Explain.

7. Suppose that a family's tax liability equalled its income multiplied by one-half, minus €10,000. Under this system, some families would pay taxes to the government, and some families would receive money from the government through a 'negative income tax'.
   a. Consider families with pre-tax incomes of €0, €10,000, €20,000, €30,000, and €40,000. Make a table showing pre-tax income, taxes paid to the government or money received from the government, and after-tax income for each family.
   b. What is the marginal tax rate in this system (i.e. out of every €1 of extra income, how much is paid in tax)? What is the maximum amount of income at which a family *receives* money from the government?
   c. Now suppose that the tax schedule is changed, so that a family's tax liability equals its income multiplied by one-quarter, minus €10,000. What is the marginal tax rate in this new system? What is the maximum amount of income at which a family receives money from the government?
   d. What is the main advantage of each of the tax schedules discussed here?

8. John and Jeremy are utilitarians. John believes that labour supply is highly elastic, whereas Jeremy believes that labour supply is quite inelastic. How do you suppose their views about income redistribution differ?

9. Do you agree or disagree with each of the following statements? What do your views imply for public policies, such as taxes on inheritance?
   a. 'Every parent has the right to work hard and save in order to give his or her children a better life.'
   b. 'No child should be disadvantaged by the sloth or bad luck of his or her parents.'

For further resources, visit
http://www.thomsonlearning.co.uk/mankiw_taylor

**7**

# TOPICS FOR
# FURTHER STUDY

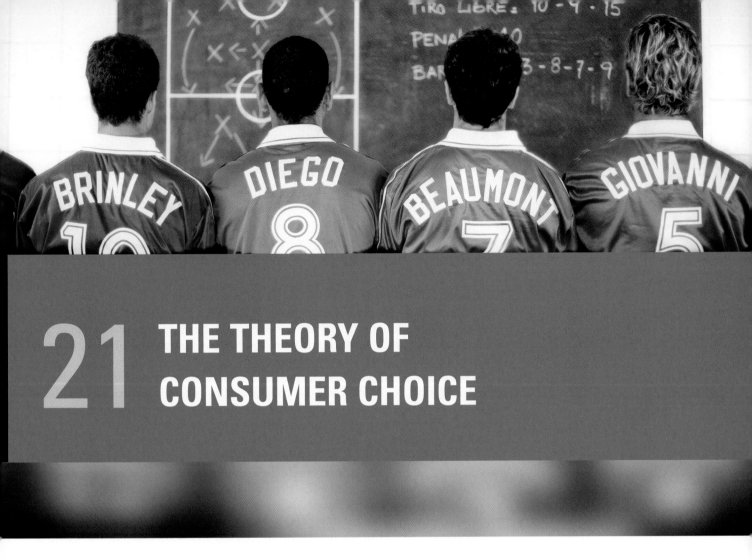

# 21 THE THEORY OF CONSUMER CHOICE

When you walk into a shop, you are confronted with thousands of goods that you might buy. Of course, because your financial resources are limited, you cannot buy everything that you want. You therefore consider the prices of the various goods being offered for sale and buy a bundle of goods that, given your resources, best suits your needs and desires.

In this chapter we develop the theory that describes how consumers make decisions about what to buy. So far throughout this book we have summarized consumers' decisions with the demand curve. As we discussed in Chapters 4 through 7, the demand curve for a good reflects consumers' willingness to pay for it. When the price of a good rises, consumers are willing to pay for fewer units, so the quantity demanded falls. We now look more deeply at the decisions that lie behind the demand curve. The theory of consumer choice presented in this chapter provides a more complete understanding of demand, just as the theory of the competitive firm in Chapter 14 provides a more complete understanding of supply.

One of the *Ten Principles of Economics* discussed in Chapter 1 is that people face trade-offs. The theory of consumer choice examines the trade-offs that people face in their role as consumers. When a consumer buys more of one good, he can afford less of other goods. When he spends more time enjoying leisure and less time working, he has lower income and can afford less consumption. When he spends more of his income in the present and saves less of it, he must accept a lower level of consumption in the future. The theory of consumer choice examines how consumers facing these trade-offs make decisions and how they respond to changes in their environment.

After developing the basic theory of consumer choice, we apply it to three questions about household decisions. In particular, we ask:

● Do all demand curves slope downward?
● How do wages affect labour supply?
● How do interest rates affect household saving?

At first, these questions might seem unrelated. But, as we will see, we can use the theory of consumer choice to address each of them.

## THE BUDGET CONSTRAINT: WHAT THE CONSUMER CAN AFFORD

Most people would like to increase the quantity or quality of the goods they consume – to take longer holidays, drive fancier cars or eat at better restaurants. People consume less than they desire because their spending is *constrained*, or limited, by their income. We begin our study of consumer choice by examining this link between income and spending.

To keep things simple, we examine the decision facing a consumer who buys only two goods: Pepsi and pizza. Of course, real people buy thousands of different kinds of goods. Yet assuming there are only two goods greatly simplifies the problem without altering the basic insights about consumer choice.

We first consider how the consumer's income constrains the amount he spends on Pepsi and pizza. Suppose that the consumer has an income of €1,000 per month and that he spends his entire income each month on Pepsi and pizza. The price of a litre of Pepsi is €2 and the price of a pizza is €10.

The table in Figure 21.1 shows some of the many combinations of Pepsi and pizza that the consumer can buy. The first line in the table shows that if the consumer spends all his income on pizza, he can eat 100 pizzas during the month,

**FIGURE 21.1**

### The Consumer's Budget Constraint

*The budget constraint shows the various bundles of goods that the consumer can afford for a given income. Here the consumer buys bundles of Pepsi and pizza. The table and graph show what the consumer can afford if his income is €1,000, the price of Pepsi is €2 and the price of pizza is €10.*

| Litres of Pepsi | Number of pizzas | Spending on Pepsi | Spending on pizza | Total spending |
| --- | --- | --- | --- | --- |
| 0 | 100 | €0 | €1,000 | €1,000 |
| 50 | 90 | 100 | 900 | 1,000 |
| 100 | 80 | 200 | 800 | 1,000 |
| 150 | 70 | 300 | 700 | 1,000 |
| 200 | 60 | 400 | 600 | 1,000 |
| 250 | 50 | 500 | 500 | 1,000 |
| 300 | 40 | 600 | 400 | 1,000 |
| 350 | 30 | 700 | 300 | 1,000 |
| 400 | 20 | 800 | 200 | 1,000 |
| 450 | 10 | 900 | 100 | 1,000 |
| 500 | 0 | 1,000 | 0 | 1,000 |

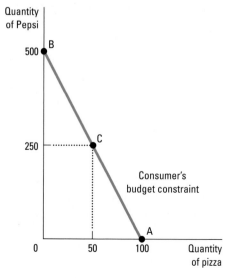

but he would not be able to buy any Pepsi at all. The second line shows another possible consumption bundle: 90 pizzas and 50 litres of Pepsi. And so on. Each consumption bundle in the table costs exactly €1,000.

The graph in Figure 21.1 illustrates the consumption bundles that the consumer can choose. The vertical axis measures the number of litres of Pepsi, and the horizontal axis measures the number of pizzas. Three points are marked on this figure. At point A, the consumer buys no Pepsi and consumes 100 pizzas. At point B, the consumer buys no pizza and consumes 500 litres of Pepsi. At point C, the consumer buys 50 pizzas and 250 litres of Pepsi. Point C, which is exactly at the middle of the line from A to B, is the point at which the consumer spends an equal amount (€500) on Pepsi and pizza. Of course, these are only three of the many combinations of Pepsi and pizza that the consumer can choose. All the points on the line from A to B are possible. This line, called the **budget constraint,** shows the consumption bundles that the consumer can afford. In this case, it shows the trade-off between Pepsi and pizza that the consumer faces.

**budget constraint**
the limit on the consumption bundles that a consumer can afford

The slope of the budget constraint measures the rate at which the consumer can trade one good for the other. Recall from the appendix to Chapter 2 that the slope between two points is calculated as the change in the vertical distance divided by the change in the horizontal distance ('rise over run'). From point A to point B, the vertical distance is 500 litres, and the horizontal distance is 100 pizzas. Because the budget constraint slopes downward, the slope is a negative number – this reflects the fact that to get one extra pizza, the consumer has to *reduce* his consumption of Pepsi by five litres. In fact, the slope of the budget constraint (ignoring the minus sign) equals the *relative price* of the two goods – the price of one good compared to the price of the other. A pizza costs 5 times as much as a litre of Pepsi, so the opportunity cost of a pizza is 5 litres of Pepsi. The budget constraint's slope of 5 reflects the trade-off the market is offering the consumer: 1 pizza for 5 litres of Pepsi.

> **Quick Quiz** Draw the budget constraint for a person with income of €1,000 if the price of Pepsi is €5 and the price of pizza is €10. What is the slope of this budget constraint?

# PREFERENCES: WHAT THE CONSUMER WANTS

Our goal in this chapter is to see how consumers make choices. The budget constraint is one piece of the analysis: it shows what combination of goods the consumer can afford given his income and the prices of the goods. The consumer's choices, however, depend not only on his budget constraint but also on his preferences regarding the two goods. Therefore, the consumer's preferences are the next piece of our analysis.

## Representing Preferences With Indifference Curves

The consumer's preferences allow him to choose among different bundles of Pepsi and pizza. If you offer the consumer two different bundles, he chooses the bundle that best suits his tastes. If the two bundles suit his tastes equally well, we say that the consumer is *indifferent* between the two bundles.

Just as we have represented the consumer's budget constraint graphically, we can also represent his preferences graphically. We do this with indifference

**indifference curve**
a curve that shows consumption bundles that give the consumer the same level of satisfaction

**marginal rate of substitution**
the rate at which a consumer is willing to trade one good for another

curves. An **indifference curve** shows the bundles of consumption that make the consumer equally happy. In this case, the indifference curves show the combinations of Pepsi and pizza with which the consumer is equally satisfied.

Figure 21.2 shows two of the consumer's many indifference curves. The consumer is indifferent among combinations A, B and C, because they are all on the same curve. Not surprisingly, if the consumer's consumption of pizza is reduced, say from point A to point B, consumption of Pepsi must increase to keep him equally happy. If consumption of pizza is reduced again, from point B to point C, the amount of Pepsi consumed must increase yet again.

The slope at any point on an indifference curve equals the rate at which the consumer is willing to substitute one good for the other. This rate is called the **marginal rate of substitution** (MRS). In this case, the marginal rate of substitution measures how much Pepsi the consumer requires in order to be compensated for a one-unit reduction in pizza consumption. Notice that because the indifference curves are not straight lines, the marginal rate of substitution is not the same at all points on a given indifference curve. The rate at which a consumer is willing to trade one good for the other depends on the amounts of the goods he is already consuming. That is, the rate at which a consumer is willing to trade pizza for Pepsi depends on whether he is more hungry or more thirsty, which in turn depends on how much pizza and Pepsi he has.

The consumer is equally happy at all points on any given indifference curve, but he prefers some indifference curves to others. Because he prefers more consumption to less, higher indifference curves are preferred to lower ones. In Figure 21.2, any point on curve $I_2$ is preferred to any point on curve $I_1$.

A consumer's set of indifference curves gives a complete ranking of the consumer's preferences. That is, we can use the indifference curves to rank any two bundles of goods. For example, the indifference curves tell us that point D is preferred to point A because point D is on a higher indifference curve than point A. (That conclusion may be obvious, however, because point D offers the consumer both more pizza and more Pepsi.) The indifference curves also tell us that point

---

**FIGURE 21.2**

**The Consumer's Preferences**

*The consumer's preferences are represented with indifference curves, which show the combinations of Pepsi and pizza that make the consumer equally satisfied. Because the consumer prefers more of a good, points on a higher indifference curve ($I_2$ here) are preferred to points on a lower indifference curve ($I_1$). The marginal rate of substitution (MRS) shows the rate at which the consumer is willing to trade Pepsi for pizza.*

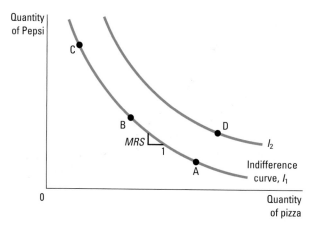

D is preferred to point C because point D is on a higher indifference curve. Even though point D has less Pepsi than point C, it has more than enough extra pizza to make the consumer prefer it. By seeing which point is on the higher indifference curve, we can use the set of indifference curves to rank any combinations of Pepsi and pizza.

## Four Properties of Indifference Curves

Because indifference curves represent a consumer's preferences, they have certain properties that reflect those preferences. Here we consider four properties that describe most indifference curves:

- *Property 1: Higher indifference curves are preferred to lower ones.* Consumers usually prefer more of something to less of it. This preference for greater quantities is reflected in the indifference curves. As Figure 21.2 shows, higher indifference curves represent larger quantities of goods than lower indifference curves. Thus, the consumer prefers being on higher indifference curves.
- *Property 2: Indifference curves are downward sloping.* The slope of an indifference curve reflects the rate at which the consumer is willing to substitute one good for the other. In most cases, the consumer likes both goods. Therefore, if the quantity of one good is reduced, the quantity of the other good must increase in order for the consumer to be equally happy. For this reason, most indifference curves slope downward.
- *Property 3: Indifference curves do not cross.* To see why this is true, suppose that two indifference curves did cross, as in Figure 21.3. Then, because point A is on the same indifference curve as point B, the two points would make the consumer equally happy. In addition, because point B is on the same indifference curve as point C, these two points would make the consumer equally happy. But these conclusions imply that points A and C would also make the consumer equally happy, even though point C has more of both goods. This contradicts our assumption that the consumer always prefers more of both goods to less. Thus, indifference curves cannot cross.

### FIGURE 21.3

**The Impossibility of Intersecting Indifference Curves**

*A situation like this can never happen. According to these indifference curves, the consumer would be equally satisfied at points A, B and C, even though point C has more of both goods than point A.*

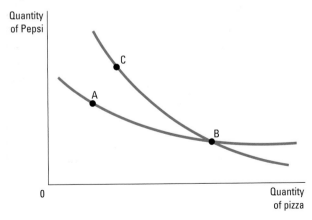

**FIGURE 21.4**

**Bowed Indifference Curves**

*Indifference curves are usually bowed inward. This shape implies that the marginal rate of substitution (MRS) depends on the quantity of the two goods the consumer is consuming. At point A, the consumer has little pizza and much Pepsi, so he requires a lot of extra Pepsi to induce him to give up one of the pizzas: the marginal rate of substitution is 6 litres of Pepsi per pizza. At point B, the consumer has much pizza and little Pepsi, so he requires only a little extra Pepsi to induce him to give up one of the pizzas: the marginal rate of substitution is 1 litre of Pepsi per pizza.*

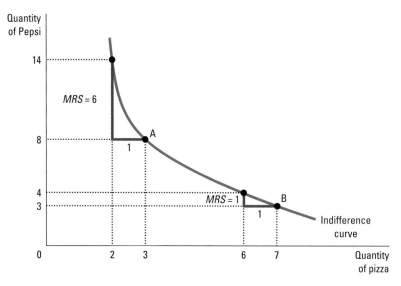

- *Property 4: Indifference curves are bowed inward.* The slope of an indifference curve is the marginal rate of substitution – the rate at which the consumer is willing to trade off one good for the other. The marginal rate of substitution (*MRS*) usually depends on the amount of each good the consumer is currently consuming. In particular, because people are more willing to trade away goods that they have in abundance and less willing to trade away goods of which they have little, the indifference curves are bowed inward. As an example, consider Figure 21.4. At point A, because the consumer has a lot of Pepsi and only a little pizza, he is very hungry but not very thirsty. To induce the consumer to give up 1 pizza, the consumer has to be given 6 litres of Pepsi: the marginal rate of substitution is 6 litres per pizza. By contrast, at point B, the consumer has little Pepsi and a lot of pizza, so he is very thirsty but not very hungry. At this point, he would be willing to give up 1 pizza to get 1 litre of Pepsi: the marginal rate of substitution is 1 litre per pizza. Thus, the bowed shape of the indifference curve reflects the consumer's greater willingness to give up a good that he already has in large quantity.

## Two Extreme Examples of Indifference Curves

The shape of an indifference curve tells us about the consumer's willingness to trade one good for the other. When the goods are easy to substitute for each other, the indifference curves are less bowed; when the goods are hard to substitute, the indifference curves are very bowed. To see why this is true, let's consider the extreme cases.

## FIGURE 21.5

### Perfect Substitutes and Perfect Complements

*When two goods are easily substitutable, such as 50p and 10p coins, the indifference curves are straight lines, as shown in panel (a). When two goods are strongly complementary, such as left shoes and right shoes, the indifference curves are right angles, as shown in panel (b).*

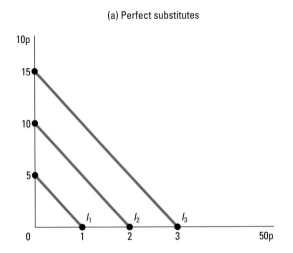

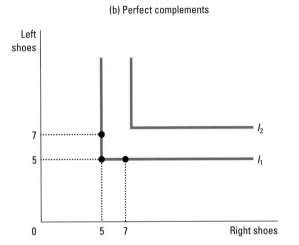

**Perfect Substitutes** Suppose that someone offered you bundles of 50p coins and 10p coins. How would you rank the different bundles?

Most probably, you would care only about the total monetary value of each bundle. If so, you would judge a bundle based on the number of 10p coins plus five times the number of 50p coins. In other words, you would always be willing to trade 1 50p coin for 5 10p coins, regardless of the number of coins in either bundle. Your marginal rate of substitution between 10p coins and 50p coins would be a fixed number: 5.

We can represent your preferences over 50p coins and 10p coins with the indifference curves in panel (a) of Figure 21.5. Because the marginal rate of substitution is constant, the indifference curves are straight lines. In this extreme case of straight indifference curves, we say that the two goods are **perfect substitutes.**

**Perfect Complements** Suppose now that someone offered you bundles of shoes. Some of the shoes fit your left foot, others your right foot. How would you rank these different bundles?

In this case, you might care only about the number of pairs of shoes. In other words, you would judge a bundle based on the number of pairs you could assemble from it. A bundle of 5 left shoes and 7 right shoes yields only 5 pairs. Getting 1 more right shoe has no value if there is no left shoe to go with it.

We can represent your preferences for right and left shoes with the indifference curves in panel (b) of Figure 21.5. In this case, a bundle with 5 left shoes and 5 right shoes is just as good as a bundle with 5 left shoes and 7 right shoes. It is also just as good as a bundle with 7 left shoes and 5 right shoes. The indifference curves, therefore, are right angles. In this extreme case of right-angle indifference curves, we say that the two goods are **perfect complements.**

In the real world, of course, most goods are neither perfect substitutes (like coins of different denominations) nor perfect complements (like right shoes and

**perfect substitutes**
two goods with straight-line indifference curves

**perfect complements**
two goods with right-angle indifference curves

left shoes). More typically, the indifference curves are bowed inward, but not so bowed as to become right angles.

**Quick Quiz** Draw some indifference curves for Pepsi and pizza. Explain the four properties of these indifference curves.

# OPTIMIZATION: WHAT THE CONSUMER CHOOSES

The goal of this chapter is to understand how a consumer makes choices. We have the two pieces necessary for this analysis: the consumer's budget constraint and the consumer's preferences. Now we put these two pieces together and consider the consumer's decision about what to buy.

## The Consumer's Optimal Choices

Consider once again our Pepsi and pizza example. The consumer would like to end up with the best possible combination of Pepsi and pizza – that is, the combination on the highest possible indifference curve. But the consumer must also end up on or below his budget constraint, which measures the total resources available to him.

Figure 21.6 shows the consumer's budget constraint and three of his many indifference curves. The highest indifference curve that the consumer can reach ($I_2$ in the figure) is the one that just barely touches the budget constraint. The point at which this indifference curve and the budget constraint touch is called

## FIGURE 21.6

**The Consumer's Optimum**

*The consumer chooses the point on his budget constraint that lies on the highest indifference curve. At this point, called the optimum, the marginal rate of substitution equals the relative price of the two goods. Here the highest indifference curve the consumer can reach is $I_2$. The consumer prefers point A, which lies on indifference curve $I_3$, but the consumer cannot afford this bundle of Pepsi and pizza. In contrast, point B is affordable, but because it lies on a lower indifference curve, the consumer does not prefer it.*

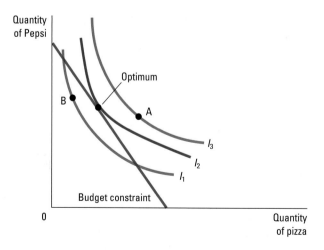

the *optimum*. The consumer would prefer point A, but he cannot afford that point because it lies above his budget constraint. The consumer can afford point B, but that point is on a lower indifference curve and, therefore, provides the consumer less satisfaction. The optimum represents the best combination of consumption of Pepsi and pizza available to the consumer.

Notice that, at the optimum, the slope of the indifference curve equals the slope of the budget constraint. We say that the indifference curve is *tangent* to the budget constraint. The slope of the indifference curve is the marginal rate of substitution between Pepsi and pizza, and the slope of the budget constraint is the relative price of Pepsi and pizza. Thus, the consumer chooses consumption of the two goods so that the marginal rate of substitution equals the relative price.

In Chapter 7 we saw how market prices reflect the marginal value that consumers place on goods. This analysis of consumer choice shows the same result in another way. In making his consumption choices, the consumer takes as given the relative price of the two goods and then chooses an optimum at which his marginal rate of substitution equals this relative price. The relative price is the

# F Y I

## Utility: An Alternative Way to Describe Preferences and Optimization

We have used indifference curves to represent the consumer's preferences. Another common way to represent preferences is with the concept of *utility*. Utility is an abstract measure of the satisfaction or happiness that a consumer receives from a bundle of goods. Economists say that a consumer prefers one bundle of goods to another if the first provides more utility than the second.

Indifference curves and utility are closely related. Because the consumer prefers points on higher indifference curves, bundles of goods on higher indifference curves provide higher utility. Because the consumer is equally happy with all points on the same indifference curve, all these bundles provide the same utility. You can think of an indifference curve as an 'equal–utility' curve.

The *marginal utility* of any good is the increase in utility that the consumer gets from an additional unit of that good. Most goods are assumed to exhibit *diminishing marginal utility:* the more of the good the consumer already has, the lower the marginal utility provided by an extra unit of that good.

The marginal rate of substitution between two goods depends on their marginal utilities. For example, if the marginal utility of good X is twice the marginal utility of good Y, then a person would need 2 units of good Y to compensate for losing 1 unit of good X, and the marginal rate of substitution equals 2. More generally, the marginal rate of substitution (and thus the slope of the indifference curve) equals the marginal utility of one good divided by the marginal utility of the other good.

Utility analysis provides another way to describe consumer optimization. Recall that at the consumer's optimum, the marginal rate of substitution equals the ratio of prices. That is:

$$MRS = P_X/P_Y$$

Because the marginal rate of substitution equals the ratio of marginal utilities, we can write this condition for optimization as:

$$MU_X/MU_Y = P_X/P_Y$$

Now rearrange this expression to become:

$$MU_X/P_X = MU_Y/P_Y$$

This equation has a simple interpretation: At the optimum, the marginal utility per euro spent on good X equals the marginal utility per euro spent on good Y. (Why? If this equality did not hold, the consumer could increase utility by spending less on the good that provided lower marginal utility per euro and more on the good that provided higher marginal utility per euro.)

When economists discuss the theory of consumer choice, they might express the theory using different words. One economist might say that the goal of the consumer is to maximize utility. Another economist might say that the goal of the consumer is to end up on the highest possible indifference curve. The first economist would conclude that, at the consumer's optimum, the marginal utility per euro is the same for all goods, whereas the second would conclude that the indifference curve is tangent to the budget constraint. In essence, these are two ways of saying the same thing.

rate at which the *market* is willing to trade one good for the other, whereas the marginal rate of substitution is the rate at which the *consumer* is willing to trade one good for the other. At the consumer's optimum, the consumer's valuation of the two goods (as measured by the marginal rate of substitution) equals the market's valuation (as measured by the relative price). As a result of this consumer optimization, market prices of different goods reflect the value that consumers place on those goods.

## How Changes in Income Affect the Consumer's Choices

Now that we have seen how the consumer makes the consumption decision, let's examine how consumption responds to changes in income. To be specific, suppose that income increases. With higher income, the consumer can afford more of both goods. The increase in income, therefore, shifts the budget constraint outward, as in Figure 21.7. Because the relative price of the two goods has not changed, the slope of the new budget constraint is the same as the slope of the initial budget constraint. That is, an increase in income leads to a parallel shift in the budget constraint.

The expanded budget constraint allows the consumer to choose a better combination of Pepsi and pizza. In other words, the consumer can now reach a higher indifference curve. Given the shift in the budget constraint and the consumer's preferences as represented by his indifference curves, the consumer's optimum moves from the point labelled 'initial optimum' to the point labelled 'new optimum'.

---

### FIGURE 21.7

**An Increase in Income**

*When the consumer's income rises, the budget constraint shifts out. If both goods are normal goods, the consumer responds to the increase in income by buying more of both of them. Here the consumer buys more pizza and more Pepsi.*

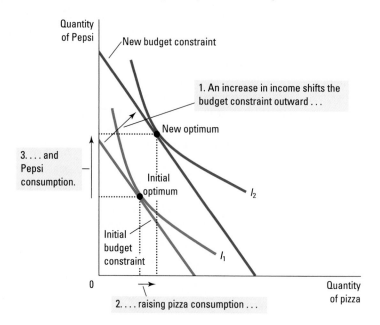

### FIGURE 21.8

**An Inferior Good**

*A good is an inferior good if the consumer buys less of it when his income rises. Here Pepsi is an inferior good: when the consumer's income increases and the budget constraint shifts outward, the consumer buys more pizza but less Pepsi.*

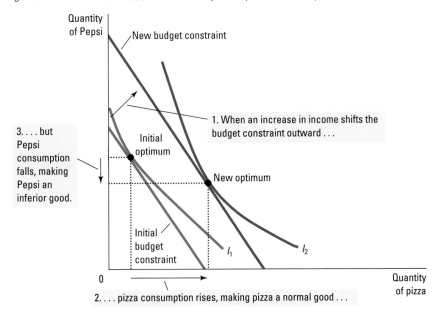

Notice that, in Figure 21.7, the consumer chooses to consume more Pepsi and more pizza. Although the logic of the model does not require increased consumption of both goods in response to increased income, this situation is the most common one. As you may recall from Chapter 4, if a consumer wants more of a good when his income rises, economists call it a **normal good.** The indifference curves in Figure 21.7 are drawn under the assumption that both Pepsi and pizza are normal goods.

Figure 21.8 shows an example in which an increase in income induces the consumer to buy more pizza but less Pepsi. If a consumer buys less of a good when his income rises, economists call it an **inferior good.** Figure 21.8 is drawn under the assumption that pizza is a normal good and Pepsi is an inferior good.

Although most goods are normal goods, there are some inferior goods in the world. One example is bus rides. High-income consumers are more likely to own cars and less likely to ride the bus than low-income consumers. Bus rides, therefore, are an inferior good.

**normal good**
a good for which, other things equal, an increase in income leads to an increase in demand

**inferior good**
a good for which, other things equal, an increase in income leads to a decrease in demand

## How Changes in Prices Affect the Consumer's Choices

Let's now use this model of consumer choice to consider how a change in the price of one of the goods alters the consumer's choices. Suppose, in particular, that the price of Pepsi falls from €2 to €1 a litre. It is no surprise that the lower price expands the consumer's set of buying opportunities. In other words, a fall in the price of any good shifts the budget constraint outward.

Figure 21.9 considers more specifically how the fall in price affects the budget constraint. If the consumer spends his entire €1,000 income on pizza, then the

**FIGURE 21.9**

**A Change in Price**

*When the price of Pepsi falls, the consumer's budget constraint shifts outward and changes slope. The consumer moves from the initial optimum to the new optimum, which changes his purchases of both Pepsi and pizza. In this case, the quantity of Pepsi consumed rises and the quantity of pizza consumed falls.*

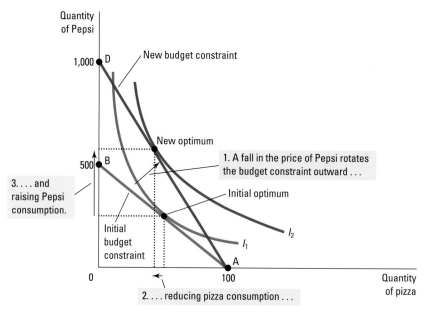

price of Pepsi is irrelevant. Thus, point A in the figure stays the same. Yet if the consumer spends his entire income of €1,000 on Pepsi, he can now buy 1,000 rather than only 500 litres. Thus, the end point of the budget constraint moves from point B to point D.

Notice that in this case the outward shift in the budget constraint changes its slope. (This differs from what happened previously when prices stayed the same but the consumer's income changed.) As we have discussed, the slope of the budget constraint reflects the relative price of Pepsi and pizza. Because the price of Pepsi has fallen to €1 from €2, while the price of pizza has remained €10, the consumer can now trade a pizza for 10 rather than 5 litres of Pepsi. As a result, the new budget constraint is more steeply sloped.

How such a change in the budget constraint alters the consumption of both goods depends on the consumer's preferences. For the indifference curves drawn in this figure, the consumer buys more Pepsi and less pizza.

## Income and Substitution Effects

The impact of a change in the price of a good on consumption can be decomposed into two effects: an **income effect** and a **substitution effect.** To see what these two effects are, consider how our consumer might respond when he learns that the price of Pepsi has fallen. He might reason in the following ways:

- 'Great news! Now that Pepsi is cheaper, my income has greater purchasing power. I am, in effect, richer than I was. Because I am richer, I can buy both more Pepsi and more pizza.' (This is the income effect.)

**income effect**
the change in consumption that results when a price change moves the consumer to a higher or lower indifference curve

**substitution effect**
the change in consumption that results when a price change moves the consumer along a given indifference curve to a point with a new marginal rate of substitution

- 'Now that the price of Pepsi has fallen, I get more litres of Pepsi for every pizza that I give up. Because pizza is now relatively more expensive, I should buy less pizza and more Pepsi.' (This is the substitution effect.)

Which statement do you find more compelling?

In fact, both of these statements make sense. The decrease in the price of Pepsi makes the consumer better off. If Pepsi and pizza are both normal goods, the consumer will want to spread this improvement in his purchasing power over both goods. This income effect tends to make the consumer buy more pizza and more Pepsi. Yet, at the same time, consumption of Pepsi has become less expensive relative to consumption of pizza. This substitution effect tends to make the consumer choose more Pepsi and less pizza.

Now consider the end result of these two effects. The consumer certainly buys more Pepsi, because the income and substitution effects both act to raise purchases of Pepsi. But it is ambiguous whether the consumer buys more pizza, because the income and substitution effects work in opposite directions. This conclusion is summarized in Table 21.1.

We can interpret the income and substitution effects using indifference curves. The income effect is the change in consumption that results from the movement to a higher indifference curve. The substitution effect is the change in consumption that results from being at a point on an indifference curve with a different marginal rate of substitution.

Figure 21.10 shows graphically how to decompose the change in the consumer's decision into the income effect and the substitution effect. When the price of Pepsi falls, the consumer moves from the initial optimum, point A, to the new optimum, point C. We can view this change as occurring in two steps. First, the consumer moves *along* the initial indifference curve $I_1$ from point A to point B. The consumer is equally happy at these two points, but at point B the marginal rate of substitution reflects the new relative price. (The dashed line through point B reflects the new relative price by being parallel to the new budget constraint.) Next, the consumer *shifts* to the higher indifference curve $I_2$ by moving from point B to point C. Even though point B and point C are on different indifference curves, they have the same marginal rate of substitution. That is, the slope of the indifference curve $I_1$ at point B equals the slope of the indifference curve $I_2$ at point C.

Although the consumer never actually chooses point B, this hypothetical point is useful to clarify the two effects that determine the consumer's decision. Notice that the change from point A to point B represents a pure change in the marginal rate of substitution without any change in the consumer's welfare. Similarly, the

## TABLE 21.1

### Income and Substitution Effects When the Price of Pepsi Falls

| Good | Income effect | Substitution effect | Total effect |
|------|--------------|---------------------|--------------|
| Pepsi | Consumer is richer, so he buys more Pepsi. | Pepsi is relatively cheaper, so consumer buys more Pepsi. | Income and substitution effects act in same direction, so consumer buys more Pepsi. |
| Pizza | Consumer is richer, so he buys more pizza. | Pizza is relatively more expensive, so consumer buys less pizza. | Income and substitution effects act in opposite directions, so the total effect on pizza consumption is ambiguous. |

*FIGURE 21.10*

**Income and Substitution Effects**

*The effect of a change in price can be broken down into an income effect and a substitution effect. The substitution effect – the movement along an indifference curve to a point with a different marginal rate of substitution – is shown here as the change from point A to point B along indifference curve I₁. The income effect – the shift to a higher indifference curve – is shown here as the change from point B on indifference curve I₁ to point C on indifference curve I₂.*

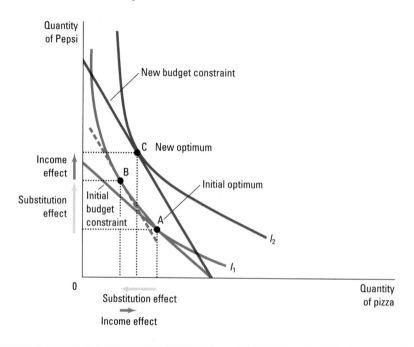

change from point B to point C represents a pure change in welfare without any change in the marginal rate of substitution. Thus, the movement from A to B shows the substitution effect, and the movement from B to C shows the income effect.

## Deriving the Demand Curve

We have just seen how changes in the price of a good alter the consumer's budget constraint and, therefore, the quantities of the two goods that he chooses to buy. The demand curve for any good reflects these consumption decisions. Recall that a demand curve shows the quantity demanded of a good for any given price. We can view a consumer's demand curve as a summary of the optimal decisions that arise from his budget constraint and indifference curves.

For example, Figure 21.11 considers the demand for Pepsi. Panel (a) shows that when the price of a litre falls from €2 to €1, the consumer's budget constraint shifts outward. Because of both income and substitution effects, the consumer increases his purchases of Pepsi from 250 to 750 litres. Panel (b) shows the demand curve that results from this consumer's decisions. In this way, the theory of consumer choice provides the theoretical foundation for the consumer's demand curve, which we first introduced in Chapter 4.

Although it is comforting to know that the demand curve arises naturally from the theory of consumer choice, this exercise by itself does not justify developing

**FIGURE 21.11**

**Deriving the Demand Curve**

*Panel (a) shows that when the price of Pepsi falls from €2 to €1, the consumer's optimum moves from point A to point B, and the quantity of Pepsi consumed rises from 250 to 750 litres. The demand curve in panel (b) reflects this relationship between the price and the quantity demanded.*

(a) The consumer's optimum

(b) The demand curve for Pepsi

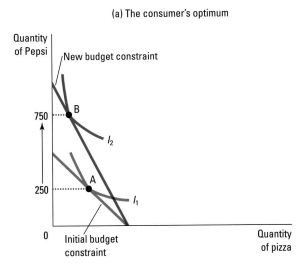
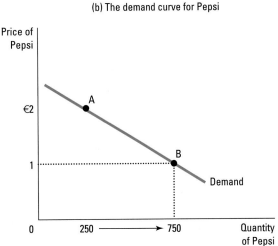

the theory. There is no need for a rigorous, analytic framework just to establish that people respond to changes in prices. The theory of consumer choice is, however, very useful. As we see in the next section, we can use the theory to delve more deeply into the determinants of household behaviour.

> **Quick Quiz** Draw a budget constraint and indifference curves for Pepsi and pizza. Show what happens to the budget constraint and the consumer's optimum when the price of pizza rises. In your diagram, decompose the change into an income effect and a substitution effect.

# THREE APPLICATIONS

Now that we have developed the basic theory of consumer choice, let's use it to shed light on three questions about how the economy works. These three questions might at first seem unrelated. But because each question involves household decision making, we can address it with the model of consumer behaviour we have just developed.

## Do All Demand Curves Slope Downward?

Normally, when the price of a good rises, people buy less of it. Chapter 4 called this usual behaviour the *law of demand*. This law is reflected in the downward slope of the demand curve.

As a matter of economic theory, however, demand curves can sometimes slope upward. In other words, consumers can sometimes violate the law of demand and buy *more* of a good when the price rises. To see how this can happen, consider Figure 21.12. In this example, the consumer buys two goods – meat and potatoes. Initially, the consumer's budget constraint is the line from point A to point B. The optimum is point C. When the price of potatoes rises, the budget constraint shifts inward and is now the line from point A to point D. The optimum is now point E. Notice that a rise in the price of potatoes has led the consumer to buy a larger quantity of potatoes.

Why is the consumer responding in a seemingly perverse way? The reason is that potatoes here are a strongly inferior good. When the price of potatoes rises, the consumer is poorer. The income effect makes the consumer want to buy less meat and more potatoes. At the same time, because the potatoes have become more expensive relative to meat, the substitution effect makes the consumer want to buy more meat and less potatoes. In this particular case, however, the income effect is so strong that it exceeds the substitution effect. In the end, the consumer responds to the higher price of potatoes by buying less meat and more potatoes.

**Giffen good**

a good for which an increase in the price raises the quantity demanded

Economists use the term **Giffen good** to describe a good that violates the law of demand. (The term is named after the British economist Robert Giffen, who first noted this possibility.) In this example, potatoes are a Giffen good. Giffen goods are inferior goods for which the income effect dominates the substitution effect. Therefore, they have demand curves that slope upward.

Economists disagree about whether any Giffen good has ever been discovered. Some historians suggest that potatoes were in fact a Giffen good during the Irish potato famine of the 19th century. Potatoes were such a large part of people's diet that when the price of potatoes rose, it had a large income effect. People responded to their reduced living standard by cutting back on the luxury of meat

## FIGURE 21.12

### A Giffen Good

*In this example, when the price of potatoes rises, the consumer's optimum shifts from point C to point E. In this case, the consumer responds to a higher price of potatoes by buying less meat and more potatoes.*

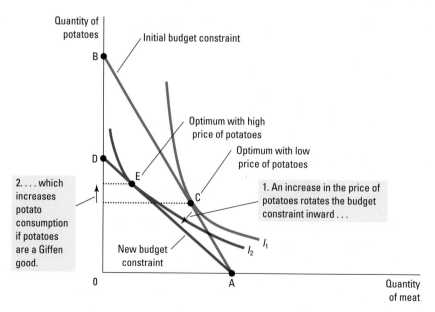

and buying more of the staple food of potatoes. Thus, it is argued that a higher price of potatoes actually raised the quantity of potatoes demanded.

Whether or not this historical account is true, it is safe to say that Giffen goods are very rare. The theory of consumer choice does allow demand curves to slope upward. Yet such occurrences are so unusual that the law of demand is as reliable a law as any in economics.

## How Do Wages Affect Labour Supply?

So far we have used the theory of consumer choice to analyse how a person decides how to allocate his income between two goods. We can use the same theory to analyse how a person decides to allocate his time between work and leisure.

Consider the decision facing Fiona, a freelance software designer. Fiona is awake for 100 hours per week. She spends some of this time enjoying leisure – riding her horse, watching television, studying economics and so on. She spends the rest of this time developing software at her computer. For every hour she spends developing software, she earns €50, which she spends on consumption goods. Thus, her wage (€50) reflects the trade-off Fiona faces between leisure and consumption. For every hour of leisure she gives up, she works one more hour and gets €50 of consumption.

Figure 21.13 shows Fiona's budget constraint. If she spends all 100 hours enjoying leisure, she has no consumption. If she spends all 100 hours working, she earns a weekly consumption of €5,000 but has no time for leisure. If she works a normal 40-hour week, she enjoys 60 hours of leisure and has weekly consumption of €2,000.

Figure 21.13 uses indifference curves to represent Fiona's preferences for consumption and leisure. Here consumption and leisure are the two 'goods' between

### FIGURE 21.13

**The Work–Leisure Decision**

*This figure shows Fiona's budget constraint for deciding how much to work, her indifference curves for consumption and leisure, and her optimum.*

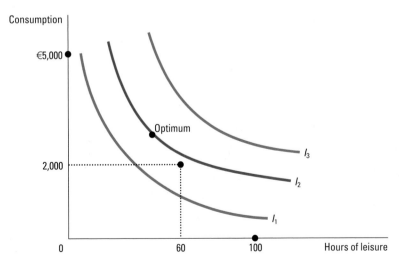

which Fiona is choosing. Because Fiona always prefers more leisure and more consumption, she prefers points on higher indifference curves to points on lower ones. At a wage of €50 per hour, Fiona chooses a combination of consumption and leisure represented by the point labelled 'optimum'. This is the point on the budget constraint that is on the highest possible indifference curve, which is curve $I_2$.

Now consider what happens when Fiona's wage increases from €50 to €60 per hour. Figure 21.14 shows two possible outcomes. In each case, the budget

## FIGURE 21.14

### An Increase in the Wage

*The two panels of this figure show how a person might respond to an increase in the wage. The graphs on the left show the consumer's initial budget constraint $BC_1$ and new budget constraint $BC_2$, as well as the consumer's optimal choices over consumption and leisure. The graphs on the right show the resulting labour supply curve. Because hours worked equal total hours available minus hours of leisure, any change in leisure implies an opposite change in the quantity of labour supplied. In panel (a), when the wage rises, consumption rises and leisure falls, resulting in a labour supply curve that slopes upward. In panel (b), when the wage rises, both consumption and leisure rise, resulting in a labour supply curve that slopes backward.*

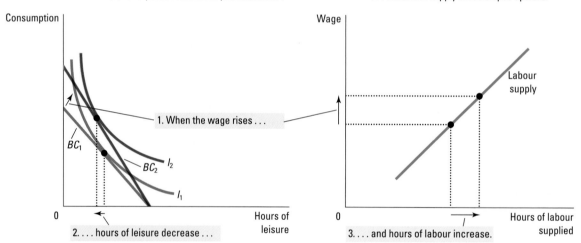

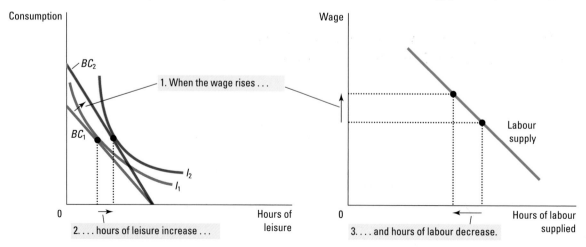

constraint, shown in the left-hand graph, shifts outward from $BC_1$ to $BC_2$. In the process, the budget constraint becomes steeper, reflecting the change in relative price: at the higher wage, Fiona gets more consumption for every hour of leisure that she gives up.

Fiona's preferences, as represented by her indifference curves, determine the resulting responses of consumption and leisure to the higher wage. In both panels, consumption rises. Yet the response of leisure to the change in the wage is different in the two cases. In panel (a), Fiona responds to the higher wage by enjoying less leisure. In panel (b), Fiona responds by enjoying more leisure.

Fiona's decision between leisure and consumption determines her supply of labour because the more leisure she enjoys, the less time she has left to work. In each panel, the right-hand graph in Figure 21.14 shows the labour supply curve implied by Fiona's decision. In panel (a), a higher wage induces Fiona to enjoy less leisure and work more, so the labour supply curve slopes upward. In panel (b), a higher wage induces Fiona to enjoy more leisure and work less, so the labour supply curve slopes 'backward'.

At first, the backward sloping labour supply curve is puzzling. Why would a person respond to a higher wage by working less? The answer comes from considering the income and substitution effects of a higher wage.

Consider first the substitution effect. When Fiona's wage rises, leisure becomes more costly relative to consumption, and this encourages Fiona to substitute consumption for leisure. In other words, the substitution effect induces Fiona to work harder in response to higher wages, which tends to make the labour supply curve slope upward.

Now consider the income effect. When Fiona's wage rises, she moves to a higher indifference curve. She is now better off than she was. As long as consumption and leisure are both normal goods, she tends to want to use this increase in well-being to enjoy both higher consumption and greater leisure. In other words, the income effect induces her to work less, which tends to make the labour supply curve slope backward.

In the end, economic theory does not give a clear prediction about whether an increase in the wage induces Fiona to work more or less. If the substitution effect is greater than the income effect for Fiona, she works more. If the income effect is greater than the substitution effect, she works less. The labour supply curve, therefore, could be either upward or backward sloping.

## CASE STUDY

### Income Effects On Labour Supply: Historical Trends, Lottery Winners, and the Carnegie Conjecture

The idea of a backward sloping labour supply curve might at first seem like a mere theoretical curiosity, but in fact it is not. Evidence indicates that the labour supply curve, considered over long periods of time, does in fact slope backwards. A hundred years ago many people in Europe and North America worked six days a week. Today five-day working weeks are the norm. At the same time that the length of the working week has been falling, the wage of the typical worker (adjusted for inflation) has been rising.

Here is how economists explain this historical pattern: over time, advances in technology raise workers' productivity and, thereby, the demand for labour. The increase in labour demand raises equilibrium wages. As wages rise, so does the reward for working. Yet rather than responding to this increased incentive by working more, most workers choose to take part of their greater prosperity

*"This will definitely affect my labour supply."*

in the form of more leisure. In other words, the income effect of higher wages dominates the substitution effect.

Further evidence that the income effect on labour supply is strong comes from a very different kind of data: winners of lotteries. Winners of large prizes in the lottery see large increases in their incomes and, as a result, large outward shifts in their budget constraints. Because the winners' wages have not changed, however, the *slopes* of their budget constraints remain the same. There is, therefore, no substitution effect. By examining the behaviour of lottery winners, we can isolate the income effect on labour supply. Nearly all the research on the effects of winning the lottery on labour supply has so far been done in the USA, but the results are striking. Of those winners who win more than $50,000, almost 25 per cent quit working within a year, and another 9 per cent reduce the number of hours they work. Of those winners who win more than $1 million, almost 40 per cent stop working. The income effect on labour supply of winning such a large prize is substantial.

Similar results were found in a study, published in the May 1993 issue of the *Quarterly Journal of Economics*, of how receiving a bequest affects a person's labour supply. The study found that a single person who inherits more than $150,000 is four times as likely to stop working as a single person who inherits less than $25,000. This finding would not have surprised the 19th-century industrialist Andrew Carnegie. Carnegie warned that 'the parent who leaves his son enormous wealth generally deadens the talents and energies of the son, and tempts him to lead a less useful and less worthy life than he otherwise would.' That is, Carnegie viewed the income effect on labour supply to be substantial and, from his paternalistic perspective, regrettable. During his life and at his death, Carnegie gave much of his vast fortune to charity.

## How Do Interest Rates Affect Household Saving?

An important decision that every person faces is how much income to consume today and how much to save for the future. We can use the theory of consumer choice to analyse how people make this decision and how the amount they save depends on the interest rate their savings will earn.

Consider the decision facing Sam, a worker planning ahead for retirement. To keep things simple, let's divide Sam's life into two periods. In the first period, Sam is young and working. In the second period, he is old and retired. When young, Sam earns €100,000. He divides this income between current consumption and saving. When he is old, Sam will consume what he has saved, including the interest that his savings have earned.

Suppose that the interest rate is 10 per cent. Then for every euro that Sam saves when young, he can consume €1.10 when old. We can view 'consumption when young' and 'consumption when old' as the two goods that Sam must choose between. The interest rate determines the relative price of these two goods.

Figure 21.15 shows Sam's budget constraint. If he saves nothing, he consumes €100,000 when young and nothing when old. If he saves everything, he consumes nothing when young and €110,000 when old. The budget constraint shows these and all the intermediate possibilities.

Figure 21.15 uses indifference curves to represent Sam's preferences for consumption in the two periods. Because Sam prefers more consumption in both periods, he prefers points on higher indifference curves to points on lower ones. Given his preferences, Sam chooses the optimal combination of consumption in both periods of life, which is the point on the budget constraint that is on the

*FIGURE 21.15*

**The Consumption–Saving Decision**

*This figure shows the budget constraint for a person deciding how much to consume in the two periods of his life, the indifference curves representing his preferences, and the optimum.*

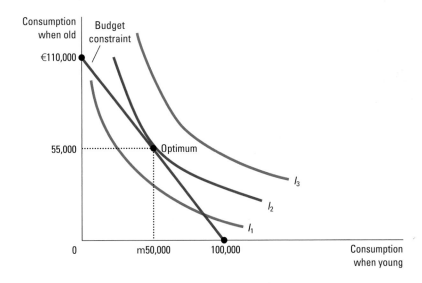

highest possible indifference curve. At this optimum, Sam consumes €50,000 when young and €55,000 when old.

Now consider what happens when the interest rate increases from 10 per cent to 20 per cent. Figure 21.16 shows two possible outcomes. In both cases, the budget constraint shifts outward and becomes steeper. At the new higher interest rate, Sam gets more consumption when old for every euro of consumption that he gives up when young.

The two panels show different preferences for Sam and the resulting response to the higher interest rate. In both cases, consumption when old rises. Yet the response of consumption when young to the change in the interest rate is different in the two cases. In panel (a), Sam responds to the higher interest rate by consuming less when young. In panel (b), Sam responds by consuming more when young.

Sam's saving, of course, is his income when young minus the amount he consumes when young. In panel (a), consumption when young falls when the interest rate rises, so saving must rise. In panel (b), Sam consumes more when young, so saving must fall.

The case shown in panel (b) might at first seem odd: Sam responds to an increase in the return to saving by saving less. Yet this behaviour is not as peculiar as it might seem. We can understand it by considering the income and substitution effects of a higher interest rate.

Consider first the substitution effect. When the interest rate rises, consumption when old becomes less costly relative to consumption when young. Therefore, the substitution effect induces Sam to consume more when old and less when young. In other words, the substitution effect induces Sam to save more.

Now consider the income effect. When the interest rate rises, Sam moves to a higher indifference curve. He is now better off than he was. As long as consumption in both periods consists of normal goods, he tends to want to use this

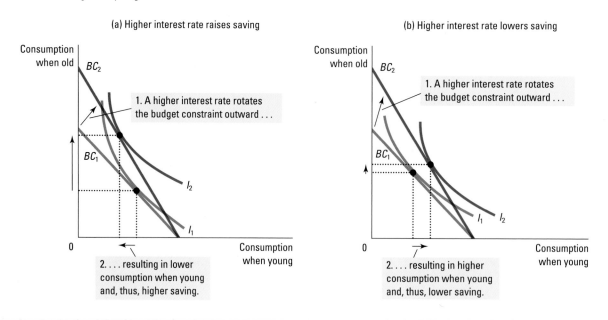

**FIGURE 21.16**

### An Increase in the Interest Rate

*In both panels, an increase in the interest rate shifts the budget constraint outward. In panel (a), consumption when young falls and consumption when old rises. The result is an increase in saving when young. In panel (b), consumption in both periods rises. The result is a decrease in saving when young.*

**(a) Higher interest rate raises saving**

Consumption when old

$BC_2$

1. A higher interest rate rotates the budget constraint outward . . .

$BC_1$

$I_2$

$I_1$

0

Consumption when young

2. . . . resulting in lower consumption when young and, thus, higher saving.

**(b) Higher interest rate lowers saving**

Consumption when old

$BC_2$

1. A higher interest rate rotates the budget constraint outward . . .

$BC_1$

$I_1$  $I_2$

0

Consumption when young

2. . . . resulting in higher consumption when young and, thus, lower saving.

increase in well-being to enjoy higher consumption in both periods. In other words, the income effect induces him to save less.

The end result, of course, depends on both the income and substitution effects. If the substitution effect of a higher interest rate is greater than the income effect, Sam saves more. If the income effect is greater than the substitution effect, Sam saves less. Thus, the theory of consumer choice says that an increase in the interest rate could either encourage or discourage saving.

Although this ambiguous result is interesting from the standpoint of economic theory, it is disappointing from the standpoint of economic policy. It turns out that an important issue in tax policy hinges in part on how saving responds to interest rates. Some economists have advocated reducing the taxation of interest and other capital income, arguing that such a policy change would raise the after-tax interest rate that savers can earn and would thereby encourage people to save more. Other economists have argued that because of offsetting income and substitution effects, such a tax change might not increase saving and could even reduce it. Unfortunately, research has not led to a consensus about how interest rates affect saving. As a result, there remains disagreement among economists about whether changes in tax policy aimed to encourage saving would, in fact, have the intended effect.

**Quick Quiz** Explain how an increase in the wage can potentially decrease the amount that a person wants to work.

# CONCLUSION: DO PEOPLE REALLY THINK THIS WAY?

The theory of consumer choice describes how people make decisions. As we have seen, it has broad applicability. It can explain how a person chooses between Pepsi and pizza, work and leisure, consumption and saving, and so on.

At this point, however, you might be tempted to treat the theory of consumer choice with some scepticism. After all, you are a consumer. You decide what to buy every time you walk into a shop. And you know that you do not decide by writing down budget constraints and indifference curves. Doesn't this knowledge about your own decision making provide evidence against the theory?

The answer is no. The theory of consumer choice does not try to present a literal account of how people make decisions. It is a model. And, as we first discussed in Chapter 2, models are not intended to be completely realistic.

The best way to view the theory of consumer choice is as a metaphor for how consumers make decisions. No consumer (except an occasional economist) goes through the explicit optimization envisioned in the theory. Yet consumers are aware that their choices are constrained by their financial resources. And, given those constraints, they do the best they can to achieve the highest level of satisfaction. The theory of consumer choice tries to describe this implicit, psychological process in a way that permits explicit, economic analysis.

The proof of the pudding is in the eating. And the test of a theory is in its applications. In the last section of this chapter we applied the theory of consumer choice to three practical issues about the economy. If you take more advanced courses in economics, you will see that this theory provides the framework for much additional analysis.

## SUMMARY

- A consumer's budget constraint shows the possible combinations of different goods he can buy given his income and the prices of the goods. The slope of the budget constraint equals the relative price of the goods.

- The consumer's indifference curves represent his preferences. An indifference curve shows the various bundles of goods that make the consumer equally happy. Points on higher indifference curves are preferred to points on lower indifference curves. The slope of an indifference curve at any point is the consumer's marginal rate of substitution – the rate at which the consumer is willing to trade one good for the other.

- The consumer optimizes by choosing the point on his budget constraint that lies on the highest indifference curve. At this point, the slope of the indifference curve (the marginal rate of substitution between the goods) equals the slope of the budget constraint (the relative price of the goods).

- When the price of a good falls, the impact on the consumer's choices can be broken down into an income effect and a substitution effect. The income effect is the change in consumption that arises because a lower price makes the consumer better off. The substitution effect is the change in consumption that arises because a price change encourages greater consumption of the good that has become relatively cheaper. The income effect is reflected in the movement from a lower to a higher indifference curve, whereas the substitution effect is reflected by a movement along an indifference curve to a point with a different slope.

- The theory of consumer choice can be applied in many situations. It can explain why demand curves can potentially slope upward, why higher wages could either increase or decrease the quantity of labour supplied, and why higher interest rates could either increase or decrease saving.

## KEY CONCEPTS

budget constraint, p. 421
indifference curve, p. 422
marginal rate of substitution, p. 422
perfect substitutes, p. 425

perfect complements, p. 425
normal good, p. 429
inferior good, p. 429
income effect, p. 430

substitution effect, p. 430
Giffen good, p. 434

## QUESTIONS FOR REVIEW

1. A consumer has income of €3,000. Wine costs €3 a glass and cheese costs €6 a kilo. Draw the consumer's budget constraint. What is the slope of this budget constraint?

2. Draw a consumer's indifference curves for wine and cheese. Describe and explain four properties of these indifference curves.

3. Pick a point on an indifference curve for wine and cheese and show the marginal rate of substitution. What does the marginal rate of substitution tell us?

4. Show a consumer's budget constraint and indifference curves for wine and cheese. Show the optimal consumption choice. If the price of wine is €3 a glass and the price of cheese is €6 a kilo, what is the marginal rate of substitution at this optimum?

5. A person who consumes wine and cheese gets a rise, so his income increases from €3,000 to €4,000. Show what happens if both wine and cheese are normal goods. Now show what happens if cheese is an inferior good.

6. The price of cheese rises from €6 to €10 a kilo, while the price of wine remains €3 a glass. For a consumer with a constant income of €3,000, show what happens to consumption of wine and cheese. Decompose the change into income and substitution effects.

7. Can an increase in the price of cheese possibly induce a consumer to buy more cheese? Explain.

## PROBLEMS AND APPLICATIONS

1. Jacqueline divides her income between coffee and croissants (both of which are normal goods). An early frost in Brazil causes a large increase in the price of coffee in France.
   a. Show the effect of the frost on Jacqueline's budget constraint.
   b. Show the effect of the frost on Jacqueline's optimal consumption bundle assuming that the substitution effect outweighs the income effect for croissants.
   c. Show the effect of the frost on Jacqueline's optimal consumption bundle assuming that the income effect outweighs the substitution effect for croissants.

2. Compare the following two pairs of goods:
   ● Coke and Pepsi
   ● skis and ski bindings.

   In which case do you expect the indifference curves to be fairly straight, and in which case do you expect the indifference curves to be very bowed? In which case will the consumer respond more to a change in the relative price of the two goods?

3. Eric consumes only cheese and bread.
   a. Could cheese and bread both be inferior goods for Eric? Explain.
   b. Suppose that cheese is a normal good for Eric while bread is an inferior good. If the price of cheese falls, what happens to Eric's consumption of bread? What happens to his consumption of cheese? Explain.

4. Oliver buys only lager and kebabs.
   a. In 2006, Oliver earns €100, lager costs €2 a pint and kebabs cost €4 each. Draw Oliver's budget constraint.

b. Now suppose that all prices increase by 10 per cent in 2007 and that Oliver's salary increases by 10 per cent as well. Draw Oliver's new budget constraint. How would Oliver's optimal combination of lager and kebabs in 2007 compare to his optimal combination in 2006?

5. Consider your decision about how many hours to work.
   a. Draw your budget constraint assuming that you pay no taxes on your income. On the same diagram, draw another budget constraint assuming that you pay a 15 per cent tax.
   b. Show how the tax might lead to more hours of work, fewer hours or the same number of hours. Explain.

6. Sarah is awake for 100 hours per week. Using one diagram, show Sarah's budget constraints if she earns €6 per hour, €8 per hour and €10 per hour. Now draw indifference curves such that Sarah's labour supply curve is upward sloping when the wage is between €6 and €8 per hour, and backward sloping when the wage is between €8 and €10 per hour.

7. Draw the indifference curve for someone deciding how much to work. Suppose the wage increases. Is it possible that the person's consumption would fall? Is this plausible? Discuss. (Hint: think about income and substitution effects.)

8. Suppose you take a job that pays €30,000 and set some of this income aside in a savings account that pays an annual interest rate of 5 per cent. Use a diagram with a budget constraint and indifference curves to show how your consumption changes in each of the following situations. To keep things simple, assume that you pay no taxes on your income.
   a. Your salary increases to €40,000.
   b. The interest rate on your bank account rises to 8 per cent.

9. As discussed in the text, we can divide an individual's life into two hypothetical periods: 'young' and 'old'. Suppose that the individual earns income only when young and saves some of that income to consume when old. If the interest rate on savings falls, can you tell what happens to consumption when young? Can you tell what happens to consumption when old? Explain.

10. (This problem is challenging.) The welfare system in industrialized countries provides income to some needy families. Typically, the maximum payment goes to families that earn no income; then, as families begin to earn income, the welfare payment declines gradually and eventually disappears. Let's consider the possible effects of a welfare system on a family's labour supply.
    a. Draw a budget constraint for a family assuming that the welfare system did not exist. On the same diagram, draw a budget constraint that reflects the existence of the welfare system.
    b. Adding indifference curves to your diagram, show how the welfare system could reduce the number of hours worked by the family. Explain, with reference to both the income and substitution effects.
    c. Using your diagram from part (b), show the effect of the welfare system on the well-being of the family.

11. (This problem is challenging.) Suppose that an individual incurred no taxes on the first €10,000 she earned and 15 per cent of any income she earned over €10,000. Now suppose that the government is considering two ways to reduce the tax burden: a reduction in the tax rate and an increase in the amount on which no tax is owed.
    a. What effect would a reduction in the tax rate have on the individual's labour supply if she earned €30,000 to start with? Explain in words using the income and substitution effects. You do not need to use a diagram.
    b. What effect would an increase in the amount on which no tax is owed have on the individual's labour supply? Again, explain in words using the income and substitution effects.

12. (This problem is challenging.) Consider a person deciding how much to consume and how much to save for retirement. This person has particular preferences: her lifetime utility depends on the lowest level of consumption during the two periods of her life. That is,
    Utility = Minimum {consumption when young, consumption when old}
    a. Draw this person's indifference curves. (Hint: recall that indifference curves show the combinations of consumption in the two periods that yield the same level of utility.)
    b. Draw the budget constraint and the optimum.
    c. When the interest rate increases, does this person save more or less? Explain your answer using income and substitution effects.

13. Economist George Stigler once wrote that, according to consumer theory, 'if consumers do not buy less of a commodity when their incomes rise, they will surely buy less when the price of the commodity rises.' Explain this statement.

# 22 FRONTIERS OF MICROECONOMICS

Economics is a study of the choices that people make and the resulting interactions they have with one another. This study has many facets, as we have seen in the preceding chapters. Yet it would be a mistake to think that all the facets we have seen make up a finished jewel, perfect and unchanging. Like all scientists, economists are always on the lookout for new areas to study and new phenomena to explain. This final chapter on microeconomics offers an assortment of three topics at the discipline's frontier to see how economists are trying to expand their understanding of human behaviour and society.

The first topic is the economics of *asymmetric information.* Many times in life, some people are better informed than others, and this difference in information can affect the choices they make and how they deal with one another. Thinking about this asymmetry can shed light on many aspects of the world, from the market for used cars to the custom of gift giving.

The second topic we examine in this chapter is *political economy.* Throughout this book we have seen many examples where markets fail and government policy can potentially improve matters. But 'potentially' is a needed qualifier: whether this potential is realized depends on how well our political institutions work. The field of political economy applies the tools of economics to understand the functioning of government.

The third topic in this chapter is *behavioural economics.* This field brings some of the insights from psychology into the study of economic issues. It offers a view of human behaviour that is more subtle and complex than that found in conventional economic theory, but this view may also be more realistic.

This chapter covers a lot of ground. To do so, it offers not a full helping of these three topics but, instead, a taste of each. One goal is to show a few of the directions economists are heading in their effort to expand knowledge of how the economy works. Another goal is to whet your appetite for more courses in economics.

# ASYMMETRIC INFORMATION

'I know something you don't know.' This statement is a common taunt among children, but it also conveys a deep truth about how people sometimes interact with one another. Many times in life, one person knows more about what is going on than another. A difference in access to relevant knowledge is called an *information asymmetry*.

Examples abound. A worker knows more than his employer about how much effort he puts into his job. A seller of a used car knows more than the buyer about the car's condition. The first is an example of a *hidden action*, whereas the second is an example of a *hidden characteristic*. In each case, the party in the dark (the employer, the car buyer) would like to know the relevant information, but the informed party (the worker, the car seller) may have an incentive to conceal it.

Because asymmetric information is so prevalent, economists have devoted much effort in recent decades to studying its effects. And, indeed, the 2001 Nobel Prize in economics was awarded to three economists (George Akerlof, Michael Spence and Joseph Stiglitz) for their pioneering work on this topic. Let's discuss some of the insights that this study has revealed.

## Hidden Actions: Principals, Agents and Moral Hazard

**moral hazard**
the tendency of a person who is imperfectly monitored to engage in dishonest or otherwise undesirable behaviour

**agent**
a person who is performing an act for another person, called the principal

**principal**
a person for whom another person, called the agent, is performing some act

**Moral hazard** is a problem that arises when one person, called the **agent**, is performing some task on behalf of another person, called the **principal.** If the principal cannot perfectly monitor the agent's behaviour, the agent tends to undertake less effort than the principal considers desirable. The phrase *moral hazard* refers to the risk, or 'hazard', of inappropriate or otherwise 'immoral' behaviour by the agent. In such a situation, the principal tries various ways to encourage the agent to act more responsibly.

The employment relationship is the classic example. The employer is the principal, and the worker is the agent. The moral-hazard problem is the temptation of imperfectly monitored workers to shirk their responsibilities. Employers can respond to this problem in various ways:

- *Better monitoring.* Parents hiring nannies have been known to plant hidden video cameras in their homes to record the nanny's behaviour when the parents are away. The aim is to catch irresponsible behaviour.
- *High wages.* According to *efficiency wages theories* (discussed in Chapter 19), some employers may choose to pay their workers a wage above the level that equilibrates supply and demand in the labour market. A worker who earns an above-equilibrium wage is less likely to shirk, because if he is caught and fired, he might not be able to find another high-paying job.
- *Delayed payment.* Firms can delay part of a worker's compensation, so if the worker is caught shirking and is fired, he suffers a larger penalty. One example of delayed compensation is the year-end bonus. Similarly, a firm may choose to pay its workers more later in their lives. Thus, the wage increases that workers get as they age may reflect not just the benefits of experience but also a response to moral hazard.

These various mechanisms to reduce the problem of moral hazard need not be used alone. Employers can use a combination of them.

Beyond the workplace, there are many other examples of moral hazard. A homeowner with fire insurance will probably buy too few smoke detectors because the homeowner bears the cost of the smoke detector while the insurance company receives much of the benefit. A family may live near a river with a high risk of flooding because the family enjoys the scenic views, while the government bears the cost of disaster relief after a flood. Many regulations are aimed at addressing the problem: an insurance company may require homeowners to buy smoke detectors, and the government may prohibit building homes on land with high risk of flooding. But the insurance company does not have perfect information about how cautious homeowners are, and the government does not have perfect information about the risk that families undertake when choosing where to live. As a result, the problem of moral hazard persists.

## Hidden Characteristics: Adverse Selection and the Lemons Problem

**Adverse selection** is a problem that arises in markets where the seller knows more about the attributes of the good being sold than the buyer does. As a result, the buyer runs the risk of being sold a good of low quality. That is, the 'selection' of goods being sold may be 'adverse' from the standpoint of the uninformed buyer.

**adverse selection**
the tendency for the mix of unobserved attributes to become undesirable from the standpoint of an uninformed party

The classic example of adverse selection is the market for used cars. Sellers of used cars know their vehicles' defects while buyers often do not. Because owners of the worst cars are more likely to sell them than are the owners of the best cars, buyers are apprehensive about getting a poor car. If you are unlucky enough to buy a poor car, then we might say that you have bought a 'lemon'. (This was the term used by Nobel prize-winner Joseph Stiglitz in his famous research article, 'The Market for Lemons': it comes from the old-fashioned fruit or gambling machines where three wheels spin and come to rest indicating a picture of a fruit that determines the payout; traditionally, a lemon was bad luck, paying out nothing). As a result of this information asymmetry, many people avoid buying vehicles in the used car market. This lemons problem can explain why a used car only a few weeks old sells for thousands of dollars less than a new car of the same type. A buyer of the used car might surmise that the seller is getting rid of the car quickly because the seller knows something about it that the buyer does not.

A second example of adverse selection occurs in the labour market. According to another efficiency wage theory, workers vary in their abilities, and they may know their own abilities better than do the firms that hire them. When a firm cuts the wage it pays, the more talented workers are more likely to quit, knowing they are better able to find other employment. Conversely, a firm may choose to pay an above-equilibrium wage to attract a better mix of workers. Or suppose that a firm is not doing so well and needs to cut the wage bill. It can do this either by reducing wages or by keeping wages where they are and laying off workers at random for a few weeks. If it cuts wages, the very best workers will quit, because they know they will be able to find a better job elsewhere. Of course, the better workers who are randomly selected when the firm chooses instead to impose layoffs may also choose to quit and find a steadier job elsewhere. But in this case only *some* of the best workers quit (since not all of them are laid off because workers were chosen randomly) while if the firms cuts wages, *all* of the best workers will quit.

A third example of adverse selection occurs in markets for insurance. For example, buyers of health insurance know more about their own health problems than do insurance companies. Because people with greater hidden health problems are more likely to buy health insurance than are other people, the price of health insurance reflects the costs of a sicker-than-average person. As a result, people in average health may be discouraged from buying health insurance by the high price.

When markets suffer from adverse selection, the invisible hand does not necessarily work its magic. In the used car market, owners of good cars may choose to keep them rather than sell them at the low price that sceptical buyers are willing to pay. In the labour market, wages may be stuck above the level that balances supply and demand, resulting in unemployment. In insurance markets, buyers with low risk may choose to remain uninsured, because the policies they are offered fail to reflect their true characteristics. Advocates of government-provided health insurance sometimes point to the problem of adverse selection as one reason not to trust the private market to provide the right amount of health insurance on its own.

## Signalling to Convey Private Information

Although asymmetric information is sometimes a motivation for public policy, it also motivates some individual behaviour that otherwise might be hard to explain. Markets respond to problems of asymmetric information in many ways. One of them is **signalling,** which refers to actions taken by an informed party for the sole purpose of credibly revealing his private information.

**signalling**
an action taken by an informed party to reveal private information to an uninformed party

We have seen examples of signalling in previous chapters. As we saw in Chapter 17, firms may spend money on advertising to signal to potential customers that they have high-quality products. As we saw in Chapter 20, students may earn university degrees in order to signal to potential employers that they are high-ability individuals. Recall that the signalling theory of education contrasts with the human capital theory, which asserts that education increases a person's productivity, rather than merely conveying information about innate talent. These two examples of signalling (advertising, education) may seem very different, but below the surface they are much the same: in both cases, the informed party (the firm, the student) is using the signal to convince the uninformed party (the customer, the employer) that the informed party is offering something of high quality.

What does it take for an action to be an effective signal? Obviously, it must be costly. If a signal were free, everyone would use it, and it would convey no information. For the same reason, there is another requirement: The signal must be less costly, or more beneficial, to the person with the higher-quality product. Otherwise, everyone would have the same incentive to use the signal, and the signal would reveal nothing.

Consider again our two examples. In the advertising case, a firm with a good product reaps a larger benefit from advertising because customers who try the product once are more likely to become repeat customers. Thus, it is rational for the firm with the good product to pay for the cost of the signal (advertising), and it is rational for the customer to use the signal as a piece of information about the product's quality. In the education case, a talented person can get through school more easily than a less talented one. Thus, it is rational for the talented person to pay for the cost of the signal (education), and it is rational for the employer to use the signal as a piece of information about the person's talent.

The world is replete with instances of signalling. Magazine advertisements sometimes include the phrase 'as seen on TV'. Why does a firm selling a product in a magazine choose to stress this fact? One possibility is that the firm is trying to convey its willingness to pay for an expensive signal (a spot on television) in the hope that you will infer that its product is of high quality. For the same reason, graduates of elite universities are always sure to put that fact on their curriculum vitaes.

# CASE STUDY

## Gifts as Signals

A man is debating what to give his girlfriend for her birthday. 'I know,' he says to himself, 'I'll give her cash. After all, I don't know her tastes as well as she does, and with cash, she can buy anything she wants.' But when he hands her the money, she is offended. Convinced he doesn't really love her, she breaks off the relationship. What's the economics behind this story?

In some ways, gift giving is a strange custom. As the man in our story suggests, people typically know their own preferences better than others do, so we might expect everyone to prefer cash to in-kind transfers. If your employer substituted merchandise for your wages, you would likely object to the means of payment. But your reaction is very different when someone who (you hope) loves you does the same thing.

One interpretation of gift giving is that it reflects asymmetric information and signalling. The man in our story has private information that the girlfriend would like to know: does he really love her? Choosing a good gift for her is a signal of his love. Certainly, picking out a gift has the right characteristics to be a signal. It is costly (it takes time), and its cost depends on the private information (how much he loves her). If he really loves her, choosing a good gift is easy because he is thinking about her all the time. If he doesn't love her, finding the right gift is more difficult. Thus, giving a gift that suits the girlfriend is one way for him to convey the private information of his love for her. Giving cash shows that he isn't even bothering to try.

The signalling theory of gift giving is consistent with another observation: people care most about the custom when the strength of affection is most in question. Thus, giving cash to a girlfriend or boyfriend is usually a bad move. But when college students receive a cheque from their parents, they are less often offended. The parents' love is less likely to be in doubt, so the recipient probably won't interpret the cash gift as a signal of lack of affection.

*"Now we'll see how much he loves me."*

## Screening to Induce Information Revelation

When an informed party takes actions to reveal his private information, the phenomenon is called signalling. When an uninformed party takes actions to induce the informed party to reveal private information, the phenomenon is called **screening.**

Some screening is common sense. A person buying a used car may ask that it be checked by a car mechanic before the sale. A seller who refuses this request reveals his private information that the car is a lemon. The buyer may decide to offer a lower price or to look for another car.

Other examples of screening are more subtle. For example, consider a firm that sells car insurance. The firm would like to charge a low premium to safe drivers and a high premium to risky drivers. But how can it tell them apart? Drivers know whether they are safe or risky, but the risky ones won't admit to it. A driver's history is one piece of information (which insurance companies in fact use), but because of the intrinsic randomness of car accidents, history is an imperfect indicator of future risks.

**screening**
an action taken by an uninformed party to induce an informed party to reveal information

The insurance company might be able to sort out the two kinds of drivers by offering different insurance policies that would induce them to separate themselves. One policy would have a high premium and cover the full cost of any accidents that occur. Another policy would have low premiums but would have, say, a €1,000 deductible. (That is, the driver would be responsible for the first €1,000 of damage, and the insurance company would cover the remaining risk.) Notice that the deductible is more of a burden for risky drivers because they are more likely to have an accident. Thus, with a large enough deductible, the low-premium policy with a deductible would attract the safe drivers, while the high-premium policy without a deductible would attract the risky drivers. Faced with these two policies, the two kinds of drivers would reveal their private information by choosing different insurance policies.

## Asymmetric Information and Public Policy

We have examined two kinds of asymmetric information – moral hazard and adverse selection. And we have seen how individuals may respond to the problem with signalling or screening. Now let's consider what the study of asymmetric information suggests about the proper scope of public policy.

The tension between market success and market failure is central in microeconomics. We learned in Chapter 7 that the equilibrium of supply and demand is efficient in the sense that it maximizes the total surplus that society can obtain in a market. Adam Smith's invisible hand seemed to reign supreme. This conclusion was then tempered with the study of externalities (Chapter 10), public goods (Chapter 11), imperfect competition (Chapters 15 through 17) and poverty (Chapter 20). These examples of market failure showed that government can sometimes improve market outcomes.

The study of asymmetric information gives us new reason to be wary of markets. When some people know more than others, the market may fail to put resources to their best use. People with high-quality used cars may have trouble selling them because buyers will be afraid of getting a lemon. People with few health problems may have trouble getting low-cost health insurance because insurance companies lump them together with those who have significant (but hidden) health problems.

Although asymmetric information may call for government action in some cases, three facts complicate the issue. First, as we have seen, the private market can sometimes deal with information asymmetries on its own using a combination of signalling and screening. Secondly, the government rarely has more information than the private parties. Even if the market's allocation of resources is not first-best, it may be second-best. That is, when there are information asymmetries, policymakers may find it hard to improve upon the market's admittedly imperfect outcome. Thirdly, the government is itself an imperfect institution – a topic we take up in the next section.

**Quick Quiz** A person who buys a life insurance policy pays a certain amount per year and receives for his family a much larger payment in the event of his death. Would you expect buyers of life insurance to have higher or lower death rates than the average person? How might this be an example of moral hazard? Of adverse selection? How might a life insurance company deal with these problems?

# POLITICAL ECONOMY

As we have seen, markets left on their own do not always reach a desirable allocation of resources. When we judge the market's outcome to be either inefficient or inequitable, there may be a role for the government to step in and improve the situation. Yet before we embrace an activist government, we need to consider one more fact: The government is also an imperfect institution. The field of *political economy* (sometimes called the field of *public choice*) applies the methods of economics to study how government works.

## The Condorcet Voting Paradox

Most advanced societies rely on democratic principles to set government policy. When a city is deciding between two locations to build a new park, for example, we have a simple way to choose: the majority gets its way. Yet, for most policy issues, the number of possible outcomes far exceeds two. A new park, for instance, could be placed in many possible locations. In this case, as an 18th century French political theorist, the Marquis de Condorcet, famously noted, democracy might run into some problems trying to choose one of the outcomes.

For example, suppose there are three possible outcomes, labelled A, B and C, and there are three voter types with the preferences shown in Table 22.1. The leader of our town council wants to aggregate these individual preferences into preferences for society as a whole. How should he do it?

At first, he might try some pairwise votes. If he asks voters to choose first between B and C, voter types 1 and 2 will vote for B, giving B the majority. If he then asks voters to choose between A and B, voter types 1 and 3 will vote for A, giving A the majority. Observing that A beats B, and B beats C, the mayor might conclude that A is the voters' clear choice.

But wait: suppose the council leader then asks voters to choose between A and C. In this case, voter types 2 and 3 vote for C, giving C the majority. That is, under pairwise majority voting, A beats B, B beats C, and C beats A. Normally, we expect preferences to exhibit a property called *transitivity*: If A is preferred to B, and B is preferred to C, then we would expect A to be preferred to C. The **Condorcet paradox** is that democratic outcomes do not always obey this property. Pairwise voting might produce transitive preferences for a society, depending on the pattern of individual preferences, but as our example in the table shows, it cannot be counted on to do so.

**Condorcet paradox**
the failure of majority rule to produce transitive preferences for society

---

**TABLE 22.1**

**The Condorcet Paradox**

*If voters have these preferences over outcomes* A, B *and* C, *then in pairwise majority voting,* A *beats* B, B *beats* C, *and* C *beats* A.

|  | Voter type | | |
|---|---|---|---|
|  | Type 1 | Type 2 | Type 3 |
| Percentage of electorate | 35 | 45 | 20 |
| First choice | A | B | C |
| Second choice | B | C | A |
| Third choice | C | A | B |

One implication of the Condorcet paradox is that the order on which things are voted can affect the result. If the council leader suggests choosing first between A and B and then comparing the winner to C, the town ends up choosing C. But if the voters choose first between B and C and then compare the winner to A, the town ends up with A. And if the voters choose first between A and C and then compare the winner to B, the town ends up with B.

There are two lessons to be learned from the Condorcet paradox. The narrow lesson is that when there are more than two options, setting the agenda (that is, deciding the order in which items are voted) can have a powerful impact on the outcome of a democratic election. The broad lesson is that majority voting by itself does not tell us what outcome a society really wants.

## Arrow's Impossibility Theorem

Since political theorists first noticed Condorcet's paradox, they have spent much energy studying voting systems and proposing new ones. For example, as an alternative to pairwise majority voting, the leader of the town council could ask each voter to rank the possible outcomes. For each voter, we could give 1 point for last place, 2 points for second to last, 3 points for third to last and so on. The outcome that receives the most total points wins. With the preferences in Table 1, outcome B is the winner. (You can do the arithmetic yourself.) This voting method is called a *Borda count*, after the 18th century French mathematician and political scientist who devised it. It is often used in polls that rank sports teams.

Is there a perfect voting system? Economist Kenneth Arrow (the winner of the 1972 Nobel Prize in Economics) took up this question in his 1951 book *Social Choice and Individual Values*. Arrow started by defining what a perfect voting system would be. He assumes that individuals in society have preferences over the various possible outcomes: A, B, C and so on. He then assumes that society wants a voting scheme to choose among these outcomes that satisfies several properties:

- *Unanimity*. If everyone prefers A to B, then A should beat B.
- *Transitivity*. If A beats B, and B beats C, then A should beat C.
- *Independence of irrelevant alternatives*. The ranking between any two outcomes A and B should not depend on whether some third outcome C is also available.
- *No dictators*. There is no person that always gets his way, regardless of everyone else's preferences.

**Arrow's impossibility theorem**
a mathematical result showing that, under certain assumed conditions, there is no scheme for aggregating individual preferences into a valid set of social preferences

These all seem like desirable properties for a voting system to have. Yet Arrow proved, mathematically and incontrovertibly, that no voting system can satisfy all of these properties. This amazing result is called **Arrow's impossibility theorem.**

The mathematics needed to prove Arrow's theorem is beyond the scope of this book, but we can get some sense of why the theorem is true from a couple of examples. We have already seen the problem with the method of majority rule. The Condorcet paradox shows that majority rule fails to produce a ranking among the outcomes that always satisfies transitivity.

As another example, the Borda count fails to satisfy the independence of irrelevant alternatives. Recall that, using the preferences in Table 22.1, outcome B wins with a Borda count. But suppose that suddenly C disappears as an alternative. If the Borda count method is applied only to outcomes A and B, then A wins. (Once again, you can do the arithmetic on your own.) Thus, eliminating alternative C changes the ranking between A and B. The reason for this change is that the result of the Borda count depends on the number of points that A and B receive, and the number of points depends on whether the irrelevant alternative, C, is also available.

Arrow's impossibility theorem is a deep and disturbing result. It doesn't say that we should abandon democracy as a form of government. But it does say that, no matter what voting scheme society adopts for aggregating the preferences of its members, in some way it will be flawed as a mechanism for social choice.

## The Median Voter Is King

Despite Arrow's theorem, voting is how most societies choose their leaders and public policies, often by majority rule. The next step in studying government is to examine how governments run by majority rule work. That is, in a democratic society, who determines what policy is chosen? In some cases, the theory of democratic government yields a surprisingly simple answer.

Let's consider an example. Imagine that society is deciding on how much money to spend on some public good, such as the army or the national parks. Each voter has his own most preferred budget, and he always prefers outcomes closer to his most preferred value to outcomes further away. Thus, we can line up voters from those who prefer the smallest budget to those who prefer the largest. Figure 22.1 is an example. Here there are 100 voters, and the budget size varies from zero to €20 billion. Given these preferences, what outcome would you expect democracy to produce?

According to a famous result called the **median voter theorem,** majority rule will produce the outcome most preferred by the median voter. The *median voter* is the voter exactly in the middle of the distribution. In this example, if you take the line of voters ordered by their preferred budgets and count 50 voters from either end of the line, you will find that the median voter wants a budget of €10 billion. By contrast, the average preferred outcome (calculated by adding the preferred outcomes and dividing by the number of voters) is €9 billion, and the modal outcome (the one preferred by the greatest number of voters) is €15 billion.

**median voter theorem**
a mathematical result showing that if voters are choosing a point along a line and each voter wants the point closest to his most preferred point, then majority rule will pick the most preferred point of the median voter

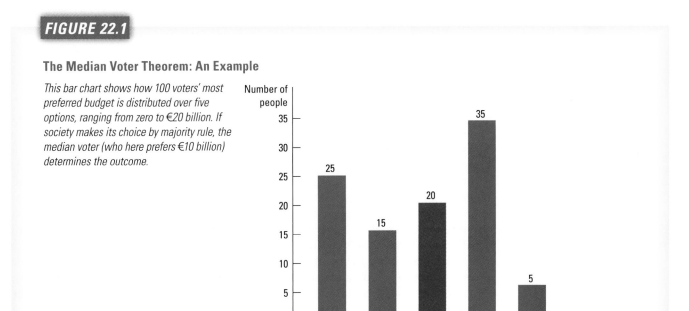

### FIGURE 22.1

**The Median Voter Theorem: An Example**

*This bar chart shows how 100 voters' most preferred budget is distributed over five options, ranging from zero to €20 billion. If society makes its choice by majority rule, the median voter (who here prefers €10 billion) determines the outcome.*

The median voter rules the day because his preferred outcome beats any other proposal in a two-way race. In our example, more than half the voters want €10 billion or more, and more than half want €10 billion or less. If someone proposes, say, €8 billion instead of €10 billion, everyone who prefers €10 billion or more will vote with the median voter. Similarly, if someone proposes €12 billion instead of €10 billion, everyone who wants €10 billion or less will vote with the median voter. In either case, the median voter has more than half the voters on his side.

What about the Condorcet voting paradox? It turns out that when the voters are picking a point along a line and each voter aims for his own most preferred point, the Condorcet paradox cannot arise. The median voter's most preferred outcome beats all comers.

One implication of the median voter theorem is that if two political parties are each trying to maximize their chance of election, they will both move their positions toward the median voter. Suppose, for example, that the Red party advocates a budget of €15 billion, while the Blue party advocates a budget of €10 billion. The Red position is more popular in the sense that €15 billion has more proponents than any other single choice. Nonetheless, the Blues get more than 50 per cent of the vote: they will attract the 20 voters who want €10 billion, the 15 voters who want €5 billion and the 25 voters who want zero. If the Reds want to win, they will move their platform toward the median voter. Thus, this theory can explain why the parties in a two-party system are similar to each other: they are both moving towards the median voter.

Another implication of the median voter theorem is that minority views are not given much weight. Imagine that 40 per cent of the population want a lot of money spent on the national parks, and 60 per cent want nothing spent. In this case, the median voter's preference is zero, regardless of the intensity of the minority's view. Such is the logic of democracy. Rather than reaching a compromise that takes into account everyone's preferences, majority rule looks only to the person in the exact middle of the distribution.

## Politicians Are People Too

When economists study consumer behaviour, they assume that consumers buy the bundle of goods and services that gives them the greatest level of satisfaction. When economists study firm behaviour, they assume that firms produce the quantity of goods and services that yields the greatest level of profits. What should they assume when they study people involved in the practice of politics?

Politicians also have objectives. It would be nice to assume that political leaders are always looking out for the well-being of society as a whole, that they are aiming for an optimal combination of efficiency and equity. Nice, perhaps, but not realistic. Self-interest is as powerful a motive for political actors as it is for consumers and firm owners. Some politicians are motivated by desire for re-election and are willing to sacrifice the national interest when doing so solidifies their base of voters. Other politicians are motivated by simple greed. If you have any doubt, you should look at the world's poor nations, where corruption among government officials is a common impediment to economic development.

This book is not the place to develop a theory of political behaviour. That topic is best left to the political scientists. But when thinking about economic policy, remember that this policy is made not by a benevolent king, but by real people with their own all-too-human desires. Sometimes they are motivated to further the national interest, but sometimes they are motivated by their own political and financial ambitions. We shouldn't be surprised when economic policy fails to resemble the ideals derived in economics textbooks.

**Quick Quiz** A local district council decides to let the people living in the area vote on how much it should spend on local schools and the resulting student–teacher ratio. A poll finds that 35 per cent of the voters want a ratio of 9:1, 25 per cent want a ratio of 10:1 and 40 per cent want a ratio of 12:1. What outcome would you expect the district to end up with?

# BEHAVIOURAL ECONOMICS

Economics is a study of human behaviour, but it is not the only field that can make that claim. The social science of psychology also sheds light on the choices that people make in their lives. The fields of economics and psychology usually proceed independently, in part because they address a different range of questions. But recently a field called *behavioural economics* has emerged in which economists are making use of basic psychological insights. Let's consider some of these insights here.

## People Aren't Always Rational

Economic theory is populated by a particular species of organism, sometimes called *homo economicus*. Members of this species are always rational. As firm managers, they maximize profits. As consumers, they maximize utility (or, equivalently, pick the point on the highest indifference curve). Given the constraints they face, they rationally weigh all the costs and benefits and always choose the best possible course of action.

Real people, however, are *homo sapiens*. Although in many ways they resemble the rational, calculating people assumed in economic theory, they are far more complex. They can be forgetful, impulsive, confused, emotional and short-sighted. These imperfections of human reasoning are the bread-and-butter of psychologists, but until recently, economists have neglected them.

Herbert Simon, one of the first social scientists to work at the boundary of economics and psychology, suggested that humans should be viewed not as rational maximizers but as *satisficers*. Rather than always choosing the best course of action, they make decisions that are merely good enough. Similarly, other economists have suggested that humans are only 'near rational' or that they exhibit 'bounded rationality'.

Studies of human decision making have tried to detect systematic mistakes that people make. Here are a few of the findings:

- *People are overconfident.* Imagine that you were asked some numerical questions, such as the number of African countries in the United Nations, the height of the tallest mountain in North America and so on. Instead of being asked for a single estimate, however, you were asked to give a 90 per cent confidence interval – a range such that you were 90 per cent confident the true number falls within it. When psychologists run experiments like this, they find that most people give ranges that are too small: the true number falls within their intervals far less than 90 per cent of the time. That is, most people are too sure of their own abilities.
- *People give too much weight to a small number of vivid observations.* Imagine that you are thinking about buying a car of brand X. To learn about its reliability, you read *Consumer Reports,* which has surveyed 1,000 owners of car X. Then you

run into a friend who owns car X and she tells you that her car is a lemon. How do you treat your friend's observation? If you think rationally, you will realize that she has only increased your sample size from 1,000 to 1,001, which does not provide much new information. But because your friend's story is so vivid, you may be tempted to give it more weight in your decision making than you should.

● *People are reluctant to change their minds.* People tend to interpret evidence to confirm beliefs they already hold. In one study, subjects were asked to read and evaluate a research report on whether capital punishment deters crime. After reading the report, those who initially favoured the death penalty said they were more sure in their view, and those who initially opposed the death penalty also said they were more sure in their view. The two groups interpreted the same evidence in exactly opposite ways.

Why, you might ask, is economics built on the rationality assumption when psychology and common sense cast doubt on it? One answer is that the assumption, even if not exactly true, is still a good approximation. For example, when we studied the differences between competitive and monopoly firms, the assumption that firms rationally maximize profit yielded many important and valid insights. Recall from Chapter 2 that economic models are not meant to replicate reality but are supposed to show the essence of the problem at hand as an aid to understanding.

Another reason that economists so often assume rationality may be that economists are themselves not rational maximizers. Like most people, they are overconfident, and they are reluctant to change their minds. Their choice among alternative theories of human behaviour may exhibit excessive inertia. Moreover, economists may be content with a theory that is not perfect but is good enough. Indeed, the model of rational man may be the theory of choice for a satisficing social scientist.

# IN THE NEWS

## False Consensus and Overconfidence

*This article discusses whether sophisticated readers of the* Financial Times *fall into the familiar traps of overconfidence and assuming most other people are like them when forming estimates of simple things like beer and tea consumption.*

**Avoid the Trap of Thinking Everyone is Just Like You: Many Marketing People Make This Mistake. But did FT readers fare any better?**
*By Andrew Gershoff and Eric Johnson*

Marketing is a social process, not simply the analysis of dry statistical reports. Whether your customers live in another country or another region, or are part of a different economic class, the heart of marketing is understanding them and their needs. Often, though, marketers and managers are very different from their customers – most products are developed by teams of like-minded people who may have little in common with the intended buyer. This can create problems for market- ers during the decision-making process – problems that have been highlighted by consumer research, behavioural economics and social psychology. Here we examine two of these pitfalls and discuss their causes and possible cures. Moreover, we shall see how a sample of *Financial Times* readers performed in making judgments like the ones we discuss.

In a 1993 study, US managers were asked to estimate various attributes of markets, including the percentage of beer sold in US supermarkets that was imported from other countries and the percentage of US households that purchased canned chilli. They were also asked how much they personally liked and purchased imported beer and canned chilli.

At the time of the study only about 2 per cent of beer sold in US supermarkets was imported. The executives, who tended to like and buy imported beer, gave an average estimate of 20 per cent. On average, the more an executive liked and purchased imported beer, the higher was his or her estimate of the amount of imported beer sold.

Canned chilli, on the other hand, is a product that was largely disliked and was rarely purchased by US executives. While 40 per cent of US households buy it in a given year, the executives' average estimate was only 28 per cent. Again, the more an executive personally shied away from canned chilli, the lower was his or her estimated purchase for the country as a whole.

The explanation for this disparity lies in a psychological phenomenon called the false consensus effect, in which people tend to think that their own attitudes are more common than they really are. When people estimate what others like and do, their own attitudes sway their responses. Since the psychologists Lee Ross, David Green and Pamela House identified this effect in 1977, a number of reasons have been suggested as to why it occurs.

One is that it is so easy for people to think of what they like and dislike that they give these preferences extra weight. Another is that when they think of other people, they think of people they know well, who tend to be similar to them. Thus their judgment is biased.

What can managers do to avoid false consensus in their estimates? Just being aware of it may not be enough. Joachim Kruger and Russell Clement, psychological researchers, found the effect can occur even when people are specifically warned about it.

But there are ways in which the effect may be reduced. Perhaps the most important is by using market research. A number of studies have found that observing real data can reduce the incidence of false consensus. Second, managers can employ diverse teams of people.

The second error lies in failing to identify what we do not know. When we asked the executives to indicate how certain they were of their estimates, they were typically overconfident.

Along with estimates, they also provided 90 per cent confidence intervals (or upper and lower bounds for their estimates), representing their belief that the true value would fall, on average, nine out of 10 times within these bounds.

Overconfidence is not universal but it does appear to be common. The best way to guard against it is to make explicit statements about how confident you are and to check how things turn out. You may start out being just as overconfident as our executives but at least you have a chance to learn from your mistakes.

So how do readers of the *Financial Times* compare with other executives? ...

We asked 274 respondents questions similar to those we had used in the past, but which we thought might tap differences between European (particularly those from the UK) and US readers. We also offered a $250 prize funded jointly by the Columbia Centre for the Decision Sciences and the Columbia Centre for Excellence in E-Business.

First, we asked readers to estimate the percentage of European beer sold in US supermarkets. According to Information Resources, which supplied recent data, European imports account for 4.1 per cent of the US market; our FT readers gave an average estimate of 24.4 per cent, more than five times as high.

Our second question asked about the average annual sum spent on tea (in bag form). Research gives a figure of $5.92 but our respondents estimated on average more than $56, off by a factor of almost 10.

These are difficult questions and FT readers may have known the perils of intuitive estimation. If so, they should have spread their confidence intervals wide, yielding – as we had hoped – answers outside their confidence intervals (that is to say, surprises) only 10 per cent of the time. However, 82 per cent of the confidence intervals for beer and 72 per cent of those for tea did not contain the right answer.

Why did this occur? One hint is that European beers made up 45 per cent of the respondents' purchases and they reported spending about $50 on tea bags every year. Once more, it looks as if FT readers thought their customers were much more like them than they really are – in spite of the incentive offered by the prize.

Of course, this task might have seemed more difficult for Europeans; and they might have felt at a handicap compared with our US entrants. They need not have worried: while they drank more European beer and purchased more tea-bags than their US counterparts, it did not affect their judgments significantly. They did no worse or better than their US counterparts.

In short, the results of the contest suggest that motivation alone cannot eliminate false consensus and overconfidence.

Source: *Financial Times*, 29 August 2003, p. 11.

## People Care About Fairness

Another insight about human behaviour is best illustrated with an experiment called the *ultimatum game.* The game works like this: two volunteers (who are otherwise strangers to each other) are told that they are going to play a game and could win a total of €100. Before they play, they learn the rules. The game begins with a flip of a coin, which is used to assign the volunteers to the roles of player A and player B. Player A's job is to propose a division of the €100 prize (in whole euros) between himself and the other player. After player A makes his proposal, player B decides whether to accept or reject it. If he accepts it, both players are paid according to the proposal. If player B rejects the proposal, both players walk away with nothing. In either case, the game then ends.

Before proceeding, stop and think about what you would do in this situation. If you were player A, what division of the €100 would you propose? If you were player B, what proposals would you accept?

Conventional economic theory assumes in this situation that people are rational wealth-maximizers. This assumption leads to a simple prediction: player A should propose that he gets €99 and player B gets €1, and player B should accept the proposal. After all, once the proposal is made, player B is better off accepting it as long as he gets something out of it. Moreover, because player A knows that accepting the proposal is in player B's interest, player A has no reason to offer him more than €1. In the language of game theory (discussed in Chapter 16), the 99–1 split is the Nash equilibrium.

Yet when experimental economists ask real people to play the ultimatum game, the results are very different from this prediction. People in the role of player B usually reject proposals that give them only €1 or a similarly small amount. Knowing this, people in the role of player A usually propose giving player B much more than €1. Some people will offer a 50–50 split, but it is more common for player A to propose giving player B an amount such as €30 or €40, keeping the larger share for himself. In this case, player B usually accepts the proposal.

What's going on here? The natural interpretation is that people are driven in part by some innate sense of fairness. A 99–1 split seems so wildly unfair to many people that they reject it, even to their own detriment. By contrast, a 70–30 split is still unfair, but it is not so unfair that it induces people to abandon their normal self-interest.

Throughout our study of household and firm behaviour, the innate sense of fairness has not played any role. But the results of the ultimatum game suggest that perhaps it should. For example, in Chapters 18 and 19 we discussed how wages were determined by labour supply and labour demand. Some economists have suggested that the perceived fairness of what a firm pays its workers should also enter the picture. Thus, when a firm has an especially profitable year, workers (like player B) may expect to be paid a fair share of the prize, even if the standard equilibrium does not dictate it. The firm (like player A) might well decide to give workers more than the equilibrium wage for fear that the workers might otherwise try to punish the firm with reduced effort, strikes or even vandalism.

To return to the ultimatum game, do you think that a sense of fairness may have its price? If the players were given, say, €1,000 to divide to the nearest hundred, and player A proposed a split of €900 to him and €100 to player B, do you think that player B would be just as likely to reject the proposal as before? What if the prize money were raised to €1 million, to be divided to the nearest €100,000?

# People Are Inconsistent Over Time

Imagine some dreary task, such as doing your laundry or tidying your room. Now consider the following questions:

1. Would you prefer (A) to spend 50 minutes doing the task immediately or (B) to spend 60 minutes doing the task tomorrow?
2. Would you prefer (A) to spend 50 minutes doing the task in 90 days or (B) to spend 60 minutes doing the task in 91 days?

When asked questions like these, many people choose B to question 1 and A to question 2. When looking ahead to the future (as in question 2), they minimize the amount of time spent on the dreary task. But faced with the prospect of doing the task immediately (as in question 1), they choose to put it off.

In some ways, this behaviour is not surprising: everyone procrastinates from time to time. But from the standpoint of the theory of rational man, it is puzzling. Suppose that, in response to question 2, a person chooses to spend 50 minutes in 90 days. Then, when the 90th day arrives, we allow him to change his mind. In effect, he then faces question 1, so he opts for doing the task the next day. But why should the mere passage of time affect the choices he makes?

Many times in life, people make plans for themselves, but then they fail to follow through. A smoker promises himself that he will quit, but within a few hours of smoking his last cigarette, he craves another and breaks his promise. A person trying to lose weight promises that he will stop eating chocolate bars, but when he gets to the checkout at the supermarket and sees the tempting array of confectionery next to the cash register, the promise is forgotten. In both cases, the desire for instant gratification induces the decision maker to abandon his own past plans.

Some economists believe that the consumption–saving decision is an important instance where people exhibit this inconsistency over time. For many people, spending provides a type of instant gratification. Saving, like passing up the cigarette or the dessert, requires a sacrifice in the present for a reward in the distant future. And just as many smokers wish they could quit and many overweight individuals wish they ate less, many consumers wish they saved more.

An implication of this inconsistency over time is that people should try to find ways to commit their future selves to following through on their plans. A smoker trying to quit may throw away his cigarettes, and a person on a diet may put a lock on the refrigerator and ask someone else to do the shopping. What can a person who saves too little do? He should find some way to lock up his money before he spends it. Some personal pension plans do exactly that. A worker can agree to have some money taken out of his salary payment before he ever sees it. The money is placed in an account and invested on his behalf by the pension company. When he retires, he can use the money to fund a pension, but the money can only be used before retirement with a penalty. This is one reason why people take out pension plans: they protect people from their own desires for instant gratification.

> **Quick Quiz** Describe at least three ways in which human decision making differs from that of the rational individual of conventional economic theory.

# CONCLUSION

This chapter has examined the frontier of microeconomics. You may have noticed that we have sketched out ideas rather than fully developing them. This is no accident. One reason is that you might study these topics in more detail in advanced courses. Another reason is that these topics remain active areas of research and, therefore, are still being fleshed out.

To see how these topics fit into the broader picture, recall the *Ten Principles of Economics* from Chapter 1. One principle states that markets are usually a good way to organize economic activity. Another principle states that governments can sometimes improve market outcomes. As you study economics, you can more fully appreciate the truth of these principles as well as the caveats that go with them. The study of asymmetric information should make you more wary of market outcomes. The study of political economy should make you more wary of government solutions. And the study of behavioural economics should make you wary of any institution that relies on human decision making – including both the market and the government.

If there is a unifying theme to these topics, it is that life is messy. Information is imperfect, government is imperfect and people are imperfect. Of course, you knew this long before you started studying economics, but economists need to understand these imperfections as precisely as they can if they are to explain, and perhaps even improve, the world around them.

## SUMMARY

- In many economic transactions, information is asymmetric. When there are hidden actions, principals may be concerned that agents suffer from the problem of moral hazard. When there are hidden characteristics, buyers may be concerned about the problem of adverse selection among the sellers. Private markets sometimes deal with asymmetric information with signalling and screening.

- Although government policy can sometimes improve market outcomes, governments are themselves imperfect institutions. The Condorcet paradox shows that majority rule fails to produce transitive preferences for society, and Arrow's impossibility theorem shows that no voting

scheme will be perfect. In many situations, democratic institutions will produce the outcome desired by the median voter, regardless of the preferences of the rest of the electorate. Moreover, the individuals who set government policy may be motivated by self-interest rather than the national interest.

- The study of psychology and economics reveals that human decision making is more complex than is assumed in conventional economic theory. People are not always rational, they care about the fairness of economic outcomes (even to their own detriment), and they can be inconsistent over time.

## KEY CONCEPTS

moral hazard, p. 446
agent, p. 446
principal, p. 446

adverse selection, p. 447
signalling, p. 448
screening, p. 449

Condorcet paradox, p. 451
Arrow's impossibility theorem, p. 452
median voter theorem, p. 453

## QUESTIONS FOR REVIEW

1. What is moral hazard? List three things an employer might do to reduce the severity of this problem.

2. What is adverse selection? Give an example of a market in which adverse selection might be a problem.

3. Define *signalling* and *screening,* and give an example of each.

4. What unusual property of voting did Condorcet notice?

5. Explain why majority rule respects the preferences of the median voter rather than the average voter.

6. Describe the ultimatum game. What outcome from this game would conventional economic theory predict? Do experiments confirm this prediction? Explain.

## PROBLEMS AND APPLICATIONS

1. Each of the following situations involves moral hazard. In each case, identify the principal and the agent, and explain why there is asymmetric information. How does the action described reduce the problem of moral hazard?
   a. Landlords require tenants to pay security deposits.
   b. Firms compensate top executives with options to buy company shares at a given price in the future.
   c. Car insurance companies offer discounts to customers who install anti-theft devices in their cars.

2. Suppose that the Live-Long-and-Prosper Health Insurance Company charges €5,000 annually for a family insurance policy. The company's president suggests that the company raise the annual price to €6,000 in order to increase its profits. If the firm followed this suggestion, what economic problem might arise? Would the firm's pool of customers tend to become more or less healthy on average? Would the company's profits necessarily increase?

3. The case study in this chapter describes how a boyfriend can signal to a girlfriend that he loves her by giving an appropriate gift. Do you think saying 'I love you' can also serve as a signal? Why or why not?

4. Some AIDS activists believe that health insurance companies should not be allowed to ask applicants if they are infected with the HIV virus that causes AIDS. Would this rule help or hurt those who are HIV-positive? Would it help or hurt those who are not HIV-positive? Would it exacerbate or mitigate the problem of adverse selection in the market for health insurance? Do you think it would increase or decrease the number of people without

health insurance? In your opinion, would this be a good policy?

5. The government is considering two ways to help the needy: giving them cash, or giving them free meals at soup kitchens. Give an argument for giving cash. Give an argument, based on asymmetric information, for why the soup kitchen may be better than the cash handout.

6. Ken walks into a restaurant.
   WAITER: Good afternoon, sir. The specials today are roast lamb and baked trout.
   KEN: I'd like the lamb, please.
   WAITER: I almost forgot. We also have lobster thermidor.
   KEN: In that case, I'll have the trout, please.
   What standard property of decision making is Ken violating? (Hint: reread the section on Arrow's impossibility theorem.) Is Ken necessarily being irrational? (Hint: what information is revealed by the fact that the chef is able to prepare lobster thermidor?)

7. Why might a political party in a two-party system choose not to move towards the median voter? (Hint: think about abstentions from voting and political contributions.)

8. Two ice cream stands are deciding where to locate along a one-mile beach. Each person sitting on the beach buys exactly one ice cream cone per day from the stand nearest to him. Each ice cream seller wants the maximum number of customers. Where along the beach will the two stands locate?

For further resources, visit
http://www.thomsonlearning.co.uk/mankiw_taylor

**ability-to-pay principle** the idea that taxes should be levied on a person according to how well that person can shoulder the burden

**absolute advantage** the comparison among producers of a good according to their productivity

**accounting profit** total revenue minus total explicit cost

**adverse selection** the tendency for the mix of unobserved attributes to become undesirable from the standpoint of an uninformed party

**agent** a person who is performing an act for another person, called the principal

**aggregate demand curve** a curve that shows the quantity of goods and services that households, firms and the government want to buy at each price level

**aggregate risk** risk that affects all economic actors at once

**aggregate supply curve** a curve that shows the quantity of goods and services that firms choose to produce and sell at each price level

**appreciation** an increase in the value of a currency as measured by the amount of foreign currency it can buy

**Arrow's impossibility theorem** a mathematical result showing that, under certain assumed conditions, there is no scheme for aggregating individual preferences into a valid set of social preferences

**automatic stabilizers** changes in fiscal policy that stimulate aggregate demand when the economy goes into a recession, without policymakers having to take any deliberate action

**average fixed cost** fixed costs divided by the quantity of output

**average revenue** total revenue divided by the quantity sold

**average tax rate** total taxes paid divided by total income

**average total cost** total cost divided by the quantity of output

**average variable cost** variable costs divided by the quantity of output

**balanced trade** a situation in which exports equal imports

**Bank of England** the central bank of the United Kingdom

**bank run** when a substantial number of depositors suspect that a bank may go bankrupt and withdraw their deposits

**benefits principle** the idea that people should pay taxes based on the benefits they receive from government services

**bond** a certificate of indebtedness

**budget constraint** the limit on the consumption bundles that a consumer can afford

**budget deficit** a shortfall of tax revenue from government spending

**budget surplus** an excess of tax revenue over government spending

**business cycle** fluctuations in economic activity, such as employment and production

**capital** the equipment and structures used to produce goods and services

**capital flight** a large and sudden reduction in the demand for assets located in a country

**cartel** a group of firms acting in unison

**catch-up effect** the property whereby countries that start off poor tend to grow more rapidly than countries that start off rich

**central bank** an institution designed to regulate the quantity of money in the economy

**circular-flow diagram** a visual model of the economy that shows how money and production inputs and outputs flow through markets among households and firms

**classical dichotomy** the theoretical separation of nominal and real variables

**closed economy** an economy that does not interact with other economies in the world

**Coase theorem** the proposition that if private parties can bargain without cost over the allocation of resources, they can solve the problem of externalities on their own

**collective bargaining** the process by which unions and firms agree on the terms of employment

**collusion** an agreement among firms in a market about quantities to produce or prices to charge

**commodity money** money that takes the form of a commodity with intrinsic value

**common currency area** a geographical area, possibly covering several countries, in which a common currency circulates as the medium of exchange

**common resources** goods that are rival but not excludable

**comparative advantage** the comparison among producers of a good according to their opportunity cost

**compensating differential** a difference in wages that arises to offset the non-monetary characteristics of different jobs

**competitive market** a market in which there are many buyers and many sellers so that each has a negligible impact on the market price

**complements** two goods for which an increase in the price of one leads to a decrease in the demand for the other

**compounding** the accumulation of a sum of money in, say, a bank account, where the interest earned remains in the account to earn additional interest in the future

**Condorcet paradox** the failure of majority rule to produce transitive preferences for society

**constant returns to scale** the property whereby long-run average total cost stays the same as the quantity of output changes

**consumer price index (CPI)** a measure of the overall cost of the goods and services bought by a typical consumer

**consumer surplus** a buyer's willingness to pay minus the amount the buyer actually pays

**consumption** spending by households on goods and services, with the exception of purchases of new housing

**cost** the value of everything a seller must give up to produce a good

**cost–benefit analysis** a study that compares the costs and benefits to society of providing a public good

**cross-price elasticity of demand** a measure of how much the quantity demanded of one good responds to a change in the price of another good, computed as the percentage change in quantity demanded of the first good divided by the percentage change in the price of the second good

**crowding out** a decrease in investment that results from government borrowing

**crowding-out effect** the offset in aggregate demand that results when expansionary fiscal policy raises the interest rate and thereby reduces investment spending

**currency** the paper banknotes and coins in the hands of the public

**customs union** a group of countries that agree not to impose any restrictions at all on trade between their own economies, but to impose the same restrictions as one another on goods imported from countries outside the group.

**cyclical unemployment** the deviation of unemployment from its natural rate

**deadweight loss** the fall in total surplus that results from a market distortion, such as a tax

**demand curve** a graph of the relationship between the price of a good and the quantity demanded

**demand deposits** balances in bank accounts that depositors can access on demand by using a debit card or writing a cheque

**demand schedule** a table that shows the relationship between the price of a good and the quantity demanded

**depreciation** a decrease in the value of a currency as measured by the amount of foreign currency it can buy

**depression** a severe recession

**diminishing marginal product** the property whereby the marginal product of an input declines as the quantity of the input increases

**diminishing returns** the property whereby the benefit from an extra unit of an input declines as the quantity of the input increases

**direct tax** a tax that is levied directly on a person's income

**discount rate** the interest rate at which the Federal Reserve lends on a short-term basis to the UK banking sector

**discrimination** the offering of different opportunities to similar individuals who differ only by race, ethnic group, sex, age or other personal characteristics

**diseconomies of scale** the property whereby long-run average total cost rises as the quantity of output increases

**diversification** the reduction of risk achieved by replacing a single risk with a large number of smaller unrelated risks

**dominant strategy** a strategy that is best for a player in a game regardless of the strategies chosen by the other players

**economic profit** total revenue minus total cost, including both explicit and implicit costs

**economics** the study of how society manages its scarce resources

**economies of scale** the property whereby long-run average total cost falls as the quantity of output increases

**efficiency** the property of society getting the most it can from its scarce resources

**efficiency wages** above-equilibrium wages paid by firms in order to increase worker productivity

**efficient markets hypothesis** the theory that asset prices reflect all publicly available information about the value of an asset

**efficient scale** the quantity of output that minimizes average total cost

**elasticity** a measure of the responsiveness of quantity demanded or quantity supplied to one of its determinants

**equilibrium** a situation in which the price has reached the level where quantity supplied equals quantity demanded

**equilibrium price** the price that balances quantity supplied and quantity demanded

**equilibrium quantity** the quantity supplied and the quantity demanded at the equilibrium price

**equity** the property of distributing economic prosperity fairly among the members of society

**European Central Bank (ECB)** the overall central bank of the 12 countries comprising the European Monetary Union

**European Economic and Monetary Union (EMU)** the European currency union that has adopted the euro as its common currency

**European Union** a family of democratic European countries, committed to working together for peace and prosperity

**Eurosystem** the system made up of the ECB plus the national central banks of each of the 12 countries comprising the European Monetary Union

**excludability** the property of a good whereby a person can be prevented from using it

**explicit costs** input costs that require an outlay of money by the firm

**exports** goods and services that are produced domestically and sold abroad

**externality** the uncompensated impact of one person's actions on the well-being of a bystander

**factors of production** the inputs used to produce goods and services

**Federal Reserve (Fed)** the central bank of the United States

**fiat money** money without intrinsic value that is used as money because of government decree

**finance** the field of economics that studies how people make decisions regarding the allocation of resources over time and the handling of risk

**financial intermediaries** financial institutions through which savers can indirectly provide funds to borrowers

**financial markets** financial institutions through which savers can directly provide funds to borrowers

**financial system** the group of institutions in the economy that help to match one person's saving with another person's investment

**fiscal federalism** a fiscal system for a group of countries involving a common fiscal budget and a system of taxes and fiscal transfers across countries

**Fisher effect** the one-for-one adjustment of the nominal interest rate to the inflation rate

**fixed costs** costs that do not vary with the quantity of output produced

**fractional-reserve banking** a banking system in which banks hold only a fraction of deposits as reserves

**free rider** a person who receives the benefit of a good but avoids paying for it

**frictional unemployment** unemployment that results because it takes time for workers to search for the jobs that best suit their tastes and skills

**fundamental analysis** the study of a company's accounting statements and future prospects in order to determine its value

**future value** the amount of money in the future that an amount of money today will yield, given prevailing interest rates

**game theory** the study of how people behave in strategic situations

**GDP deflator** a measure of the price level calculated as the ratio of nominal GDP to real GDP times 100

**Giffen good** a good for which an increase in the price raises the quantity demanded

**government purchases** spending on goods and services by local, state and national governments

**gross domestic product (GDP)** the market value of all final goods and services produced within a country in a given period of time

**horizontal equity** the idea that taxpayers with similar abilities to pay taxes should pay the same amount

**human capital** the accumulation of investments in people, such as education and on-the-job training

**idiosyncratic risk** risk that affects only a single economic actor

**implicit costs** input costs that do not require an outlay of money by the firm

**import quota** a limit on the quantity of a good that can be produced abroad and sold domestically

**imports** goods and services that are produced abroad and sold domestically

**income effect** the change in consumption that results when a price change moves the consumer to a higher or lower indifference curve

**income elasticity of demand** a measure of how much the quantity demanded of a good responds to a change in consumers' income, computed as the percentage change in quantity demanded divided by the percentage change in income

**indexation** the automatic correction of a money amount for the effects of inflation by law or contract

**indifference curve** a curve that shows consumption bundles that give the consumer the same level of satisfaction

**indirect tax** a tax that is levied on goods and services bought

**inferior good** a good for which, other things equal, an increase in income leads to a decrease in demand

**inflation** an increase in the overall level of prices in the economy

**inflation rate** the percentage change in the price index from the preceding period

**inflation tax** the revenue the government raises by creating money

**informationally efficient** reflecting all available information in a rational way

**in-kind transfers** transfers to the poor given in the form of goods and services rather than cash

**internalizing an externality** altering incentives so that people take account of the external effects of their actions

**investment** spending on capital equipment, inventories and structures, including household purchases of new housing

**investment fund** an institution that sells shares to the public and uses the proceeds to buy a portfolio of stocks and bonds

**job search** the process by which workers find appropriate jobs given their tastes and skills

**labour force** the total number of workers, including both the employed and the unemployed

**labour force participation rate** the percentage of the adult population that is in the labour force

**law of demand** the claim that, other things equal, the quantity demanded of a good falls when the price of the good rises

**law of supply** the claim that, other things equal, the quantity supplied of a good rises when the price of the good rises

**law of supply and demand** the claim that the price of any good adjusts to bring the quantity supplied and the quantity demanded for that good into balance

**liberalism** the political philosophy according to which the government should choose policies deemed to be just, as evaluated by an impartial observer behind a 'veil of ignorance'

**libertarianism** the political philosophy according to which the government should punish crimes and enforce voluntary agreements but not redistribute income

**life cycle** the regular pattern of income variation over a person's life

**liquidity** the ease with which an asset can be converted into the economy's medium of exchange

**lump-sum tax** a tax that is the same amount for every person

**macroeconomics** the study of economy-wide phenomena, including inflation, unemployment and economic growth

**marginal changes** small incremental adjustments to a plan of action

**marginal cost** the increase in total cost that arises from an extra unit of production

**marginal product** the increase in output that arises from an additional unit of input

**marginal product of labour** the increase in the amount of output from an additional unit of labour

**marginal rate of substitution** the rate at which a consumer is willing to trade one good for another

**marginal revenue** the change in total revenue from an additional unit sold

**marginal tax rate** the extra taxes paid on an additional unit of income

**market** a group of buyers and sellers of a particular good or service

**market economy** an economy that allocates resources through the decentralized decisions of many firms and households as they interact in markets for goods and services

**market failure** a situation in which a market left on its own fails to allocate resources efficiently

**market for loanable funds** the market in which those who want to save supply funds and those who want to borrow to invest demand funds

**market power** the ability of a single economic agent (or small group of agents) to have a substantial influence on market prices

**maximin criterion** the claim that the government should aim to maximize the well-being of the worst-off person in society

**median voter theorem** a mathematical result showing that if voters are choosing a point along a line and each voter wants the point closest to his most preferred point, then majority rule will pick the most preferred point of the median voter

**medium of exchange** an item that buyers give to sellers when they want to purchase goods and services

**menu costs** the costs of changing prices

**microeconomics** the study of how households and firms make decisions and how they interact in markets

**model of aggregate demand and aggregate supply** the model that most economists use to explain short-run fluctuations in economic activity around its long-run trend

**monetary neutrality** the proposition that changes in the money supply do not affect real variables

**monetary policy** the set of actions taken by the central bank in order to affect the money supply

**money** the set of assets in an economy that people regularly use to buy goods and services from other people

**money market** the market in which the commercial banks lend money to one another on a short-term basis

**money multiplier** the amount of money the banking system generates with each unit of reserves

**money supply** the quantity of money available in the economy

**monopolistic competition** a market structure in which many firms sell products that are similar but not identical

**monopoly** a firm that is the sole seller of a product without close substitutes

**moral hazard** the tendency of a person who is imperfectly monitored to engage in dishonest or otherwise undesirable behaviour

**multiplier effect** the additional shifts in aggregate demand that result when expansionary fiscal policy increases income and thereby increases consumer spending

**Nash equilibrium** a situation in which economic actors interacting with one another each choose their best strategy given the strategies that all the other actors have chosen

**national saving (saving)** the total income in the economy that remains after paying for consumption and government purchases

**natural monopoly** a monopoly that arises because a single firm can supply a good or service to an entire market at a smaller cost than could two or more firms

**natural-rate hypothesis** the claim that unemployment eventually returns to its normal, or natural, rate, regardless of the rate of inflation

**natural rate of unemployment** the normal rate of unemployment around which the unemployment rate fluctuates

**natural resources** the inputs into the production of goods and services that are provided by nature, such as land, rivers and mineral deposits

**negative income tax** a tax system that collects revenue from high-income households and gives transfers to low-income households

**net capital outflow** the purchase of foreign assets by domestic residents minus the purchase of domestic assets by foreigners

**net exports** the value of a nation's exports minus the value of its imports; also called the trade balance

**nominal exchange rate** the rate at which a person can trade the currency of one country for the currency of another

**nominal GDP** the production of goods and services valued at current prices

**nominal interest rate** the interest rate as usually reported without a correction for the effects of inflation

**nominal variables** variables measured in monetary units

**normal good** a good for which, other things equal, an increase in income leads to an increase in demand

**normative statements** claims that attempt to prescribe how the world should be

**oligopoly** a market structure in which only a few sellers offer similar or identical products

**open economy** an economy that interacts freely with other economies around the world

**open-market operations** the purchase and sale of non-monetary assets from and to the banking sector by the central bank

**opportunity cost** whatever must be given up to obtain some item

**optimum currency area** a group of countries for which it is optimal to adopt a common currency and form a currency union

**outright open-market operations** the outright sale or purchase of non-monetary assets to or from the banking sector by the central bank without a corresponding agreement to reverse the transaction at a later date

**perfect complements** two goods with right-angle indifference curves

**perfect substitutes** two goods with straight-line indifference curves

**permanent income** a person's normal income

**Phillips curve** a curve that shows the short-run trade-off between inflation and unemployment

**physical capital** the stock of equipment and structures that are used to produce goods and services

**Pigovian tax** a tax enacted to correct the effects of a negative externality

**positive statements** claims that attempt to describe the world as it is

**present value** the amount of money today that would be needed to produce, using prevailing interest rates, a given future amount of money

**price ceiling** a legal maximum on the price at which a good can be sold

**price discrimination** the business practice of selling the same good at different prices to different customers

**price elasticity of demand** a measure of how much the quantity demanded of a good responds to a change in the price of that good, computed as the percentage change in quantity demanded divided by the percentage change in price

**price elasticity of supply** a measure of how much the quantity supplied of a good responds to a change in the price of that good, computed as the percentage change in quantity supplied divided by the percentage change in price

**price floor** a legal minimum on the price at which a good can be sold

**principal** a person for whom another person, called the agent, is performing some act

**prisoners' dilemma** a particular 'game' between two captured prisoners that illustrates why cooperation is difficult to maintain even when it is mutually beneficial

**private goods** goods that are both excludable and rival

**private saving** the income that households have left after paying for taxes and consumption

**producer price index** a measure of the cost of a basket of goods and services bought by firms

**producer surplus** the amount a seller is paid for a good minus the seller's cost

**production function** the relationship between quantity of inputs used to make a good and the quantity of output of that good

**production possibilities frontier** a graph that shows the combinations of output that the economy can possibly produce given the available factors of production and the available production technology

**productivity** the quantity of goods and services produced from each hour of a worker's time

**profit** total revenue minus total cost

**progressive tax** a tax for which high-income taxpayers pay a larger fraction of their income than do low-income taxpayers

**proportional tax** a tax for which high-income and low-income taxpayers pay the same fraction of income

**public goods** goods that are neither excludable nor rival

**public saving** the tax revenue that the government has left after paying for its spending

**purchasing power parity** a theory of exchange rates whereby a unit of any given currency should be able to buy the same quantity of goods in all countries

**quantity demanded** the amount of a good that buyers are willing and able to purchase

**quantity equation** the equation $M \times V = P \times Y$, which relates the quantity of money, the velocity of money, and the dollar value of the economy's output of goods and services

**quantity supplied** the amount of a good that sellers are willing and able to sell

**quantity theory of money** a theory asserting that the quantity of money available determines the price level and that the growth rate in the quantity of money available determines the inflation rate

**random walk** the path of a variable whose changes are impossible to predict

**rational expectations** the theory according to which people optimally use all the information they have, including information about government policies, when forecasting the future

**real exchange rate** the rate at which a person can trade the goods and services of one country for the goods and services of another

**real GDP** the production of goods and services valued at constant prices

**real interest rate** the interest rate corrected for the effects of inflation

**real variables** variables measured in physical units

**recession** a period of declining real incomes and rising unemployment

**refinancing rate** the interest rate at which the European Central Bank lends on a short-term basis to the eroa area banking sector

**regressive tax** a tax for which high-income taxpayers pay a smaller fraction of their income than do low-income taxpayers

**repo rate** the interest rate at which the Bank of England lends on a short-term basis to the UK banking sector

**repurchase agreement (repo)** the sale of a non-monetary asset together with an agreement to repurchase it at a set price at a specified future date

**reserve ratio** the fraction of deposits that banks hold as reserves

**reserve requirements** regulations on the minimum amount of reserves that banks must hold against deposits

**reserves** deposits that banks have received but have not loaned out

**risk averse** exhibiting a dislike of uncertainty

**rivalry** the property of a good whereby one person's use diminishes other people's use

**sacrifice ratio** the number of percentage points of annual output lost in the process of reducing inflation by 1 percentage point

**scarcity** the limited nature of society's resources

**screening** an action taken by an uninformed party to induce an informed party to reveal information

**shoeleather costs** the resources wasted when inflation encourages people to reduce their money holdings

**shortage** a situation in which quantity demanded is greater than quantity supplied

**signalling** an action taken by an informed party to reveal private information to an uninformed party

**Single European Market** a (still-not-complete) EU-wide market throughout which labour, capital, goods and services can move freely

**social security** government benefits that supplement the incomes of the needy

**stagflation** a period of falling output and rising prices

**stock** a claim to partial ownership in a firm

**store of value** an item that people can use to transfer purchasing power from the present to the future

**strike** the organized withdrawal of labour from a firm by a union

**structural unemployment** unemployment that results because the number of jobs available in some labour markets is insufficient to provide a job for everyone who wants one

**substitutes** two goods for which an increase in the price of one leads to an increase in the demand for the other

**substitution effect** the change in consumption that results when a price change moves the consumer along a given indifference curve to a point with a new marginal rate of substitution

**sunk cost** a cost that has already been committed and cannot be recovered

**supply curve** a graph of the relationship between the price of a good and the quantity supplied

**supply schedule** a table that shows the relationship between the price of a good and the quantity supplied

**supply shock** an event that directly alters firms' costs and prices, shifting the economy's aggregate supply curve and thus the Phillips curve

**surplus** a situation in which quantity supplied is greater than quantity demanded

**tariff** a tax on goods produced abroad and sold domestically

**tax incidence** the manner in which the burden of a tax is shared among participants in a market

**technological knowledge** society's understanding of the best ways to produce goods and services

**theory of liquidity preference** Keynes's theory that the interest rate adjusts to bring money supply and money demand into balance

**total cost** the market value of the inputs a firm uses in production

**total revenue (for a firm)** the amount a firm receives for the sale of its output

**total revenue (in a market)** the amount paid by buyers and received by sellers of a good, computed as the price of the good times the quantity sold

**trade balance** the value of a nation's exports minus the value of its imports; also called net exports

**trade deficit** an excess of imports over exports

**trade policy** a government policy that directly influences the quantity of goods and services that a country imports or exports

**trade surplus** an excess of exports over imports

**Tragedy of the Commons** a parable that illustrates why common resources get used more than is desirable from the standpoint of society as a whole

**transaction costs** the costs that parties incur in the process of agreeing and following through on a bargain

**unemployment insurance** a government programme that partially protects workers' incomes when they become unemployed

**unemployment rate** the percentage of the labour force that is unemployed

**union** a worker association that bargains with employers over wages and working conditions

**unit of account** the yardstick people use to post prices and record debts

**utilitarianism** the political philosophy according to which the government should choose policies to maximize the total utility of everyone in society

**utility** a measure of happiness or satisfaction

**value of the marginal product** the marginal product of an input times the price of the output

**variable costs** costs that vary with the quantity of output produced

**velocity of money** the rate at which money changes hands

**vertical equity** the idea that taxpayers with a greater ability to pay taxes should pay larger amounts

**welfare economics** the study of how the allocation of resources affects economic well-being

**willingness to pay** the maximum amount that a buyer will pay for a good

**world price** the price of a good that prevails in the world market for that good